T0281496

Lecture Notes in Computer Science 13950

Founding Editors

Gerhard Goos
Juris Hartmanis

Editorial Board Members

Elisa Bertino, *Purdue University, West Lafayette, IN, USA*
Wen Gao, *Peking University, Beijing, China*
Bernhard Steffen ⓘ, *TU Dortmund University, Dortmund, Germany*
Moti Yung ⓘ, *Columbia University, New York, NY, USA*

The series Lecture Notes in Computer Science (LNCS), including its subseries Lecture Notes in Artificial Intelligence (LNAI) and Lecture Notes in Bioinformatics (LNBI), has established itself as a medium for the publication of new developments in computer science and information technology research, teaching, and education.

LNCS enjoys close cooperation with the computer science R & D community, the series counts many renowned academics among its volume editors and paper authors, and collaborates with prestigious societies. Its mission is to serve this international community by providing an invaluable service, mainly focused on the publication of conference and workshop proceedings and postproceedings. LNCS commenced publication in 1973.

Foteini Baldimtsi · Christian Cachin

Editors

Financial Cryptography and Data Security

27th International Conference, FC 2023
Bol, Brač, Croatia, May 1–5, 2023
Revised Selected Papers, Part I

 Springer

Editors
Foteini Baldimtsi (iD)
George Mason University
Fairfax, VA, USA

Christian Cachin (iD)
University of Bern
Bern, Switzerland

ISSN 0302-9743   ISSN 1611-3349 (electronic)
Lecture Notes in Computer Science
ISBN 978-3-031-47753-9   ISBN 978-3-031-47754-6 (eBook)
https://doi.org/10.1007/978-3-031-47754-6

© International Financial Cryptography Association 2024
Chapter "Optimally-Fair Exchange of Secrets via Delay Encryption and Commutative Blinding" is licensed under the terms of the Creative Commons Attribution 4.0 International License (http://creativecommons.org/licenses/by/4.0/). For further details see license information in the chapter.

This work is subject to copyright. All rights are reserved by the Publisher, whether the whole or part of the material is concerned, specifically the rights of translation, reprinting, reuse of illustrations, recitation, broadcasting, reproduction on microfilms or in any other physical way, and transmission or information storage and retrieval, electronic adaptation, computer software, or by similar or dissimilar methodology now known or hereafter developed.
The use of general descriptive names, registered names, trademarks, service marks, etc. in this publication does not imply, even in the absence of a specific statement, that such names are exempt from the relevant protective laws and regulations and therefore free for general use.
The publisher, the authors, and the editors are safe to assume that the advice and information in this book are believed to be true and accurate at the date of publication. Neither the publisher nor the authors or the editors give a warranty, expressed or implied, with respect to the material contained herein or for any errors or omissions that may have been made. The publisher remains neutral with regard to jurisdictional claims in published maps and institutional affiliations.

This Springer imprint is published by the registered company Springer Nature Switzerland AG
The registered company address is: Gewerbestrasse 11, 6330 Cham, Switzerland

Paper in this product is recyclable.

Preface

The 27th International Conference on Financial Cryptography and Data Security, FC 2023, was held from May 1 to May 5, 2023, at the Bluesun Hotel Elaphusa in Bol, on the island of Brač, Croatia. The conference is organized annually by the International Financial Cryptography Association (IFCA).

We received 182 papers (165 regular ones and 17 short papers) by the submission deadline for the conference, which was October 19th, 2022. Of these, 41 were accepted (39 regular papers and two short papers), resulting in an acceptance rate of 22.5%. The present proceedings volume contains revised versions of all the papers presented at the conference.

The review process lasted approximately two months and was double-blind. Each paper received a minimum of three reviews. The Program Committee used the HotCRP system to organize the reviewing process. The merits of each paper were discussed thoroughly and intensely on the online platform as we converged to the final decisions. In the end, a number of worthy papers still had to be rejected owing to the limited number of slots in the conference program.

The Program Committee (PC) consisted of 64 members with expertise in various aspects of financial cryptography, including representatives from both industry and academia. The PC additionally solicited reviews from 58 external reviewers. We are deeply grateful to all the members of the PC and the external reviewers for their dedication and thorough work. Their valuable insights and constructive feedback considerably strengthened the overall quality of the final program.

The main conference program lasted for four days. A half-day tutorial on the topic of "Constant Function Market Makers" took place a day before the main conference and a series of one-day workshops were held the day after the main conference. The main conference started with an invited keynote talk by George Danezis, University College London and Mysten Labs, titled "Combining broadcast and consensus in a production blockchain system." The accepted papers were presented in 10 sessions and there was also a Rump Session and a General Meeting. Finally, two posters were presented during the poster session.

We are grateful to the general chairs, Ray Hirschfeld and Carla Mascia, for an excellent organization. Additionally, we appreciate the dedication of the IFCA directors and Steering Committee for their service. We would also like to express our thankfulness to the conference sponsors whose generous support made this event possible. Our Platinum Sponsors: a16z Crypto Research, Casper Association, Chainlink Labs and Mysten Labs. Our Silver Sponsors: Evertas and Zcash Foundation. Finally, we would like to thank our sponsors in kind: the Croatian National Tourist Board, the Split-Dalmatia Tourist Board, the Bol Tourist Board, and Worldpay.

Lastly, our sincere gratitude goes to all the authors who submitted their papers to this conference, as well as to all the attendees who contributed to making this event a truly intellectually stimulating experience through their active participation. Their support is the most important factor for the success of the conference.

August 2023   Foteini Baldimtsi
                                                               Christian Cachin

Organization

General Chairs

Rafael Hirschfeld	Unipay Technologies, The Netherlands
Carla Mascia	University of Trento, Italy

Steering Committee

Joseph Bonneau	New York University and a16z Crypto Research, USA
Sven Dietrich	City University of New York, USA
Rafael Hirschfeld	Unipay Technologies, The Netherlands
Andrew Miller	University of Illinois at Urbana-Champaign, USA
Monica Quaintance	Zenia Systems, USA
Burton Rosenberg	University of Miami, USA
Kazue Sako	Waseda University, Japan

Program Committee Chairs

Foteini Baldimtsi	George Mason University, USA
Christian Cachin	University of Bern, Switzerland

Program Committee

Ghada Almashaqbeh	University of Connecticut, USA
Zeta Avarikioti	Technical University of Vienna, Austria
Christian Badertscher	Input Output, Switzerland
Massimo Bartoletti	University of Cagliari, Italy
Rainer Böhme	University of Innsbruck, Austria
Joseph Bonneau	New York University and a16z Crypto Research, USA
Benedikt Bünz	Stanford University and Espresso Systems, USA
L. Jean Camp	Indiana University, USA
Srdjan Čapkun	ETH Zurich, Switzerland
Kostas Chalkias	Mysten Labs, USA
T.-H. Hubert Chan	University of Hong Kong, China
Panagiotis Chatzigiannis	Visa Research, USA

Jeremy Clark	Concordia University, Canada
Vanesa Daza	Universitat Pompeu Fabra, Spain
Rafael Dowsley	Monash University, Australia
Stefan Dziembowski	University of Warsaw, Poland
Karim Eldefrawy	SRI International, USA
Kaoutar Elkhiyaoui	IBM Research, Switzerland
Zeki Erkin	TU Delft, The Netherlands
Chaya Ganesh	Indian Institute of Science, Bangalore, India
Christina Garman	Purdue University, USA
Peter Gaži	Input Output, Slovakia
Rosario Gennaro	Protocol Labs, USA
Arthur Gervais	University College London, UK
Ethan Heilman	BastionZero, USA
Ari Juels	Cornell Tech, USA
Aniket Kate	Purdue University and Supra Research, USA
Lefteris Kokoris-Kogias	IST Austria, Austria
Evgenios M. Kornaropoulos	George Mason University, USA
Duc V. Le	University of Bern, Switzerland
Andrew Lewis-Pye	London School of Economics, UK
Ben Livshits	Imperial College and Brave Software, UK
Giorgia Azzurra Marson	NEC Labs Europe, Germany
Shin'ichiro Matsuo	Georgetown University, USA
Patrick McCorry	Infura, UK
Ian Miers	University of Maryland, USA
Andrew Miller	University of Illinois at Urbana-Champaign, USA
Pedro Moreno-Sanchez	IMDEA Software Institute, Spain
Kartik Nayak	Duke University, USA
Valeria Nikolaenko	a16z Crypto Research, USA
Anca Nitulescu	Protocol Labs, France
Giorgos Panagiotakos	Input Output, UK
Dimitris Papadopoulos	Hong Kong University of Science and Technology, China
Charalampos Papamanthou	Yale University, USA
Alexandros Psomas	Purdue University, USA
Elizabeth A. Quaglia	Royal Holloway, University of London, UK
Ling Ren	University of Illinois at Urbana-Champaign, USA
Ori Rottenstreich	Technion, Israel
Abhi Shelat	Northeastern University, USA
Alberto Sonnino	Mysten Labs, UK
Alessandro Sorniotti	IBM Research, Switzerland
Alexander Spiegelman	Aptos Labs, USA
Chrysoula Stathakopoulou	Chainlink Labs, Switzerland

Vanessa Teague	Thinking Cybersecurity and Australian National University, Australia
Marie Vasek	University College London, UK
Roger Wattenhofer	ETH Zurich, Switzerland
Edgar Weippl	University of Vienna and SBA Research, Austria
Fan Zhang	Yale University, USA
Haibin Zhang	Beijing Institute of Technology, China
Ren Zhang	Cryptape Co. Ltd. and Nervos, China
Yupeng Zhang	Texas A&M University, USA
Hong-Sheng Zhou	Virginia Commonwealth University, USA
Dionysis Zindros	Stanford University, USA
Aviv Zohar	Hebrew University, Israel

Additional Reviewers

Hamza Abusalah
Amit Agarwal
Jannik Albrecht
Balaji Arun
Judith Beestermöller
Adithya Bhat
Matteo Campanelli
Kevin Choi
Sandro Coretti-Drayton
Xiaohai Dai
Sourav Das
Yepeng Michael Ding
Fatima Elsheimy
Zhiyong Fang
Rati Gelashvili
Tiantian Gong
Florian Grötschla
Lioba Heimbach
Javier Herranz
Yanxue Jia
Aljosha Judmayer
Dimitris Karakostas
David Lehnherr
Rujia Li
Yunqi Li
Yujie Lu
Zhichun Lu
Nikos Makriyannis
Easwar Vivek Mangipudi
Deepak Maram

Joël Mathys
Subhra Mazumdar
Liam Medley
Jovana Micic
Atsuki Momose
Muhammad Haris Mudgees
Kamilla Nazirkhanova
Ben Riva
Schwinn Saereesitthipitak
Philipp Schindler
Peiyao Sheng
Srivatsan Sridhar
Shravan Srinivasan
Christo Stefo
Nicholas Stifter
Ertem Nusret Tas
Benjamin Terner
Athina Terzoglou
Phuc Thai
Giorgos Tsimos
Sarisht Wadhwa
Chenghong Wang
Weijie Wang
Zhuolun Xiang
Yuting Xiao
Tom Yurek
Yuncong Zhang
Ren Zhijie
Zhelei Zhou

Contents – Part I

Decentralized Finance

Contents – Part II

Consensus

Executing and Proving Over Dirty Ledgers

Christos Stefo[1,2(✉)], Zhuolun Xiang[3], and Lefteris Kokoris-Kogias[1,4]

[1] IST Austria, Klosterneuburg, Austria
xristostefo98@gmail.com
[2] National Technical University of Athens, Athens, Greece
[3] Aptos Labs, Palo Alto, USA
[4] Mysten Labs, Palo Alto, USA

Abstract. Scaling blockchain protocols to perform on par with the expected needs of Web3.0 has been proven to be a challenging task with almost a decade of research. In the forefront of the current solution is the idea of separating the execution of the updates encoded in a block from the ordering of blocks. In order to achieve this, a new class of protocols called rollups has emerged. Rollups have as input a total ordering of valid and invalid transactions and as output a new valid state-transition.

If we study rollups from a distributed computing perspective, we uncover that rollups take as input the output of a Byzantine Atomic Broadcast (BAB) protocol and convert it to a State Machine Replication (SMR) protocol. BAB and SMR, however, are considered equivalent as far as distributed computing is concerned and a solution to one can easily be retrofitted to solve the other simply by adding/removing an execution step before the validation of the input.

This "easy" step of retrofitting an atomic broadcast solution to implement an SMR has, however, been overlooked in practice. In this paper, we formalize the problem and show that after BAB is solved, traditional impossibility results for consensus no longer apply towards an SMR. Leveraging this we propose a distributed execution protocol that allows reduced execution and storage cost per executor ($O(\frac{log^2 n}{n})$) without relaxing the network assumptions of the underlying BAB protocol and providing censorship-resistance. Finally, we propose efficient non-interactive light client constructions that leverage our efficient execution protocols and do not require any synchrony assumptions or expensive ZK-proofs.

1 Introduction

The rise of blockchain technology has lead to the rapid development of a variety of solutions for the State Machine Replication (SMR) problem. Nodes running an SMR algorithm need to both order a set of transactions as well as execute them to update their local state, two separate responsibilities that are usually conflated into a single consensus protocol. Recently, the idea of separating the total ordering of transactions from the execution has shown tremendous promise on increasing the scalability of blockchains [9,14,27] however all existing research focuses on the ordering layer assuming that after ordering every participant can locally execute the transactions and update the state.

ⓒ International Financial Cryptography Association 2024
F. Baldimtsi and C. Cachin (Eds.): FC 2023, LNCS 13950, pp. 3–20, 2024.
https://doi.org/10.1007/978-3-031-47754-6_1

In this work, we investigate the question of "how to scale execution after the ordering is done". In other words, given that transactions are ordered, how scalable can an execution protocol be. Currently there exist two proposed solutions. The first and most prevalent is that every consensus-node also executes and adds a commitment to the new-state on a succeeding block [9,11,30]. The second relies on a semi-trusted executor node that runs a "rollup" protocol [26]. The executor proposing a new state after locally executing the ordered transactions either provides a sufficiently large dispute window for some honest executor to challenge the proposal with a fraud proof [2,4,7], or a zk-proof [1,10] of correct execution. Neither of these solutions are built from first principles, the former is merely a synchrony assumption breaking the model of the underlying ordering-layer [11,12,17,21,22] whereas the later is proposed as a remedy to that assumption which forces mostly inefficient and non-general purpose zero-knowledge proof usage as well as allows for the executor to censor transactions.

In this paper, we take a step back and design from first principles. As a first contribution we merely point out that decoupling of ordering from execution is nothing more than taking a Byzantine Atomic Broadcast (BAB) [15], i.e. ensuring the total ordering of sent messages, and a deterministic execution engine [3,16,18] to solve the SMR problem. In blockchain systems, the BAB layer is called a *dirty* ledger because transactions are not checked for validity. The nodes taking part in the network, which we call *consensus nodes*, commit transactions without validation and only make sure the ledger is growing consistently.

Once we define our problem we propose a novel protocol for the execution layer of an underlying dirty ledger for both the permissioned and the Proof-of-Stake settings. Our protocol works in an asynchronous environment, making no extra assumptions and does not use zk-proving machinery. We merely assume the existence of a dirty ledger, that ensures both the total ordering and the availability of the transactions committed to it. Then, for the execution layer, we use a set of nodes that we call *executors*. They validate transactions and update the state of the system and can be a subset of the consensus nodes or external. Surprisingly an honest majority is sufficient for the executors even though we have no timing assumptions and only a poly-logarithmic number of them needs to execute every block. As a result our solution provides both better fault tolerance ($f \leq (1 - \epsilon)\frac{n}{2}$ instead of $f < \frac{n}{3}$) and significantly better scalability in two dimensions, execution and storage, with expected $O(\frac{log^2 n}{n})$ (instead of $O(1)$) cost per executor per block meaning that the system can be truly scalable and decentralized.

Our Approach

Our protocol can be roughly split into two steps. In the first step, we *elect* on expectation one executor per round by computing a VRF [25]. Then the executor *votes* by computing state commitments for the next $O(log^2 n)$ rounds. Hence every round will have an $O(log^2 n)$ number of executors. Their task is to construct verifiable certificates of the state such that a user (*executor* or light client) can be convinced about the state without execution. At first glance, that problem seems related to the consensus problem [23] since executors need to agree on the state, but unlike the consensus problem, in each round all honest nodes have the same input, an ordered list of transactions. Therefore, as long as honest executors bootstrap in the correct state, a state commitment can be considered valid if and only if at least one honest executor has voted on it.

Since nodes update the state in a distributed fashion, we must guarantee its availability. More specifically, in each round, only the elected nodes obtain the state. However, to vote for the following $O(log^2 n)$ rounds, elected executors must acquire the state of the previous round. For that reason, every node stores the state of the rounds it has executed and provides it upon request.

A final general challenge for dirty ledgers is to define light client constructions. Straightforward solutions such as providing inclusion proofs for the transactions committed to the ledger are not sufficient since the transactions can be invalid. To solve this challenge, we present the first non-interactive light client construction for dirty ledgers in the asynchronous model. In a nutshell, light clients learn information about the state by verifying the certificates produced by the executors, i.e., the valid state commitments, along with inclusion proofs.

Our paper has the following contributions.

- We formalize the SMR problem by separating it into ordering and execution.
- We propose a solution for the SMR execution layer with $O(\frac{log^2(n)}{n})$ cost per executor and near-optimal fault tolerance $f < (1 - \epsilon)n/2$, assuming the existence of the ordering layer.
- We extend our protocol for the proof-of-stake settings.
- We introduce the first non-interactive light client for dirty ledgers.

The structure of the paper is as follows. In Sect. 2 we present the related work, model and assumptions, as well as the problem definition of scaling execution. In Sect. 3, we overview our solutions for different settings, present the detailed solution of Horizontal Sampling in Sect. 4, and defer the solutions of deterministic and Proof-of-Stake in the full version of the paper [28]. Section 5 discusses the light client protocol and Sect. 6 discusses the data availability problem. We provide a summary of terminologies in Sect. 7, and all proofs of the protocols are deferred to the full version of the paper [28] due to space constraints.

2   Preliminaries

In this section, we give an overview of the related work on two components, separating the ordering and execution of transactions and defining light client constructions for dirty ledgers. Then, we define the model and the assumptions that our protocols build upon. Last, we define formally an SMR architecture composed of an ordering and an execution layer and the light client constructions.

2.1 Related Work

The natural way to separate the ordering from the execution is to let each node execute every round and add the state commitment to a subsequent block, leading to an average cost per block execution $O(1)$ [9,11,30]. The other promising approach to moving the computation of the state off-chain is employing a *rollup* protocol where a coordinator, updates the state of the system locally and only posts the state commitment on the main chain. There are two directions to verify the state commitments, *optimistic rollups* [5] and *ZK-rollups* [6].

In *optimistic rollups*, there is a dispute period during which executors can prove that a state commitment posted on the main chain is invalid. However, this technique requires synchrony assumptions and average cost per block execution $O(1)$ to guarantee that only valid state commitments are posted on the main chain. On the other hand, in *ZK-rollups*, the coordinator commits the state commitment along with a zero-knowledge proof (ZK-STARK) indicating that a specific set of transactions has been applied to the state. Nevertheless, *ZK-rollups* are not *censorship-resistant* since the coordinator can just not include some valid transactions in this set. Furthermore, computing ZK-STARKs is a computationally heavy for the users, and scaling general-purpose applications is challenging due to the difficulty to express general computation.

Finally, on the light-client for dirty ledgers domain, Tas et al. [29] proposed the first such solution in the synchronous model. In that work, a number of nodes, which are called *full nodes*, are in charge of updating the state of the system and providing state commitments to the light clients, proving their validity through an interactive game (bisection game). Unlike this solution we propose a light-client construction that is non-interactive, third-party verifiable (i.e., if a node is convinced it can convince other nodes as well) and works in the asynchronous model. This however, comes at the cost that we require an honest majority of executors that cannot be bribed or adaptively corrupted (for the probabilistic solution). We can also employ a fall-back mode in the protocol where any client not happy with the assumption above, but who assumes synchrony waits for any of the elected executors to provide a fraud-proof [8] or ask an honest full-node for the correctness of a state-commitment through bisection games. Both approaches have an honest minority assumption which will always be true with overwhelming probability. As a result, our proposal can easily be adapted to a flexible model [24] for heterogeneous clients.

2.2 Model and Assumptions

Communication Model: We assume an asynchronous environment, where any message sent can be delayed for an unspecified, but finite, amount of time. The link between every two honest nodes is reliable, namely when an honest node sends a message to another honest node, the message will eventually arrive.

Cryptographic Primitives: We use κ to denote the security parameter. We assume a large number of participants and let the security parameter be a function of that number as we will discuss. We assume the adversary is computationally bounded, the communication channels are cryptographically secure, and the existence of hash functions, signatures, and encryption schemes. We use a computationally hiding and perfectly binding commitment scheme: $(Compute_{cmt}, Verify_{cmt})$. We require the commitment scheme to be deterministic and provide inclusion proofs, e.g., it can be a Merkle tree. Moreover, users employ a Verifiable Random function (VRF) [25].

Permissioned Setting: We consider a fixed number of n nodes with their public keys known to every participant in the network. A genesis block G which describes the initial state of the system is provided both to the executors and to the clients. The adversary is static and can corrupt up to $f \leq (1 - \epsilon)\frac{n}{2}$ nodes in a Byzantine fashion before the protocol starts.

Proof of Stake: With the term node we refer to each identity that has an account on the system. The point of reference in the proof-of-stake system is a unit coin, which is the smallest amount of money existing. Each coin is a unique string linked to its owner. We assume each node is equipped with a private-public key pair. A genesis block G which contains the initial stake distribution is accessible to all nodes. The stake distribution is dynamic, namely the coins might change hands over time. We assume that the total amount of stake is fixed and equal to W in every round. The adversary is static and can corrupt a portion of the stake holders holding at most f coins, such that $f \leq (1 - \epsilon)\frac{W}{2}$ where $0 < \epsilon < \frac{1}{2}$, in a Byzantine fashion.

2.3   Problem Definition

Cohen et al. [13] introduced a modular SMR architecture, separating the data dissemination, ordering, and execution and they investigated solutions for the dissemination part. In this paper, we formulate the State Machine Replication (SMR) problem by diving it into an ordering and an execution layer. Solutions for the ordering layer include Blockchain protocols such as Byzantine Atomic Broadcast (BAB) [11,12,21,31], in which the nodes only agree on the order of the blocks without executing them. Our protocols are solutions for the execution layer.

State Machine Replication (SMR): A state machine consists of a set of state variables that encode its current state. External identities, users of the system, can issue commands to the state machine. The state machine executes the commands sequentially using a transition function to update the state of the system. Furthermore, the state machine might generate an output after executing each command. To provide fault-tolerant behavior, the state machine replicates in multiple copies. An SMR protocol aims to maintain synchronization between the replicas. In this paper, we illustrate that an SMR solution can be a composition of a protocol Π_1 for the *ordering layer* and a protocol Π_2 for the *execution layer*. Below, we define the *ordering* and the *execution* layers.

Ordering Layer: Consider a number of nodes, some of which can be adversarial, receiving transactions from external identities. The nodes organize the transactions in blocks. Furthermore, they employ a protocol Π_1 to agree on an order of the blocks. Each node i commits locally to a finalized ledger of blocks.

We denote the ledger to which node i commits in the round r by T_r^i. The output of the ordering protocol, i.e. the order of the blocks in which the nodes reach, is a ledger $T = b_0 \leftarrow b_1 \leftarrow ... \leftarrow b_i$. We introduce the properties that an ordering protocol must satisfy:

- *O-Safety*: There is no round r for which exist two honest nodes i, j s.t. $T_r^i \neq T_r^j$.
- *O-Liveness*: If an honest node receives an input tx, then all honest nodes will eventually include tx in a block of their local ledger.

Execution Layer: Consider a number of nodes where some of them can be adversarial. Moreover, consider the ledger of blocks $T = b_0 \leftarrow b_1 \leftarrow ... \leftarrow b_i$ output by the ordering layer, accessible to everyone. Each block might contain invalid transactions. The validity of a transaction depends on the logic of the application. The nodes are responsible for applying only the valid transactions within the blocks committed to the ledger T. The invalid transactions within the blocks are disregarded. Each node updates the state of the system. We denote the state of the system in the round r according to node's i view by S_r^i.

State: As a blockchain state, we denote a structure keeping track of each user's possessions. The content of the state depends on the type of transactions committed to the ledger. For instance, in Ethereum, the state captures the balance accounts of the users, while in Bitcoin the UTXO model is adopted. Furthermore, the state can contain fragments of code, e.g., smart contracts.

Ideal Functionality Π: We illustrate the correctness of the state of the system by introducing an ideal functionality Π. The functionality Π receives as input the ledger $T = b_0 \leftarrow b_1 \leftarrow ... \leftarrow b_i$ which is an output by the ordering layer. Π updates the state by applying all (and only) the valid transactions within the blocks committed to the ledger T. We denote the state of the system stored by Π for the round r by S_r^*. The initial state of the system S_0^* equal to the genesis block, $S_0^* = G$. To update the state in each round, Π uses the deterministic transition function *apply*. The inputs are the state of the previous round and the block to be executed in the current round. More specifically, in the round r, $S_r^* \leftarrow apply(b_r, S_{r-1}^*) = S_{r,len(b_r)}$ where

$$S_{r,j} = \begin{cases} S_{r-1}^* & \text{if } j = 0 \\ \text{apply\_tx}(S_{r,j-1}, tx_j) & \text{if } 1 \leq j \leq len(b_r) \end{cases}$$ and $b_r = [tx_1, ..., tx_{len(b_r)}]$. The

state applied to the function *apply_tx* remains unchanged when the input tx is an invalid transaction, namely $apply\_tx(S,tx)=S$. Therefore, for the ledger T, there exists a unique sequence of states $S_0^*, S_1^*, ..., S_i^*$ defined by the state transition function above.

In practice, nodes can employ any execution engine M that simulates the ideal functionality Π. When receiving as inputs the correct state of r and the block $r + 1$, the engine M outputs the correct state of $r + 1$.

An execution layer guarantees that the honest nodes simulate the ideal functionality Π. We proceed with defining the properties of an execution layer:

- *E-Safety*: There is no round r for which exists an honest node i that commits on a state S_r^i s.t. $S_r^i \neq S_r^*$.

- *E-Liveness*: For any round r where an honest node i commits a state S_r^i, there exists a round $r' > r$ where node i eventually commits a state $S_{r'}^i$ s.t. $S_r^i \neq S_{r'}^i$.

Since nodes keep updating their state without deviating from the ideal functionality Π, an execution protocol is *Censorship Resistant*, namely it satisfies the following property:

- *Censorship Resistance:* Every valid transaction tx committed to the ledger T will eventually be applied in the state.

Note that the liveness property ensures only that each honest node will eventually update its state. Since not all nodes execute for every round essentially, we do not require that the honest nodes update their states in the same rounds. **State Machine Replication:** Finally, we formulate the SMR problem on top of the ordering and execution layers. More specifically, transactions issued by external identities constitute the input of the SMR. An SMR protocol consists of an ordering layer protocol Π_1 and an execution layer protocol Π_2 satisfying the properties *O-Safety*, *O-Liveness* and *E-Safety*, *E-Liveness* respectively. Nodes participating in those protocols may or may not be the same. The output of Π_1 which is a ledger of blocks T is the input of Π_2. The output of the machine is the output of Π_2, namely an ever-growing state sequence $S_0, S_1, S_2, ..., S_i$.
Light Client. Consider an execution layer Π_e with input a ledger T and the average size of the state that the ideal functionality Π outputs in any round $|S|$. The execution layer supports light client constructions. Light clients request succinct proofs from the participating nodes to learn desired information about the state of the system. We capture this idea by defining the *state proof* certificates.

- A *state proof* π_S for the round r is a succinct proof indicating that the state S is the correct state of the round r. Proof π_S is correct if and only if $S = S_r^*$, where S_r^* is the output of the functionality Π for the round r.
- A *state proof* π for the round r is succinct if it contains asymptotically less data than the history of states, namely if $\frac{len(\pi)}{r|S|} = o(1)$

Assume that the light client lc_i receives a *state proof* π_S for the round r without necessarily receiving the state S. Lc_i evaluates whether the proof is correct, in its perception, using a predicate $accept_{lc_i}(\pi_S, r)$ which yields either True or False. The light client lc_i accepts π_S if and only if $accept_{lc_i}(\pi_S, r) = True$. The properties which a light client execution layer protocol must satisfy are the following:

- *LC-Safety*: There is no round r for which exists a light client lc_i that receives a proof π_S for the round r s.t. $accept_{lc_i}(\pi_S, r) = True$ and $S \neq S_r^*$.
- *LC-Liveness*: A light client bootstrapping in the round r will eventually receive a proof $\pi_{S_{r'}}$ for a round $r', r' \geq r$ s.t. $accept_{lc_i}(\pi_{S'}, r') = True$.

Additional Assumptions: We assume the existence of an underlying ledger T as an output of an *ordering layer* Π that satisfies the properties of *O-Safety*, *O-Liveness*. The ledger T is accessible to every node. Furthermore, we assume that there are no duplicate transactions committed to T. Finally, we assume that for each round a random seed is provided by the dirty ledger, similarly to Algorand [19], or DAG-based BFT protocols [14,20,21].

3   Overview of the Protocols

In our proposed protocols, executors update the state of the system in a distributed fashion. We decompose the protocols in two phases, an *election phase* and a *voting phase*. The *election phase* will select a set of executors for every round. Then, in the *voting phase* the elected executors of that round compute and broadcast their signed state commitments. The *voting phase* outputs *valid* state commitments, as defined:

- A state commitment is considered to be valid if and only if either it is signed by at least one honest node or it is the genesis block.

The goal is to ensure that only *correct* state commitments, defined below, will become *valid*.

- A state commitment *cmt* is the *correct* state commitment of round r if and only if $cmt = compute_{cmt}(S_r^*)$, where S_r^* is state of round r defined by the ideal functionality of the execution layer as in Sect. 2.

There are two challenges when solving the problem. The first is to ensure that there is provably at least one honest node that has voted a state commitment to guarantee its validity. The second is to ensure that when elected nodes enter the *voting phase*, they have the state of the previous round available. Below we explain how we tackle these challenges for different settings.

Permissioned and Deterministic. First, we present a straightforward deterministic protocol for the permissioned settings to lay the foundation of our other solutions. We consider a total number of $n = 2f+1$ executors (instead of $n > 3f$), with f executors corrupted by a static adversary. Every node executes for each round, i.e., each executor starts from the genesis block and updates the state by applying the valid transactions of the dirty ledger. For every round, executors compute, sign, and broadcast the corresponding state commitment. A state commitment is valid if it is signed by at least $f + 1$ nodes so that at least one honest node is included.

Probabilistic Solutions. The straightforward deterministic solution requires every executor to run for every round, which is not scalable. For better scalability, we propose probabilistic protocols for the permissioned and the Proof-of-Stake settings. We assume up to $f \leq (1 - \epsilon)\frac{n}{2}$ executors can be corrupted by a static adversary, where ϵ is some constant. Our protocols guarantee the validity of a state commitment by requiring a threshold of executors to sign the state commitment. To ensure safety, the number of adversarial nodes executing in each round must be less than this threshold. To ensure liveness, in each round, there must be enough honest nodes executing to form a valid state commitment. We set the threshold for the valid state commitment to be $1/2$ of the number of elected executors, and demonstrate that the aforementioned property is satisfied with a overwhelming probability in the security parameter by electing only a poly-logarithmic number of nodes per round.

Vertical vs Horizontal Sampling. The straightforward probabilistic solution is to elect a *committee* of poly-logarithmic size per round who broadcasts signed state commitments. A state commitment is considered valid if it is signed by at least half of the committee members. We call this approach *Vertical Sampling*. Each node is elected on average once per $O(\frac{n}{polylogn})$ rounds and executes for only the respective rounds. Instead, we adopt an approach we call *Horizontal Sampling*, in which only expected constant number (e.g. one) of nodes are elected per round. In that solution, every node is elected on average every n rounds and executes for $O(polylogn)$ rounds. In both cases the cost per block execution is $O(\frac{polylogn}{n})$. However, since nodes update their execution states in a distributed fashion, elected nodes may need to retrieve the previous execution state from other nodes in order to execute the current round, which incurs high communication overhead. In *Horizontal Sampling*, in comparison to the *Vertical Sampling*, nodes request the state less frequently, resulting in a more scalable solution.

Permissioned and Randomized. First, we present the *Horizontal Sampling* protocol for the permissioned settings. During the *election phase*, each executor computes the VRF locally in each round. Only one node on average is elected per round. The elected node starts from the state of the previous round, computes and broadcasts state commitments for the following $O(polylogn)$ rounds. Hence, with only one executor elected per round, a poly-logarithmic number of nodes will vote for each round. State commitments signed by at least half of the elected nodes are considered valid.

Proof-of-Stake (PoS). We then extend the *Horizontal Sampling* protocol for the Proof-of-Stake settings. In the permissioned settings, each node computes a VRF for the *election phase*. In PoS, the adversary can create numerous accounts to increase the probability of being elected. To make the protocol Sybil Resistant, each node's election probability is proportional to its stake. Concretely, nodes compute the VRF for all of their coins in the *election phase*. In the *voting phase*, elected nodes compute and broadcast their signed state commitments, as in the permissioned protocol.

An extra challenge in the PoS protocol is that the stake distribution changes over time. In every round, each node keeps track of its own stake and only the elected nodes execute the state. Therefore, elected nodes must prove the ownership of elected coins to the rest of the nodes. To this end, they construct and broadcast inclusion proofs along with their signed state commitments.

State Availability. In the probabilistic protocols, not all nodes execute for every round to acquire the respective the state of every round. For liveness, our protocol must guarantee state availability, i.e., any node is able to acquire the state of the previous round every time when it executes the current round.

Since any valid state commitment is signed by at least one honest node, the corresponding state will eventually be available to any node requesting it.

Light Clients. Lastly, we introduce a non-interactive light client construction for our protocols. We assume that at any given time, each light client is connected to at least one honest executor. Briefly, a non-interactive light client can learn information about the state of the system after receiving a valid state commitment from an executor, along with an inclusion proof (e.g. Merkle proof).

4   Protocols

In this section, we present our asynchronous execution layer protocols on top of an underlying dirty ledger. First, in the permissioned settings, we present the deterministic protocol demonstrating how to construct verifiable certificates that correspond to the correct state, i.e., the valid state commitments. The deterministic protocol suggests that a majority of honest nodes is a necessary and sufficient condition to construct valid state commitments. Due to its simplicity, we omit the details here and refer the reader to the full version of the paper [28]. However, in the deterministic protocol, every node executes for every round resulting in cost per block execution O(1). Next, we define a probabilistic scalable protocol called Horizontal Sampling, where in every round we select only a poly-logarithmic number of nodes to execute so that the majority of them are honest with overwhelming probability. Due to space limitations, we only present the details of the horizontal sampling protocol and some intuitive descriptions for the Proof-of-Stake protocol in Sect. 4.2 in the main paper, and leave other protocol details in the full version of the paper [28].

4.1   Horizontal Sampling

In the deterministic protocol, all nodes execute in every round and broadcast their state commitments. Now, we proceed with building an efficient probabilistic protocol, called *Horizontal Sampling*, illustrated in Algorithm 1. We assume up to $f \leq (1 - \epsilon)\frac{n}{2}$ executors can be corrupted by a static adversary where ϵ is some constant, and we choose the security parameter $\kappa = O(\log^2 n)$ for this section. Nodes first download the genesis block G which holds the initial state. In each round, every node checks whether it is elected (Algorithm 1, line 28). Elected nodes propose state commitments during the *voting phase*. The *voting phase* outputs valid state commitments, which are state commitments signed by enough executors.

Election Phase: In each round, every node computes the VRF using its private key, the round number, and the corresponding random seed. This computation returns two values, a hash value of length $|h|$ and a proof of authenticity certifying this hash value (Algorithm 1, line 27). We refer to this proof as the *proof of election* of the leaders. All nodes with hash value in round r of less than

$$X_r = \begin{cases} \kappa \frac{2^{|h|}}{n}, & \text{if } r = 1 \\ \frac{2^{|h|}}{n}, & \text{if } r > 1 \end{cases}$$ are elected (Algorithm 1, line 28). In that way, in the

first round there will be expected κ elected nodes constituting the *bootstrap committee*, while for $r > 1$ there will be only one node in expectation, which is called the leader.

Validity of a Commitment: For the first κ rounds only the members of the *bootstrap committee* are voting. For any round $r \geq \kappa + 1$ all the elected nodes in the interval $[r - \kappa + 1, r]$ compute the state commitments. In the full version of the paper [28], we prove that the *bootstrap committee* consists of at least $\frac{\kappa}{2}$ honest nodes and at most $\frac{\kappa}{2} - 1$ adversarial nodes with overwhelming probability in n (we choose $\kappa = O(\log^2 n)$). The same property holds for the elected nodes in any interval of κ consecutive rounds. As a result, in each round, at least $\frac{\kappa}{2}$ honest and at most $\frac{\kappa}{2} - 1$ adversarial nodes will be responsible for voting. Therefore, a state commitment corresponding to a round r can be considered as valid if it is signed by at least $\frac{\kappa}{2}$ nodes among those that are elected to execute during the interval of rounds $[max(1, r - \kappa + 1), r]$ or if it is the genesis block. In Fig. 1, on the left side we present an example of the leaders' votes in the interval $[r, r + 3]$ where the malicious leader L_{r+2} votes for incorrect state commitment for rounds $r + 2, r + 3$; on the right side we present an example of the committee members voting for the execution state commitments of different rounds, and the malicious nodes try to create a fork on the execution state.

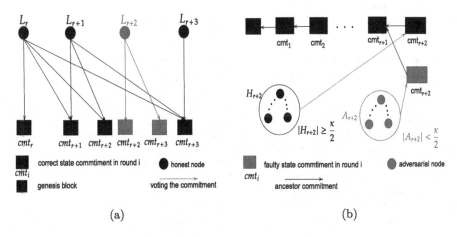

(a)   (b)

Fig. 1. Figure (a) illustrates the elected leaders' votes in the round interval $[r, r + 3]$, resulting in the fork in the chain of the proposed state commitments illustrated in figure (b). The set H_i (or A_i) consists of the votes of the honest (or adversarial) elected leaders in the interval $[r - \kappa + 3, r + 2]$.

Voting Phase: For the first κ rounds, the *bootstrap committee* members form the respective valid state commitments. To update the state, they apply the transactions committed to the ledger for all these rounds starting from the genesis block. For every round, they compute and broadcast their signed state commitments along with their proof of election.

Now consider node p_i, an elected leader in some round $r \geq 2$ during the *voting phase* (Algorithm 1, Procedure Execute). First, p_i waits until witnessing

---

Algorithm 1: Horizontal Sampling: Node p_i with public key pk_i and secret key sk_i

---

1   $state(0) \leftarrow G$ `// genesis block`

2   `threshold` $\leftarrow \frac{\kappa}{2}, state\_com \leftarrow \{\}$

3   $r_{cur} \leftarrow 1$ `// current round`

    `/* verify the election proof with public key` p_k `in the round` r `*/`

4   **Predicate** $TimeToExecute(p_k, r, u, \pi)$:

5       $target \leftarrow \frac{2^{|h|}}{n}\kappa$ **if** $r = 1,$ **else** $\frac{2^{|h|}}{n}$ `// threshold for the election` process

6   **return** $VerifyVRF_{p_k}(u, \pi, seed_r||r) \wedge u \leq Target(r)$

    `/* check whether` cmt `comes from a valid leader of round` r_l `that is` `responsible for executing in round` r `*/`

7   **Predicate** $AcceptCommitment(p_k, r_l, u, \pi, r, \sigma, cmt)$:

8   **return** $\neg(r_l > 1 \wedge r \leq \kappa) \wedge (r_l \leq r \leq$ $r_l + \kappa - 1) \wedge Verify(\sigma, p_k, cmt||r) \wedge TimeToExecute(p_k, r_l, u, \pi)$

    `/* acquiring the state of round` r `*/`

9   **Procedure** $AcquireState(r)$:

10   **Wait** until $\exists (cmt, r) \; s.t. |state\_com[(cmt, r)]| \geq threshold$

11   **if** $state(r) = null$ **then**

12   **request** $state(r)$

13   **wait** until receiving $state$ s.t. $Compute_{cmt}(state) = cmt$

14          $state(r) \leftarrow state$

    `/* compute and broadcast the signed state commitments for all the` `intermediate rounds within the interval` $[r_l, r_l + \kappa - 1]$ `*/`

15   **Procedure** $Execute(r_l, (u, \pi))$:

16      $AcquireState(r_l - 1)$ **if** $r_l > 1$

17   **for** $r = r_l, ..., r_l + \kappa - 1$ **do**

18   **download** $data(r)$ `// data within the block with height` r

19          $state(r) \leftarrow apply(state(r - 1), data(r))$

20   **continue if** $r_l > 1 \wedge r \leq \kappa$ `// only bootstrap committee votes`

21          $cmt \leftarrow Compute_{cmt}(state(r))$

22          $\sigma \leftarrow Sign(cmt||r, pk_i, sk_i)$

23          $state\_com[(r, cmt)].add((pk_i, r_l, u, \pi, \sigma))$

24   Send $("state\ cmt", cmt, r_l, r, \sigma, u, \pi)$ to all nodes

    `/* Main loop, run leader election for each round`   `*/`

25   **while** $True$ **do**

26      $(u, \pi) \leftarrow VRF_{sk}(seed_{r_{cur}}||r_{cur})$

27   **if** $u \leq Target(r_{cur})$ **then**

28          $Execute(r_{cur}, (u, \pi))$

29      $r_{cur} \leftarrow r_{cur} + 1$

30   **Upon** $receiving("state\ cmt", cmt, r_l, r, \sigma, u, \pi)$ *from the node with public key* pk_j *for the first time for round* r_l **do** :

31   **if** $AcceptCommitment(pk_j, r_l, u, \pi, r, \sigma, cmt)$ **then**

32          $state\_com[(r, cmt)].add((pk_j, r_l, u, \pi, \sigma))$

---

a valid state commitment for the round $r - 1$. After receiving the valid state, the leader acquires the corresponding state. If the state is not available from a previous execution, p_i requests it from all the nodes that have signed the commitment (Algorithm 1, lines 13–14) (more on data availability in Sect. 6). Then, p_i downloads the data committed to the ledger for the intermediate rounds and applies it sequentially to obtain the state of the round $r+\kappa-1$. For each round, it constructs and signs the respective state commitment. Finally, p_i broadcasts the signed state commitments along with the proof of its election to the rest of the nodes. We note again that only *bootstrap committee* members vote for the first κ rounds (Algorithm 1 line 21). The rest of the nodes accept the received commitments only after confirming $p_i's$ signature and proof of election (Algorithm 1, lines 8–9).

Due to space limitation, we defer the correctness proof of the Horizontal Sampling algorithm to the full version of the paper [28].

4.2   Proof-of-Stake Settings

Now we extend the *Horizontal Sampling* protocol to the proof-of-stake setting. Participating nodes have accounts holding stake/coins, and we use W to denote the total amount of the stake in the system. New nodes can dynamically join the system, and we demonstrate bootstrapping later. We assume up to $f \leq (1-\epsilon)\frac{W}{2}$ stake can be corrupted by a static adversary, where ϵ is some constant, and we choose the security parameter $\kappa = O(\log^2 W)$ for this section.

First, all nodes download the genesis block G which contains the initial stake distribution. The stake distribution can change over time. More specifically, we decompose the protocol into the following phases. In each round, every node participates in the *election phase* to check whether any of its coins is elected. During the *voting phase*, nodes with at least one elected coin compute state commitments like in the permissioned protocol.

Tracking Wealth: The stake distribution changes over time and the nodes do not necessarily acquire the execution state of each round. Hence the challenge for a node is to check whether the transactions it receives are successful or not. In our protocol, the node requests a *proof of payment* certificate from the payer, (see Sect. 5), to verify that its state has changed as expected and therefore the transaction was successful.

Election Phase: In each round, every node computes the VRF using its owned coins and the randomness seed coming from the dirty ledger to generate *proofs of election* for the elected coins. Similarly to the permissioned protocol, the PoS protocol elects a *bootstrap committee* for the first round, and elects on average one coin per round for every round $r > 1$. To keep the threshold of a valid state commitment identical for every round, only the *bootstrap committee* members are voting for the first κ rounds, while for $r \geq 2$ the owner of an elected coin in round r can vote for every round in the interval $[max(r, \kappa + 1), r + \kappa - 1]$. A state commitment for the round r is valid if it is signed by the owners of at least $\frac{\kappa}{2}$ of the elected coins during the interval of rounds $[max(1, r - t + 1), r]$ or if it is the genesis block.

Proof of Ownership: Since nodes track only their own stake, the elected nodes must prove that they own the elected coins. Hence, they provide inclusion proofs for their elected coins using the valid state commitment of the previous round, e.g., the commitment can be the Merkle root in a Merkle proof. We call these certificates *proofs of ownership* and the corresponding state commitment *parent commitment.* To be able to verify the *proofs of payment* in order to track its stake, and to compute the *proofs of ownership* in case of election, each node waits for the valid state commitment of the previous round before participating in the election phase.

Voting Phase: The *voting phase* is similar to the permissioned protocol. First, the *bootstrap committee* members compute and broadcast their signed state commitments for every round $r \leq \kappa$ to form the respective valid state commitment. Then, every node with an elected coin in the round r, can start from the state corresponding to the valid state commitment of the round $r - 1$. Moreover, the node uses the valid state commitment to construct the *proof of ownership* for its elected coin. Finally, the elected node computes and broadcasts the signed state commitments for all the intermediate rounds along with the *proof of election* and the *proof of ownership* in the round r. To accept a signed state commitment, nodes first verify the related certificates. Especially for *proofs of ownership*, nodes wait until the *parent commitment* becomes valid.

Bootstrapping: Consider *Bob*, a node that wishes to join the network in the round r. We assume that *Bob* is connected to at least one honest executor. Bob has received from many nodes a data structure called *chain* that contains the state commitments signed by the elected nodes along with the respective certificates (signatures, proofs of election, and proofs of ownership) for each round.

Bob downloads the genesis block G first. For each *chain*, *Bob* applies the following approach to evaluate whether it is the correct one. For the first round, *Bob* verifies only the *proofs of election* of the *bootstrap committee* members since the initial stake distribution is contained in G. Then, for each vote up to round r, he verifies the signatures, the *proof of ownership*, and the *proof of election* of the elected nodes. When *Bob* receives the correct *chain*, it acquires the last valid state commitment in the *chain* and requests the corresponding state (Sect. 6).

5   Light Clients Protocol

Once we have a system where executors can verify that a payment has been made, it is simple to transform it to the first non-interactive, asynchronous light-client for dirty ledgers. In this section, we demonstrate how a light client can learn the state of the system. First, we discuss how a light client can acquire and verify a *state proof.* Then, we use *state proofs* as a building block to prove that a change in the state occurred.

Assumptions: Each light client has access to the random seed for each round through the dirty ledger, in order to verify the leader election. In addition, each light client is connected to at least one honest executor. An executor uses a gossip protocol to obtain information necessary to react to a light client's requests, such as the state that corresponds to a valid state commitment.

Bootstrapping: Assume that the height of the dirty ledger equals h and a light client lc_i bootstraps in the round $r \leq h$. First, we illustrate how lc_i can verify a *state proof*. A validity proof of the state commitment corresponding to the state S constitutes the *state proof* π_S. The light client then chooses how to connect to the network. One option is to receive the corresponding state and derive the desired information after downloading and applying the data committed to the ledger on its own. Otherwise, lc_i can reconnect to the network whenever it needs a *proof of payment* certificate.

State Proof - Permissioned Settings: To bootstrap in the round r, lc_i waits to receive a valid state commitment for some round greater than or equal to the round r. In the *deterministic protocol*, lc_i verifies that a state commitment is signed by at least $f + 1$ nodes. In the *Horizontal Sampling protocol*, a valid state commitment in a round r' is voted by at least $\frac{\kappa}{2}$ elected leaders in the interval $[max(1, r' - \kappa + 1), r']$. Each leader's vote includes their signature and proof of election. Lc_i verifies this using the Predicate *AcceptStateProof* in Algorithm 2.

Algorithm 2: Light Client protocol - Horizontal Sampling

1   threshold $\leftarrow \frac{\kappa}{2}$
    /* check whether there are at least $\frac{\kappa}{2}$ signatures for *cmt* by leaders
      of rounds $[r - t + 1, r]$ in Σ */
2   **Predicate** *AcceptStateProof(cmt, r, Σ))* :
3   Remove duplicates in Σ
4   **return**
         $|AcceptCommitment(p_k, r_l, u, \pi, r, \sigma, cmt) : (p_k, r_l, u, \pi, \sigma) \in \Sigma| \geq threshold$
5   **Predicate** *PaymentProof(cmt, r, Σ, $\pi_{inclusion\_proof}$)* :
6   **return** AcceptStateProof(cmt, r, Σ)$\wedge$ state change occurred according to
         the $\pi_{inclusion\_proof}$

State Proof - Proof-of-Stake Settings: The light client bootstraps as explained in Sect. 4.2. In a nutshell, for each round, lc_i requires and verifies the signatures, the *proof of ownership*, and the *proof of election* coming from the owners of the elected coins that have voted for the valid state commitments.

Proofs of Payment: We now demonstrate how to provide certificates for successful transactions. Consider Alice and Bob, two light clients using our system. Bob wishes to purchase a product from Alice, triggering a transaction that will be logged in the dirty ledger. Alice needs a proof that the payment is successful before providing the merchandise to Bob.

Assume that the transaction of Bob paying Alice is committed at round r. The certificate with which Bob proves that Alice's state is changed in round r is called *proof of payment*. More specifically, the certificate constitutes of a valid state commitment for any round greater than r and a short inclusion proof (e.g. a Merkle proof) indicating Alice's new state. Alice uses the Predicate PaymentProof in Algorithm 2 to verify first the validity of the state commitment and then the inclusion proof, using the valid state commitment, to extract her new state. If the transaction is successful, Alice's state is changed during this interval.

6   Data Availability

In this section, we discuss what data executors store locally to support the proposed protocols.

State Availability: Nodes responsible for executing in a particular round need to acquire first the state of a previous round. It is also required by the *Proof of payment* and bootstrapping in the proof-of-stake settings (Sect. 4.2).

We let the executors store every state they executed. In all of the proposed protocols, each valid state commitment is signed by at least one honest node which has stored the state with overwhelming probability. An executor requests the state that corresponds to a *valid* state commitment from all the nodes that have signed the respective state commitment. The honest node that has signed the state commitment will eventually provide it to the executor. The executor will verify that the state indeed corresponds to the valid state commitment.

Certificate Availability: To support bootstrapping protocols, executors store the certificates related to the valid state commitments. In the deterministic protocol, they only store the signed state commitments. In the Horizontal Sampling protocol, executors store the signed valid state commitments along with the leaders' proofs of election (Algorithm 1 lines: 24, 33), and in the proof-of-stake settings, they additionally keep the *proofs of ownership* of the elected coins.

7   Summary of Terminologies

We summarize the terminologies used in this paper in Table 1.

Table 1. Terminologies

Notation	Description
n	total number of nodes in the permissioned settings
f	number of adversarial nodes (or coins held by adversarial nodes) in the permissioned settings (or in PoS)
W	total amount of stake in PoS
proof of election	proofs coming from the VRF computation of the elected nodes in the probabilistic protocols
proof of ownership with parent commitment cmt	inclusion proof with hash header cmt demonstrating that a node p_i owns a particular coin in PoS

8   Conclusion

In this paper, we demonstrated how *Horizontal Sampling* converts an atomic broadcast (BAB) solution to an SMR (or how to execute the state on top of a dirty ledger). To this end, *Horizontal Sampling* is an efficient distributed execution protocol that consists of two phases. First, there is a voting phase where a constant number of nodes are selected. Second, the selected nodes execute and propose state commitments for the following polylogn rounds during the voting phase. *Horizontal Sampling* is a censorship-resistant solution that does not violate the network assumptions of the underlying ledger. Lastly, we illustrated how to leverage *Horizontal Sampling* for defining non-interactive light clients that learn the state of the system.

Acknowledgements. Eleftherios Kokoris-Kogias is partially supported by Austrian Science Fund (FWF) grant No: F8512-N.

References

1. Bringing the World to Ethereum | Polygon. www.polygon.technology
2. Fuel Network. www.fuel.network
3. Neon Team. Neon EVM. www.neon-labs.org/Neon_EVM.pdf. Accessed 3 Aug 2022
4. Optimism. www.optimism.io
5. Optimistic rollups: How they work and why they matter (2021). www.medium.com/stakefish/optimistic-rollups-how-they-work-and-why-they-matter-3f677a504fcf
6. What is a zero-knowledge (ZK) rollup? (2022). www.zebpay.com/blog/what-is-a-zero-knowledge-rollup-zk
7. Al-Bassam, M.: LazyLedger: a distributed data availability ledger with client-side smart contracts. arXiv preprint arXiv:1905.09274 (2019)
8. Al-Bassam, M., Sonnino, A., Buterin, V.: Fraud proofs: maximising light client security and scaling blockchains with dishonest majorities. arXiv preprint arXiv: 1809.09044, 160 (2018)
9. Androulaki, E., et al.: Hyperledger fabric: a distributed operating system for permissioned blockchains. In: Proceedings of the Thirteenth EuroSys Conference, pp. 1–15 (2018)
10. Bertoni, G., Daemen, J., Peeters, M., Van Assche, G.: On the indifferentiability of the sponge construction. In: Smart, N. (ed.) EUROCRYPT 2008. LNCS, vol. 4965, pp. 181–197. Springer, Heidelberg (2008). https://doi.org/10.1007/978-3-540-78967-3_11
11. Buchman, E.: Tendermint: Byzantine fault tolerance in the age of blockchains. Ph.D. thesis, University of Guelph (2016)
12. Castro, M., Liskov, B., et al.: Practical byzantine fault tolerance. In: OSDI, vol. 99, pp. 173–186 (1999)
13. Cohen, S., Goren, G., Kokoris-Kogias, L., Sonnino, A., Spiegelman, A.: Proof of availability & retrieval in a modular blockchain architecture. Cryptology ePrint Archive (2022)
14. Danezis, G., Kokoris-Kogias, L., Sonnino, A., Spiegelman, A.; Narwhal and Tusk: a DAG-based mempool and efficient BFT consensus. In: Proceedings of the Seventeenth European Conference on Computer Systems, pp. 34–50 (2022)

15. Défago, X., Schiper, A., Urbán, P.: Total order broadcast and multicast algorithms: taxonomy and survey. ACM Comput. Surv. (CSUR) **36**(4), 372–421 (2004)
16. Faleiro, J.M., Abadi, D.J.: Rethinking serializable multiversion concurrency control. arXiv preprint arXiv:1412.2324 (2014)
17. Gelashvili, R., Kokoris-Kogias, L., Sonnino, A., Spiegelman, A., Xiang, Z.: Jolteon and Ditto: network-adaptive efficient consensus with asynchronous fallback. In: Eyal, I., Garay, J. (eds.) Financial Cryptography and Data Security, FC 2022. LNCS, vol. 13411, pp. 296–315. Springer, Cham (2022). https://doi.org/10.1007/978-3-031-18283-9_14
18. Gelashvili, R., et al.: Block-STM: scaling blockchain execution by turning ordering curse to a performance blessing. arXiv preprint arXiv:2203.06871 (2022)
19. Gilad, Y., Hemo, R., Micali, S., Vlachos, G., Zeldovich, N.: Algorand: scaling Byzantine agreements for cryptocurrencies. In: Proceedings of the 26th Symposium on Operating Systems Principles, pp. 51–68 (2017)
20. Giridharan, N., Kokoris-Kogias, L., Sonnino, A., Spiegelman, A.: Bullshark: DAG BFT protocols made practical. arXiv preprint arXiv:2201.05677 (2022)
21. Keidar, I., Kokoris-Kogias, E., Naor, O., Spiegelman, A.: All you need is DAG. In: Proceedings of the 2021 ACM Symposium on Principles of Distributed Computing, pp. 165–175 (2021)
22. Kogias, E.K., Jovanovic, P., Gailly, N., Khoffi, I., Gasser, L., Ford, B.: Enhancing bitcoin security and performance with strong consistency via collective signing. USENIX Association (2016)
23. Lamport, L., Shostak, R., Pease, M.: The Byzantine generals problem. In: Concurrency: The Works of Leslie Lamport, pp. 203–226 (2019)
24. Malkhi, D., Nayak, K., Ren, L.: Flexible Byzantine fault tolerance. In: Proceedings of the 2019 ACM SIGSAC Conference on Computer and Communications Security, pp. 1041–1053 (2019)
25. Micali, S., Rabin, M., Vadhan, S.: Verifiable random functions. In: 40th Annual Symposium on Foundations of Computer Science (cat. No. 99CB37039), pp. 120–130. IEEE (1999)
26. Polynya: Rollups, data availability layers & modular blockchains: introductory meta post (2021). www.polynya.medium.com/rollups-data-availability-layers-modular-blockchains-introductory-meta-post-5a1e7a60119d
27. Stathakopoulou, C., David, T., Pavlovic, M., Vukolić, M.: Mir-BFT: high-throughput robust BFT for decentralized networks. arXiv preprint arXiv:1906.05552 (2019)
28. Stefo, C., Xiang, Z., Kokoris-Kogias, L.: Executing and proving over dirty ledgers. Cryptology ePrint Archive (2022)
29. Tas, E.N., Zindros, D., Yang, L., Tse, D.: Light clients for lazy blockchains. arXiv preprint arXiv:2203.15968 (2022)
30. The DiemBFT Team: State machine replication in the diem blockchain (2021). www.developers.diem.com/docs/technical-papers/state-machine-replication-paper
31. Yin, M., Malkhi, D., Reiter, M.K., Gueta, G.G., Abraham, I.: HotStuff: BFT consensus with linearity and responsiveness. In: Proceedings of the 2019 ACM Symposium on Principles of Distributed Computing, pp. 347–356 (2019)

Byzantine Generals in the Permissionless Setting

Andrew Lewis-Pye[1]([⊠]) [iD] and Tim Roughgarden[2,3] [iD]

[1] London School of Economics, London, UK
a.lewis7@lse.ac.uk
[2] Columbia University, New York, USA
[3] a16z Crypto, New York, USA
troughgarden@a16z.com

Abstract. Consensus protocols have traditionally been studied in the *permissioned* setting, where all participants are known to each other from the start of the protocol execution. What differentiates the most prominent blockchain protocol Bitcoin [15] from these previously studied protocols is that it operates in a *permissionless* setting, i.e. it is a protocol for establishing consensus over an unknown network of participants that anybody can join, with as many identities as they like in any role. The arrival of this new form of protocol brings with it many questions. Beyond Bitcoin and other proof-of-work (PoW) protocols, what can we prove about permissionless protocols in a general sense? How does the recent stream of work on permissionless protocols relate to the well-developed history of research on permissioned protocols?

To help answer these questions, we describe a formal framework for the analysis of both permissioned and permissionless systems. Our framework allows for "apples-to-apples" comparisons between different categories of protocols and, in turn, the development of theory to formally discuss their relative merits. A major benefit of the framework is that it facilitates the application of a rich history of proofs and techniques for permissioned systems to problems in blockchain and the study of permissionless systems. Within our framework, we then address the questions above. We consider a programme of research that asks, "Under what adversarial conditions, and for what types of permissionless protocol, is consensus possible?" We prove several results for this programme, our main result being that *deterministic* consensus is not possible for permissionless protocols.

Keywords: Consensus · Proof-of-Work · Proof-of-Stake · Proof-of-Space

1 Introduction

The Byzantine Generals Problem [14,18] was introduced by Lamport, Shostak and Pease to formalise the problem of reaching consensus in a context where faulty processors may display arbitrary behaviour. The problem has subsequently become a central topic in distributed computing. Of particular relevance to us

© International Financial Cryptography Association 2024
F. Baldimtsi and C. Cachin (Eds.): FC 2023, LNCS 13950, pp. 21–37, 2024.
https://doi.org/10.1007/978-3-031-47754-6_2

here are the seminal works of Dwork, Lynch and Stockmeyer [8], who considered the problem in a range of synchronicity settings, and the result of Dolev and Strong [7] showing that, even in the strongly synchronous setting of reliable next-round message delivery with PKI, $f + 1$ rounds of interaction are necessary to solve the problem if up to f parties are faulty.

The Permissionless Setting (and The Need for a Framework). This rich history of analysis considers the problem of consensus in the *permissioned* setting, where all participants are known to each other from the start of the protocol execution. More recently, however, there has been significant interest in a number of protocols, such as Bitcoin [15] and Ethereum [3], that operate in a fundamentally different way. What differentiates these new protocols is that they operate in a *permissionless* setting, i.e. these are protocols for establishing consensus over an unknown network of participants that anybody can join, with as many identities as they like in any role. Interest in these new protocols is such that, at the time of writing, Bitcoin has a market capitalisation of over \$400 billion.[1] Given the level of investment, it seems important to put the study of permissionless protocols on a firm theoretical footing.

Since results for the permissioned setting rely on bounding the number of faulty participants, and since there may be an *unbounded* number of faulty participants in the permissionless setting, it is clear that classical results for the permissioned setting will not carry over to the permissionless setting directly. Consider the aforementioned proof of Dolev and Strong [7] that $f + 1$ rounds are required if f many participants may be faulty, for example. If the number of faulty participants is unbounded, then the apparent conclusion is that consensus is not possible. To make consensus possible in the permissionless setting, some substantial changes to the setup assumptions are therefore required. Bitcoin approaches this issue by introducing the notion of 'proof-of-work' (PoW) and limiting the computational (or hashing) power of faulty participants. A number of papers [9,10,16] consider frameworks for the analysis of Bitcoin and other PoW protocols. The PoW mechanism used by Bitcoin is, however, just one approach to defining permissionless protocols. As has been well documented [2], proof-of-stake (PoS) protocols, such as Ouroboros [13] and Algorand [6], are a form of permissionless protocol with very different properties, and face a different set of design challenges. As we will expand on here, there are a number of reasons why PoS protocols do not fit into the previously mentioned frameworks for the analysis of Bitcoin. The deeper question remains, how best to understand permissionless protocols more generally?

Defining a Framework. Our first aim is to describe a framework that allows one to formally describe and analyse both permissioned and permissionless protocols in a general sense, and to compare their properties. To our knowledge, our framework is the first capable of modelling all significant features of PoW and PoS protocols simultaneously, as well as other approaches like proof-of-space [19].

---

[1] See www.coinmarketcap.com for a comprehensive list of cryptocurrencies and their market capitalisations.

This allows us to prove general impossibility results for permissionless protocols. The framework is constructed according to two related design principles:

1. Our aim is to establish a framework capable of dealing with permissionless protocols, but which is as similar as possible to the standard frameworks in distributed computing for dealing with permissioned protocols. As we will see in Sects. 3 and 4, a major benefit of this approach is that it facilitates the application of classical proofs and techniques in distributed computing to problems in 'blockchain' and the study of permissionless protocols.
2. We aim to produce a framework which is as accessible as possible for researchers in blockchain without a strong background in security. To do so, we blackbox the use of cryptographic methods where possible, and isolate a small number of properties for permissionless protocols that are the key factors in determining the performance guarantees that are possible for different types of protocol (such as availability and consistency in different synchronicity settings).

In Sect. 2 we describe a framework of this kind, according to which protocols run relative to a *resource pool*. This resource pool specifies a *resource balance* for each participant over the duration of the execution (such as hashrate or stake in the currency), which may be used in determining which participants are permitted to make broadcasts updating the state.

Byzantine Generals in the Permissionless Setting. Our second aim is to address a programme of research that looks to replicate for the permissionless setting what papers such as [7,8,14] achieved for the permissioned case. Our framework allows us to formalise the question, "Under what adversarial conditions, under what synchronicity assumptions, and for what types of permissionless protocol (proof-of-work/proof-of-stake/proof-of-space), are solutions to the Byzantine Generals Problem possible?" In fact, the theory of consensus for permissionless protocols is quite different than for the permissioned case. Our main theorem establishes one such major difference. All terms in the statement of Theorem 1 below will be formally defined in Sects. 2 and 3. Roughly, the adversary is q-bounded if it always has at most a q-fraction of the total resource balance (e.g. a q-fraction of the total hashrate).

Theorem 1. *Consider the synchronous and permissionless setting, and suppose $q \in (0, 1]$. There is no deterministic protocol that solves the Byzantine Generals Problem for a q-bounded adversary.*

The positive results that we previously mentioned for the permissioned case concerned deterministic protocols. So, Theorem 1 describes a fundamental difference in the theory for the permissioned and permissionless settings. With Theorem 1 in place, we then focus on probabilistic solutions to the Byzantine Generals Problem. We leave the details until Sects. 3 and 4, but highlight below another theorem of significant interest, which clearly separates the functionalities that can be achieved by PoW and PoS protocols.

Separating PoW and PoS Protocols. The resource pool will be defined as a function that allocates a resource balance to each participant, depending on time and on the messages broadcast by protocol participants. One of our major concerns is to understand how properties of the resource pool may influence the functionality of the resulting protocol. In Sects. 2, 3 and 4 we will be concerned, in particular, with the distinction between scenarios in which the resource pool is given as a protocol input, and scenarios where the resource pool is unknown. We refer to these as the *sized* and *unsized* settings, respectively. PoS protocols are best modelled in the sized setting, because the way in which a participant's resource balance depends on the set of broadcast messages (such as blocks of transactions) is given from the start of the protocol execution. PoW protocols, on the other hand, are best modelled in the unsized setting, because one does not know in advance how a participant's hashrate will vary over time. The fundamental result when communication is partially synchronous is that no PoW protocol gives a probabilistic solution to the Byzantine Generals Problem:

Theorem 3. *There is no permissionless protocol giving a probabilistic solution to the Byzantine Generals Problem in the unsized setting with partially synchronous communication.*

In some sense, Theorem 3 can be seen as an analogue of the CAP Theorem [1,11] for our framework, but with a trade-off now established between 'consistency' and weaker notion of 'availability' than considered in the CAP Theorem (and with the unsized setting playing a crucial role in establishing this tradeoff). For details see Sect. 4.

1.1   Related Work

In the interests of conserving space, we describe here the most relevant related papers and refer the reader to Appendix 1 for a more detailed account.[2]

The Bitcoin protocol was first described in 2008 [15]. Since then, a number of papers (see, for example, [10,12,16,17]) have considered frameworks for the analysis of PoW protocols. These papers generally work within the UC framework of Canetti [4], and make use of a random-oracle (RO) functionality to model PoW. As we shall see in Sect. 2, however, a more general form of oracle is required for modelling PoS and other forms of permissionless protocol. With a PoS protocol, for example, a participant's apparent stake (and their corresponding ability to update state) depends on the set of broadcast messages that have been received, and *may therefore appear different from the perspective of different participants* (i.e. unlike hashrate, measurement of a user's stake is user-relative). In Sect. 2 we will also describe various other modelling differences that are required to be able to properly analyse a range of attacks, such as 'nothing-at-stake' attacks, on PoS protocols.

In [9], the authors considered a framework with similarities to that considered here, in the sense that ability to broadcast is limited by access to a

---

[2] For appendices, see the arXiv version: https://arxiv.org/abs/2101.07095.

restricted resource. In particular, they abstract the core properties that the resource-restricting paradigm offers by means of a *functionality wrapper*, in the UC framework, which when applied to a standard point-to-point network restricts the ability to send new messages. However, the random oracle functionality they consider is appropriate for modelling PoW rather than PoS protocols, and does not reflect, for example, the sense in which resources such as stake can be user relative (as discussed above), as well as other significant features of PoS protocols discussed in Sect. 2.3.

In [20], a model is considered which carries out an analysis somewhat similar to that in [10], but which blackboxes all probabilistic elements of the process by which processors are selected to update state. Again, the model provides a potentially useful way to analyse PoW protocols, but does not reflect PoS protocols in certain fundamental regards. In particular, the model does not reflect the fact that stake is user relative (i.e. the stake of user x may appear different from the perspectives of users y and z). The model also does not allow for analysis of the 'nothing-at-stake' problem, and does not properly reflect timing differences that exist between PoW and PoS protocols, whereby users who are selected to update state may delay their choice of block to broadcast upon selection. These issues are discussed in more depth in Sect. 2.

As stated in the introduction, Theorem 3 can be seen as a recasting of the CAP Theorem [1,11] for our framework. CAP-type theorems have previously been shown for various PoW frameworks [12,17].

2   The Framework

2.1   The Computational Model

Informal Overview. We use a very simple computational model, designed to be as similar as possible to standard models from distributed computing (e.g. [8]), while also being adapted to deal with the permissionless setting.[3] Processors are specified by state transition diagrams. A *permitter oracle* is introduced as a generalisation of the random oracle functionality in the Bitcoin Backbone paper [10]: It is the permitter oracle's role to grant *permissions* to broadcast messages. The duration of the execution is divided into timeslots. Each processor enters each timeslot t in a given *state* x, which determines the instructions for the processor in that timeslot – those instructions may involve broadcasting messages, as well as sending *requests* to the permitter oracle. The state x' of the processor at the next timeslot is determined by the state x, together with the messages and permissions received at t.

Formal Description. For a list of commonly used variables and terms, see Table 1 in Appendix 2.[4] We consider a (potentially infinite) system of *processors*,

---

[3] There are a number of papers analysing Bitcoin [10,16] that take the approach of working within the language of the UC framework of Canetti [4]. Our position is that this provides a substantial barrier to entry for researchers in blockchain who do not have a strong background in security, and that the power of the UC framework remains largely unused in the subsequent analysis.

[4] For the appendix, see https://arxiv.org/abs/2101.07095.

some of which may be *faulty*. Each processor is specified by a state transition diagram, for which the number of states may be infinite. At each timeslot t of its operation, a processor p *receives* a pair (M, M^*), where either or both of M and M^* may be empty. Here, M is a finite set of *messages* (i.e. strings) that have previously been *broadcast* by other processors. We refer to M as the *message set* received by p at t, and say that each message $m \in M$ is received by p at t. M^* is a potentially infinite set of pairs (m, t'), where each m is a message and each t' is a timeslot. M^* is referred to as the *permission set* received by p at t. If $(m, t') \in M^*$, then receipt of the permission set M^* means that p is able to broadcast m at step t': Once M^* has been received, we refer to m as being *permitted* for p at t'. To complete the instructions for timeslot t, p then broadcasts a finite set of messages M' that are permitted for p at t, makes a finite *request set* R, and then enters a new state x', where x', M' and R are determined by the present state x and (M, M^*), according to the state transition diagram. The form of the request set R will be described shortly, together with how R determines the permission set received at the next timeslot.

Amongst the states of a processor are a non-empty set of possible *initial states*. The *inputs* to p determine which initial state it starts in. If a variable is specified as an input to p, then we refer to it as *determined* for p, referring to the variable as *undetermined* for p otherwise. If a variable is determined/undetermined for all p, we simply refer to it as determined/undetermined. To define outputs, we consider each processor to have a distinguished set of *output states*, a processor's output being determined by the first output state it enters. Amongst the inputs to p is an *identifier* U_p, which can be thought of as a name for p, and which is unique in the sense that $\mathsf{U}_p \neq \mathsf{U}_{p'}$ when $p \neq p'$. A principal difference between the permissionless setting (as considered here) and the permissioned setting is that, in the permissionless setting, the number of processors is undetermined, and U_p is undetermined for p' when $p' \neq p$.

We consider a real-time clock, which exists outside the system and measures time in natural number timeslots. We also allow the inputs to p to include messages, which are thought of as having been received by p at timeslot $t = 0$. A *run* of the system is described by specifying the initial states for all processors and by specifying, for each timeslot $t \geq 1$: (1) The messages and permission sets received by each processor at that timeslot, and; (2) The instruction that each processor executes, i.e., what messages it broadcasts, what requests it makes, and the new state it enters.

We require that each message is received by p at most once for each time it is broadcast, i.e. at the end of the run it must be possible to specify an injective function d_p mapping each pair m, t, such that m is received by p at timeslot t, to a triple (p', m, t'), such that $t' < t$, $p' \neq p$ and such that p' broadcast m at t'.

In the *authenticated* setting, we assume the existence of a signature scheme (without PKI), see Appendix 3 for formal details. We let m_U denote the message m signed by U. We consider standard versions (see Appendix 3) of the *synchronous* and *partially synchronous* settings (as in [8]) – the version of the partially synchronous setting we consider is that in which the determined upper bound Δ on message delay holds after some undetermined stabilisation time.

2.2   The Resource Pool and the Permitter

Informal Motivation. Who should be allowed to create and broadcast new Bitcoin blocks? More broadly, when defining a permissionless protocol, who should be able to broadcast new messages? For a PoW protocol, the selection is made depending on computational power. PoS protocols are defined in the context of specifying how to run a currency, and select identifiers according to their stake in the given currency. More generally, one may consider a scarce resource, and then select identifiers according to their corresponding resource balance.

We consider a framework according to which protocols run relative to a *resource pool*, which specifies a resource balance for each identifier over the duration of the run. The precise way in which the resource pool is used to determine identifier selection is then black boxed through the use of what we call the *permitter oracle*, to which processors can make requests to broadcast, and which will respond depending on their resource balance. To model Bitcoin, for example, we simply allow each identifier (or rather, the processor allocated the identifier) to make a request to broadcast a block at each step of operation. The permitter oracle then gives a positive response with probability depending on their resource balance, which in this case is defined by hashrate. So, this gives a straightforward way to model the process, without the need for a detailed discussion of hash functions and how they are used to instantiate the selection process.

Formal Specification. At each timeslot t, we refer to the set of all messages that have been received or broadcast by p at timeslots $\leq t$ as the *message state* M of p. Each run happens relative to a (determined or undetermined) *resource pool*,[5] which in the general case is a function $\mathcal{R} : \mathcal{U} \times \mathbb{N} \times \mathcal{M} \to \mathbb{R}_{\geq 0}$, where $\mathcal{U}$ is the set of all identifiers and $\mathcal{M}$ is the set of all possible sets of messages (so, $\mathcal{R}$ can be thought of as specifying the resource balance of each identifier at each timeslot, possibly relative to a given message state).[6] For each t and M, we suppose: (a) If $\mathcal{R}(\mathtt{U}, t, M) \neq 0$ then $\mathtt{U} = \mathtt{U}_p$ for some processor p; (b) There are finitely many $\mathtt{U}$ for which $\mathcal{R}(\mathtt{U}, t, M) \neq 0$, and; (c) $\sum_{\mathtt{U}} \mathcal{R}(\mathtt{U}, t, M) > 0$.

After receiving messages and a permission set at timeslot t, suppose p's message state is M_0 and that, for each t', $M^*(t')$ is the set of all messages that are permitted for p at timeslots $\leq t'$. We consider two *settings* – the *timed* and *untimed* settings. The form of each request $r \in R$ made by p at timeslot t depends on the setting, as specified below. While the following definitions might

---

[5] As described more precisely in Sect. 2.3, whether the resource pool is determined or undetermined will decide whether we are in the *sized* or *unsized* setting.

[6] For a PoW protocol like Bitcoin, the resource balance of each identifier will be their (relevant) computational power at the given timeslot (and hence independent of the message state). For PoS protocols, such as Ouroboros [13] and Algorand [6], however, the resource balance will be determined by 'on-chain' information, i.e. information recorded in the message state M.

initially seem a little abstract, we will shortly give some concrete examples to make things clear.

- **The untimed setting**. Here, each request r made by p must be[7] of the form (M, A), where $M \subseteq M_0 \cup M^*(t)$, and where A is some (possibly empty) extra data. The permitter oracle will respond with a (possibly empty) set M^* of pairs of the form $(m, t + 1)$. The value of M^* will be assumed to be a probabilistic function[8] of the determined variables, (M, A), and of $\mathcal{R}(\mathsf{U}_p, t, M)$, subject to the condition that $M^* = \emptyset$ if $\mathcal{R}(\mathsf{U}_p, t, M) = 0$. (If modelling Bitcoin, for example, M might be a set of blocks that have been received by p, or that p is already permitted to broadcast, while A specifies a new block extending the 'longest chain' in M. If the block is valid, then the permitter oracle will give permission to broadcast it with probability depending on the resource balance of p at time t. We will expand on this example below.)
- **The timed setting**. Here, each request r made by p must be of the form (t', M, A), where t' is a timeslot, $M \subseteq M_0 \cup M^*(t')$ and where A is as in the untimed setting. The permitter oracle will respond with a set M^* of pairs of the form (m, t'). M^* will be assumed to be a probabilistic function of the determined variables,[9] (t', M, A), and of $\mathcal{R}(\mathsf{U}_p, t', M)$, subject to the condition that $M^* = \emptyset$ if $\mathcal{R}(\mathsf{U}_p, t', M) = 0$.

If the set of requests made by p at timeslot t is $R = \{r_1, \dots, r_k\}$, and if the permitter oracle responds with $M_1^*, \dots, M_k^*$ respectively, then $M^* := \cup_{i=1}^{k} M_i^*$ is the permission set received by p at its next step of operation.

By a *permissionless protocol* we mean a pair (S, O), where S is a state transition diagram to be followed by all non-faulty processors, and where O is a permitter oracle, i.e. a probabilistic function of the form described above. It should be noted that the roles of the resource pool and the permitter oracle are different, in the following sense: While the resource pool is a variable (meaning that a given protocol will be expected to function with respect to all possible resource pools consistent with the setting), the permitter is part of the protocol description.

How to Understand the Form of Requests (Informal). To help explain these definitions, we consider how to model some simple protocols.

Modelling Bitcoin. To model Bitcoin, we work in the untimed setting, and we define the set of possible messages to be the set of possible *blocks* (in this paper, we use the terms 'block' and 'chain' in an informal sense, for the purpose of giving

---

[7] To model a perfectly co-ordinated adversary, we will later modify this definition to allow the adversary to make requests of a slightly more general form (see the Appendix 5).

[8] See Appendix 5 for a detailed explanation of what it means to be a 'probabilistic function'.

[9] In the authenticated setting the response of the permitter is now allowed to be a probabilistic function also of U_p. See Appendix 3 for details.

examples). We then allow p to make a single request of the form (M, A) at each timeslot. Here M will be a set of blocks that have been received by p, or that p is already permitted to broadcast. The entry A will be data (without PoW attached) that specifies a block extending the 'longest chain' in M. If A specifies a valid block, then the permitter oracle will give permission to broadcast the block specified by A with probability depending on the resource balance of U_p at time t (which is p's hashrate, and is independent of M). So, if each timeslot corresponds to a short time interval (one second, say), then the model 'pools' all attempts by p to find a nonce within that time interval into a single request. The higher U_p's resource balance at a given timeslot, the greater the probability p will be able to mine a block at that timeslot.[10] Note that the resource pool is best modelled as undetermined here, because one does not know in advance how the hashrate attached to each identifier (or even the total hashrate) will vary over time.

Modelling PoS Protocols. The first major difference for a PoS protocol is that the resource balance of each participant now depends on the message state, and may also be a function of time.[11] So, the resource pool is a function $\mathcal{R} : \mathcal{U} \times \mathbb{N} \times \mathcal{M} \to \mathbb{R}_{\geq 0}$. A second difference is that $\mathcal{R}$ is determined, because one knows from the start how the resource balance of each participant depends on the message state as a function of time. Note that advance knowledge of $\mathcal{R}$ *does not* mean that one knows from the start which processors will have large resource balances throughout the run, unless one knows which messages will be broadcast. A third difference is that, with PoS protocols, processors can generally look ahead to determine their permission to broadcast at future timeslots, when their resource balance may be different than it is at present. This means that PoS protocols are best modelled in the timed setting, where processors can make requests corresponding to timeslots t' other than the current timeslot t. To make these ideas concrete, let us consider a simple example.

There are various ways in which 'standard' PoS selection processes can work. Let us restrict ourselves, just for now and for the purposes of this example, to considering blockchain protocols in which the only broadcast messages are blocks, and let us consider a longest chain PoS protocol which works as follows: For each broadcast chain of blocks C and for all timeslots in a set $T(C)$, the protocol being modelled selects precisely *one* identifier who is permitted to produce blocks extending C, with the probability each identifier is chosen being

---

[10] So, in this simple model, we don't deal with any notion of a 'transaction'. It is clear, though, that the model is sufficient to be able to define what it means for blocks to be *confirmed*, to define notions of *liveness* (roughly, that the set of confirmed blocks grows over time with high probability) and *consistency* (roughly, that with high probability, the set of confirmed blocks is monotonically increasing over time), and to prove liveness and consistency for the Bitcoin protocol in this model (by importing existing proofs, such as that in [10]).

[11] It is standard practice in PoS blockchain protocols to require a participant to have a currency balance that has been recorded in the blockchain for at least a certain minimum amount of time before they can produce new blocks, for example. So, a given participant may not be permitted to extend a given chain of blocks at timeslot t, but may be permitted to extend the same chain at a later timeslot t'.

proportional to their wealth, which is a time dependent function of C. To model a protocol of this form, we work in the timed and authenticated setting. We consider a resource pool which takes any chain C and allocates to each identifier U_p their wealth according to C as a function of t. Then we can consider a permitter oracle which chooses one identifier U_p for each chain C and each timeslot t' in $T(C)$, each identifier U_p being chosen with probability proportional to $\mathcal{R}(U_p, t', C)$. The owner p of the chosen identifer U_p corresponding to C and t', is then given permission to broadcast blocks extending C whenever p makes a request $(t', C, \emptyset)$. This isolates a fourth major difference from the PoW case: For the PoS protocol, the request to broadcast and the resulting permission is not block specific, i.e. requests are of the form (t', M, A) for $A = \emptyset$, and the resulting permission is to broadcast *any* from the range of appropriately timestamped and valid blocks extending C. If one were to make requests block specific, then users would be motivated to churn through large numbers of blocks, making the protocol best modelled as partly PoW.

To model a BFT PoS protocol like Algorand, the basic approach will be very similar to that described for the longest chain PoS protocol above, except that certain other messages might be now required in M (such as authenticated votes on blocks) before permission to broadcast is granted, and permission may now be given for the broadcast of messages other than blocks (such as votes on blocks).

2.3 Defining the Timed/Untimed, Sized/Unsized and Single/Multi-permitter Settings

In the previous section we isolated four qualitative differences between PoW and PoS protocols. The first difference is that, for PoW protocols, the resource pool is a function $\mathcal{R} : \mathcal{U} \times \mathbb{N} \to \mathbb{R}_{\geq 0}$, while for PoS protocols, the resource pool is a function $\mathcal{R} : \mathcal{U} \times \mathbb{N} \times \mathcal{M} \to \mathbb{R}_{\geq 0}$. Then there are three differences in the *settings* that are appropriate for modelling PoW and PoS protocols. We make the following formal definitions:

1. **The timed and untimed settings.** This difference between the timed and untimed settings was specified in Sect. 2.2.
2. **The sized and unsized settings.** We call the setting *sized* if the resource pool is determined. By the *total resource balance* we mean the function $\mathcal{T} : \mathbb{N} \times \mathcal{M} \to \mathbb{R}_{>0}$ defined by $\mathcal{T}(t, M) := \sum_U \mathcal{R}(U, t, M)$. For the unsized setting, $\mathcal{R}$ and $\mathcal{T}$ are undetermined, with the only restrictions being:
   (i) $\mathcal{T}$ only takes values in a determined interval $[\alpha_0, \alpha_1]$, where $\alpha_0 > 0$ (meaning that, although α_0 and α_1 are determined, protocols will be required to function for all possible $\alpha_0 > 0$ and $\alpha_1 > \alpha_0$, and for all undetermined $\mathcal{R}$ consistent with α_0, α_1, subject to (ii) below).[12]

---

[12] We consider resource pools with range restricted in this way, because it turns out to be an overly strong condition to require a protocol to function without *any* further conditions on the resource pool, beyond the fact that it is a function to $\mathbb{R}_{\geq 0}$. Bitcoin will certainly fail if the total resource balance over all identifiers decreases sufficiently quickly over time, or if it increases too quickly, causing blocks to be produced too quickly compared to Δ.

(ii) There may also be bounds placed on the resource balance of identifiers owned by the adversary.

3. **The multi-permitter and single-permitter settings**. In the *single-permitter* setting, each processor may submit a single request of the form (M, A) or (t, M, A) (depending on whether we are in the timed setting or not) at each timeslot, and it is allowed that $A \neq \emptyset$. In the *multi-permitter* setting, processors can submit any finite number of requests at each timeslot, but they must all satisfy the condition that $A = \emptyset$.[13]

We do not define the general classes of PoW and PoS protocols (although we will be happy to refer to specific protocols as PoW or PoS). Such an approach would be too limited, being overly focussed on the step-by-step operations. In our impossibility results, we assume nothing about the protocol other than basic properties of the resource pool and permitter, as specified by the various settings above. We model PoW protocols in the untimed, unsized, and single permitter settings, with $\mathcal{R} : \mathcal{U} \times \mathbb{N} \to \mathbb{R}_{\geq 0}$. We model PoS protocols in the timed, sized, multi-permitter and authenticated settings, and with $\mathcal{R} : \mathcal{U} \times \mathbb{N} \times \mathcal{M} \to \mathbb{R}_{\geq 0}$. Appendix 4 expands on the reasoning behind these modelling choices. In the following sections, we will see that whether a protocol operates in the sized/unsized, timed/untimed, or multi/single-permitter settings is a key factor in determining the performance guarantees that are possible (such as availability and consistency in different synchronicity settings).

2.4   The Adversary

Appendix 5 gives an expanded version of this subsection and also considers the meaning of probabilisitic statements in detail. In the permissionless setting, we generally consider Byzantine faults, thought of as being carried out with malicious intent by an *adversary*. The adversary controls a fixed set of faulty processors - in formal terms, the difference between faulty and non-faulty processors is that the state transition diagram for faulty processors might not be S, as specified by the protocol. In this paper, we consider a static (i.e. non-mobile) adversary that controls a set of processors that is fixed from the start of the protocol execution. We do this to give the strongest possible form of our impossibility results. We place no bound on the *size* of the set of processors controlled by the adversary. Rather, placing bounds on the power of the adversary in the permissionless setting means limiting their resource balance. For $q \in [0, 1]$, we say the adversary is *q-bounded* if their total resource balance is always at most a q fraction of the total, i.e. for all $M, t, \sum_{p \in P_A} \mathcal{R}(\mathsf{U}_p, t, M) \leq q \cdot \sum_{p \in P} \mathcal{R}(\mathsf{U}_p, t, M)$, where P_A is the set of processors controlled by the adversary.

---

[13] The names 'single-permitter' and 'multi-permitter' come from the sizes of the resulting permission sets when modelling blockchain protocols. For PoW protocols the the permission set received at a single step will generally be of size at most 1, while this is not generally true for PoS protocols.

2.5   The Permissioned Setting

So that we can compare the permissioned and permissionless settings, it is useful to specify how the permissioned setting is to be defined within our framework. According to our framework, the permissioned setting is exactly the same as the permissionless setting that we have been describing, but with the following differences:

- The finite number n of processors is determined, together with the identifier for each processor.
- All processors are automatically permitted to broadcast all messages, (subject only to the same rules as formally specified in Appendix 2 for the authenticated setting).[14]
- Bounds on the adversary are now placed by limiting the *number* of faulty processors – the adversary is *q-bounded* if at most a fraction q of all processors are faulty.

3   Byzantine Generals in the Synchronous Setting

Recall from Sect. 2.2 that we write m_U to denote the message m signed by U. We consider protocols for solving a version of 'Byzantine Broadcast' (BB). A distinguished identifier U*, which does not belong to any processor, is thought of as belonging to the *general*. Each processor p begins with a protocol input in_p, which is a set of messages from the general: either $\{0_{U*}\}$, $\{1_{U*}\}$, or $\{0_{U*}, 1_{U*}\}$. All non-faulty processors p must give the same output $o_p \in \{0,1\}$. In the case that the general is 'honest', there will exist $z \in \{0,1\}$, such that $in_p = \{z_{U*}\}$ for all p, and in this case we require that $o_p = z$ for all non-faulty processors.

As we have already stipulated, processors also take other inputs beyond their *protocol input* as described in the last paragraph, such as their identifier and Δ – to distinguish these latter inputs from the protocol inputs, we will henceforth refer to them as *parameter inputs*. The protocol inputs and the parameter inputs have different roles, in that the form of the outputs required to 'solve' BB only depend on the protocol inputs, but the protocol will be required to produce correct outputs for all possible parameter inputs.

3.1   The Impossibility of Deterministic Consensus
in the Permissionless Setting

In Sect. 2.2, we allowed the permitter oracle O to be a probabilistic function. In the case that O is deterministic, i.e. if there is a single output for each input, we will refer to the protocol (S, O) as deterministic.

---

[14] It is technically convenient here to allow that processors can still submit requests, but that requests always get the same response (the particular value then being immaterial).

In the following proof, it is convenient to consider an infinite set of processors. As always, though, (see Sect. 2.2) we assume for each t and M, that there are finitely many U for which $\mathcal{R}(\mathtt{U}, t, M) \neq 0$, and thus only finitely many corresponding processors given permission to broadcast. All that is really required for the proof to go through is that there are an unbounded number of identifiers that can participate *at some timeslot* (such as is true for Bitcoin, or in any context where the adversary can transfer their resource balance to an unbounded number of possible public keys), and that the set of identifiers with non-zero resource balance can change quickly. In particular, this means that the adversary can broadcast using new identifiers at each timeslot. Given this condition, one can then adapt the proof of [7], that a permissioned protocol solving BB for a system with t many faulty processors requires at least $t + 1$ many steps, to show that a deterministic protocol in the permissionless setting cannot always give correct outputs. Adapting the proof, however, is highly non-trivial, and requires establishing certain compactness conditions on the space of runs, which are straightforward in the permissioned setting but require substantial effort to establish in the permissionless setting.

Theorem 1. *Consider the synchronous setting and suppose $q \in (0, 1]$. There is no deterministic permissionless protocol that solves BB for a q-bounded adversary.*

Proof. See Appendix 6 (in the arXiv version).

Theorem 1 limits the kind of solution to BB that is possible in the permissionless setting. In the context of a blockchain protocol (for state machine replication), however, one is (in some sense) carrying out multiple versions of (non-binary) BB in sequence. One approach to circumventing Theorem 1 would be to accept some limited centralisation: One might have a fixed circle of participants carry out each round of BB (involving interactions over multiple timeslots according to a permissioned protocol), only allowing in new participants after the completion of each such round. While this approach clearly does *not* involve a decentralised solution to BB, it might well be considered sufficiently decentralised in the context of state machine replication.

3.2 Probabilistic Consensus

In light of Theorem 1, it becomes interesting to consider permissionless protocols giving *probabilistic* solutions to BB. To this end, from now on, we consider protocols that take an extra parameter input $\varepsilon > 0$, which we call the *security parameter*. Now we require that, for any value of the security parameter input $\varepsilon > 0$, it holds with probability $> 1 - \varepsilon$ that all non-faulty processors give correct outputs.

Appendix 7 explains which questions remain open for probabilistic permissionless protocols in the synchronous setting. For now, in the interests of conserving space, we just briefly mention another negative result:

Theorem 2. *Consider the synchronous and unauthenticated setting. If $q \geq \frac{1}{2}$, then there is no permissionless protocol giving a probabilistic solution to BB for a q-bounded adversary.*

Proof. See Appendix 7.

4 Byzantine Generals with Partially Synchronous Communication

We note first that, in this setting, protocols giving a probabilistic solution to BB will not be possible if the adversary is q-bounded for $q \geq \frac{1}{3}$ – this follows easily by modifying the argument presented in [8], although that proof was given for deterministic protocols in the permissioned setting. For $q < \frac{1}{3}$ and working in the sized setting, there are multiple PoS protocols, such as Algorand,[15] which work successfully when communication is partially synchronous.

The fundamental result with respect to the *unsized* setting with partially synchronous communication is that there is no permissionless protocol giving a probabilistic solution to BB. So, PoW protocols cannot give a probabilistic solution to BB when communication is partially synchronous.[16]

Theorem 3. *There is no permissionless protocol giving a probabilistic solution to BB in the unsized setting with partially synchronous communication.*

Proof. See Appendix 8.

As stated previously, Theorem 3 can be seen as an analog of the CAP Theorem for our framework. While the CAP Theorem asserts that (under the threat of unbounded network partitions), no protocol can be both available and consistent, it *is* possible to describe protocols that give a solution to BB in the partially synchronous setting [8]. The crucial distinction is that such solutions are not required to give outputs until after the undetermined stabilisation time has passed. The key idea behind the proof of Theorem 3 is that, in the unsized and partially synchronous setting, this distinction disappears. Network partitions are now indistinguishable from waning resource pools. In the unsized setting, the requirement to give an output can therefore force participants to give an output before the stabilisation time has passed.

---

[15] For an exposition of Algorand that explains how to deal with the partially synchronous setting, see [5].

[16] Of course, it is crucial to our analysis here that PoW protocols are being modelled in the unsized setting. It is also interesting to understand why Theorem 3 does not contradict the results of Sect. 7 in [10]. In that paper, they consider the form of partially synchronous setting from [8] in which the delay bound Δ always holds, but is undetermined. In order for the 'common prefix property' to hold in Lemma 34 of [10], the number of blocks k that have to be removed from the longest chain is a function of Δ. When Δ is unknown, the conditions for block confirmation are therefore also unknown. It is for this reason that the Bitcoin protocol cannot be used to give a probabilistic solution to BB in the partially synchronous and unsized setting.

5 Concluding Comments

We close with some questions.

Question 1. What are the results for the timed/untimed, sized/unsized, and the single/multi-permitter settings other than those used to model PoW and PoS protocols? What happens, for example, when communication is partially synchronous and we consider a variant of PoW protocols for which the total resource balance (see Sect. 2.3) is determined?

While we have defined the single-permitter and multi-permitter settings, we didn't analyse the resulting differences in Sects. 3 and 4. In fact, this is the distinction between PoS and PoW protocols which has probably received the most attention in the previous literature (but not within the framework we have presented here) in the form of the 'nothing-at-stake' problem [2]. In the framework outlined in Sect. 2, we did not allow for a mobile adversary (who can make non-faulty processors faulty, perhaps for a temporary period). It seems reasonable to suggest that the difference between these two settings becomes particularly significant in the context of a mobile adversary:

Question 2. What happens in the context of a mobile adversary, and how does this depend on whether we are working in the single-permitter or multi-permitter settings? Is this a significant advantage of PoW protocols?

In the framework we have described here, we have followed much of the classical literature in not limiting the length of messages, or the finite number of messages that can be sent in each timeslot. While the imagined network over which processors communicate does have message delays, it apparently has infinite bandwidth so that these delays are independent of the number and size of messages being sent. While this is an appropriate model for some circumstances, in looking to model such things as sharding protocols [21] it will be necessary to adopt a more realistic model:

Question 3. How best to modify the framework, so as to model limited bandwidth (and protocols such as those for implementing sharding)?

In this paper we have tried to follow a piecemeal approach, in which new complexities are introduced one at a time. This means that there are a number of differences between the forms of analysis that normally take place in the blockchain literature and in distributed computing that we have not yet addressed. One such difference is that it is standard in the blockchain world to consider a setting in which participants may be late joining. A number of papers [12,17] have already carried out an analysis of some of the nuanced considerations to be had here, but there is more to be done:

Question 4. What changes in the context of late joining? In what ways is this different from the partially synchronous setting, and how does this relate to Question 3? How does all of this depend on other aspects of the setting?

References

1. Brewer, E.A.: Towards robust distributed systems. In: PODC, Portland, OR, vol. 7, pp. 343477–343502 (2000)
2. Brown-Cohen, J., Narayanan, A., Psomas, A., Weinberg, S.M.: Formal barriers to longest-chain proof-of-stake protocols. In: Proceedings of the 2019 ACM Conference on Economics and Computation, pp. 459–473 (2019)
3. Buterin, V.: What is Ethereum? Ethereum Official webpage. www.ethdocs.org/en/latest/introduction/what-is-ethereum.html. Accessed 14 2018
4. Canetti, R.: Universally composable security: a new paradigm for cryptographic protocols. In: Proceedings 42nd IEEE Symposium on Foundations of Computer Science, pp. 136–145. IEEE (2001)
5. Chen, J., Gorbunov, S., Micali, S., Vlachos, G.: ALGORAND AGREEMENT: super fast and partition resilient Byzantine agreement. IACR Cryptol. ePrint Arch. **2018**, 377 (2018)
6. Chen, J., Micali, S.: Algorand. arXiv preprint arXiv:1607.01341 (2016)
7. Dolev, D., Strong, H.R.: Authenticated algorithms for Byzantine agreement. SIAM J. Comput. **12**(4), 656–666 (1983)
8. Dwork, C., Lynch, N.A., Stockmeyer, L.: Consensus in the presence of partial synchrony. J. ACM **35**(2), 288–323 (1988)
9. Garay, J., Kiayias, A., Ostrovsky, R.M., Panagiotakos, G., Zikas, V.: Resource-restricted cryptography: revisiting MPC bounds in the proof-of-work era. In: Canteaut, A., Ishai, Y. (eds.) EUROCRYPT 2020. LNCS, vol. 12106, pp. 129–158. Springer, Cham (2020). https://doi.org/10.1007/978-3-030-45724-2_5
10. Garay, J.A., Kiayias, A., Leonardos, N.: The bitcoin backbone protocol: analysis and applications (2018)
11. Gilbert, S., Lynch, N.: Brewer's conjecture and the feasibility of consistent, available, partition-tolerant web services. ACM SIGACT News **33**(2), 51–59 (2002)
12. Guo, Y., Pass, R., Shi, E.: Synchronous, with a chance of partition tolerance. In: Boldyreva, A., Micciancio, D. (eds.) CRYPTO 2019. LNCS, vol. 11692, pp. 499–529. Springer, Cham (2019). https://doi.org/10.1007/978-3-030-26948-7_18
13. Kiayias, A., Russell, A., David, B., Oliynykov, R.: Ouroboros: a provably secure proof-of-stake blockchain protocol. In: Katz, J., Shacham, H. (eds.) CRYPTO 2017. LNCS, vol. 10401, pp. 357–388. Springer, Cham (2017). https://doi.org/10.1007/978-3-319-63688-7_12
14. Lamport, L., Shostak, R., Pease, M.: The Byzantine generals problem. ACM Trans. Program. Lang. Syst. (TOPLAS) **4**(3), 382–401 (1982)
15. Nakamoto, S., et al.: Bitcoin: a peer-to-peer electronic cash system (2008)
16. Pass, R., Seeman, L., shelat, a.: Analysis of the blockchain protocol in asynchronous networks (2016). https://eprint.iacr.org/2016/454.pdf
17. Pass, R., Shi, E.: Rethinking large-scale consensus. In: 2017 IEEE 30th Computer Security Foundations Symposium (CSF), pp. 115–129. IEEE (2017)
18. Pease, M., Shostak, R., Lamport, L.: Reaching agreement in the presence of faults. J. ACM (JACM) **27**(2), 228–234 (1980)

19. Ren, L., Devadas, S.: Proof of space from stacked expanders. In: Hirt, M., Smith, A. (eds.) TCC 2016. LNCS, vol. 9985, pp. 262–285. Springer, Heidelberg (2016). https://doi.org/10.1007/978-3-662-53641-4_11

20. Terner, B.: Permissionless consensus in the resource model. IACR Cryptol. ePrint Arch. **2020**, 355 (2020)

21. Zamani, M., Movahedi, M., Raykova, M.: Rapidchain: scaling blockchain via full sharding. In: Proceedings of the 2018 ACM SIGSAC Conference on Computer and Communications Security, pp. 931–948 (2018)

The Unique Chain Rule and Its Applications

Adithya Bhat[1(✉)], Akhil Bandarupalli[1], Saurabh Bagchi[1], Aniket Kate[1], and Michael K. Reiter[2]

[1] Purdue University, West Lafayette, IN 47906, USA
{abhatk,abandaru,sbagchi,aniket}@purdue.edu
[2] Duke University, Durham, NC 27708, USA
michael.reiter@duke.edu

Abstract. Most existing Byzantine fault-tolerant State Machine Replication (SMR) protocols rely explicitly on either equivocation detection or quorum certificate formations to ensure protocol safety. These mechanisms inherently require $O(n^2)$ communication overhead among n participating servers. This work proposes the Unique Chain Rule (UCR), a simple rule for hash chains where extending a block by including its hash in the next block, is treated as a vote for the proposed block *and its ancestors*. When a block obtains a vote from at least one correct server, we can commit the block and its ancestors. While this idea was used implicitly earlier in conjunction with equivocation detection or quorum certificate generation, this work employs it explicitly to show safety. We present three applications of UCR. We design *Apollo*, and *Artemis*: two novel synchronous SMR protocols with linear best-case communication complexity using round-robin, and stable leaders, respectively as the first two applications. Next, we employ UCR in a black-box fashion toward making any SMR commits publicly verifiable, where clients will no longer have to wait for $2t + 1$ confirmations on every block, where t is the number of Byzantine faults tolerated by the protocol, but can instead collect a UCR proof consisting of $\min(\kappa, t) + 1$ extensions on a block, where κ is a security parameter. This results in faster syncing times for clients as the publicly verifiable proofs can also be gossiped with every new block extension confirming a new block.

1 Introduction

State Machine Replication (SMR) [33] is a fundamental distributed-computing primitive that is receiving renewed attention due to its potential to support blockchains. At its core, an SMR protocol coordinates a set of n servers running a deterministic service so that they collectively implement the abstraction of a single, correct server, even when a subset of servers turns malicious (or Byzantine). Most SMR protocols [1–4,9,12,14–16,18,23,26,27,29,34–36,39]

An extended version is available at https://eprint.iacr.org/2021/180.

© International Financial Cryptography Association 2024
F. Baldimtsi and C. Cachin (Eds.): FC 2023, LNCS 13950, pp. 38–55, 2024.
https://doi.org/10.1007/978-3-031-47754-6_3

achieve this coordination of forming a sequence/chain of blocks (of instructions/transactions) using a *leader* server that the other servers follow, with provisions to change this leader in response to some faults or regularly by design.

In the standard (bounded) synchronous communication setting with the worst-case network delay of Δ for messages, publicly-verifiable Byzantine fault-tolerant (BFT) SMR protocols can tolerate up to one-half Byzantine faults[1]. Many synchronous SMR protocols [2,3,14,16,23,34] achieve this resilience primarily using the lack of equivocation in $O(\Delta)$ time; here, confirming lack of equivocation for a message (or a block) requires sending the message to all the servers and then not hearing any complaints in 2Δ time. Other synchronous protocols [16,34] that avoid the above equivocation detection use the fact that at most one message can obtain $3n/4$ votes. Nevertheless, they still require certificates with $O(n)$ signatures, and incur quadratic in n communication.

This work explores a significantly different approach towards SMR, which is reminiscent of proof-of-work SMR systems [31,38] such as Bitcoin. The Bitcoin networks follow an informal rule that after observing six blocks of transactions extending a block B, the block B is deemed as final; i.e., the probability of the block B being rejected and replaced with another block by another correct server is considered to be small enough. We observe that if we can ensure that no alternate chain of blocks is possible in the permissioned SMR systems, i.e., the SMR chain we have is unique, then we can use the *unique chain* to commit blocks. Subsequently, we ask the following question: *How many blocks do we need to observe before we are sure that a block B is final, in a permissioned network?* The answer turns out to be γ for a protocol if: (i) the γ blocks contain blocks from at least one correct server, (ii) there is only one server that proposes a block for a height, (iii) correct block proposals are always accepted, and (iv) we use a tamper-resistant chain (e.g., hash-chain, where every block contains the hash of the previous block). Based on these observations, we develop a consensus rule called the *Unique Chain Rule (UCR)* (Sect. 3) and its three applications: two novel SMR protocols: Apollo (Sect. 4) and Artemis (Sect. 5), and a protocol to make any SMR publicly verifiable (Sect. 6).

At network speed with delay δ, our protocols commit a block every δ time, with a constant[2] per-block commit latency of $(\min(\kappa, t) + 1)\delta$, and rely on Δ only to detect crashed leader(s). Our protocols are the first synchronous SMR protocols with certificate-free optimistically linear communication when the leader(s) behave correctly. It also produces $2\times$ more blocks as the time between two successive produced blocks, i.e., block period is $1/2$ of the state-of-the-art protocols due to the lack of a round-trip communication to form quorum certificates. Our protocols are efficient in terms of cryptography (see Table 1), making it a suitable candidate for SMR in resource-restricted environments.

---

[1] It is possible for SMR protocols to tolerate more than 1/2 faults. However, these SMR protocols cannot safely convince any external observer of statements regarding the latest state of the system due to the dishonest majority [30].

[2] Many related works claim constant latency [1,3]. The correct term should be $(\min(\kappa, t) + 1)$ as leader randomization is inherently assumed and for small t round-robin protocols are sufficient.

Finally, we can apply UCR to make any SMR commit *publicly verifiable*, i.e., any server that observes the SMR commit data can non-interactively confirm the correctness of the commit. Such publicly verifiable commits can be leveraged to efficiently disseminate the state and prove the state to the clients instead of requesting $2t + 1$ acknowledgments (of which at least $t + 1$ are guaranteed to be from correct servers) from the servers for every block.

1.1   An Informal Exposition of Key Ideas

Unique Chain Rule (UCR). As an example, consider a system of n servers with up to t Byzantine servers, where the blocks proposed in every round are from a round-robin among all the servers. Assume that the blocks use a hash-chain, i.e., a block B proposed in round r includes the hash of its parent block from the previous round $r-1$. Implicitly, this proposer is voting for all the blocks in rounds $\{r, \ldots, 0\}$. In contrast to existing SMR protocols where quorum certificates (i.e., a vector of signatures from more than 50% or 66.67% of the servers) were built for every block of every round, we can use these implicit votes to form certificates for blocks. A traditional certificate guaranteed that no other block for the same height can get certified, while our implicit certificates guarantee that no other chain with the same prefix can form, making the prefix a *unique chain*. We present the resulting commit rule as the Unique Chain Rule (UCR).

Apollo Protocol. Using UCR, we then develop an SMR protocol. We use random leader selection to ensure that at least one leader is correct in any sequence of $\kappa + 1$ rounds. We add a constraint that a server must extend a block from the previous round unless it can obtain a certificate consisting of $n/2 + 1$ signatures claiming Byzantine behavior. We use this to ensure that a block proposed by a correct server cannot be skipped by Byzantine servers. Now, if any server (including the client) observes a chain that is $\kappa + 1$ long, it knows that one of those servers is correct, and its block will never be skipped. Therefore, the chain is unique and final; thus, it can be committed.

In the optimistic conditions, i.e., when the leader(s) is correct, Apollo protocol creates new blocks to increase the length of the chain and thus commit blocks without equivocation detection. In this setting, it is sufficient for all the servers to forward the latest block to the next leader. This gives us certificate-free optimistic linearity and allows responsive commits, i.e., speeds independent of Δ.

Round-robin protocols are efficient in distributing the system load across all the participating servers and are also used to ensure chain quality, i.e., the majority of the chain is from the correct servers. However, Byzantine servers can slow the progress of the SMR by crashing and slowing down the pipeline.

Artemis Protocol. In order to overcome this, we present a stable leader-based SMR protocol: Artemis protocol. In a nutshell, in Artemis protocol, there is a dedicated leader server that creates blocks. The other servers run a modified version of Apollo using the latest leader's blocks. If the leader crashes, the protocol changes the *view* and elects a new leader. Since the latest block is used, a slow proposer in the inner Apollo protocol may stall for some time, but when the next correct server proposes, it will propose the latest block thus effectively catching up with all the servers to the highest block.

Publicly Verifiable SMR. In several permissioned widely-deployed SMR implementations, committed blocks or states are downloaded by clients by connecting to the servers and waiting for $t + 1$ acknowledgments for the block [6,17,32,37]. This incurs a significant overhead on the servers for large numbers of clients. If the chain is ℓ blocks long, the cost incurred by the servers is $O(\ell t)$.

A typical approach to solving this is to add another step of quorum certificate generation after committing in every round, and gossip this quorum certificate to all the clients. This approach incurs $O(1)$ signature generation overheads and $O(t)$ signature verification overheads for all the servers in the system. It also incurs $O(1)$, and $O(t)$ certificate verification overheads respectively, with and without the usage of threshold signatures, for the clients.

Using UCR, we can make the servers gossip a signed message after committing, in every round. On collecting *any* increasing sequence of $\kappa + 1$ such signed state messages, any client (without talking to the servers) can verify that the state is correct leading to $O(1)$ signature generation overhead, $O(1)$ signature verification overheads, for all the servers in the system, and $O(\kappa)$ signature verification overheads for the clients, irrespective of the usage of threshold signatures. This application provides a trade-off to the publicly verifiable SMR problem with fewer overheads on the servers and more overheads to the clients.

1.2 Related Work

Recently, several permissioned SMR protocols have emerged, in the standard synchrony [3,5,14,16,34], weak synchrony [3,23], partial synchrony [10,15,20, 21,35,36,39], and asynchronous models [18,26,27,29][3]. Permissionless systems such as Proof-of-Stake (PoS) blockchain protocols require a rotating leader based SMR, where the leader is generally chosen randomly with probability of being a leader for an epoch/round being directly proportional to the amount of stake invested. Therefore, permissioned consensus protocols are of interest in this area. We discuss the landscape of Proof-of-Work and Proof-of-Stake protocols.

PoW and PoS. In retrospect to this work, UCR can be viewed as being implicitly applied in Proof-of-Work [31,38] and Proof-of-Stake [10,19] based systems, which use the fact that votes on hash-chain or checkpoints in the directed acyclic hash graph of blocks also serve as votes for prior checkpoints or blocks. In particular, Casper [10] uses the fact that if a validator vote for two conflicting checkpoints then its stake is slashed. Here, the conflicting checkpoint is implicitly determined by checking two votes that differ in their ancestors.

In the next part of our literature review, we focus on works that are similar to our work and use standard synchrony assumptions.

---

[3] This list is not exhaustive.

BFT-SMR Protocols. The applications of UCR in the literature have always been in secondary roles as a helper mechanism to equivocation or quorum certificate based commit rules [1–3,10,18,20,26,27,29,31,34,35]. For instance, the idea of using a vote on a block in a hash-chain as votes for all its parents has been used implicitly in [2,3,16,34]. In Sync-Hotstuff [3], Abraham et al. mention that for a hash-chain *"the voting step on a block also serves as a voting step for all its ancestor blocks that have not been committed"*. While several protocols [1–3,10,18,20,26,27,29,34,35] use this for committing ancestors of a committed block, none of them build an explicit protocol out of this observation. They use a UCR-like idea whereby adding extra markers to vote messages for a block B, the vote messages are used as endorsements (a vote) for that block and its ancestors, and when an ancestor gets x endorsements it becomes x-strong. We present an extended related work comparison in the full version of our draft [7].

Table 1. Comparison of the best case (i.e., all the servers are correct) and worst case of Apollo with the related synchronous SMR works. Here κ is $\min(f, \kappa)$.

Protocol	Best Case				Worst Case		
	Commit Latency	#Sign	CC	Block Period	Latency	#Sign	CC
Dfinity [2,24]	$6\Delta + 2\delta$	$O(n)$	$O(n^2)$	2Δ	$O^\star(\kappa\Delta)$	$O(\kappa n^2)$	$O(\kappa n^3)$
PiLi [16]	26δ	$O(n)$	$O(n^2)$	2δ	$O(\kappa\Delta)$	$O(\kappa n)$	$O(\kappa n^2)$
Sync HS [3]	6δ	$O(n)$	$O(n^2)$	2δ	$O(p^\star\Delta) + O(\kappa\Delta)$	$O(\kappa n)$	$O(\kappa n^2)$
Rot. SMR [5]	$2\Delta + 2\delta$	$O(n)$	$O(n^2)$	2δ	$O(\kappa\Delta)$	$O(\kappa n)$	$O(\kappa n^2)$
Streamlet [14]	$8\Delta + 8\delta$	$O(n)$	$O(n^2)$	2Δ	$O(\kappa\Delta)$	$O(\kappa n)$	$O(\kappa n^2)$
$1 - \Delta$ SMR [4]	$1\Delta + 2\delta$	$O(n)$	$O(n^2)$	2δ	$O(p^\star\Delta) + O(\kappa\Delta)$	$O(\kappa n)$	$O(\kappa n^2)$
OptSync [34]	2δ	$O(n)$	$O(n^2)$	2δ	$O(p^\star\Delta) + O(\kappa\Delta)$	$O(\kappa n)$	$O(\kappa n^2)$
Apollo	$(\kappa + 1)\delta$	$O(1)$	$O(n)$	δ	$O(\kappa\Delta)$	$O(\kappa n)$	$O(\kappa n^2)$
Artemis	$(\kappa + 2)\delta$	$O(1)$	$O(n)$	0	$O(\kappa\Delta)$	$O(\kappa n)$	$O(\kappa n^2)$

#Sign is the number of signature generated by all the servers per proposal/block. The number of verification operations for each protocol is n times the signing complexity as every signed message is verified by all the servers. **CC** stands for Communication Complexity of the protocol. **Block Period** is defined as the time between two successive block proposals. $O^\star(g)$ denotes $O(g)$ with high probability. $p^\star$ denotes the number blocks proposed before the leader crashes. In Sync-HotStuff [3] and OptSync [34], a leader is blamed only if p blocks are not proposed in $(2p + 4)\Delta$ time. If p' blocks are proposed by time T, then the servers wait for $p^\star = (2p' + 4)\Delta - T$ time before blaming the leader.

2 Preliminaries

Our system consists of a set $\mathcal{N} := \{p_1, \ldots, p_n\}$ of n servers with $t < n/2$ Byzantine servers with static corruptions[4]. A server is *correct* if it is never Byzantine.

---

[4] Our protocol is adaptively secure, but a different randomization protocol will be needed. There is a trade-off between constant latency and increased signature complexity using [11], or $O(f\delta)$ latency and constant signature complexity using round-robin.

Setup. We assume secure $(n, n/2+1)$-threshold digital signatures (e.g., BLS [8]) and denote signed messages from p_i by $\langle \cdot \rangle_{p_i}$, and the aggregated threshold signature on the same message m as a (quorum) certificate $\mathcal{C}(m)$ similar to most other SMR protocols (such as [3,15,16,24,34,39]). We assume that all the servers use the same genesis block before starting the protocol which can be derived from a Common Reference String (CRS) setup. We also use the CRS to randomize our leaders as done by existing works [1–3].

We assume a fully connected standard (bounded) synchronous network which assumes a public worst-case network delay Δ, i.e., if a correct server sends a message to another correct server, then the message is received by the latter within Δ time from when it was sent by the former. Similar to most recent synchronous SMR protocols, we use two delays: Δ and δ. Δ refers to the synchrony bound, i.e., the *worst case network delay*, and δ refers to the optimistic (actual/real) network speed[5]. A *multicast* means a send-all operation where a server p_i sends a message to all servers $\mathcal{N}$.

State Machine Replication—SMR. An SMR protocol (Definition 1) executes transactions from clients using a state machine replicated across different servers. Clients are nodes that can be the servers themselves. The SMR protocol is typically implemented by generating a linearizable log of transactions. A secure SMR protocol guarantees two properties: *safety*, and *liveness*. Safety, in a broad sense, ensures that the states of the servers must be consistent, i.e., no two correct servers output different states at any point. Liveness, in a broad sense, argues that the system can never go into a deadlock.

Definition 1 (SMR *[3]).* *Assume a system of n servers $\mathcal{N} := \{p_1, \ldots, p_n\}$, t of which are Byzantine. The SMR protocol implements a linearizable log of transactions from clients with the following properties:*

1. ***Safety.*** *If two correct servers p_i, $p_j \in \mathcal{N}$ commit transaction tx and tx', respectively, at the same log height k, then $tx = tx'$.*
2. ***Liveness.*** *Each client transaction is eventually processed by the system.*

Chains and Blocks. The servers agree on a *chain* $\mathcal{C} := \{B_0, \ldots, B_\ell\}$, which we define as a list of blocks[6], where blocks contain client transactions. The height of a block is the index in this list or the chain. A block at height k is B_k. In particular, the first block B_0 is the genesis block with height 0. A block $B_k := \langle h_k, \mathsf{cmds} \rangle_L$ includes the hash of B_{k-1} as $h_k = H(B_{k-1})$ along with a list of transactions cmds. B_{k-1} and B_k share a parent-child relationship. h_k is the parent hash or pointer. Block $B_{k'}$ at height $k' < k$ is an ancestor of B_k as long as they have valid parent hashes linking them.

The genesis block is always *valid*. The child B_k of a valid block B_{k-1} is valid, if h_k is correct, and it satisfies other validity conditions imposed on cmds. A valid

---

[5] In practice, δ varies between pairs of servers, instances of time, and size of the message. However, the analysis here assumes that a single δ value is the optimistic delay time, a violation of which implies that we are not in the optimistic scenario.

[6] We use the notation from Python.

chain $\mathcal{C} := \{B_0, \ldots, B_\ell\}$ is a list of valid blocks starting with the genesis block B_0. The chain size is the highest height of blocks in the chain, i.e., $\ell = \mathsf{height}(\mathcal{C}[-1])$.

Tamper-Resistance. Since the blocks in a chain are hash-linked, it is not possible to change a block in the chain without changing all the blocks after it. We call this the *tamper-resistance* property of the chain.

3   Unique Chain Rule (UCR)

A quorum [28] is a subset of servers. In distributed protocols, we typically need a certain number of acknowledgements on a message to ensure that the other servers are in sync. We typically deal with $t + 1$ sized quorums in standard synchrony (e.g., [1,2,4,34]) or $n - t$ quorums in non-synchronous[7] networks (e.g., [9,10,13–15,39]). In these quorums, the names of servers are not as important, when compared to their count. A quorum certificate is a publicly verifiable message consists of these specified number of signatures from a quorum, typically instantiated with threshold signatures.

Synchronous SMR protocols [1,3,14,16,34] typically improve the fault tolerance from $n > 3t$ to $n > 2t$ by adding equivocation detection which involves $O(\Delta)$ waits due to the message delivery guarantees [14]. We observe that, in a hash chain, equivocation is a chain fork (multiple valid chains), and resolving equivocations translates into a fork-resolution problem. If we want to avoid equivocation detection, we need a mechanism to resolve chain forks.

For a system tolerating t Byzantine servers, $t + 1$ quorum certificate on a block is insufficient to remove equivocation detection of the block. A Byzantine proposer p_L can propose two blocks B and $B^\star$. If two correct servers vote for B and $B^\star$ respectively, without being aware of the existence of the other block, then with the votes from the t Byzantine servers, both the blocks can obtain a quorum certificate.

Unique Chains. Let γ be a parameter such that in any sequence of γ rounds, there is at least one correct leader. Consider a protocol that uses round-robin leaders who propose one block in every round using hash chains. Trivially, this protocol has $\gamma \leftarrow t+1$. Consider that a server votes for a block by extending it in its turn to propose, instead of the traditional approach of voting for every block and building quorum certificates and detecting equivocation for them. Let *chain weight* of a block be the number of unique servers extending a block. Finally, if we can ensure that a correct proposer's block for a round is always extended by the correct servers, i.e., a Byzantine leader cannot propose a block without extending the block from the previous round if the previous leader was correct, then observe that when this chain weight exceeds γ for a block, no other valid chain can be formed that does not extend this block. Intuitively, if this was not true, then the Byzantine servers managed to overwrite a correct proposer's block thus leading to a contradiction.

---

[7] Non-synchronous includes partial synchrony, asynchronous networks, etc. that are not standard synchrony.

We can ensure that a correct server's block for a round is always extended by the correct servers by changing the rejection condition: a valid block can be rejected only if there are $n/2 + 1$ explicit complaints against it. By explicit complaints, we mean $n/2 + 1$ signed (blame) messages for the round.

In the consensus literature so far, certificates consisted of signatures on a particular message/block, and used $O(1)$ such quorum certified blocks in the commit rules. The examples include $3n/4$ quorum with 1 certified block [3, 16, 34], $2n/3$ quorum with 3 blocks [13, 39], and $n/2 + 1$ quorum with 6, 13 blocks [14, 16]. However, we can look at the γ weighted chain suffix as equivalent to the $t + 1$ quorum certificate for the prefix of the chain, thereby leading to implicit certificates of size $O(\gamma) = O(\kappa)$. Using this certificate, we can ensure that the block, and thus the corresponding chain referenced by the block is *unique*, i.e., no alternate chain can form by the protocol. Definition 2 specify the requirements formally. We state the Unique Chain Rule formally in Theorem 1 as the Unique Chain Rule (UCR). In the rest of the paper, unless otherwise specified, we use $\gamma \leftarrow t + 1$.

Definition 2 (γ-UCR requirements). *The requirements to apply γ-UCR in a protocol: (1) the chains built are tamper-resistant, (2) blocks are proposed by servers such that there is at least one correct server in any sequence of γ rounds, and (3) a correct server's blocks are always accepted by all the correct servers.*

Theorem 1 (Unique Chain Rule). *Consider a protocol for n servers tolerating t Byzantine faults, and satisfying Definition 2. Then, on observing a valid chain $\mathcal{C} := \{B_0, \ldots, B_\ell\}$ of size ℓ (with $\ell > \gamma$), commit the prefix chain $\mathcal{C}[: \ell - \gamma]$.*

4   Apollo Protocol

In this section, we present the Apollo protocol which uses UCR (Theorem 1) to build a pipelined, linear SMR protocol in the bounded synchrony model.

Proposer Set. We define a proposer set $\mathcal{P}$ consisting of all (or $t+1$) servers $\mathcal{N}$. Let R be a random number chosen in the setup. We use a well-known technique [14, 16] and use $H(R, i)$ to randomly elect the leaders from $\mathcal{P}$ in every round. As servers agree on *misbehavior* from leaders (by committing blocks that contain proof of equivocation/no progress of leaders), we remove (or replace) the servers from the proposer set. This allows us to eventually stabilize on a set of leaders of size at least $t + 1$ (even if $n \neq 2t + 1$) that are correct.

4.1   Overview

We give an overview of Apollo in Fig. 1 and the technical details in Fig. 2. The protocol proceeds in rounds. p_1 is the leader for the first round and performs the *Propose* Step (Step 1 and blue lines) at time $T = 0$. It proposes a block B_1 extending the genesis block since it is the first proposer, but generally the servers extend the block proposed by the leader for the previous round. At time $T = \delta$, p_2 proposes the next block B_2 on receiving the block B_1. Note that this gives us $\gamma \leftarrow \kappa + 1$ except with negligible probability.

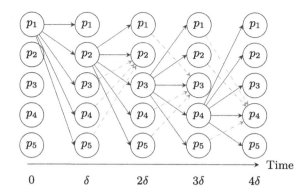

Fig. 1. Overview of the Apollo Protocol in the optimistic case, when all the leaders are correct. The blue messages are block proposals. The dotted lines are relay messages. The proposer for round $r + 1$ can immediately propose as soon as it receives the block for round r. Hence, Apollo has a block period of δ, as it does not have to collect votes and certificates for the previous block unlike existing protocols. (Color figure online)

A Byzantine leader can try to slow down the protocol or may not send its proposal to the next leader. To ensure that a correct leader is always able to propose, all correct servers also forward the proposals of the current round to the next leader (Step 2 and gray lines).

The Propose Step and the Relay Step follow each other with different leaders drawn from $\mathcal{P}$. Additionally, in every round, the correct servers commit blocks after removing the top κ blocks from their local chains.

4.2 Handling Faults

Next, we give an intuition of fault-handling in Apollo and present a concise technical description in Fig. 3.

Block Equivocation. A leader can equivocate by sending different blocks to different correct servers. Unlike existing synchronous SMR protocols [1,3], Apollo does not need to detect equivocation to preserve *safety* or *liveness*.

Consider a leader L_r equivocating in round r. At least one of the blocks reaches the next leader L_{r+1} through the *Relay* step. It will immediately propose the next block. In general, an equivocation is detected by correct servers in two ways: (1) A correct server whose head of the chain is $B_{k'}$ obtains a block B_k from some leader L_r with $k' < k$ and an unknown parent hash. It will immediately request all the blocks $B_{k'}, \ldots, B_{k-1}$ until B_k connects to the server's local chain. If L_r cannot provide valid ancestors within 2Δ, then the correct server blames L_r by sending a blame message. A correct L_r can always respond to such queries and therefore not get blamed by correct servers. When the parent block is received, a correct server may realize equivocations due to conflicts with the local chain. (2) A correct server gets two different blocks during the *Relay* Step (Step 2).

Let L_r be the leader of round r. Let κ be the security parameter.

1. **Propose.** On receiving block B_{k-1} for round $r-1$, the leader L_r for round r proposes a block $B_r := \langle h_k, \mathsf{cmds} \rangle_L$ by multicasting $\langle \mathsf{propose}, B_k \rangle_{L_r}$ extending the previous block B_{k-1} from the previous leader.

2. **Relay.** On receiving a *valid* proposal for round r, forward it to the next leader L_{r+1}, set timer $\mathsf{blTimer}(r+1)$ to 4Δ and start counting down (refer Fig. 3). Cancel all timers for lower rounds.

3. **(Non-blocking) Commit.** On receiving a *valid* chain of blocks $\mathcal{C} := \{B_0, \ldots, B_\ell\}$ commit blocks $\mathcal{C}[: \ell - \kappa]$ if $\ell > \kappa$.

Fig. 2. Rounds in Apollo protocol.

In both of these cases, the correct servers multicast the equivocations to all the other servers if it detected it directly, or via forwarding the blame from others. All the correct servers include the equivocation blame as a meta-transaction in their future proposals until it is committed.

It is not secure to update the proposer set or punish the Byzantine server on obtaining a blame certificates, until it is committed. This is because we do not use timing guarantees, i.e., rely on Δ, to ensure that all correct servers have detected and agreed on the equivocation. On committing a block containing the blame certificates, we know that sufficient correct servers have extended the block, thereby ensuring all the other correct servers will learn about the Byzantine server.

Crashed Leader(s). Consider leaders L_r and L_{r+1} for rounds r and $r+1$ respectively. Let L_r not propose any block. Now, the correct servers could be processing/waiting for blocks at different rounds $\leq r-1$. The first correct server to finish processing the block B_k for round $r-1$, will wait for 4Δ time (we will describe soon why to wait for 4Δ) after relaying B_k before blaming L_r. Upon timing out, a correct server cannot be sure if all the correct servers are waiting for a proposal for round r, since our protocol can proceed at network speed. Therefore, different correct servers could be waiting for blocks from rounds $r' < r$. This case can also occur if the Byzantine leaders send the proposals to some correct servers, who will then be ahead in round number when compared to the servers that did not receive the proposals.

In any case, a correct server on timeout for round r, sends the latest block B_k to all the correct servers in order to synchronize all the correct servers up to round $r-1$. This multicast is not done during the steady state in order to obtain the desired linearity in the steady state as this step has a communication complexity of $O(n^2)$ when $t = O(n)$ servers time out. We know that within another 4Δ all servers will relay the proposal to L_r and then blame when it does not respond. On collecting $t+1$ such blame messages, all the correct servers build a virtual block for round r. Using threshold signatures, this block has $O(1)$ size. From this point, we continue with the relay (Step 2) of this virtual block to L_{r+1} just as though we received a proposal with this virtual block from L_r.

Round-Relative Timers. Apollo uses *round-relative* timers, i.e., blame based on the latest round. Earlier works [3,34] use stable leaders and *view-relative*

Let L_r and L_{r+1} be the leaders of rounds r and $r + 1$ respectively.

1. **Blames.** The server p_i always does the following:

– **No-progress Blame.** If blTimer(r) expires and no *valid* block was proposed by leader L_r, then multicast $\langle r, \mathsf{NPBlame} \rangle_i$ along with the latest known local block B_k for round $r - 1$. Wait for a blame certificate $\mathcal{C}(r, \mathsf{NPBlame})$. Treat the blame certificate as a virtual block for round r and continue with the Relay Step (Step 2) of Fig. 2. Multicast the certificate $\mathcal{C}(r, \mathsf{NPBlame})$ to all the servers.

– **Equivocation.** If there exists two valid blocks B and $B^\star$ proposed by server $p_j \in \mathcal{N}$ in any round $r^\star$ for the first time, obtained directly or indirectly, multicast a $\langle r, \mathsf{EQBlame} \rangle$ message and the two equivocating blocks B and $B^\star$ with signatures.

2. **Remove Leader (Optional).** On committing a block with blame certificates $\langle r, \mathsf{EQBlame} \rangle_i$ or $\mathcal{C}(r, \mathsf{NPBlame})$, remove the leader from the proposer set $\mathcal{P}$.

Fig. 3. Handling Byzantine behavior in Apollo protocol.

timers, where in a view v, the condition for triggering a no-progress blame is to not receive p blocks in $(2p + 4)\Delta$ time. Assume that the first 1000 proposals are made at network speed after which the leader crashes. In Sync-HotStuff [3] and OptSync [34], the servers needlessly wait for 2004Δ before blaming the leader. We overcome this, since our timers are always rooted at the last received block. **Why is 4Δ Timeout Sufficient?** Say p_i is the first server that enters round r at time T. It relays the previous block to the current leader L_r which will reach L_r by time $T + \Delta$. A correct leader L_r may not recognize this chain, and request the full chain. This request will reach p_i by time $T + 2\Delta$. A correct leader will then immediately propose since it has a valid chain to extend. This proposal will reach p_i by time $T + 4\Delta$. Therefore, waiting for a total of 4Δ after relaying the block is always sufficient for a correct server to propose, and thus ensure that a correct leader is never blamed a correct server.

Security Analysis. We state the security theorems here without proofs and defer the security analysis [7].

Theorem 2 (Apollo Safety). *For any height $k \geq 0$, if two correct servers commit to blocks B and $B^\star$, then $B = B^\star$.*

Theorem 3 (Apollo Liveness). *Assuming standard synchrony, Apollo always makes progress, and commits blocks with a period of at most 12Δ.*

5   Artemis Protocol

Round-robin protocols working at the network speed can be slower than stable leader protocols since a slow leader can slow the system, while a stable leader may make faster progress as evidenced in practical implementations [25]. In this section, we construct Artemis which uses a view leader that coordinates the chain, and still allows applying UCR by running a Apollo sub-protocol on the chain produced by the view leader.

Views. Like stable-leader SMR [3,9,13,34,39], our Artemis uses a view number v to represent a period with a stable leader L_v. A change in view number indicates a leader change.

Artemis uses two leaders: *view leader* L_v and *round leader* L_r. The view leader L_v of view v creates *blocks* and builds a chain. The round leader L_r for round r runs Apollo sub-protocol by creating proposals called *votes* containing the hash of the latest block from the view leader.

5.1 Steady-State Protocol

We present an overview in Fig. 4. The view leader L_v signs blocks B_1 to B_8. p_i signs vote messages $V_i = \langle \text{vote}, v, r, H(B) \rangle_i$. Intuitively, we can visualize Artemis as using L_v to build a chain of blocks, and simultaneously using Apollo on vote messages using round leaders L_r. The vote messages form a tamper-resistant chain, and the round leaders are chosen akin to Apollo (Fig. 5).

The view leader L_v of view v collects transactions from the clients and creates a chain of blocks. Like related works [3,15,16,34,39], we assume that there are always sufficient transactions available[8]. Thus, every server must receive p blocks in $p\Delta$ time from L_v. Due to synchrony assumptions, if block B_k is received at time T, then B_{k+1} must be received within time $T + \Delta$. This is because L_v does not need any interaction to create blocks in the steady-state, unlike related works [3,5,34,39] which requires every block to contain a quorum certificate and thus requiring a round-trip of communication.

The round-leaders can be viewed as running Apollo sub-protocol. A vote is a block for the Apollo sub-protocol. A series of vote messages for consecutive rounds forms a vote chain. A vote at round r for block B_k connects indirectly to the vote at round $r + 1$ for block B_{k+1} via the hash pointers between B_k and B_{k+1} ensuring tamper-resistance.

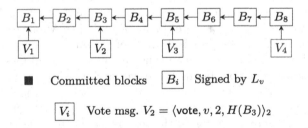

■ Committed blocks $\boxed{B_i}$ Signed by L_v

$\boxed{V_i}$ Vote msg. $V_2 = \langle \text{vote}, v, 2, H(B_3) \rangle_2$

Fig. 4. High-level overview of Artemis (n = 5). V_i are vote messages proposed by servers p_i. We apply UCR using the vote messages resulting in block commits (in blue). (Color figure online)

---

[8] This assumption can be removed by slightly changing the blaming mechanism to not blame if the local transaction buffer is empty and attempting to send transactions to L_v on timeout first, and then blaming. An example of this implementation can be found in Concord-BFT [22].

Let L_v be the view leader for the view v. **View Leader.** L_v creates blocks $B_k :=$ $\langle b_k, H(B_{k-1}) \rangle_{L_v}$ and multicasts the chain of blocks to all the servers. The servers p_i do the following in round r:

1. **Update chain.** On receiving valid blocks from L_v add them to the locally stored chain. Set blameViewLeader $\leftarrow \Delta$.
2. **Vote.** If $p_i = L_r$ for the round r in view v, then it multicasts $\langle \text{vote}, v, r, H(B_k) \rangle_i$ where B_k is the highest height block known to the server.
3. **Relay.** On receiving $\langle \text{vote}, v, r, H(B_k) \rangle_{L_r}$ for a valid chain containing B_k, forward the vote message to L_{r+1} along with the latest known block B_k. Set blTimer$(r+1)$ to 4Δ and cancel all timers for rounds $r' \leq r$.

(Non-blocking) Commit. On receiving a *valid* chain of votes $\mathcal{C}^\star := \{V_0, \ldots, V_\ell\}$ commit all ancestors of the block referred by the vote $V_{\ell-\kappa}$ if $\ell > \kappa$.

Fig. 5. Steady-state protocol for Artemis.

A key difference between blocks in Apollo and in Artemis is that vote messages can produce and commit multiple blocks between each proposal. When the view leader is correct, Byzantine servers do not affect the throughput of the system, as the fast correct servers will collect more blocks while the Byzantine servers slow the system down, and include the highest hash in its turn to send the vote message. This will eventually result in committing a large volume of transactions. In the example illustration in Fig. 4, the vote message V_4 results in the block B_3 and its ancestors having $\kappa + 1 = t + 1 = 3$ children and hence results in committing them. Artemis retains the round-relative blaming property for the view leader from Apollo which improves the worst-case performance of Artemis over the state-of-the-art related works [34].

5.2 Handling Byzantine Behavior

Figure 6 describes the protocol to handle Byzantine behavior in Artemis. We discuss three cases: (i) L_v is correct, (ii) L_v crashes, and (iii) L_v is Byzantine. *Case (i).* When L_v is correct, the vote chain is exactly like Apollo except that the blocks are detached from the proposals and come from L_v. A Byzantine server cannot forge alternate blocks, and can thus only crash or send messages slowly. In the former case, we simply blame the server and use a blame certificate as a virtual block for round r. The latter case does not affect throughput as other correct servers will keep downloading the chain and proposing them during their turn to propose, thereby ensuring all the servers catch-up to the latest chain. *Case (ii).* When L_v crashes at time T, the round-relative timer kicks in for all correct servers by time $T + \Delta$. By time $T + 2\Delta$, all the correct servers will blame and by $T + 3\Delta$ obtain $\mathcal{C}(\text{Blame}, L_v, v)$, and thus quit the view v. By time $T + 6\Delta$ all the correct servers enter the view $v + 1$. The extra 3Δ wait is used to ensure that all servers stop processing vote messages in the view v and synchronize their highest chains.

In the new view $v + 1$, all the correct servers lock on to the highest block known from the view v. From the safety properties of Apollo, we know that

Let L_v and L_{v+1} be the leaders for views v and $v+1$. The server p_i does the following:

- **Round Leader Equivocation.** If two equivocating votes are observed from a server p_j directly or indirectly, then multicast $\langle \mathsf{Blame}, j \rangle_i$, the equivocating votes, and the latest vote received.
- **Slow Round Leader.** If $\mathsf{blTimer}(r)$ expires for a round r, multicast $\langle \mathsf{Blame}, L_r \rangle_i$ and the latest vote message received.
- **Blame Certificates for Round Leaders.** On collecting $n/2 + 1$ blame messages or a blame certificate for server p_j, multicast the blame certificate and include it in the next vote message. On committing a block with vote containing a blame certificate, optionally remove p_i from $\mathcal{P}$.
- **View Leader Equivocation.** If two equivocating blocks are observed from L_v directly or indirectly, then multicast $\langle \mathsf{Blame}, L_v, v \rangle_i$ and the equivocating blocks. Quit view v and stop processing messages in view v.
- **Slow View Leader.** If $\mathsf{blameViewLeader}$ expires, multicast $\langle \mathsf{Blame}, L_v, v \rangle_i$.
- **Quit View.** On receiving $t + 1$ $\langle \mathsf{Blame}, L_v, v \rangle$ messages or $\mathcal{C}(\mathsf{Blame}, L_v, v)$, stop voting in view v if we haven't already. Multicast $\mathcal{C}(\mathsf{Blame}, L_v, v)$, and the highest known vote, and wait 3Δ to enter view $v + 1$.
- **New View.** Perform the following steps:
  (i) Lock on to the block B_{lck} referred by the highest vote in view v. Send the head of the local chain and the highest vote to L_{v+1} and wait for 5Δ for the first block in view $v + 1$.
  (ii) L_{v+1} waits for 3Δ and requests missing blocks (if any), and then sends $\langle B_k, v + 1, V_r \rangle_{L_v}$ where B_k is a block extending the highest block from view v, V_r is the highest view v vote received. Collect $t + 1$ votes, and include $\mathcal{C}(\mathsf{newView}, v + 1, H(B_k))$ in the next block.
  (iii) For the first block in view $v + 1$ send $\langle \mathsf{newView}, v + 1, H(B_k) \rangle_i$ if B_k extends B_{lck} block (equal to or longer than). Send $\langle \mathsf{newView}, v + 1, H(B_k) \rangle_i$ to L_{v+1} and wait for 4Δ. Ensure that the next block contains $\mathcal{C}(\mathsf{newView}, v + 1, H(B_{k-1}))$ and continue the steady-state.

Fig. 6. Handling Byzantine faults in Artemis.

if a correct server commits a block, then all possible chains must extend the committed block. The servers then send their highest view v block to L_{v+1}. By time $T + 7\Delta$, L_{v+1} receives all the chains, and by time $T + 9\Delta$, L_{v+1} has all the chains and proposes the first block for the view $v + 1$ which will reach all correct servers by time $T + 10\Delta$ well within the 5Δ timer for the first block from L_{v+1} by the other correct servers. We ensure that the second block in the view $v + 1$ must be certified, which guarantees that the chain selected by L_{v+1} extends at least one honest server's locked block and has provided a convincing vote message from view v. The latter guarantees that the highest committed block must be extended in the new view $v + 1$.

Case (iii). If L_v is Byzantine and tries to equivocate (via vote message or directly sending B_k and $B_k^\star$ to different servers), it will be detected by all correct servers within $O(\kappa\Delta)$ and thus trigger view-change. This does not affect the safety as at least one vote in the vote chain is from a correct server whose vote pins the blocks at that height, akin to Apollo.

During the view-change, Byzantine servers may add votes with the help of L_v and send them to only some correct servers. In the worst case, Byzantine servers can add up to t more vote messages. This is not a concern, since all the servers lock on to blocks that extends the highest known vote message. Thus, any chain in the next view $v + 1$ is guaranteed to result in committing of the highest committed block in view v.

Security Analysis. Using Theorem 4 and Theorem 5 we prove that Artemis is a secure SMR protocol in standard synchrony. See [7] for proofs.

Theorem 4 (Artemis Safety). *If two correct servers commit blocks B_k and $B_k^\star$ at height k, then $B_k = B_k^\star$.*

Theorem 5 (Artemis Liveness). *Assuming standard synchrony, Artemis always makes progress, and commits blocks with a period of at most $O(\kappa\Delta)$.*

6   Publicly Verifiable SMR

A publicly verifiable SMR allows the clients to verify the state of the SMR protocol without having to contact the servers that run the protocol. Prominent blockchain protocols [10,31,38] are naturally publicly verifiable as their commit rules are properties of their chains[9]. However, not all protocols can use the quorum certificates generated for agreement to convince the clients that it is the accepted block. For instance, in Sync-HotStuff [3], multiple quorum certificates could be generated for a round without the correct clients having heard them; by contacting a Byzantine server, a correct client can be convinced of an incorrect state.

Permissioned protocols [3,13,34] can be made publicly verifiable (if not already) by building quorum certificates on the state for every height. Now, the clients can obtain the state verifiably using the state quorum certificate. For a chain of length ℓ, this incurs a signature complexity of $O(\ell t)$ for the SMR servers.

We can use UCR to design an improved protocol to ensure public verifiability for any SMR. Intuitively, we can run Apollo (Fig. 1) protocol with the SMR commits as input without the fault tolerance. The liveness property of the underlying SMR automatically guarantees progress. This results in a signature complexity for a chain of length ℓ to $O(\ell + \kappa)$.

Consider any SMR protocol that implements Definition 1 with n servers tolerating t faults. Then every log position $r > 0$ has some state S_r attached to it. Committing blocks is an agreement on S_r, and clients of SMR protocols need S_{latest}, where, the latest means that a state that can only be up to Δ time old for synchronous systems[10].

---

[9] In Proof-of-Stake protocols, the stake is defined by the chain, and thus the leaders are publicly verifiable. However, the public verifiability of the chain depends on the underlying SMR used in the protocol.

[10] We cannot discuss it in terms of block heights because any number of blocks might be successfully committed within Δ because of the responsiveness of our protocols.

Servers. For every round r, if $H(R, r)$ mod $n = j$, then the server p_j gossips $v_r :=$ $\langle H(S_{r-1}), S_r \rangle_j$ (or some digest of S_r).

Clients. Any external client commits S_r if all the following are satisfied: (a) collects valid $(v_{r_1}, v_{r_2}, \ldots, v_{r_f})$, (b) $r \leq r_1 < r_2 < \cdots < r_{\kappa+1}$, (c) obtains $H(S_{r_i}), H(S_{r_{i-1}})$ for $r_1 \leq i \leq r_{\kappa+1}$, and (d) downloads S_r. Here, by valid we mean that all the messages are correctly signed.

Fig. 7. Publicly verifiable SMR.

We present a simple UCR-based publicly verifiable SMR protocol in Fig. 7 that is agnostic to the underlying details of the SMR. In this new protocol, we first chain the states together by including the hash of the parent state using state tuples $v_r = \langle H(S_{r-1}), S_r \rangle$ for the log position r. A designated server with id $i = H(R, r)$ mod n signs and sends this to all the active clients. We can also use gossip networks to diffuse this message as done by Bitcoin [31].

A client obtaining any $\kappa + 1$ such signed v_j for $j > i$, from any external source, is guaranteed that S_r is committed (see Lemma 1, [7] for proofs). Note that, unlike Apollo, here we do not blame the server with id i if no v_r are received. The protocol can still continue because the hash chain and $\kappa + 1$ implicit votes guarantee that no other root state S_r can get committed.

To ensure safety, we show in Lemma 1 that the commits made by any client with access to information about the chain and v_i must be the same as the state committed by the correct servers in the underlying SMR protocol. We state the security lemma here and defer the formal proof to [7].

Lemma 1 (Commit Safety). *If a correct client commits S_r using Fig. 7 for round r, then all the correct SMR servers must have committed S_r.*

Acknowledgements. We thank Ling Ren and Ittai Abraham for helpful feedback on the applications of UCR, Kartik Nayak for discussions regarding good-case latency, Nibesh Shrestha for feedback on the draft, and Manish Nagaraj for early discussions. This work was supported in part by NIFA award number 2021-67021-34252, the National Science Foundation (NSF) under grant CNS1846316, the United States Department of Agriculture, and the Army Research Lab Contract number W911NF-2020-221.

References

1. Abraham, I., Devadas, S., Dolev, D., Nayak, K., Ren, L.: Synchronous Byzantine agreement with expected $O(1)$ rounds, expected $O(n^2)$ communication, and optimal resilience. In: Goldberg, I., Moore, T. (eds.) FC 2019. LNCS, vol. 11598, pp. 320–334. Springer, Cham (2019). https://doi.org/10.1007/978-3-030-32101-7_20

For partially synchronous systems it is not possible to guarantee any form of the latest state before GST.

2. Abraham, I., Malkhi, D., Nayak, K., Ren, L.: Dfinity Consensus, Explored. IACR Cryptology ePrint Archive, Report 2018/1153 (2018). www.eprint.iacr.org/2018/1153
3. Abraham, I., Malkhi, D., Nayak, K., Ren, L., Yin, M.: Sync HotStuff: simple and practical synchronous state machine replication. In: 2020 IEEE Symposium on Security and Privacy (SP), Oakland, May 2020, pp. 106–118. IEEE (2020)
4. Abraham, I., Nayak, K., Ren, L., Xiang, Z.: Good-case latency of Byzantine broadcast. In: Proceedings of the 2021 ACM Symposium on Principles of Distributed Computing, July 2021, pp. 331–341. ACM, New York (2021)
5. Abraham, I., Nayak, K., Shrestha, N.: Optimal good-case latency for rotating leader synchronous BFT. In: Bramas, Q., Gramoli, V., Milani, A. (eds.) 25th International Conference on Principles of Distributed Systems, OPODIS 2021. Leibniz International Proceedings in Informatics (LIPIcs), vol. 217, pp. 27:1–27:19. Schloss Dagstuhl – Leibniz-Zentrum für Informatik, Dagstuhl, Germany (2022)
6. Baudet, M., et al.: State machine replication in the libra blockchain (2019). www.developers.diem.com/papers/diem-consensus-state-machine-replication-in-the-diem-blockchain/2020-05-26.pdf
7. Bhat, A., Bandarupalli, A., Bagchi, S., Kate, A., Reiter, M.: Unique chain rule and its applications (2021). www.eprint.iacr.org/2021/180, full version of this draft
8. Boneh, D., Lynn, B., Shacham, H.: Short signatures from the weil pairing. J. Cryptol. **17**(4), 297–319 (2004)
9. Buchman, E., Kwon, J., Milosevic, Z.: The latest gossip on BFT consensus (2019)
10. Buterin, V., Griffith, V.: Casper the friendly finality gadget (2019)
11. Cachin, C., Kursawe, K., Shoup, V.: Random Oracles in Constantinople: practical asynchronous Byzantine agreement using cryptography. J. Cryptol. **18**(3), 219–246 (2005)
12. Castro, M., Liskov, B.: Practical Byzantine fault tolerance and proactive recovery. ACM Trans. Comput. Syst. (TOCS) **20**(4), 398–461 (2002)
13. Castro, M., Liskov, B.: Practical Byzantine fault tolerance and proactive recovery. ACM Trans. Comput. Syst. **20**(4), 398–461 (2002)
14. Chan, B.Y., Shi, E.: Streamlet: textbook streamlined blockchains. In: Proceedings of the 2nd ACM Conference on Advances in Financial Technologies, AFT 2020, New York, October 2020, pp. 1–11. Association for Computing Machinery (2020)
15. Chan, T.H.H., Pass, R., Shi, E.: PaLa: a simple partially synchronous blockchain. IACR Cryptology ePrint Archive, Paper 2018/981 (2018)
16. Chan, T.H.H., Pass, R., Shi, E.: PiLi: an extremely simple synchronous blockchain. IACR Cryptology ePrint Archive, Paper 2018/980 (2018)
17. GitHub - vmware/concord-bft: concord Byzantine fault tolerant state machine replication library (2021). www.github.com/vmware/concord-bft
18. Danezis, G., Kogias, E.K., Sonnino, A., Spiegelman, A.: Narwhal and Tusk: A DAG-based Mempool and Efficient BFT Consensus, vol. 1. Association for Computing Machinery (2021)
19. David, B., Gaži, P., Kiayias, A., Russell, A.: Ouroboros Praos: an adaptively-secure, semi-synchronous proof-of-stake blockchain. In: Nielsen, J.B., Rijmen, V. (eds.) EUROCRYPT 2018. LNCS, vol. 10821, pp. 66–98. Springer, Cham (2018). https://doi.org/10.1007/978-3-319-78375-8_3
20. Duan, S., Meling, H., Peisert, S., Zhang, H.: BChain: Byzantine replication with high throughput and embedded reconfiguration. In: Aguilera, M.K., Querzoni, L., Shapiro, M. (eds.) OPODIS 2014. LNCS, vol. 8878, pp. 91–106. Springer, Cham (2014). https://doi.org/10.1007/978-3-319-14472-6_7

21. Gelashvili, R., Kokoris-Kogias, L., Sonnino, A., Spiegelman, A., Xiang, Z.: Jolteon and Ditto: network-adaptive efficient consensus with asynchronous fallback. arXiv arxiv.org/abs/2106.10362, June 2021
22. Golan Gueta, G., et al.: SBFT: a scalable and decentralized trust infrastructure. In: 2019 49th Annual IEEE/IFIP International Conference on Dependable Systems and Networks (DSN), June 2019, pp. 568–580. IEEE (2019)
23. Guo, Y., Pass, R., Shi, E.: Synchronous, with a chance of partition tolerance. In: Boldyreva, A., Micciancio, D. (eds.) CRYPTO 2019. LNCS, vol. 11692, pp. 499–529. Springer, Cham (2019). https://doi.org/10.1007/978-3-030-26948-7_18
24. Hanke, T., Movahedi, M., Williams, D.: DFINITY technology overview series, consensus system (2018)
25. Hot-Stuff: hot-stuff/libhotstuff (2021). www.github.com/hot-stuff/libhotstuff
26. Keidar, I., Kokoris-Kogias, E., Naor, O., Spiegelman, A.: All you need is DAG. In: Proceedings of the 2021 ACM Symposium on Principles of Distributed Computing, New York, July 2021, pp. 165–175. ACM (2021)
27. Keidar, I., Naor, O., Shapiro, E.: Cordial miners: blocklace-based ordering consensus protocols for every eventuality, August 2022
28. Lamport, L., Shostak, R., Pease, M.: The Byzantine generals problem. ACM Trans. Program. Lang. Syst. **4**(3), 382–401 (1982)
29. Malkhi, D., Szalachowski, P.: Maximal Extractable Value (MEV) Protection on a DAG. arXiv arXiv:2208.00940, September 2022
30. Momose, A., Ren, L.: Multi-threshold Byzantine fault tolerance. In: Proceedings of the 2021 ACM SIGSAC Conference on Computer and Communications Security, CCS 2021, New York, November 2021, pp. 1686–1699. Association for Computing Machinery (2021)
31. Nakamoto, S.: Bitcoin: a peer-to-peer electronic cash system. Technical report. Manubot (2019)
32. ConsenSys/quorum, September 2021. www.github.com/ConsenSys/quorum. Original-date: 2016–11-14T05:42:57Z
33. Schneider, F.B.: Implementing fault-tolerant services using the state machine approach: a tutorial. ACM Comput. Surv. **22**(4), 299–319 (1990)
34. Shrestha, N., Abraham, I., Ren, L., Nayak, K.: On the optimality of optimistic responsiveness. In: Proceedings of the 2020 ACM SIGSAC Conference on Computer and Communications Security, New York, October 2020, pp. 839–857. ACM (2020)
35. Spiegelman, A., Giridharan, N., Sonnino, A., Kokoris-Kogias, L.: Bullshark: DAG BFT protocols made practical. In: Proceedings of the 2022 ACM SIGSAC Conference on Computer and Communications Security, CCS 2022, New York, November 2022, pp. 2705–2718. Association for Computing Machinery (2022)
36. The DFINITY Team: The Internet Computer for Geeks (2022). https://eprint.iacr.org/2022/087
37. Tendermint: tendermint/tendermint: Tendermint core (BFT consensus) in Go. www.github.com/tendermint/tendermint
38. Wood, G., et al.: Ethereum: a secure decentralised generalised transaction ledger. Ethereum Project Yellow Paper, 151, 1–32 (2014)
39. Yin, M., Malkhi, D., Reiter, M.K., Gueta, G.G., Abraham, I.: HotStuff: BFT consensus with linearity and responsiveness. In: Proceedings of the 2019 ACM Symposium on Principles of Distributed Computing, PODC 2019, New York, July 2019, pp. 347–356. Association for Computing Machinery (2019)

Player-Replaceability and Forensic Support Are Two Sides of the Same (Crypto) Coin

Peiyao Sheng[1]([✉])[iD], Gerui Wang[1,2][iD], Kartik Nayak[3]([✉])[iD],
Sreeram Kannan[4][iD], and Pramod Viswanath[5][iD]

[1] University of Illinois at Urbana-Champaign, Champaign, IL, USA
`psheng2@illinois.edu`
[2] Beijing Academy of Blockchain and Edge Computing, Beijing, China
`wanggerui@baec.org.cn`
[3] Duke University, Durham, NC, USA
`kartik@cs.duke.edu`
[4] University of Washington at Seattle, Seattle, WA, USA
`ksreeram@ece.uw.edu`
[5] Princeton University, Princeton, NJ, USA
`pramodv@princeton.edu`

Abstract. *Player-replaceability* is a property of a blockchain protocol that ensures every step of the protocol is executed by an unpredictably random (small) set of players; this guarantees security against a fully adaptive adversary and is a crucial property in building permissionless blockchains. *Forensic Support* is a property of a blockchain protocol that provides the ability, with cryptographic integrity, to identify malicious parties when there is a safety violation; this provides the ability to enforce punishments for adversarial behavior and is a crucial component of incentive mechanism designs for blockchains. Player-replaceability and strong forensic support are both desirable properties, yet, none of the existing blockchain protocols have *both* properties. Our main result is to construct a new BFT protocol that is player-replaceable *and* has maximum forensic support. The key invention is the notion of a "transition certificate", without which we show that natural adaptations of extant BFT and longest chain protocols do not lead to the desired goal of simultaneous player-replaceability and forensic support. (The full version of paper is available in https://eprint.iacr.org/2022/1513.)

1 Introduction

Byzantine fault tolerant state machine replication (BFT SMR) protocols allow a group of parties to agree on a common sequence of values submitted by external clients. The core security guarantee provided by BFT SMR is that as long as a certain fraction of parties are honest, i.e., follow the protocol, then these parties achieve consensus with respect to a time evolving ledger regardless of the actions of the remaining Byzantine parties that deviate from the protocol. Of particular

© International Financial Cryptography Association 2024
F. Baldimtsi and C. Cachin (Eds.): FC 2023, LNCS 13950, pp. 56–74, 2024.
https://doi.org/10.1007/978-3-031-47754-6_4

interest are secure and efficient BFT SMR protocols: efficiency is measured in terms of commit latency and communication complexity [1,4,13,21,22,30], and security is measured by tolerating the maximum number of Byzantine parties under various network and cryptographic assumptions [2,13–16,18,24].

Security guarantee of BFT protocols is one-sided, addressing the scenario when the number of Byzantine parties is less than a certain threshold. *Forensic support* addresses the other side: what happens when the number of Byzantine parties exceeds the allowable threshold? Several recent works focus on designing secure BFT protocols that also have an additional goal of accountability, i.e., the ability to detect faulty behavior through an irrefutable proof upon security violation [6,11,25,26,29]. A recent work [28] has formally defined forensic support of BFT protocols, providing a unified framework to compare and contrast different designs; [28] provides a detailed analysis of canonical BFT protocols (e.g., PBFT [7,8], HotStuff [30], VABA [3], and Algorand [9,10,17]) with respect to their support for forensics on detecting Byzantine behavior. A key takeaway from this work is that, while forensic support depends heavily on the implementation details of the protocol, deterministically secure protocols with poly(n) communication complexity (here, n is the number of parties in the protocol) have protocol variants with maximum forensic support, i.e., the maximum number of Byzantine parties can be identified irrefutably using simply the transcript available at one of the honest parties.

An entirely different aspect of BFT protocols has emerged with the advent of blockchains and the desire to support the participation of a very large number of players ("permissionless" participation): communication-efficiency (i.e., have sub-quadratic communication complexity) combined with security against a fully adaptive adversary; e.g., Algorand [9] and Ouroboros Praos [12]. Such protocols are commonly referred to as "player-replaceable" since they rely on verifiably selecting small subgroups of truly random parties in each round, thus achieving adaptive security and communication efficiency. Of specific interest are secure blockchain protocols that offer both desired properties: forensic support *and* player-replaceability. We begin by observing that no extant blockchain protocols offer both properties. For instance, HotStuff excels in efficiency and forensic support but is not player-replaceable; Algorand is player-replaceable but has non-existent forensic support [28]. Indeed, no extant blockchain protocol appears to have both player-replaceability and strong forensic support.

Could this status-quo be not coincidental? Player replaceability implies security even though different players are corrupted at different rounds of the protocol; perhaps this strong property inherently rules out the ability to identify malicious parties when security is violated? Understanding the core relationships between player-replaceability and forensic support properties of BFT protocols is the main goal of this paper. Our main result is dissenting: we construct a new BFT protocol that is player-replaceable *and* has strong forensic support (i.e., detecting the maximum number of Byzantine nodes with the minimum number of honest transcripts).

In this paper, we divide our investigation based on two stylistically different families of player-replaceable protocols: BFT protocols and longest-chain protocols. A summary of our results is presented in Table 1.

Table 1. Comparison of forensic properties among different protocols

	Protocol	Byzantine threshold (t)	Player replaceability	Forensic support	(d)
BFT Protocols	Algorand [9]	$n/3$	Yes	None	0
	HotStuff [30]		No	Strong	$\lceil n/3 \rceil$
	Player-replaceable HotStuff (§3.1)		Yes	None	0
Longest-chain Protocols	OBFT [19]	$n/3$	No	Moderate	$n - 2f$
	Ouroboros [20]	$n/2$①	No		$< (n-2f)\kappa/n$
	Ouroboros Praos [12]		Yes		$< (n-2f)\kappa/n - T(n,\kappa)$②
Our Result	Algorithm 3	$n/3$	Yes	Strong	$\lceil \lambda/3 \rceil$③

① In Ouroboros and Praos, forensic support is discussed even when $f < t$.
② κ is a parameter for longest-chain confirmation, $T(n,\kappa) > 0$.
③ λ is the expected size of committee.

Main Result: A Player-Replaceable BFT Protocol with Strong Forensic Support. We first present a novel player-replaceable BFT protocol with strong forensic support in the partially synchronous setting, where "strong" implies that the most number of Byzantine nodes can be detected with the least number of honest transcripts. In particular, we show that when the total fraction of Byzantine parties is less than $(1-\epsilon)2/3$ (ϵ is a positive constant) and the expected committee size is λ, our forensic protocol can detect at least $\lceil \lambda/3 \rceil$ Byzantine parties when safety violations occur. Due to idiosyncratic constraints imposed by player-replaceability, traditional analyses of forensic support [28] do not immediately apply. For instance, a core component of the forensic support analysis of existing BFT protocols relies on identifying parties that perform two or more actions that are incompatible with each other with respect to the protocol specification [28]. The forensic protocol determines appropriate quorums and uses quorum intersection arguments to identify culpable parties. However, with player replaceability, when n is large, *it is extremely unlikely that the same player will be selected twice; thus access to incompatible actions performed by the same player, especially across different rounds (or views) of the protocol, may be unavailable.* One of our key innovations is the notion of "transition certificates", maintained and shared by each party in each round – this ensures that if Byzantine parties vote incorrectly in a round resulting in a safety violation, there is sufficient information to detect misbehavior.

Forensic Analysis for Longest-Chain Protocols. Bitcoin, the prototypical longest-chain protocol, demonstrates ideal player-replaceability: not only is the next proposer not predictable, but also the mined block safe from any later tampering. Indeed, the longest chain rule has inspired both BFT and proof-of-stake (PoS) based player-replaceable blockchain protocols, e.g., Ouroboros family, including Ouroboros BFT (OBFT), Ouroboros, and Ouroboros Praos (referred to simply as Praos in this paper). We first prove that OBFT, as a binary consensus protocol, can hold $n - 2f$ replicas culpable where n and f represent the total number of replicas and the number of actual faults respectively. On the other hand, the number of Byzantine parties detected in Ouroboros and Praos is bounded by $2\kappa(n - 2f)/n$ where κ is the confirmation depth. The bound is a result of the randomized leader election process in the two protocols. It is noteworthy that there is no forensic support when $f > n/2$. However, even if Ouroboros and Praos have Byzantine threshold $t < n/2$, the random election results in possible executions with safety violation when $f < t$. We observe that the safety violation of longest chain protocols can be identified when an honest replica finalizes two conflicting blocks and observes more than one longest chain. In the case of Ouroboros family, this is used to identify malicious leaders who propose more than one valid block in the same round.

Outline. We describe the security model and definitions in §2. §3 contains our main result: the construction of a new BFT protocol endowed with both player-replaceability and strong forensic support. Longest-chain protocols are naturally aligned with the player-replaceability property and we explore their forensic support properties in §4. §5 concludes the paper with a discussion of the relationship between player-replaceability and forensic support. The topic of this paper has not been broached in any prior work, to the best of the authors' knowledge. Works, other than those already referenced, are tangential to the core content here; the connections are discussed for completeness in Appendix A. The practicality and parameter choices of our protocol are formally described in Appendix B.

2   Model and Definitions

We consider a network with n nodes interacting via all-to-all communication. Prior to the protocol execution, each node generates its key pair honestly and sends its public key to all other nodes. The adversary can adaptively corrupt nodes at any time during the protocol execution after the trusted setup. Nodes that are never corrupted are referred to as honest. The total number of nodes corrupted by the adversary in an execution is denoted as f. The maximum number of corrupted nodes the protocols can tolerate is denoted as t.

Network Setting. We consider synchronous and partially synchronous network settings. In a synchronous protocol, a message sent at time T by a sender node is guaranteed to arrive at the receiver node by time $T + \Delta$, where Δ is a bounded network delay. In a partially synchronous protocol, there exists an unknown global stabilization time (GST), after which all transmissions between two honest nodes arrive within a bounded network delay Δ [15].

Blockchains and State Machine Replication (SMR). The goal of blockchains (state machine replication [27]) is to build a public ledger that provides clients a totally ordered sequence of transactions. The key security properties a blockchain protocol should provide are those of safety and liveness. Safety: no two honest nodes finalize two different blocks at the same position in the ledger. Liveness: every valid transaction is eventually finalized by every honest node. We use blockchain and SMR interchangeably and refer to nodes that run blockchain protocols as "replicas" or "players".

Player-Replaceability is a property of blockchain protocols. As presented by Chen and Micali [9], a protocol is player-replaceable if each step of the protocol execution is conducted by an independently and randomly selected subset of players. A player-replaceable protocol achieves both adaptivity and communication efficiency since the adaptive adversary cannot predict the committee membership ahead of time and only a subset of parties (typically sublinear) need to communicate in each round (hence the communication complexity is subquadratic).

Forensic Support for Blockchains. The notion of forensic support for Byzantine Agreement (BA) was introduced by [28]. Forensic support refers to the ability to identify misbehaving replicas whenever there is a safety violation (two honest replicas finalize different blocks at the same position). The number of replicas that can be held culpable when $t < f \leq m$ is captured by the parameter d. Here, m denotes the bound on Byzantine replicas under which the forensic support can be provided. In BA, transcripts of honest parties are needed to obtain irrefutable proof of culprits *after* clients detect a safety violation. The number of transcripts to decide culpability of replicas is denoted by k. In the blockchain setting, we adapt the definition of k to denote the number of transcripts required to detect safety violations and construct the culpability proof.

Definition 1 (m, k, d)-Forensic Support [28]. *If $t < f \leq m$ and there is a safety violation, then using the transcripts of all messages received from k honest replicas during the protocol, a client can provide an irrefutable proof of culpability of at least d Byzantine replicas.*

Cryptographic Primitives. All protocols we discuss in this paper use collision resistant cryptographic hash functions and digital signatures (that are adaptively secure for achieving player-replaceability). $\langle x \rangle$ denotes the signed message x. The intersection of two aggregated signatures refers to the set of replicas who sign both messages. We use verifiable random functions (VRFs) [23] to choose a random subset of replicas to be the leader or committee in a round. In our model, VRF has two functions: $\mathtt{VRF}(x)$ and $\mathtt{VerifyVRF}_{pk}(msg, x)$. $\mathtt{VRF}(x)$ returns two values: a *hash* and a proof π. The hash is a *HASHLEN*-bit value, normalized by $2^{HASHLEN}$, i.e., $hash \in [0, 1)$. It is uniquely determined by sk and x, and indistinguishable from a random value to anyone that does not know sk. The proof π enables anyone that knows pk to verify the value by $\mathtt{VerifyVRF}_{pk}$. In our protocol, $(hash, \pi)$ is always appended to a message and hence not explicitly specified. $\mathtt{VerifyVRF}_{pk}(msg, x)$ verifies that $hash$ is the correct value computed from x by using π. The appended $hash$ value is denoted by $msg.vrf$. We omit the notation of sk, pk and the appended $(hash, \pi)$ when the context is clear. In some of the protocols, VRFs may be used to elect leaders and/or committees to obtain player-replaceability, i.e., every step of the protocol is executed by a potentially new set of parties. This approach was pioneered in [9] to construct protocols secure under fully adaptive adversaries that are also efficient, i.e., subquadratic communication complexity.

3   Main Results

Our main result is the first player-replaceable BFT protocol that has strong (maximum) forensic support. In particular, we construct a partially synchronous, player-replaceable BFT protocol (§3.2) that tolerates $t = (1 - \epsilon)n/3$ Byzantine faults for safety and liveness while providing forensic support with $t < f \leq (1 - \epsilon)2n/3$, where ϵ is a positive constant.

We start with a warm-up protocol (§3.1) that makes HotStuff [30] player-replaceable using ideas in Algorand [9] but it is shown to lack forensic support. Inspired by the learnings, we design our protocol which is equipped with an additional step, called *certified transition*, to obtain both player-replaceability and strong forensic support. We provide the forensic protocol and formally prove that when there is a safety violation, the protocol can hold at least $\lceil \lambda/3 \rceil$ Byzantine replicas culpable with irrefutable proof (§3.3).

3.1   Warmup: HotStuff Made Player-Replaceable

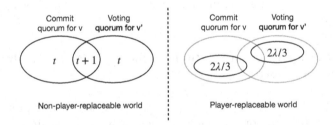

Fig. 1. Comparison of non-player-replaceable and player-replaceable worlds.

The most intuitive approach to obtain both properties is to start with a protocol with strong forensic support and make it player-replaceable. For instance, we can start with HotStuff [30] (or Tendermint [5]) and make it player-replaceable using techniques from Algorand [9]. Specifically, in each round of voting, replicas perform cryptographic sortition to determine whether they are eligible to vote in the current round. Such a sortition is publicly verifiable and produces a randomly and independently selected voting committee in each round.

While the use of sortition enables player-replaceability, the protocol still falls short of providing forensic support. In HotStuff with forensic support, when there is a safety violation, the forensic support protocol can always map it back to a set of culpable parties that have performed (at least) two contradictory actions, thus not following the protocol. Such behavior is observable even in non-trivial violations that happen across rounds. In particular, in a non-player-replaceable world, since a majority of honest parties guard the safety of the commit, there does not exist enough votes for a different value when $f \leq t$. When $f > t$, it has been shown in [28] that we can detect $t + 1$ such parties whenever there is a safety violation. Intuitively, the idea uses a quorum intersection between the $2t + 1$ parties that send a commit message for the first committed value v and a specific set of $2t+1$ parties that vote on a different value v' later (cf. left figure in Fig. 1), where the voting quorum for a different value consists of honest parties who hold stale states, and Byzantine parties trying to violate the safety.

Unfortunately, with player-replaceable protocols, such an argument does not apply. Since only a small λ-sized fraction (λ is a security parameter) of parties are chosen each time, it is highly likely that a replica is elected in the committee only once. As is shown in Fig. 1 on the right, the quorums from the committee in two distinct rounds are mutually exclusive with high probability, due to which the continuity of participation of a single replica is lost. In other words, we cannot distinguish between Byzantine replicas from honest replicas with stale states since in any of the cases, since Byzantine replicas can deliberately mimic the behavior of honest replicas who suffer long message delays. By contradiction, suppose forensic support is possible in some case, i.e., some Byzantine replicas voting for a different value are made accountable, there must exist a corresponding scenario where these accountable replicas are honest (and their behaviors are simulated by Byzantine parties in the first case). Thus, we may not have any forensic support under this circumstance when $f > t$ while still being safe and live when $f \leq t$.

3.2 Construction of a Player-Replaceable BFT Protocol with Strong Forensic Support

Intuition. To address the above concern, the intuition of our protocol is to enforce replicas to wait for enough messages (2/3 of the committee size) to form a *transition certificate (TC)* of each round r before entering round $r + 1$. Waiting for messages of round r ensures that a replica's state is up-to-date at the beginning of round $r + 1$, then the scenario where honest parties are blamed due to message delays are no longer possible. Therefore, no honest replicas have stale states and we can distinguish honest replicas who suffer long message delays from Byzantine replicas, and have strong forensic support. Starting from this intuition, we design the protocol with safety and liveness properties as well as strong forensic support.

Protocol Overview. The protocol proceeds in a sequence of consecutive rounds where each round lasts for at least 4Δ time (as measured by each replica's own clock). In each round, a set of leaders and a committee will be self-selected from all replicas using cryptographic sortition. The role of a leader is to collect *votes* from committee members and generate a *quorum certificate (QC)* from the votes. It then proposes a *block* that contains the QC to all replicas. The role of a committee member is to wait for the leader's proposal and, if it is valid, to vote for it. We first describe the sortition process used for election, then define the data structures used in the protocol, and finally present the protocol.

Cryptographic Sortition. We use cryptographic sortition to choose a random subset of parties as leaders or committee members, by using VRF [23]. A replica determines its eligibility to be the next leader or the committee member by computing VRF from the random seed, the round, and the role ("*leader*" or "*committee*"), i.e., $\mathsf{VRF}(seed\|curRound\|role)$, $role \in \{\text{"leader"}, \text{"committee"}\}$. If the VRF hash value is smaller than a threshold, the replica is eligible and when it fulfills its role by broadcasting a message, it accompanies the VRF output (hash value and proof) thus allowing other replicas to verify its eligibility. For a message m, we denote the accompanied VRF hash value as $m.vrf$. The threshold is set to τ/n for leader and λ/n for committee where τ and λ are the expected number of leaders and the committee size, respectively. Hence, to validate cryptographic sortition of a message m, a replica calls $\mathsf{VerifyVRF}$ and checks whether $m.vrf < \tau/n$ or λ/n appropriately. To ensure that some block is proposed in each round with high probability, parameter τ should be chosen much larger than 1, e.g., Algorand [17] chooses $\tau = 26$. We denote $t_H \leftarrow \lceil 2\lambda/3 \rceil$ as the number of votes used to form a QC.

Cryptographic sortition enables player-replaceability in a straightforward manner. In each round, a new leader and committee are elected privately, i.e., only the elected parties know their eligibility before they fulfill their roles. To be resilient to strongly adaptive adversaries, the protocol can use ephemeral keys as in Algorand [10]. For simplicity, we use the same random seed in the genesis block for cryptographic sortition in all rounds. The protocol can be enhanced with a frequently refreshing random seed, as in Algorand [17]. Cryptographic sortition also works in a proof-of-stake setting if eligibility is weighted by stakes.

Blocks and Quorum Certificates. Client requests are batched into *blocks*. Each block references its predecessor (parent) with the exception of the genesis block which has no predecessor. A block proposed in round r, denoted b_r, has the following format: $b_r := (cmd, parent, justify)$. cmd denotes client commands to be committed, *parent* denotes the hash of the parent block of block b_r, and *justify* stores the quorum certificate (QC) for the parent block. A QC for a block b_r consists of at least t_H vote messages. A QC contains the hash, the round number of the block, and metadata such as signatures and accompanying VRF outputs of the vote messages. Notice that we abuse the notation $qc.block$ to refer to the actual block instead of the block hash when the context is clear. A block is said to be valid if its parent is valid (genesis block is always valid) and client requests in the block meet application-level validity conditions. A block b_r extends a block $b_{r'}$ if $b_{r'}$ is an ancestor of b_r. Note that a block extends itself. Two blocks b_r and $b'_{r'}$ are conflicting if they do not extend one another.

Full Protocol. Each replica maintains a lock denoted as *lockedQC* initialized as $qc_{genesis}$, and a set of $(id, lockedQC)$ pairs for every round, where id is the replica identifier. Each round proceeds as follows. (The full protocol is also presented in Algorithm 3, Appendix C.)

- **Propose.** A replica checks its potential leader eligibility using cryptographic sortition (line 7). Leader can construct a new QC and update its own lock once receiving t_H votes for the same block. Then the leader collects commands and proposes a new block extending from *lockedQC.block*.
- **Process proposals.** Unlike HotStuff, a replica waits for a fixed length period (period $[0, 2\Delta)$) for proposals in case there are multiple leaders eligible to propose (line 13). When a replica receives multiple proposals, it chooses the one with the smallest VRF hash (line 15). At time 2Δ of this round, all replicas check the validity of the block and the *safety rule* to ensure the new block extends from *lockedQC.block* (line 17). If the block is valid and safe, replicas will update *lockedQC, TC* properly. When two consecutive QCs are formed, the block is *directly* finalized, and all its previous blocks on the same chain will also be finalized *indirectly* (line 35).
- **Vote and timeout.** Then every replica checks its eligibility to vote for the round (line 20). The vote message is denoted as $\langle \text{VOTE}, r, b, lockedQC, TC[r - 1] \rangle$, where r is the current round number, b is the hash of the block the committee replica votes for, $TC[r - 1]$ is the set of locks collected from the last round (line 21). When $b = \emptyset$, the vote message serves as a timeout message and meanwhile contains the lock of the committee replica. When b is not empty, it is required that $b.justify = lockedQC$. For each round, replicas selected as committee broadcast their votes to all replicas.
- **Wait for locks.** All replicas cannot enter a round r until they receive t_H locks reported by the committee in round $r - 1$. If a vote message in r is received from a replica whose lock has not been received in this round, the lock is added into a set $TC[r]$, and if the lock is more up-to-date, the replica updates its own lock (line 26). The replicas will also update $TC[r - 1]$ given $TC^*[r - 1]$ contained in the vote. At time 4Δ or later of a round r, replicas enter the next round $r + 1$ if $|TC[r]| \geq t_H$.

Communication Complexity. The communication complexity of Algorithm 3 is $O(n \cdot poly(\lambda))$ where λ is a security parameter denoting the committee size. In each round, only λ replicas in the committee broadcast messages and the TC in messages is $O(\lambda)$-sized.

3.3   Forensic Protocol and Proof of Forensic Support

When $f < (1 - \epsilon)n/3$, the safety and liveness of Algorithm 3 are formally stated in Appendix C. When $f \geq (1 - \epsilon)n/3$, it is possible that safety is violated, at which time the following forensic protocol in Algorithm 1 can provide forensic support proved in Theorem 1.

Theorem 1 *When $f \geq (1 - \epsilon)n/3$, if two honest replicas finalize conflicting blocks, Algorithm 1 provides $((1 - \epsilon)2n/3, 2, \lceil \lambda/3 \rceil)$-forensic support.*

Algorithm 1. Forensic protocol for Algorithm 3

1: **upon receiving** conflicting blocks finalized by two honest replicas **do**
2:    query the entire blockchain from the two honest replicas
3:    find the first block finalized by consecutive QCs in each chain, denoted by $b_r, b_{r'}$
4:    swap $b_r, b_{r'}$ if $r' < r$ ▷ make sure $r \leq r'$
5:    **if** $r + 2 > r'$ **then**
6:        find two $QC_{r'}$ on each chain
7:        return the intersection of two $QC_{r'}$
8:    **else**
9:        query $TC[r + 1]$ from either of the honest replicas
10:       **if** all $lockedQC$ in $TC[r + 1]$ has round $< r$ **then**
11:           find QC_{r+1} that makes b_r be committed
12:           return the intersection of $TC[r + 1]$ and QC_{r+1}
13:       **else**
14:           find block b_{r^*} s.t.
                  (1) $r + 2 \leq r^* \leq r'$, and
                  (2) $b_{r'}$ extends b_{r^*}, and
                  (3) b_r conflicts with b_{r^*}, and
                  (4) r^* is the smallest round satisfying the above 3 conditions
15:           find QC for b_{r^*}, denoted by QC_{r^*}, return all replicas in QC_{r^*}

Proof Suppose two conflicting blocks are finalized by two honest replicas, let $b_r, b_{r'}$ be the first directly finalized blocks that are conflicting, w.l.o.g., suppose $r \leq r'$.

Case $r + 2 > r'$.
Culpability. If $r \leq r' < r + 2$, there are two quorums formed in r', these two $\overline{QC_{r'}}$ intersect in $\lceil \lambda/3 \rceil$ replicas. These replicas should be Byzantine since the protocol requires a replica to vote for at most one block in a round.
Witnesses. In this case, the culpability proof can be constructed from two QCs generated in the same round (line 5–7, Algorithm 3).

Case $r + 2 \leq r'$.
Culpability. Since b_r is directly finalized in round $r + 2$ (by QC_{r+1}), it must be the case that at least t_H committee replicas are locked on at least QC_r (if they are honest), and broadcast their votes with lock to all replicas. Then consider the first block b_{r^*} (possibly $b_{r'}$) that is conflicting with b_r and proposed after $r + 1$. On the one hand, b_{r^*} must be extended from a block older than b_r since this is the first conflicting block proposed after r. On the other hand, only those replicas whose locks are staler than QC_r can vote for b_{r^*}. Remember that in round $r + 1$, at least t_H committee replicas broadcast lock QC_r (or higher lock). And for committee replicas in r^* to vote, they must collect a set $TC[\cdot]$ consisting of at least t_H locks from the committee in every round $< r^*$. If the lock of any one of them is still staler than QC_r, the intersection ($\lceil \lambda/3 \rceil$ replicas) of QC_{r+1} and $TC[r + 1]$ is the set of committee replicas who equivocate in round $r + 1$ hence are Byzantine (line 10–12, Algorithm 3). Otherwise all the committee replicas who vote for b_{r^*} must be Byzantine (line 13–15, Algorithm 3).

Witnesses. In this case, there are two possible scenarios. (i) QC_{r+1} intersects $TC[r+1]$ in $\lceil \lambda/3 \rceil$ replicas, who are culpable since their votes in QC_{r+1} and $TC[r+1]$ are incompatible. (ii) All replicas in QC_{r^*} (at least t_H in total) are Byzantine because they should have received $TC[r+1]$ containing QC_r and update their locks to be at least QC_r, but they vote for a conflicting block b_{r^*} extending from a block older than r. These two cases indicate that with same-round safety violation, the witnesses can detect $\lceil \lambda/3 \rceil$ replicas. If same-round safety violation does not exist, at least t_H culprits can be detected.

4   Forensic Analysis for Player-Replaceable Longest-Chain Protocols

Longest-chain based protocols such as Bitcoin and Ouroboros are another family of SMR protocols. Compared to BFT protocols, they do not have explicit voting procedure and finalization of a block is probabilistic. In this section, we show that forensic support for longest-chain protocols targets leader proposals, and we investigate how player-replaceability influences the forensic properties by analyzing the Ouroboros protocol family, including Ouroboros BFT (OBFT) [19], Ouroboros [20], and Ouroboros Praos [12] (referred to as Praos).

4.1   Protocol Description

Ouroboros is a proof-of-stake blockchain protocol which tolerates up to $1/2$ Byzantine stake under a synchronous network. Building on Ouroboros, Praos is a player-replaceable protocol secure under an adaptive adversary. On the other hand, OBFT is a deterministic permissioned derivative of Ouroboros for ledger consensus. We start with a general simplified description of Ouroboros family.

Each of the n replicas maintain the longest blockchain $C = b_0 \cdots b_r$ (b_0 is the genesis block and round number $r \geq 0$) containing a sequence of blocks. The length of a blockchain is the number of blocks on the chain, and the height of a block b_r is the length of chain $b_0 \cdots b_r$. Each block $b_r := (data, parent, proof)$ proposed in round r contains block data $data$, the hash of the parent block $parent$, and a block proof $proof$ that replicas can use to verify the validity of the block. The block is valid if its data and parent are valid, and it is signed by a certified round leader. The protocol proceeds in rounds, in round j, replica i performs the following.

- **Blockchain update.** The replica collects chains diffused by all valid leaders in the current round as set $\mathbb{C}$. Denote the longest valid chain (does not fork from C more than κ blocks) among $\mathbb{C}$ as C'. It updates its local longest chain C with C' if C' is strictly longer.
- **Blockchain extension.** If the replica is a leader in the current round, it generates a new block with a proof of leader (stored in $proof$). After the new block is appended to the local longest chain, the replica diffuses the new chain to other replicas.

Algorithm 2. Forensic protocol for OBFT

1: **upon receiving** conflicting outputs from two honest replicas **do**
2:     query the entire blockchain from the two honest replicas
3:     $r, r' \leftarrow$ minimum / maximum round number among all blocks
4:     $S \leftarrow \emptyset$
5:     **for** $i = r, r + 1, \cdots, r'$ **do**
6:         **if** two conflicting blocks are generated in round i by a valid leader **then**
7:             add leader j of round i into S $\triangleright j - 1 = (i - 1) \mod n$ in OBFT
8:     return S

The key distinguishing factors between the protocols we consider are the leader election process and the confirmation depth κ. We describe these in more detail for each of the three protocols below. Observe that we omit details related to message verification, stake distribution, randomness generation, etc. in our analysis since they do not matter in terms of forensic support. In terms of stake distribution, for our analysis we assume the stake of each of the parties are equal, although our analysis should be generalizable when the stakes are not equal.

4.2 Forensic Support for OBFT

We start with the simplest of the three protocols, OBFT, which is a deterministic permissioned protocol. In OBFT, leaders are elected in a round-robin manner, i.e., in round j, if $i - 1 = (j - 1) \mod n$, replica i is the round leader. Moreover, a block is committed if it is on the longest chain that is $\kappa = 3t + 1$ blocks deep.

Security Analysis. The key property satisfied by OBFT is that the blockchain is not forkable during a period of execution where the fraction of Byzantine leaders over all rounds is $< 1/3$ [19, Proposition 3.7]. Furthermore, under covert adversaries (who do not leave any verifiable evidence of misbehavior), the threshold of Byzantine leaders' fraction becomes $1/2$.

First, observe that the adversary can simply behave as covert adversary to fork the chain when $f > n/2$, in which case no cryptographic evidence will be left behind and therefore there is no forensic support (formally stated in Theorem 1). Thus, we argue about forensic support only when $n/3 \leq f < n/2$. In such a situation, the adversary can undertake multiple malicious actions such as not extending any chain when it is the leader, extending a smaller chain, extending more than one chain, etc. Among these, the only detectable action is when a Byzantine leader proposes two or more blocks in the same round. Thus, given a safety violation (i.e., two or more chains of depth κ), if any leader proposes two different blocks in these chains in the same round, it is a Byzantine replica. The proof to hold it culpable are the two signed blocks.

The key part of our forensic analysis is to determine the minimum number of rounds that must equivocate to violate safety for an execution. The following lemma formally presents a bound on equivocating rounds (see proof in Appendix E.1).

Lemma 1 $\forall i \in [r, r']$, we define

$$\omega_i = \begin{cases} 0 & \text{the leader of block in round } i \text{ is unique and honest} \\ 1 & \text{otherwise} \end{cases}$$

If there exist two or more longest chains that diverge from height h until $h+l-1$, define $R_{\mathcal{H}} = |\{\omega_i = 0 | r \leq i \leq r'\}|$ as the number of rounds whose leader is unique and honest (where r, r' are the minimum/maximum round number among all blocks with height between h and $h + l - 1$), $R_{\mathcal{A}} = |\{\omega_i = 1 | r \leq i \leq r'\}|$ as the number of rounds that possibly equivocate (generate more than one block).

Denote the number of rounds whose leader generates two or more blocks (for each chain) as X, then we have $X \geq R_{\mathcal{H}} - R_{\mathcal{A}}$.

Applying the above lemma to an execution of binary consensus version of OBFT, where the protocol terminates after $2n$ rounds and the majority bits of the first n rounds of blocks will be output (the first n blocks are finalized by κ-deep rule when $n = 3t + 1$), we can get the following theorem.

Theorem 2 *When $n/3 \leq f < n/2$, if two honest replicas output conflicting values, Ouroboros BFT has $(n/2, 2, n - 2f)$-forensic support.*

Proof Suppose safety fails, i.e., when protocol terminates, there exist two longest chains finalized by honest replicas, whose majority bits among the first n rounds are different. Since OBFT uses round-robin leader election, we can apply Lemma 1 with $R = r' - r + 1 = n$, $R_{\mathcal{H}} = n - f$ and $R_{\mathcal{A}} \leq f$ (since some Byzantine replicas may stay silent), then $d = R_{\mathcal{H}} - R_{\mathcal{A}} \geq n - 2f$.

Notice that in Theorem 2, $d = n - 2f = 0$ when $f = n/2$, thus $m = n/2$. And two honest replicas are required to provide two different longest chains for irrefutable proof, thus $k = 2$. With two different chains, the forensic protocol to detect Byzantine leaders is to find these rounds whose leaders have proposed more than one values (Algorithm 2). Further, the impossibility for $f > n/2$ is formally stated in Appendix D.

4.3   Forensic Support for Ouroboros and Praos

In Ouroboros and Praos, the leader election process is randomized. In Ouroboros, in each round, a unique leader is elected randomly among the n replicas. In Praos, each replica evaluates a round dependent VRF independently. The probability of a replica i with relative stake α_i to be selected as a round leader is

$$\Pr[i \text{ is a leader}] = \phi_w(\alpha_i) = 1 - (1 - w)^{\alpha_i}$$

where w is the probability of electing a replica in a round when it holds all the stake. The probability of electing a leader with lesser stake is scaled as described above; due to this, zero, one or multiple leaders may be elected in a round.

Since the leader election process is randomized, "forkability" of the chain is not deterministic. However, when considering a single execution after safety is violated, since they are executed under the same longest chain rule, a similar intuition as in OBFT is still applicable for forensic support. Even though these protocols tolerate $t < n/2$ w.h.p., there may be executions with safety violation when the fraction of adversarial rounds is $< 1/2$ independent of f.[1] We formally discuss this in the following theorem.

Theorem 3 *For a given execution, if during rounds $[r, r + R - 1]$, two honest replicas finalize two conflicting blocks at height h (i.e., there exist two longest chains that diverge from height h to $h + \kappa - 1$), then* Ouroboros *has $(n/2, 2, d)$-forensic support where $d = (1 - \epsilon)\left(n\left(1 - (1 - 1/n)^R\right) - 2fR/n\right)$ except with $\exp(-\Omega(R))$ probability.*

We provide a short proof here, with complete proof in Appendix E.2. According to Lemma 1, the expected number of rounds whose leader equivocates $E[X] \geq E[R_{\mathcal{H}} - R_{\mathcal{A}}] \geq (n - 2f)R/n$. However, some of these rounds may have the same leaders, denote D as the number of rounds whose leader has been selected before, then $E[d] \geq E[X - D] \geq (n - 2f)R/n - (R - n\left(1 - (1 - 1/n)^R\right))$. Finally, using a Chernoff bound, we have $d = (1 - \epsilon)\left(n\left(1 - (1 - 1/n)^R\right) - 2fR/n\right)$ for $\epsilon > 0$ except with $\exp(-\Omega(R))$ probability.

Corollary 1 *When $R/n = o(1)$,* Ouroboros *has $(n/2, 2, d)$-forensic support where $d = (1 - \epsilon)(n - 2f)\kappa/n$ except with $\exp(-\Omega(\kappa))$ probability.*

Proof When $R/n = o(1)$, by binomial approximation, $E[D] \sim 0$. With $R \geq \kappa$, we have $E[d] \geq (n - 2f)\kappa/n$. Using a Chernoff bound, we have $d = (1 - \epsilon)(n - 2f)\kappa/n$ for $\epsilon > 0$ except with $\exp(-\Omega(\kappa))$ probability.

The random leader election process of Ouroboros adds some uncertainty to the forensic analysis due to possibly duplicated equivocating leaders, which slightly impairs the forensic ability (though when κ/n is very small, this effect will be negligible). In comparison, since in Praos multiple leaders may be elected in a round, there may be equivocation even when all of them are honest. In this case, if multiple honest leaders are elected in round i, $\omega_i = 1$ per the definition in Lemma 1, the round may contribute to the violation of safety. But such leaders in these rounds should not be held culpable by the forensic protocol.

Recall the probability for any replica i to be elected as a leader in a round is defined as $\phi_w(\alpha_i)$. Observe that the probability that no one is elected as a leader in some round is

$$p_0 = \Pr[\text{no leader is elected}] = \prod_{i=1}^{n}(1 - w)^{1/n} = 1 - w$$

---

[1] Our paper discusses the forensic ability after a safety violation happens. In particular, we ignore *when* such a violation happens. The probability of such a safety violation has been shown in Ouroboros [20, Figure 8].

And the probability that only one honest or adversarial leader is elected is

$$p_1^{\mathcal{H}} = \Pr[\text{one honest leader}] = (n - f)(1 - (1 - w)^{1/n})(1 - w)^{1-1/n} = (n - f)g(n)$$

$$p_1^{\mathcal{A}} = \Pr[\text{one adversarial leader}] = f(1 - (1 - w)^{1/n})(1 - w)^{1-1/n} = fg(n)$$

where $g(n) = (1 - (1 - w)^{1/n})(1 - w)^{1-1/n}$. Therefore,

$$\Pr[\text{multiple leaders are elected}] = p_2 = 1 - p_0 - p_1^{\mathcal{H}} - p_1^{\mathcal{A}} = w - ng(n)$$

Based on the analysis above, **Praos** has the following forensic support.

Theorem 4 *For a given execution, if during rounds $[r, r + R - 1]$, two honest replicas finalize two conflicting blocks at height h (i.e. there exist two longest chains that diverge from height h until $h+\kappa-1$). Ouroboros **Praos** has $(n/2, 2, d)$-forensic support where $d = (1 - \epsilon)((n - 2f)g(n)R - T(n, R))$ except with $\exp(-\Omega(R))$ probability, and $T(n, R) = 2(w - ng(n))R + (R - n + n(1 - g(n))^R) > 0$.*

Corollary 2 Ouroboros **Praos** *has $(n/2, 2, d)$-forensic support where*

$$d = (1 - \epsilon)((w - w^2)(n - 2f)\kappa/n - (1 - w + 3w^2)\kappa)$$

when $R/n = o(1)$, except with $\exp(-\Omega(\kappa))$ probability.

The complete proof of Theorem 4 and Corollary 2 are presented in Appendix E.3 and E.4 respectively.

5   Discussion and Conclusion

We begin with two observations about the forensic properties for player-replaceable protocols in both families.

First, compared to quadratic complexity protocols analyzed in [28], player-replaceable protocols require fewer replicas to send messages; correspondingly, only fewer replicas ($O(\lambda)$ or $O(\kappa)$) can be held culpable when there is a safety violation even if the total number of Byzantine replicas are far higher ($O(n)$). For BFT style protocols, whenever forensic support is available, the number of culpable replicas is in the same proportion to the quorum size as in the non player-replaceable setting. Moreover, this number is independent of f. When there is no forensic support, no replica may be held culpable. On the other hand, since longest-chain style protocols are synchronous and can tolerate $t < n/2$, our detection is applicable in the regime $n/3 \leq f < n/2$. Safety violation is still possible since these protocols are randomized. In this case, we observe that the number of culpable replicas decreases linearly as f increases.

Second, qualitatively, the key difficulty with holding replicas culpable is related to potentially having a different set of replicas participating in each round. In BFT protocols, voting rules stipulate how previous actions impose restrictions on current behavior. Due to player-replaceability, voters' behaviors across rounds are less traceable, which can be utilized by adversary to conceal evidence of deviation. Thus, to construct a protocol with strong forensic support, we need to reconnect across-rounds actions. In our protocol, transition certificates serve as the link that the forensic protocol can use to identify culpable behavior. In longest-chain protocols, extending blocks are also used to certify the previous blocks. However, there is no evidence if a Byzantine replica appends blocks to a shorter chain. Thus the only culpable behavior our forensic protocol can detect is when a leader double proposes blocks (equivocates) in a round. As a consequence, the forensic analysis for longest-chain protocols only focuses on the same-round behavior. Player-replaceability can still adversely affect forensic analysis if multiple leaders are allowed to be elected in the same round. However, as seen in Corollary 2, this has a limited effect when κ/n is small.

Blockchain protocols perform two distinct roles: first, they are secure against adversarial behavior (by a fraction of participating nodes). Second, they are imbibed with incentives that encourage participation, and furthermore via honest behavior (i.e., following protocol). In this paper, forensic support of protocols serves the implicit role of incentives (identification of Byzantine action with cryptographic integrity strongly discourages deviation from following protocol). By studying both strong security (i.e., against fully adaptive adversaries) and strong forensic support (i.e., identifying the maximum number of Byzantine nodes from just the transcripts of two honest nodes) we are considering both sides of the blockchain protocol (resistance to Byzantine behavior as well as incentives to promote honest behavior). Further, the identification of BFT protocols with both strong security and strong forensic support properties allows us to construct blockchain protocols with implicitly built incentive mechanisms. It is in these two senses that the title of this manuscript is constructed.

Appendix

Appendix is available online in https://eprint.iacr.org/2022/1513.

Algorithm 3. A player-replaceable, partially synchronous SMR protocol

1: $t_H \leftarrow \lceil 2\lambda/3 \rceil$
2: $TC[0] \leftarrow \emptyset$, $Votes[0] \leftarrow \emptyset$
3: $lockedQC \leftarrow qc_{genesis}$ ▷ the lock variable
4: **for** $curRound \leftarrow 1, 2, \dots$ **do**
    ▷ At time 0 of $curRound$
5:    $TC[curRound] \leftarrow \emptyset$
6:    $Votes[curRound] \leftarrow \emptyset$
7:    **if** $\mathrm{VRF}(seed \| curRound \| \text{``leader''}) < \tau/n$ **then**   ▷ as the leader of $curRound$
8:        **if** $\exists h, s.t. | Votes[curRound-1][h] | \geq t_H \leftarrow \emptyset$ **then**
9:            $lockedQC \leftarrow$ QC generated from $Votes[curRound-1][h]$
10:        create block b^* where $b^*.justify \leftarrow lockedQC$; $b^*.cmd \leftarrow$ commands from clients; $b^*.parent \leftarrow lockedQC.block$
11:        broadcast $\langle \mathrm{PROPOSAL}, curRound, b^*, TC[curRound-1] \rangle$
12:    $m \leftarrow \emptyset$
13:    **upon receiving** $m' \leftarrow \langle \mathrm{PROPOSAL}, curRound, b^*, TC[curRound-1] \rangle$ from a leader whose cryptographic sortition is valid **do**
14:        **if** $(m = \emptyset) \vee (m'.vrf < m.vrf)$ **then**
15:            $m \leftarrow m'$ ▷ m is the proposal with the min VRF hash
    ▷ At time 2Δ of $curRound$
16:    $blockHash = \emptyset$
17:    **if** m is not empty and $m.b^*$ extends from $lockedQC.block$ **then**
18:        $\mathrm{PROCESSPROPOSAL}(m)$ (line 30)
19:        $blockHash = H(m.b^*)$
20:    **if** $\mathrm{VRF}(seed \| curRound \| \text{``committee''}) < \lambda/n$ **then**▷ as a committee member of $curRound$
21:        broadcast $\langle \mathrm{VOTE}, curRound, blockHash, lockedQC, TC[curRound-1] \rangle$
22:    **while** $|TC[curRound]| < t_H$ or before 4Δ of $curRound$ **do**
23:        wait for $\langle \mathrm{VOTE}, curRound, h^*, lockedQC, TC[curRound-1] \rangle$ whose cryptographic sortition is valid
    ▷ At any time (triggered by receiving a vote)
24: **upon receiving** $\langle \mathrm{VOTE}, r, h^*, lockedQC^*, TC^*[r-1] \rangle$ s.t. sender's cryptographic sortition is valid **do**
25:    add VOTE message to set $Votes[r][h^*]$
26:    **if** sender id has no entry in $TC[r]$ **then**
27:        $TC[r] \leftarrow TC[r] \cup \{(id, lockedQC^*)\}$
28:        $lockedQC \leftarrow \max_{round}\{lockedQC^*, lockedQC\}$ ▷ do not update in case of a draw
29:    $TC[r-1] \leftarrow TC[r-1] \cup TC^*[r-1]$▷ do not update in case an entry for an id exists
30: **procedure** $\mathrm{PROCESSPROPOSAL}(\langle \mathrm{PROPOSAL}, r, b^*, TC^*[r-1] \rangle)$
31:    $lockedQC \leftarrow \max_{round}\{b^*.justify, lockedQC\}$ ▷ do not update in case of a draw
32:    $TC[r-1] \leftarrow TC[r-1] \cup TC^*[r-1]$▷ do not update in case an entry for an id exists
33:    $b' \leftarrow b^*.parent$, $b \leftarrow b'.parent$
34:    **if** b, b', b^* are in consecutive rounds **then**
35:        finalize block b (directly) and all blocks before b (indirectly), execute commands in the finalized blocks

References

1. Abraham, I., et al.: Communication complexity of Byzantine agreement, revisited. In: Proceedings of the 2019 ACM Symposium on Principles of Distributed Computing, pp. 317–326 (2019)
2. Abraham, I., Devadas, S., Dolev, D., Nayak, K., Ren, L.: Synchronous Byzantine agreement with expected $O(1)$ rounds, expected $O(n^2)$ communication, and optimal resilience. In: Goldberg, I., Moore, T. (eds.) FC 2019. LNCS, vol. 11598, pp. 320–334. Springer, Cham (2019). https://doi.org/10.1007/978-3-030-32101-7_20
3. Abraham, I., Malkhi, D., Spiegelman, A.: Asymptotically optimal validated asynchronous Byzantine agreement. In: Proceedings of the 2019 ACM Symposium on Principles of Distributed Computing, pp. 337–346 (2019)
4. Abraham, I., Nayak, K., Ren, L., Xiang, Z.: Good-case latency of Byzantine broadcast: a complete categorization. arXiv preprint arXiv:2102.07240 (2021)
5. Buchman, E., Kwon, J., Milosevic, Z.: The latest gossip on BFT consensus. arXiv preprint arXiv:1807.04938 (2018)
6. Buterin, V., Griffith, V.: Casper the friendly finality gadget. arXiv preprint arXiv:1710.09437 (2017)
7. Castro, M., Liskov, B.: Practical Byzantine fault tolerance and proactive recovery. ACM Trans. Comput. Syst. (TOCS) 20(4), 398–461 (2002)
8. Castro, M., Liskov, B., et al.: Practical Byzantine fault tolerance. In: OSDI, vol. 99, pp. 173–186 (1999)
9. Chen, J., Gorbunov, S., Micali, S., Vlachos, G.: ALGORAND AGREEMENT: super fast and partition resilient byzantine agreement. IACR Cryptology ePrint Archive, Paper 2018/377 (2018)
10. Chen, J., Micali, S.: Algorand: a secure and efficient distributed ledger. Theoret. Comput. Sci. 777, 155–183 (2019)
11. Civit, P., Gilbert, S., Gramoli, V.: Polygraph: accountable Byzantine agreement. IACR Cryptology ePrint Archive, Paper 2019/587 (2019)
12. David, B., Gaži, P., Kiayias, A., Russell, A.: Ouroboros Praos: an adaptively-secure, semi-synchronous proof-of-stake blockchain. In: Nielsen, J.B., Rijmen, V. (eds.) EUROCRYPT 2018. LNCS, vol. 10821, pp. 66–98. Springer, Cham (2018). https://doi.org/10.1007/978-3-319-78375-8_3
13. Dolev, D., Reischuk, R.: Bounds on information exchange for Byzantine agreement. J. ACM (JACM) 32(1), 191–204 (1985)
14. Dolev, D., Strong, H.R.: Authenticated algorithms for Byzantine agreement. SIAM J. Comput. 12(4), 656–666 (1983)
15. Dwork, C., Lynch, N., Stockmeyer, L.: Consensus in the presence of partial synchrony. J. ACM (JACM) 35(2), 288–323 (1988)
16. Fischer, M.J., Lynch, N.A., Merritt, M.: Easy impossibility proofs for distributed consensus problems. Distrib. Comput. 1(1), 26–39 (1986)
17. Gilad, Y., Hemo, R., Micali, S., Vlachos, G., Zeldovich, N.: Algorand: scaling Byzantine agreements for cryptocurrencies. In: Proceedings of the 26th Symposium on Operating Systems Principles, pp. 51–68 (2017)
18. Katz, J., Koo, C.-Y.: On expected constant-round protocols for Byzantine agreement. In: Dwork, C. (ed.) CRYPTO 2006. LNCS, vol. 4117, pp. 445–462. Springer, Heidelberg (2006). https://doi.org/10.1007/11818175_27
19. Kiayias, A., Russell, A.: Ouroboros-BFT: a simple Byzantine fault tolerant consensus protocol. IACR Cryptology ePrint Archive, Paper 2018/1049 (2018)

20. Kiayias, A., Russell, A., David, B., Oliynykov, R.: Ouroboros: a provably secure proof-of-stake blockchain protocol. In: Katz, J., Shacham, H. (eds.) CRYPTO 2017. LNCS, vol. 10401, pp. 357–388. Springer, Cham (2017). https://doi.org/10.1007/978-3-319-63688-7_12

21. Kotla, R., Alvisi, L., Dahlin, M., Clement, A., Wong, E.: Zyzzyva: speculative Byzantine fault tolerance. In: Proceedings of Twenty-First ACM SIGOPS Symposium on Operating Systems Principles, pp. 45–58 (2007)

22. Lamport, L., Shostak, R., Pease, M.: The Byzantine generals problem. ACM Trans. Program. Lang. Syst. 4(3), 382–401 (1982)

23. Micali, S., Rabin, M., Vadhan, S.: Verifiable random functions. In: 40th Annual Symposium on Foundations of Computer Science (cat. No. 99CB37039), pp. 120–130. IEEE (1999)

24. Mostefaoui, A., Moumen, H., Raynal, M.: Signature-free asynchronous Byzantine consensus with $t < n/3$ and $o(n^2)$ messages. In: Proceedings of the 2014 ACM Symposium on Principles of Distributed Computing, pp. 2–9 (2014)

25. Neu, J., Tas, E.N., Tse, D.: Ebb-and-flow protocols: a resolution of the availability-finality dilemma. arXiv preprint arXiv:2009.04987 (2020)

26. Neu, J., Tas, E.N., Tse, D.: Snap-and-chat protocols: system aspects. arXiv preprint arXiv:2010.10447 (2020)

27. Schneider, F.B.: Implementing fault-tolerant services using the state machine approach: a tutorial. ACM Comput. Surv. 22(4), 299–319 (1990). https://doi.org/10.1145/98163.98167

28. Sheng, P., Wang, G., Nayak, K., Kannan, S., Viswanath, P.: BFT protocol forensics. In: Proceedings of the 2021 ACM SIGSAC Conference on Computer and Communications Security, pp. 1722–1743 (2021)

29. Stewart, A., Kokoris-Kogia, E.: GRANDPA: a Byzantine finality gadget. arXiv preprint arXiv:2007.01560 (2020)

30. Yin, M., Malkhi, D., Reiter, M.K., Gueta, G.G., Abraham, I.: HotStuff: BFT consensus with linearity and responsiveness. In: Proceedings of the 2019 ACM Symposium on Principles of Distributed Computing, pp. 347–356 (2019)

Cryptographic Protocols

Synchronous Perfectly Secure Message Transmission with Optimal Asynchronous Fallback Guarantees

Giovanni Deligios[1(✉)] and Chen-Da Liu-Zhang[2]

[1] ETH Zurich, Zurich, Switzerland
`giovanni.deligios@inf.ethz.ch`
[2] HSLU and Web3 Foundation, Zug, Switzerland
`chen-da.liuzhang@hslu.ch`

Abstract. Secure message transmission (SMT) constitutes a fundamental network-layer building block for distributed protocols over incomplete networks. More specifically, a sender S and a receiver R are connected via ℓ disjoint paths, a subset of which are controlled by the adversary.

Perfectly-secure SMT protocols in synchronous and asynchronous networks are resilient up to $\ell/2$ and $\ell/3$ corruptions respectively. In this work, we ask whether it is possible to achieve a perfect SMT protocol that simultaneously tolerates $t_s < \ell/2$ corruptions when the network is synchronous, and $t_a < \ell/3$ when the network is asynchronous.

We completely resolve this question by showing that perfect SMT is possible if and only if $2t_a + t_s < \ell$. In addition, we provide a concretely round-efficient solution for the (slightly worse) trade-off $t_a + 2t_s < \ell$.

As a direct application of these results, following the recent work by Appan, Chandramouli, and Choudhury [PODC'22], we obtain an n-party perfectly-secure multi-party computation protocol with asynchronous fallback over any network with connectivity ℓ, as long as $t_a + 3t_s < n$ and $2t_a + t_s < \ell$.

1 Introduction

1.1 Motivation

Secure message transmission (SMT) is a fundamental building block that allows to run more complex distributed protocols over incomplete networks (e.g. consensus protocols, secret-sharing, or secure computation protocols). It allows a sender S and a receiver R of an incomplete network of point-to-point channels to communicate securely [9]. Justified by the fact that in a ℓ-connected graph there are at least ℓ disjoint paths among any two nodes [15], one often considers the abstraction in which S and R are simply connected via ℓ channels (also called wires), representing vertex-disjoint paths in the network graph. Assuming

C.-D. Liu-Zhang—This work was partially carried out while the author was at Carnegie Mellon University, USA. Supported in part by the NSF award 1916939, DARPA SIEVE program, a gift from Ripple, a DoE NETL award, a JP Morgan Faculty Fellowship, a PNC center for financial services innovation award, and a Cylab seed funding award.

© International Financial Cryptography Association 2024
F. Baldimtsi and C. Cachin (Eds.): FC 2023, LNCS 13950, pp. 77–93, 2024.
https://doi.org/10.1007/978-3-031-47754-6_5

an adversary that can corrupt at most t parties in the network, this translates to at most t of the ℓ wires being under the control of the adversary (the ones containing a corrupted node), while the remaining $\ell - t$ wires can be considered secure channels. In other words, the secure message transmission problem asks to construct a secure channel between $\mathbf{S}$ and $\mathbf{R}$ from ℓ channels of which an unknown subset of t is under full control of the adversary.

Protocols for SMT can be classified with respect to the underlying communication model. Two prominent models in the literature are the synchronous and asynchronous models. In the synchronous model, channels are guaranteed to deliver messages within a known delay. In contrast, in the asynchronous model, the delivery of messages can be delayed arbitrarily by the adversary. As a consequence, parties cannot wait to receive messages from all parties to proceed in the protocol execution, as there is no way to distinguish a corrupted party who does not send a message from an honest party whose message is delayed.

Perfectly secure SMT can be achieved in the synchronous model if up to $t_s < \ell/2$ wires are corrupted [8,9,13], while perfectly secure SMT in the asynchronous model can only tolerate up to $t_a < \ell/3$ corrupted wires. It is therefore natural to investigate whether there is a protocol that achieves (simultaneously) security guarantees in both network models. More concretely, we ask the following question:

> Under what conditions does there exist a perfectly-secure message transmission protocol that tolerates up to t_s wires to be corrupted if the network is synchronous, and also up to t_a if the network is asynchronous?

We completely resolve this question by providing several feasibility and impossibility results. More concretely, we show that $2t_a + t_s < \ell$ is necessary and sufficient for a perfectly-secure message transmission protocol that tolerates up to t_s (resp. t_a) corrupted wires if the network is synchronous (resp. asynchronous).

Together with the result by Appan, Chandramouli, and Choudhury [1] on perfectly-secure synchronous multi-party computation (MPC) with asynchronous fallback, we obtain an n-party perfectly-secure synchronous MPC with asynchronous fallback over any network with connectivity ℓ, as long as $t_a + 3t_s < n$ and $2t_a + t_s < \ell$.

Finally, as a result of independent interest, we show that assuming the slightly worse trade-off[1] of $t_a + 2t_s < \ell$, we can achieve a similar perfectly secure message transmission protocol, but that runs in 3 rounds when the network is synchronous. This round complexity is essentially optimal, given that in the purely synchronous setting the optimal number of rounds is 2 [17,19].

1.2   Technical Overview

Feasibility. Our feasibility result has three main ingredients:

---

[1] This trade-off is worse given that $t_a \leq t_s$. Note that any protocol with asynchronous security is also secure when run over a synchronous network.

- A *compiler*, which given black-box access to a synchronous (enhanced) secure message transmission protocol and an asynchronous one, provides a protocol with security in both synchronous (up to t_s corruptions) and asynchronous (up to $t_a \le t_s$ corruptions) networks, assuming the trade-off $2t_a + t_s < \ell$. Intuitively, the synchronous (respectively asynchronous) protocol should provide most of the security guarantees if the network is synchronous (respectively asynchronous). The synchronous protocol either runs successfully or guarantees that the sender detects that the network is asynchronous, and can fallback on the asynchronous protocol. The main challenge is ensuring that, if the network is synchronous, the adversary cannot convince the sender to run the asynchronous protocol, which only tolerates a lower corruption threshold.
- A *Synchronous* SMT *protocol* with the additional guarantees that, if the network is asynchronous, either the protocol succeeds or the sender *is sure* that the network is asynchronous. The construction is round-based. Intuitively, the sender tries to send a secret pad to the receiver by secret sharing the pad and sending each share over one of the ℓ wires. If too many errors were introduced by the adversary, the receiver cannot reconstruct the pad, but can inform the sender (via a reliable public channel that also needs to be constructed, which we denote by RMT). The sender can then detect a faulty wire and repeat the process excluding this wire (with a fresh pad and a lower degree sharing). If the sender and the receiver successfully share a secret pad, the actual message can be one-time-pad encrypted and sent over the public channel.

  The main challenge to overcome is properly dealing with erasures (that can originate from faulty wires or by delays on honest wires). In our model when the network is asynchronous, the adversary can convince the sender to exclude an honest wire by simply delaying a message along this wire by longer than the round time. If the sender excludes too many (honest) wires and decreases the degree of the sharing accordingly, eventually the shares on the t_a *actually corrupted* wires determine the secret pad, and secrecy is lost. This is where the trade-off comes into play: we only allow the sender to eliminate up to $t_s - t_a$ wires. This fixes the problem in the asynchronous setting because the starting degree is t_s, so after removing $t_s - t_a$ wires, the remaining degree is still $t_s - (t_s - t_a) = t_a$. Moreover, if the network is synchronous, it is guaranteed that the protocol succeeds at the latest after the last wire is excluded: there are $\ell - (t_s - t_a) = \ell - t_s + t_a$ non-excluded wires (among which t_a are corrupted), and the sharing has degree $t_s - (t_s - t_a) = t_a$. Since $2t_a < \ell - t_s$, the reconstruction is successful. In turn, if at this point the protocol does not succeed, the sender *is sure* that the network is asynchronous. Therefore, the resulting protocol runs in at most $t_s - t_a$ rounds when the network is synchronous.
- An *Asynchronous* SMT *protocol*. This protocol does not require any additional properties for the higher synchronous corruption threshold of t_s, and therefore any protocol from the literature can be used in a black-box fashion. Due to space constraints, we report a known construction (using our notation) and prove its security only in the full version of this paper [7].

Impossibility. We prove that our feasibility result is tight, by showing that the trade-off assumption $2t_a + t_s < \ell$ on the corruption thresholds we made up to this point is not only sufficient, but also necessary to achieve secure message transmission in this hybrid model. Towards contradiction, consider $2t_a + t_s = n$. Partition the channels into three sets K, A, B of sizes $|A| = |B| = t_a$ and $|K| = t_s$. At a high level, the idea is as follows: the information travelling over the channels in A and B must completely determine the message being transmitted (even if no information is transmitted over K). This is because in the synchronous setting, the transmission succeeds when there are t_s corruptions. However, if the network is asynchronous, the adversary can delay all the information via the channels in K, and control *half* of the remaining channels, which are enough to tamper with the output of the receiver. Proving this precisely requires a carefully designed scenario-based argument, that can be found in the full version of this paper [7].

Round-Efficient Synchronous SMT with Sub-optimal Trade-Off. We slightly strengthen these assumptions to $t_a + 2t_s < n$ to achieve a protocol that almost achieves the optimal round complexity of protocols in the purely synchronous model. Intuitively, the stronger trade-off helps for the following reason: if the network is asynchronous, the adversary can delay messages on up to t_s-wires (and change those on up to t_a), and the receiver can still not be sure the network is asynchronous (the t_s erasures could also originate on wires in a synchronous network). During the transmission of a secret pad, this results in $t_s + t_a$ *actual* wrong shares. Under the stronger assumption, $t_s + t_a < n - t_s$, which is the number of wrong shares that can be tolerated (in the sense of at least detected) in the purely synchronous setting. Therefore, erasures can simply be treated as wrong values, greatly reducing the need for interaction between **S** and **R**.

1.3   Related Work

Synchronous Protocols with Asynchronous Fallback. A recent line of works [1–4,6,11,16] has investigated the feasibility and efficiency of distributed protocols (consensus and secure computation protocols) that are secure in both synchronous and asynchronous networks. All these works assume a complete network of point-to-point channels among the parties. Our work expands upon this line by considering the simplest building block for distributed protocols over incomplete networks.

Secure Message Transmission. The problem of SMT in synchronous networks has been widely investigated [9,10,14,18–20]. Perfectly-secure SMT can be achieved, allowing multiple rounds of interaction between the sender and the receiver, if and only if $t < \ell/2$ channels are under control of the adversary [9]. Several works focused on improving the round complexity, achieving optimal 2-round constructions [17,19]. In the asynchronous model, the number of corrupted channels tolerated decreases to $t < n/3$ for perfect security, but interestingly it is still possible up to $t < \ell/2$ corruptions [5] when allowing a small probability of error. In [12] the authors investigate SMT in a model where some channels are synchronous and some are asynchronous. They prove that PSMT in this model is impossible *unless the synchronous channels alone already allow* for PSMT. This is in contrast to our model in which the parties are unaware of the network conditions at execution time. The argument they use is similar to the one in Sect. 4.

2   Preliminaries

2.1   Model

Adversary. We consider an active threshold adversary which is allowed to adaptively (based on the information gathered during the execution of the protocol) corrupt a subset of at most t of the parties (in the secure message transmission abstraction, this amounts to corrupting t channels). We assume that the adversary is computationally unbounded and we consider information theoretic security for our protocols.

Network Topology. We consider an incomplete network of point-to-point secure channels among parties. We identify the network as a graph, where parties represent vertices and channels represent edges. We say a graph is ℓ-connected if ℓ is the minimum number of edges that must be removed in order to disconnect any two vertices in the graph (two vertices are disconnected if there is no path with these vertices as endpoints). The connectivity ℓ is equal to the number of disjoint paths between any two given vertices [15]. We assume that the network topology is fixed and known to the parties before executing a protocol.

Communication Model. We consider a model in which parties have access to local clocks and are not a priori aware of the network conditions when executing a protocol. We distinguish two possibilities: the *synchronous model* and the *asynchronous model*.

In the synchronous model, the local clocks are synchronized, and messages are guaranteed to be delivered within some known time bound Δ. The communication can then naturally be described as proceeding in rounds, where for $\mathbb{N} \ni r \geq 1$, each message received in the time slot $[r\Delta, (r+1)\Delta)$ (according to the local clock of each party) is regarded as a round r message.

In the asynchronous model, parties do not have access to synchronized clocks. The adversary is allowed to schedule the delivery of messages arbitrarily, but each message sent by honest parties must eventually be delivered (this guarantee is needed if one wishes to make statements about protocol termination). In this setting, one describes protocols in a message-driven fashion. This means that, upon receiving a message, a party adds this message to a pool of received messages and checks weather a list of conditions specified from the protocol is satisfied to decide on its next action (sending a message, producing output, terminating, etc.).

In our model, both descriptions can be adopted. In a round-based protocol, if a message is received outside of the time allocated for a certain round, it is ignored. In the secure message transmission abstraction, the assumptions on the communication network directly translate into assumptions on the ℓ wires connecting $\mathbf{S}$ and $\mathbf{R}$. However, the assumed maximum delay on the resulting channels needs to account for the delays of all channels in the corresponding paths (meaning each wire will have a delay of $d \cdot \Delta$, where d denotes the diameter of the network graph).

2.2 Definitions

A secure message transmission protocol allows two parties, connected by multiple channels (wires), to communicate securely even when a subset of the channels is under the control of an adversary.

This abstraction captures the scenario in which two parties part of an incomplete network of secure channels wish to communicate securely. Disjoint paths in the network graph serve as channels. A channel is corrupted if at least one of the parties (nodes) on the path is corrupted. Notice that all guarantees are lost if either the sender or the receiver do not follow the protocol.

We slightly deviate from usual definitions by requiring that the sender protocol also produces a Boolean output. Intuitively, the output is 1 if the sender *knows* the protocol succeeded. Similarly, the receiver is allowed to output a value $\perp$. Intuitively, this means they could not produce a valid output.

Definition 1 *(Secure Message Transmission). Let Π be a protocol executed between $\mathbf{S}$ (the sender) with input $m \in \mathbb{F}$ and randomness r_1 and output $b \in \{0,1\}$ and $\mathbf{R}$ (the receiver) with randomness r_2 and output $v \in \mathbb{F} \cup \{\perp\}$, connected by channels $(c_1, \ldots, c_\ell)$. We say Π is a protocol for SMT achieving:*

- *(t-**correctness**) if whenever up to t channels are under control of the adversary, if $\mathbf{S}$ has input m, then $\mathbf{R}$ outputs $v = m$ and $\mathbf{S}$ outputs $b = 1$;*
- *(t-**perfect**[2] **privacy**) if for all m, m', for all $k \geq 1$, for all $\mathcal{I} \subseteq \{1, \ldots, \ell\}$ such that $|\mathcal{I}| \leq t$, the distributions of $T_{\mathcal{I},m}^k$ and $T_{\mathcal{I},m'}^k$ are equal, where $T_{\mathcal{I},m}^k$ denotes the random variable whose values are the k-th messages travelling on the channels $\{c_i\}_{i \in \mathcal{I}}$ when the sender has input m;*
- *(t-**termination**) if whenever up to t channels are under control of the adversary, $\mathbf{S}$ and $\mathbf{R}$ terminate;*
- *(t-**weak correctness**) if whenever up to t channels are under control of the adversary, if $\mathbf{S}$ has input m, then*
  - *$\mathbf{R}$ outputs m or $\perp$;*
  - *$\mathbf{R}$ outputs m or $\mathbf{S}$ outputs 0.*

If Π achieves t-correctness, t-perfect privacy and t-termination, we say that Π is t-perfectly secure.

---

[2] By requiring the distributions $T_{\mathcal{I},m}^k$ and $T_{\mathcal{I},m'}^k$ to be statistically close or computationally indistinguishable one obtains the notion of statistical security and computational security. In this paper, we are only concerned with perfect security.

In what follows, unless otherwise stated, an SMT protocol is to be understood as *perfectly* secure. Depending on the assumptions made on the channels c_i, we will consider two cases. If the channels are synchronous (cf. Sect. 2.1), we will talk about synchronous SMT (sSMT); if the channels are asynchronous we will talk about asynchronous SMT (aSMT).

3   Secure Message Transmission with Fallback

Throughout this section, we work in the abstract setting of an honest sender and receiver connected by ℓ channels, t of which are under full control of the adversary, and the remaining $\ell - t$ are secure channels.

We show an SMT protocol which is secure regardless of whether the sender and the receiver are connected by synchronous or asynchronous channels. The protocol tolerates up to $t_s < \ell/2$ channels to be under the control of the adversary if the channels are synchronous, and up to $t_a < \ell/3$ if the channels are asynchronous, under optimal trade-offs on the corruption thresholds $2t_a + t_s < \ell$ (optimality of the trade-offs is discussed in Sect. 4).

3.1   Compiler

First, we present a compiler that combines a synchronous sSMT protocol and an asynchronous aSMT protocol to obtain a protocol that is secure in both communication models. The synchronous component needs to provide certain guarantees even the channels are asynchronous, while the asynchronous one does not require any additional guarantees. More specifically let $\Pi_{\mathsf{sSMT}} = (\mathbf{S}_s, \mathbf{R}_s)$ be an SMT protocol with the following properties:

- If $(c_1, ..., c_\ell)$ are synchronous channels: t_s-security.
- If $(c_1, ..., c_\ell)$ are asynchronous channels: t_a-(perfect) privacy, t_a-weak correctness, t_a-termination.

Moreover, let $\Pi_{\mathsf{aSMT}} = (\mathbf{S}_a, \mathbf{R}_a)$ be an SMT protocol with the following properties:

- If $(c_1, ..., c_\ell)$ are asynchronous channels: t_a-security.

The sender and the receiver first run the synchronous protocol. If the network is synchronous, then t_s-security guarantees that the protocol succeeds. In this case, the asynchronous protocol is not run. If the network is asynchronous, t_a-weak correctness guarantees that any output by the receiver matches the message sent by the sender. However, in this case the protocol might also fail and the receiver might not produce output. If this happens, t_a-weak correctness of the synchronous protocol comes to the rescue again: the sender can detect that something went wrong and run the asynchronous protocol. Asynchronous secure message transmission does not require interaction: if the receiver has already produced output while running the synchronous protocol, they simply ignore any further messages. Otherwise, t_a-security of the asynchronous component guarantees that the protocol terminates successfully. Notice that even when the network is asynchronous, the synchronous protocol still t_a-provides privacy. This idea is formalized in the following protocol. Lemmas 1 and 2 are proven in the full version of this paper.

Protocol $\Pi_{\mathsf{hSMT}}(\Pi_{\mathsf{sSMT}}, \Pi_{\mathsf{aSMT}})$

Code for $\mathbf{S}_h(m, r_1)$:

1: $b \leftarrow \mathbf{S}_s(m, r_1)$;
2: **if** $b = 1$ **then**
3:     **return** b;
4: **else**
5:     $b \leftarrow \mathbf{S}_a(m, r_1)$;
6:     **return** b;
7: **end if**

Code for $\mathbf{R}_h(r_2)$:

1: $v \leftarrow \mathbf{R}_s(r_2)$;
2: **if** $v \neq \perp$ **then**
3:     **return** v;
4: **else**
5:     $v \leftarrow \mathbf{R}_a(r_2)$;
6:     **return** v;
7: **end if**

Lemma 1. *If $(c_1, ..., c_\ell)$ are synchronous channels and at most t_s channels are under control of the adversary, then Π_{sSMT} achieves t_s-security.*

Lemma 2. *If $(c_1, ..., c_\ell)$ are asynchronous channels and at most t_a channels are under control of the adversary then Π_{hSMT} achieves t_a-security.*

3.2 Synchronous RMT with Asynchronous Detection

Before describing our construction for Π_{sSMT}, it will be useful to discuss the weaker primitive of *Robust Message Transmission* (RMT). Intuitively, an RMT protocol is an SMT protocol that provides no privacy guarantees (i.e. a public channel between the sender and the receiver that the adversary cannot tamper with). More formally, an RMT protocol is a protocol satisfying the correctness and termination properties of Definition 1. In the context of secure message transmission, such a primitive is often referred to as *broadcast*.

Consider the scenario where a sender $\mathbf{S}$ and a receiver $\mathbf{R}$ are connected by ℓ channels $(c_1, \ldots, c_\ell)$ of which at most $t < \ell/2$ under control of the adversary and the remaining $\ell - t$ are secure channels. Here RMT can be achieved by $\mathbf{S}$ sending the same message over all channels, and $\mathbf{R}$ taking a majority decision over the received messages (this is the same as encoding and decoding using an $(1, \ell)$-repetition code).

We use RMT as a building block in our synchronous sSMT protocols. To provide the security guarantees we are after in our synchronous model with asynchronous fallback, we require enhanced RMT protocols. More specifically, when the channels are asynchronous and up to t_a are under control of the adversary, we still require that either $\mathbf{S}'s$ message is correctly delivered to $\mathbf{R}$, or that $\mathbf{S}$ detects that something went wrong. This is formalized in the following protocol and lemmas. Please refer to the full version of this paper for proofs [7].

Protocol $\Pi_{\mathsf{sRMT}}^{t_s}$

Code for S(m):

Initialize $b := 0$;
Round 1: send m over c_i for all $1 \leq i \leq \ell$;
Round 2: if ok is received over at least $t_s + 1$ channels, set $b := 1$; output b and terminate;

Code for R():

Initialize $v := \bot$;
Round 1: if there is $m \in \mathbb{F}$ received over at least $t_s + 1$ channels, set $v := m$ and send ok over c_i for all $1 \leq i \leq \ell$;
Round 2: output v and terminate;

Lemma 3. *Assume that $t_a \leq t_s < \ell/2$. If $(c_1, ..., c_\ell)$ are synchronous channels and at most t_s channels are under control of the adversary, then Π_{sRMT} achieves t_s-correctness and t_s-termination.*

Lemma 4. *Assume that $t_a \leq t_s < \ell/2$. If $(c_1, ..., c_\ell)$ are asynchronous channels and at most t_a channels are under control of the adversary, then Π_{sRMT} achieves t_a-weak correctness and t_a-termination.*

3.3 Synchronous SMT with Asynchronous Detection

We show a sSMT protocol which is t_s-secure when the network is synchronous and t_a-secure when the network is asynchronous, under the (provably optimal) trade-off assumption $2t_a + t_s < \ell$.

The protocol takes after one of the first synchronous constructions introduced by Dolev et al. [9]. The idea is the following: the sender $\mathbf{S}$ selects a random pad and secret shares it using a (ℓ, t_s)-threshold secret sharing scheme, sending each share over a distinct channel. The receiver $\mathbf{R}$ tries to reconstruct the secret from the received shares. If reconstruction fails because too many shares were tampered with by the adversary, the receiver $\mathbf{R}$ sends the received messages back to $\mathbf{S}$ via sRMT (the roles of sender and receiver are reversed in this sub-protocol). The sender $\mathbf{S}$ identifies at least one corrupted channel, and the process is then repeated (with a fresh pad and a lower degree sharing) excluding this faulty channel.

In a purely synchronous setting, in each round of interaction the number of corrupted channels strictly decreases, so that after at most $(t_s + 1)$-rounds $\mathbf{R}$ receives a pad correctly. Once a pad has been transmitted successfully, in the following round $\mathbf{S}$ can use the pad to one-time-pad encrypt the message and send it to $\mathbf{R}$ via sRMT.

In our setting things are more complicated. If the channels are asynchronous, the adversary could convince $\mathbf{S}$ that a certain channel is corrupted by simply delaying the message on this channel by longer than the round time Δ. By doing so, the adversary can force $\mathbf{S}$ to eliminate honest channels one-at-a-time, until the degree of the sharing of the pad is low enough that the t_a known shares determine the secret pad, thus violating privacy.

To overcome this problem, one must keep $\mathbf{S}$ from removing too many channels (at most $t_s - t_a$), so that the degree of the sharing is never smaller than t_a. This solves a problem but creates others: since now we can never eliminate all the corrupted channels even if the network is synchronous, how do we guarantee correctness? Our trade-off assumption $2t_a + t_s < \ell$ plays a crucial role here. To be consistent with the rest of the presentation, we explain the protocol using the language of error-correcting codes. Lemma 9 guarantees that, for all ℓ and $i < \ell$ there exists a pair $(\mathcal{C}^{(i)}, \mathbf{h}^{(i)})$ where $\mathcal{C}^{(i)}$ is an $(\ell - i, t_s + 1 - i, \ell - t_s)$-linear MDS code such that for all $\mathbf{x} \in \mathcal{C}^{(i)}$ the scalar product $\mathbf{h}^{(i)}\mathbf{x}^T$ is uniformly random in $\mathbb{F}$ even when up to $t_s - i$ symbols of $\mathbf{x}$ are known. Let $\mathrm{decode}_{\mathcal{C}^{(i)}}(\mathbf{y})$ be an (efficient) decoding algorithm for $\mathcal{C}^{(i)}$ returning a pair $(b, \mathbf{x})$. If decoding is successful, then $b = 1$ and $\mathbf{x} \in \mathcal{C}$, otherwise $b = 0$. To ease the notation, we consider that the sRMT protocol runs in 1 round. Lemmas 5 and 6 are proven in the full version of this paper [7].

Protocol $\Pi_{\mathsf{sSMT}}^{t_s, t_a}\left(\Pi_{\mathsf{sRMT}}^{t_s}, \left\{\mathcal{C}^{(k)}, \mathbf{h}^{(k)}\right\}_{k=1}^{t_s - t_a}\right)$

Code for $\mathbf{S}(m, r_1)$

```
 1: elimChannels ← ∅;
 2: b ← 0;  // records success of pad transmission
    Round 2r − 1, for r ≥ 1 :
 3: k ← #elimChannels;
 4: if k > t_s − t_a then  // prevents sender from eliminating too many channels
 5:     return b;
 6: end if
 7: b̄ ← Π_sRMT(elimChannels);  // tell R what channels to consider
 8: if b̄ = 0 then
 9:     return b̄;
10: end if
11: x ←$ C^(k);
12: c_i ← x_i;  // send i-th symbol of x along c_i
    Round 2r:
13: y' ← Π_sRMT()^a;
14: if y' = ok then
```

```
15:      e ← m + h^(k)x^T; // one-time-pad encryption
16:      b ← Π_sRMT(e);
17:      return b;
18: end if
19: if y' = ⊥ then
20:      return b;
21: end if
22: p ← smallest index such that y' ≠ x; // find one corrupted channel
23: elimChannels ← elimChannels ∪ {p};
```

Code for R()

```
24: v ← 0;
25: b' ← 0; // true only successfully communicating ok to the sender// true only
        after successful decoding
```

Round 2r − 1, for r ≥ 1:

```
25: elimChannels' ← Π_sRMT();
26: if elimChannels' ≠ ⊥ then
27:      k' ← #elimChannels';
28:      for i ∉ elimChannels' do
29:          y_i ← c_i; // only read values on good channels
30:      end for
31:      if y_j ≠ ⊥ for all j ∉ elimChanels' then
32:          (v, x') ← decode_{c_0}(y);
33:      end if
34: end if
```

Round 2r:

```
35: if b' = 1 then
36:      e' ← Π_sRMT();
37:      if e' ≠ ⊥ then
38:          m' ← e' − h^(k')x'; // one-time-pad decryption
39:          return m';
40:      end if
41:      if e' = ⊥ then
42:          return e'
43:      end if
44: end if
45: if v=1 then
46:      b' ← Π_sRMT(ok);
47: end if
48: if v = 0 then
49:      b' ← Π_sRMT(y); // information to identify corrupted channels
50: end if
```

---

[a] By Π_sRMT() we denote running the protocol as the receiver.

Lemma 5. *Assume $2t_a + t_s < \ell$, $t_a \leq t_s$, and $t_s < \ell/2$. Then, if the channels $(c_1, \ldots, c_\ell)$ are synchronous and at most t_s are under control of the adversary, protocol $\Pi_{sSMT}^{t_a, t_s}$ achieves t_s-security.*

Lemma 6. *Assume* $2t_a + t_s < \ell$, $t_a \leq t_s$, *and* $t_s < \ell/2$. *If the channels* $(c_1, \ldots, c_\ell)$ *are synchronous and at most* t_s *are under control of the adversary, protocol* $\Pi_{\mathsf{sSMT}}^{t_a, t_s}$ *achieves* t_a-*weak correctness,* t_a-*perfect privacy, and* t_a-*termination.*

3.4   Asynchronous SMT

We need a protocol that can be used as the asynchronous protocol Π_{aSMT} in the compiler Π_{hSMT} of Sect. 3.1. Since we do not require any ad-hoc properties, we can employ any protocol from the literature in a black-box fashion, but we briefly describe a protocol here, and defer a more formal description of the protocol and a proof of its security to the full version of this paper [7]. The idea is simple: the sender secret shares their input with a (ℓ, t_a)-threshold secret sharing scheme sending each share along a distinct channel. The receiver waits until they have received $2t_a + 1$ consistent shares, and then reconstructs the secret. The idea might seem overwhelmingly simple, but the lower number of corrupted channels substantially simplifies matters.

4   Impossibility Result

We justify the trade-off assumptions made in the SMT constructions from previous sections, and show that the trade-off $2t_a + t_s < \ell$, together with the trivial constraints $t_a \leq t_s$ and $t_s < \ell/2$, is necessary to achieve perfectly secure message transmission in our hybrid model. The following Lemma is inspired by proofs in [2,4,5], from which we also borrow some notation. Due to space constraints, please refer to the full version of this paper for the proof [7].

Lemma 7. *Let* $t_a \leq t_s$. *There exists no SMT protocol that is both* t_s-*perfectly secure if the channels are synchronous and* t_a-*perfectly secure if the channels are asynchronous, for* $t_s + 2t_a \geq \ell$.

5   Round-Efficient Synchronous SMT with Sub-optimal Trade-Off

Assuming the trade-off $t_a + 2t_s < \ell$, we show a protocol Π_{sSMT} with the properties required for the compiler presented in Sect. 3.1 and that runs in 3 rounds when the network is synchronous. This (almost) matches the optimal round complexity of purely synchronous protocols (2 rounds). Our construction adapts known ideas (cf. [17,19]) to the context of security with fallback. Due to space constraints, we assume that the reader is familiar with the basic theory of error correcting codes. More details can be found in the full version of this paper [7]. Below, we report some facts that will be needed in our constructions: once again, we refer the reader to [7] for proofs.

Lemma 8 ([19], Lemma 2). *Let $\mathcal{C}$ be an (ℓ, k, d)-linear code over $\mathbb{F}_q$. Let $\mathbf{H}$ be the parity-check matrix of $\mathcal{C}$. Let E be a linear subspace of $\mathbb{F}_q^n$ such that $w(e) < d$ for all $e \in E$. Then*

$$\sigma|_E : E \to \mathbb{F}_q^{\ell - k}$$

$$e \mapsto \mathbf{H}e^T$$

is injective.

Definition 2. *Let $\mathcal{Y} \subseteq \mathbb{F}_q^n$. A pseudo-basis of $\mathcal{Y}$ is a subset $\mathcal{W} \subseteq \mathcal{Y}$ such that $\sigma(\mathcal{W})$ is a basis of the linear subspace $\langle \sigma(\mathcal{Y}) \rangle$ of $\mathbb{F}_q^{n-k}$.*

Let U denote a uniformly distributed random variable over $\mathbb{F}_q$, and let $\mathbf{X} = (X_1, \ldots, X_\ell)$ denote a uniformly distributed random variable over $\mathcal{C}$.

Lemma 9. *There exists an $(\ell, t_s + 1, \ell - t_s)$-linear code $\mathcal{C}$ and a vector $\mathbf{h} \in \mathbb{F}_q^n$ such that, for all $I \subseteq \{1, \ldots, \ell\}$ with $|I| \leq t_s$, the joint distributions $((X_i)_{i \in I}, U)$ and $((X_i)_{i \in I}, \mathbf{h}\mathbf{X}^T)$ are equal.*

The intuition is the following: the receiver $\mathbf{R}$ picks ℓ random field elements, encodes them using an $(\ell, t_s, t_s + t_a + 1)$ MDS code, and then sends the i-th coordinate of the each code-word to the sender via channel c_i. The sender receives these code-words with errors introduced by the adversary. Notice that, if the network is asynchronous, the adversary can modify up to t_a symbols of a code-word *and* erase up to t_s symbols. However, we can still ensure that the $t_s + t_a$ errors occur at the same coordinates for all words: if the coordinates at which erasures happen exceed t_s, then the sender knows that the channels are asynchronous.

Once the error versions of the code-words have been received, the sender $\mathbf{S}$ computes a pseudo-basis, and communicates it to $\mathbf{R}$ via RMT together with the syndromes of the errors introduced on code-words that are *not* in the pseudo-basis. With this information receiver $\mathbf{R}$ can now compute all the errors introduced by the adversary on *all* the code-words sent to $\mathbf{S}$. The code-words in the pseudo-basis have been revealed to the adversary, but the remaining words can now be used as shared secret randomness between $\mathbf{S}$ and $\mathbf{R}$ to one-time-pad encrypt messages and communicate them via RMT, as their syndromes leak no information about them.

In general, error-correcting codes need not give any privacy guarantees. For our purposes, however, the knowledge that the adversary gains by seeing up to t_s coordinates of a code-word must not completely determine the code-word (the remaining entropy can be extracted to use as an encryption pad). Considering appropriate codes solves this issue: it is well-known that certain classes of codes are equivalent to threshold-secret sharing schemes. Lastly, in order for $\mathbf{R}$ to correctly compute the errors introduced by the adversary, the minimum distance of the code used must be greater than $t_s + t_a$. Lemma 9 shows how to construct a code with all the required properties, under the assumption that $t_a + 2t_s < \ell$.

Let $\mathsf{PseudoBasis}_{\mathcal{C}} \left(\mathbf{y}^{(1)}, \ldots, \mathbf{y}^{(q)} \right)$ be an algorithm that, given q vectors as input with $q \geq \ell - \dim(\mathcal{C})$, efficiently computes a pseudo-basis for these vectors.

Let $\mathsf{ComputeErrors}_{\mathcal{C}}\left(\mathcal{W}, \mathbf{x}^{(1)}, \ldots, \mathbf{x}^{(q)}, \sigma, p\right)$ be an algorithm that, given a pseudo-basis of some corrupted versions of $\mathbf{x}^{(1)}, \ldots, \mathbf{x}^{(q)}$, computes the error introduced on $\mathbf{x}^{(p)}$ from the syndrome $\sigma = \sigma(\mathbf{e}^{(p)})$. Such an algorithm can be found in the full version of this paper [7]. Let $\mathcal{C}$ and $\mathbf{h}$ be as in Lemma 9. Lemmas 10 and 11 are proven in [7].

Protocol $\Pi_{\mathsf{sSMT}}^{t_s, t_a}(\mathcal{C}, \mathbf{h})$

Code for $\mathbf{S}(m)$:

1: $b \leftarrow 0$;

Round 1:

2: $\mathsf{erasureCounter} \leftarrow 0$;

3: **for** $1 \leq i \leq \ell$ **do**

4:     $\left(y_i^{(1)}, \ldots, y_i^{(t_s+1)}\right) \leftarrow c_i$;

5:     **if** $y_i^{(j)}$ missing for some j **then**

6:         $\mathsf{erasureCounter} \leftarrow \mathsf{erasureCounter} + 1$;

7:     **end if**

8: **end for**

9: **if** $\mathsf{erasureCounter} \geq t_s + 1$ **then**

10:     **return** b;

11: **end if**

12: **for** $1 \leq j \leq t_s + 1$ **do**

13:     $\mathbf{y}^{(j)} \leftarrow \left(y_1^{(j)}, \ldots, y_\ell^{(j)}\right)$;

14: **end for**

15: $\mathcal{W} \leftarrow \mathsf{PseudoBasis}_{\mathcal{C}}\left(\mathbf{y}^{(1)}, \ldots, \mathbf{y}^{(q)}\right)$;

16: $\mathbf{y}^{(p)} \leftarrow \left\{\mathbf{y}^{(j)}\right\}_{j=1}^{t_s+1} \setminus \mathcal{W}$; // find vector *not* in the pseudo-basis

17: $\sigma \leftarrow \mathbf{H}(\mathbf{y}^{(p)})^T$; // the syndrome of $\mathbf{y}^{(p)}$

18: $pad \leftarrow \mathbf{h}(\mathbf{y}^{(p)})^T$; // the pad to use for encryption

Round 2, 3:

12: $b \leftarrow \Pi_{\mathsf{sRMT}}\left(\mathcal{W}, s, m + pad\right)$;

13: **return** b;

Code for $\mathbf{R}(r_2)$:

14: $v \leftarrow \perp$;

Round 1:

15: $\mathbf{x}^{(1)}, \ldots, \mathbf{x}^{(t_s+1)} \leftarrow_\$ \mathcal{C}$;

16: **for** $1 \leq i \leq \ell$ **do**

17:     $c_i \leftarrow \left(x_i^{(1)}, \ldots, x_i^{(t_s+1)}\right)$;

18: **end for**

Round 2,3:

19: $(\mathcal{W}', \sigma', m') \leftarrow \Pi_{\mathsf{sRMT}}()$;

20: **if** $(\mathcal{W}', \sigma', m') \neq \perp$ **then**

21:     $p' \leftarrow$ index not in $\mathcal{W}'$;

```
22:     e'^{(p')} ← ComputeErrors_C (W', x^{(1)}, ..., x^{(t_s+1)}, σ', p');
23:     y'^{(p')} = x^{(p')} + e'^{(p')};
24:     pad' ← h(y'^{(p')})^T;
25:     v ← m' − pad';
26:     return v;
27: else
28:     return v;
29: end if
```

Lemma 10. *Assume $t_a + 2t_s < \ell$ and $t_a \leq t_s$. If $(c_1, ..., c_\ell)$ are synchronous channels and at most t_s channels are under control of the adversary, then protocol $\Pi_{sSMT}^{t_s,t_a}(\mathcal{C}, \mathbf{h})$ achieves t_s-security.*

Lemma 11. *Assume $t_a + 2t_s < \ell$ and $t_a \leq t_s$. If $(c_1, ..., c_\ell)$ are asynchronous channels and at most t_a channels are under control of the adversary, then protocol $\Pi_{sSMT}^{t_s,t_a}(\mathcal{C}, \mathbf{h})$ achieves t_a-weak correctness and t_a-perfect privacy.*

6   Conclusions

6.1   Putting Things Together

We have investigated the feasibility and optimality of perfectly secure message transmission protocols that achieve security in both synchronous and asynchronous networks. The following corollaries summarize the main results.

Corollary 1. *There exists a perfectly secure SMT protocol that is t_s-secure when run over a synchronous network, and t_a-secure when run over an asynchronous network if and only if $2t_a + t_s < \ell$.*

Corollary 2. *There exists a perfectly secure SMT protocol that is t_s-secure when run over a synchronous network, t_a-secure when run over an asynchronous network, and runs in 3 rounds when the network is synchronous, if $t_a + 2t_s < \ell$.*

Using Theorem 6.1 from [1], combined with our SMT protocol from Corollary 1, we obtain an n-party perfectly-secure MPC protocol over networks with ℓ-connectivity, for any $t_a \leq t_s$ satisfying $3t_s + t_a < n$ and $2t_a + t_s < \ell$.

Corollary 3 ([1], Theorem 6.1; restated for incomplete networks). *Let n be the number of parties and ℓ be the connectivity of the network. Let $t_a \leq t_s$, such that $3t_s + t_a < n$ and $2t_a + t_s < \ell$. Moreover, let $f : \mathbb{F}^n \to \mathbb{F}$ be a function represented by an arithmetic circuit over a field $\mathbb{F}$. Then, there is an n-party MPC protocol evaluating f over any network with ℓ connectivity, such that:*

- *Correctness: (a) When the network is synchronous and there are up to t_s corruptions, all honest parties correctly evaluate the function (with all honest inputs taken into account), and (b) when the network is asynchronous and there are up to t_a corruptions, all honest parties correctly evaluate the function (with $n - t_s$ inputs taken into account).*

- *Privacy: The view of the adversary is independent of the inputs of the honest parties.*

Acknowledgments. The authors would like to thank Martin Hirt for some very insightful discussions related to the material in this work.

References

1. Appan, A., Chandramouli, A., Choudhury, A.: Perfectly- secure synchronous MPC with asynchronous fallback guarantees. In: ACM Symposium on Principles of Distributed Computing (2022)
2. Blum, E., Katz, J., Loss, J.: Synchronous consensus with optimal asynchronous fallback guarantees. In: Hofheinz, D., Rosen, A. (eds.) TCC 2019. LNCS, vol. 11891, pp. 131–150. Springer, Cham (2019). https://doi.org/10.1007/978-3-030-36030-6_6
3. Blum, E., Katz, J., Loss, J.: TARDIGRADE: an atomic broadcast protocol for arbitrary network conditions. In: Tibouchi, M., Wang, H. (eds.) ASIACRYPT 2021. LNCS, vol. 13091, pp. 547–572. Springer, Cham (2021). https://doi.org/10.1007/978-3-030-92075-3_19
4. Blum, E., Liu-Zhang, C.-D., Loss, J.: Always have a backup plan: fully secure synchronous MPC with asynchronous fallback. In: Micciancio, D., Ristenpart, T. (eds.) CRYPTO 2020. LNCS, vol. 12171, pp. 707–731. Springer, Cham (2020). https://doi.org/10.1007/978-3-030-56880-1_25
5. Choudhury, A., et al.: Secure message transmission in asynchronous networks. J. Parallel Distrib. Comput. **71**, 1067–1074 (2011)
6. Deligios, G., Hirt, M., Liu-Zhang, C.-D.: Round-efficient Byzantine agreement and multi-party computation with asynchronous fallback. In: Nissim, K., Waters, B. (eds.) TCC 2021. LNCS, vol. 13042, pp. 623–653. Springer, Cham (2021). https://doi.org/10.1007/978-3-030-90459-3_21
7. Deligios, G., Liu-Zhang, C.-D.: Synchronous perfectly secure message transmission with optimal asynchronous fallback guarantees. Cryptology ePrint Archive, Paper 2022/1397. https://eprint.iacr.org/2022/1397.2022
8. Desmedt, Y., Wang, Y.: Perfectly secure message transmission revisited. In: Knudsen, L.R. (ed.) EUROCRYPT 2002. LNCS, vol. 2332, pp. 502–517. Springer, Heidelberg (2002). https://doi.org/10.1007/3-540-46035-7_33
9. Dolev, D., et al.: Perfectly secure message transmission. J. ACM **40**(1), 17–47 (1993)
10. Garay, J., Givens, C., Ostrovsky, R.: Secure message transmission by public discussion: a brief survey. In: Chee, Y.M., et al. (eds.) IWCC 2011. LNCS, vol. 6639, pp. 126–141. Springer, Heidelberg (2011). https://doi.org/10.1007/978-3-642-20901-7_8
11. Ghinea, D., Liu-Zhang, C.-D., Wattenhofer, R.: Optimal synchronous approximate agreement with asynchronous fallback. In: ACM Symposium on Principles of Distributed Computing. Springer (2022)
12. Kishore, R., Inumella, A., Srinathan, K.: Perfectly secure message transmission over partially synchronous networks. In: ICDCN 2019, Bangalore, India, pp. 302–306. Association for Computing Machinery (2019). isbn: 9781450360944. https://doi.org/10.1145/3288599.3288612

13. Kurosawa, K., Suzuki, K.: Almost secure (1-round, n-channel) message transmission scheme. IEICE Trans. Fundam. Electron. Commun. Comput. Sci. **92**(1), 105–112 (2009)

14. Kurosawa, K., Suzuki, K.: Truly efficient 2-round perfectly secure message transmission scheme. In: Smart, N. (ed.) EUROCRYPT 2008. LNCS, vol. 4965, pp. 324–340. Springer, Heidelberg (2008). https://doi.org/10.1007/978-3-540-78967-3_19

15. Menger, K.: Zur allgemeinen kurventheorie. Fund. Math. **10**, 96–1159 (1927)

16. Momose, A., Ren, L.: Multi-threshold Byzantine fault tolerance. In: Proceedings of the 2021 ACM SIGSAC Conference on Computer and Communications Security, CCS 2021, Virtual Event, Republic of Korea, pp. 1686–1699. Association for Computing Machinery (2021). isbn: 9781450384544. https://doi.org/10.1145/3460120.3484554

17. Resch, N., Yuan, C.: Two-round perfectly secure message transmission with optimal transmission rate. Cryptology ePrint Archive, Report 2021/158 (2021)

18. Md Sayeed, H., Abu-Amara, H.: Efficient perfectly secure message transmission in synchronous networks. Inf. Comput. **126**(1), 53–61 (1996)

19. Spini, G., Zémor, G.: Perfectly secure message transmission in two rounds. In: Hirt, M., Smith, A. (eds.) TCC 2016. LNCS, vol. 9985, pp. 286–304. Springer, Heidelberg (2016). https://doi.org/10.1007/978-3-662-53641-4_12

20. Srinathan, K., Narayanan, A., Rangan, C.P.: Optimal perfectly secure message transmission. In: Franklin, M. (ed.) CRYPTO 2004. LNCS, vol. 3152, pp. 545–561. Springer, Heidelberg (2004). https://doi.org/10.1007/978-3-540-28628-8_33

Optimally-Fair Exchange of Secrets via Delay Encryption and Commutative Blinding

Ivo Maffei$^{(\boxtimes)}$ and Andrew W. Roscoe

Department of Computer Science, University of Oxford, Oxford, UK
{ivo.maffei,bill.roscoe}@cs.ox.ac.uk

Abstract. We propose a new fair exchange protocol that takes advantage of delay encryption and commutative encryption to achieve optimal partial fairness among all protocols involving one-way messages. Our protocol consists of 3 setup messages and $2N + 1$ exchange messages and it is fair against covert adversaries with probability $1 - \frac{1}{2N}$. We prove that this is optimal up to shortening the setup phase which is notably more efficient than existing protocols.

Keywords: Fair Exchange · Timed-Release Encryption · Partial Fairness · Commutative Blinding

1 Introduction

A fair exchange protocol allows two parties to exchange secrets fairly without mutual trust. Given its practical importance, this problem has been studied extensively in different contexts. Many solutions using Trusted Third Parties as mediators (e.g. [10]) or judges (e.g. [1]) have been proposed. When in lack of a TTP, fair exchange was first shown to be impossible by Even and Yacobi [9] in 1980 and later by Pagnia and Gärtner [21]. Garbinato and Rickebusch [11] analysed this result further to provide a finer classification when some trust is present in the network. While their result is very interesting in the setting where multiple parties are involved, in our 2-party context they conclude that one party must be trusted.

Similar problems such as multi-party coin flipping or exchange of signatures were also proved impossible, respectively, by Cleve [5] and by Even and Yacobi [9]. As a result, researchers tried to design protocols that either achieve weaker fairness properties or take advantage of stronger assumptions. For instance, under the assumption that both parties have similar computational power, bit commitments schemes [7] can be used to achieve weaker fairness where a party's

---

This research was funded in whole, or in part, by UKRI 2421791 and Crypto.com. For the purpose of Open Access, the author has applied a CC BY public copyright licence to any Author Accepted Manuscript (AAM) version arising from this submission.

© The Author(s) 2024
F. Baldimtsi and C. Cachin (Eds.): FC 2023, LNCS 13950, pp. 94–111, 2024.
https://doi.org/10.1007/978-3-031-47754-6_6

knowledge is at most one bit more than the other party's knowledge. Using the weaker assumption that both parties have similar sequential computational power, Boneh and Naor [3] proposed a protocol where bit commitments were replaced with timed commitments. Alternatively, Ben-Or et al.[2] proposed a fair exchange of signatures where the probability that one party is committed to a contract while the other is not can be arbitrarily small. Following the same trend of using probabilistic definitions of fairness, Gordon and Katz [16] introduced the concept of partial fairness for secure two-party computations.

A very similar concept was used in the context of two-party fair exchange by Roscoe and Ryan [24] and later refined by Couteau et al. [6]. We follow their approach and propose a fair exchange protocol where the probability of an unfair run is almost inversely proportional to the number of messages exchanged. This fairness is achieved against covert adversaries, i.e. the malicious entity will not perform actions for which they can be blamed. We achieve a stronger form of fairness and better bounds than the protocols of [6,16]. In particular, Gordon and Katz [16] show that general 2 party computations cannot be performed with polynomial partial fairness when parties are allowed to early abort the protocol and only polynomial running time. Couteau et al. [6] escape this impossibility result using timed-release encryption and show that any 2 party functionality can achieve partial fairness by designing a partially fair exchange protocol.

1.1   Our Contribution and Related Work

The key idea used in the protocol by Couteau et al. as well as in [16] is to hide the secret among a set of dummy values, then exchange them one by one. In this paper, we explore the theoretical limits of this approach by proving an upper bound on the partial fairness that can be achieved and then building a protocol that reaches it. In this paper, the results and protocols of that approach are improved significantly.

In the protocol analysed by Couteau et al., the probability that Alice receives Bob's secret is at most $\frac{2}{N}$ greater than Bob's chances of receiving Alice's secret (and vice versa), where N is the number of messages in the exchange phase of their protocol. However, each party could get roughly a $\frac{1}{4}$ probability of receiving the other party's secret without revealing theirs. In our protocol, the latter probability is bounded above by $\frac{1}{N-1}$.

Similarly, Gordon and Katz's [16] protocol hides the correct output of the computation among a list of other random values. Our protocol improves on theirs in three distinct ways. Firstly, in [16] each party has immediate access to all the value already exchanged. Therefore, if a malicious entity had access to some information on the value of the correct output, they could recognise some random values as such. Hence, their decision on when to abort will no longer be uniformly random. We solve this by encrypting the secrets to exchange and only work with encryption keys. Assuming that the honest party picks truly random keys, the adversary cannot distinguish which key is used for the secrets until the ciphertext is available at the end of the protocol. Secondly, we propose a concrete setup phase consisting of only 3 messages, of which the last will be sent together with the first exchange message. In [16], the sub-protocol preceding the exchange phase is only described abstractly. Finally, we achieve better fairness, i.e. we halve the probability of an unfair run of the protocol.

Like those of [6,24], our protocol relies on the unusual assumptions of the existence of delay encryption (often called Timed-Release Encryption) [23] and a commutative blinding scheme. The former assumption is what let our protocol circumvent the impossibility result proved by Gordon and Katz [16]. Only a few delay encryption schemes have been proposed in the past 30 years. We believe exponentiation modulo a prime [18] is a viable option in our case since it relies only on the assumption that repeated squaring is inherently sequential and that both parties have a somewhat similar sequential computation power. This is much more reasonable assumptions than similarity in general (i.e. parallel) computational power.

In Sect. 2, we present the preliminary definitions of each cryptographic primitive used in the fair exchange protocol. The next section is dedicated to the description of our protocol. In Sect. 4, we analyse the fairness of the proposed protocol as well as showing its optimality.

2   Preliminaries

In this section, we lay out the definitions of the cryptographic primitives that will be used in the fair exchange protocol.

2.1   Notation

In this paper we will use the following notation:

- $\mathbb{Z}_N$ is the *set* $\{0, \ldots, N-1\}$
- vectors are written in bold. $\boldsymbol{v}[i]$ is the ith entry of $\boldsymbol{v}$ starting from 0.
- $(a_i)_{i \in X}$ is a vector of length $|X|$ whose entries are a_i
- If $\boldsymbol{v} \in X^N$ and $f : X \to Y$, we write $f(\boldsymbol{v})$ for $(f(\boldsymbol{v}[i]))_{i \in \mathbb{Z}_N} \in Y^N$.
- $x \xleftarrow{\$} X$ means that x is sampled uniformly from the set X.
- mod is the usual binary function $\mathbb{Z} \times \mathbb{N}^+ \to \mathbb{N}$ such that $a \bmod b \in \mathbb{Z}_b$.
- $a\|b$ is the concatenation of a and b by interpreting them as binary strings.

2.2   Symmetric Encryption and Hashing

We use standard symmetric encryption (KGen, Enc, Dec) [15,17] and only require it to be secure against ciphertext-only attacks. We write $\mathsf{Enc}_k(m)/\mathsf{Dec}_k(m)$ to mean the encryption/decryption of message/ciphertext m under the key k.

Our protocol takes advantage of cryptographic hashing (H : $\{0,1\}^* \to \{0,1\}^n$) [15,17] as a commitment scheme. Therefore, both preimage resistant and second preimage resistant are required.

2.3 Delay Encryption

Delay encryption (sometimes called Timed-Release Encryption) is an unusual cryptographic primitive whose aim is not to provide confidentiality of a message from other parties, but to hide the message from anyone for some predefined amount of time. For the reader accustomed with Timed-Release Encryption, what we use and define is a "delay" time-lock-puzzle-based encryption scheme rather than time-specific schemes using trusted third parties. This is justified because, in the presence of a TTP, the fair exchange problem becomes trivial.

More formally, a delay encryption scheme is a triple of algorithms and associated sets $\mathcal{M}, \mathcal{C}, \mathcal{P}$:

$$\mathsf{Pgen} \colon \{1\}^* \times \mathbb{N} \to \mathcal{P} \qquad \mathsf{delay} \colon \mathcal{M} \times \mathcal{P} \to \mathcal{C} \qquad \mathsf{open} \colon \mathcal{C} \times \mathcal{P} \to \mathcal{M}$$

Intuitively, $\mathsf{Pgen}(1^\lambda, T)$ generates public parameters $\mathfrak{p}$ that are used to delay a message for time T. $\mathsf{delay}_T(m)$ will mean that the algorithm is used on m to delay it for elapsed time T. Similarly, we omit $\mathfrak{p}$ and write $\mathsf{open}(c)$. Practically speaking, $\mathsf{delay}_T(m)$ will create a puzzle c so that $\mathsf{open}(c)$ can solve the puzzle and obtain m only after at least T (sequential) time. A honest party with moderate computational power should be able to run $\mathsf{open}(c)$ in sequential time not much longer than T. In order for our scheme to make sense, we set the following requirement

$$\forall m \in M \ \forall T \in \mathbb{N} \quad \mathsf{open}(\mathsf{delay}_T(m)) = m$$

We say that a delay encryption is COA-secure if for any family of circuits $\mathcal{A}$ of conceivable size and depth at most λT, we have

$$\Pr_{\substack{m \xleftarrow{\$} \mathcal{M} \\ T \xleftarrow{\$} \mathbb{N}}} \left[m \leftarrow \mathcal{A}(c, T, \mathfrak{p}) \ \middle| \ c \leftarrow \mathsf{delay}_T(m) \wedge \mathfrak{p} \leftarrow \mathsf{Pgen}(1^\lambda, T) \right] < \frac{1}{|\mathcal{M}|} + \mathsf{negl}\,(\lambda)$$

Intuitively, a COA-secure delay encryption scheme correctly hides encrypted messages for the expected amount of time. We remark that the size of such circuits will depend on the current state of technology. As noted in [18], allowing all polynomially-sized circuits could lead to misleading results with circuits much larger than what is feasible at the time of writing.

2.4 Commutative Blinding

A feature of our protocol is the use of commutative blinding that enables two parties to jointly shuffle a deck of cards in such a way that neither know where a given card is. Usually a blinding scheme is nothing but an encryption scheme, however the usual definition of a commutative encryption scheme is stricter than what we need. As a result, we define a commutative blinding scheme as a tuple of algorithms $(\mathsf{KGen}_1, \mathsf{KGen}_2, \mathsf{Blind}_1, \mathsf{Blind}_2, \mathsf{Unblind}_1, \mathsf{Unblind}_2)$ with sets $(\mathcal{M}, \mathcal{K}_1, \mathcal{K}_2, \mathcal{C}_{\mathrm{int}}, \mathcal{C})$ such that

$$\mathsf{KGen}_1 \colon \{1\}^* \to \mathcal{K}_1 \qquad \mathsf{Blind}_1 \colon \mathcal{M} \times \mathcal{K}_1 \to \mathcal{C}_{\mathrm{int}} \qquad \mathsf{Unblind}_1 \colon \mathcal{C} \times \mathcal{K}_1 \to \mathcal{C}_{\mathrm{int}}$$
$$\mathsf{KGen}_2 \colon \{1\}^* \to \mathcal{K}_2 \qquad \mathsf{Blind}_2 \colon \mathcal{C}_{\mathrm{int}} \times \mathcal{K}_2 \to \mathcal{C} \qquad \mathsf{Unblind}_2 \colon \mathcal{C}_{\mathrm{int}} \times \mathcal{K}_2 \to \mathcal{M}$$

In order for the scheme to make sense we require

$$\forall k_1 \in \mathcal{K}_1 \ \forall k_2 \in \mathcal{K}_2 \ \forall m \in \mathcal{M}$$
$$\mathsf{Unblind}_2\left(\mathsf{Unblind}_1\left(\mathsf{Blind}_2\left(\mathsf{Blind}_1\left(m, k_1\right), k_2\right), k_1\right), k_2\right) = m$$

If these functions were used in other contexts, these names could be misleading. In particular, $\mathsf{Unblind}_1$ and Blind_1 are not necessarily inverses, nor are $\mathsf{Unblind}_2$ and Blind_2. In most practical scenarios, the blinding and unblinding will be inverses as well as $\mathsf{Blind}_1 = \mathsf{Blind}_2$ and $\mathsf{Unblind}_1 = \mathsf{Unblind}_2$. However, this is not required and constructions using homomorphic encryption are likely to need the full generality of our definition.

We say that Blind_1 is COA-secure if for any PPT adversary $\mathcal{A}$ we have

$$\Pr_{\substack{m \xleftarrow{\$} \mathcal{M} \\ k \xleftarrow{\$} \mathsf{KGen}_1(1^\lambda)}} \left[m \leftarrow \mathcal{A}(c) \ \middle| \ c \leftarrow \mathsf{Blind}_1(m, k) \right] < \frac{1}{|\mathcal{M}|} + \mathsf{negl}\left(\lambda\right)$$

The remaining security requirements are described in Figs. 1, 2 and 3.

We say that an adversary wins the N-KPA game (Fig. 1) if $m' = m_{N+1}$. In the $(N, \mathcal{P})$-CPA game, we note that $\mathcal{P}$ is a set of permutations of N-dimensional vectors. We say that an adversary wins the $(N, \mathcal{P})$-CPA game if $\sigma' = \sigma$. In other words, if we are presented a blinded permutation of known distinct messages, we should not be able to tell which message corresponds to which. Finally, we say that an adversary wins the KIND game if $b' = b$.

We say that Blind_1 is N-KPA secure if for any PPT adversary $\mathcal{A}$, the probability that $\mathcal{A}$ wins the N-KPA game is at most $\frac{1}{|\mathcal{M}|-N} + \mathsf{negl}\left(\lambda\right)$.

We say that Blind_2 is $(N, \mathcal{P})$-CPA secure if for any PPT adversary $\mathcal{A}$, the probability that $\mathcal{A}$ wins the $(N, \mathcal{P})$-CPA game is at most $\frac{1}{|\mathcal{P}|} + \mathsf{negl}\left(\lambda\right)$.

We say that Blind_2 is KIND secure if for any PPT adversary $\mathcal{A}$, the probability that $\mathcal{A}$ wins the KIND game is at most $\frac{1}{2} + \mathsf{negl}\left(\lambda\right)$.

Explanations for these requirements will be discussed in Sect. 3.2 after we present our protocol.

2.5 Fair Exchange

We say that a protocol Π is an ideal fair exchange of secrets between two parties Alice and Bob if it achieves the same result as performing the exchange in an ideal world where there is a TTP collecting the secrets and exchanging them. Intuitively, the exchange is *fair* if Alice learns Bob's s secret if and only if Bob learns Alice's secret. As noted in the introduction, an ideal fair exchange protocol is not possible without a TTP or some very strong assumptions on the network of parties. As a result, our fair exchange protocol achieves fairness only in a probabilistic way.

Definition 1. *We say that a probabilistic protocol Π achieves p-partial fairness if the probability of an unfair run is at most p.*

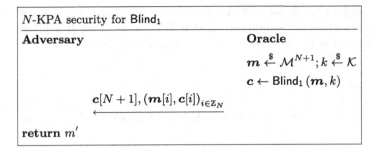

Fig. 1. N-KPA game

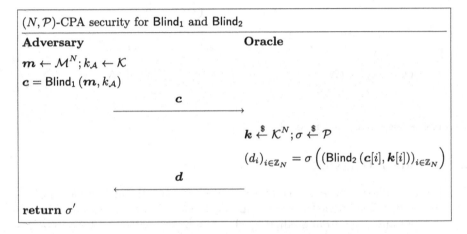

Fig. 2. $(N, \mathcal{P})$-CPA game

```
KIND security for Blind₂
```

Adversary	Oracle
	$m \stackrel{\$}{\leftarrow} \mathcal{M}^2; k_O \stackrel{\$}{\leftarrow} \mathcal{K}$
	$c \leftarrow \mathsf{Blind}_1(m, k_O)$
	$\xleftarrow{\quad c \quad}$
$k \stackrel{\$}{\leftarrow} \mathcal{K}^2; d \leftarrow (\mathsf{Blind}_2(c[i], k[i]))_{i \in \{0,1\}}$	
	$\xrightarrow{\quad d \quad}$
	$e \leftarrow \mathsf{Unblind}_1(d, k_O); b \stackrel{\$}{\leftarrow} \{0,1\}$
	$\xleftarrow{\quad e_b \quad}$
return b'	

Fig. 3. KIND game

In other words, a malicious entity can obtain the other party's secret without revealing theirs with probability at most p. We also say that Π achieves fairness with probability p to mean that it is $(1 - p)$-partially fair.

3 Protocol

Firstly, we define a few permutations that will be used in the protocol.

$$\sigma_d : \mathbb{Z}_N \to \mathbb{Z}_N \qquad\qquad \sigma_d^e : \mathbb{Z}_{N+1} \to \mathbb{Z}_{N+1}$$

$$x \mapsto x + d \mod N \qquad\qquad x \mapsto \begin{cases} \sigma_d(x) & \text{if } 0 \le x < N \\ N & \text{if } x = N \end{cases}$$

$$\tau_N^b : X^N \to X^N \qquad\qquad \pi^b : X^{N+1} \to X^{N+1}$$

$$\boldsymbol{v} \mapsto \left(\boldsymbol{v}[i(-1)^b + (N-1)b]\right)_{i \in \mathbb{Z}_N} \qquad \boldsymbol{v} \mapsto \left(\boldsymbol{v}[(i - b) \mod (N+1)]\right)_{i \in \mathbb{Z}_{N+1}}$$

Figure 4 is the exchange protocol.

3.1 Protocol Overview

Our protocol follows the idea used by Roscoe and Ryan [24] and Couteau et $al.$[6], i.e. Alice and Bob will hide their secret among a set of dummy messages. The aim is to prevent any party from predicting when the secrets will be exchanged or distinguish when they have sent or received a secret until all exchanges should have finished. A key component to achieve this is delay encryption. The delayed messages D_A, D_B fulfil two different purposes. Firstly, they guarantee the exchanged secrets cannot be computed as soon as the keys $\boldsymbol{k}^A[0], \boldsymbol{k}^B[0]$ are received, but only at the end of the protocol. Secondly, they behave as a timed commitment to each player's strategy. This is used to detect any active cheater[1]. Most of the complexity of the protocol lies in the three setup messages that are used to hide $\boldsymbol{k}^A[0]$ and $\boldsymbol{k}^B[0]$ among dummy keys. The shuffling process proceeds as follow:

1. Each party places their secret among a list of N values and permutes it. Alice places an extra dummy value at the end of her list.
2. After exchanging these lists, each party permutes the received list.
3. Bob decides whether to place Alice's extra dummy at the start or end of Alice's list.
4. Alice decides whether to reflect each list around their midpoint or not.

---

[1] For example, if its initially declared and committed strategy obliges A to send its own secret in message x, then not doing so would be a detectable abuse even if the protocol is terminated before its end.

Optimally Fair Exchange Protocol

Alice	**Bob**

$\dots\dots\dots\dots\dots\dots\dots\dots\dots\dots\dots\dots\dots$ Setup phase $\dots\dots\dots\dots\dots\dots\dots\dots\dots\dots$

$d_A \xleftarrow{\$} \mathbb{Z}_N; \boldsymbol{k^A} \xleftarrow{\$} \mathcal{K}^{N+1}$

$\boldsymbol{B^A} \xleftarrow{\$} \mathcal{BK}^N; B_c^A \xleftarrow{\$} \mathcal{BK}$

$\boldsymbol{c^A} \leftarrow \left(\mathsf{Blind}_1(\boldsymbol{k^A}[\sigma_{d_A}^e(i)], B_c^A) \right)_{i \in \mathbb{Z}_{N+1}}$

$D_A \leftarrow \mathsf{delay}\left(\mathsf{Enc}_{\boldsymbol{k^A}[0]}(s_A) \| \mathsf{H}(\boldsymbol{k^A}) \| \boldsymbol{B^A} \| d_A \| b_A \right)$

$S_1:$ $\qquad\qquad \xrightarrow{\quad D_A, \mathsf{H}\left(\mathsf{open}\left(D_A\right)\right), \boldsymbol{c^A} \quad}$

$\qquad\qquad\qquad d_B \xleftarrow{\$} \mathbb{Z}_N; \boldsymbol{k^B} \xleftarrow{\$} \mathcal{K}^N$

$\qquad\qquad\qquad \boldsymbol{B^B} \xleftarrow{\$} \mathcal{BK}^{N+1}; B_c^B \xleftarrow{\$} \mathcal{BK}$

$\qquad\qquad\qquad \boldsymbol{c^B} \leftarrow \left(\mathsf{Blind}_1(\boldsymbol{k^B}[\sigma_{d_B}(i)], B_c^B) \right)_{i \in \mathbb{Z}_N}$

$\qquad\qquad\qquad \boldsymbol{d} \leftarrow \pi^{b_B}\left(\left(\mathsf{Blind}_2(\boldsymbol{c^A}[\sigma_{d_B}^e(i)], \boldsymbol{B^B}[i]) \right)_{i \in \mathbb{Z}_{N+1}} \right)$

$\qquad\qquad\qquad D_B \leftarrow \mathsf{delay}\left(\mathsf{Enc}_{\boldsymbol{k^B}[0]}(s_B) \| \mathsf{H}(\boldsymbol{k^B}) \| \boldsymbol{B^B} \| d_B \| b_B \right)$

$S_2:$ $\qquad\qquad \xleftarrow{\quad D_B, \mathsf{H}\left(\mathsf{open}\left(D_B\right)\right), \boldsymbol{c^B}, \boldsymbol{d} \quad}$

$\boldsymbol{c^{BA}} \leftarrow \left(\mathsf{Blind}_2(\boldsymbol{c^B}[\sigma_{d_A}(i)], \boldsymbol{B^A}[i]) \right)_{i \in \mathbb{Z}_N}$

$\boldsymbol{e^B} \leftarrow \tau_N^{b_A}\left(\boldsymbol{c^{BA}} \right); \boldsymbol{e^A} \leftarrow \tau_{N+1}^{b_A}\left(\boldsymbol{d} \right)$

$\boldsymbol{m^A} \leftarrow \left(\mathsf{Unblind}_1(\boldsymbol{e^A}[i], B_c^A) \right)_{i \in \mathbb{Z}_{N+1}}$

$S_3:$ $\qquad\qquad \xrightarrow{\qquad\qquad \boldsymbol{e^B} \qquad\qquad}$

$\qquad\qquad\qquad \boldsymbol{m^B} \leftarrow \left(\mathsf{Unblind}_1(\boldsymbol{e^B}[i], B_c^B) \right)_{i \in \mathbb{Z}_N}$

$\dots\dots\dots\dots\dots\dots\dots\dots\dots\dots\dots\dots$ Exchange phase $\dots\dots\dots\dots\dots\dots\dots\dots\dots$

$E_{2r+1}:$ $\qquad\qquad \xrightarrow{\qquad\qquad \boldsymbol{m^A}[r] \qquad\qquad}$

$E_{2r+2}:$ $\qquad\qquad \xleftarrow{\qquad\qquad \boldsymbol{m^B}[r] \qquad\qquad}$

$\dots\dots\dots\dots\dots\dots\dots\dots\dots\dots\dots\dots$ Disclosure $\dots\dots\dots\dots\dots\dots\dots\dots\dots\dots\dots$

$O_1:$ $\qquad\qquad \xleftarrow{\qquad\qquad \mathsf{open}\left(D_B\right) \qquad\qquad}$

$O_2:$ $\qquad\qquad \xrightarrow{\qquad\qquad \mathsf{open}\left(D_A\right) \qquad\qquad}$

Fig. 4. Main protocol

In the first two steps, we restrict the permutations to rotations. This makes the permutations commute without affecting the probability distribution of where the secrets are. After step 2, we obtain two lists where the secrets are in the same position. This in not enough to achieve optimality since the relative order of the secrets is fixed. If the messages were exchanged in their form after step 2, the secrets were in position r and Alice were the first at sending the rth blinded value, then Bob's secret would follow Alice's. This would achieve a sub-optimal fairness probability of roughly $1 - \frac{1}{N}$.

The last two steps have the effect of shuffling the relative order of the secrets. If Bob places the extra dummy at the start of Alice's list, then he is effectively moving Alice's secret after his. Alice's action changes the relative order of any pair of messages. At the end of step 4, the relative order of the secrets is uniformly random and unknown to the parties. In particular, this represents the optimal distribution, i.e. no probability distribution of the 2 secret messages leads to a fairer exchange.

The last two messages $\mathbf{O_1}, \mathbf{O_2}$ are entirely optional and only used for computational optimisation, so that opening the delay encryption is made unnecessary. More specifically, they contain all the information needed to retrieve the secrets from the list of $\mathbf{E_i}$'s. Therefore, a party needs to undergo the expensive computation to open the delayed messages only if the exchange is not terminated or the other party actively cheated.

3.2   Security Requirements

After explaining the protocol, we can justify the need for the security parameters we set. The requirements on the delay encryption and symmetric encryption should be straight forward. These two primitives are only meant to hide the messages encrypted. The hash function is used as a commitment scheme, therefore the need for second preimage resistance. Collision resistance is not strictly needed but preimage resistance is required to avoid revealing something about the committed value.

The commutative blinding scheme must satisfy more complex requirements since it is the cornerstone of the setup phase. The scheme is required to hide the blinded values as well as hiding the shuffling. As a result, the simple COA requirement only ensures that nothing can be extracted from c^A or c^B. The KPA requirement is needed if the protocol is aborted early before the actual secrets are exchanged. In this scenario, after the opening of the delay message, both parties can unblind the messages exchanged obtaining some of the dummy k^A's (or k^B's). Moreover, the delayed messages reveal the shuffling used, so a malicious party can perform a KPA on the values c^A (respectively c^B).

The CPA requirements, using the set of permutations $\{\pi^b \circ \sigma_d \mid d \in \mathbb{Z}_N, b \in \{0,1\}\}$ (notation abuse), is needed to guarantee that Alice can't guess d_B, b_B from d. Similarly, the CPA requirement with permutations $\{\tau_N^b \circ \sigma_d \mid b \in \{0,1\}, d \in \mathbb{Z}_N\}$ prevents Bob from guessing d_A, b_A from e^B. It is worth pointing out that our choice of using rotations instead of arbitrary permutations results in stronger requirements for the commutative blinding. On the other side, arbitrary permutations do not commute, therefore the setup phase will need to be extended in order to keep the secrets next to each other.

Finally, the key indistinguishability requirement is used to guarantee that no information is leaked during the exchange phase. In particular, note that $m^B[i]$ is blinded using a key which is chosen entirely upon on b_A. Therefore, Alice can unblind messages as she receives them. However, she can't check if the message received contain the correct key (since the encryption of the secret is delayed) and the KPA requirement prevents her from obtaining information from c^B. On the other side, $m^A[i]$ is blinded using a key dependent on b_A and b_B. Therefore, Bob doesn't know a priori which key is used. If he were to discover which key is used to blind $m^A[i]$, then he would discover b_A. This gives Bob knowledge of whether $k_A[0]$ precedes or succeeds $k_B[0]$, which is an unfair advantage.

3.3   Commutative Blinding and Why It Is Needed

The commutative blinding scheme is the most complex primitive used in our protocol. Quite a few options are available for commutative encryptions: ElGamal, SRA, Pohlig-Hellman, Massay-Omura, etc. However, most do not satisfy our requirements. For instance, ElGamal is not secure against our strong CPA requirement since each ciphertext is paired with a "tag" that encapsulates the random nonce used in the encryption process. On the other hand, we believe that the Pohlig-Hellman cipher satisfies our requirements, provided it is used carefully.[2]

It is important to note that all these cited commutative encryptions are based on the hardness of either the integer factorisation problem or the discrete logarithm problem. Since both are known to be vulnerable to quantum computers, the interesting question of finding post-quantum blindings arises. Most literature on post-quantum commutative encryption (e.g. [8,19]) is based on generalising the discrete logarithm problem to non-abelian groups. However, this approach may be flawed [20,27]. Other quantum resistant commutative encryption schemes might arise from group action on sets of isogenous elliptic curves as attempted by Stolbunov [26] or similarly to the CSIDH protocol [4]. As noted during the definition of the commutative blinding, we believe homomorphic encryption could be used to construct this primitive. The most trivial implementation would require the outer blinding Blind$_1$ to be the homomorphic encryption, while the inner blinding Blind$_2$ can be a simple Vernam cipher. Since Blind$_2$ is always used with unique keys, the overall construction's security should follow from the security of the homomorphic encryption. In this regard, we wish to point out that most fully homomorphic encryption schemes rely on the hardness of the Learning With Errors problem (or its ring variant) which was proved to be at least as hard as some worst case lattice problems [22] such as the Shortest Vector Problem. As

---

[2] In particular, we need to prevent the ciphertexts from being recognised from their order. Thus, the modulus picked should be a safe prime $p = 2q + 1$ and all plaintexts should be forced to be in the same subgroup of prime order q.

a result, these schemes are good candidates for building quantum-safe blinding schemes.

Given the complexity of commutative blinding, a natural question is whether we can achieve the same results without its use. Therefore, we feel the need to briefly justify its use. Our problem of hiding the secret messages among a list of other dummy messages is similar to the issue of shuffling a deck of cards for an online game of poker. No single party must know the whole shuffle and both need to contribute to it. This "mental poker" problem is often solved using commutative blinding, oblivious transfer or by generating cards on the fly. [12–14,25] The last option is clearly not an option in our context. On the other hand, the use of oblivious transfer is appealing yet we believe this is only possible (without greatly increasing the round complexity of the protocol) if the shuffling phase can be split into two sub-shuffles each performed independently by the two parties. We could not find such a split, therefore we consider the existence an efficient setup phase without commutative blinding an open question.

4   Analysis

A protocol Π^{M+1} is a sequence of messages $\langle m_0, \ldots, m_M \rangle$. A time point t in the protocol Π^M is an integer $t \in \mathbb{Z}_M$. We say that messages m_i with $i \leq t$ happens before t. We write T_A (and T_B) for the time point after which Alice (respectively Bob) is guaranteed to obtain s_B (respectively s_A). For instance, $m_0 = \mathsf{Enc}_k(s_A) \wedge m_3 = k \implies T_B \leq 3$. A subtler example is: $m_0 = \mathsf{Enc}_k(s_A) \wedge m_4 = \mathsf{delay}(k) \implies T_B \leq 4$. Using this simple model, we can analyse the fairness of our protocol against passive adversaries. In this context, we define a passive adversary as one that is only allowed to go offline unexpectedly.

In this section, we write $s_A \in \boldsymbol{m}^A[i]$ to mean that $\boldsymbol{m}^A[i]$ is the blinding of $\boldsymbol{k}^A[0]$. Essentially, $\boldsymbol{m}^A[i]$ is the only important message in $\boldsymbol{m}^A$. The analogue notation $s_B \in \boldsymbol{m}^B[i]$ will also be used.

4.1   Adversarial Model

In our adversarial model, the enemy can control Alice or Bob (but not both) and they are allowed only to perform actions that do not reveal them as a bad actor. We define this kind of adversary as a *covert adversary*. We assume communications channels are authenticated, guarantee integrity and confidentiality and are secure against reordering and replay attacks. Therefore receiving a malformed message signed by the adversary constitute a proof of their misbehaviour, however, aborting communication is not assumed to be a malicious action. To prove the security of our protocol, we first show that it is secure against *passive* adversaries which are only allowed to perform side computations and abort communication. We then show that any covert adversary is restricted to behave like a passive adversary.

4.2   Fairness

We will show that the protocol of Fig. 4 achieves $\frac{1}{2N}$-partial fairness. The key idea is that T_A and T_B are kept next to each other so that there is only one successful early-termination attack among the $2N$ possible. Due to the use of delay encryption, we see that $T_A = i + 2$ if and only if E_i is the blinding of $\boldsymbol{k}^B[0]$. Similarly, $T_B = i + 2$ if and only if E_i is the blinded $\boldsymbol{k}^A[0]$. Therefore, we compute the distribution of T_A, T_B by looking at the distribution of $\boldsymbol{k}^A[0]$ and $\boldsymbol{k}^B[0]$.

Theorem 1. *Let Π be the fair exchange protocol from Fig. 4. Then*

$$\Pr\left[s_A \in \boldsymbol{m}^A[i] \wedge s_B \in \boldsymbol{m}^B[j]\right] = \begin{cases} \frac{1}{2N} & \text{if } i = j \vee i = j + 1 \\ 0 & \text{otherwise} \end{cases} \tag{1}$$

Proof. Note that

$$\boldsymbol{m}^A[i] = \mathsf{Blind}_2\left(\boldsymbol{k}^A[\sigma_{d_A + d_B}^e((i(-1)^{b_A} + Nb_A - b_B) \bmod (N+1))],\right.$$

$$\left. \boldsymbol{B}^B[(i(-1)^{b_A} + Nb_A - b_B) \bmod (N+1)]\right) \tag{2}$$

$$\boldsymbol{m}^B[i] = \mathsf{Blind}_2\left(\boldsymbol{k}^B[(i(-1)^{b_A} + (N-1)b_A + d_A + d_B) \bmod N],\right.$$

$$\left. \boldsymbol{B}^A[i(-1)^{b_A} + (N-1)b_A]\right) \tag{3}$$

So

$$s_A \in \boldsymbol{m}^A[i] \iff 0 = \sigma_{d_A + d_B}^e((i(-1)^{b_A} + Nb_A - b_B) \bmod (N+1))$$

$$s_B \in \boldsymbol{m}^B[i] \iff 0 = (i(-1)^{b_A} + (N-1)b_A + d_A + d_B) \bmod N$$

Hence

$$\Pr\left[s_B \in \boldsymbol{m}^B[i]\right] = \Pr_{\substack{b_a \xleftarrow{\$} \{0,1\} \\ d_A, d_B \xleftarrow{\$} \mathbb{Z}_N}} \left[0 = (i(-1)^{b_A} + (N-1)b_A + d_A + d_B) \bmod N\right]$$

$$= \frac{1}{2}\left(\Pr_{d \xleftarrow{\$} \mathbb{Z}_N}[0 = (i + d) \bmod N] + \right.$$

$$\left. \Pr_{d \xleftarrow{\$} \mathbb{Z}_N}[0 = (N - 1 - i + d) \bmod N]\right) = \frac{1}{N}$$

Assume $s_B \in \boldsymbol{m}^B[j]$, that is:

$$0 = (j(-1)^{b_A} + (N-1)b_A + d_A + d_B) \bmod N$$

We will show that s_A is either in $\boldsymbol{m}^A[j]$ or $\boldsymbol{m}^A[j+1]$ by analysing the four cases $(b_A, b_B) \in \{0, 1\}^2$

1. $b_A = b_B = 0$

$$s_B \in m^B[j] \implies \sigma^e_{d_A+d_B}(j) = (j + d_A + d_B) \bmod N = 0 \implies s_A \in m^A[j]$$

2. $b_A = b_B = 1$

$$s_B \in m^B[j] \implies \sigma^e_{d_A+d_B}(N - 1 - j) = (N - 1 - j + d_A + d_B) \bmod N = 0$$
$$\implies s_A \in m^A[j]$$

3. $b_A = 0 \wedge b_B = 1$

$$s_B \in m^B[j] \implies \sigma^e_{d_A+d_B}(j + 1 - b_B) = (j + d_A + d_B) \bmod N = 0$$
$$\implies s_A \in m^A[j + 1]$$

4. $b_A = 1 \wedge b_B = 0$

$$s_B \in m^B[j] \implies$$
$$\sigma^e_{d_A+d_B}(N - (j + 1)) = (N - j - 1 + d_A + d_B) \bmod N = 0$$
$$\implies s_A \in m^A[j + 1]$$

As a result,

$$\Pr_{b_A, b_B \overset{\$}{\leftarrow} \{0,1\}} \left[s_A \in m^A[i] \,\middle|\, s_B \in m^B[j] \right] = \begin{cases} \frac{1}{2} & \text{if } i = j \vee i = j + 1 \\ 0 & \text{otherwise} \end{cases}$$

The statement of the theorem follows directly from the equation

$$\Pr\left[s_A \in m^A[i] \wedge s_B \in m^B[j] \right] =$$
$$\Pr\left[s_A \in m^A[i] \,\middle|\, s_B \in m^B[j] \right] \Pr\left[s_B \in m^B[j] \right]$$

$\square$

Corollary 1. *Let Π be the protocol from Fig. 4. Let $\mathcal{A}$ be a computationally bounded passive adversary. Then $\mathcal{A}$ can successfully obtain the other party's secret without revealing theirs with probability $\frac{1}{2N}$.*

Proof (Sketch). First, recall Eq. 1. All we have to prove is that $\mathcal{A}$ cannot obtain any knowledge that gives them any better probability distribution. The parameters $\mathfrak{p}$ which determines the distributions are d_A, d_B, b_A, b_B. In Sect. 3.2, we have described what role each security requirement plays in guaranteeing the fairness of the protocol, but here we report briefly the key points.

Note that message $\mathbf{S_1}, \mathbf{S_2}, \mathbf{S_3}$ don't reveal anything about $\mathfrak{p}$ until the delays open *after* the protocol termination. This is given by the properties: delay-COA, H-preimage resistance, Blind$_1$-COA and Blind$_2$-CPA. The messages $\mathbf{E_{2r-1}}$ and $\mathbf{E_{2r}}$ do not reveal anything about $\mathfrak{p}$ since Blind$_2$ is key-indistinguishable and Blind$_1$ is KPA secure. Therefore, $\mathcal{A}$ only knows the parameters they picked and these are not enough to skew the probability distribution of Eq. 1.

Say that $\mathcal{A}$ stops after message $\mathbf{S_i}$, then they will obtain the other party's secret with probability 0. Say that $\mathcal{A}$ stops after message $\mathbf{E_i}$, then they will successfully cheat if $\mathbf{E_i}$ contains the other party's secret and $s_A \in \mathbf{E_j}$ with $j > i$. By Eq. 1 this happens with probability $\frac{1}{2N}$. Stopping during the disclosure phase is pointless as s_A is already transmitted. $\qquad\square$

4.3   Optimality

In the protocol from Fig. 4, we hide the secrets s_A, s_B among the messages $\mathbf{E_i}$'s and use delay encryption to guarantee that $T_A = i + 2 \iff s_B \in \mathbf{E_i}$ (and similarly for Bob). Note that the $+2$ is needed to account for the setup phase. Hence, T_A and T_B are also hidden for the entire duration of the exchange phase.

Here, we prove that our construction is "optimal", meaning that no exchange phase of M messages can achieve fairness greater than $1 - \frac{1}{M-1}$. However, this leaves open the question of whether our setup phase can be shortened. In this regard, we point out that messages $\mathbf{S_3}$ and $\mathbf{E_1}$ can be sent as one. Therefore, the proposed protocol achieves $\frac{1}{M-1}$-partial fairness using $M + 2$ messages.

Lemma 1. *A receives a message at time T_A.*

Proof. Assume for a contradiction that m_{T_A} is a message from Alice to Bob. It follows that Alice can compute m_{T_A} from $\{m_1, \ldots, m_{T_A-1}\}$. As a result, everything that Alice can compute from $\{m_1, \ldots, m_{T_A}\}$ can be done from $\{m_1, \ldots, m_{T_A-1}\}$. Therefore T_A is not minimal. $\qquad\square$

Lemma 2. *In the absence of third parties, $T_A \neq T_B$.*

Proof. This follows directly from Lemma 1. $\qquad\square$

Lemma 3. *Assume there is no third party. If in Π messages do not alternate between Alice and Bob, then there is another protocol Π' which is as fair as Π in which the messages alternate.*

Proof. Let Π be a protocol where the messages between Alice and Bob do not alternate. Construct Π' from Π by collapsing consecutive messages from the same party into one. After this process, append "dummy" messages so that Π' and Π have the same length. In this process, the fairness of Π is left untouched. In particular, note that the optimal strategy of any adversary could have not been to stop between consecutive messages and it is definitely not to stop after dummy messages. $\qquad\square$

Theorem 2. *Let Π be a fair exchange protocol between Alice and Bob in absence of third parties. If Π consists of $M + 1$ messages, then there is an unfair run with probability $\frac{1}{M}$*

Proof. By Lemma 3 we can assume that $\Pi = \langle m_0, \ldots, m_M \rangle$ where Alice sends the messages with even index, and Bob those with odd index. There are m possible attacks on the protocol by early abortion: stop the protocol after i messages where $0 < i \leq M$. By Lemma 2 we know that at least one of these attacks would be successful. So, the probability of an unfair run is at least $\frac{1}{M}$. $\square$

4.4   Catching Active Cheaters

So far we have analysed the fairness of our protocol when the adversary is passive. We now look at the case where the adversary can alter the messages they send. Our aim is to show that any such adversary will be caught. That is, our protocol allows the honest party to demonstrate the misbehaviour of the other party. Since channels are authenticated a transcript of the protocol constitute a proof of misbehaviour. Hence, covert adversary can only behave like passive adversaries.

Theorem 3. *If a party misbehaves, the other can prove it (unless both misbehaved).*

Proof. Firstly, note that inconsistencies between the delayed messages and the shuffling "sub-messages" c^A, c^B, d, e^B will result in inconsistent $\mathbf{E_i}$'s. We assume that Alice and Bob have agreed on predicates (i.e. boolean functions) $\mathsf{Exp}_A, \mathsf{Exp}_B$ to indicate what they expect to receive. Recall Eqs. 2 and 3 and assume that both parties have knowledge of the content of the delayed messages D_A, D_B, which they eventually will. Therefore, both parties have complete knowledge of the permutations used. Each exchange messages $\mathbf{E_i}$ can be unblinded and reordered so that they are expected to match $\mathsf{H}(k^A[j])$ (or $\mathsf{H}(k^B[j])$) for some j. Finally, the secrets can be retrieved and checked against Exp_A or Exp_B. Assume that $m^A[i]$ is not correct, then Bob could be responsible only if they have wrongly computed d. However, note that the function $c^A \mapsto d$ is entirely determined by (d_B, b_B, B^B). Therefore, one can verify the computation of d and, if this is correct, prove that Alice was responsible for the issue with $m^A[i]$. Similarly, Alice's computation $c^B \mapsto e^B$ is determined by (d_A, b_A, B^A). It follows that anyone holding a transcript of the protocol (and $\mathsf{Exp}_A, \mathsf{Exp}_B$) can check if each $\mathbf{E_i}$ is correct and determine who introduced any eventual error.   □

5   Conclusion and Future Research

In this paper, we have presented a fair exchange protocol which achieves fairness against covert adversaries with probability $1 - \frac{1}{2N}$ in $2N + 1$ exchange messages and 3 setup messages. We proved that the protocol is optimally fair up to shortening the already-short setup phase. This impossibility result holds in a general model which only assumes that the involved parties are not computationally unbounded. The cryptographic primitives that allow the design of the optimally-fair protocol are delay encryption and commutative blinding. The use of delay encryption introduces the reasonable assumption that both parties have somewhat similar sequential computational power, a considerable improvement on the results of [7] where similar (parallel) computing power was needed. Nevertheless, we limited the use of delay encryption to a single message which will be opened only when a party suspects misbehaviour. This gives some leeway to use less efficient algorithms. We showed that our protocol is secure against covert adversaries without the need of expensive constructions and point out that all the primitive used can be quantum safe. We overcome the bounds of [16] by extending the cryptographic palette and achieve a stronger fairness than [6] by careful choice of the blinding strategy. Despite the substantial contribution of our paper, more research is needed in the field of fair exchange. The only drawback of our protocol is the need for a strong commutative blinding. Therefore, it raises the interesting question of whether our protocol can be modified so as not to use commutative encryption without increasing the message complexity of the setup phase. On the more practical side, an interesting problem to consider is the scenario where the malicious party aborts the exchange and, if the secrets are not exchanged, they begin another exchange with the same party and same secrets. This seems a plausible scenario in real-world applications since the honest party is likely to need the exchange to succeed, and they will try again if network failures seem the cause of abortion. However, the fairness of the protocol is different since multiple runs of the same protocol must be taken into account.

References

1. Asokan, N., Schunter, M., Waidner, M.: Optimistic protocols for multi-party fair exchange. IBM Research Division (1996)
2. Ben-Or, M., Goldreich, O., Micali, S., Rivest, R.L.: A fair protocol for signing contracts. IEEE Trans. Inf. Theory **36**(1), 40–46 (1990). https://doi.org/10.1109/18.50372
3. Boneh, D., Naor, M.: Timed commitments. In: Bellare, M. (ed.) CRYPTO 2000. LNCS, vol. 1880, pp. 236–254. Springer, Heidelberg (2000). https://doi.org/10.1007/3-540-44598-6_15
4. Castryck, W., Lange, T., Martindale, C., Panny, L., Renes, J.: CSIDH: an efficient post-quantum commutative group action. In: Peyrin, T., Galbraith, S. (eds.) ASIACRYPT 2018. LNCS, vol. 11274, pp. 395–427. Springer, Cham (2018). https://doi.org/10.1007/978-3-030-03332-3_15
5. Cleve, R.: Limits on the security of coin flips when half the processors are faulty. In: Proceedings of the Eighteenth Annual ACM Symposium on Theory of Computing (STOC 1986), pp. 364–369. Association for Computing Machinery, New York (1986). https://doi.org/10.1145/12130.12168
6. Couteau, G., Roscoe, A.W., Ryan, P.Y.A.: Partially-fair computation from timed-release encryption and oblivious transfer. In: Baek, J., Ruj, S. (eds.) ACISP 2021. LNCS, vol. 13083, pp. 330–349. Springer, Cham (2021). https://doi.org/10.1007/978-3-030-90567-5_17
7. Damgård, I.B.: Practical and provably secure release of a secret and exchange of signatures. J. Cryptol. **8**(4), 201–222 (1995). https://doi.org/10.1007/BF00191356
8. Dmitriy, M.: Non-commutative finite groups as primitive of public key cryptosystems. Quasigroups Related Syst. **18**(2), 165–176 (2010)
9. Even, S., Yacobi, Y.: Relations among public key signature systems. Report, TECHNION - Israel Istitute of Technology (1980)
10. Franklin, M., Tsudik, G.: Secure group barter: multi-party fair exchange with semi-trusted neutral parties. In: Hirchfeld, R. (ed.) FC 1998. LNCS, vol. 1465, pp. 90–102. Springer, Heidelberg (1998). https://doi.org/10.1007/BFb0055475
11. Garbinato, B., Rickebusch, I.: Impossibility results on fair exchange. In: Eichler, G., Kropf, P., Lechner, U., Meesad, P., Unger, H. (eds.) 10th International Conference on Innovative Internet Community Systems (I2CS) (Jubilee Edition 2010), pp. 507–518. Gesellschaft für Informatik e.V, Bonn (2010)

12. Goldreich, O., Micali, S., Wigderson, A.: How to play any mental game. In: Proceedings of the Nineteenth Annual ACM Symposium on Theory of Computing (STOC 1987), pp. 218–229. Association for Computing Machinery, New York (1987). https://doi.org/10.1145/28395.28420

13. Goldwasser, S., Micali, S.: Probabilistic encryption & how to play mental poker keeping secret all partial information. In: Proceedings of the Fourteenth Annual ACM Symposium on Theory of Computing (STOC 1982), pp. 365–377. Association for Computing Machinery, New York (1982). https://doi.org/10.1145/800070.802212

14. Golle, P.: Dealing cards in poker games. In: International Conference on Information Technology: Coding and Computing (ITCC 2005) - Volume II, vol. 1, pp. 506–511 (2005). https://doi.org/10.1109/ITCC.2005.119

15. Gollmann, D.: Computer Security. Wiley Textbooks, Chichester (2011)

16. Gordon, S.D., Katz, J.: Partial fairness in secure two-party computation. In: Gilbert, H. (ed.) EUROCRYPT 2010. LNCS, vol. 6110, pp. 157–176. Springer, Heidelberg (2010). https://doi.org/10.1007/978-3-642-13190-5_8

17. Kaufman, C., Perlman, R., Speciner, M.: Network Security: Private Communication in a Public World, 2nd edn [electronic resource]. Prentice Hall PTR (2002)

18. Maffei, I., Roscoe, A.W.: Delay encryption by cubing (2022). https://doi.org/10.48550/ARXIV.2205.05594

19. Moldovyan, A.A., Moldovyan, D.N., Moldovyan, N.A.: Post-quantum commutative encryption algorithm. Comput. Sci. J. Moldova **27**, 299–317 (2019)

20. Myasnikov, A.D., Ushakov, A.: Quantum algorithm for the discrete logarithm problem for matrices over finite group rings. Cryptology ePrint Archive, Report 2012/574 (2012)

21. Pagnia, H., Gärtner, F.C.: On the impossibility of fair exchange without a trusted third party. Darmstadt University of Technology, Technical Report (1999)

22. Regev, O.: On lattices, learning with errors, random linear codes, and cryptography. In: Proceedings of the Thirty-Seventh Annual ACM Symposium on Theory of Computing (STOC 2005), pp. 84–93. Association for Computing Machinery, New York (2005). https://doi.org/10.1145/1060590.1060603

23. Rivest, R.L., Shamir, A., Wagner, D.A.: Time-Lock Puzzles and Timed-Release Crypto. Report, Massachusetts Institute of Technology (1996)

24. Roscoe, A.W., Ryan, P.Y.A.: Auditable PAKEs: approaching fair exchange without a TTP. In: Stajano, F., Anderson, J., Christianson, B., Matyáš, V. (eds.) Security Protocols 2017. LNCS, vol. 10476, pp. 278–297. Springer, Cham (2017). https://doi.org/10.1007/978-3-319-71075-4_31

25. Shamir, A., Rivest, R.L., Adleman, L.M.: Mental poker. In: The Mathematical Gardner, pp. 37–43. Springer, Boston (1981). https://doi.org/10.1007/978-1-4684-6686-7_5

26. Stolbunov, A.: Constructing public-key cryptographic schemes based on class group action on a set of isogenous elliptic curves. Adv. Math. Commun. 4(2), 215–235 (2010)

27. Yanlong, M.: Cryptanalysis of the cryptosystems based on the generalized hidden discrete logarithm problem. Cryptology ePrint Archive, Report 2021/1701 (2021)

Open Access This chapter is licensed under the terms of the Creative Commons Attribution 4.0 International License (http://creativecommons.org/licenses/by/4.0/), which permits use, sharing, adaptation, distribution and reproduction in any medium or format, as long as you give appropriate credit to the original author(s) and the source, provide a link to the Creative Commons license and indicate if changes were made.

The images or other third party material in this chapter are included in the chapter's Creative Commons license, unless indicated otherwise in a credit line to the material. If material is not included in the chapter's Creative Commons license and your intended use is not permitted by statutory regulation or exceeds the permitted use, you will need to obtain permission directly from the copyright holder.

Witness-Authenticated Key Exchange, Revisited: Extensions to Groups, Improved Models, Simpler Constructions

Matteo Campanelli[1]([☒]) [iD], Rosario Gennaro[1,2]([☒]) [iD], Kelsey Melissaris[2,3]([☒]) [iD], and Luca Nizzardo[1] [iD]

[1] Protocol Labs, San Francisco, USA
{matteo,rosario.gennaro,luca}@protocol.ai
[2] The City University of New York, New York, USA
[3] Aarhus University, Aarhus, Denmark
kelsey@cs.au.dk

Abstract. We study *witness-authenticated key exchange* (WAKE), in which parties authenticate through knowledge of a witness to any NP statement. WAKE achieves generic authenticated key exchange in the absence of trusted parties; WAKE is most suitable when a certificate authority is either unavailable or undesirable, as in highly decentralized networks. In practice WAKE approximates witness encryption, its elusive non-interactive analogue, at the cost of minimal interaction.

This work is the first to propose, model and build witness-authenticated key exchange amongst *groups* of more than two parties, as well as the first to provide *practical* and *provably secure* constructions in the two-party case for *general* NP statements. Specifically our contributions are:

1. both game-based and universally composable (Canetti, FOCS '01) definitions for WAKE along with equivalence conditions between the two definitions,
2. a highly general compiler that introduces witness-authentication to any key exchange protocol along with, as a direct consequence, a three-round group WAKE protocol from DDH and signatures of knowledge (SOK), and
3. an optimized two-round group WAKE construction from DDH and SOK along with experimental benchmarks to demonstrate concrete practicality.

Additionally, we study the specialized two-party case and provide a critique of prior work on this topic (Ngo et al., Financial Crypto '21) by pinpointing nontrivial weaknesses in the model, constructions and security proofs seen therein. We rectify those limitations with this work, significantly diverging in our techniques, design and approach.

Keywords: Witness-based primitives · Authentication · Key Exchange

K. Melissaris—Work done while affiliated with The City University of New York.

© International Financial Cryptography Association 2024
F. Baldimtsi and C. Cachin (Eds.): FC 2023, LNCS 13950, pp. 112–128, 2024.
https://doi.org/10.1007/978-3-031-47754-6_7

1 Introduction

Public-Key cryptography, as introduced in the seminal paper by Diffie and Hellman, allows two parties that have never met to confidentially exchange information. This can be achieved *non-interactively* via encryption, with which messages are encrypted under a receiver's public key [29], or *interactively* via key exchange [12]. Traditionally these parties' identities are endorsed by a trusted certificate authority (CA) via e.g. digital signatures which bind each public key to a corresponding identity and are published in a public key infrastructure. Beyond this, in both the non-interactive and interactive cases there are more flexible ways to designate the intended recipients of secure communications. For example, in *identity-based* cryptography [31] public keys are replaced by arbitrary identity strings and in *attribute-based* cryptography [30] certain policies define the set of attributes that parties must satisfy. Critically, both of these primitives employ a trusted party to issue certificates or keys corresponding to a party's claimed identity or attributes and therefore can be considered to assume the existence of a CA.

Arguably, witness-based cryptography is the most general way to specify the intended recipient of an encrypted message. With Witness Encryption (WE) [17] a message can be encrypted to a statement ϕ, an instance of some NP language L, such that if $\phi \in L$ then that message can be efficiently decrypted with a witness w to ϕ. With WE one can encrypt a message under a Sudoku puzzle such that it is efficiently decryptable with any solution to that puzzle. Remarkably, WE does not require any trusted party to certify and issue keys; in WE the secret decryption key is the uncertified witness. Despite recent progress [1] practical WE for all of NP from standard assumptions remains elusive.

In this work we turn our attention to a new witness-based primitive that *(i)* similarly to WE, can be used in several applications where an *arbitrary* secret enables secure communication,[1] yet *(ii)* differently from WE, can be concretely and efficiently realized under computational assumptions *held today*. We achieve this by allowing an extremely low amount of interaction – in some cases only two messages. We refer to this primitive, the interactive process by which parties mutually authenticate with respect to knowledge of a witness to an NP statement, as *witness-authenticated key exchange* (WAKE). We argue that this interactive abstraction deserves to be studied in its own right due to its utility and generality.

Just as WE is the most general form of encryption, the interactive WAKE subsumes all efficiently verifiable means of authentication for key exchange as special cases.

Contributions. This work is the first to propose, model and build witness-authentication amongst *groups* of authenticated parties. We are also the first to provide *practical* and *provably secure* protocols between two-parties authenticating under *general* statements. Our contributions are as follows:

---

[1] That is, not requiring certification by an authority and not the output of a specific key generation algorithm.

(1) We revisit witness-authentication: we identify shortcomings of witness-key-agreement, as proposed by [26]—the model's applicability, the construction's practicality, and the proof of security. Our discussion demonstrates a need for new models and constructions in the two-party case, a specialization of our general model for groups of parties.

(2) We define WAKE via both a modular and intuitive game-based formalization and a universally composable (UC) ideal functionality. UC is the most desirable security guarantee for authenticated key exchange and we prove the satisfaction of the strongest variant of our game-based definition equivalent composability.

(3) We construct new protocols for group WAKE. First, we show a *general compiler* that transforms any *passively* secure key exchange protocol into a witness-authenticated key exchange. The main features of this general construction are it's conceptual simplicity, modularity and efficiency. The compiler relies on strongly simulation-extractable signatures of knowledge [20], the properties of which can be leveraged to provide our security and efficiency guarantees. Concretely we apply our compiler to the group key exchange protocol of Burmester and Desmedt, giving a practical 3-round WAKE protocol.

(4) We optimize the 3-round protocol above to a 2-round *concretely efficient* group WAKE protocol. The improved solution achieves UC security, a property which does not follow from the security of the above compiler and demands particular care in proving. We show that the optimized protocol remains practical with our estimated benchmarks in Sect. 4.

THE GENERAL PROTOCOL IN A NUTSHELL. We begin with the Katz-Yung [23] approach to authenticated group key exchange and replace their digital signature authentication mechanism with simulation-extractable signatures of knowledge (SOK) [20], a primitive that enables a signer to verifiably claim knowledge of a particular secret. The idea is fundamentally simple but modeling WAKE and proving security of our protocols require care and should be considered our main technical contributions.

Applications. The main application of WAKE is the establishment of secure communication channels between groups of parties contingent upon the information those parties provably know. The absence of a trusted CA renders WAKE especially compelling for decentralized applications that require parties to confidentially connect based on arbitrary and dynamic policies. Decoupling authentication and identity permits flexible, deniable and anonymous authentication. We present several examples of applications for WAKE. Estimated benchmarks for parties authenticating in both the dark pool and retrieval market applications can be found in Sect. 4.

DARK POOL TRANSACTIONS. The primary motivation for the predecessor to WAKE [26], dark pool transactions allow for confidential and anonymous negotiation. In this scenario Alice is selling an item and wants to confidentially negotiate with any party holding enough funds to purchase that item. Alice determines a minimum balance B and any party Bob can establish a key with Alice if, for a public commitment c to his private balance b, the following relation is satisfied

$\mathcal{R}\big((B,c),(b,r)\big) = \big(c = \mathsf{comm}(b;r) \wedge b \geq B\big)$. Alice can remain unauthenticated, as in *unilateral* WAKE, or Bob may wish that Alice authenticates her ownership of the item for sale. Given our group WAKE this dark pools scenario can be extended, providing a group chat between many parties that satisfy the condition of holding enough funds to participate.

RETRIEVAL MARKETS. In decentralized storage systems such as Filecoin [27] and IPFS [28] files are stored by providers and addressed with *content identifiers (CID)*, typically the cryptographic hash of a file, which additionally serve as commitments. A provider can authenticate to any client interested in retrieving a file if the provider in fact holds the private file associated to the public CID. Similarly providers storing the same file can establish a confidential group channel via group WAKE.

CHAT WITH THE SAME WALLET. Several services are offered that allow parties to create chatrooms and schedule meetings amongst parties that hold similar tokens in a blockchain (e.g. [25,32]). A group WAKE can be used for these tasks. Thanks to the inherent flexibility of WAKE, existing schemes can be extended to more general conditions, e.g. confidential group chatrooms between owners of NFTs by a particular artist.

DECENTRALIZED ANONYMOUS ROUTING. Several proposals have been put forward for decentralized naming and routing protocols over the internet (see e.g. [22] and [15]). WAKE can play an important role in securing such protocols by providing a method by which parties can authenticate without a CA.

Table 1. Comparison to related work. `Model/GB`: game-based model. `Model/UC`: UC-based model. `Model/All NP`: supports any efficiently computable relation. `Model/No CA`: no certifying authority. `Model/ML`: supports multi-lateral authentication. `Model/grp`: supports more than two parties. `Protocol/O(1)-rnd`: constant round protocol. `Protocol/All NP`: protocol supports any efficiently computable relation.

Primitive	Model						Protocol	
	GB	UC	All NP	No CA	ML	Groups	$O(1)$-rnd	All NP
PAKE [2]	✓	✓		✓	✓		✓	
CAKE [7]		✓	✓		✓			
ABKE [24]		✓	✓				✓	✓
LAKE [21]		✓	✓	✓	✓		✓	
WKA* [26]	✓		✓	✓				
WAKE	✓	✓	✓	✓	✓	✓	✓	✓

Related Work. The relevant generalizations of authenticated key exchange are summarized in Table 1. Credential-authenticated and attribute-based key exchange (CAKE [7] and ABKE [24]), respectively, model bilateral and unilateral authentication on the basis of efficiently computable relations over certified credentials. Thus, both CAKE and ABKE assume a CA to issue these certificates (CA) and depend upon the strong assumption of unanimous trust in an incorruptible CA. Beyond this impracticality and the inherent certificate governance issues, no CA could possibly certify every arbitrary property potentially desirable for authentication; any CA is a limitation against a truly general key exchange.

In the absence of a CA, password-authenticated key exchange (PAKE) permits parties to boost shared low entropy passwords into a high entropy key [2] and has been generalized to noisy, approximately-equal passwords [14]. Even closer to the goal of witness-authentication is language-authenticated key exchange (LAKE [21]), with which two parties establish a shared key if each participant has knowledge of a word that lies in a language defined by their partner. Notably, the language and the word remain secret with LAKE. In contrast, WAKE does not *straightforwardly* guarantee secrecy of the statement or language, as modeled. As the model closest to our goal, it is important to note that the LAKE protocol exclusively supports self-randomizable algebraic languages, the subset of languages which admit smooth projective hash functions [11]. Therefore the LAKE protocol cannot support all of NP.[2]

Finally, in comparison to generic multiparty computation (MPC) or fully homomorphic encryption, the state-of-the-art SNARKs we employ are both mature and efficient. One primary observation that we wish to communicate is the simplicity of our solutions. A custom protocol for WAKE, as in Sect. 4, is both lighter and simpler than employing the heavy hammer that is MPC.

Analysis of Witness Key Agreement (WKA) [26]. We briefly discuss witness-key-agreement (WKA) [26], which inspired our work and proposed interesting applications.[3] We identify three primary shortcomings of WKA, that we discuss at length in the full version of our paper.[4]

LIMITATIONS OF THE WKA MODEL. A standard security requirement for key exchange is that an adversary should not be able to learn anything about the session key from the transcript of the interaction—a random key should be *indistinguishable* from the real key output by the participants in the protocol. Against active adversaries the [26] definition requires *unpredictability* in lieu of indistinguishability. As a consequence this model may consider a construction in which an active adversary *is able* to distinguish keys secure. As modeled, active adversaries are unrealistically weak: they can leverage *only a single session* in

---

[2] If every language in NP admits a smooth projective hash function then the polynomial hierarchy collapses.

[3] First, a note on terminology: WAKE and WKA aim at modeling similar settings but the models in our work are more general. In light of the observations in this section we chose to reflect these major differences in approach by further differentiating WAKE from WKA in name.

[4] A full version of our paper can be found on eprint: https://eprint.iacr.org/2022/382.

their attack. Furthermore, confidentiality in WKA neglects the case that an adversary has some relevant witness as auxiliary input.[5]

QUESTIONABLE PROOF OF WKA PROTOCOL SECURITY. Security of the WKA scheme in [26] requires a more elaborate proof under stricter assumptions than those acknowledged currently. The construction in [26] can be seen as a designated-verifier proof system, adapted from the ideas in [4] in which soundness is proven from the IND-CPA security of a linear-only encryption (LOE) scheme where LOE ciphertexts are contained in a CRS. WKA augments the CRS with encryptions of the randomness used to generate the ciphertexts that appear in the CRS. As such, WKA requires a stronger variant of IND-CPA security that accounts for randomness-dependent message (RDM) security [3], yet the proof sketch does not discuss RDM security. A concrete instantiation of the protocol would require a LOE scheme which is simultaneously IND-CPA and RDM secure. We are not aware of any such schemes.

IMPRACTICALITY OF THE WKA PROTOCOL. A primary limitation of WKA is that a trusted setup is required *each time* a new party wants to initiate the key exchange.[6] Every time a party aims to initiate an exchange the authority must be invoked to distribute a secret (tantamount to a verification key in a designated-verifier SNARK) for the key exchange. The trusted authority is invoked at least once per party in the system. Such an exchange is highly impractical. Beyond this, it is undesirable to have a trusted CA producing—and potentially leaking—trapdoors that enable impersonation. If relied on frequently this can compromise the entire system. On the other hand, our protocols can rely on no trusted setup [10], one trusted setup generated per given computation (reusable in all relevant key exchanges) [20] or a single trusted setup generated once and for all [16].

2 WAKE: Game-Based Definition

We provide both a game-based definition and a universally composable (UC) ideal functionality [9] for WAKE and prove the two equivalent under certain conditions. These two approaches offer a tradeoff: game-based definitions are modular and make explicit the security properties one intuitively expects of a WAKE protocol whereas composable ideal functionalities are secure under arbitrary composition with arbitrary protocols, thereby guaranteeing that the output key can be employed arbitrarily as is desirable for key exchange.

The objective of WAKE, and our primary modeling challenge, is that any set of participants should terminate with a shared key if each participant *has knowledge of a witness* to their own efficiently verifiable statement. Clearly, witness

---

[5] If Alice and Bob authenticate using witness w the adversary should not learn their key even with knowledge of w. Our definition models this case while the definition of WKA is silent.

[6] If the same party wants to run multiple key agreements for the same relation this setup could potentially be reused.

encryption is not a very useful starting point for this interactive setting; WE's nonintuitive security-correctness gap explicitly requires semantic security only for statements *not in the language* and correctness only for statements in the language. This is at odds with the aforementioned goal. Instead, our approach draws inspiration from the group key exchange of [23] modified to the unique and more general case of witness-authentication.

In public key infrastructure (PKI), such as that required by [23], a participant's certified public key is synonymous with their e.g. identity. Again a direct analogue to the witness-based setting is not straightforward and erroneously conflates knowledge of a witness with identity. The first incongruency is redundancy; as opposed to identities statements are not necessarily unique. Secondly, a WAKE protocol is required to guarantee secrecy of the witnesses whereas a PKI is necessarily public. This zero-knowledge style guarantee implies that all parties associated to the same statement are indistinguishable. Crucially, any meaningful notion of personal identity is absent in WAKE; witness-authentication remains agnostic to the true identity of a sender and, instead, exclusively asks: *were these protocol messages generated with knowledge of a witness?*

NOTATION. The concatenation of two strings, $a, b \in \{0, 1\}^*$ or two vectors $a, b \in \mathbb{F}^*$ is denoted $a \| b$. We write $x \leftarrow X$ to denote sampling the element x either uniformly at random from the set X or according to the distribution X and $x \leftarrow A(y)$ to denote running algorithm A on input y to get output x. The security parameter is denoted by λ. A function f is negligible if $|f(\lambda)| = \lambda^{-\omega(1)}$. PPT is used to denote probabilistic polynomial time. For an oracle $\mathcal{O}$ we use $A^{\mathcal{O}}$ to denote that algorithm A has oracle access to $\mathcal{O}$.

The transcript trans of a protocol execution is defined as the concatenation of all messages sent and received by any party in that execution, and can be subscripted to denote the transcript according to a specific party. The view of party P_i is written view_{P_i} and is defined to be the entire state of that party, including trans_{P_i}. A participant P_i is initialized with input input using square brackets. A protocol execution between a set of ℓ parties generating transcript trans is written as $(\mathsf{trans}, \mathsf{out}_1, \ldots, \mathsf{out}_\ell) \leftarrow \langle P_1[\mathsf{input}_1], \ldots, P_\ell[\mathsf{input}_\ell] \rangle$.

SIGNATURES OF KNOWLEDGE. A signature of knowledge (SOK) [10] is a witness-based generalization of a traditional digital signature. Consider security parameter λ, NP relation $\mathcal{R}$, statement ϕ, witness w and message m. A SOK has three main algorithms: $\mathsf{SSetup}(1^\lambda, \mathcal{R}) \to pp$ is a randomized relation-specific setup outputting public parameters pp, $\mathsf{SSign}(pp, \phi, w, m) \to \sigma$ is a randomized signing algorithm outputting signature σ and $\mathsf{SVerify}(pp, \phi, m, \sigma) \to \{0, 1\}$ is a deterministic verification algorithm outputting 1 for acceptance.[7]

Correctness requires that verification will accept a signature if it was generated with a valid witness. Security requires that a signature of knowledge be simulation-extractable. This property, at a high level, requires that there exists a simulator which can output public parameters that are indistinguishable from those output by the real SSetup, along with a trapdoor τ that can then be used to simulate signatures without witnesses. An efficient adversary with access to

---

[7] An ideal functionality for SOK can be found in the full version of our paper.

simulated signatures cannot forge a verifying signature without knowledge of a witness. Knowledge of a witness is modeled via the existence of an efficient extractor that can output a witness from the view of any forging adversary.

THE MODEL. We consider a set of participants $\mathcal{P}$ of size $\ell = \ell(\lambda)$ authenticating with respect to the fixed NP relation $\mathcal{R}$. Each $P \in \mathcal{P}$ is associated with the public statement ϕ_P and has an additional private input as the string w_P. The entire public statement vector is $\Phi = \langle \phi_1, \ldots, \phi_\ell \rangle$. We assume a distribution over witnesses $\mathcal{D}_\Phi$ such that each $\mathsf{w} \leftarrow \mathcal{D}_\Phi$ is a vector of witnesses $\mathsf{w} = \langle w_1, \ldots, w_\ell \rangle$ corresponding to the statements in Φ.[8]

Each $P \in \mathcal{P}$ participates in a polynomial number of protocol sessions with arbitrary subsets of $\mathcal{P}$. This is modelled via single-execution instances: Π_P^i is the ith instance of participant P. In addition to the inputs $(\Phi, \phi_P, \mathsf{w}_P)$ each instance stores a boolean acc_P^i indicating acceptance, a session identifier sid_P^i that is set to trans_{P^i}, and the session key sk_P^i. First, relation-specific public parameters are generated via a setup algorithm: $\mathsf{pp} \leftarrow \mathsf{SetUp}(1^\lambda, \mathcal{R})$.[9] **Correctness** requires that for all NP relations $\mathcal{R}$ and sets of participants $\mathcal{P}$, all instances terminate with a shared key if all parties have as input valid witnesses to their associated statements and the instances store matching session identifiers.[10]

ADVERSARIES. An adversary controls all communication between parties in the network via three oracles: $\mathsf{Send}(P, i, M)$ sends, i.e. inputs, message M to instance Π_P^i and returns it's response, $\mathsf{Execute}(P_{i_1}, j_1, \ldots, P_{i_K}, j_K)$ returns the transcript of an honest execution of the protocol between the queried instances $\{\Pi_{i_k}^{j_k}\}_{1 \leq k \leq K}$ and $\mathsf{Reveal}(P, i)$ outputs the session key sk_P^i stored by instance Π_P^i. A *passive* adversary uses the $\mathsf{Execute}$ oracle to play as a wire, essentially forwarding messages between parties, and attempts to learn information about a session key from the session transcript. An *active* adversary additionally can participate in the exchange, using the Send oracle to inject messages into a session that were not output by any party, and attempts to authenticate to any actual party in the exchange. Notably, a passive adversary trivially convinces every party in the exchange to accept the session by merely forwarding protocol messages between parties with valid witnesses, but does not do so *adversarially*. Therefore, we must clearly define what adversarial behavior is admissible.

A **forwarding adversary** engages in passive behavior. A forwarding adversary is such that for every Send query with input message M and instance Π_Q^j (except the first) there exists a preceding call to Send which output that message M as a response. Moreover, the query which output message M must have

---

[8] Our subscript notation is overloaded for ease of understanding; it is convenient to associate participants P_i, statements ϕ_i and witnesses w_i with the same index i when listing or assigning values, but it is also often convenient to index statements ϕ_P and witnesses w_P by the associated participant P when discussing a single instance.

[9] Our syntax requires one setup per relation but can easily be extended to a single universal setup [19].

[10] As the session identifier is the transcript of the session, two parties store matching session identifiers if those instances have recorded the same transcript, i.e. received the same messages, and therefore were participating in the same session.

taken as input an instance Π_P^i with a matching session identifier $\mathsf{sid}_P^i \equiv \mathsf{sid}_Q^j$. For each instance Π_P^i we define the **impersonation set** of that instance $\mathcal{I}(P, i)$ as the set of instances to which the adversary *impersonated* Π_P^i by injecting a message "from" Π_P^i that was not output by a corresponding query $\mathsf{Send}(P, i, \cdot)$. By definition a passive adversary does not have access to the Send oracle and therefore cannot be forwarding. Queries to Reveal can also trivially compromise session keys; no adversary should have access to the challenge session key. This motivates a freshness requirement: an instance is considered **fresh** if the adversary has neither revealed the session key stored by that instance nor any instance participating in the same session.[11]

An **admissible adversary** is an adversary that does not trivially compromise the session key. An adversary $\mathcal{A}$ is considered admissible for an experiment if $\mathcal{A}$ outputs a fresh challenge (P, i) upon which $\mathcal{A}$ is not forwarding. We reiterate that a passive adversary cannot be forwarding; an passive adversary is only required to output a fresh challenge instance to be considered admissible.

$\mathbf{Exp}_{\Pi,\mathcal{A}}^{\mathsf{WAKE-confid}}(\lambda, \mathcal{R}, \Phi, \mathcal{D}_\Phi):$

$b \leftarrow_\$ \{0,1\}$
$pp \leftarrow \mathsf{SetUp}(1^\lambda, \mathcal{R})$
$W \leftarrow \mathcal{D}_\Phi$
$\mathcal{P} \leftarrow \{P_i([\phi_i, w_i])\}_{i=1}^n$
$(C, i) \leftarrow \mathcal{A}^{\mathsf{Execute},\mathsf{Reveal}}(pp, \Phi, W)$
if $\mathsf{acc}_C^i = \mathsf{FALSE} : \mathbf{output}\ b$
$k_1 \leftarrow \mathsf{sk}_C^i, k_0 \leftarrow_\$ \{0,1\}^\lambda$
$b' \leftarrow \mathcal{A}^{\mathsf{Execute},\mathsf{Reveal}}(k_b)$
output $b == b'$

$\mathbf{Exp}_{\Pi,\mathcal{A},\mathcal{E}_*}^{\mathsf{WAKE-auth}}(\lambda, \mathcal{R}, \Phi, \mathcal{D}_\Phi):$

$pp, \tau \leftarrow \mathsf{SimSetUp}(1^\lambda, \mathcal{R})$
$\mathsf{w} \leftarrow \mathcal{D}_\Phi; \mathcal{P} \leftarrow \{P_i[\phi_i, \mathsf{w}_i]\}_{i=1}^n$
$(C, i, P) \leftarrow \mathcal{A}^{\mathsf{Send},\mathsf{Reveal}}(pp, \Phi)$
assert $(P \in \mathcal{I}(C, i))$
$b_{\mathsf{imp}} \leftarrow \mathsf{acc}_C^i$
$\mathsf{w}' \leftarrow \mathcal{E}_\mathcal{A}(\mathsf{view}_\mathcal{A}); \ \mathsf{w}' \leftarrow \mathcal{E}_\tau(\mathsf{trans}_\mathcal{A})$
$b_{\mathsf{ext}} \leftarrow (\phi_P, \mathsf{w}') \in \mathcal{R}$
output $(b_{\mathsf{imp}} \wedge \bar{b}_{\mathsf{ext}})$

$\mathbf{Exp}_{\Pi,\mathcal{A}}^{\mathsf{WAKE-sim}}(\lambda, \mathcal{R}):$

$b \xleftarrow{\$} \{0,1\}; \mathcal{P} \leftarrow \emptyset; c \leftarrow 0$
$pp_0 \leftarrow \mathsf{SetUp}(1^\lambda, \mathcal{R})$
$(pp_1, \tau) \leftarrow \mathsf{SimSetUp}(1^\lambda, \mathcal{R})$
$b' \leftarrow \mathcal{A}^{\mathsf{Send}^b,\mathsf{Reveal},\mathsf{SetKeys}}(pp_b)$
output $b == b'$

$\mathsf{SetKeys}(\phi, w):$

assert $(\phi, w) \in \mathcal{R}$
$\mathcal{P} \leftarrow \mathcal{P} \cup P_c[\phi, w]$
$c \leftarrow c + 1$

$\mathsf{Send}_{pp_0}^0(P, j, m):$

The real party: $P_{\phi,w} \leftarrow \mathcal{P}$
output $\mathsf{Send}(P_{\phi,w}, j, m)$

$\mathsf{Send}_{pp_1,\tau}^1(P, j, m):$

The simulated party.
output $\mathsf{Sim}_\tau(P, j, m)$

Fig. 1. WAKE confidentiality, authenticity and simulatability security experiments.

---

[11] Instances are participating in the same protocol session if the stored session identifiers agree on the first round messages.

SECURITY. Minimally a WAKE protocol should be secure in the standard unauthenticated key exchange sense. Confidentiality, Definition 1, is that standard passive security notion. Confidentiality guarantees that an eavesdropping adversary with access to a polynomial number of honest transcripts and session keys cannot distinguish a random string from the real challenge session key associated to the adversarially-chosen challenge transcript. In the confidentiality experiment, $\mathsf{Exp}_{\Pi,\mathcal{A}}^{\mathsf{WAKE\text{-}confid}}$ in Fig. 1, the adversary is given access to Execute and Reveal and the entire vector of witnesses. This formulation strengthens confidentiality to additionally provide forward secrecy.[12]

Definition 1 (Confidentiality). *Consider the experiment* $\mathsf{Exp}_{\Pi,\mathcal{A}}^{\mathsf{WAKE\text{-}confid}}$ *in Fig. 1. A WAKE protocol Π is confidential if for all NP relations $\mathcal{R}$, for all statement vectors Φ, for all distributions over witnesses $\mathcal{D}_\Phi$ and for all admissible non-uniform PPT $\mathcal{A}$:*

$$\left| 2 \cdot \Pr[\mathbf{Exp}_{\Pi,\mathcal{A}}^{\mathsf{WAKE\text{-}confid}}(\lambda, \mathcal{R}, \Phi, \mathcal{D}_\Phi)] - 1 \right| \leq \mathsf{negl}(\lambda) \tag{1}$$

Simulatability, Definition 2, is the requirement that messages exchanged in a protocol hide any witnesses used to generate them. This implies that an adversary cannot learn anything about a party's witness from the messages sent by that party. The simulatability experiment $\mathsf{Exp}_{\Pi,\mathcal{A}}^{\mathsf{WAKE\text{-}sim}}$ is seen in Fig. 1. Simulatability stipulates the existence of a two part simulator: $\mathcal{S} = \{\mathsf{SimSetUp}, \mathsf{Sim}\}$. The simulated setup algorithm SimSetUp takes as input the security parameter and the relation $\mathcal{R}$ and outputs a trapdoor τ along with simulated public parameters that are indistinguishable from those output by SetUp. The simulated party algorithm Sim_τ is a stateful simulator that uses the trapdoor τ to output messages which are indistinguishable from those generated by real parties with knowledge of witnesses. Simulatability requires that no efficient adversary can distinguish between access to the simulated parameters and parties via $\mathsf{Send}_{pp_1,\tau}^1$ from access to real parameters and parties via $\mathsf{Send}_{pp_0}^0$. The adversary is permitted to use the SetKeys oracle to determine which statements and witnesses are used for authentication.

Definition 2 (Simulatability). *Consider the experiment* $\mathsf{Exp}_{\Pi,\mathcal{A}}^{\mathsf{WAKE\text{-}sim}}$ *in Fig. 1,* $\mathsf{Exp}_{\Pi,\mathcal{A}}^{\mathsf{WAKE\text{-}sim}}$. *A WAKE protocol Π is simulatable if there exist efficient algorithms* (SimSetUp, Sim) *(the latter stateful) such that for all relations $\mathcal{R}$ and for all non-uniform PPT $\mathcal{A}$:*

$$\left| 2 \cdot \Pr[\mathbf{Exp}_{\Pi,\mathcal{A}}^{\mathsf{WAKE\text{-}sim}}(\lambda, \mathcal{R})] - 1 \right| \leq \mathsf{negl}(\lambda) \tag{2}$$

Authenticity, Definition 3, is the requirement that an unauthenticated party cannot convince another party to accept the execution. In the authenticity experiment, seen in Fig. 1, the active adversary is given access to Send and Reveal with the goal of authenticating to at least one instance of one other participant.

---

[12] Observe that this is a perhaps a slightly stronger variant of forward secrecy than that modelled via the corruption oracle in [23].

Authenticity guarantees that if an adversary can authenticate then is either through forwarding (and therefore inadmissible) or knowledge of a witness. The adversary can be said to know a witness if there exists an efficient extractor that can output a witness from that adversary and wins the experiment if the extractor fails.

We define two variants of authenticity that differ exclusively in the style of extraction. In summary our authenticity definition provides the following tradeoff: the stronger sl-BB authenticity is equivalent to UC security while the weaker nBB authenticity admits practical protocols. The corresponding authenticity experiments are $\mathsf{Exp}_{\Pi,\mathcal{A},\mathcal{E}_*}^{\mathsf{WAKE-auth}}$ in Fig. 1.

A straightline-black-box extractor (sl-BB) must produce a valid witness only given access to the adversary's transcript and a simulation trapdoor τ, and is therefore *black-box* in the adversary. A protocol admitting such an extractor satisfies the *stronger* notion of authenticity which is ultimately proven, in conjunction with the other WAKE security properties, to be equivalent to UC-security in Theorem 1. In contrast, an nBB extractor outputs a witness from the *entire view* of the adversary and is therefore a weaker security requirement – in part because an nBB extractor is adversarially-dependent. Fortunately, such an extractor ultimately permits efficiency as discussed further in Sect. 4.

Definition 3 (Authenticity). *Consider the experiments* $\mathsf{Exp}_{\Pi,\mathcal{A},\mathcal{E}_*}^{\mathsf{WAKE-auth}}$ *in Fig. 1. A WAKE protocol Π is* nBB-*witness-authenticated if for all admissible non-uniform PPT $\mathcal{A}$ there exists a PPT extractor $\mathcal{E}_{\mathcal{A}}$, such that for all relations $\mathcal{R}$, for all statement vectors Φ and for all witness distributions $\mathcal{D}_{\Phi}$:*

$$\Pr[\mathbf{Exp}_{\Pi,\mathcal{A},\mathcal{E}_{\mathcal{A}}}^{\mathsf{WAKE-nBB-auth}}(\lambda, \mathcal{R}, \Phi, \mathcal{D}_{\Phi})] \leq \mathsf{negl}(\lambda) \qquad (3)$$

A WAKE protocol Π is sl-BB-*witness-authenticated if there exists a straightline PPT extractor $\mathcal{E}_{\tau}$ such that for all admissible non-uniform PPT $\mathcal{A}$, for all relations $\mathcal{R}$, for all statement vectors Φ and for all witness distributions $\mathcal{D}_{\Phi}$:*

$$\Pr[\mathsf{Exp}_{\Pi,\mathcal{A},\mathcal{E}_{\tau}}^{\mathsf{WAKE-sl-BB-auth}}(\lambda, \mathcal{R}, \Phi, \mathcal{D}_{\Phi})] \leq \mathsf{negl}(\lambda) \qquad (4)$$

A WAKE protocol is **passively secure** if it satisfies confidentiality. We observe that the confidentiality-only security requirement corresponds to passive security in classical key exchange, though with different syntax. A WAKE protocol achieves **full security** if it is passively secure and additionally satisfies authenticity and simulatability. A WAKE protocol satisfying nBB-extraction is also specified as nBB-WAKE secure, whereas a protocol satisfying sl-BB extraction is sl-BB-WAKE secure. As a sl-BB extractor is also a nBB extractor we note that any sl-BB-WAKE secure protocol Π is also nBB-WAKE secure.

We remark that unilateral authentication in the two party case, and the generalization where an arbitrary subset of the participants are *unauthenticated* in the group case, is modeled by requiring that subset of parties are associated to trivial or empty statements.[13]

---

[13] This can also be seen as an adaptation of Unilaterally Authenticated Key Exchange [13] to the witness-based setting, and is further explored in the full version of our paper.

UNIVERSALLY COMPOSABLE WAKE. In the UC framework a cryptographic task is defined with respect to an ideal functionality $\mathcal{F}$, essentially a trusted party that behaves ideally with access to every secret. Proving that a protocol Π is indistinguishable from the ideal functionality then guarantees that the protocol is *just as good* as that ideal functionality. [14] We provide a definition for WAKE as a UC ideal functionality $\mathcal{F}_{\mathsf{WAKE}}$ in addition to our game-based definition and prove that UC-security is equivalent to our game-based definition of WAKE with sl-BB authenticity. UC-security ensures that our WAKE protocol remains secure when composed with any protocol, for example symmetric encryption, as is ideal.

Theorem 1. *Let Ω be a fully secure group WAKE protocol achieving* sl-BB *authenticity. Then there exists a simple protocol Π_Ω which UC-realizes $\mathcal{F}_{\mathsf{WAKE}}$ in the presence of static, malicious adversaries without the assumption of authenticated channels.*

3   A General Compiler to Witness-Authentication

In Fig. 2 we describe a general compiler from any passively-secure key exchange protocol Π_{KE} to a fully-secure witness-authenticated key exchange protocol Π_{WAKE}. Our compiler adapts that presented in [23] and can be applied to any arbitrary passively-secure key exchange protocol. Given Π_{KE}, a key exchange protocol between set of parties $\mathcal{P}$, a strongly simulation-extractable signature of knowledge Σ can be used to transform that protocol into Π_{WAKE} which satisfies full WAKE security.

SETUP

   $pp_{\mathsf{KE}} \leftarrow \Pi_{\mathsf{KE}}.\mathsf{SetUp}(1^\lambda, \mathcal{R})$

   $pp_\Sigma \leftarrow \Sigma.\mathsf{SetUp}(1^\lambda, \mathcal{R})$

   $pp_{\mathsf{WAKE}} := (pp_{\mathsf{KE}}, pp_\Sigma)$

PARTY i: ROUND 1

   Input: $(pp_{\mathsf{WAKE}}, \mathcal{R}, \Phi, w_i)$

   $r_i \leftarrow_\$ \{0,1\}^\lambda$

   Send $(P_i||0||r_i) \rightarrow \mathcal{P}$

   Receive $\{(P_j||0||r_j)\}_{j \neq i; 1 \leq j \leq \ell}$

   $\mathsf{sid} := (P_1||r_1||\ldots||P_\ell||r_\ell)$

PARTY i: ROUND $k = 2, \ldots K$

   Receive $\{(M_j = (P_j, k_j, m_j, \mathsf{sid}_j), \sigma_j)\}_{j \neq i; 1 \leq j \leq \ell}$

   $\forall k > 2 : \forall j$ // verify messages and signatures

     assert $(k_j = k - 1) \wedge (\mathsf{sid}_j = \mathsf{sid})$

     assert $\Sigma.\mathsf{Verify}(pp_\Sigma, \phi_j, M_j, \sigma_j)$

   $\forall k < K :$ // reply according to Π_{KE}

     $m \leftarrow \Pi_{\mathsf{KE}}(\{m_j\}_{j \neq i; 1 \leq j \leq \ell})$

     $M := (P||k||m||\mathsf{sid})$

     $\sigma \leftarrow \Sigma.\mathsf{SSign}(pp_\Sigma, \phi_i, w_i, M)$

     Send $(M, \sigma) \rightarrow \mathcal{P}$

   $k = K :$ // output key according to Π_{KE}

     Output: $\mathsf{sk} \leftarrow \Pi_{\mathsf{KE}}(\{m_j\}_{j \neq i; 1 \leq j \leq \ell})$

Fig. 2. Compiler from passively secure key exchange Π_{KE} to WAKE.

Each party P_i receives input (ϕ_i, w_i, Φ) and uses the passively secure key exchange Π_{KE} as a black box to transform Π_{KE} to a WAKE protocol in which

[14] The UC framework is discussed in detail in the full version of our paper.

parties $\mathcal{P}$ authenticate with respect to statements Φ under relation $\mathcal{R}$. Compilation comes at the expense of an additional round in which parties exchange random nonces to define a session identifier. After that preliminary round parties proceed according to Π_{KE}, following two additional steps: (1) each message sent by P_i according to Π_{KE} is concatenated with the session identifier and signed with a signature of knowledge under ϕ_i, and (2) all received message-signature pairs are first verified against $(\Phi, \mathcal{R})$ upon receipt before P_i proceeds again according to Π_{KE}. A full proof of Theorem 2 appears in the full version of our paper.

Theorem 2. *If Π_{KE} is a passively secure key exchange and Σ is a strongly simulation-extractable signature of knowledge then the protocol Π_{WAKE} in Fig. 2 is a fully secure nBB-WAKE protocol for relation $\mathcal{R}$.*

4   Two-Round Group WAKE

SETUP
$$\mathcal{R}' := \mathcal{R} \times \mathcal{R}_{\mathsf{DLP}}^{(\mathbb{G},g)}$$
$$pp \leftarrow \mathsf{SOK.SSetup}(1^\lambda, \mathcal{R}')$$

PARTY i: ROUND 1
Input: $(pp, \mathcal{R}', \Phi, \phi_i, w_i)$
$x_i \leftarrow_\$ \mathbb{Z}_q^*, z_i := g^{x_i}$
$w_i' := (w_i, x_i)$
Send $(P_i \| z_i) \to \mathcal{P}$

PARY i: ROUND 2
Receive $\{(P_j \| z_j)\}_{j \neq i; 1 \leq j \leq \ell}$
$\forall j : \phi_j' := (\phi_j, z_j)$
$\mathsf{sid} := (P_1 \| z_1 \| \ldots \| P_\ell \| z_\ell)$
$Z_i \leftarrow (z_{i+1}/z_{i-1})^{x_i}$
$m_i := (P_i \| Z_i \| \mathsf{sid})$
$\sigma_i \leftarrow \mathsf{SOK.SSign}(pp, \phi_i', w_i', m_i)$
Send $(P_i \| Z_i \| \sigma_i) \to \mathcal{P}$
Receive $\{(P_j \| Z_j \| \sigma_j)\}_{j \neq i; 1 \leq j \leq \ell}$
$\forall j \neq i : m_j := (P_j \| Z_j \| \mathsf{sid})$

PARTY i: KEY COMPUTATION
if $\bigwedge_{j \neq i; 1 \leq j \leq \ell} \mathsf{SOK.Verify}(pp, \phi_j', m_j, \sigma_j) \neq 1$: **Output:** $sk \leftarrow_\$ \{0,1\}^\lambda$
Output: $sk := (z_{i-1})^{\ell x_i} \cdot Z_i^{\ell-1} \cdot Z_{i+1}^{\ell-2} \cdots Z_{i+\ell-2}$

Fig. 3. $\Pi_{\text{2-WAKE}}$: optimized two-round multiparty WAKE protocol.

The two round protocol $\Pi_{\text{2-WAKE}}$ presented in Fig. 3 is provably UC-secure when the parties are given access to the ideal functionalities for signatures of knowledge, $\mathcal{F}_{\mathsf{SOK}}$ and common reference strings $\mathcal{F}_{\mathsf{CRS}}$. When our protocol is instantiated with a *succinct* simulation-extractable signature of knowledge it is possible to achieve efficiency at the expense of weakening security to nBB-WAKE from sl-BB-WAKE, and sacrificing provable universal composability. The two round protocol $\Pi_{\text{2-WAKE}}$ directly achieves **session authenticity**, the guarantee that senders are consistent throughout the exchange. Security is stated in Theorem 3, which is proven in the full version of our paper.

Most notably, the second round of $\Pi_{2\text{-WAKE}}$ requires each participant to *simultaneously authenticate with respect to their statement and knowledge of the discrete log of their first round message*; party P_i signs their second message m_i with a signature of knowledge under statement ϕ_i and the ephemeral Diffie-Hellman value z_i sent in the first round: $\phi_i' = (\phi_i, z_i)$ with witness (w_i, x_i). The signature of knowledge is initialized with relation $\mathcal{R}' = \mathcal{R} \times \mathcal{R}_{\text{DLP}}$ at setup, where $\mathcal{R}_{\text{DLP}}$ is the discrete logarithm relation $\mathcal{R}_{\text{DLP}}^{(\mathbb{G}, g)} := \{(h = g^x, x) \mid h \in \mathbb{G}, x \in \text{ord}(h)\}$.

Theorem 3. *For any NP relation $\mathcal{R}$ the protocol $\Pi_{2\text{-WAKE}}$ UC-realizes $\mathcal{F}_{\text{WAKE}}$ in the $(\mathcal{F}_{\text{CRS}}, \mathcal{F}_{\text{SOK}})$-hybrid model against malicious adaptive adversaries in the unauthenticated, asynchronous setting.*

Table 2. Authenticated party runtime estimation (seconds, rounded to ceil).

Setting	$\mathcal{R} \in \mathsf{NP}$	ϕ	w	T(s)
Dark Pools	$\bar{c} = \mathsf{Comm}(\mathsf{s}; \rho) \wedge \mathsf{s} \geq \bar{\mathbf{B}}$	$\bar{c}, \bar{\mathbf{B}}$	(ρ, s)	4
IPFS	$\bar{h} = \mathsf{blake3hash}(\mathbf{F})$	$\bar{h}$	$\mathbf{F}$	68
ZKCP	$\mathsf{solvesSudoku}(\mathsf{sol}, \overline{pzl})$	$\overline{pzl}$	sol	1
Bug bounty	$C_{\mathsf{buggy}}(\mathbf{bug}) \wedge \neg C_{\mathsf{expect}}(\mathbf{bug})$	$C_{\{\mathsf{buggy}, \mathsf{expect}\}}$	$\mathbf{bug}$	58

Estimated benchmarks for the above protocol are presented in Table 2. The *authenticated party running time* can be found in the last column. The timings refer to our protocol instantiated through *Snarky Signature* [20].[15] Our *communication complexity* is constant and estimated to be below $0.5\,\mathsf{KB}$ in total for the unilateral two-party case and of approximately N KB for the group authenticated case with N parties. When using BLS12-381 [5] as the concrete curve a signature is 224 bytes.[16] We remark that an additional *offline-online* optimization of our protocol can be applied to migrate a majority of the online running time, i.e. the signature, to an offline phase. This example is further discussed in the unilaterally-authenticated two-party case in the full version of our paper.

We briefly describe detail one more application scenario we benchmarks in our table, that of *Zero-Knowledge Contingent Payment (ZKCP)*, where a seller wants to initiate a channel with any party claiming to have a digital good that satisfies a certain property to negotiate a price for that good prior to a ZKCP protocol [8,18]. We benchmark the ZKCP case of payments for Sudoku Solutions (also used in prior work [8,18] and for the case of bug bounties. In the latter, the software producer of a (potentially buggy) program C_{buggy} can incentivize users to find bugs **bug** in it. These can be checked through additional program

---

[15] See the full version of our paper for more information on the experimental setting.
[16] More specifically, 192 bytes for the group elements and 32 bytes for the SHA256.

C_{expect}, guaranteeing an expected condition for an input the program accepts (which will be violated by the bug, a false positive).[17]

References

1. Barta, O., Ishai, Y., Ostrovsky, R., Wu, D.J.: On succinct arguments and witness encryption from groups. In: Micciancio, D., Ristenpart, T. (eds.) CRYPTO 2020. LNCS, vol. 12170, pp. 776–806. Springer, Cham (2020). https://doi.org/10.1007/978-3-030-56784-2_26
2. Bellovin, S.M., Merritt, M.: Encrypted key exchange: password-based protocols secure against dictionary attacks. In: 1992 IEEE Computer Society Symposium on Research in Security and Privacy, Oakland, CA, USA, 4–6 May 1992, pp. 72–84. IEEE Computer Society (1992). https://doi.org/10.1109/RISP.1992.213269
3. Birrell, E., Chung, K.-M., Pass, R., Telang, S.: Randomness-dependent message security. In: Sahai, A. (ed.) TCC 2013. LNCS, vol. 7785, pp. 700–720. Springer, Heidelberg (2013). https://doi.org/10.1007/978-3-642-36594-2_39
4. Bitansky, N., Chiesa, A., Ishai, Y., Paneth, O., Ostrovsky, R.: Succinct non-interactive arguments via linear interactive proofs. In: Sahai, A. (ed.) TCC 2013. LNCS, vol. 7785, pp. 315–333. Springer, Heidelberg (2013). https://doi.org/10.1007/978-3-642-36594-2_18
5. BLS12-381 curve. www.electriccoin.co/blog/new-snark-curve/
6. Bug in primes testing in swiss post voting system. www.gitlab.com/swisspost-evoting/crypto-primitives/crypto-primitives/-/issues/13
7. Camenisch, J., Casati, N., Gross, T., Shoup, V.: Credential authenticated identification and key exchange. In: Rabin, T. (ed.) CRYPTO 2010. LNCS, vol. 6223, pp. 255–276. Springer, Heidelberg (2010). https://doi.org/10.1007/978-3-642-14623-7_14
8. Campanelli, M., Gennaro, R., Goldfeder, S., Nizzardo, L.: Zero-knowledge contingent payments revisited: attacks and payments for services. In: Thuraisingham, B., Evans, D., Malkin, T., Xu, D. (eds.) Proceedings of the 2017 ACM SIGSAC Conference on Computer and Communications Security, CCS 2017, Dallas, TX, USA, 30 October–03 November 2017, pp. 229–243. ACM (2017). https://doi.org/10.1145/3133956.3134060
9. Canetti, R.: Universally composable security: a new paradigm for cryptographic protocols. IACR Cryptology ePrint Archive, Paper 2000/067 (2000). https://eprint.iacr.org/2000/067
10. Chase, M., Lysyanskaya, A.: On signatures of knowledge. In: Dwork, C. (ed.) CRYPTO 2006. LNCS, vol. 4117, pp. 78–96. Springer, Heidelberg (2006). https://doi.org/10.1007/11818175_5
11. Cramer, R., Shoup, V.: A practical public key cryptosystem provably secure against adaptive chosen ciphertext attack. In: Krawczyk, H. (ed.) CRYPTO 1998. LNCS, vol. 1462, pp. 13–25. Springer, Heidelberg (1998). https://doi.org/10.1007/BFb0055717

---

[17] As an example consider a prime-testing program C_{buggy}. Here, the bug could consist of an even number greater than 2 that the program erroneously recognizes as a prime. In this case we could have for example $C_{\text{expect}}(z) :=$ "z is odd $\vee z = 2$". Anything not satisfying the latter would be a false positive. This is not just a toy setting but it is relevant in real world systems [6].

12. Diffie, W., Hellman, M.E.: New directions in cryptography. IEEE Trans. Inf. Theor. **22**(6), 644–654 (1976). https://doi.org/10.1109/TIT.1976.1055638
13. Dodis, Y., Fiore, D.: Unilaterally-authenticated key exchange. In: Kiayias, A. (ed.) FC 2017. LNCS, vol. 10322, pp. 542–560. Springer, Cham (2017). https://doi.org/10.1007/978-3-319-70972-7_31
14. Dupont, P.-A., Hesse, J., Pointcheval, D., Reyzin, L., Yakoubov, S.: Fuzzy password-authenticated key exchange. In: Nielsen, J.B., Rijmen, V. (eds.) EURO-CRYPT 2018. LNCS, vol. 10822, pp. 393–424. Springer, Cham (2018). https://doi.org/10.1007/978-3-319-78372-7_13
15. Ethereum Name Service. www.ens.domains/
16. Ganesh, C., Khoshakhlagh, H., Kohlweiss, M., Nitulescu, A., Zajac, M.: What makes Fiat-Shamir zkSNARKs (updatable SRS) simulation extractable? Cryptology ePrint Archive, Report 2021/511 (2021). www.ia.cr/2021/511
17. Garg, S., Gentry, C., Sahai, A., Waters, B.: Witness encryption and its applications. In: Boneh, D., Roughgarden, T., Feigenbaum, J. (eds.) Symposium on Theory of Computing Conference, STOC 2013, Palo Alto, CA, USA, 1–4 June 2013, pp. 467–476. ACM (2013). https://doi.org/10.1145/2488608.2488667
18. Greg Maxwell's zero knowledge contingent payment (bitcoin Wiki). www.en.bitcoin.it/wiki/Zero_Knowledge_Contingent_Payment
19. Groth, J., Kohlweiss, M., Maller, M., Meiklejohn, S., Miers, I.: Updatable and universal common reference strings with applications to zk-SNARKs. In: Shacham, H., Boldyreva, A. (eds.) CRYPTO 2018. LNCS, vol. 10993, pp. 698–728. Springer, Cham (2018). https://doi.org/10.1007/978-3-319-96878-0_24
20. Groth, J., Maller, M.: Snarky signatures: minimal signatures of knowledge from simulation-extractable SNARKs. In: Katz, J., Shacham, H. (eds.) CRYPTO 2017. LNCS, vol. 10402, pp. 581–612. Springer, Cham (2017). https://doi.org/10.1007/978-3-319-63715-0_20
21. Ben Hamouda, F., Blazy, O., Chevalier, C., Pointcheval, D., Vergnaud, D.: Efficient UC-secure authenticated key-exchange for algebraic languages. In: Kurosawa, K., Hanaoka, G. (eds.) PKC 2013. LNCS, vol. 7778, pp. 272–291. Springer, Heidelberg (2013). https://doi.org/10.1007/978-3-642-36362-7_18
22. Handshake: Decentralized naming and certificate authority. www.handshake.org
23. Katz, J., Yung, M.: Scalable protocols for authenticated group key exchange. In: Boneh, D. (ed.) CRYPTO 2003. LNCS, vol. 2729, pp. 110–125. Springer, Heidelberg (2003). https://doi.org/10.1007/978-3-540-45146-4_7
24. Kolesnikov, V., Krawczyk, H., Lindell, Y., Malozemoff, A.J., Rabin, T.: Attribute-based key exchange with general policies. In: Weippl, E.R., Katzenbeisser, S., Kruegel, C., Myers, A.C., Halevi, S. (eds.) Proceedings of the 2016 ACM SIGSAC Conference on Computer and Communications Security, Vienna, Austria, 24–28 October 2016, pp. 1451–1463. ACM (2016). https://doi.org/10.1145/2976749.2978359
25. MeetWallet: The Meet JS SDK Library for MEET.ONE Client. www.meet-common.gitlab.io/fe/meet-js-sdk/classes/meetwallet.html
26. Ngo, C.N., Massacci, F., Kerschbaum, F., Williams, J.: Practical witness-key-agreement for blockchain-based dark pools financial trading. In: Borisov, N., Diaz, C. (eds.) FC 2021. LNCS, vol. 12675, pp. 579–598. Springer, Heidelberg (2021). https://doi.org/10.1007/978-3-662-64331-0_30
27. Protocol Labs: Filecoin. www.filecoin.io/
28. Protocol Labs: IPFS: Interplanetary file system. www.ipfs.io

29. Rivest, R.L., Shamir, A., Adleman, L.M.: A method for obtaining digital signatures and public-key cryptosystems. Commun. ACM **21**(2), 120–126 (1978). https://doi.org/10.1145/359340.359342
30. Sahai, A., Waters, B.: Fuzzy identity-based encryption. In: Cramer, R. (ed.) EURO-CRYPT 2005. LNCS, vol. 3494, pp. 457–473. Springer, Heidelberg (2005). https://doi.org/10.1007/11426639_27
31. Shamir, A.: Identity-based cryptosystems and signature schemes. In: Blakley, G.R., Chaum, D. (eds.) CRYPTO 1984. LNCS, vol. 196, pp. 47–53. Springer, Heidelberg (1985). https://doi.org/10.1007/3-540-39568-7_5
32. CWEB3. www.npmjs.com/package/cweb3

On the Correlation Complexity of MPC with Cheater Identification

Nicholas Brandt[1]([⊠]) [iD], Sven Maier[2] [iD], Tobias Müller[3],
and Jörn Müller-Quade[4]

[1] ETH Zurich, Zurich, Switzerland
`nicholas.brandt@inf.ethz.ch`
[2] CNRS, IRIF, Université de Paris, Paris, France
`sven.maier@irif.fr`
[3] Karlsruhe, Germany
[4] Karlsruhe Institute of Technology, Karlsruhe, Germany
`joern.mueller-quade@kit.edu`

Abstract. Composable protocols for Multi-Party Computation that provide security with Identifiable Abort against a dishonest majority require some form of setup, e.g. correlated randomness among the parties. While this is a very useful model, it has the downside that the setup's randomness must be *programmable*, otherwise security becomes provably impossible. Since programmability is more realistic for smaller setups (in terms of number of parties), it is crucial to minimize the correlation complexity (degree of correlation) of the setup's randomness.

We give a tight tradeoff between the correlation complexity β and the corruption threshold t. Our bounds are strong in that β-wise correlation is sufficient for statistical security while $\beta - 1$-wise correlation is insufficient even for computational security. In particular, for strong security, i.e., $t < n$, full n-wise correlation is necessary. However, for any constant fraction of honest parties, we provide a protocol with *constant* correlation complexity which tightens the gap between the theoretical model and the setup's implementation in the real world. In contrast, previous state-of-the-art protocols require full n-wise correlation regardless of t.

1 Introduction

Secure Multi-Party Computation (MPC) is a powerful notion that allows multiple mutually distrustful parties to perform a joint computation that—loosely speaking—ensures the privacy of the inputs and the correctness of the output. The currently strongest security notion—that is not ruled out by some impossibility result [10]—is called security with Identifiable Abort (IA) [21]. It allows an adversary to abort the protocol (this is unavoidable) but then the honest parties can identify the common identity of at least one malicious party. This acts as

Work done while the first author was supported by ERC Project PREP-CRYPTO 724307, the second author was at the Karlsruhe Institute of Technology, Germany, and the third author was at the FZI Research Center for Information Technology, Germany.

ⓒ International Financial Cryptography Association 2024
F. Baldimtsi and C. Cachin (Eds.): FC 2023, LNCS 13950, pp. 129–146, 2024.
https://doi.org/10.1007/978-3-031-47754-6_8

a deterrent against cheating by coupling cheater identification to some form of penalty mechanism. This is especially useful in the context of blockchains where one could require all parties to initially commit to some coins s.t. an identified cheater's coins are redistributed to the other parties or the cheater's coins are rendered void by publishing the evidence of cheating.

In the dishonest majority settings, $t \geq n/2$, protocols such as the one of Ostrovsky, and Zikas [21] that achieve IA require a setup that distributes correlation randomness to each party in the protocol. In fact, for $t \geq n/2$, a setup is provably necessary for general MPC protocols that can be composed arbitrarily, e.g. in the Universal Composability (UC) framework [7]. Moreover, for the security proof to work the setup needs to be *programmable* to realize certain functionalities such as commitments [8]. That is, the setup information may not leak directly to the environment, instead, in the security proof the simulator must be able to embed a trapdoor into the setup information to extract or equivocate the committed message. Indeed, if the setup is *global*, the setup information leaks directly to the environment, then many functionalities become *provably impossible* [9,25]. In particular, if in practice the setup information is extracted from some public source, like stock market data, then the security guarantee provided by the ID-MPC protocol is void. This leaves the option to generate the correlated randomness via some physical means, like noisy or quantum channels, or secure hardware assumptions. However, for such a means of generating randomness the correlation complexity (CC) is the most important parameter.

As shown in [21] the correlated randomness setup for n-parties suffices to statistically securely realize any other functionality (or setup) of cardinality n (with n-participants). Therefore, we equate the correlation complexity with the minimal complete cardinality (MCC)[1] as introduced by Fitzi et al. [16].

For $t < n/2$ pairwise correlation (even pairwise channels) suffice [3,26], while for $t \geq n/2$ protocols like [21] are quite conservative in that they require (maximal) n-wise correlation; even for $t = n/2$. Our work closes this gap between $t = n/2$ and $t = n - 1$ by answering the question:

"What is the correlation complexity of MPC with a dishonest majority?"

We settle this question with tight bounds for the correlation complexity $\beta \approx 2n/(n-t)$ depending on the max. number of corrupted parties t.

While theoretically interesting[2], our results offer also two practical insights:

- If one requires maximal security $t < n$, then n-wise correlation is necessary, i.e., the CC is $\beta = n$. Hence protocols like [21] are optimal w.r.t. the CC.
- If one is willing to accept any constant fraction of malicious parties $t \leq (1-\varepsilon)n$ for any $\varepsilon > 0$, then the CC is only constant $\beta \approx 2/\varepsilon$.

---

[1] Throughout the paper, we require a setup among each subset of parties of size β.

[2] To our knowledge this is the first full characterization of Identifiable Abort in the dishonest majority setting.

Table 1. Exemplary overview of the correlation complexity (CC)/minimal complete cardinality (MCC) β and respective supported number of parties n vs. malicious parties t for UC-secure ID-MPC given broadcast. The limitation of the overall number of parties is only to achieve polynomial-time protocols, for more parties the protocols remain correct and secure but require the parties to have superpolynomial runtime. The case $(*)$ also covers an honest majority of parties treated in early works [3,26].

Max. malicious parties t	Max. supported parties n	CC/MCC β
$n-1$	$\text{poly}(\lambda)$	n
$n-2$	$\text{poly}(\lambda)$	$n-2$
$n-c \leq n-3$	$\Theta(\ln \lambda)$	$\approx 2n/c$
$n - \Theta(\ln n)$	$\mathcal{O}(\ln(\lambda) \ln \ln(\lambda)/ \ln \ln \ln(\lambda))$	$\Theta(n/\ln n)$
$n - \Theta(\sqrt{n})$	$\mathcal{O}(\ln^2(\lambda)/ \ln^2 \ln(\lambda))$	$\Theta(\sqrt{n})$
$n - \Theta(n/\ln n)$	$\mathcal{O}(\exp \sqrt{\ln \lambda})$	$\Theta(\ln n)$
$\Theta(n)$	$\text{poly}(\lambda)$	$\Theta(1)$
$(n+1)/2$	$\text{poly}(\lambda)$	3
$\leq n/2^{(*)}$	$\text{poly}(\lambda)$	2

Especially the latter case has practical implications. Due to the aforementioned *provable impossibility* of composable MPC with a global setup, the setups must be realized by non-cryptographic means such as trusted hardware [18,27] or noisy/quantum channels [12,14]. There, the CC (the number of setup participants) is a critical parameter. To illustrate this, consider the following example: Suppose a group of people can generate correlated randomness via some trusted hardware in their smartphones while being online simultaneously. However, the runtime of this supposed setup computation is exponential in the number of parties involved. In this scenario, if a protocol relies on a single setup of cardinality n, then all parties must be online together for an exponential time. In contrast, if a protocol could be based on (polynomially) many setup instances between a constant number of people (as is the case for our protocols for any $t \leq (1-\varepsilon)n$), then a) being online at the same time as a constant number of parties much more realistic and b) the runtime is only polynomial in the number of people (Table 1).

The above example showcases that our results are particularly interesting for applications in which mobile clients (which are not always online) perform decentralized operations and store a common state on some form of blockchain (which allows for monetary penalties for cheating).

1.1   Contributions and Techniques

Correlation Complexity/ID-MPC from Small Setups. Due to the completeness of the correlated randomness setup [21], we can substitute any setup functionality of some cardinality by the correlated randomness functionality of the same cardinality. To minimize the correlation complexity we concentrate on constructing n-party ID-MPC from the smallest possible (arbitrary) setups. In other words, we can answer the question of the CC by determining the minimal complete cardinality (MCC)[3] in the sense of [16], i.e., the number of participants of a setup functionality. As a sidenote, in the full version we deal with some definitorial issues that arise when the number of parties grows with the security parameter which is not the case in [16]. As our main result we establish tight bounds on the minimal complete cardinality β for general ID-MPC (given broadcast). We assume that each subset of parties (of cardinality β) has access to a setup functionality. Furthermore, we only require these setups to guarantee security with Identifiable Abort—unlike many other works which don't allow the setups to be aborted at all. For a formal description of our setting see our full version.

Theorem 1 (Correlation complexity bounds). *The correlation complexity for UC-secure Multi-Party Computation with Identifiable Abort (given broadcast) is $\beta := \min(n, \lfloor n/(n-t) \rfloor + \lceil n/(n-t) \rceil - 2) \approx 2n/(n-t)$ where n is the overall number of parties and t is an upper bound on the number of malicious parties.*

In other words, for any n-party functionality with Identifiable Abort there exists a protocol that uses hybrid functionalities of cardinality β and broadcast, but there exists an n-party functionality with Identifiable Abort which cannot be realized by any protocol that uses hybrid functionalities of cardinality $\beta - 1$ and broadcast.

Identification via Conflicts. Towards our main result we formalize an intuitive mechanism for cheater identification that is also used in various other works [1,2,19,21,23,28,29] in different contexts. In our application, all parties maintain a global data structure, namely a graph with one vertex per party where each party can remove incident edges (we call missing edges "conflicts") but never add edges. Following Wan et al. [29] we call this structure "Trust Graph" (TG). With it, we provide a ruleset for its usage which we call *abort-respecting* that ensures that the Trust Graph exhibits certain useful properties: On an intuitive level, a disconnected subgraph corresponds to an aborted setup and vice-versa while a disconnected overall TG corresponds to the honest parties' ability to abort by identifying malicious parties.

Lemma 1 (Informal conflict reporting). *Any protocol that securely realizes an ideal functionality $\mathcal{F}$ in some hybrid model can be modified such that*

1. *all honest parties keep a (common) Trust Graph,*
2. *if the Trust Graph is disconnected, then all honest parties can identify the same malicious parties,*
3. *upon abort of the protocol its Trust Graph is disconnected,*

---

[3] As a side note we generalize the notion of the minimal complete cardinality (MCC) from [16] to the setting where the number of parties varies in the security parameter λ. This was not captured by the original definition of MCC in [16] and—to the best of our knowledge—not formally addressed in previous literature.

4. *after abort of any setup (hybrid functionality on some subset of parties*[4]*) in the protocol the corresponding subgraph of the Trust Graph becomes disconnected,*

and the modified protocol still securely realizes the same functionality.

As a consequence, the impossibility of any abort-respecting protocol implies the impossibility of any protocol. On the other hand, if some protocol for a given functionality exists, then so does an abort-respecting protocol. In consequence, we only need to consider abort-respecting protocols.

For the lower and the upper bound, we prove two complementing graph-theoretical lemmas that link the connectivity of the overall TG to the connectivity of its subgraphs. In a nutshell, a connected graph of cardinality n can have "many" disconnected subgraph of cardinality $\beta - 1$ but only "few" disconnected subgraphs of cardinality β.

For our lower bound we devise a strategy for the adversary such that it can abort many setups of cardinality $\beta - 1$ while the overall Trust Graph remains connected. Following the proof strategy of Canetti and Fischlin [8] we can show that against such an adversary any protocol for a commitment must violate either the hiding or the binding property. For our upper bound we know that any adversary can only abort "few" setups. Thus the honest parties can rely on some "guaranteed" setups to perform the protocol.

1.2 Related and Concurrent Work

There are many works that share common aspects with this paper, among others [1,2,16,17,19–21,23,28,29]. Here we pick only the most closely related ones and describe their relation to this work.

- Fitzi et al. [16] initialize the study of the minimal complete cardinality (MCC)—the cardinality of the smallest setup (least number of participants) that suffices to securely realize any n-party functionality.
- Ishai, Ostrovsky, and Seyalioglu [20] rule out pairwise setups plus broadcast for statistically secure ID-MPC.
- Ishai, Ostrovsky, and Zikas [21] formally define Identifiable Abort (IA), introduce the Correlated-Randomness model for IA and give a computationally secure construction from any adaptively secure OT protocol.
- Wan et al. [29] use the almost identical idea of maintaining a "Trust Graph" (TG) in the context of *constructing* Byzantine broadcast (BB) while we assume a broadcast to construct general ID-MPC. Specifically, Wan et al. [29] give lower bounds for the round-complexity of BB. From the different applications arises the slight difference in the two concepts, in [29] each party maintains its own copy of the TG whereas in our work it is crucial that all parties have a common view of the TG. Nevertheless, we use very similar graph properties as Wan et al. [29]. Their idea is to limit the distance that

---

[4] Throughout the paper we assume that each subset of parties of the appropriate cardinality has access to a setup.

information can travel within a graph in a given number of round, if the graph's diameter is too large, then a sender's message may not be able to reach all other parties. Their upper bound for the TG's diameter d matches our tight bound for the CC, i.e., $\beta = \lfloor n/(n-t) \rfloor + \lceil n/(n-t) \rceil - 2 = d+1$ where $t \geq n-2$ is a lower bound on the number of honest parties.

We think there are interesting connections[5] between our paper and [29]. While [29] assumes pairwise channels, we assume a full broadcast. We maintain the view that both [29] and our paper can be generalized along the dimension of the setup size, i.e., assuming a partial broadcast of size $2 \leq k \leq n$. Regarding the round-complexity of BB, it seems that the round-complexity decreases as k increases because the sender's message travels farther in each round. Regarding the correlation complexity, it seems that the CC increases as k increases because for larger partial broadcasts reaching a consensus on a identified cheater seems easier.

- Simkin, Siniscalchi, and Yakoubov [28] essentially study the same question as our paper. They give a weaker upper bound $\beta \leq t+2 \leq n-2$ of the CC/MCC, although in the stand-alone model whereas our result holds in the UC framework.

  They construct n-party MPC from correlation of degree $n-1$ and broadcast. For this reason their work supports polynomially many parties $n \in \text{poly}(\lambda)$ only for $n - t \in \Theta(1)$. For larger expansions the supported number of parties drops rapidly since the overall runtime grows exponentially in the number of recursive applications of the protocol. This is not the case for our work; see the full version for a discussion.

  Their approach uses an new form of identifiable secret-sharing with public and private shares. There, one party P is chosen and the remaining $n-1$ parties obtain correlated randomness, i.e., secret-shares of their randomness, from the setup oracle. Then the parties send their shares to the excluded party P who reconstructs its randomness. If reconstruction fails to due faulty shares sent by malicious parties, then party P detects whose shares where faulty and declares conflicts with these parties. These conflicts are then used in the next iteration. That is, conflicting parties do not obtain shares from the setup.

  It seems unclear how the approach of [28] could be generalized to setups of cardinality $n-2$ without the disadvantageous recursion blowup.

- Finally, much work [4–6,11,24] has gone into reducing the necessary length of correlated randomness. This is highly relevant in practice. Nevertheless, to the best of our knowledge, in these works all parties need to participate in the correlation generation simultaneously. That is, although the overall length of the correlated randomness is short, the degree of the correlation is maximal—which is where our work steps in. We'd like to emphasize that our protocols are compatible with approaches to reduce the length of the correlated strings,

---

[5] In particular, Claim 3.1 in [29] and our Lemma 3 share the same core idea but are stated in different terms with different applications in mind.

Table 2. Overview of related work on the foundations of Multi-Party Computation with Identifiable Abort in the dishonest majority setting with broadcast. SA stands for stand-alone, UC stands for Universal Composability [7], t is the max. number of corrupted parties, and $\beta := \min(n, \lfloor n/(n-t) \rfloor + \lceil n/(n-t) \rceil - 2)$. π_{OT} denotes any adaptively secure Oblivious Transfer (OT) protocol, $\mathcal{F}_{\mathsf{CRS}}^n$ is the Common Reference String (CRS) functionality from [8], $\mathcal{F}_{\mathsf{Corr},\mathcal{D}}^n$ is the Correlated-Randomness functionality from [21]. $\mathcal{F}_{\mathsf{COM},1:1}^n$ is a one-to-one commitment and $\mathcal{F}_{\mathsf{SFE},f}^n$ is the Secure Function Evaluation functionality; both defined in the full version. Note that the impossibility 6) does not contradict 3) because 6) does not assume a CRS.

No	Reference	Model	Result	Technique
1)	[20]	SA	$\{\mathcal{F}^2, \mathcal{F}_{\mathsf{BC}}^n\} \overset{stat}{\not\leadsto}_{2n/3} \mathcal{F}_{\mathsf{SFE},f}^n$	Secret-Sharing
2)	[21]	UC, SA	$\mathcal{F}_{\mathsf{Corr},\mathcal{D}}^n \overset{stat}{\leadsto}_n \mathcal{F}_{\mathsf{SFE},f}^n$	Setup+Commit+Prove
3)	[21]	UC, SA	$\{\pi_{\mathsf{OT}}, \mathcal{F}_{\mathsf{CRS}}^n\} \overset{comp}{\leadsto}_n \mathcal{F}_{\mathsf{Corr},\mathcal{D}}^n$	Setup+Commit+Prove
4)	[28]	SA	$\{\mathcal{F}_{\mathsf{Corr},\mathcal{D}}^{n-1}, \mathcal{F}_{\mathsf{BC}}^n\} \overset{stat}{\leadsto}_{n-2} \mathcal{F}_{\mathsf{Corr},\mathcal{D}}^n$	Secret-Sharing
5)	This work	UC	$\{\mathcal{F}_{\mathsf{Corr},\mathcal{D}}^{\beta}, \mathcal{F}_{\mathsf{BC}}^n\} \overset{stat}{\leadsto}_t \mathcal{F}_{\mathsf{SFE},f}^n$	Trust Graph
6)	This work	UC	$\{\mathcal{F}_{\mathsf{Corr},\mathcal{D}}^{\beta-1}, \mathcal{F}_{\mathsf{BC}}^n\} \overset{comp}{\not\leadsto}_t \mathcal{F}_{\mathsf{COM},1:1}^n$	Trust Graph

and they can be used in conjunction to reduce both the length as well as the degree of correlation.

Our results subsume or improve upon all previously listed constructions and impossibilities in a unified way. For the minimal complete cardinality (MCC) it holds that:

- The lower bound of 3 from [20] for $t \geq 2n/3$ is raised to $\min(n, 5)$.
- The upper bound of $n-1$ from [28] reduced to the optimal $n-2$ for $t \leq n-2$.
- The upper bound of n from [21] is shown to be tight for $t = n-1$.

These (and more) results are summarized in Table 2. In the following we use the short notation $F \leadsto_t \mathcal{F}$ for the fact that the ideal functionality $\mathcal{F}$ can be realized by some protocol in the F-hybrid model with up to t malicious parties.

1.3   Technical Overview

We state our results in the standard UC-framework (see [7]) in terms ideal functionalities and protocols that realize them. Due to the large notational and conceptual overhead of rigorous statements about MPC and the given space limitations, we decided to give most of the formal definitions and statements in the appendices, and instead try to convey the core idea behind our techniques in this overview and how they are combined to obtain our main results.

The main idea behind the usage of the Trust Graph (TG) is that if the TG is disconnected, then there are at least two partitions A and B such that all parties in A distrust all parties in B. Now, if honest parties always trust each other (as is the case throughout this paper), then all honest parties must be in the same connected component. W.l.o.g. let all honest parties be in A, then they can jointly identify B and abort with $(\texttt{abort}, B)$. In this sense the disconnectivity of the TG is equivalent to the identification of malicious parties, and hence the abort of a ID-MPC protocol.

To simplify our analysis we formally introduce an ideal functionality $\mathcal{F}_{\mathsf{TG}}^{n}$ for n parties in the full version. This functionality stores an (initially complete) graph with one vertex per party. Any party P can announce "conflicts" by sending $(\texttt{conflict}, \mathsf{P}')$ to $\mathcal{F}_{\mathsf{TG}}^{n}$. Consequently, the edge $(\mathsf{P}, \mathsf{P}')$ is irrevocably removed from the TG—we say P and P' are *in conflict*. Any party can also query the currently stored graph $G = (P, E)$ (typically at the onset of each round); such that all parties have a consistent view of the TG in each round. The functionality $\mathcal{F}_{\mathsf{TG}}^{n}$ can be viewed as syntactical sugar, as it can be perfectly securely realized using only broadcast

Now, we give a high-level intuition of a particular set of protocol rules that will prove useful in our results for the correlation complexity. We call this set of six rules "abort-respecting" . One can view it as a kind of manual for how to utilize the Trust Graph. Informally, abort-respecting protocols ensure in particular the following properties:

- Honest parties are never in conflict.
- Whenever some party has strictly more than t conflicts, it must be malicious.
- Whenever some setup of cardinality β is aborted[6], the subTG on the participants of the setup becomes disconnected.
- When the protocol aborts (with $(\texttt{abort}, C)$ where C is a set of malicious parties), the overall TG is disconnected.
- When the overall TG becomes disconnected, the protocol aborts (with $(\texttt{abort}, C)$ where C is a set of malicious parties).

Intuitively, from these rules and the usage of $\mathcal{F}_{\mathsf{TG}}^{n}$ follows Lemma 1. More formally, it states that any secure protocol for some functionality in some F-hybrid model can be transformed into a secure and abort-respecting protocol for the same functionality in the $F \cup \{\mathcal{F}_{\mathsf{TG}}^{n}\}$-hybrid model. As a corollary, we note that to rule out *all* ID-MPC protocol for some functionality it suffices to rule out all abort-respecting protocols. We will use this fact in the proof of our lower bound on the CC.

Before, we want to elaborate a bit on the third property. When a setup with Identifiable Abort is aborted, all participants P obtain the message $(\texttt{abort}, C)$ where $C \subseteq P$ is some set of malicious participants. Then all honest parties declare conflicts with C via the $\mathcal{F}_{\mathsf{TG}}^{n}$ functionality. In the next round either a) all parties $P \setminus C$ declared conflicts with the identified parties C, or b) there are some "loyalists" $L \subseteq P \setminus C$ who did not declare conflicts with *all* identified parties C. In the first case the subTG is clearly disconnected between $P \setminus C$ and C. In the second case b) note that loyalists noticeably deviate from the abort-respecting rules; thus the honest parties add the loyalists L to the identified parties C and repeat the procedure. Since in each iteration at least one loyalist

---

[6] Recall that we only assume setups to have security with Identifiable Abort.

gets added to the identified parties, the overall procedure terminates within at most n iterations.

Lower Bound on the Correlation Complexity. Eventually, we show that no protocol in the $\{\mathcal{F}_{\mathsf{BC}}^n, \mathcal{F}^{\beta-1}\}$-hybrid model for any functionality $\mathcal{F}^{\beta-1}$ of cardinality $\beta - 1$ can securely realize an ideal commitment functionality where n is the overall number of parties, t is a upper bound on the malicious parties and $\beta := \min(n, \lfloor n/(n - t)\rfloor + \lceil n/(n - t)\rceil - 2)$. Towards this end, we prove a graph-theoretical lemma that relates the connectivity of the overall TG to the connectivity of its subgraphs. More concretely, the lemma constructs a connected graph that has "many" disconnected subgraphs of the cardinality $\beta - 1$. With the intuition that aborts of setups correspond to disconnected subTGs (via the abort-respecting property), this graph-theoretical lemma translates into a strategy for the adversary to abort many setups in a clever way such that the overall TG remains connected, i.e., the overall protocol cannot abort. However, after these many setups are aborted, we follow the idea of Canetti and Fischlin [8] to prove that any protocol that only relies on the remaining setups must either violate the hiding or the binding property. We note that this proof strategy only works because we want to rule out composable commitment protocols.

The high-level idea is as follows: Because "many" setups are aborted, the sender cannot "directly" commit towards the receiver via some setup that contains both the sender *and* the receiver. Consequently, in order to be committed towards the receiver (binding), the sender has to send the message (information-theoretically) to intermediate parties—even when all parties act honestly (relative to their view of the Trust Graph given the aborted setups) in the commitment phase. However, this set of intermediate parties is small enough that an alternative environment can corrupt it (because $t \geq n/2$) and thus extract the message of an honest sender during the commitment phase (not hiding).

Lemma 2 (Connected graph $\implies$ many disconnected $\beta-1$-subgraphs). *Let $n, t \in \mathbb{N}$ s.t. $n/2 \leq t \leq n-1$, and let $\beta := \min(n, \lfloor n/(n-t)\rfloor + \lceil n/(n-t)\rceil - 2)$. Furthermore, let V be a set of n vertices and let $v, v' \in V : v \neq v'$ be two different vertices. There exist some edges $E \subseteq \binom{V}{\leq 2}$ s.t.*

1. *$G := (V, E)$ is an undirected, reflexive and connected graph,*
2. *$\forall \{u, u'\} \in E : |N_G(u) \cap N_G(u')| \geq n - t$,*
3. *for each $V' \in M$ the subgraph $G' := (V', E \cap \binom{V'}{\leq 2})$ is disconnected*

where

$$N_u := \begin{cases} \{u\} & , \text{ if } t = n - 1 \\ N_G(u) & , \text{ else} \end{cases}$$

is the set of "effective" neighbors of any vertex u, and

$$M := \{V' \subseteq V \mid V' \cap N_v \neq \emptyset \ \wedge \ V' \cap N_{v'} \neq \emptyset \ \wedge \ |V'| < \beta\}$$

is the set of relevant subsets of vertices that contain both an effective neighbor of v and an effective neighbor of v'.

The proof is contained in the full version. For $t = n - 1$ the lemma states that there exists some graph whose subgraphs G' that contain both v and v' are disconnected, yet the overall graph is connected. For $t \leq n - 2$ the lemma states that there exists some graph whose subgraphs G' that contain both a neighbor[7] of v and a neighbor of v' are disconnected while the overall graph is connected.

Application to ID-MPC. Throughout, we denote the security parameter by λ. In the context of our impossibility proof, the graph G takes the role of the Trust Graph, $v = \mathsf{S}$ will be the sender, and $v' = \mathsf{R}$ will be the receiver. As such, the lemma translates to the statement that all setups in which the sender and the receiver (or their neighbors respectively) participate jointly can be aborted by the adversary without causing the overall TG to become disconnected, thus evading identification. The proof is essentially just a constructive description of the graph G alongside a proof of its properties. This graph-theoretic statement translates into the context of ID-MPC protocols as follows:

Corollary 1. *Let $n = n(\lambda), t = t(\lambda), \beta = \min(n, \lfloor n/(n-t) \rfloor + \lceil n/(n-t) \rceil - 2)$ s.t. $0 \leq t < n$. For any security parameter $\lambda \in \mathbb{N}$ let P_λ be a set of n parties, and let $v_\lambda, v'_\lambda \in P_\lambda$ be two different parties. Furthermore, let π^F be any abort-respecting protocol for some functionality $\mathcal{F}^n$ in some F-model s.t. $\mathcal{F}^n_{\mathsf{BC}} \in F$. An adversary for π^F that corrupts t parties can abort all setups of cardinality at most $\beta - 1$ in which any effective neighbor of v_λ and any effective neighbor of v'_λ participate, without disconnecting the overall Trust Graph G.*

For $t \geq n/2$ this follows from Lemma 2 (aborted setups correspond to disconnected subgraphs). Also, for $t < n/2$ it follows that $\beta = 1$, hence Corollary 1 follows trivially. Finally, we get the formal statement.

Theorem 2 (No transmitted commitment). *Let $n = n(\lambda), t = t(\lambda), \beta := \min(n, \lfloor n/(n-t) \rfloor + \lceil n/(n-t) \rceil - 2)$ s.t. $n/2 \leq t < n$ and $\binom{n}{\beta} \in \mathrm{poly}(\lambda)$. No $\{\mathcal{F}^2, ..., \mathcal{F}^{\beta-1}, \mathcal{F}^n_{\mathsf{BC}}\}$-hybrid protocol can securely UC-realize $\mathcal{F}^n_{\mathsf{COM},1:1}$ against environments that (maliciously) corrupt up to t parties. Formally, we get*

$$\{\mathcal{F}^2, ..., \mathcal{F}^{\beta-1}, \mathcal{F}^n_{\mathsf{BC}}\} \overset{\mathrm{comp}}{\not\rightsquigarrow}_t \mathcal{F}^n_{\mathsf{COM},1:1} \tag{1}$$

where $\mathcal{F}^2, ..., \mathcal{F}^{\beta-1}$ stand for arbitrary functionalities of the respective cardinality, and $\mathcal{F}^n_{\mathsf{COM},1:1}$ is defined in the full version.
Consequently, the correlation complexity for UC-secure ID-MPC is at least β.

The proof is contained in the full version.

Corollary 2. *Let $n = n(\lambda)$. In particular, we find $\{\mathcal{F}^2, ..., \mathcal{F}^{n-3}, \mathcal{F}^n_{\mathsf{BC}}\} \overset{\mathrm{comp}}{\not\rightsquigarrow}_{n-2} \mathcal{F}^n_{\mathsf{COM},1:1}$ where $\mathcal{F}^2, ..., \mathcal{F}^{n-3}$ stand for arbitrary functionalities of the respective cardinality. This shows that the result $\{\mathcal{F}^{n-1}_{\mathsf{Corr},\mathcal{D}}, \mathcal{F}^n_{\mathsf{BC}}\} \overset{\mathrm{stat}}{\rightsquigarrow}_{n-2} \mathcal{F}^n_{\mathsf{Corr},\mathcal{D}}$ from [28] is tight up to a constant of 1.[8]*

---

[7] Note that is vertex is their own neighbor because the graph is reflexive.
[8] We note that [28] state their results in the stand-alone model.

Upper Bound on the Correlation Complexity. Towards our construction, we first prove a complementary graph-theoretical lemma that relates the connectivity of the overall TG to the connectivity of its subgraphs. More concretely, the lemma states that any graph with "many" disconnected subgraphs of the cardinality β must be disconnected.

Lemma 3 (Connected graph $\Longrightarrow$ few disconnected β-subgraphs). *Let $n, t \in \mathbb{N}$ s.t. $n/2 \leq t \leq n - 2$, and let $\beta := \lfloor n/(n-t) \rfloor + \lceil n/(n-t) \rceil - 2$. Let V be a set of n vertices and let $v, v' \in V : v \neq v'$ be two different vertices. Moreover, let $E \subseteq \binom{V}{\leq 2}$ be a set of edges s.t. $G := (V, E)$ is an undirected, reflexive graph, and let $N_u := \mathrm{N}_G(u)$ be the set of neighbors of any vertex u, let*

$$M := \{V' \subseteq V \mid \quad V' \cap N_v \neq \emptyset \quad \wedge \quad V' \cap N_{v'} \neq \emptyset \quad \wedge \quad |V'| = \beta\}$$

be the set of relevant subsets of vertices that contain both a neighbor of v and a neighbor of v', and let

$$E^* := \{\{u, u'\} \in E \mid |N_u \cap N_{u'}| \geq n - t\}$$

be the set of postprocessed[9] edges. If for all $V' \in M$ the subgraph $G' := (V', E \cap \binom{V'}{\leq 2})$ is disconnected, then $G^* := (V, E^*)$ is disconnected. Furthermore, the map $\phi : G \mapsto G^*$ is efficiently computable.

This lemma tightly complements Lemma 2. It states that as soon as all subgraphs G' that contain both a neighbor of v and a neighbor of v' are disconnected, the overall postprocessed graph G^* must be disconnected as well. The proof is contained in the fullversion.

Application to ID-MPC. In the context of our construction, the graph G takes the role of the TG, $v = \mathsf{S}$ will be the sender, and $v' = \mathsf{R}$ will be some receiver. As such, the lemma translates to the statement that at least one (not necessarily fixed) setup in which the sender and the receiver (or their neighbors respectively) participate jointly *cannot* be aborted by the adversary without causing the overall TG to become disconnected. This "guaranteed" setup can then reliably perform the commitment (resp. OT) between the sender and the receiver (resp. their neighbors).

The proof is by contradiction. Suppose all subgraphs G' are disconnected, yet G^* were connected. Then there must be a path W from any neighbor $u \in N_v$ to any neighbor $u' \in N_{v'}$ with length $\Delta_{G^*}(u, u') > \beta$. Note that, by definition of E^*, all adjacent parties in G^* must have at least $n - t$ common neighbors. This means that the parties along the path W must have many auxiliary neighbors. Counting the overall number of parties yields a contradiction. We formalize this in the full version. This graph-theoretic statement translates into the context of ID-MPC protocols as follows:

---

[9] The postprocessing ϕ corresponds to removing edges from parties with strictly more than t conflicts.

Corollary 3. *Let* $n = n(\lambda), t = t(\lambda), \beta := \lfloor n/(n-t) \rfloor + \lceil n/(n-t) \rceil - 2$ *s.t.* $n/2 \leq t \leq n-2$. *For any security parameter* $\lambda \in \mathbb{N}$ *let* P_λ *be a set of* n *parties, and let* $v_\lambda, v'_\lambda \in P_\lambda$ *be two different parties. Furthermore, let* π^F *be any abort-respecting protocol for some functionality* $\mathcal{F}^n$ *in some* F-*model s.t.* $\mathcal{F}^n_{\mathsf{BC}} \in F$. *If an adversary for* π^F *that corrupts at most* t *parties aborts all setups of cardinality* β *in which any neighbor of* v_λ *and any neighbor of* v'_λ *participate, then the overall Trust Graph becomes disconnected, i.e., the protocol* π^F *aborts.*

This follows from Lemma 3 (aborted setups correspond to disconnected subgraphs).

In particular, in our protocols we require all honest parties to locally postprocess $G^* = \phi(G)$ from Lemma 3 when querying the TG G from $\mathcal{F}^n_{\mathsf{TG}}$. Moreover, we require all parties to abort according to G^* instead of G. This modification of the abort condition is justified because the additional (specific) conflicts introduced by the postprocessing ϕ preserve the invariant that no two honest parties are in conflict.

Committed Oblivious Transfer. Before we proceed with a more detailed description of our protocols we have to introduce a committed variant of Oblivious Transfer (OT) [13,15] where the sender, the receiver and some witnesses participate. We call this variant Fully Committed Oblivious Transfer (FCOT). As in the standard 1-out-of-2 OT, the sender inputs two messages and the receiver inputs a choice bit, then the receiver obtains its chosen message while the receiver remains oblivious to the choice bit. The committed variant additionally allows the sender and the receiver to later open their inputs to all other parties (called witnesses).

The purpose of this FCOT can be state as follows.

Lemma 4 (Completeness of committed OT (informal)). *There is a protocol in the* $\mathcal{F}^n_{\mathsf{FCOT}}$-*hybrid model that realizes any ideal* n-*party functionality.*

We can replace the standard OT setups in the IPS-compiler [22]. The IPS-compiler is an OT-hybrid protocol in the client-server-model that realizes general MPC guaranteeing security with (non-identifiable) abort against malicious (active) adversaries. In this protocol each party sets up a watchlist for each server such that other parties can monitor a small subsets of servers to detect tampering with overwhelming probability. Once a party detects misbehavior on some server it announces a complaint and all parties abort the protocol (without identifying malicious parties). For this reason, the standard IPS-compiler only enjoys security with (non-identifiable) abort. Substituting all calls to classical OT setups with calls to FCOT setups allows the parties to open all messages regarding the server in question. This way all parties can retrace which party misbehaved, thus identifying at least one malicious party, hence the resulting protocol enjoys security with Identifiable Abort.

We continue with a high-level overview of our two protocols that utilize the guaranteed setups mentioned above. The two constructions are

- n-party commitment from β-party commitments and n-party broadcast, and
- n-party FCOT from β-party FCOT, n-party commitments and broadcast.

Commitment Expansion

Theorem 3 (COM expansion). *Let $n = n(\lambda), t = t(\lambda), \beta := \lfloor n/(n-t) \rfloor + \lceil n/(n-t) \rceil - 2$ s.t. $n/2 \leq t \leq n-2$ and $\binom{n}{\beta} \in \mathrm{poly}(\lambda)$. There is an efficient protocol π_{COM} that statistically securely UC-realizes $\mathcal{F}^n_{\mathsf{COM}}$ in the $\{\mathcal{F}^2_{\mathsf{SMT}}, \mathcal{F}^\beta, \mathcal{F}^n_{\mathsf{BC}}\}$-hybrid model against environments that (maliciously) corrupt up to t parties. Formally,*

$$\{\mathcal{F}^2_{\mathsf{SMT}}, \mathcal{F}^\beta, \mathcal{F}^n_{\mathsf{BC}}\} \overset{\mathrm{stat}}{\leadsto}_t \mathcal{F}^n_{\mathsf{COM}} \ . \tag{2}$$

On a high level our one-to-many commitment protocol follows a commit-and-prove approach. Without going into too much detail, we outline the idea of the protocol. The sender inputs its message m—in the form of a threshold sharing μ—into all setups[10] and gives (secret-shared) masks ξ^j to its neighbors $R_j \in N_G(S)$ who, in turn, also commit to their sharings in all commitment setups. Additionally, the sender broadcasts the message's sharing μ masked with the masks' sharings $\sigma := \mu \oplus \bigoplus_{R_j \in N(S)} \xi^j$. Subsequently, all parties broadcast some randomly drawn "probing indices" on which the sender (resp. neighbors) broadcast the resp. share and open the setup commitment for the resp. share. Then all parties check for inconsistencies. Indeed, all setups (intended for the same value) contain sharings of the *same* (possibly masked) value with overwhelming probability. If shares differ significantly, this discrepancy will be detected with overwhelming probability; then the affected setup is considered aborted by identifying the committer as malicious. If shares differ only on a few indices, then the sharing's error-detection will allow the parties to notice that the shares are invalid. Again, the affected setup is considered aborted by identifying the committer as malicious. Moreover, due to the privacy of the secret-sharing opening a few shares does not reveal anything about the encoded value.

Lemma 3 guarantees that at least one setup of cardinality β that contains both a neighbor of the sender and a neighbor of the receiver must succeed. Otherwise, if all such setups are aborted, then the TG becomes disconnected by Lemma 3 and the honest parties can abort the protocol.

To open the message, all parties open all commitment setups and at least one honest receiver is able to recover the message either directly from the sender's sharing μ of the message, or from the opened masks ξ^j and the previously broadcasted masked sharing σ. Those receivers then broadcast the recovered message. Any honest receiver that did not receive any opening information—because all its setups have been aborted—then it outputs the majority of its neighbors' broadcasted messages. To see why such "cut-off" receivers output the correct message we have to see the following fact. Whenever all setups containing both a neighbor of the sender *and* a neighbor of the receiver are aborted, then an

---

[10] The sender inputs the same shares into each setup that it participates in.

honest receiver has a majority of honest neighbors that could reconstruct the message. This statement follows from graph-theoretical considerations. An intuitive explanation is that if all such setups are aborted, then the sender and the cut-off receiver have a large distance of at least β in the TG. In that case the cut-off receiver cannot have too many malicious neighbors, yet honest parties always remain neighbors.

Skipping ahead to the proof of security, the simulator will extract the committed message from the sharings input into the partial commitment setups. As the verification step ensures consistency among the committed messages the simulator's extracted message is uniquely defined and correct.

Committed OT Expansion

Theorem 4 (FCOT expansion). *Let* $n = n(\lambda), t = t(\lambda), \beta := \lfloor n/(n - t) \rfloor + \lceil n/(n - t) \rceil - 2$ *s.t.* $n/2 \leq t \leq n - 2$ *and* $\binom{n}{\beta} \in \mathrm{poly}(\lambda)$. *There is an efficient protocol* π_{FCOT} *that statistically securely UC-realizes* $\mathcal{F}^n_{\mathsf{FCOT}}$ *in the* $\{\mathcal{F}^2_{\mathsf{SMT}}, \mathcal{F}^\beta_{\mathsf{SFE},f}, \mathcal{F}^n_{\mathsf{COM}}, \mathcal{F}^n_{\mathsf{BC}}\}$-*hybrid model against environments that (maliciously) corrupt up to* t *parties. Formally, for some specific functionality* $\mathcal{F}^\beta$ *we get*

$$\{\mathcal{F}^2_{\mathsf{SMT}}, \mathcal{F}^\beta, \mathcal{F}^n_{\mathsf{COM}}, \mathcal{F}^n_{\mathsf{BC}}\} \overset{\mathrm{stat}}{\leadsto}_t \mathcal{F}^n_{\mathsf{FCOT}} \ . \tag{3}$$

Recall that in the FCOT functionality there exists a sender, a receiver and $n-2$ witnesses. Let $\mathcal{F}^\beta_{\mathsf{SFE},f}$ be some Secure Function Evaluation (SFE) setup for β-parties for some function f_{OT} that allows for an FCOT but whose details we omit at this point. In our FCOT protocol the sender and the receiver try to perform the global FCOT *directly*, i.e., via some setup in which both the sender and the receiver and $n - \beta$ witnesses (w.r.t. the overall FCOT) are left out. To ensure consistency with the excluded witnesses the sender and the receiver globally commit to their inputs (again as secret-sharings) via $\mathcal{F}^n_{\mathsf{COM}}$. Accordingly, the setup $\mathcal{F}^\beta_{\mathsf{SFE},f}$ also takes the same sharing as inputs. As in the commitment protocol the sender and the receiver open their shares, in the $\mathcal{F}^\beta_{\mathsf{SFE},f}$ setup and the global commitments, on some random probing indices to detect inconsistencies.

To open, the sender and the receiver can simply open the global commitments to their respective inputs.

In the security proof the simulator extracts the sender's messages and the receiver's choice bit from their inputs to their global commitments. Again, the verification step (commit-then-prove by probing random shares) guarantees that the simulator's extracted inputs match the ones output be the honest parties in the real protocol execution with overwhelming probability.

As in the previous construction, we leverage Lemma 3 which guarantees essentially that some such "direct" SFE setup must not be aborted, if the protocol is not to abort. Here lies the technical difficulty of our protocol because Lemma 3 only guarantees such a setup between a neighbor of the sender and a neighbor of the receiver (not the sender and the receiver themselves). To remedy this issue we make the following observation: In the seemingly hopeless scenario where the adversary chooses to abort the setups in such a way that the sender and the receiver themselves are not able to perform the direct setup, then one of them (the honest one) has many honest neighbors. In this case the sender and receiver use their neighbors respectively to carry out the OT for them. Here, the sender and the receiver secret-share their inputs to retain their privacy and distribute them to their neighbors. While for the sender's messages the sharing seems straightforward (additive sharing), it may not be obvious how the receiver's choice bit can be shared s.t. the receiver obtains its chosen message. To this end we invoke a technique akin to the one used by Wolf and Wullschleger [30] which they used to show the symmetry of OT. This allows the receiver to only distribute additive shares of its choice bit (ensuring privacy) but still obtain the chosen message.

Equivalence of SFE-Complete Setups. In the full version we prove that the setups Fully Committed Oblivious Transfer (FCOT) $\mathcal{F}_{\text{FCOT}}^n$, Secure Function Evaluation (SFE) $\mathcal{F}_{\text{SFE},f}^n$, and Correlated-Randomness from [21] $\mathcal{F}_{\text{Corr},\mathcal{D}}^n$ can be efficiently realized from each other with statistical security; so we can substitute one with the other by the Universal Composability Theorem of [7].

Putting the Results Together. For brevity we use the short notation $F \leadsto_t \mathcal{F}$ to describe the construction of UC-secure protocols for the ideal functionality $\mathcal{F}$ in the F-hybrid model against at most t corruptions.

Corollary 4 (Composition of constructions). *The correlation complexity for UC-secure ID-MPC is at most β. We observe*

$$\{\mathcal{F}_{\text{FCOT}}^\beta\} \overset{\text{stat}}{\leadsto}_\beta \mathcal{F}_{\text{SFE},f}^\beta \tag{4}$$

$$\{\mathcal{F}_{\text{SMT}}^2, \mathcal{F}_{\text{SFE},f}^\beta, \mathcal{F}_{\text{BC}}^n\} \overset{\text{stat}}{\leadsto}_t \mathcal{F}_{\text{FCOT}}^n \tag{5}$$

$$\overset{\text{stat}}{\leadsto}_n \mathcal{F}^n \tag{6}$$

where $\mathcal{F}^n$ is any arbitrary functionality. Equation (5) follows from the combination of Theorems 3 and 4, and Eqs. (4) and (6) follows from the ID-MPC-completeness of FCOT. For statistical security we get

$$\{\mathcal{F}_{\text{Corr},\mathcal{D}}^\beta\} \overset{\text{stat}}{\leadsto}_\beta \mathcal{F}_{\text{FCOT}}^\beta \tag{7}$$

$$\implies \{\mathcal{F}_{\text{SMT}}^2, \mathcal{F}_{\text{Corr},\mathcal{D}}^\beta, \mathcal{F}_{\text{BC}}^n\} \overset{\text{stat}}{\leadsto}_t \mathcal{F}^n \tag{8}$$

where $\mathcal{F}^n$ is any arbitrary functionality. Equation (7) follows from the ID-MPC-completeness of the correlated randomness setup (Theorem 6 in [21]). For computational security we get

$$\{\pi_{\text{OT}}, \mathcal{F}_{\text{CRS}}^\beta, \mathcal{F}_{\text{BC}}^\beta\} \overset{\text{comp}}{\leadsto}_\beta \mathcal{F}_{\text{FCOT}}^\beta \tag{9}$$

$$\implies \{\pi_{\text{OT}}, \mathcal{F}_{\text{SMT}}^2, \mathcal{F}_{\text{CRS}}^\beta, \mathcal{F}_{\text{BC}}^n\} \overset{\text{comp}}{\leadsto}_t \mathcal{F}^n \tag{10}$$

where $\mathcal{F}^n$ is any arbitrary functionality, π_{OT} is any adaptively secure OT protocol and $\mathcal{F}_{\text{CRS}}^\beta$ is the Common Reference String functionality from [8]. Equation (9) follows from the computational construction in Theorem 12 in [21].

144   N. Brandt et al.

For ID-MPC with statistical security this reduces the required correlation complexity from n to β. For ID-MPC with computational security this reduces the required cardinality of the CRS for the computationally secure offline phase of the construction in [21] from n to β.

Theorem 1 (Correlation complexity bounds). *The correlation complexity for UC-secure Multi-Party Computation with Identifiable Abort (given broadcast) is $\beta := \min(n, \lfloor n/(n-t) \rfloor + \lceil n/(n-t) \rceil - 2) \approx 2n/(n-t)$ where n is the overall number of parties and t is an upper bound on the number of malicious parties.*

In other words, for any n-party functionality with Identifiable Abort there exists a protocol that uses hybrid functionalities of cardinality β and broadcast, but there exists an n-party functionality with Identifiable Abort which cannot be realized by any protocol that uses hybrid functionalities of cardinality $\beta - 1$ and broadcast.

Proof. The theorem follows directly from Theorem 2 and Corollary 4.   □

References

1. Baum, C., Orsini, E., Scholl, P.: Efficient secure multiparty computation with identifiable abort. In: Hirt, M., Smith, A. (eds.) TCC 2016, Part I. LNCS, vol. 9985, pp. 461–490. Springer, Heidelberg (2016). https://doi.org/10.1007/978-3-662-53641-4_18
2. Baum, C., Orsini, E., Scholl, P., Soria-Vazquez, E.: Efficient constant-round MPC with identifiable abort and public verifiability. In: Micciancio, D., Ristenpart, T. (eds.) CRYPTO 2020, Part II. LNCS, vol. 12171, pp. 562–592. Springer, Cham (2020). https://doi.org/10.1007/978-3-030-56880-1_20
3. Beaver, D.: Multiparty protocols tolerating half faulty processors. In: Brassard, G. (ed.) CRYPTO 1989. LNCS, vol. 435, pp. 560–572. Springer, New York (1990). https://doi.org/10.1007/0-387-34805-0_49
4. Boyle, E., et al.: Compressing vector OLE. In: Lie, D., et al. (eds.) ACM CCS 2018, pp. 896–912. ACM Press, October 2018
5. Boyle, E., et al.: Correlated pseudorandom functions from variable-density LPN. In: 61st FOCS, pp. 1069–1080. IEEE Computer Society Press, November 2020
6. Boyle, E., Couteau, G., Gilboa, N., Ishai, Y., Kohl, L., Scholl, P.: Efficient pseudorandom correlation generators: silent OT extension and more. In: Boldyreva, A., Micciancio, D. (eds.) CRYPTO 2019, Part III. LNCS, vol. 11694, pp. 489–518. Springer, Cham (2019). https://doi.org/10.1007/978-3-030-26954-8_16
7. Canetti, R.: Universally composable security: a new paradigm for cryptographic protocols. In: 42nd FOCS, pp. 136–145. IEEE Computer Society Press, October 2001
8. Canetti, R., Fischlin, M.: Universally composable commitments. In: Kilian, J. (ed.) CRYPTO 2001. LNCS, vol. 2139, pp. 19–40. Springer, Heidelberg (2001). https://doi.org/10.1007/3-540-44647-8_2
9. Canetti, R., Dodis, Y., Pass, R., Walfish, S.: Universally composable security with global setup. In: Vadhan, S.P. (ed.) TCC 2007. LNCS, vol. 4392, pp. 61–85. Springer, Heidelberg (2007). https://doi.org/10.1007/978-3-540-70936-7_4
10. Cleve, R.: Limits on the security of coin flips when half the processors are faulty (extended abstract). In: 18th ACM STOC, pp. 364–369. ACM Press, May 1986

11. Couteau, G., Rindal, P., Raghuraman, S.: Silver: silent VOLE and oblivious transfer from hardness of decoding structured LDPC codes. In: Malkin, T., Peikert, C. (eds.) CRYPTO 2021, Part III. LNCS, vol. 12827, pp. 502–534. Springer, Cham (2021). https://doi.org/10.1007/978-3-030-84252-9_17

12. Crépeau, C.: Efficient cryptographic protocols based on noisy channels. In: Fumy, W. (ed.) EUROCRYPT 1997. LNCS, vol. 1233, pp. 306–317. Springer, Heidelberg (1997). https://doi.org/10.1007/3-540-69053-0_21

13. Crépeau, C.: Verifiable disclosure of secrets and applications (abstract). In: Quisquater, J.-J., Vandewalle, J. (eds.) EUROCRYPT 1989. LNCS, vol. 434, pp. 150–154. Springer, Heidelberg (1990). https://doi.org/10.1007/3-540-46885-4_17

14. Crépeau, C., Kilian, J.: Achieving oblivious transfer using weakened security assumptions (extended abstract). In: 29th FOCS, pp. 42–52. IEEE Computer Society Press, October 1988

15. Crépeau, C., van de Graaf, J., Tapp, A.: Committed oblivious transfer and private multi-party computation. In: Coppersmith, D. (ed.) CRYPTO 1995. LNCS, vol. 963, pp. 110–123. Springer, Heidelberg (1995). https://doi.org/10.1007/3-540-44750-4_9

16. Fitzi, M., Garay, J.A., Maurer, U., Ostrovsky, R.: Minimal complete primitives for secure multi-party computation. In: Kilian, J. (ed.) CRYPTO 2001. LNCS, vol. 2139, pp. 80–100. Springer, Heidelberg (2001). https://doi.org/10.1007/3-540-44647-8_5

17. Gennaro, R., Ishai, Y., Kushilevitz, E., Rabin, T.: On 2-round secure multiparty computation. In: Yung, M. (ed.) CRYPTO 2002. LNCS, vol. 2442, pp. 178–193. Springer, Heidelberg (2002). https://doi.org/10.1007/3-540-45708-9_12

18. Goyal, V., Ishai, Y., Sahai, A., Venkatesan, R., Wadia, A.: Founding cryptography on tamper-proof hardware tokens. In: Micciancio, D. (ed.) TCC 2010. LNCS, vol. 5978, pp. 308–326. Springer, Heidelberg (2010). https://doi.org/10.1007/978-3-642-11799-2_19

19. Ishai, Y., Kushilevitz, E., Paskin, A.: Secure multiparty computation with minimal interaction. In: Rabin, T. (ed.) CRYPTO 2010. LNCS, vol. 6223, pp. 577–594. Springer, Heidelberg (2010). https://doi.org/10.1007/978-3-642-14623-7_31

20. Ishai, Y., Ostrovsky, R., Seyalioglu, H.: Identifying cheaters without an honest majority. In: Cramer, R. (ed.) TCC 2012. LNCS, vol. 7194, pp. 21–38. Springer, Heidelberg (2012). https://doi.org/10.1007/978-3-642-28914-9_2

21. Ishai, Y., Ostrovsky, R., Zikas, V.: Secure multi-party computation with identifiable abort. In: Garay, J.A., Gennaro, R. (eds.) CRYPTO 2014, Part II. LNCS, vol. 8617, pp. 369–386. Springer, Heidelberg (2014). https://doi.org/10.1007/978-3-662-44381-1_21

22. Ishai, Y., Prabhakaran, M., Sahai, A.: Founding cryptography on oblivious transfer – efficiently. In: Wagner, D. (ed.) CRYPTO 2008. LNCS, vol. 5157, pp. 572–591. Springer, Heidelberg (2008). https://doi.org/10.1007/978-3-540-85174-5_32

23. Ishai, Y., et al.: Zero-knowledge from secure multiparty computation. In: Johnson, D.S., Feige, U. (eds.) 39th ACM STOC, pp. 21–30. ACM Press, June 2007

24. Orlandi, C., Scholl, P., Yakoubov, S.: The rise of paillier: homomorphic secret sharing and public-key silent OT. In: Canteaut, A., Standaert, F.-X. (eds.) EUROCRYPT 2021, Part I. LNCS, vol. 12696, pp. 678–708. Springer, Cham (2021). https://doi.org/10.1007/978-3-030-77870-5_24

25. Pass, R.: On deniability in the common reference string and random oracle model. In: Boneh, D. (ed.) CRYPTO 2003. LNCS, vol. 2729, pp. 316–337. Springer, Heidelberg (2003). https://doi.org/10.1007/978-3-540-45146-4_19

26. Rabin, T., Ben-Or, M.: Verifiable secret sharing and multiparty protocols with honest majority (extended abstract). In: 21st ACM STOC, pp. 73–85. ACM Press, May 1989

27. Sadeghi, A.-R., Schneider, T., Winandy, M.: Token-based cloud computing. In: Acquisti, A., Smith, S.W., Sadeghi, A.-R. (eds.) Trust 2010. LNCS, vol. 6101, pp. 417–429. Springer, Heidelberg (2010). https://doi.org/10.1007/978-3-642-13869-0_30

28. Simkin, M., Siniscalchi, L., Yakoubov, S.: On sufficient oracles for secure computation with identifiable abort. In: Galdi, C., Jarecki, S. (eds.) SCN 2022. LNCS, vol. 13409, pp. 494–515. Springer, Cham (2022). https://doi.org/10.1007/978-3-031-14791-3_22

29. Wan, J., Xiao, H., Shi, E., Devadas, S.: Expected constant round byzantine broadcast under dishonest majority. In: Pass, R., Pietrzak, K. (eds.) TCC 2020, Part I. LNCS, vol. 12550, pp. 381–411. Springer, Cham (2020). https://doi.org/10.1007/978-3-030-64375-1_14

30. Wolf, S., Wullschleger, J.: Oblivious transfer is symmetric. In: Vaudenay, S. (ed.) EUROCRYPT 2006. LNCS, vol. 4004, pp. 222–232. Springer, Heidelberg (2006). https://doi.org/10.1007/11761679_14

TALUS: Reinforcing TEE Confidentiality with Cryptographic Coprocessors

Dhiman Chakraborty$^{(\boxtimes)}$, Michael Schwarz, and Sven Bugiel

CISPA Helmholtz Center for Information Security, Saarbruecken, Germany
{dhiman.chakraborty,michael.schwarz,bugiel}@cispa.de

Abstract. Platforms are nowadays typically equipped with trusted execution environments (TEEs), such as Intel SGX or ARM TrustZone. However, recent microarchitectural attacks on TEEs repeatedly broke their confidentiality guarantees, including the leakage of long-term cryptographic secrets. These systems are typically also equipped with a cryptographic coprocessor, such as a TPM or Google Titan. These coprocessors offer a unique set of security features focused on safeguarding cryptographic secrets. Still, despite their simultaneous availability, the integration between these technologies is practically nonexistent, which prevents them from benefitting from each other's strengths.

In this paper, we propose *TALUS*, a general design and a set of three main requirements for a secure symbiosis between TEEs and cryptographic coprocessors. We implement a proof-of-concept of *TALUS* based on Intel SGX and a hardware TPM. We show that with *TALUS*, the long-term secrets used in the SGX life cycle can be moved to the TPM. We demonstrate that our design is robust even in the presence of transient execution attacks, preventing an entire class of attacks due to the reduced attack surface on the shared hardware.

1 Introduction

The need for stronger protection of data and computations has led to the advent of *secure enclaves*, CPU-provided isolated *Trusted Execution Environments* (TEE) that secure general-purpose computations. Prevalent technologies are Intel SGX [16,20,27], ARM TrustZone [1], or Keystone [42] and MI6 [5] for RISC-V.

The security offered by these *secure enclaves* for code and data isolation depends on several high value cryptographic credentials (e.g., Launch and Provisioning Key for Intel SGX, AMD PSP infrastructure key for AMD SEV, manufacturer root keys for ARM TrustZone). Enclave programs, in turn, depend on credentials derived from those long-term secrets, e.g., for secure storage of enclave data. Unfortunately, enclave technology shares hardware, e.g., CPU cores, between trusted and untrusted code, opening an attack surface. Especially for Intel SGX, this attack surface has been exploited in microarchitectural attacks [49], some of which leak confidential data from CPU buffers [4,7,63,64,72].

© International Financial Cryptography Association 2024
F. Baldimtsi and C. Cachin (Eds.): FC 2023, LNCS 13950, pp. 147–165, 2024.
https://doi.org/10.1007/978-3-031-47754-6_9

Our key observation is that virtually all platforms today are additionally equipped with specialized cryptographic or security-oriented coprocessors that protect cryptographic credentials, access control secure storage, or monotonically count. For instance, Trusted Platform Modules (TPM) [68] are available on effectively all desktop and server machines, and more solutions become available, such as Google's Titan, Microsoft's Cerberus, or AMD's PSP [76]. In contrast to general purpose application processors with security extensions for TEEs, those coprocessors have been designed for the primary goal to safeguard cryptographic credentials and secret data. Integration between secure enclaves and cryptographic coprocessors creates a stronger security solution in which enclaves can use the complementary coprocessor features. Concrete use-cases would benefit from this integration, e.g., impeding microarchitectural attacks against enclaves based on TPM features. Unfortunately, such an integration is currently, if it exists, very limited. We ask the following fundamental questions: *Which security guarantees does the combination of CPU-provided TEEs with secure coprocessors provide that each of the technologies cannot provide on their own? What are the requirements to combine the advantages of both technologies without introducing new security problems or large performance overheads?*

To answer these questions, we introduce a hardware/software co-design, *TALUS*, to combine CPU-provided TEEs with cryptographic coprocessors. Enclave code can directly invoke the coprocessor *only* via the CPU firmware and bus connections to make use of the coprocessor's facilities, such as counters or key management. We identify three core requirements to realize our idea: a *secure communication channel* between processors and coprocessors, *vertical access control* to distinguish between enclave and non-enclave code, and *horizontal access control* to distinguish between different enclaves. To understand how SGX can be integrated with an on-board hardware TPM, we built a proof-of-concept integration between Intel SGX and a hardware TPM on commodity hardware. We show that a combination of Intel SGX (emulated through KVM-SGX [34] and QEMU-SGX [35]) with hardware TPM is feasible with firmware changes and demonstrate through different use cases the security benefits of this symbiosis.

We show that TPM fills a gap in the trusted-computing features of SGX that is due to a lack of replay-protected secure non-volatile memory. Several previously published defenses for attacks against SGX provide their full strength only if such building blocks are available [13,57,65]. Furthermore, preventing recent microarchitectural attacks against TEEs [7,63,64,75], including undervolting [38,56,61] is only effective if an enclave can store a persistent state to limit the number of attack attempts. In addition to the possibility of preventing attacks against enclaves, we demonstrate that all high-value secrets used during the lifetime of enclaves can be safely stored in the TPM without ever reaching a shared hardware element. We can actively mitigate existing attacks and harden an enclave against potential future attacks by reducing the amount of high-value secrets stored in the enclave. Our proof-of-concept implementation shows that the expected overhead of an average 21.6% is amortized in typical use cases, as only rarely used operations suffer from a slowdown of several milliseconds.

In summary, we make the following contributions:

1. We introduce *TALUS*, a hardware/software co-design to combine CPU-provided TEEs with cryptographic coprocessors.
2. We show that *TALUS* provides extended features, like rollback protected TPM NV-storage for persistent counters to limit execution control attacks against enclaves.
3. We demonstrate that *TALUS* significantly reduces the attack surface for microarchitectural attacks.
4. We analyze *TALUS* for real use cases, showing that its performance overhead is amortized in many use cases while providing strong security guarantees.

2 Background

2.1 Intel Software Guard eXtension (SGX)

SGX is an extension to the x86 instruction set that allows a user-space process to create and manage a protected isolated memory region called an *enclave* within its own address space, even protected from OS and hypervisor access [26,48]. SGX assumes that the CPU, including its microcode, is the only trusted element in the system. Enclave data are stored encrypted in DRAM and unencrypted in the CPU caches and registers. An external party can verify an enclave by (remote) attestation of the enclave code and meta-data [6,66].

Intel supplies two infrastructure enclaves, the *launch enclave* (LE) and *quoting enclave* (QE), on which SGX is heavily dependent. The LE is responsible for handling and launching user-space enclaves with a token called EINITTOKEN that is generated using i) the measurement of the static content of the enclave (MRENCLAVE) and ii) the enclave-author validation (MRSIGNER). The LE requires a 128-bit *Launch Key* (LK) to derive the EINITTOKEN. The QE is designed to validate local attestation reports by enclaves generated with an asymmetric private key that a remote verifier can verify. Both the LE and the QE are entrusted with long-term high-value cryptographic credentials.

2.2 Trusted Platform Module (TPM)

TPM by the Trusted Computing Group is the most widely deployed trusted computing technology on commodity platforms used by, e.g., Microsoft Windows management instrumentation, Intel Trusted eXecution Technology (TXT) [31], Microsoft Bitlocker [51], or Google Chrome [19]. A TPM contains a small non-volatile memory block, a set of platform configuration registers (PCR), an onboard processor to execute TPM code in isolation from the other hardware, co-processing for standard cryptographic algorithms, a secure clock, and a random number generator. TPMs can reliably report internal data to a third-party verifier, i.e., remote attestation based on a pre-installed endorsement key. Typically, a TPM is available as a hardware chip soldered to the mainboard, traditionally connected via the Low Pin Count (LPC) bus or on newer platforms via the SPI bus, making it only available through memory-mapped I/O (MMIO) registers protected by the chipset. Intel also implements a firmware TPM called Platform Trust Technology (Intel-PTT) [25] housed inside Intel CSME [28].

3 Requirements Analysis

In this section, we define three fundamental requirements for a secure integration of CPU-provided Trusted Execution Environments with onboard secure coprocessors: *secure communication channel*, *horizontal access control*, and *vertical access control*. We systematically compare how SGX and TPM meet those requirements and how well these two technologies can be integrated, as demonstrated later by our proof-of-concept implementation. In the full technical report [11], we have extended this comparison further to other secure coprocessors and TEEs.

Communication Channel (CC). For a secure integration between the security coprocessor and the application processor (AP), the communication channel between them must be secured from eavesdropping even in case of physical attacks, e.g., bus sniffing (**CC1**), and there should not be any dependencies on buffers vulnerable to microarchitectural attacks that can leak sensitive data transferred via the channel (**CC2**). TPM and SGX fulfill **CC1** since TPM and Intel CPUs support end-to-end encryption of the communication between them [17,31,68]. However, this channel does not avoid insecure buffers, and decrypted data on the CPU side might still pass through such buffers. As demonstrated by recent attacks, none of the TEEs, including SGX, is free of insecure buffers. Therefore, SGX inherently fulfills **not CC2**, and we show in Sect. 5 how we overcome this limitation in combination with TPM.

Horizontal Access Control (HC). TEEs can host multiple tenants. For example, SGX supports multiple (parallel) enclaves. Horizontal access control ensures that the AP and the coprocessor can distinguish between requests from mutually untrusted tenants inside a TEE. For instance, one enclave should not be able to access another enclave's data within the coprocessor. A trusted entity, such as an AP, must create access or identity tokens that can identify TEE tenants. The tokens must be securely communicated to the coprocessor. The coprocessor must also understand those tokens to control access to managed data and secrets. Hardware TPM and firmware TPM employ extended authorization policies (EAP) that can use these access tokens for access control to TPM-managed objects, like TPM-internal storage and keys. All AP-based TEEs can fulfill this requirement because they can uniquely identify the different enclave codes they host. They can provide this information on calls to the coprocessor. For example, in SGX, this would be the code measurement of the enclave by the CPU.

Vertical Access Control (VC). AP-based TEE technologies and the coprocessor should support access control based on different security levels (e.g., application, OS, or hardware) to prevent non-enclave code from accessing enclave-owned entities in the coprocessor. The access token to distinguish between different security levels needs to be generated and handled by a secure piece of code and be securely communicated to the coprocessor. Hardware and firmware TPM offer *Locality* to distinguish between TPM commands originating from different security levels. Still, the locality of a command must be communicated to the TPM by the CPU or firmware. Furthermore, SGX registers when it executes in enclave mode, but this security level is only used CPU-internally and not for Locality.

TALUS: Integrating Intel SGX and Hardware TPM. The main issue of vanilla SGX is the lack of confidentiality- and integrity-protected tamper-resistant storage. As we are unaware of any non-volatile memory inside a CPU, we do not see how SGX can be improved by only updating the firmware and without adding new components (like a TPM) to the TCB. Vanilla SGX can use PTT for certain trusted computing use cases. However, PTT is housed inside the CSME [28] and connected through the DMI interface without any security around the communication channel. Moreover, although CSME employs its own OS with its own security ring, completely segregated from the platform security, the command buffer for PTT is configured by untrusted software, such as the OS, and PTT recently suffered from access control errors [29,30] that completely undermine its security and are currently unfixable in production devices. Additionally, secrets typically flow through the memory hierarchy on the CPU where untrusted code can run in parallel, observing side effects of the secret processing, e.g., when unsealing data from disk. Furthermore, in SGX, support for counters depends on the Platform Service Enclave and Intel ME, which are often not available in SGX production deployments and have already been deprecated [32]. Moreover, these counters can be reset by reinstalling the SGX platform software [46]. As SGX stores counters inside the BIOS flash storage, they do not persist across system resets [46]. The unavailability of integrity-protected, tamper-resistant storage does not allow SGX to store a secure counter, which limits the possibility of enclaves to enforce a number of enclave executions, as exploited in interrupt-based attacks [7].

Based on our requirements analysis, we found that the combination of SGX with hardware TPM is highly amenable for integration and allows to fill those gaps in SGX with TPM functionality. Due to the historical relationships between Intel CPUs and TPM, they can create an encrypted channel between them. Additionally, SGX can identify (i.e., measure) enclave code while TPM can use this identity in its access control policies. Therefore, our proof-of-concept implementation for our TALUS design is based on SGX and a **hardware** TPM.

4   High-Level TALUS Overview

Our systematization (Sect. 3) underlines the intuition that the TPM, when integrated as a coprocessor with SGX, can provide desirable features to secure enclaves, such as physically isolated processing of cryptographic secrets, a secure clock, or persistent counters. The basic idea is to retrofit SGX with a *direct* communication channel to the TPM chip *without* going through the host OS. With such a communication channel, enclaves can leverage the TPM facilities as building blocks, e.g., to implement secure monotonic counters (cf. Sect. 5). This section provides more details on the security benefits, requirements, and challenges of integrating SGX enclaves with a TPM. The high-level overview of *TALUS* is available in the extended version of the paper [11].

4.1 Threat Model

The threat model for *TALUS* is the union of the coprocessor and enclave threat model. Only the coprocessor (including firmware) and the processor (including microcode) are trusted. We assume that the coprocessor does not suffer from implementation [54] or platform integration flaws [22]. Similarly, we assume that the enclaves are not malicious [50] and are free of classical software vulnerabilities [14,43,71,74]. Microarchitectural attacks [69], such as classical side channels and transient execution attacks, are in scope. We allow physical attacks in line with the TPM and SGX specifications, e.g., bus tapping, bus sniffing, or similar physical layer attacks [3,37,40]. We exclude physical attacks outside of a reasonable attacker model for SGX and consumer-grade hardware, such as bus snooping on high-speed or address buses [41], against which SGX also fails to defend.

4.2 Design of TALUS

Integrating a coprocessor (e.g., TPM) with a secure enclave technology, such as SGX, poses both security (SC) and functional (FC) challenges. In this section, we detail the challenges and how we design *TALUS* to solve these challenges.

SC1. Secure Communication Channel. CPU and coprocessor must exchange data securely. Ideally, the coprocessor is physically integrated with the CPU package (e.g., similar to AMD PSP), and the communication channel is physically secured against eavesdropping. If the coprocessor is an additional hardware element, a secure connection via the usually insecure bus is required. For TPM and SGX, TPM is connected to the CPU via the unprotected LPC or SPI bus. Thus, *TALUS* relies on symmetric authenticated cryptography to establish a secure channel between the coprocessor and the CPU while ensuring confidentiality and integrity despite an untrusted OS and a physical attacker.

SC2. Authorization of Commands. A coprocessor, such as TPM, is often shared between various entities on the system, such as firmware, OS, and user-space applications. Further, the enclave technology might support multiple mutually-untrusted tenants. Thus, the coprocessor has to manage the credentials for different enclaves (differentiated using, e.g., MRSIGNER, MRENCLAVE, PRODID and SVN). Moreover, the coprocessor is also used by non-enclave code, e.g., the OS, firmware, or user-space application. Consequently, it is crucial to have authorization of coprocessor commands to control access to coprocessor entities (like keys or NVM) to ensure that every enclave and non-enclave code only ever has access to its own coprocessor entities. *TALUS* with SGX and TPM ensures authorization using locality and EAP. Authorization to TPM entities between different actors in the system, e.g., OS, third-party software, or hardware, is based on the TPM locality. Different enclaves running on the same system authorize via their identities through TPM EAP [11].

SC3. Avoiding Shared Hardware. It is often necessary to securely (SC1) send secret data, e.g., session keys, to the CPU while reducing the amount of shared hardware involved in the communication. Recent transient-execution attacks showed that a software-only attacker can read stale entries in various internal CPU buffers [7,9,62–64]. Thus, *TALUS* provides strict isolation of coprocessor-released data, ensuring that data does not pass (in plaintext) through shared hardware elements with (known) vulnerabilities. *TALUS* implements the entire communication using only CPU registers as storage.

Besides those security challenges, we identify the following functional challenges (FC) that influence *TALUS*.

FC1. Functionality Mapping. Enclave functionalities require a corresponding faithful command mapping offered by the coprocessor, e.g., to generate and use keys with the same authorization policies. The coprocessor driver logic for these commands can be implemented in CPU microcode [33] without requiring hardware changes. The microcode changes have to support only minimal amounts of ephemeral storage for policy sessions and session handles, both of which can be stored in the insecure BIOS flash.

FC2. Attestation. Enclaves depend on attestation to convince (remote) parties that they are communicating with the intended enclave. If the coprocessor supports attestation and management of attestation secrets, the attestation can be outsourced to the coprocessor. Thus, attestation secrets are never stored in shared hardware. A TPM supports remote attestation of TPM internal data. However, this poses the challenge of faithfully integrating the TPM attestation protocols with SGX. *TALUS* achieves this by extending TPM PCR21 with a measurement of an SGX secret (e.g., measurement of the QE). PCR21 is protected using EAP to ensure that only the microcode can access it, and the PCR21 measurement is attested through TPM-based attestation to a remote verifier.

FC3. Asynchronous Execution. When outsourcing cryptographic commands to a potentially much slower coprocessor, we face the problem that the coprocessor execution is asynchronous to the enclave execution. For example, the enclave might be interrupted before the coprocessor finishes executing an issued command by the enclave. Thus, *TALUS* ensures proper scheduling between enclave execution and coprocessor execution to handle asynchronous execution by storing secrets in the special-purpose registers and encrypting them during interrupts, preventing the register content from leaking through unprotected buffers. Interrupts already require a significant amount of microcode execution in the CPU, e.g., SGX stores registers in the SSA and resets the register values to non-secret values. Hence, adding encryption is feasible in microcode.

5   TALUS Implementation

This section briefly introduces the implementation details of a proof-of-concept of *TALUS* based on SGX and a hardware TPM. An in-depth discussion is available in the extended version [11]. We show the functionality and all the security guarantees using the Intel SGX emulator [45] and a hardware TPM, allowing us to implement the entire design of *TALUS*. For the performance evaluation, we instead use a hardware SGX enclave in combination with the same hardware TPM, with the limitation that the communication channel is not protected against a malicious OS. All evaluations are performed on an Intel i7-7820X running Ubuntu 16.04.04 with kernel 5.0.0. As the TPM, we use an Infineon SLB 9670 that supports TPM 2.0 (HTPM). The size of the enclave used for performance evaluation is 52 kB.

5.1   Connecting SGX and TPM

Channel Between SGX and TPM (SC1). Typically, the OS provides the TPM as an MMIO device to the system and user-space software. However, *TALUS cannot* rely on the untrusted OS for communication. For our proof-of-concept implementation, we rely on the end-to-end encrypted programmed I/O channel between the CPU and the hardware TPM. To prevent untrusted system software from interfering with the channel, we distinguish between MMIO and DMA requests. The channel is controlled by Intel TXT using an access control mechanism called *Locality* offered by the TPM through *TPM Locality Address Mapping* [31]. TPM localities indicate the source of the command within the platform. Locality 0 is full public access, locality 1 is the OS, and higher localities (up to locality 4) correspond to the highest privilege levels, *i.e.*, hardware and microcode, including SGX. In *TALUS*, localities ensure the vertical access control to the TPM (e.g., software, OS), while command authorization (cf. Sect. sec:integration) ensures the horizontal access control (*i.e.*, different enclaves).

The channel directly stores data in the CPU registers. Cole and Prakash [15] showed that, in addition to general-purpose registers, sensitive data can also be stored in the Intel MPX bnd registers. As Linux or GCC no longer supports Intel MPX [60], these registers can be used by an enclave without conflicting with any other existing software.

Interrupt Handling (FC3). On an interrupt, SGX performs an *Asynchronous Enclave Exit* (AEX) to save the enclave execution state in the *State Save Area* (SSA) before invoking the OS exception handling. Although architecturally secure, RIDL [63], ZombieLoad [64], and ÆPIC [4] showed that storing registers in the SSA leaves copies of the values in internal CPU buffers from where they can be leaked. Forcing SGX to dump registers to the SSA is always possible, as an attacker can inject interrupts at any time during enclave execution [70].

TALUS does not allow the registers (BND0-BND3) holding potentially secret data to be saved directly to the SSA. In our proof-of-concept implementation, we encrypt the registers on EEXIT, EREMOVE, or AEX before storing them. We use

AES in counter mode, with the SGX sealing key as the encryption key and the number of asynchronous exits as the counter. Using the number of asynchronous exits as a counter has the advantage that an attacker has only one shot at leaking the (encrypted) secret, and the attacker cannot even detect if the secret has changed between two interrupts [44].

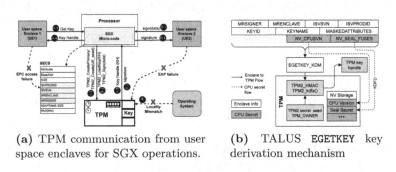

(a) TPM communication from user space enclaves for SGX operations.

(b) TALUS EGETKEY key derivation mechanism

Fig. 1. Design and implementation of TALUS

As computations with secrets often require multiple general-purpose or SIMD registers [18,55], it is also beneficial to prevent other registers from spilling secrets into the SSA. Similarly to protecting enclaves from traditional side-channel attacks, we see that responsibility with the enclave developer. Without *TALUS*, a developer cannot write code so that secrets are not leaked through transient-execution attacks. If TSX is available, it is possible to protect intermediate results from spilling into the architectural domain by relying on a compiler extension [21]. However, since TSX is deprecated, transient execution can be used as a (less efficient) alternative, as shown in recent work [64,73,77].

5.2 Porting SGX Functionality to TPM

In this section, we demonstrate that SGX functionality can be mapped to the TPM using command authorization.

TPM Command Mapping (FC1). Figure 1.a shows the *TALUS* workflow to use the TPM as the backend for the SGX SDK functions that handle keys. Other operations, such as reading a persistent counter from the TPM, follow the same idea. For persistent secure storage of the wrapped keys, an enclave can rely on the OS to store the data on the hard disk. Creating and using counters is similar to key handling. As TPM counters are implemented in the TPM's NVM, creating a new counter equals creating a new dedicated NVM space with TPM_NVDefineSpace and returning a handle to the enclave. Via this handle, the enclave can read or increment the TPM-managed counter. To retrieve the time, TPM's GetTime or Readclock can be used. TPM provides a secure clock signal with the granularity of 30 ns (LPC bus bandwidth is 33 MHz).

For key handling, TPM offers adequate secrets and functionalities to achieve the same bindings of keys as SGX (cf. Fig. 1.b). For example, TPM's TPM2_OWNERSHIP can replace the SGX OWNERSHIP or the CPU can share the CPUSVN with the TPM that can be used as KDF input (Fig. 1.b). TPM-generated keys can be bound to the specific TPMs through TPM secret seeds (i.e., TPM2_CreatePrimary or TPM2_Create for non-migratable keys). To bind generated keys in *TALUS* to both CPU and TPM, SGX sends a secret derived from SEAL_FUSES to the TPM as input to the TPM key generation. Other enclave-related information are available in the SECS created by SGX for every enclave. More details on the command mapping between SGX and TPM are available in the extended version [11].

Enclave Authorization (SC2). *TALUS* uses TPM's extended authorization policies (EAP) to ensure that one enclave cannot have unauthorized access to another enclave's TPM entities. EAP policies are set during the creation of a TPM entity, such as a key. The CPU in *TALUS* dictates the EAP of newly created TPM entities. It handles the policy sessions with the TPM, supplying the necessary information for authorization from the key-derivation material. With EAP, we can represent the same policies reflected in the key-derivation material selection in default SGX. For example, if a key is created with MRSIGNER selected but not MRENCLAVE, *i.e.*, it can be derived by all enclaves of the same developer, we represent this in an EAP that requires the enclave's MRSIGNER value. When using the key, the CPU supplies the current enclave's MRSIGNER value to the TPM policy session. Only if it matches the value set in the EAP at key creation time can that enclave use the key.

5.3   Limitations of the TALUS Implementation

Our proof-of-concept implementation demonstrates that TPM and SGX are very amenable for integration, leading to improved enclave security (cf. Sect. 6). Our security discussion motivates further research into more secure integration of coprocessors with CPUs. In our proof-of-concept implementation, the CPU uses an end-to-end encrypted channel with pre-shared keys to the TPM (TPM_TakeOwnership). Hence, we rely on a non-compromised chipset to, e.g., prevent cuckoo attacks [58]. A coprocessor physically integrated into the CPU, such as Microsoft Pluton [52], can remove the dependency on the chipset for a secure, authenticated connection. While we did not attempt such a tighter integration for the proof-of-concept in this paper, we provide functional objectives and requirements for a secure integration between a coprocessor and an enclave. More details are available in the extended version [11].

6   Case Studies

In this section, we present two case studies using *TALUS*. We demonstrate how *TALUS* protects the enclave life cycle by storing all long-term secrets in the TPM. We also show how to strengthen mitigations against microarchitectural attacks by reducing the amount of data to protect and limiting enclave restarts.

6.1   TALUS-Backed Enclave Management

Enclave Creation. Figure 2.a shows the two-step process of TPM-backed enclave creation: (i) allocating enclave pages in EPC and addition of code and data to those pages, and (ii) measuring page contents (MRENCLAVE) and verification of the measurement against a signed reference value. With *TALUS*, the TPM creates and verifies MRSIGNER and MRENCLAVE. These operations require hashing of MRSIGNER using TPM commands like TPM2_HashSequenceStart, TPM2_HashSequenceUpdate and lastly TPM2_HashSequenceComplete. The TPM returns the hash of the measured enclave pages, *i.e.*, MRENCLAVE. SGX verifies the measurement of the enclave code (using the command TPM2_VerifySignature) with the reference value signed by the creator of the enclave using the creator's public key. If the values are the same, the enclave creation is successful.

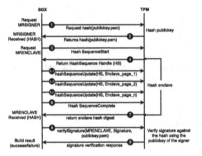

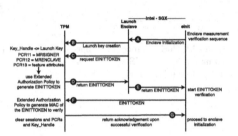

(a) TPM communication from user space enclaves for SGX operations.

(b) TALUS EGETKEY key derivation mechanism

Fig. 2. Enclave-related use-cases for TALUS

Enclave Launch. A successfully created enclave is launched using the EINIT command. Vanilla SGX employs a complex launch-control mechanism involving the LE, which requires a launch key (LK) [16]. By default, the LK is derived using the same key derivation used for sealing keys, and transferred between the trusted runtime and LE via microarchitectural buffers. Transient-execution attacks [7,64] attacked these buffers to extract the launch key. *TALUS* replaces this unprotected buffer transfer by encapsulating the key inside the TPM and releasing it upon successful authorization. We implement the launch control using TPM (cf. Fig. 2.b). The launch process starts when EINIT requests an enclave initialization (cf. Fig. fig:usecaseenclacveverification.b) from the LE. The LE issues an LK request to the TPM with the TPM2_CreatePrimary command. Note that this process can also be ported to Intel DCAP.

The related enclave information from Enclave SECS is passed to the TPM. The TPM creates a key using the EINITTOKEN KDM as supplied by the CPU. SGX also resets TPM PCRs and extends the enclave information into those PCRs (e.g., PCR 11–13). The PCR extension is a well-known procedure used in, e.g., Flicker [47], other solutions for proof-of-execution [59], and measured boot mechanisms [31]. After the TPM returns a key handle, an EINITTOKEN generation request is issued, wrapped in an EAP session using the enclave identity information as policy. Therefore, the authorization succeeds only if the correct enclave information was extended into the PCRs. The TPM creates the EINITTOKEN, an HMAC of the enclave identity information, using the launch key loaded into the TPM. The EINITTOKEN is returned to EINIT (**D**) from the LE. EINIT receives the EINITTOKEN and sends it to the TPM for verification (**F**). After verification, the TPM returns an acknowledgment of success to EINIT (**G**) to proceed, setting the enclave's INIT attribute to true. This enables a ring 3 application to execute the enclave's code using SGX instructions. The used PCRs are reset to their predefined values, which is possible because the code runs at locality 4.

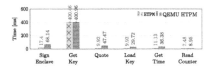

(a) TPM Performance of different SGX commands for TALUS with TPM (average time and standard error).

(b) Performance comparison (in *ms*): enclave management of SGX against TALUS.

Fig. 3. TALUS performance evaluation

Performance of Enclave Management Using *TALUS*. Figure 3.b shows the performance of the TPM-backed functions. Enclave creation, which includes allocating enclave pages, measuring page contents, and verifying the measurements, takes on average 624.16 ms with *TALUS* and a hardware TPM (QEMU-HTPM). Compared to vanilla SGX, which also takes 97.75 ms, this is only an overhead of 526.41 ms. Given that the creation of an enclave is a one-time event in the life cycle of an enclave and does not affect any operation at runtime, this overhead is likely amortized over the runtime of the enclave.

SGX Attestation (FC2). For SGX, attestation is implemented in the QE. SGX employs local attestation to prove an enclave's identity to the QE. The QE uses the attestation keys provisioned to the platform to attest the platform information and the attested enclave's MRENCLAVE. A TPM naturally supports attestation using attestation keys, however, only of TPM-internal data (e.g., PCR values or TPM entities). With *TALUS*, we adapt the mechanism implemented by Intel and AMD for DRTM/Late-launch, where the platform attests with the TPM a small piece of code measured by the CPU. DRTM uses PCR17 of the TPM for measurement attestation. The CPU can only reset PCR17 at locality 4. Hence, a verifier is assured that the attested measurement in PCR17 can only come from the CPU during DRTM. In *TALUS*, we designate PCR21 for SGX attestation and set an EAP on this PCR that allows only locality 4 to read, extend, and reset this PCR. The TPM can attest this policy to a remote verifier to ensure them about this policy. During SGX attestation, the microcode resets PCR21 and extends it with the measurement of the QE (i.e., MRENCLAVE of the QE) and the report generated by the QE. A remote verifier can use the attested PCR21 value to check for a trusted QE and the proper report, *i.e.*, MRENCLAVE and optionally supplied data to the report. Note that the EPID attestation used by SGX [66] is an extended version of TPM's DAA and can be modeled entirely using DAA [6]. Simply extending the enclave MRENCLAVE into a PCR and attesting this PCR is insufficient without ensuring that the MRENCLAVE is correct and reported by a trusted entity.

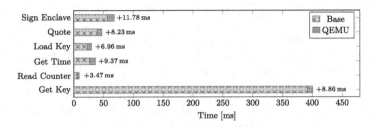

Fig. 4. The total runtime of the commands split into base execution time and the overhead added by QEMU.

Performance of Other Co-processor Functions We evaluate the runtime of Sign Enclave, Get Key, Quote, Load key, Get Time and Read Counter provided by *TALUS*. As a baseline, we measure the time it takes the hardware TPM (HTPM) to execute these primitives. Figure 3.a shows the average execution time over 1000 measurements and a 95 % confidence interval. Communication between the TPM and SGX adds a small average overhead between 0.49 ms (generating a 2048-bit RSA key) and 50.77 ms (enclave signing).

TALUS running with a hardware TPM adds an average overhead of 98.61 ms ± 1.95 ms. Note that the overall runtime overhead of an enclave depends on its workload, *i.e.*, how often these commands are executed.

Data Encryption using TALUS. We evaluate a real-world use case that encrypts data using AES without leaking the key, even in the presence of transient execution attacks (cf. Sect. 6.2). Our application uses a 128-bit AES key securely stored in the TPM, only fetched when encrypting user-provided data. To ensure no leakage of round keys via the SSA [64], we execute the round-key derivation and encryption within a hardware transaction [21]. The total runtime of encrypting 4 kB of data and cleaning up any secret state is 1.66 μs±0.001 μs, excluding fetching the key from the TPM. The overhead from *TALUS*, *i.e.*, securely getting the key, is 58.43 ms±1.45 ms. As a baseline, we compare the runtime to a variant where the key is not fetched from the TPM but unsealed from the disk. This (insecure) variant has an average runtime of 199.21 μs±0.45 μs. Note that the one-time overhead is amortized if the enclave runtime increases, e.g., if larger amounts of data are encrypted.

Since only Intel can implement a native version of *TALUS*, and there is no cycle-accurate emulator that supports SGX, we can only provide an estimate for such a version. Figure 4 shows the overhead added by QEMU for the *TALUS* commands, adding an overhead between 5 ms to 10 ms (avg. of 6.82 ms). This overhead constitutes between 2.21% to 38.77% (avg. of 21.60 %). We assume that commands in a native *TALUS* implementation are around 20 % faster.

6.2   Impeding Microarchitectural Attacks

SGX enclaves are a constant target of microarchitectural attacks [49,69]. The property that enclaves can be started arbitrarily often makes it challenging to write side-channel-resilient code [49]. Furthermore, with transient-execution attacks such as Foreshadow [7], Spectre [39], RIDL [63], ZombieLoad [64], and architectural vulnerabilities such as ÆPIC [4], attackers can leak sensitive data from internal CPU buffers despite side-channel-resilient code.

Preventing Transient-Execution Attacks. TPMs are assumed to be resilient against other forms of microarchitectural attacks since no untrusted code can access the hardware of a TPM. Further, by design, TPM does not release any secret keys managed by TPM to the outside, but only *key handles*. However, sometimes the TPM needs to release secret data to the enclave (e.g., a decrypted symmetric key). With *TALUS*, data is loaded directly into CPU registers. No transient-execution attack against CPU general-purpose registers has been demonstrated [8]. Note that Meltdown attacks were only shown against system registers [8,23] and floating-point and the upper half of SIMD registers in specific scenarios [24,53,67]. Hence, as long as a secret is only stored in, e.g., an MPX register (BND0-BND3), it cannot be leaked using a transient-execution attack. Otherwise, Meltdown mitigations, such as KPTI, would also be ineffective.

Proof-of-Concept Evaluation. As a proof of concept, we reproduce the AES-NI encryption from ZombieLoad [64]. With *TALUS*, we can load the AES key from the TPM directly into the CPU registers without requiring a memory load. Hence, the attack vector used by Schwarz et al. [64] is mitigated. To mitigate the remaining attack vector, the storing and loading of the XMM registers in the SSA, we rely on Cloak [21] to not leak any intermediate results from the registers to memory. We verify that the plain AES key is never stored in memory by inspecting the memory. Further, we are certain that the key is not stored in any vulnerable microarchitectural element used for interacting with the memory, such as the store buffer or line-fill buffer, preventing leakage via transient-execution attacks. However, we cannot exclude the existence of unknown buffers that are on the data path in Cloak [21] and that might become vulnerable in the future.

Limiting Precise Execution Control & Strengthening Countermeasures. Due to the strong attacker model, SGX enclaves can be interrupted at an arbitrary point, allowing precise execution control [49]. With SGX-step [70], enclaves can be interrupted after every instruction, allowing to amplify side-channel leakage. Constant interruptions result in constantly storing and loading of the enclave state, resulting in more reliable transient-execution attacks [7,64]. By design, *TALUS* does not store secrets stored in the MPX registers in plain memory, preventing leakage of these values (cf. Sect. 5.1). While *TALUS* cannot directly prevent precise execution control, its persistent storage can track how often an enclave was interrupted. Although enclaves can detect interrupts via overwritten values in the SSA [12,57], they cannot store this information across enclave restarts. With *TALUS*, an enclave can track the number of interrupts across enclave restarts. Due to this persistent storage, an enclave can refuse to start if it suffers from an excessive number of interrupts.

Generally, *TALUS* allows enclaves to keep information across restarts, strengthening state-of-the-art countermeasures against microarchitectural attacks. T-SGX [65], Varys [57], or Déjà Vu [13] drastically reduce the observable leakage during one enclave run. However, since they cannot prevent arbitrary enclave restarts, leakage is still possible [36]. Using secure counters of *TALUS* strengthens such countermeasures to prevent an enclave from starting if too many abnormal events have been observed during execution.

Proof-of-Concept Evaluation. We implement the restart limitation in the sample enclave of T-SGX [65]. The enclave first increments a counter stored in the TPM and retrieves the current value. This value is the number of times the enclave has been started. Only if the current counter value is below an enclave-defined threshold the enclave continues to provision the secrets. The limit can be obtained from a remote server to increase the number of allowed executions over time gradually. Contrary to the number of enclave executions, storing this threshold in a sealed data blob is possible. A rollback attack would only decrease the number of remaining enclave executions, providing no advantages to an attacker. As the check only happens once at enclave startup, this is a one-time overhead. With T-SGX, the time it takes to create and launch the enclave is $19.66\,\text{ms} \pm 0.016\,\text{ms}$ ($n = 1000$). Increasing, reading, and comparing the timer with *TALUS* takes on average $17.45\,\text{ms} \pm 0.23\,\text{ms}$.

7   Other Platforms

TALUS shows how a co-processor can be integrated with a TEE on x86. Other platforms, such as ARM and RISC-V, can also benefit from our requirement analysis. For example, ARM TrustZone supports co-processors such as Google Titan or Apple T2 but with limited use cases such as disk encryption, key generation or encryption. On RISC-V, Keystone Enclaves and RoCC (Rocket chip coprocessor) are available on the Boom core [10] and Rocket core [2]. Hence, also on RISC-V, integrating the co-processor with enclaves can provide better security guarantees. A detailed discussion on how other platform can benefit from a TALUS implementation is available in the extended version [11].

8   Conclusion

We showed that secure enclaves, such as SGX, can benefit from secure coprocessors, such as a TPM, if they are securely integrated. With *TALUS*, we presented a design that supports secure side-channel-resilient communication between TEEs and cryptographic coprocessors. We presented a proof-of-concept implementation based on a hardware TPM and SGX, demonstrating how a TPM can protect the SGX infrastructure credentials during enclave building and launching, and how such a design impedes microarchitectural attacks on SGX. From our prototype, we derive crucial requirements for secure integration between TEEs and coprocessors. We believe that the identified and solved challenges leading to our design of *TALUS* are valuable for future systems, such as integrating Microsoft's Pluton with enclaves, and can be transferred to other combinations of enclave technology and coprocessors, such as AMD PSP or ARM TrustZone.

References

1. Arm Limited: The trustzone hardware architecture (2021). https://developer. arm.com/documentation/100935/0100/The-TrustZone-hardware-architecture-? lang=en. Accessed 05 Jan 2021
2. Asanović, K., et al.: The rocket chip generator. Tech. rep., EECS Department, University of California, Berkeley, April 2016. http://www2.eecs.berkeley.edu/Pubs/ TechRpts/2016/EECS-2016-17.html
3. Boone, J.: Tpm genie: attacking the hardware root of trust for less than $50 (2018). Acessed 13 Feb 2019
4. Borrello, P., et al.: ÆPIC Leak: Architecturally leaking uninitialized data from the microarchitecture. In: USENIX Security 22 (2022)
5. Bourgeat, T., et al.: Mi6: Secure enclaves in a speculative out-of-order processor. In: MICRO '52 (2019)
6. Brickell, E., Li, J.: Enhanced privacy id: a direct anonymous attestation scheme with enhanced revocation capabilities. IEEE Trans. Dependable Secure Comput. (2012)
7. Bulck, J.V., et al.: Foreshadow: extracting the keys to the intel SGX kingdom with transient out-of-order execution. In: 27th USENIX Security Symposium (USENIX Security 18) (2018)
8. Canella, C., et al.: A systematic evaluation of transient execution attacks and defenses. In: USENIX Security Symposium (2019)
9. Canella, C., et al.: Fallout: Leaking data on meltdown-resistant cpus. In: CCS (2019)
10. Celio, C., et al.: Boom v2: an open-source out-of-order risc-v core. Tech. rep., EECS Department, University of California, Berkeley, September 2017. http:// www2.eecs.berkeley.edu/Pubs/TechRpts/2017/EECS-2017-157.html
11. Chakraborty, D., Schwarz, M., Bugiel, S.: Talus: Reinforcing tee confidentiality with cryptographic coprocessors (technical report) (2023)
12. Chen, G., et al.: Defeating Speculative-Execution Attacks on SGX with HyperRace. In: Dependable and Secure Computing (DSC) (2019)
13. Chen, S., Zhang, X., Reiter, M.K., Zhang, Y.: Detecting privileged side-channel attacks in shielded execution with déjà vu. In: AsiaCCS (2017)
14. Cloosters, T., Rodler, M., Davi, L.: Teerex: discovery and exploitation of memory corruption vulnerabilities in {SGX} enclaves. In: USENIX Security Symposium (2020)

15. Cole, M., Prakash, A.: Simplex: repurposing intel memory protection extensions for information hiding. arXiv:2009.06490 (2020)
16. Costan, V., Devadas, S.: Intel sgx explained. IACR Cryptology ePrint Archive (2016)
17. Futral, W., Greene, J.: Intel Trusted Execution Technology for Server Platforms: A Guide to More Secure Datacenters, 1st edn. Apress, Berkely, CA, USA (2013)
18. Garmany, B., Müller, T.: PRIME: private RSA infrastructure for memory-less encryption. In: ACSAC (2013)
19. Google: Tpm usage - the chromium project (2019). https://www.chromium.org/developers/design-documents/tpm-usage
20. Greene, James: Intel® smi transfer monitor (stm) user guide (2016). https://firmware.intel.com/content/smi-transfer-monitor-stm
21. Gruss, D., et al.: Strong and efficient cache side-channel protection using hardware transactional memory. In: USENIX Security Symposium (2017)
22. Han, S., Shin, W., Park, J.H., Kim, H.: A bad dream: subverting trusted platform module while you are sleeping. In: USENIX Security 18 (2018)
23. Intel: Rogue system register read (2018). https://software.intel.com/content/www/us/en/develop/articles/software-security-guidance/advisory-guidance/rogue-system-register-read.html
24. Intel: Vector Register Sampling/CVE-2020-0548/INTEL-SA-OO329 (2020). https://software.intel.com/content/www/us/en/develop/articles/software-security-guidance/advisory-guidance/vector-register-sampling.html
25. Intel Corporation: Strengthening security with intel®platform trust technology (2014). https://www.intel.com/content/dam/www/public/us/en/documents/white-papers/enterprise-security-platform-trust-technology-white-paper.pdf
26. Intel Corporation: Intel® 64 and ia-32 architectures software developer's manual (2016).   https://www.intel.com/content/dam/www/public/us/en/documents/manuals/64-ia-32-architectures-software-developer-instruction-set-reference-manual-325383.pdf
27. Intel Corporation: Intel® software guard extensions (intel sgx) (2016). https://software.intel.com/en-us/sgx. Accessed 15 July 2019
28. Intel Corporation: Intel converged security and management engine (intel csme) (2020). https://www.intel.com/content/dam/www/public/us/en/security-advisory/documents/intel-csme-security-white-paper.pdf
29. Intel Corporation: Intel-sa-00219 sgx sw developer guidance (2020). https://www.intel.com/content/dam/www/public/us/en/security-advisory/documents/the-intel-csme-dam-vulnerability-cve-2018-3659-and-cve-2018-3643-whitepaper.pdf. Accessed 11 Dec 2021
30. Intel Corporation: The intel® converged security and management engine iommu hardware issue - cve-2019-0090 and cve-2020-0566 (2020). https://www.intel.com/content/dam/www/public/us/en/security-advisory/documents/cve-2019-0090-whitepaper.pdf. Accessed 11 Dec 2021
31. Intel Corporation: Intel® trusted execution technology (intel® txt) software development guide measured launch environment developer's guide (2021). http://www.intel.com/content/www/us/en/software-developers/intel-txt-software-development-guide.html
32. Intel Corporation: Unable to find alternatives to monotonic counter application programming interfaces (apis) in intel® software guard extensions (intel® sgx) for linux* to prevent sealing rollback attacks (2021). https://www.intel.com/content/www/us/en/support/articles/000057968/software/intel-security-products.html. Accessed 10 Jan 2022

33. Intel Corporation: Xucode: An innovative technology for implementing complex instruction flows (2021). https://software.intel.com/content/www/us/en/develop/articles/software-security-guidance/secure-coding/xucode-implementing-complex-instruction-flows.html
34. Intel Corporation: Kvm sgx (2022). https://github.com/intel/kvm-sgx. Accessed 01 June 2020
35. Intel Corporation: Qemu sgx (2022). https://github.com/intel/qemu-sgx. Accessed 01 June 2020
36. Jiang, J., Soriente, C., Karame, G.: Monitoring performance metrics is not enough to detect side-channel attacks on intel sgx. arXiv:2011.14599 (2020)
37. Kauer, B.: Oslo: improving the security of trusted computing. In: Proceedings 16th USENIX Security Symposium (SEC '07). USENIX Association (2007)
38. Kenjar, Z., et al.: V0LTpwn: attacking x86 processor integrity from software. In: USENIX Security Symposium (2020)
39. Kocher, P., et al.: Spectre attacks: exploiting speculative execution. In: 2019 IEEE Symposium on Security and Privacy (SP) (2019)
40. Lawson, N.: Tpm hardware attacks July 2007. https://rdist.root.org/2007/07/16/tpm-hardware-attacks/. Accessed 06 Aug 2018
41. Lee, D., Jung, D., Fang, I.T., Tsai, C.C., Popa, R.A.: An off-chip attack on hardware enclaves via the memory bus. In: USENIX Security 20 (2020)
42. Lee, D., Kohlbrenner, D., Shinde, S., Asanović, K., Song, D.: Keystone: an open framework for architecting trusted execution environments. In: Proceedings of the Fifteenth European Conference on Computer Systems (2020). https://dl.acm.org/doi/abs/10.1145/3342195.3387532
43. Lee, J., et al.: Hacking in darkness: return-oriented programming against secure enclaves. In: USENIX Security Symposium (2017)
44. Li, M., Zhang, Y., Wang, H., Li, K., Cheng, Y.: CIPHERLEAKS: breaking constant-time cryptography on AMD SEV via the ciphertext side channel. In: USENIX Security Symposium (2021)
45. M., J.: Virtualizing intel® software guard extensions with kvm and qemu (2019). https://software.intel.com/en-us/articles/virtualizing-intel-software-guard-extensions-with-kvm-and-qemu. Accessed 01 June 2020
46. Matetic, S., et al.: ROTE: rollback protection for trusted execution. In: Proceedings 26th USENIX Security Symposium (SEC' 17). usenix (2017)
47. McCune, J.M., Parno, B.J., Perrig, A., Reiter, M.K., Isozaki, H.: Flicker: An execution infrastructure for tcb minimization. SIGOPS Oper. Syst, Rev (2008)
48. McKeen, F., et al.: Innovative instructions and software model for isolated execution. Hasp@ isca 10(1) (2013)
49. Michael Schwarz, D.G.: How trusted execution environments fuel research on microarchitectural attacks. In: Security & Privacy (2020)
50. Schwarz, M., Samuel Weiser, D.G.: Practical enclave malware with intel SGX. In: DIMVA (2019)
51. Microsoft Corporation: Bitlocker (2018). https://docs.microsoft.com/en-us/windows/security/information-protection/bitlocker/bitlocker-overview
52. Microsoft Corporation: Meet the microsoft pluton processor - the security chip designed for the future of windows pcs (2021). https://www.microsoft.com/security/blog/2020/11/17/meet-the-microsoft-pluton-processor-the-security-chip-designed-for-the-future-of-windows-pcs/
53. Moghimi, D., et al.: Medusa: microarchitectural data leakage via automated attack synthesis. In: USENIX Security Symposium (2020)

54. Moghimi, D., et al.: TPM-FAIL: TPM meets timing and lattice attacks. In: 29th USENIX Security Symposium (USENIX Security 20) (2020)
55. Müller, T., Freiling, F.C., Dewald, A.: Tresor runs encryption securely outside ram. In: USENIX Security Symposium (2011)
56. Murdock, K., et al.: Plundervolt: software-based fault injection attacks against Intel SGX. In: S&P (2020)
57. Oleksenko, O., Trach, B., Krahn, R., Silberstein, M., Fetzer, C.: Varys: protecting SGX enclaves from practical side-channel attacks. In: USENIX ATC (2018)
58. Parno, B.: Bootstrapping trust in a "trusted" platform. In: Proceedings of the 3rd Conference on Hot Topics in Security. HOTSEC'08 (2008)
59. Perez, R., Sailer, R., van Doorn, L., et al.: vtpm: virtualizing the trusted platform module. In: USENIX Security 06, pp. 305–320 (2006)
60. Phoronix: Intel MPX Support Is Dead With Linux 5.6 (2020). https://www.phoronix.com/scan.php?page=news_item&px=Intel-MPX-Is-Dead
61. Qiu, P., Wang, D., Lyu, Y., Qu, G.: Voltjockey: breaching trustzone by software-controlled voltage manipulation over multi-core frequencies. In: Proceedings of the 2019 ACM CCS 2019 (2019)
62. Ragab, H., et al.: CrossTalk: speculative data leaks across cores are real. In: S&P (2021)
63. van Schaik, S., et al.: RIDL: Rogue in-flight data load. In: S&P, May 2019
64. Schwarz, M., et al.: ZombieLoad: cross-privilege-boundary data sampling. In: CCS (2019)
65. Shih, M.W., Lee, S., Kim, T., Peinado, M.: T-SGX: eradicating controlled-channel attacks against enclave programs. In: NDSS (2017)
66. Johnson, S., Scarlata, V., Rozas, C., Brickell, E., Mckeen, F.: Intel software guard extensions: epid provisioning and attestation services (2016). https://software.intel.com/sites/default/files/managed/57/0e/ww10-2016-sgx-provisioning-and-attestation-final.pdf
67. Stecklina, J., Prescher, T.: LazyFP: leaking FPU register state using microarchitectural side-channels (2018). arXiv:1806.07480
68. Trusted Computing Group: Tpm 2.0 library specification (2016). https://trustedcomputinggroup.org/resource/tpm-library-specification/
69. Van Bulck, J.: Microarchitectural Side-Channel Attacks for Privileged Software Adversaries. Ph.D. thesis, KU Leuven (2020)
70. Van Bulck, J., Piessens, F., Strackx, R.: Sgx-step: a practical attack framework for precise enclave execution control. In: SysTEX'17 (2017)
71. Van Bulck, J., et al.: A tale of two worlds: assessing the vulnerability of enclave shielding runtimes. In: CCS (2019)
72. Van Bulck, J., et al.: LVI: hijacking transient execution through microarchitectural load value injection. In: S&P (2020)
73. Wampler, J., Martiny, I., Wustrow, E.: Exspectre: hiding malware in speculative execution. In: NDSS (2019)
74. Weichbrodt, N., Kurmus, A., Pietzuch, P., Kapitza, R.: AsyncShock: exploiting synchronisation bugs in intel SGX enclaves. In: ESORICS (2016)
75. Xu, Y., Cui, W., Peinado, M.: Controlled-channel attacks: deterministic side channels for untrusted operating systems. In: ssp15. IEEE Computer Society (2015)
76. Zhang, F., Zhang, H.: Sok: a study of using hardware-assisted isolated execution environments for security. In: Proceedings of the Hardware and Architectural Support for Security and Privacy 2016, HASP 2016 (2016)
77. Zhang, T., Koltermann, K., Evtyushkin, D.: Exploring branch predictors for constructing transient execution trojans. In: ASPLOS (2020)

Practical Construction for Secure Trick-Taking Games Even with Cards Set Aside

Rohann Bella[1] , Xavier Bultel[1] , Céline Chevalier[2]([✉]) ,
Pascal Lafourcade[3] , and Charles Olivier-Anclin[1,3,4]

[1] INSA Centre Val de Loire, Laboratoire d'informatique fondamental d'Orléans,
Bourges, France
[2] CRED, Université Paris-Panthéon-Assas and DIENS, École normale supérieure,
PSL Université, CNRS, INRIA, Paris, France
`celine.chevalier@ens.fr`
[3] Université Clermont-Auvergne, CNRS, Clermont-Auvergne-INP, LIMOS,
Clermont-Ferrand, France
`pascal.lafourcade@uca.fr`
[4] be ys Pay, Paris, France

Abstract. Trick-taking games are traditional card games played all over the world. There are many such games, and most of them can be played online through dedicated applications, either for fun or for betting money. However, these games have an intrinsic drawback: each player plays its cards according to several secret constraints (unknown to the other players), and if a player does not respect these constraints, the other players will not realize it until much later in the game.

In 2019, X. Bultel and P. Lafourcade proposed a cryptographic protocol for Spades in the random oracle model allowing peer-to-peer trick-taking games to be played securely without the possibility of cheating, even by playing a card that does not respect the secret constraints. However, to simulate card shuffling, this protocol requires a custom proof of shuffle with quadratic complexity in the number of cards, which makes the protocol inefficient in practice. In this paper, we improve their work in several ways. First, we extend their model to cover a broader range of games, such as those implying a set of cards set aside during the deal (for instance Triomphe or French Tarot). Then, we propose a new efficient construction for Spades in the standard model (without random oracles), where cards are represented by partially homomorphic ciphertexts. It can be instantiated by any standard generic proof of shuffle, which significantly improves the efficiency. We demonstrate the feasibility of our approach by giving an implementation of our protocol, and we compare the performances of the new shuffle protocol with the previous

This study was partially supported by the French ANR project ANR-18-CE39-0019 (MobiS5). Other programs also fund to write this paper, namely the French government research program "Investissements d'Avenir" through the IDEX-ISITE initiative 16-IDEX-0001 (CAP 20-25) and the IMobS3 Laboratory of Excellence (ANR-10-LABX-16-01). Finally, the French ANR project DECRYPT (ANR-18-CE39-0007) and SEVERITAS (ANR-20-CE39-0009) also subsidize this work.

© International Financial Cryptography Association 2024
F. Baldimtsi and C. Cachin (Eds.): FC 2023, LNCS 13950, pp. 166–181, 2024.
https://doi.org/10.1007/978-3-031-47754-6_10

one. Finally, we give a similar protocol for French Tarot, with comparable efficiency.

1   Introduction

Trick-Taking Games. With the development of computers, many traditional games have been adapted into electronic versions. The emergence of the Internet has naturally made it possible to play these games online with opponents from all over the world. This is particularly the case for card games, and it is now possible to play Poker, Bridge, Blackjack, Ramis, Triomphe, Écarté, Euchre or Tarot with human opponents at any time and any place, thanks to the use of dedicated applications on computers or smartphones. While these applications allow users to play for fun, many of them offer to play for money. In this case, there are several security issues to consider, since an application that allows players to cheat would illegitimately make honest players lose money. For this reason, several works, initiated in the seminal paper of Goldwasser and Micali [13], have proposed cryptographic protocols allowing to play cards securely.

Trick-taking games are a family of card games that all have the same structure: the cards are dealt to the players, then the game is divided into several rounds; in each round, players take turns playing a card, and the player with the highest value card wins the round. However, players cannot play any card from their hand and must follow several constraints defined by the rules. For example, in Whist and its variant Spades (which appeared in the 40's), players must play a card of the same suit as the first card of the round if they can. There are many popular trick-taking games around the world such as Belote, Bridge, Tarot, Skat or Whist. Some of them are gambling, and can be played in online casinos, such as Spades, Bourré or Oh Hell Stackpot (a gambling version of Oh Hell).

Unlike other card games, trick-taking games allow players to cheat without it being immediately detectable: since the players' cards are hidden, it is not possible to know if a player respects the rules at the time it plays its card. The cheating is detected later in the game, when the cheater plays a card it is not supposed to have. In this case, the game is cancelled at the detriment of the other players which have lost time and energy. In addition, trick-taking games are often played in teams, and the cheater's teammates must then take responsibility of the cheater's behavior. While this may be embarrassing in the presence of the other players, it is much easier to deal with online when players are anonymous. To avoid this situation, online trick-taking game applications prevent illegal plays. However, to do this control, the application must have access to the cards of all players, which must therefore trust the application by assuming that it is not rigging the games.

Since such cheating is possible with a physical deck of cards, the classical cryptographic card game protocols do not prevent it. In [5], Bultel and Lafourcade introduce the secure trick-taking game protocols, which allows to detect when a player does not respect the rules of the game, without learning anything from its cards. Such protocols have the following properties:

Unpredictability: the cards are dealt at random.

Theft and cheating resistance: a player cannot play a card that is not in its hand, and cannot play a card that does not follow the rules of the game.

Hand and game privacy: players do not know the hidden cards of their adversaries at the beginning of the game, then at each step of the game, the protocol does not reveal anything else than the cards that have been played.

Unfortunately, the security model from [5] cannot be applied to games in which not all cards are used by the players, because the challenger deduces the opponent's hand from the knowledge of the honest players' hands, which is not possible if cards are discarded. This excludes some very famous games, such as the well-known French Tarot, the Skat game, considered as the national card game of Germany, as well as one of the oldest trick-taking games, Triomphe, which dates back to the 15th century and is at the origin of both the word *trump* and many other games, like Écarté and Euchre. As with Spades, for sake of clarity, we choose to focus here on Tarot, but our approach is easily generalized.

Furthermore, the card distribution mechanism of the protocol in [5] suffers from two drawbacks inherent to its design. In a nutshell, each player chooses a secret key sk and computes the corresponding public key pk for each of its cards. It then alters its public key (and other parameters) using a random value, and shuffles the generator/key pairs (with a proof of correctness). At the end of this step, each generator/key pair is assigned a random card thanks to a random value the players need to agree on. The first issue is that this approach is highly dependent on the random oracle model, the second is that the shuffle proof proposed in [5] is not efficient since its complexity is in $\mathcal{O}(n^2)$ in the number of cards, which is 32, 54, 78 or even 104 cards depending on the game.

Contributions. In this paper, we first extend the security model from [5] to cover the French Tarot (see Sect. 4). French Tarot being the most complex of the games with Cards Set Aside, it is easy to simplify our model to adapt it to other games having this property.

Then, we propose two new secure Trick-taking protocols based on a common idea (as in [5], for the sake of clarity, we base one of our protocols on Spades, but it can be adapted to any game having the same structure, such as Whist, Bridge, *etc.*, the other is based on Tarot for similar reasons). Their card representations differ from [5] (and is closer to classical cryptographic card game protocols), which allows us to address both of the above drawbacks. Each card is encrypted by a key shared by all players using a partially homomorphic public key encryption scheme, such that all shares are needed to decrypt a card. To shuffle the deck, the players randomise and shuffle these encrypted cards in turn, then each player is given its encrypted cards, and each player uses its key share to partially decrypt the other players' cards. Thus, at the end of this process, the cards are only encrypted by their owner's key share. This method has the advantage of shuffling the cards directly instead of shuffling keys associated with cards assigned *a posteriori*, so it is no longer necessary to use a random oracle to assign the cards randomly. Moreover, the shuffle is done on a partially homomorphic encryption scheme, and there are many efficient generic zero-knowledge proofs to prove the correctness of such a shuffle in the literature with linear complexity in the number of ciphertexts [2,11,15]. This allows us to instantiate our protocols much more efficiently than in [5], and to propose practical yet secure trick-taking protocols. Details are given in Sect. 5 and proofs are presented in the full version [3]. We also give a protocol for Tarot, with similar complexity (see Sect. 6 and the full version [3]).

The goal is to reduce this additional cost to a point where cryptographic operations would no longer cause delays during the game. The efficiency of our Trick-taking protocols is assessed in [3], along with an implementation in Rust to demonstrate their practicality. Most of the complexity cost comes from the proofs (that everything was done correctly), and especially in the shuffle phase (Proof 1 in Sect. 5). A first improvement is that we can implement two designs for this proof. In order to show the advantage of our approach, we evaluate the performance of our protocols when instantiated either with a specific proof built from the same method (and a similar execution time) as [5] (5.64 s for the proof and 5.72 s for the verification), or with the efficient generic proof proposed by Groth in [15] (234.70 ms for the proof and 175.23 ms for the verification), which is unapplicable to [5]. Provided with a linear execution time, usage of this design makes our protocol practical even if used with more cards and/or more players as its overall complexity is linear in the number of cards and in the number of players.

Related Work. There are several cryptographic protocols in the literature for securing online card games [1,4,8–10,13,16,18,20], but most of them do not prevent illegal moves in trick-taking games. To the best of our knowledge, the only protocol with this property is [5]. It is also possible to use generic tools to obtain similar properties such as multiparty computation [7] or proofs of circuits [12], but these approaches are too generic and inefficient. Finally, another line of research, complementary to ours, studies ways to detect cheating in trick-taking games by analysing the behavior of players [19]. The idea is to determine if a player knows its opponent's cards by analysing its playing style.

2 Technical Overview

2.1 Rules of Trick-Taking Games: The Example of Spades

The traditional version of Spades is played by 4 players divided into two teams of 2 players, but the rules can be adapted for more players. It uses the traditional deck of 52 cards divided into the 4 Latin suits, which are swords (spades ♠), cups (hearts ♡), coins (diamonds ◇) and clubs (♣) and its rules are as follows:

Draw. All 52 cards are handed out equally to each player for a total of 13 cards each. Each player then bids on the number of tricks it plans to win.
A round. The first player of a new game is chosen randomly, the others following in a determined order. The game consists of a sequence of rounds, requiring all 4 players to play a card in turn. In each round, the suit of the first card

played is called the *leading suit* and the player that plays the highest card wins the tricks (the 4 cards played), and starts the next round.

Rank of cards. The cards of the same suit are ranked from highest to lowest as follows: Ace, King, Queen, Jack, 10, 9, 8, 7, 6, 5, 4, 3, 2. The cards of the spade suit have a higher value than the cards of the leading suit.

Priority of cards. A player *must play a card from the leading suit if it can.* Otherwise, it can play any card it wants. Note that since the players' cards are hidden, the other players cannot check if a player is following this rule at the moment it plays the card. We address this limitation (among others) with our secure trick-taking game protocol.

Objective. If the number of tricks exceeds a team's bet, its players win 10 points per trick, plus 1 point for each additional trick, otherwise 0 points.

Most trick-taking games, including Bridge, Whist, Belotte, Bourré, Coinche, Pinochle, Ho Hell and many others follow the same structure as Spades. The differences are in the number of players or cards, the way scores are calculated, the ranking and the priority of the cards. The rules of priority can be complex, requiring cards of higher and higher values for a given suit, or requiring a particular suit when a player does not have a card of the leading suit. However, as a general rule, at the time the card is played, it is always possible to determine which cards should have been played first if the player had them. Our protocol is based only on this property, so it can be easily generalized.

2.2 The Particularity of French Tarot

By describing Spades, we have given a quite general framework, powerful enough to be adapted to almost any trick-taking game. But one particular case has never been addressed: the case where a set of cards is set aside during the deal, such as the dog (*chien*) in French Tarot. The dealing of this game generates another hand: While played with 4 players, 6 cards are put aside in a fifth hand until the bets are over. Once the cards are dealt, the *bids* start. The *taker* (the player that bets the highest) then plays against the 3 other players and needs to obtain a certain amount of points in its tricks to win. A player that does not bid *passes*. If all players pass, new cards are dealt. Presented below in increasing importance, the bids implies various dealing procedures for the dog:

Petite ("small"): the "dog" is revealed to all players and added to the hand of the taker. The latter confidentially sets aside the same number of cards from its hand and puts them aside to form the beginning of its score pile.

Garde ("guard"): same as *petite*, and points earned by the taker are double.

Garde sans ("guard without" the dog): the dog goes directly into the taker's score pile, no one gets to see it. The point multiplier is set to four.

Garde contre ("guard against" the dog): the dog goes directly into the opposing score pile. The score is worth six times the base score.

The deck in Tarot consists of 78 cards of 3 types: 52+4 normal cards (Ace, King, Queen, *Knight*, Jack, 10 down to 2, nearly as in Spades) and 22 *trumps* (from 1 to 21, and an *Excuse*). Excuse, 1 (*Petit*) and 21 of trumps are special

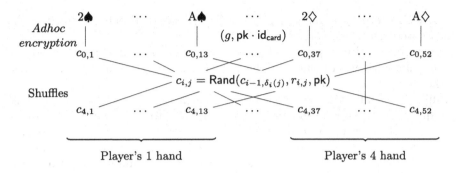

Fig. 1. Dealing cards in our trick-taking protocol. id : cards, pk : a public key, $r_{i,j}$: random numbers, permutations $\delta_i(j) \in [\![1, 52]\!]$ for all $i \in [\![0, 3]\!]$, $j \in [\![1, 52]\!]$.

cards and called the *oudlers*. On a *petite* or *garde*, the taker may not set aside in the dog a king or a trump, except if it cannot discard anything else; In this case, the trumps put in the dog must be displayed. In any case, it is forbidden to discard oudler trumps. Without entering into details of the game, Tarot follows the general rule that at the time the card is played, it is always possible to determine which cards should have been played first if the player had them.

Note that unlike Tryomphe or Euchre, this game has very specific rules giving rise to several particular cases. We treat the case of the French Tarot because its model and protocol can be adapted easily to other games with cards set aside.

2.3   An Overview of Our Protocols

To ensure that honest users can play online while no cheater can proceed for more than one round, our trick-taking protocols (formally presented in Definitions 3 and 4) require the following properties: First, at each step of the game, the previous plays should have been valid for the rounds to continue. Secondly, no player or central authority must have been trusted to reach the first requirement. Finally, maybe the most important of the conditions, the algorithm has to be practical, since a significant computational overhead would prevent any attempt of a player to play the game. To achieve this level of security, we choose a model in which at each round, for each of the played cards, the players must provide a proof for each of their actions, that their fellows verify before proceeding. These proofs have to be *zero-knowledge*, *i.e.*, reveal nothing about the players' hands.

Card Dealing. Before playing, the cards must have been shuffled and drawn (proofs ensuring each player that everything was executed correctly). We use randomisable encryption (that allows to randomise the ciphertext). A first phase (graphically represented in Fig. 1, for a standard set of cards) allows to give each player its (encrypted) hand. A second phase allows it to recover its hand.

Setup. Each player P_i starts the game by (1.i) generating a key pair $(\mathsf{pk}_i, \mathsf{sk}_i)$ from which a global public key pk is generated. The canonical deck (with predefined order) is denoted as $D = (\mathsf{id}_1, \ldots, \mathsf{id}_{52})$. Proofs ensure that the keys were generated correctly.

Generation of the Ciphertexts. Each player (1.ii) computes on his side *ad hoc* randomisable (ElGamal) ciphertexts $(c_{0,j})_{j=1,\ldots,52}$ of all cards in D with the common public key pk.

Shuffle. To shuffle this set of encrypted cards, each player P_i in turn (1.iii) sequentially applies a random permutation $(\delta_{i,j})$ to the ciphertexts and randomise them using a secret random vector $(r_{i,j})$ and the randomisation algorithm of ElGamal presented in Sect. 2.3. Each of these steps is associated with a proof. Cards are now shuffled and distributed in between the players. For $i \in \{1, 2, 3, 4\}$, player P_i receives the ciphertexts of indices in $\{13 \cdot (i - 1) + 1, 13 \cdot i\}$.

Hand Recovery. All players (2.i) broadcast some values $\theta_{i,j}$ (beside a proof) for the 39 ciphertexts they have not been attributed. This allows each player P_i to (2.ii) remove the randomness on the other players' keys on the ciphertexts to recover a vector of ciphertexts only encrypted by pk_i. Its cards remain oblivious to the other players as they are still encrypted with its key. It can finally obtain its cards by decrypting these values using sk_i.

Dog Generation. The rules of a trick-taking game may require some cards to be set aside during the shuffle. To keep these cards secret, some ciphertext indices are associated to the dog and the matching $\theta_{i,j}$ may not be revealed by the players. Unrevealed cards form the dog, based on the rules, they can later be revealed (through a similar process as part 2 of the shuffle), permuted or shuffled with some other cards (as in 1.iii). All outputs of these operations are produced alongside the associated proofs. As highlighted in Sect. 2.2, in French Tarot, kings and trumps may not be placed in the dog unless it is impossible to proceed otherwise. For later use, we define a set $\mathsf{O} \subset D \in \mathsf{Deck}$ composed of the cards id that may not be discarded. To guaranty that rules are followed, one has to prove that none of the cards placed in the dog do belong to O.

Card Playing. How a card is picked is not specified in our protocol, but it ensures that it follows the rules of the game. When player P_i picks one of its cards to be played, it first proves that the played card is indeed in its hand (by showing it matches one of its ciphertexts). Then it shows that the played card follows the rules of the game: if it does not follow the leading suit, it has to prove that none of its remaining ciphertexts encrypt cards that could have followed this suit. Immediate verification of the proofs by the other players remove all potential doubts on the validity of the new play.

3   Cryptographic Tools

First we recall the Decision Diffie-Hellman hypothesis (DDH): Let $\mathbb{G}$ be a group. The DDH assumption states that given $(g, g^a, g^b, g^z) \in \mathbb{G}^4$, there exists no polynomial-time algorithm able to decide whether $z = a \cdot b$ or not. Our schemes uses the ElGamal encryption scheme defined by the following algorithms:

KeyGen($\mathfrak{K}$): Picks dk $\xleftarrow{\$} \mathbb{Z}_q^*$ (draw uniformly in the specified set) and computes ek $= g^{dk}$. Returns (ek, dk).

Enc(m, ek): Draws $y \xleftarrow{\$} \mathbb{Z}_q^*$, returns $c = (c_1 = g^y, c_2 = m \cdot ek^y)$.

Dec(c, dk): Parses c as (c_1, c_2) and returns $m = c_2 \cdot c_1^{-dk}$.

ElGamal is IND-CPA secure (indistinguishable under chosen plaintext attack) under DDH [17], moreover it is *partially homomorphic* and *randomizable*, which means that there exists an algorithm Rand that changes a ciphertext c into a new ciphertext c' of the same plaintext:

Rand(c, r, ek): Parses c as (c_1, c_2) and returns $c' = (c_1' = c_1 \cdot g^r, c_2' = c_2 \cdot ek^r)$.

Our construction also uses Non-Interactive Zero-Knowledge Proofs of Knowledge (NIZKP) [14]. Let $\mathcal{R}$ a binary relation and s, w two elements verifying $(s, w) \in \mathcal{R}$. A (NIZKP) is a cryptographic primitive allowing a prover knowing a witness w to show that w and s verify the relation $\mathcal{R}$ leaking no information on w. Throughout this paper, we use the Camenisch and Stadler notation [6], *i.e.*, ZK$\{w : (w, s) \in \mathcal{R}\}$ denotes the proof of knowledge of w for the statement s and the relation $\mathcal{R}$, and Ver(s, π) returns 1 if the proof π is correct, 0 otherwise.

Let $\mathcal{L}$ be a language such that $s \in \mathcal{L} \Leftrightarrow (\exists w, (s, w) \in \mathcal{R})$. A NIZKP is said to be *sound* when there is no polynomial-time adversary $\mathcal{A}$ such that $\mathcal{A}(\mathcal{L})$ outputs (s, π) such that Ver(s, π) = 1 and $s \notin \mathcal{L}$ with non-negligible probability. It is said to be *extractable* when there exist a polynomial-time knowledge *extractor* Ext and a negligible function ϵ_{SoK} such that, for any algorithm $\mathcal{A}^{Sim(\cdot, \cdot)}$ that outputs a fresh statement (s, π) with Ver(s, π) = 1 such that $\mathcal{A}$ has access to a simulator that forges proofs for chosen statements, Ext$^{\mathcal{A}}$ outputs w such that $(s, w) \in \mathcal{R}$ having access to $\mathcal{A}$ with probability $1 - \epsilon_{extract}$. It is said to be *Zero-knowledge* when a proof leaks no information, *i.e.*, there exists a polynomial-time algorithm Sim called the *simulator* such that ZK$\{w : (s, w) \in \mathcal{R}\}$ and Sim(s) follow the same probability distribution.

4   Models for Trick-Taking Game Revisited

4.1   Formal Definitions of Trick-Taking Scheme and Protocol

Trick-taking schemes and protocols were formalised in [5], but their definitions miss the French Tarot. Here we extend them to cover this additional game while staying consistent with the existing. We introduce a new definition covering both the existing and our work, for that we merge algorithms DeckGen and GKeyGen as it could have been in [5]. Only DeckGen is kept for the shuffle. In order to cover the dog in French Tarot, we also add up an algorithm named MakeDog.

Trick-Taking Game Scheme. In trick-taking games, a card is defined based on two attributes: a suit and a number, such that id = (suit, val) $\in$ Suits $\times$ Values is a card. A *deck* of k *cards* is modeled by a k-tuple $D = (id_1, \ldots, id_k)$, where $\forall i, j \in [\![1, k]\!]$, $id_i \neq id_j$. The set of all possible decks is denoted by Decks. A deck D might contains a subset O of cards that may not be discarded in the dog.

We first define trick-taking schemes, which contain all the algorithms that are used by the players. KeyGen allows each player to generate its public/secret key. DeckGen is a protocol that distributes the cards. MakeDog allows to manipulate a dog. GetHand determines the hand of a given player from its secret key and the game key. Play allows a player to play a card, and to prove that it follows the rules of the game. Verif allows the other players to check this proof. Finally, GetSuit returns the leading suit of the current round. Formally:

Definition 1. *A* trick-taking *scheme* W, *definied as a tuples composed of algorithms* (Init, KeyGen, VerifKey, DeckGen, GetHand, Play, Verif, GetSuit) *executed between m participants is defined as follows:*

Init($\mathfrak{K}$): *It returns a setup parameter* **setup**.

KeyGen(*setup*): *It returns a key pair* (pk, sk).

DeckGen: *It is a m-party protocol, where for all $i \in [\![1, m]\!]$ the ith party, denoted as P_i, takes as input* (sk$_i$, {pk$_l$}$_{1 \leq l \leq m}$). *This protocol returns a deck D and a game public key* PK, *or the bottom symbol* $\perp$.

GetHand(n, sk, pk, PK): *It returns a set of cards $H \subset D$ called* a hand *if the player index n matches the keys.*

Play(n, id, sk, pk, st, PK): *It takes as input a player index $n \in [\![1, m]\!]$, a card* id, *a pair of secret/public key, a global state* st *that stores the relevant information about the previous plays, the game public key* PK *and returns a proof Π, and the updated global state* st′.

Verif(n, id, Π, pk, st, st′, PK): *It takes as input a player index $n \in [\![1, m]\!]$, a card identity* id, *a proof Π generated by the algorithm* Play, *the global state* st *and the updated global state* st′, *the game public key* PK *and returns a bit b. If $b = 1$, we say that Π is valid.*

GetSuit(st): *It returns a suit* suit $\in$ Suits *from the current global state of the game* st, *where* suit *is the leading suit for the current turn.*

An additional algorithm can be added to trick-taking schemes to support a dog:

MakeDog(n, PK): *This is an m-party protocol outputting an updated game public key* PK *based on the previously derived key and a player index n.*

Trick-Taking Protocol. We now present the trick-taking protocol, which defines the order of execution of the above algorithms. It is divided into three phases: keys generation, shuffle and splitting of the card, and finally the game phase.

Definition 2. *Let W be a trick-taking scheme potentially with a* MakeDog *algorithm and $\mathfrak{K} \in \mathbb{N}$ be a security parameter. Let $P_1, \ldots, P_m$ be m polynomial-time algorithms. The* trick-taking protocol *instantiated by W between $P_1, \ldots, P_m$ is the following protocol:*

Keys generation phase: P_1 *runs* setup $\leftarrow$ Init($\mathfrak{K}$) *and broadcasts* setup. *The players set* st $= \perp$. *Each player P_i runs* (pk$_i$, sk$_i$) $\leftarrow$ KeyGen(*setup*) *and broadcasts* pk$_i$.

Shuffle phase: *All the players start by checking the other players' proofs. Then* P_1 *generates a deck* $D \in$ Decks *and broadcasts it. The players generate* PK *by running the protocol* DeckGen *together. For all* $i \in [\![1, m]\!]$, P_i *runs* $H_i \leftarrow$ GetHand$(n, \mathsf{sk}, \mathsf{pk}, \mathsf{PK})$. *Then if instantiated, the players run* MakeDog *based on the derived game public key* PK *and for a common index* n.

Game phase: *This phase is composed of* k *(sequential) steps (corresponding to the number of cards played in a game). The players initialize the current player index* $p = 1$. *At each turn,* P_p *designates the player which plays. Each step proceeds as follows:*

- P_p *chooses* id $\in H_p$, *then runs* $(\Pi, \mathsf{st}') \leftarrow$ Play$(p, \mathsf{id}, \mathsf{sk}_p, \mathsf{pk}_p, \mathsf{st}, \mathsf{PK})$.
- *For all* $i \in [\![1, m]\!] \setminus \{p\}$, P_p *sends* $(\mathsf{id}, \Pi, \mathsf{st}')$ *to* P_i.
- *Each* P_i *then checks that* Verif$(p, \mathsf{id}, \Pi, \mathsf{pk}_p, \mathsf{st}, \mathsf{st}', \mathsf{PK}) = 1$, *otherwise,* P_i *sends* error *to* P_p, *which repeats this step.*
- *If* Verif$(p, \mathsf{id}, \Pi, \mathsf{pk}_p, \mathsf{st}, \mathsf{st}', \mathsf{PK}) = 1$, *all players update the state* $\mathsf{st} := \mathsf{st}'$, *and update the index* p *that points to the next player according to the rule of the game.*

4.2   Security Properties

We now recall the security model of trick-taking protocols introduced in [5]. We give a high-level description of its properties, the full formalism is given in the full version [3]. Note that we adjusted some parts to make them more generic to cover both the protocol of [5] and our Spades protocol (the model proposed in [5] being too specific to the design of the related protocol). To formalise the security of our French Tarot protocol, that does not fall within the general model, an *ad hoc* model is depicted at the end of this section and detailed in [3].

In general, we consider a security experiment where a challenger interacts with an adversary. The adversary simulates the behaviour of a malicious player and its teammate, which we will refer to as an *accomplice* (we therefore consider strong attacks where the adversary colludes with its teammate). The adversary chooses the secret key of the malicious player and shares its public key after the challenger has sent the public keys of the other three players, then the adversary chooses its accomplice, and the challenger reveals the key of the accomplice to the adversary. They then perform the shuffle phase, where the adversary plays the role of the malicious user and its accomplice, and the challenger simulates the behaviour of the other two players. Note that the challenger knows the secret keys of three players, so it can determine their hands, and thus deduce the hand of the malicious user. Finally, the adversary and the challenger simulate the game phase, where the adversary plays the role of the malicious user and its accomplice, and the challenger plays the role of the other two honest players. Of course, the security properties we describe must be proven regardless of the algorithm the challenger uses to simulate the two honest players.

Theft and Cheating Resistance: A protocol is *theft-resistant* when a player cannot play a card that is not in its hand. To attack the theft-resistance, the adversary must make the challenger accept a card that is not in the hand of the malicious player during the experiment with non-negligible probability. A protocol is *cheating-resistant* when a player cannot play a card that does not follow the rules of the game. To attack the cheating-resistance in a trick-taking protocol, the adversary must make the challenger accept a card that is not of the leading suit from the malicious player during the experiment with non-negligible probability, even though it has such cards in its hand.

Unpredictability: The *unpredictability* ensures that the cards are dealt at random. The adversary breaks this property if it can alter the shuffle in such a way that a card chosen at the beginning of the experiment ends up in one chosen hand with a significantly different probability than the usual distribution. Thus, unpredictable holds if no adversary succeeds this attack for any chosen card with a significant advantage. We have slightly modified this property to achieve a stronger version that the one originally presented in [5]. Here, our adversary chooses the card and the hand where it expects the card to be distributed.

Hand-Privacy: The *hand-privacy* ensures that the players do not know the hand of the other players at the beginning of the game. This time, the adversary has no accomplice, and the original experiment is truncated before the game phase. The challenger then chooses two out of the three honest players, and randomly picks one of their cards. To break the hand-privacy, the adversary must guess which player owns this card with a non-negligible advantage.

Game-Privacy: A protocol is *game-private* when at each step of the game phase, the players learn nothing else than the previously played cards. This property is defined by a real/simulated experiment. In the real setting, the adversary plays the real protocol with a challenger as in the experiment described above (again, the adversary has no accomplice). In the ideal one, the protocol is simulated using the public parameters of the honest users only. If there is a simulator such that the adversary cannot distinguish whether it is playing a real or simulated experiment with a non-negligible advantage, then the protocol is game-private. Intuitively, this means that a player could have simulated the protocol itself convincingly, which means that an adversary does not learn anything private during the game. Note that the combination of hand-privacy and game-privacy shows that the players have no information about the other players' hands except for all the cards they have already played.

Particularity of Dog's Security. One would expect a dog (or any set of card set aside in general) to behave as one of the player's hands: it should not be possible to steal (covered by theft resistance), to predict (unpredictability), to influence (theft-resistance) nor learn the cards in the dog (hand and game privacy) at the end of the shuffle. Despite fitting the model in terms of required properties, games with dogs do not allow us to rely completely on what exists. As specified above, the challenger must deduce the adversary's hand from its knowledge of the other three. With the dog, since some cards are not in the players' hands, this is no longer possible. The model must therefore be refined, at the expense of its genericity. Since the hand can no longer be implicitly inferred, we need to add an extractable NIZK of the players' secret keys to the formal definition to allow the challenger to explicitly retrieve the hand of the adversary. A less *ad hoc* model is left as an open problem.

In addition, to empower our adversary we let it decide which player takes and its bet. A second accomplice is also granted. Based on the rules of the Tarot game, the security of the dog should be insured through an additional property. The rules disallow to place some cards in the dog during the MakeDog algorithm. The latter is ensured through a property that we call *Dog security*.

5   Our Spades Protocol

We first define our new Spades protocol based on the randomisation of ElGamal. Here the deck D contains 52 cards, and each of the 4 players hands 13 cards.

Definition 3. *Algorithms of our Spades scheme are instantiated as follows:*

Init($\mathfrak{K}$): *It generates a group $\mathbb{G}$ of prime order q, a generator $g \in \mathbb{G}$ and returns* setup $= (\mathbb{G}, q, g)$.

KeyGen(setup): *It picks* dk $\xleftarrow{\$} \mathbb{Z}_q^*$ *and computes* ek $= g^{\mathsf{dk}}$. *Then a proof of knowledge* $\Pi_{\mathsf{ek}} = \mathsf{ZK}\{\mathsf{dk}: \mathsf{ek} = g^{\mathsf{dk}}\}$ *is computed and* (sk $=$ dk, pk $=$ (ek, Π_{pk})) *is returned.*

DeckGen: *It is a 4-party protocol, where for all $i \in [\![1,4]\!]$ the ith party is denoted as P_i, and takes as input his/her secret keys sk_i and the public keys of all the players $\{\mathsf{pk}_l\}_{1 \le l \le 4}$. This protocol returns a game public key PK, or $\perp$.*
Phase 1:
  - *The canonical deck $D \in$ Decks is initialized by each player.*
  - *Each user parses $D = (\mathsf{id}_1, \ldots, \mathsf{id}_{52})$ and computes* pk $= \prod_{i=1}^{4} \mathsf{ek}_i$, *then for all $j \in [\![1,52]\!]$ each player computes $c_{0,j} \leftarrow (g, \mathsf{pk} \cdot \mathsf{id}_j)$ and set $c_0 \leftarrow (c_{0,j})_{1 \le j \le 52}$.*
  - *For each $i \in \{1,2,3,4\}$, each P_i does in turn: it picks at random a permutation $\delta_i \in [\![1,52]\!]^{52}$, and $(r_{i,j})_{1 \le j \le 52} \xleftarrow{\$} (\mathbb{Z}_q^*)^{52}$. P_i then computes $c_{i,j} \leftarrow \mathsf{Rand}(c_{i-1,\delta_i(j)}, r_{i,j}, \mathsf{pk})$ and generates a proof*

$$\pi_{i,1} \leftarrow \mathsf{ZK}\left\{(\delta_i, (r_{i,j})_{1 \le j \le 52}) : c_{i,j} = \mathsf{Rand}(c_{i-1,\delta_i(j)}, r_{i,j}, \mathsf{pk})\right\}. \quad (1)$$

  Finally, P_i sets $c_i \leftarrow (c_{i,j})_{1 \le j \le 52}$ and broadcasts $(c_i, \pi_{i,1})$.
  - *Each player verifies the proofs $(\pi_{i,1})_{1 \le i \le 4}$.*
Phase 2:
  - *For all $i \in [\![1,4]\!]$, player P_i parses $c_4 = (c_{4,j})_{1 \le j \le 52}$ and $c_{4,j} = (x_j, y_j)$.*
  - *For all $j \in [\![1,52]\!] \backslash [\![13 \cdot (i-1) + 1, 13 \cdot i]\!]$, each P_i computes $\theta_{(i,j)} = x_j^{\mathsf{sk}_i}$,*

$$\pi_{i,2} \leftarrow \mathsf{ZK}\left\{\mathsf{sk}_i : \bigwedge_{j \in [\![1,52]\!] \backslash [\![13 \cdot (i-1)+1, 13 \cdot i]\!]} \theta_{(i,j)} = x_j^{\mathsf{sk}_i} \wedge \mathsf{pk}_i = g^{\mathsf{sk}_i}\right\}, \quad (2)$$

  then P_i broadcasts $(\theta_{(i,j)})_{j \in [\![1,52]\!] \backslash [\![13 \cdot (i-1)+1, 13 \cdot i]\!]}$ and $\pi_{i,2}$.

- *For all* $i \in [\![1,4]\!]$, *for all* $l \in [\![1,4]\!]$, *for all* $j \in [\![13 \cdot (l-1)+1, 13 \cdot l]\!]$, *each* P_i *computes* $c_j^* \leftarrow \left(x_j, \frac{y_j}{\prod_{1 \leq \gamma \leq 4; \gamma \neq l} \theta_{(\gamma,j)}} \right)$, *and verifies the proofs* $(\pi_{\gamma,2})_{\gamma \in [\![1,4]\!] \backslash \{i\}}$.
- *Each player returns* $\mathsf{PK} \leftarrow (c_j^*)_{1 \leq j \leq 52}$.

$\mathsf{GetHand}(n, \mathsf{sk}, \mathsf{pk}, \mathsf{PK})$: *The algorithm parses* PK *as* $(c_j^*)_{1 \leq j \leq 52}$ *and returns a hand* $H \leftarrow \{\mathsf{Dec}_{\mathsf{sk}}(c_j^*)\}_{j \in [\![13 \cdot (n-1)+1, 13 \cdot n]\!]}$.

$\mathsf{Play}(n, \mathsf{id}, \mathsf{sk}, \mathsf{pk}, \mathsf{st}, \mathsf{PK})$: *It parses* $\mathsf{PK} = (c_j^*)_{1 \leq j \leq 52}$ *and the state element* $\mathsf{st} = (\alpha, \mathsf{suit}, U_1, U_2, U_3, U_4)$. *If* $\mathsf{st} = \perp$ *it sets four empty sets* U_1, U_2, U_3 *and* U_4. *Let* $t \in [\![13 \cdot (n-1)+1, 13 \cdot n]\!]$ *be the integer such that* $\mathsf{id} = \mathsf{Dec}_{\mathsf{sk}}(c_t^*)$. *It sets* $U_n' = U_n \cup \{t\}$. *Note that at each step of the game, the set* U_n *contains the indices of all the* $(c_j^*)_{j \in [\![13 \cdot (n-1)+1, 13 \cdot n]\!]}$ *that have already been used by player* n *to play a card. For all* $i \in [\![1,4]\!] \backslash \{n\}$, *it sets* $U_i' = U_i$.

If $\alpha = 4$ *or* $\mathsf{st} = \perp$ *then it sets* $\alpha' = 1$ *and* $\mathsf{suit}' = \mathsf{id.suit}$. *Else it sets* $\alpha' = \alpha + 1$ *and* $\mathsf{suit}' = \mathsf{suit}$. *The index* α *states how many players have already played this round, so if* $\alpha = 4$, *players start a new round. Moreover,* suit *states which suit is the leading suit of the round, given by the first card played in the round. This algorithm sets* $\mathsf{st}' = (\alpha', \mathsf{suit}', U_1', U_2', U_3', U_4')$. *It generates*

$$\Pi_0 = \mathsf{ZK} \{ \mathsf{sk} : \mathsf{id} = \mathsf{Dec}_{\mathsf{sk}}(c_t^*) \}, \tag{3}$$

which proves that the played card id *matches one of the ciphertexts in* PK *attributed to the player* n. *Let* $L \subset [\![1, 52]\!]$ *be a set such that for all* $l \in L$, $\mathsf{suit}' \neq \mathsf{id}_l.\mathsf{suit}$, *i.e.,* L *is the set of the indices of the cards that are not of the leading suit this round. Then it produces:*
- *If* $\mathsf{suit}' = \mathsf{id.suit}$ *or if* $|U_n \cup \{t\}| = 13$, *it sets* $\Pi_1 \leftarrow \perp$ *(if the card* id *is of the leading suit, then the player can play it in any case).*
- *If* $\mathsf{suit}' \neq \mathsf{id.suit}$ *and* $|U_n \cup \{t\}| < 13$, *it generates*

$$\Pi_1 = \mathsf{ZK} \left\{ \mathsf{sk} : \bigwedge_{\substack{j \in [\![13 \cdot (n-1)+1, 13 \cdot n]\!] \\ j \notin U_n \cup \{t\}}} \bigvee_{l \in L} \mathsf{id}_l = \mathsf{Dec}_{\mathsf{sk}}(c_j^*) \right\}. \tag{4}$$

Which proves that the player n *cannot play a card of the leading suit. Finally, it returns the proof* $\Pi = (t, \Pi_0, \Pi_1)$, *and the updated value* st'.

$\mathsf{Verif}(n, \mathsf{id}, \Pi, \mathsf{pk}, \mathsf{st}, \mathsf{st}', \mathsf{PK})$: *It parses* st *as* $(\alpha, \mathsf{suit}, U_1, U_2, U_3, U_4)$, st' *as* $(\alpha', \mathsf{suit}', U_1', U_2', U_3', U_4')$, *the key* PK *as* $(c_j^*)_{1 \leq j \leq 52}$, *and* Π *as* (t, Π_0, Π_1). *First checks if* $t \in [\![13 \cdot (n-1)+1, 13 \cdot n]\!]$, *if not return* 0. *If* $\mathsf{st} = \perp$, *it sets four empty sets* U_1, U_2, U_3 *and* U_4. *Let* $L \subset [\![1, 52]\!]$ *be a set such that for all* $l \in L$, $\mathsf{suit}' \neq \mathsf{id}_l.\mathsf{suit}$, *i.e.,* L *is the set of the indices of the cards that are not of the leading suit. This algorithm first checks that the state* st *is correctly updated:*
- *If there exists* $i \in [\![1,4]\!] \backslash \{n\}$ *such that* $U_i' \neq U_i$, *then it returns* 0.
- *If* $t \in U_n$ *or* $U_n \cup \{t\} \neq U_n'$, *then it returns* 0.
- *If* $\alpha = 4$ *or* $\mathsf{st} = \perp$, *and* $\alpha' \neq 1$ *or* $\mathsf{suit}' \neq \mathsf{id.suit}$, *then it returns* 0.
- *If* $\alpha \neq 4$ *and* $\mathsf{suit} \neq \perp$, *and* $\alpha' \neq \alpha + 1$ *or* $\mathsf{suit}' \neq \mathsf{suit}$, *then it returns* 0.

This algorithm then verifies the ZKP to check that the player does not cheat by playing a card it has not, or by playing a card that is not of the leading suit even though it could play a card of the leading suit.

- *If Π_0 is not valid then it returns 0.*
- *If* suit$'$ $\neq$ id.suit *and there exists an integer $j \in [\![1, 13]\!]$ such that $(13 \cdot (n - 1) + j) \notin U_n$ and Π_1 is not valid then it returns 0.*

If none of the previous checks fails, then this algorithm returns 1.

GetSuit(st)*: It parses* st *as* $(\alpha, \text{suit}, U_1, U_2, U_3, U_4)$ *and returns* suit.

Security. This Spades protocol relies on the unpredictability of the randomness introduced by the players, security of the ZKP and the DDH hypothesis.

Theorem 1. *Given proofs of knowledge with soundness, extractability and zero-knowledge, our protocol is theft-resistant, cheating-resistant, hand-private, unpredictable, and game-private under the DDH assumption.*

For lack of space, the proof of this theorem is given in the full version [3].

6   Our French Tarot's Protocol

We now show how to achieve a protocol that contains a dog through highlighting an instantiation of a Tarot protocol. Adapted from our previously presented Spades scheme of Sect. 5, we need to address the MakeDog algorithm based on the rules of this game. We present this protocol for 4 players and a regular deck of 78 cards. Based on the rules this leads to 18 cards for each player and a dog composed 6 cards. We assume that cards indexed by $i \in [\![73, 78]\!]$ are reserved for the dog and that O contains the cards that may not be discarded in the dog.

Definition 4. *Our French Tarot protocol is defined similarly to Definition 3 (the few differences are implied trivially by the specificity of the rules) except for the algorithm* MakeDog *defined as follows (see the full version [3] for details).*

MakeDog*: It is a 4-party protocol taking as input the index n of a player.*
- *For all $i \in [\![1, 4]\!]$, player P_i parses $c_4 = (c_{4,j})_{1 \leq j \leq 78}$ and $c_{4,j} = (x_j, y_j)$.*
- *For all $j \in [\![73, 78]\!]$, each P_i send $\theta_{(i,j)} = x_j^{\mathsf{sk}_i}$, as well as a proof $\pi'_{i,2} \leftarrow$ $\mathsf{ZK}\left\{ \mathsf{sk}_i : \bigwedge_{j \in [\![73,78]\!]} \theta_{(i,j)} = x_j^{\mathsf{sk}_i} \wedge \mathsf{pk}_i = g^{\mathsf{sk}_i} \right\}$.*
- *For all $i \in [\![1, 4]\!]$, $j \in [\![73, 78]\!]$, each P_i recovers $\mathsf{id}_j^* \leftarrow \left(\frac{y_j}{\prod_{1 \leq \gamma \leq 4} \theta_{(\gamma, j)}} \right)$, the cards of the dog, and verifies the proofs $(\pi'_{\gamma,2})_{\gamma \in [\![1,4]\!] \setminus \{i\}}$.*
- *P_n shuffles its cards with the dog: first sets $c_j^* = (g, \mathsf{pk} \cdot \mathsf{id}_j)$ for $j \in [\![73, 78]\!]$, then let $\mathsf{K} = [\![18 \cdot (n - 1) + 1, 18 \cdot n]\!] \cup [\![73, 78]\!]$. It picks a permutation $\delta \in \mathsf{K}^{24}$, and $(r_j)_{j \in \mathsf{K}} \xleftarrow{\$} (\mathbb{Z}_q^*)^{24}$, computes $c_{5,j} \leftarrow \mathsf{Rand}(c_{\delta(j)}^*, r_j, \mathsf{pk})$ for $j \in \mathsf{K}$ and a proof $\pi_5 \leftarrow \mathsf{ZK}\left\{ (\delta, (r_j)_{j \in \mathsf{K}}) : c_{5,j}^* = \mathsf{Rand}(c_{\delta(j)}^*, r_j, \mathsf{pk}) \right\}$. For all $j \in [\![1, 78]\!] \setminus \mathsf{K}$, set $c_{5,j} \leftarrow c_j^*$. Player P_n sets $c^* \leftarrow (c_{5,j})_{1 \leq j \leq 78}$.*
- *P_n shows that it follows the rules and did not put unauthorized card in the dog by producing the proof:*

$$\Pi_n \leftarrow \mathsf{ZK}\left\{ \mathsf{sk}_n : \bigwedge_{j \in [\![73,78]\!]} \bigvee_{l \notin \mathsf{O}} \mathsf{id}_l = \mathsf{Dec}_{\mathsf{sk}_n}(c_{5,j}) \right\}, \tag{5}$$

then it sends (c^*, π_5, Π_n). If P_n has no choice but to put l trumps in the dog, then it cannot produce this proof. Let $j_1, \ldots, j_l \in [\![73, 78]\!]$ be the indices of these cards. In this case, P_n produces the tokens $\theta_{j_k} = x_{j_k}^{\mathsf{sk}_n}$ and the proofs $\pi_{j_k} \leftarrow \mathsf{ZK}\left\{\mathsf{sk}_n : \theta_{j_k} = x_{j_k}^{\mathsf{sk}_n} \wedge \mathsf{pk}_i = g^{\mathsf{sk}_i}\right\}$ for $1 \leq k \leq l$. It also proves than it cannot proceed otherwise:

$$\Pi'_n \leftarrow \mathsf{ZK}\left\{\mathsf{sk}_n : \bigwedge_{j \in [\![18 \cdot (j-1)+1, 18 \cdot j]\!]} \bigvee_{l \in \mathsf{O}} \mathsf{id}_l = \mathsf{Dec}_{\mathsf{sk}_n}(c_{5,j})\right\}, \qquad (6)$$

and then produces proof 5, with $j \in [\![73, 78]\!] \setminus \{j_1, \ldots, j_l\}$. Player P_n then broadcasts (c^*, π_5, Π_n) and $(\Pi'_n, \{\theta_{j_k}, \pi_{j_k}\}_{1 \leq k \leq l})$.

- Each P_i for $i \in [\![1, 4]\!] \setminus \{n\}$, checks all the received proofs and checks that for all $j \in [\![1, 78]\!] \setminus \mathsf{K}$, $c_{5,j} = c_l^*$. In case P_n has revealed a card, P_i computes $\mathsf{id}_{j_k} \leftarrow y_{j_k}/\theta_{j_k}$ and checks id_{j_k} is an authorised oudler.
- Each player returns $\mathsf{PK} \leftarrow c^*$.

Theorem 2. *Given proofs of knowledge with soundness, extractability and zero-knowledge, our tarot protocol is theft-resistant, cheating-resistant, hand-private, unpredictable, game-private and dog-secure under the DDH assumption.*

This theorem is based on similar arguments as exposed in Sect. 5. The proof is available in the full version [3].

7   Conclusion

In this paper, we modify and expand the security model for trick-taking games. It encompasses the security for a broader range of protocols and enables to put aside some cards after the shuffle and appoint them to a player later in the game. Two new trick-taking schemes with security in the standard model are proposed. These protocols can be instantiated with any proof of shuffle on partially homomorphic encryption, which makes them efficient and usable.

Future work would consist in implementing them in real conditions, with real and not simulated interactions between the players.

References

1. Barnett, A., Smart, N.P.: Mental poker revisited. In: Paterson, K.G. (ed.) Cryptography and Coding 2003. LNCS, vol. 2898, pp. 370–383. Springer, Heidelberg (2003). https://doi.org/10.1007/978-3-540-40974-8_29
2. Bayer, S., Groth, J.: Efficient zero-knowledge argument for correctness of a shuffle. In: Pointcheval, D., Johansson, T. (eds.) EUROCRYPT 2012. LNCS, vol. 7237, pp. 263–280. Springer, Heidelberg (2012). https://doi.org/10.1007/978-3-642-29011-4_17
3. Bella, R., Bultel, X., Chevalier, C., Lafourcade, P., Olivier-Anclin, C.: Practical construction for secure trick-taking games even with cards set aside. Cryptology ePrint Archive, Paper 2023/309 (2023). https://eprint.iacr.org/2023/309

4. Bentov, I., Kumaresan, R., Miller, A.: Instantaneous decentralized poker. In: Takagi, T., Peyrin, T. (eds.) ASIACRYPT 2017. LNCS, vol. 10625, pp. 410–440. Springer, Cham (2017). https://doi.org/10.1007/978-3-319-70697-9_15

5. Bultel, X., Lafourcade, P.: Secure trick-taking game protocols - how to play online spades with cheaters. In: Goldberg, I., Moore, T. (eds.) FC 2019. Springer, Heidelberg (2019). https://eprint.iacr.org/2019/375

6. Camenisch, J., Stadler, M.: Efficient group signature schemes for large groups. In: Kaliski, B.S. (ed.) CRYPTO 1997. LNCS, vol. 1294, pp. 410–424. Springer, Heidelberg (1997). https://doi.org/10.1007/BFb0052252

7. Damgård, I., Pastro, V., Smart, N., Zakarias, S.: Multiparty computation from somewhat homomorphic encryption. In: Safavi-Naini, R., Canetti, R. (eds.) CRYPTO 2012. LNCS, vol. 7417, pp. 643–662. Springer, Heidelberg (2012). https://doi.org/10.1007/978-3-642-32009-5_38

8. David, B., Dowsley, R., Larangeira, M.: 21 - bringing down the complexity: fast composable protocols for card games without secret state. In: Susilo, W., Yang, G. (eds.) ACISP 2018. LNCS, vol. 10946, pp. 45–63. Springer, Cham (2018). https://doi.org/10.1007/978-3-319-93638-3_4

9. David, B., Dowsley, R., Larangeira, M.: Kaleidoscope: An efficient poker protocol with payment distribution and penalty enforcement. In: 21st International Conference, FC (2018)

10. David, B., Dowsley, R., Larangeira, M.: ROYALE: a framework for universally composable card games with financial rewards and penalties enforcement. In: Goldberg, I., Moore, T. (eds.) FC 2019. LNCS, vol. 11598, pp. 282–300. Springer, Cham (2019). https://doi.org/10.1007/978-3-030-32101-7_18

11. Furukawa, J., Sako, K.: An efficient scheme for proving a shuffle. In: Kilian, J. (ed.) CRYPTO 2001. LNCS, vol. 2139, pp. 368–387. Springer, Heidelberg (2001). https://doi.org/10.1007/3-540-44647-8_22

12. Giacomelli, I., Madsen, J., Orlandi, C.: Zkboo: faster zero-knowledge for boolean circuits. In: Proceedings of the 25th USENIX Conference on Security Symposium. USENIX Association (2016)

13. Goldwasser, S., Micali, S.: Probabilistic encryption & how to play mental poker keeping secret all partial information. In: Proceedings of the Fourteenth Annual ACM Symposium on Theory of Computing. STOC. ACM (1982)

14. Goldwasser, S., Micali, S., Rackoff, C.: The knowledge complexity of interactive proof systems. SIAM J. Comput. (1989)

15. Groth, J.: A verifiable secret shuffle of homomorphic encryptions. In: Journal of Cryptology. Springer (2010)

16. Stamer, H.: Bibliography on mental poker. https://www.nongnu.org/libtmcg/MentalPoker.pdf

17. Tsiounis, Y., Yung, M.: On the security of ElGamal based encryption. In: Imai, H., Zheng, Y. (eds.) PKC 1998. LNCS, vol. 1431, pp. 117–134. Springer, Heidelberg (1998). https://doi.org/10.1007/BFb0054019

18. Wei, T.J.: Secure and practical constant round mental poker. In: Information Sciences (2014)

19. Yan, J.: Collusion detection in online bridge. In: Proceedings of the Twenty-Fourth AAAI Conference on Artificial Intelligence, AAAI. AAAI Press (2010). http://www.aaai.org/ocs/index.php/AAAI/AAAI10/paper/view/1942

20. Zhao, W., Varadharajan, V., Mu, Y.: A secure mental poker protocol over the internet. In: ACSW frontiers. Conferences in research and practice in information technology, Australian Computer Society (2003)

Signature for Objects: Formalizing How to Authenticate Physical Data and More

Ryuya Hayashi[1,2]([✉]), Taiki Asano[3], Junichiro Hayata[4], Takahiro Matsuda[2], Shota Yamada[2], Shuichi Katsumata[2,5], Yusuke Sakai[2], Tadanori Teruya[2], Jacob C. N. Schuldt[2], Nuttapong Attrapadung[2], Goichiro Hanaoka[2], Kanta Matsuura[1], and Tsutomu Matsumoto[2,6]

[1] The University of Tokyo, Tokyo, Japan
`{rhys,kanta}@iis.u-tokyo.ac.jp`
[2] National Institute of Advanced Industrial Science and Technology, Tokyo, Japan
`{t-matsuda,yamada-shota,yusuke.sakai,tadanori.teruya,jacob.schuldt,`
`n.attrapadung,hanaoka-goichiro,matsumoto.tsutomu}@aist.go.jp`
[3] GMO Cybersecurity by Ierae, Inc., Tokyo, Japan
`asano@gmo-cybersecurity.com`
[4] Deloitte Tohmatsu Cyber LLC, Tokyo, Japan
`junichiro.hayata@tohmatsu.co.jp`
[5] PQShield Ltd, Oxford, UK
`shuichi.katsumata@pqshield.com`
[6] Yokohama National University, Yokohama, Kanagawa, Japan

Abstract. While the integrity of digital data can be ensured via digital signatures, ensuring the integrity of physical data, i.e., objects, is a more challenging task. For example, constructing a digital signature on data extracted from an object does not necessarily guarantee that an adversary has not tampered with the object or replaced this with a cleverly constructed counterfeit. This paper proposes a new concept called *signatures for objects* to guarantee the integrity of objects cryptographically. We first need to consider a mechanism that allows us to mathematically treat objects which exist in the physical world. Thus, we define a model called an *object setting* in which we define physical actions, such as a way to extract data from objects and test whether two objects are identical. Modeling these physical actions via oracle access enables us to naturally enhance probabilistic polynomial-time algorithms to algorithms having access to objects—we denote these *physically enhanced algorithms* (PEAs). Based on the above formalization, we introduce two security definitions for adversaries modeled as PEAs. The first is unforgeability, which is the natural extension of EUF-CMA security, meaning that any adversary cannot forge a signature for objects. The second is confidentiality, which is a privacy notion, meaning that signatures do not leak any information about signed objects. With these definitions in hand, we show two generic constructions: one satisfies unforgeability by signing extracted data from objects; the other satisfies unforgeability and confidentiality by combining a digital signature with obfuscation.

© International Financial Cryptography Association 2024
F. Baldimtsi and C. Cachin (Eds.): FC 2023, LNCS 13950, pp. 182–199, 2024.
https://doi.org/10.1007/978-3-031-47754-6_11

1   Introduction

Cryptography provides a formal ground to authenticate and secure *digital* data. For instance, by using a signature scheme to sign a (digital) message, the verifier can detect fraudulent activities such as message injections and impersonation attacks, while further providing a mechanism to hold the signer accountable for the message.

On the other hand, authenticating *physical* data (or what we simply call *objects*) are much more challenging. Consider a hardware vendor shipping a microchip to a client. While the client may hold a digital receipt of the transaction, this does not prevent an adversary from substituting the product from a counterfeit. Unless the counterfeit is obviously non-functional, it would be difficult for an average consumer to detect the authenticity of the received product. Moreover, even if the product was non-functional, the client would not know if it was an inferior vendor or if a substitution attack occurred since the sender of the product cannot be held accountable by cryptographic means.

The inability to authenticate objects has had a grave economic impact. This is exacerbated by the globalization of supply chains: since each component of a product can be made in different regions and countries, protecting against substitution attacks becomes increasingly difficult. The OECD and the EU's Intellectual Property Office report that 3.3% of global trade, which amounts to 509 Billion USD, is counterfeit or pirated goods [23] out of which the market for counterfeit electronic is 169 Billion USD according to Havocscope [1]. In 2019, the United States Department of Homeland Security reports the estimated manufacture's suggested retail price (MSRP) for seized electronic goods to be 106 Billion USD [2]. The amount of damage could be amplified if we consider indirect consequences of such counterfeit electronics. For example, a tiny microchip was injected in the server's motherboard of Elemental during manufacturing [27]; the server was obliviously used by the Department of Defense data centers, the CIA's drone operations, and the onboard networks of Navy warships.

While various countermeasures are taken by companies and state actors to digitally and physically secure the global supply chains, there is still much to be improved. In the above example, once a counterfeit makes it into the supply chain and received by a consumer, it seems difficult to detect such substitution within the current systems. An ambitious goal would be to cryptographically secure the supply chains by authenticating objects as we do digital data. In other words, can we use cryptography to formally *prove* that it is difficult for adversaries to modify an object without being detected, while further holding the sender of an object accountable? This is the question we tackle in this work.

1.1   Our Contribution

In this work, we lay the foundation of digitally authenticating objects (i.e., physical data) and propose a new concept called *signatures for objects* (SfO). The combination of a SfO and a standard signature for digital data brings us one step closer to the sought-after goal of cryptographically securing the entire global supply chain: any injection of forged objects and digital data become detectable and the original signer (i.e., sender) of these objects and digital data can be held accountable.

Concretely, we first introduce new tools to formally handle objects in a cryptographically sound manner. To give an idea, an object exists in the physical world while a signature produced by a Turing machine (or a probabilistic polynomial-time (PPT) algorithm) exists in the digital world. Therefore, at the minimum, there needs to be a mechanism to translate objects into digital data which a Turing machine can operate on. While there have been several research aiming to bridge the digital world and the physical world (e.g., [15, 24, 30]) , we are the first to formalize *physically-enhanced algorithms* (PEA)—a new computational model that enhances standard PPT algorithms by physical properties.

With PEA formalized, we define a signature of objects with an intuitive unforgeability security notion analogous to standard digital signatures. That is, (informally) an adversary should not be able to forge a signature on an object that has not been signed before. We then provide a simple and efficient generic construction based on any standard signature scheme. We further explore a potentially relevant security notion of *confidentiality*—again analogous to those considered for standard signature schemes [8]—and construct an SfO scheme satisfying this security notion based on obfuscation [3,4]. We elaborate on our contributions below.

How to Treat Objects. To treat physical object in a cryptographically sound manner, we need to answer the following fundamental questions: (A) how to capture objects in a well-defined way, (B) how to translate objects into digital data, and (C) how to enhance the definition of PPT algorithms to handle objects. Answering these questions will be the main theoretical contribution of our work.

We first define an *object setting* to answer the questions (A) and (B). Informally, an object setting is defined with respect to a *relation function* and a *sensing function*. At a high level, the (possibly non-efficient) relation function decides whether two objects are the same, e.g., two laptops may be considered the same object if they are the same model, or they may be considered different with different MAC addresses for each individual. A sensing function on the other hand takes an object as input and outputs a digital digest of the object. For instance, a sensing function could be a photograph of an object along with its weight, size, and color. The concrete definition of an object setting is necessarily application dependent.

We then define *physically-enhanced algorithms* (PEAs) to answer the question (C). A PEA should capture all the intuitive and natural capability of an algorithm having access to an object. Continuing with the above example, given a laptop, we can consider taking some pieces out from the laptop. Formally, we capture these capabilities by enhancing the definition of a PPT algorithm by further giving it oracle access that embeds an object. For instance, a PPT algorithm can query a bit string that represents, say "open a laptop", to the oracle and the oracle will modify the embedded laptop accordingly. Importantly, only giving handles to objects and not the object itself is what allows to naturally enhance PPT algorithms to PEAs. We also introduce a sub-class of PEAs that we call *sensing algorithms*, whose only physical action is to use the sensing function. More details are provided in Sect. 3.2. With object settings and PEAs formally defined, we are ready to modify standard cryptographic primitives defined against PPT algorithms to PEAs.

How to Sign Physical Data: Signature for Objects. In this work, we propose a new cryptographic primitive called signature for objects (SfO). At a high level, it is defined analogously to standard digital signatures, where the difference is that signing and verification is done with respect to objects. To formally define such an idea, we rely on an object setting, PEAs, and sensing algorithms as defined above. Specifically, the signing algorithm of a SfO is a sensing algorithm, instead of the usual PPT algorithm, which has oracle access to a sensing function: given an object, the signing algorithm can query the sensing function to obtain a digital digest of the object and finally outputs a *digital* signature.[1] The verification algorithm, which is also a sensing algorithm, is defined similarly. It takes a digital signature along with an object as input and verifies the validity of the signature.

Correctness of SfO is defined using the relation function defined above. If the two objects that the signing and verification algorithms take as input are identical under the relation function, then the signature should verify. In particular, unlike digital data where equivalence is easy to check (i.e., check if the bit strings are identical), we require relation functions to check equivalence of objects.

Security of SfO is captured by *existential unforgeability under chosen-object attacks* (EUF-COA security), which is analogous to existential unforgeability against chosen-message attacks (EUF-CMA) for an ordinary digital signature scheme. The adversary is a PEA and we allow it to query for signatures on different objects. However, the definition requires subtle care since we cannot allow the adversary to query arbitrary objects. For instance, we can consider an adversary that queries a device solving factorization in polynomial time. While such a pathological adversary can break any cryptographic scheme based on the hardness of factorization, it does not appropriately capture a practical adversary. To remove these pathological adversaries, we restrict the adversary so that it can obtain signatures on objects that can be obtained by performing some *action* (e.g., turning in some other direction, heating it up) on the challenge object. Specifically, the adversary can only perform actions on the challenge object by means of oracle calls, where the set of allowed actions will be defined by the object setting. In reality, this reflects the intuition that a counterfeit can be created through modifying the original product.

Finally, once all the definitions of a SfO are formalized, the construction of a SfO is simple and intuitive. We provide an efficient generic construction of an SfO signature scheme that satisfies EUF-COA security, based on any standard

---

[1] Recall that the input and output of a sensing algorithm are the same as PPT. The only difference is that it also has oracle access to sensing functions, which allows to indirectly operate on objects.

digital signature scheme. See Sect. 3.2 for the definition of sensing algorithms and PEAs, Sect. 3.3 for the definitions for SfO, and Sect. 3.4 for the construction.

Adding Confidentiality. In some applications of SfO, it is possible that the signature on a particular object gets leaked to the public. If the object being signed is sensitive, e.g., an unpublicized hardware, then we would like the signature to leak no information of the object.

To this end, we consider an additional security notion for SfO called *confidentiality under chosen-object attacks* (Conf-COA security). This is a simulation-based security definition, similar to the semantic security of public-key encryption [13] and virtual black-box security of obfuscation [3,4]. Informally, we say that a SfO scheme is Conf-COA secure if for any PEA adversary $\mathcal{A}$ that, given a signature of some object, tries to guess some information about the data of object being signed, there exists a PEA simulator $\mathcal{S}$ that can succeed the guess without seeing the signature. We then show a generic construction and instantiation of an EUF- and Conf-COA secure scheme by combining a standard signature and an obfuscation. See Sect. 4 for the details.

1.2   Related Works

Relationship to Existing Digital Signature Schemes. Some existing works considered confidentiality for standard signature schemes [8,10]. In our setting, data to be signed is fuzzy (i.e., sensing outputs can be different every time), so there are challenges in applying these technologies to our model. There also exist some works that use fuzzy data for creating signing keys [20,31,33]. However, we sign on fuzzy data rather than generating signing keys from it, so our model is orthogonal to theirs.

Relationship to Existing Physical Cryptographic Protocols. Some works have proposed cryptographic protocols that consider physical actions (e.g., position based cryptography [7], physical zero-knowledge [9], card-based cryptography [21]). These works construct protocols using physical information, but they do not formalize physical things in a cryptographically sound manner. Another related work by Ishai et al. [15] studied sensing as a cryptographic function. We again note that we are the first to formalize physical actions cryptographically.

Implementation of Sensing and Identification of Objects. To realize a signature for objects scheme, we need to implement a *sensing* function which allows us to extract data from objects (e.g., photographic images) with which we can identify objects. We can use object detection/recognition tools as sensing, which have been proposed since the recent progress of machine learning (e.g., [14,18,19,25,26]). Another candidate technique to realize sensing and identification of objects is via a physically unclonable function (PUF) [12,24]. (See the paragraph *Examples.* in Sect. 3.1.)

Supply Chain Security. There has been much interest in supply chain security. Lee et al. [17] showed that a safer supply chain could be achieved at a lower cost by re-designing appropriate management and operational design using information technology. In recent years, research has been conducted using the latest technologies, such as blockchain (e.g., [16,22,28]) and machine learning (e.g., [5,29,32]), to configure more secure supply chains. However, discussions of security in these studies are heuristic and typically there are no formal security models and/or proofs.

2 Preliminaries

In this section, we review basic notation and existing cryptographic notions used in this paper.

Basic Notation. $\mathbb{N}$, $\mathbb{Z}$, and $\mathbb{R}$ denote the sets of all natural numbers, integers, and real numbers, respectively. For $n \in \mathbb{N}$, we define $[n] := \{1, \ldots, n\}$. For a set S, $|S|$ denotes its size. For two strings x and y, $(x \overset{?}{=} y)$ is defined to be 1 if $x = y$ and 0 otherwise. For a probabilistic algorithm A, we write $x \leftarrow \mathsf{A}(y)$ to mean that A on input y outputs x, and when we need to make the randomness r used by A explicit, we write $x \leftarrow \mathsf{A}(y; r)$ (in which case the computation of A is deterministic with respect to the inputs y and r). We say that a non-negative function $f : \mathbb{N} \to \mathbb{R}$ is negligible if for all $c \in \mathbb{N}$ there exists $\lambda_0 \in \mathbb{N}$ such that $f(\lambda) \leq \lambda^{-c}$ for all $\lambda \geq \lambda_0$. "negl" denotes an unspecified negligible function, and "poly" denotes an unspecified positive polynomial. PPT stands for *probabilistic polynomial-time*.

2.1 Digital Signature

Here we briefly recall the definition of an ordinary digital signature scheme. A digital signature scheme DS consists of the following three PPT algorithms.

$\mathsf{DS.KG}(1^\lambda) \to (\mathsf{vk}, \mathsf{sk})$: This is the key generation algorithm, which takes the security parameter 1^λ as input, and outputs a verification/signing key pair $(\mathsf{vk}, \mathsf{sk})$.

$\mathsf{DS.Sign}(\mathsf{sk}, m) \to \sigma$: This is the algorithm for generating a signature, which takes a signing key sk and a message m as input, and outputs a signature σ.

$\mathsf{DS.Ver}(\mathsf{vk}, m, \sigma) \to 1/0$: This is the algorithm for verifying a signature, which takes a verification key vk, a message m, and a signature σ as input, and outputs 1 (accept) or 0 (reject).

As the correctness condition, we require that for all $\lambda \in \mathbb{N}$, $(\mathsf{vk}, \mathsf{sk}) \leftarrow \mathsf{DS.KG}(1^\lambda)$, $m \in \{0,1\}^*$, and $\sigma \leftarrow \mathsf{DS.Sign}(\mathsf{sk}, m)$, we have $\mathsf{DS.Ver}(\mathsf{vk}, m, \sigma) = 1$.

We recall the definition of existential unforgeability under chosen-message attacks (EUF-CMA security). For a digital signature scheme DS = (DS.KG, DS.Sign, DS.Ver) and a PPT adversary $\mathcal{A}$, we consider the following experiment:

$$\mathsf{Expt}_{\mathsf{DS},\mathcal{A}}^{\mathsf{EUF\text{-}CMA}}(\lambda) : \begin{bmatrix} \mathsf{Msg} \leftarrow \emptyset; \quad (\mathsf{vk}, \mathsf{sk}) \leftarrow \mathsf{DS.KG}(1^\lambda); \\ (m', \sigma') \leftarrow \mathcal{A}^{\mathsf{DS.Sign}(\mathsf{sk},\cdot)}(\mathsf{vk}); \\ \text{If } \mathsf{DS.Ver}(\mathsf{vk}, m', \sigma') = 1 \wedge m' \notin \mathsf{Msg} \\ \text{then return 1 else return 0} \end{bmatrix}$$

$$\begin{array}{l|l}
\mathsf{Expt}_{\mathsf{Obf},\mathcal{A},\mathcal{P}}^{\mathsf{dVBB\text{-}Real}}(\lambda): & \mathsf{Expt}_{\mathsf{Obf},\mathcal{S},\mathcal{P}}^{\mathsf{dVBB\text{-}Sim}}(\lambda): \\
\quad C \leftarrow \mathcal{D}_\lambda & \quad C \leftarrow \mathcal{D}_\lambda \\
\quad \widetilde{C} \leftarrow \mathsf{Obf}(1^\lambda, C) & \quad g \leftarrow \mathcal{S}^C(1^\lambda, |C|) \\
\quad g \leftarrow \mathcal{A}(1^\lambda, \widetilde{C}) & \quad \text{Return } (\mathcal{P}(C) \overset{?}{=} g). \\
\quad \text{Return } (\mathcal{P}(C) \overset{?}{=} g). &
\end{array}$$

Fig. 1. The experiments for defining distributional VBB security of an obfuscator Obf. In the simulator's experiment $\mathsf{Expt}_{\mathsf{Obf},\mathcal{S},\mathcal{P}}^{\mathsf{dVBB\text{-}Sim}}(\lambda)$, $\mathcal{S}^C$ means that $\mathcal{S}$ has oracle access to the circuit C.

where $\mathsf{DS.Sign}(\mathsf{sk}, \cdot)$ is the signing oracle that takes a message m as input and operates as follows: it updates Msg by $\mathsf{Msg} \leftarrow \mathsf{Msg} \cup \{m\}$, computes a signature $\sigma \leftarrow \mathsf{DS.Sign}(\mathsf{sk}, m)$, and returns σ to $\mathcal{A}$.

Definition 1 (EUF-CMA). *We say that a digital signature scheme* DS *is EUF-CMA secure if for any PPT adversary* $\mathcal{A}$, *we have* $\mathsf{Adv}_{\mathsf{DS},\mathcal{A}}^{\mathsf{EUF\text{-}CMA}}(\lambda) := \Pr[\mathsf{Expt}_{\mathsf{DS},\mathcal{A}}^{\mathsf{EUF\text{-}CMA}}(\lambda) = 1] = \mathsf{negl}(\lambda)$.

2.2 Obfuscation

Here, we recall the definitions for obfuscation (for circuits) [4] that we use in this paper.

Let $\mathcal{C} = \{\mathcal{C}_\lambda\}_{\lambda \in \mathbb{N}}$ be a class of polynomial-size circuits. Let Obf be a PPT algorithm that takes the security parameter 1^λ and a circuit $C \in \mathcal{C}_\lambda$ as input, and outputs some circuit $\widetilde{C}$ (called an "obfuscated circuit"). Obf is said to be an obfuscator for $\mathcal{C}$ if it satisfies the following functional requirements: For all $\lambda \in \mathbb{N}$ and $C \in \mathcal{C}_\lambda$, we have

- *(Correctness (a.k.a. functionality preservation):)* If $\widetilde{C} \leftarrow \mathsf{Obf}(1^\lambda, C)$, we have that $C(x) = \widetilde{C}(x)$ for all inputs x (in the domain of C).
- *(Polynomial slowdown:)* $|\widetilde{C}| = \mathsf{poly}(\lambda, |C|)$.

For a security notion for obfuscation, we will consider *distributional virtual black-box (VBB) security* [3], which is sufficient for our purpose.

Definition 2 (Distributional Virtual Black-Box Security). *Let* Obf *be an obfuscator for a circuit class* $\mathcal{C} = \{\mathcal{C}_\lambda\}_{\lambda \in \mathbb{N}}$. *Let* $\mathcal{D} = \{\mathcal{D}_\lambda\}_{\lambda \in \mathbb{N}}$ *be a class of distributions such that* $\mathcal{D}_\lambda$ *is a distribution over* $\mathcal{C}_\lambda$ *for each* $\lambda \in \mathbb{N}$. *We say that* Obf *is distributional virtual black-box (VBB) secure for* $\mathcal{D}$ *if the following holds: For any PPT adversary* $\mathcal{A}$, *there exists a PPT simulator* $\mathcal{S}$ *such that for any PPT predicate* $\mathcal{P}$, *we have* $\mathsf{Adv}_{\mathsf{Obf},\mathcal{A},\mathcal{S},\mathcal{P}}^{\mathsf{dVBB}}(\lambda) := |\Pr[\mathsf{Expt}_{\mathsf{Obf},\mathcal{A},\mathcal{P}}^{\mathsf{dVBB\text{-}Real}}(\lambda) = 1] - \Pr[\mathsf{Expt}_{\mathsf{Obf},\mathcal{S},\mathcal{P}}^{\mathsf{dVBB\text{-}Sim}}(\lambda) = 1]| = \mathsf{negl}(\lambda)$, *where the real experiment* $\mathsf{Expt}_{\mathsf{Obf},\mathcal{A},\mathcal{P}}^{\mathsf{dVBB\text{-}Real}}(\lambda)$ *and the simulator's experiment* $\mathsf{Expt}_{\mathsf{Obf},\mathcal{S},\mathcal{P}}^{\mathsf{dVBB\text{-}Sim}}(\lambda)$ *are defined as in Fig. 1.*

3   Signature for Objects: Definition and Basic Construction

This section provides the definitions for signature for objects (SfO). An SfO scheme enables us to generate a signature on an object and to detect a replacement for a fake one by verifying a signature.

We note that in order for this type of signature primitive to be possible, there must first exist some mechanism to (1) extract some digital data from an object, and (2) judge whether two objects are the same or not. (For example, imagine a setting of identifying objects based on photographic images of the objects (taken by a camera) by using some technology of image recognition and machine learning.) In this paper, we assume that such a mechanism is given, and define an SfO scheme on top of such a mechanism. Therefore, we first formalize such a mechanism for extracting digital data of objects as well as identifying objects as an *object setting*, and then give a formalization for SfO. For defining the security of SfO, we would like to consider a class of adversaries that can perform some physical actions on objects. To this end, we also introduce the notion of *physically-enhanced algorithms* (PEAs) that captures such a class of adversaries.

The rest of this section is as follows: In Sect. 3.1, we give a formalization for an object setting. In Sect. 3.2, we give definitions for a class of algorithms that can handle objects. Then, in Sect. 3.3, we give definitions for an SfO scheme. Finally, in Sect. 3.4, we show our basic construction of SfO as well as its proof of security.

3.1   Object Setting

Here, we give the definition for an object setting in which (1) how to extract data from an object, and (2) how to identify two objects, are defined. Looking ahead, an SfO scheme as well as the class of adversaries for it will be based on top of this setting.

Definition 3 (Object Setting). *An object setting $\mathcal{OS}$ consists of $(\mathbb{X}, \mathbb{V}, \mathcal{X}, \mathbb{D},$ $\mathsf{Sen}, R_{\mathbb{X}}, R_{\mathbb{D}}, \mathbb{C})$, each of which is defined as follows:*

$\mathbb{X}$: *This is the set of all objects that can be treated by the sensing function Sen explained below.*

$\mathbb{V}$ $(\subseteq \mathbb{X})$: *This is a subset of $\mathbb{X}$. We will refer to the elements in $\mathbb{V}$ as* valid *and will require that for the sensing function Sen defined below, it holds that $\mathsf{Sen}(x) \neq \bot$ if and only if $x \in \mathbb{V}$.*

$\mathcal{X}$: *This is a distribution over $\mathbb{V}$. When a new object is created, it follows this distribution.*

$\mathbb{D}$ $(\subseteq \{0,1\}^*)$: *This is the set of all (digital) data that could be generated by the sensing function Sen explained below.*

Sen: *This is a "sensing" function that takes an object $x \in \mathbb{X}$ as input, and outputs data $D \in \mathbb{D}$ or the special invalid symbol $\bot \notin \mathbb{D}$. This models some device* *that "extracts" digital information from an object.*

As highlighted above, we require that for all $x \in \mathbb{V}$ we have $\mathsf{Sen}(x) \neq \bot$ whereas for all $x \in \mathbb{X} \setminus \mathbb{V}$, we have $\mathsf{Sen}(x) = \bot$.

$R_\mathbb{X} : \mathbb{X} \times \mathbb{X} \to \{0, 1\}$*: This is a relation between two objects for identifying if two objects are identical. That is, $x, x' \in \mathbb{X}$ are considered the same objects if and only if $R_\mathbb{X}(x, x') = 1$.*

(We note that such a relation may not be efficiently computable in general, depending on a setting.)

We require $R_\mathbb{X}(x, x) = 1$ for all $x \in \mathbb{X}$.

$R_\mathbb{D} : \mathbb{D} \times \mathbb{D} \to \{0, 1\}$*: This is a relation between data.*

We require that this is computable by a deterministic PT algorithm. We also require that for all $x, x' \in \mathbb{V}$, we have $R_\mathbb{X}(x, x') = R_\mathbb{D}(\mathsf{Sen}(x), \mathsf{Sen}(x'))$.

$\mathbb{C}$*: This is the set of "command" functions, which models physical actions to objects. A command function may be a probabilistic function, and takes an object (or multiple objects[2]) as input, and outputs a new object $x' \in \mathbb{X} \cup \{\bot\}$ and some auxiliary (digital) information $z \in \{0, 1\}^*$ about x and x'. Put differently, if $\mathsf{cmd} \in \mathbb{C}$, then $\mathsf{cmd} : \mathbb{X}^* \to (\mathbb{X} \cup \{\bot\}) \times \{0, 1\}^*$.*

Note that Sen can be naturally cast as a command function that takes an object $x \in \mathbb{X}$ as input, and outputs (no object and) data $D \in \mathbb{D}$ as auxiliary information of x, and with this interpretation, we require that $\mathbb{C}$ contain Sen. We also require that $\mathbb{C}$ contain the special command Create that, when invoked, generates and returns a new object $x \in \mathbb{V}$ by $x \leftarrow \mathcal{X}$ (and no auxiliary information).

On the Relationship Between $R_\mathbb{X}$ and $R_\mathbb{D}$. Note that we require that for all $x, x' \in \mathbb{V}$, we have $R_\mathbb{X}(x, x') = R_\mathbb{D}(\mathsf{Sen}(x), \mathsf{Sen}(x'))$. This might seem a somewhat too idealized condition, say if we think of a setting where objects are identified by some image recognition technology based on machine learning, which may not necessarily support error-less identification of two objects by their corresponding data. One possible interpretation of our treatment is that we implicitly assume the identification of objects using solely their corresponding data taken via Sen. For simplicity, we stick to the above treatment, but it will be interesting to investigate whether some relaxation for the relation between $R_\mathbb{X}$ and $R_\mathbb{D}$ can be introduced.

Examples. Here, we give some examples of an object setting. Consider a setting where electric chips are manufactured in a factory. Suppose the chips can be identified with some photographic images taken by a camera using some technology of image recognition (say, based on machine learning). Then, the set of valid objects $\mathbb{V}$ corresponds to the chips produced in the factory, and Sen corresponds to the camera for taking a photographic image. The set of all data $\mathbb{D}$ is then photographic images that can be generated by the camera (i.e., Sen). $R_\mathbb{X}$

---

[2] We assume that the arity of an input is specified for each command function.

identifies two chips x and x' iff x and x' are the same chip, and $R_{\mathbb{D}}$ judges if they are the same in the images taken by Sen. $\mathcal{X}$ corresponds to the way a new chip is produced in the factory. $\mathbb{C}$ may contain any action that can be physically performed on a chip, say turning in some other direction, heating it up, and cutting it into two, etc. (Note that $\mathbb{C}$ could contain actions that destroy an object.)

In another example, where an electric chip admits a physically unclonable function (PUF) [12,24] that can be used for identifying two objects, Sen corresponds to obtaining the PUF-value of a given chip, and $R_{\mathbb{D}}$ will identify two objects to be identical if the given PUF-values are "close" (where the features of the PUF will determine the closeness). Other components will remain the same.

3.2   Algorithms that Can Interact with Physical Objects

As a preparation for defining SfO, we introduce two types of algorithms that can treat physical objects, a *sensing algorithm* and a *physically-enhanced algorithm*, which are both associated with an object setting $\mathcal{OS}$. Informally, a sensing algorithm models an algorithm that can extract digital data from a physical object via a sensing function Sen supported in $\mathcal{OS}$. On the other hand, a physically enhanced algorithm (PEA) models an algorithm that can indirectly interact with objects via command functions cmd $\in \mathbb{C}$ supported in $\mathcal{OS}$.

Our main idea behind the formalization here is that interactions between algorithms and physical objects are done only via the sensing function (in the case of a sensing algorithm) or command functions (in the case of a PEA), and are conducted outside algorithms. Looking ahead, sensing algorithms are a class of algorithms to which the signing and verification algorithms for an SfO scheme belong, while PEAs are a class of algorithms to which an adversary against the security of an SfO scheme belongs.

The formal definitions of these notions are as follows.

Definition 4 (Sensing Algorithm and Physically-Enhanced Algorithm). *Let $\mathcal{OS} = (\mathbb{X}, \mathbb{V}, \mathcal{X}, \mathbb{D}, \mathsf{Sen}, R_{\mathbb{X}}, R_{\mathbb{D}}, \mathbb{C})$ be an object setting.*

- *A* sensing algorithm *with respect to $\mathcal{OS}$ is a PPT algorithm that has access to an object $x \in \mathbb{X}$ given as an input via the sensing function Sen with which data $D \in \mathbb{D}$ from the object x can be extracted.*
  In order to distinguish an object from ordinary (digital) inputs given as an input to a sensing algorithm, we will use the boxed notation. For example, if A is a sensing algorithm and is given an object $x \in \mathbb{X}$ as an input, we write $\mathsf{A}(\boxed{x})$.
- *A* physically-enhanced algorithm *(PEA) with respect to $\mathcal{OS}$ is a PPT algorithm that has access to the command oracle $\mathcal{O}_{\mathbb{C}}$ explained next.*
  The command oracle $\mathcal{O}_{\mathbb{C}}$ maintains a counter c (initially 0) and an ordered list $L_{\mathbb{X}}$ of objects (initially empty). $\mathcal{O}_{\mathbb{C}}$ accepts a "command" query consisting of (the name of) a command function cmd $\in \mathbb{C}$ and optionally a set of indices $(i_1, \ldots, i_n) \in [c]^n$ (where n is the number of inputs that is specified by cmd). Then, it sets $c \leftarrow c+1$, computes $(x_c, z_c) \leftarrow \mathsf{cmd}(x_{i_1}, \ldots, x_{i_n})$, appends x_c to the end of the list $L_{\mathbb{X}}$, and returns z_c to the caller.

We will omit "with respect to $\mathcal{OS}$" when it is clear from context.

3.3   Signature for Objects

Let $\mathcal{OS} = (\mathbb{X}, \mathbb{V}, \mathcal{X}, \mathbb{D}, \mathsf{Sen}, R_\mathbb{X}, R_\mathbb{D}, \mathbb{C})$ be an object setting. A signature for objects (SfO) scheme SfO with respect to $\mathcal{OS}$ consists of the following algorithms.

$\mathsf{SfO.KG}(1^\lambda) \to (\mathsf{VK}, \mathsf{SK})$: This is a PPT algorithm for key generation. It takes the security parameter 1^λ as input, and outputs a key pair $(\mathsf{VK}, \mathsf{SK})$.

$\mathsf{SfO.Sign}(\mathsf{SK}, \boxed{x}) \to \sigma$: This is a sensing algorithm for generating a signature. It takes as input a signing key SK and an object $x \in \mathbb{X}$ as input, and outputs a signature σ.

$\mathsf{SfO.Ver}(\mathsf{VK}, \boxed{x}, \sigma) \to 1/0$: This is a sensing algorithm for verifying a signature. It takes a verification key VK, an object $x \in \mathbb{X}$, and a signature σ as input, and outputs 1 (accept) or 0 (reject).

As the correctness condition, we require that for all $\lambda \in \mathbb{N}$, $x, x' \in \mathbb{V}$ such that $R_\mathbb{X}(x, x') = 1$, $(\mathsf{VK}, \mathsf{SK}) \leftarrow \mathsf{SfO.KG}(1^\lambda)$, and $\sigma \leftarrow \mathsf{SfO.Sign}(\mathsf{SK}, \boxed{x})$, we have $\mathsf{SfO.Ver}(\mathsf{VK}, \boxed{x'}, \sigma) = 1$.

Basic Security Definition: Unforgeability. Here, we introduce a natural adoption of EUF-CMA security for ordinary signatures to the setting of SfO schemes, which we call *existential unforgeability under chosen-objects attacks* (EUF-COA security). Similarly to EUF-CMA security for an ordinary signature scheme, EUF-COA security guarantees that it is hard for any PEA adversary to forge a signature on objects for which they have never obtained signatures. Note that a PEA adversary may generate a new object via queries to the command oracle $\mathcal{O}_\mathbb{C}$, and it is allowed to obtain signatures for any objects in the object list $L_\mathbb{X}$ maintained in $\mathcal{O}_\mathbb{C}$.

Formally, the EUF-COA security for an SfO scheme is defined as follows. Let $\mathcal{OS} = (\mathbb{X}, \mathbb{V}, \mathcal{X}, \mathbb{D}, \mathsf{Sen}, R_\mathbb{X}, R_\mathbb{D}, \mathbb{C})$ be an object setting, and let $\mathsf{SfO} = (\mathsf{SfO.KG}, \mathsf{SfO.Sign}, \mathsf{SfO.Ver})$ be an SfO scheme with respect to $\mathcal{OS}$. Consider the following experiment $\mathsf{Expt}_{\mathsf{SfO}, \mathcal{A}}^{\mathsf{EUF\text{-}COA}}(\lambda)$ in which a PEA adversary $\mathcal{A}$ is executed[3]:

$$\mathsf{Expt}_{\mathsf{SfO}, \mathcal{A}}^{\mathsf{EUF\text{-}COA}}(\lambda) : \left[\begin{array}{l} c \leftarrow 0; \quad L_\mathbb{X} \leftarrow \emptyset; \quad \mathsf{Ind} \leftarrow \emptyset; \\ (\mathsf{VK}, \mathsf{SK}) \leftarrow \mathsf{SfO.KG}(1^\lambda); \quad (i', \sigma') \leftarrow \mathcal{A}^{\mathcal{O}_\mathbb{C}, \mathcal{O}_{\mathsf{Sign}}}(\mathsf{VK}); \\ \text{If } \mathsf{SfO.Ver}(\mathsf{VK}, \boxed{x_{i'}}, \sigma') = 1 \wedge \forall j \in \mathsf{Ind} : R_\mathbb{X}(x_{i'}, x_j) = 0 \\ \text{then return 1 else return 0} \end{array} \right]$$

where $\mathcal{O}_\mathbb{C}$ is the command oracle for $\mathcal{A}$ defined in Definition 4 (which updates the counter c and the object list $L_\mathbb{X}$ upon a query from $\mathcal{A}$), and $\mathcal{O}_{\mathsf{Sign}}$ is the signing oracle that takes an index $i \in [c]$ as input, and operates as follows: it updates Ind by $\mathsf{Ind} \leftarrow \mathsf{Ind} \cup \{i\}$, computes a signature $\sigma \leftarrow \mathsf{SfO.Sign}(\mathsf{SK}, \boxed{x_i})$, and returns σ.

---

[3] We remind the reader that as defined in Definition 4, a PEA has access to the command oracle $\mathcal{O}_\mathbb{C}$ that internally maintains the counter c and the object list $L_\mathbb{X}$, which we use for defining $\mathcal{A}$'s winning condition here.

SfO.KG(1^λ) :	SfO.Sign(SK, $\boxed{x}$) :	SfO.Ver(VK, $\boxed{x'}$, σ) :
(VK, SK) $\leftarrow$ DS.KG(1^λ)	$D \leftarrow$ Sen(x)	If $\sigma = \bot$ then return 0.
Return (VK, SK).	If $D = \bot$ then return $\sigma := \bot$.	$D' \leftarrow$ Sen(x')
	$\sigma_D \leftarrow$ DS.Sign(SK, D)	Parse σ as (D, σ_D).
	Return $\sigma := (D, \sigma_D)$.	If $\bot \in \{D', D\}$ then return 0.
		If DS.Ver(VK, D, σ_D) = 1
		and $R_\mathbb{D}(D', D) = 1$
		then return 1 else return 0.

Fig. 2. The SfO scheme SfO$_1$.

Definition 5 (EUF-COA). *We say that an SfO scheme* SfO *with respect to an object setting* $\mathcal{OS}$ *is EUF-COA secure if for any PEA adversary* $\mathcal{A}$*, we have* $\mathsf{Adv}_{\mathsf{SfO}, \mathcal{A}}^{\mathsf{EUF\text{-}COA}}(\lambda) := \Pr[\mathsf{Expt}_{\mathsf{SfO}, \mathcal{A}}^{\mathsf{EUF\text{-}COA}}(\lambda) = 1] = \mathsf{negl}(\lambda)$.

On Security of Ordinary (Non-physical) Cryptographic Primitives Against PEA Adversaries. In this paper, we will construct an SfO scheme using ordinary (non-physical) cryptographic primitives as building blocks, and in the security proof, we would like to reduce the security of the proposed signature for objects schemes to that of the building blocks. However, one can quickly realize that there is a subtle technical problem: Although the security of an SfO scheme is defined with respect to PEA adversaries, that of ordinary cryptographic primitives is defined with respect to standard PPT adversaries that cannot deal with physical objects, and thus there is a mismatch regarding the class of adversaries. To circumvent this subtle problem, we simply assume that the ordinary cryptographic primitives used as building blocks are secure against PEA adversaries. We believe that this is a reasonable assumption, since ordinary cryptographic primitives are defined (and their security are proved) independently of any object setting. (It will be a ground-breaking finding if there is a cryptographic primitive whose security is defined with respect to PPT adversaries can be attacked if an adversary can perform some physical action.)

3.4   Basic Construction

Here we show our first construction SfO$_1$, which is constructed by simply combining an ordinary digital signature scheme DS and the relation function $R_\mathbb{D}$ supported in an underlying object setting $\mathcal{OS}$.

$\mathcal{OS} = (\mathbb{X}, \mathbb{V}, \mathcal{X}, \mathbb{D}, \mathsf{Sen}, R_\mathbb{X}, R_\mathbb{D}, \mathbb{C})$ be an object setting. Let DS = (DS.KG, DS.Sign, DS.Ver) be an ordinary digital signature scheme. Then, using DS as a building block, we construct an SfO scheme SfO$_1$ as described in Fig. 2.

It is straightforward to see that SfO$_1$ satisfies correctness. By the property of $R_\mathbb{X}$ and $R_\mathbb{D}$, if $x \in \mathbb{V}$ used in signing and $x' \in \mathbb{V}$ used in verification satisfy $R_\mathbb{X}(x', x) = 1$, we have $R_\mathbb{D}(D', D) = 1$, where $D \leftarrow$ Sen(x) and $D' \leftarrow$ Sen(x'). As long as the digital signature scheme DS satisfies correctness, we always have DS.Ver(VK, D, σ_D) = 1, where (VK, SK) $\leftarrow$ DS.KG(1^λ) and $\sigma_D \leftarrow$ DS.Sign(SK, D).

The security of SfO_1 is guaranteed by the following theorem, which is also straightforward to prove.

Theorem 1. *If the digital signature scheme* DS *is EUF-CMA secure against PEA adversaries with respect to* $\mathcal{OS}$, *then* SfO_1 *is EUF-COA secure.*

We defer the formal proof of this theorem to the full version. Informally, if a PEA adversary $\mathcal{A}$ attacking the EUF-COA security wins, then it outputs a valid signature for data extracted from unqueried objects. Therefore, we can construct another adversary attacking the EUF-CMA security of DS using $\mathcal{A}$.

4 Conf-COA Security and Construction

In this section, we introduce a security definition for SfO concerning privacy of objects that we call *confidentiality under chosen object attacks* (Conf-COA security). This security notion ensures that given a signature on an object that is generated according to the distribution $\mathcal{X}$ supported in an object setting, it is hard to gain any information on the data corresponding to the object. This security notion is naturally desirable in a supply chain scenario where an object being signed is a product of a company which itself and/or its corresponding data could contain some confidential information, and a signer would like to prevent its information from leaking from a signature to those who are outside the supply chain and need not verify the signature. We note that this security notion is orthogonal to EUF-COA security.

This section provides the security definition of Conf-COA in Sect. 4.1 and a provably secure construction that satisfies EUF-COA and Conf-COA using an obfuscation in Sect. 4.2. Moreover, we consider an instantiation of our scheme in Sect. 4.3.

4.1 Security Definition: Conf-COA

Here, we give a formal definition of Conf-COA security.

Let $\mathcal{OS} = (\mathbb{X}, \mathbb{V}, \mathcal{X}, \mathbb{D}, \mathsf{Sen}, R_{\mathbb{X}}, R_{\mathbb{D}}, \mathbb{C})$ be an object setting, and let $\mathsf{SfO} = (\mathsf{SfO.KG}, \mathsf{SfO.Sign}, \mathsf{SfO.Ver})$ be an SfO scheme with respect to $\mathcal{OS}$. For PEA algorithms $\mathcal{A}$, $\mathcal{S}$, and a predicate $\mathcal{P}$, consider the real experiment $\mathsf{Expt}_{\mathsf{SfO},\mathcal{A},\mathcal{P}}^{\mathsf{Conf\text{-}COA\text{-}Real}}(\lambda)$ and the simulated experiment $\mathsf{Expt}_{\mathsf{SfO},\mathcal{S},\mathcal{P}}^{\mathsf{Conf\text{-}COA\text{-}Sim}}(\lambda)$ as described in Fig. 3. In the experiments, where $\mathcal{O}_{\mathbb{C}}$ and $\mathcal{O}_{\mathsf{Sign}}$ are the command oracle and signing oracle, respectively, that are defined in the same way as in the EUF-CMA experiment. We stress that the "challenge object" x^* is not included in the object list $L_{\mathbb{X}}$ maintained in $\mathcal{O}_{\mathbb{C}}$ in both experiments, and thus $\mathcal{A}$ and $\mathcal{S}$ have no control over it as well as the data D^* extracted from x^*.

Definition 6 (Conf-COA). *We say that an SfO scheme* SfO *with respect to an object setting* $\mathcal{OS}$ *is Conf-COA secure if for any PEA adversary* $\mathcal{A}$, *there exists a PEA simulator* $\mathcal{S}$ *such that for any PPT-computable predicate* $\mathcal{P}$, *we have* $\mathsf{Adv}_{\mathsf{SfO},\mathcal{S},\mathcal{A},\mathcal{P}}^{\mathsf{Conf\text{-}COA}}(\lambda) := |\Pr[\mathsf{Expt}_{\mathsf{SfO},\mathcal{A},\mathcal{P}}^{\mathsf{Conf\text{-}COA\text{-}Real}}(\lambda) = 1] - \Pr[\mathsf{Expt}_{\mathsf{SfO},\mathcal{S},\mathcal{P}}^{\mathsf{Conf\text{-}COA\text{-}Sim}}(\lambda) = 1]| = \mathrm{negl}(\lambda).$

$$\mathsf{Expt}_{\mathsf{SfO},\mathcal{A},\mathcal{P}}^{\mathsf{Conf\text{-}COA\text{-}Real}}(\lambda):$$
$\quad c \leftarrow 0; \quad L_{\mathbb{X}} \leftarrow \emptyset$
$\quad x^* \leftarrow \mathcal{X}; \quad D^* \leftarrow \mathsf{Sen}(x^*)$
$\quad (\mathsf{VK},\mathsf{SK}) \leftarrow \mathsf{SfO.KG}(1^\lambda)$
$\quad \sigma^* \leftarrow \mathsf{SfO.Sign}(\mathsf{SK}, \boxed{x^*})$
$\quad g \leftarrow \mathcal{A}^{\mathcal{O}_{\mathsf{C}}, \mathcal{O}_{\mathsf{Sign}}}(\mathsf{VK}, \sigma^*)$
$\quad$ Return $(\mathcal{P}(D^*) \stackrel{?}{=} g)$.

$$\mathsf{Expt}_{\mathsf{SfO},\mathcal{S},\mathcal{P}}^{\mathsf{Conf\text{-}COA\text{-}Sim}}(\lambda):$$
$\quad c \leftarrow 0; \quad L_{\mathbb{X}} \leftarrow \emptyset$
$\quad x^* \leftarrow \mathcal{X}; \quad D^* \leftarrow \mathsf{Sen}(x^*)$
$\quad g \leftarrow \mathcal{S}^{\mathcal{O}_{\mathsf{C}}}(1^\lambda)$
$\quad$ Return $(\mathcal{P}(D^*) \stackrel{?}{=} g)$.

Fig. 3. The experiments for defining Conf-COA security for an SfO scheme SfO.

$\mathsf{SfO.KG}(1^\lambda):$	$\mathsf{SfO.Sign}(\mathsf{SK}, \boxed{x}):$	$\mathsf{SfO.Ver}(\mathsf{VK}, \boxed{x'}, \sigma):$
$(\mathsf{VK},\mathsf{SK}) \leftarrow \mathsf{DS.KG}(1^\lambda)$	$D \leftarrow \mathsf{Sen}(x)$	If $\sigma = \bot$ then return 0.
Return $(\mathsf{VK},\mathsf{SK})$.	If $D = \bot$ then return $\sigma = \bot$.	$D' \leftarrow \mathsf{Sen}(x')$
	Let $R_D(\cdot) := R_{\mathbb{D}}(\cdot, D)$.	Parse σ as $(\widetilde{R}, \sigma_{\widetilde{R}})$.
	$\widetilde{R} \leftarrow \mathsf{Obf}(1^\lambda, R_D)$	If $\bot \in \{D', \widetilde{R}\}$ then return 0.
	$\sigma_{\widetilde{R}} \leftarrow \mathsf{DS.Sign}(\mathsf{SK}, \widetilde{R})$	If $\mathsf{DS.Ver}(\mathsf{VK}, \widetilde{R}, \sigma_{\widetilde{R}}) = 1$
	Return $\sigma := (\widetilde{R}, \sigma_{\widetilde{R}})$.	and $\widetilde{R}(D') = 1$
		then return 1 else return 0.

Fig. 4. The SfO scheme SfO_2.

4.2 Our Construction Based on Obfuscation

Here we show our second construction SfO_2. This is a simple variant of our first construction SfO_1, where instead of directly signing the data D in the signing algorithm, we now sign an obfuscated circuit $\widetilde{R} \leftarrow \mathsf{Obf}(1^\lambda, R_{\mathbb{D}}(\cdot, D))$, and the relation $R_{\mathbb{D}}$ over the data D contained in a signature and D' computed in the verification is now done using an obfuscated circuit $\widetilde{R}$.

Formally, our construction is as follows. Let $\mathcal{OS} = (\mathbb{X}, \mathbb{V}, \mathcal{X}, \mathbb{D}, \mathsf{Sen}, R_{\mathbb{X}}, R_{\mathbb{D}},$ $\mathbb{C})$ be an object setting. Let $\mathcal{R}$ be the class of circuits $\{R_D(\cdot) := R_{\mathbb{D}}(\cdot, D)\}_{D \in \mathbb{D}}$, where $R_{\mathbb{D}}(\cdot, D)$ denotes a circuit which has D hardwired, and takes some data D' as input, and returns $R_{\mathbb{D}}(D', D)$. We assume that there is a one-to-one correspondence between a circuit $R_D \in \mathcal{R}$ and $D \in \mathbb{D}$, and D can be extracted in the clear from R_D. Let Obf be an obfuscator for $\mathcal{R}$, and let $\mathsf{DS} = (\mathsf{DS.KG},$ $\mathsf{DS.Sign}, \mathsf{DS.Ver})$ be an ordinary digital signature scheme. Then, using Obf and DS as building blocks, we construct an SfO scheme SfO_2 as described in Fig. 4.

The correctness of SfO_2 can be seen similarly to SfO_1. As explained earlier, the only essential difference of SfO_2 from SfO_1 is that in the former, the check of $R_{\mathbb{D}}(D', D)$ is done using the obfuscated circuit $\widetilde{R}$ which is computed as $\widetilde{R} \leftarrow \mathsf{Obf}(1^\lambda, R_D)$ and $R_D(\cdot) := R_{\mathbb{D}}(\cdot, D)$. Then the correctness of Obf ensures that if $R_{\mathbb{D}}(D', D) = 1$ then $\widetilde{R}(D') = 1$. The rest is unchanged from SfO_1.

We now show how the EUF-COA and Conf-COA security of SfO_2 can be established.

Theorem 2. *If the digital signature scheme* DS *is EUF-CMA secure against PEA adversaries, then* SfO_2 *is EUF-COA secure.*

We defer the formal proof of this theorem to the full version. Informally, if a PEA adversary $\mathcal{A}$ attacking the EUF-COA security wins, then it outputs the index i^* of an object x_{i^*} and a valid signature for an obfuscated circuit $\widetilde{R}$ such that $\widetilde{R}(D^*) = 1$ where $D^* \leftarrow \mathsf{Sen}(x_{i^*})$. From the winning condition for $\mathcal{A}$, we have $\widetilde{R}_j(D^*) = 0$ for all $j \in \mathsf{Ind}$, which means that $\mathcal{A}$ does not know any signature of $\widetilde{R}$ that it obtained via signing queries. Therefore, we can construct another adversary attacking the EUF-CMA security of DS using $\mathcal{A}$.

For the Conf-COA security of SfO_2, we need the property that the distribution of the data taken from a newly generated object via Sen, namely $\{x \leftarrow \mathcal{X}; D \leftarrow \mathsf{Sen}(x) : D\}$, has sufficient amount of entropy, so that for any data $D' \in \mathbb{D}$, the probability that $R_{\mathbb{D}}(D, D') = 1$ occurs is sufficiently small. Following [3,11], we call such a property of a distribution *evasive*, and define it as a property of an object setting.

Definition 7 (Evasiveness). *We say that an object setting $\mathcal{OS} = (\mathbb{X}, \mathbb{V}, \mathcal{X},$ $\mathbb{D}, \mathsf{Sen}, R_{\mathbb{X}}, R_{\mathbb{D}}, \mathbb{C})$ is ϵ-evasive if for any $D' \in \mathbb{D}$, $\Pr[x \leftarrow \mathcal{X}; D \leftarrow \mathsf{Sen}(x) :$ $R_{\mathbb{D}}(D, D') = 1] \leq \epsilon$.*

Theorem 3. *If the obfuscator Obf satisfies distributional VBB security for the distribution $\{x \leftarrow \mathcal{X}; D \leftarrow \mathsf{Sen}(x) : D\}$ against PEA adversaries[4], and the distribution $\{x \leftarrow \mathcal{X}; D \leftarrow \mathsf{Sen}(x) : D\}$ is ϵ-evasive for some negligible $\epsilon = \epsilon(\lambda)$, then SfO_2 is Conf-COA secure.*

The formal proof of this theorem is given in the full version. We briefly give a proof sketch. From a Conf-COA adversary $\mathcal{A}$, we construct an adversary $\mathcal{B}$ against the distributional VBB security of Obf. $\mathcal{B}$ is initially given as input an obfuscated program $\widetilde{R}^*$ that is generated as $x^* \leftarrow \mathcal{X}$, $D^* \leftarrow \mathsf{Sen}(x^*)$, and $\widetilde{R}^* \leftarrow \mathsf{Obf}(1^\lambda, R_{D^*})$, and perfectly simulates the real Conf-COA experiment for $\mathcal{A}$. Due to the distributional VBB security of Obf, there exists a simulator $\mathcal{S}_{\mathcal{B}}$ such that its output distribution is negligibly close to that of $\mathcal{B}$ (and hence that of $\mathcal{A}$). Then, from $\mathcal{S}_{\mathcal{B}}$, we construct a simulator $\mathcal{S}$ for $\mathcal{A}$. The $\mathcal{S}_{\mathcal{B}}$ is a simulator and can submit a query to the circuit $R_{D^*}(\cdot)$, but the evasiveness of the distribution allows $\mathcal{S}$ to answer it to always 0, which ensures that the distribution of the output of $\mathcal{S}_{\mathcal{B}}$ and that of $\mathcal{S}$ are negligibly close. Then, combining all the arguments, we can conclude that the output distribution of $\mathcal{A}$ is negligibly close to that of $\mathcal{S}$.

4.3 Instantiation

Unfortunately, no obfuscator can obfuscate all polynomial-sized circuits with (worst-case) VBB security [4]. However, this impossibility result does not rule

---

[4] When we consider distributional VBB security for an obfuscator against PEA adversaries, we consider not only an adversary but also a simulator to be PEA algorithms.

out the existence of an obfuscator for a particular class of circuits, in particular the one considered in the previous subsection.[5]

For example, Galbraith and Zobernig [11] showed a distributionally VBB secure obfuscator for "fuzzy Hamming distance" predicates (from the hardness of so-called the decisional distributional modular subset product problem). Here, a fuzzy Hamming distance predicate is a circuit $R_D(\cdot)$ such that $R_D(D') = 1$ iff the Hamming distance of the input D' is close (within some pre-determined distance r) to the value D that is hardcorded in the circuit R_D. By using their obfuscator, our construction $\mathsf{SfO_2}$ yields a Conf-COA secure SfO scheme for an object setting where the relation $R_{\mathbb{D}}$ just tests the closeness of the inputs by the Hamming distance.

We do not claim this scheme can be used in a realistic scenario (such as a supply-chain scenario), but hopefully techniques of obfuscation will be developed and more complicated classes of circuits can be obfuscated with distributionally VBB security in the future, so that our Conf-COA secure construction can be instantiated for a wider class of object settings.

Acknowledgements. The authors would like to thank the anonymous referees for their valuable comments and helpful suggestions. This work was partially supported by JSPS KAKENHI Grant Number JP19H01109, JST AIP Acceleration Research JPMJCR22U5, and JST CREST Grant Number JPMJCR22M1, Japan.

References

1. Havocscope. https://havocscope.com/. Accessed 22 Aug 2022
2. Intellectual Property Rights Seizure Statistics — Fiscal Year 2019. Homeland Security (2019). https://www.iprcenter.gov/file-repository/trade-fy2017-ipr-seiz ures.pdf/view. Accessed 22 Aug 2022
3. Barak, B., Bitansky, N., Canetti, R., Kalai, Y.T., Paneth, O., Sahai, A.: Obfuscation for evasive functions. In: Lindell, Y. (ed.) TCC 2014. LNCS, vol. 8349, pp. 26–51. Springer, Heidelberg (2014). https://doi.org/10.1007/978-3-642-54242-8_2
4. Barak, B., et al.: On the (Im)possibility of obfuscating programs. In: Kilian, J. (ed.) CRYPTO 2001. LNCS, vol. 2139, pp. 1–18. Springer, Heidelberg (2001). https://doi.org/10.1007/3-540-44647-8_1
5. Baryannis, G., Dani, S., Antoniou, G.: Predicting supply chain risks using machine learning: the trade-off between performance and interpretability. Futur. Gener. Comput. Syst. **101**, 993–1004 (2019). https://doi.org/10.1016/j.future.2019.07.059
6. Brakerski, Z., Rothblum, G.N.: Virtual black-box obfuscation for all circuits via generic graded encoding. In: Lindell, Y. (ed.) TCC 2014. LNCS, vol. 8349, pp. 1–25. Springer, Heidelberg (2014). https://doi.org/10.1007/978-3-642-54242-8_1
7. Chandran, N., Goyal, V., Moriarty, R., Ostrovsky, R.: Position based cryptography. In: Halevi, S. (ed.) CRYPTO 2009. LNCS, vol. 5677, pp. 391–407. Springer, Heidelberg (2009). https://doi.org/10.1007/978-3-642-03356-8_23

---

[5] Another possibility to bypass the impossibility result of [4] is to resort to an idealized model: Brakerski and Rothblum [6] showed that we can construct a (worst-case, and hence distributionally) VBB secure obfuscator for circuits in the generic graded encoding model. Unfortunately, as far as we know, all candidates of graded encodings are broken and hence cannot be used to securely instantiate the obfuscator of [6].

8. Dent, A.W., Fischlin, M., Manulis, M., Stam, M., Schröder, D.: Confidential signatures and deterministic signcryption. In: Nguyen, P.Q., Pointcheval, D. (eds.) PKC 2010. LNCS, vol. 6056, pp. 462–479. Springer, Heidelberg (2010). https://doi.org/10.1007/978-3-642-13013-7_27

9. Fisch, B., Freund, D., Naor, M.: Physical zero-knowledge proofs of physical properties. In: Garay, J.A., Gennaro, R. (eds.) CRYPTO 2014, Part II. LNCS, vol. 8617, pp. 313–336. Springer, Heidelberg (2014). https://doi.org/10.1007/978-3-662-44381-1_18

10. Fleischhacker, N., Günther, F., Kiefer, F., Manulis, M., Poettering, B.: Pseudorandom signatures. In: Chen, K., Xie, Q., Qiu, W., Li, N., Tzeng, W.G. (eds.) ASIACCS 2013, pp. 107–118. ACM Press, May 2013

11. Galbraith, S.D., Zobernig, L.: Obfuscated fuzzy hamming distance and conjunctions from subset product problems. In: Hofheinz, D., Rosen, A. (eds.) TCC 2019, Part I. LNCS, vol. 11891, pp. 81–110. Springer, Cham (2019). https://doi.org/10.1007/978-3-030-36030-6_4

12. Gassend, B., Clarke, D.E., van Dijk, M., Devadas, S.: Silicon physical random functions. In: Atluri, V. (ed.) ACM CCS 2002, pp. 148–160. ACM Press, November 2002. https://doi.org/10.1145/586110.586132

13. Goldwasser, S., Micali, S.: Probabilistic encryption. J. Comput. Syst. Sci. **28**(2), 270–299 (1984)

14. He, K., Gkioxari, G., Dollár, P., Girshick, R.: Mask R-CNN. In: 2017 IEEE International Conference on Computer Vision (ICCV), pp. 2980–2988 (2017). https://doi.org/10.1109/ICCV.2017.322

15. Ishai, Y., Kushilevitz, E., Ostrovsky, R., Sahai, A.: Cryptographic sensing. In: Boldyreva, A., Micciancio, D. (eds.) CRYPTO 2019, Part III. LNCS, vol. 11694, pp. 583–604. Springer, Cham (2019). https://doi.org/10.1007/978-3-030-26954-8_19

16. Kshetri, N., Loukoianova, E.: Blockchain adoption in supply chain networks in Asia. IT Prof. **21**(1), 11–15 (2019). https://doi.org/10.1109/MITP.2018.2881307

17. Lee, H.L., Whang, S.: Higher supply chain security with lower cost: lessons from total quality management. Int. J. Prod. Econ. **96**(3), 289–300 (2005). https://doi.org/10.1016/j.ijpe.2003.06.003, quality in Supply Chain Management and Logistics

18. Lin, T.Y., Dollar, P., Girshick, R., He, K., Hariharan, B., Belongie, S.: Feature pyramid networks for object detection. In: Proceedings of the IEEE Conference on Computer Vision and Pattern Recognition (CVPR), July 2017. https://doi.org/10.1109/CVPR.2017.106

19. Liu, W., et al.: SSD: single shot multibox detector. In: Leibe, B., Matas, J., Sebe, N., Welling, M. (eds.) ECCV 2016. LNCS, vol. 9905, pp. 21–37. Springer, Cham (2016). https://doi.org/10.1007/978-3-319-46448-0_2

20. Maji, H.K., Prabhakaran, M., Rosulek, M.: Attribute-based signatures. In: Kiayias, A. (ed.) CT-RSA 2011. LNCS, vol. 6558, pp. 376–392. Springer, Heidelberg (2011). https://doi.org/10.1007/978-3-642-19074-2_24

21. Mizuki, T., Shizuya, H.: A formalization of card-based cryptographic protocols via abstract machine. Int. J. Inf. Secur. **13**(1), 15–23 (2013). https://doi.org/10.1007/s10207-013-0219-4

22. Moosavi, J., Naeni, L.M., Fathollahi-Fard, A.M., Fiore, U.: Blockchain in supply chain management: a review, bibliometric, and network analysis. Environ. Sci. Pollut. Res. (2021). https://doi.org/10.1007/s11356-021-13094-3

23. OECD/EUIPO: Global Trade in Fakes: A Worrying Threat. Illicit Trade, OECD Publishing, Paris (2021)

24. Pappu, R., Recht, B., Taylor, J., Gershenfeld, N.: Physical one-way functions. Science **297**(5589), 2026–2030 (2002). https://doi.org/10.1126/science.1074376

25. Redmon, J., Divvala, S., Girshick, R., Farhadi, A.: You only look once: unified, real-time object detection. In: 2016 IEEE Conference on Computer Vision and Pattern Recognition (CVPR), pp. 779–788 (2016). https://doi.org/10.1109/CVPR.2016.91
26. Ren, S., He, K., Girshick, R., Sun, J.: Faster R-CNN: towards real-time object detection with region proposal networks. In: Proceedings of the 28th International Conference on Neural Information Processing Systems, NIPS 2015, vol. 1, pp. 91–99. MIT Press, Cambridge (2015)
27. Robertson, J., Riley, M.: The Big Hack: How China Used a Tiny Chip to Infiltrate U.S. Companies. Bloomberg, October 2018. https://www.bloomberg.com/news/features/2018-10-04/the-big-hack-how-china-used-a-tiny-chip-to-infiltrate-america-s-top-companies. Accessed 22 Aug 2022
28. Saberi, S., Kouhizadeh, M., Sarkis, J., Shen, L.: Blockchain technology and its relationships to sustainable supply chain management. Int. J. Prod. Res. **57**(7), 2117–2135 (2019). https://doi.org/10.1080/00207543.2018.1533261
29. Sharma, R., Kamble, S.S., Gunasekaran, A., Kumar, V., Kumar, A.: A systematic literature review on machine learning applications for sustainable agriculture supply chain performance. Comput. Oper. Res. **119**, 104926 (2020). https://doi.org/10.1016/j.cor.2020.104926
30. Sun, H., Sun, K., Wang, Y., Jing, J.: TrustOTP: transforming smartphones into secure one-time password tokens. In: Ray, I., Li, N., Kruegel, C. (eds.) ACM CCS 2015, pp. 976–988. ACM Press, October 2015. https://doi.org/10.1145/2810103.2813692
31. Takahashi, K., Matsuda, T., Murakami, T., Hanaoka, G., Nishigaki, M.: A signature scheme with a fuzzy private key. In: Malkin, T., Kolesnikov, V., Lewko, A.B., Polychronakis, M. (eds.) ACNS 2015. LNCS, vol. 9092, pp. 105–126. Springer, Cham (2015). https://doi.org/10.1007/978-3-319-28166-7_6
32. Tirkolaee, E.B., Sadeghi, S., Mooseloo, F.M., Vandchali, H.R., Aeini, S.: Application of machine learning in supply chain management: a comprehensive overview of the main areas. Math. Probl. Eng. **2021**, 1476043 (2021). https://doi.org/10.1155/2021/1476043
33. Yang, P., Cao, Z., Dong, X.: Fuzzy identity based signature. Cryptology ePrint Archive, Report 2008/002 (2008). https://eprint.iacr.org/2008/002

The Superlinearity Problem
in Post-quantum Blockchains

Sunoo Park[1]([⊠]) and Nicholas Spooner[2]([⊠])

[1] Columbia University, New York, USA
sunoo@csail.mit.edu
[2] University of Warwick, Coventry, UK
nicholas.spooner@warwick.ac.uk

Abstract. The *proof of work* mechanism by which many blockchain-based protocols achieve consensus may be undermined by the use of quantum computing in mining—even when all cryptographic primitives are replaced with post-quantum secure alternatives. First, we offer an impossibility result: we prove that quantum (Grover) speedups in solving a large, natural class of proof-of-work puzzles cause an inevitable incentive incompatibility in mining, by distorting the reward structure of mining in proof-of-work-based protocols such as Bitcoin. We refer to such distortion as the Superlinearity Problem. Our impossibility result suggests that for robust post-quantum proof-of-work-based consensus, we may need to look beyond standard cryptographic models. We thus propose a proof-of-work design in a random-beacon model, which is tailored to bypass the earlier impossibility. We conclude with a discussion of open problems, and of the challenges of integrating our new proof-of-work scheme into decentralised consensus protocols under realistic conditions.

1 Introduction

Blockchain-based technologies have gained remarkable traction since the proposal of the Bitcoin protocol in 2009 [37]. Today, blockchains and cryptocurrencies are familiar topics in mainstream media and among government regulators (e.g., [6,21,28,31]), and the top two cryptocurrencies' collective market cap is around 500 billion U.S. dollars [19].

At the same time, progress in quantum computing has been rapidly advancing. Recent experiments have shown that quantum computers can perform certain (contrived) tasks faster than the largest classical supercomputers available [3].

Much has been written on the potential impact of quantum computing on blockchain-based technologies [1,10,25], primarily focused on the fact that existing blockchains tend to rely on *pre-quantum* cryptography (primarily signature schemes) that is breakable using sufficiently powerful quantum computers [33].

Certainly, today's blockchains would become insecure if a sufficiently powerful quantum computer were developed. This will not happen overnight: quantum computers that can break today's pre-quantum cryptography are widely believed

© International Financial Cryptography Association 2024
F. Baldimtsi and C. Cachin (Eds.): FC 2023, LNCS 13950, pp. 200–217, 2024.
https://doi.org/10.1007/978-3-031-47754-6_12

to be more than a decade away [36]. Moreover, this is an aspect of a much broader phenomenon, relevant not only to blockchains but to all of the essential Internet infrastructure that relies on pre-quantum cryptography, including protocols such as HTTPS and SSL that are used for viewing most websites, and to secure online banking and shopping. As such, secure and efficient *post-quantum* alternatives to such pre-quantum cryptography are already well studied, and implementation and standardization processes are well underway [38]. These processes are designed to ensure that by the time that quantum computers become viable, any infrastructure that relies on pre-quantum cryptography will have replaced it with secure, standardized post-quantum alternatives.

However, quantum computing poses another lesser studied but potentially more impactful threat to many existing blockchain technologies. The *proof of work* mechanism by which many blockchain-based protocols achieve the crucial property of consensus may be undermined by protocol participants' (miners') use of quantum computers. In a nutshell, a proof of work is a *moderately hard* computational puzzle, which many protocol participants (*miners*) attempt until someone "wins" by finding a solution to the latest puzzle for a given blockchain. The "winning" miner then appends some information (a *block*) to the blockchain.

Proofs of work rely on cryptographic hash functions, which are believed to already be post-quantum secure, so they would remain moderately hard (as intended) for quantum computers. However, the *relative* power of different miners in a blockchain network would change impactfully if some or all of them had quantum computers. This causes two key problems.

I. Quantum Advantage Problem (Nearer Future). Efficient quantum computers would speed up quantum miners' production of proofs of work compared to classical miners,[1] likely discouraging those without quantum computers from participating in mining. However, this would not be problematic if and when quantum computers become widely available.

II. Quantum Superlinearity Problem (Farther Future). Because the quantum speedup is *quadratic*, more computationally powerful quantum miners would gain a disproportionate speedup, eliminating the incentive for less powerful quantum miners — as well as those who lack quantum computers entirely—to participate at all. The result could be a destablising concentration of network control among just the most computationally powerful miners in proof-of-work-based blockchains, weakening the networks' security and consensus properties, as well as undermining the vision of fairness and distributed governance that motivate many blockchain-based systems today. As a concrete example, the famous "51% attack" on Bitcoin — thus named because it requires control of 51% of network hash power — would become possible through control of just over a quarter of hash power, under certain conditions.[2]

---

[1] *Classical* means computing without quantum computers.

[2] Classical network takeover attacks are also possible with the collusion of much less than half of mining power [24]. The Quantum Superlinearity Problem worsens those attacks too: basically, an attack that requires a certain fraction of classical mining power may require a much smaller fraction of quantum mining power.

The Quantum Superlinearity Problem has a natural classical variant, which we call the Classical Superlinearity Problem: namely, similar problems arise when more powerful *classical* miners have a disproportionate advantage over less powerful *classical* miners. Bitcoin and other major blockchains that use proofs of work are designed to yield mining advantage *proportionate* to miners' hash power. Even so, significant (and much critiqued) concentration of power has already occurred in existing proof-of-work-based blockchains due to economies of scale, specialized mining hardware, geographic disparities, and other factors [12,14,27,34,48], due to which some larger miners' advantage is *disproportionate* in terms of economic investment even if it is proportionate in terms of their hash power. Our results suggest that the impact of quantum superlinearity could be an order of magnitude worse than the classical counterparts, as discussed in more detail below.

We write simply Superlinearity Problem when referring to both the Quantum and Classical Superlinearity Problems.

These problems raise a natural question, which is the focus of this paper:

Can we design a proof of work that avoids the Quantum Advantage and Quantum Superlinearity Problems, and thus preserve the incentive structure that currently supports proof-of-work-based systems such as Bitcoin?

We answer this question in the *negative* for a large and natural class of proofs of work encompassing all prior constructions to our knowledge, as summarized in the informal theorem below. Then, we highlight several potential directions for *positive* results outside the scope of our impossibility, and provide a partial *positive* result: a new proof-of-work construction that provably avoids the Quantum Advantage and Quantum Superlinearity problems, in a random beacon model.

Theorem (Informal). For a large, natural class of proofs of work (which includes the Hashcash [4] and Equihash [8] methods that underlie Bitcoin and most proof-of-work blockchains today):

– the Quantum Superlinearity Problem is inherent (i.e., unavoidable), and
– the Quantum Advantage Problem is not solvable without exacerbating the Classical Superlinearity Problem.

Interpreting this impossibility in light of prior theoretical and empirical analyses of centralization in Bitcoin, it appears that the impact from widespread quantum computing could be an order of magnitude worse than the effects of superlinearity already present in the classical setting. Gencer et al. estimated recently that more than 50% of Bitcoin mining power is controlled by eight miners, and 90% is controlled by sixteen miners [27]—already a concerning centralization trend. However, Arnosti and Weinberg's theoretical model of the impact of superlinear rewards [2], together with our results, indicates that the equilibrium number of miners in the post-quantum setting may be *just two* for the large class of proof-of-work protocols this paper considers.

Our impossibility results suggest that to design a proof of work that avoids the Quantum Advantage and Quantum Superlinearity Problems, we may need to look beyond standard cryptographic models. We analyze our impossibility theorem in detail to highlight seven potential research directions towards post-quantum blockchains that do not suffer from the Quantum Advantage and Quantum Superlinearity Problems. Then, focusing on one of these seven directions, we propose a proof-of-work design in a random-beacon model, tailored to bypass the above impossibilities. Finally, we prove the security of our proof-of-work construction, and discuss the significant challenges that seem to remain to integrate a proof of work like ours into a realistic blockchain protocol.

Proof-of-Work Alternatives. Given that the Quantum Advantage and Superlinearity Problems are inherent to a large class of proofs of work, it is also natural to consider whether alternatives to proofs of work could resolve these problems. That is: *can we develop alternative consensus mechanisms not involving proofs of work, that preserve the incentive structure that currently supports proof-of-work-based systems such as Bitcoin, even in the presence of quantum computers?*

This paper's main focus is to examine what is possible and impossible within the proof-of-work approach. As such, we make just a few remarks on proof-of-work alternatives, and leave this question open as an important direction for future work. Despite significant environmental and efficiency concerns about proof-of-work-based consensus (e.g., [9,32,42,50,52]), it remains the dominant consensus model in blockchains today. The main competing approach of *proof of stake* [30,41] has not yet gained traction competitive with Bitcoin's original proof-of-work model. However, this may be changing, with the very recent shift (in early 2022) of the second-biggest cryptocurrency, Ethereum, to a proof-of-stake model [15,23]. Yet other alternatives to proof of work exist as well, with much less adoption than proof of stake (e.g., [18,43–45,47,51]).

Existing efficient implementations of proofs of stake rely on pre-quantum cryptography much more advanced[3] than the cryptography typically used in proof-of-work blockchains. While post-quantum alternatives to these advanced cryptographic tools exist in theory, current standalone constructions would entail impractical computational overhead (e.g., in the order of 1000–10000× for certain operations [13]). An key research direction to make proof-of-stake blockchains practical for post-quantum use is to improve this overhead.

Prior Work on the Quantum Advantage Problem. Past research has considered the extent to which the Quantum Advantage Problem is an issue and how it can be mitigated. Aggarwal et al. [1] conclude that the Hashcash proof of work used by Bitcoin is "relatively resistant to substantial speedup by quantum computers in the next 10 years". This is because, even given optimistic estimates about the near-term development of quantum computers, classical ASIC mining will continue to outperform quantum mining despite the quadratic speedup offered by Grover search. Nonetheless, in the medium term it remains possible that quantum computers will comprise a significant portion of mining power. Aggarwal et al. suggest a potential mitigation using an alternative proof of work called Momentum, which is based on finding collisions in

---

[3] E.g., verifiable random functions and verifiable delay functions.

a hash function. This is a more "quantum-resistant" proof of work, in the sense that there is a classical algorithm for finding collisions in a random function $\{0,1\}^m \to \{0,1\}^n$ in time $T = O(2^{n/2})$, whereas any quantum algorithm requires at least $\Omega(2^{n/3}) = \Omega(T^{2/3})$ queries, giving a somewhat smaller speedup than for the Hashcash proof of work. However, this proposal has a significant drawback. The best algorithms for finding collisions [46] have the property that the probability of finding a collision increases quadratically in the running time of the algorithm. As a result, the Momentum proof of work suffers from the Superlinearity Problem in both the quantum and the classical settings.

Behnia et al. [7] proposes an alternative to Momentum based on the fact that the best known classical and quantum algorithms for the problem of finding a short vector in a lattice (in certain parameter regimes) have similar time complexities: 1.22^n and 1.20^n, respectively. Unlike for preimage and collision finding, the success probability of the "sieving" algorithms achieving these complexities has not been analysed as a function of running time. Nonetheless, it is easily seen that this function is at least quadratic.

Cojocaru et al. [20] give a formal asymptotic analysis of the security of the "Bitcoin backbone" protocol against quantum adversaries. They conclude that the protocol remains secure so long as malicious quantum parties control a very small fraction of the total computing power. We note that this fraction actually becomes *smaller* as the puzzle becomes more difficult, suggesting that an increase in *classical* computational power may help quantum attackers.

Prior Work on the Superlinearity Problem. We are not aware of any prior work that considers the Quantum Superlinearity Problem. However, prior work has considered why superlinearity *in general* is a problem in blockchain protocols. Chen, Papadimitriou, and Roughgarden [17] conduct a game-theoretic analysis of *allocation rules* in proof-of-work blockchains. An allocation rule is *proportional* if each miner (in expectation) receives reward proportional to their contribution relative to total network power. They show that the proportional allocation rule is the unique rule which satisfies both sybil- and collusion-resistance.

Nerem and Gaur [39] give another analysis of the impact of quantum mining on Bitcoin. Their analysis considers a simple Markov model of a single quantum miner Q competing with classical miners, and shows that when Q holds a very small fraction of total network power, Q only has a *linear* speedup over classical mining. They note that this analysis arises from an approximation that holds only if Q is weak compared to the network; that is, a quantum computer with a constant fraction of network power can still get superlinear rewards.

1.1   Technical Overview

Next, we briefly summarise the techniques underlying our results.

Impossibility Result. First, recall the Hashcash proof of work, and why it is subject to superlinear quantum attack. A Hashcash challenge consists of a hash function $h\colon \{0,1\}^\lambda \to \{0,1\}^\lambda$ and a target set $S \subseteq \{0,1\}^\lambda$. A proof π is some

x such that $h(x) \in S$. If h is pseudorandom, then by evaluating h at t random points, we find such an x with probability roughly $t|S|/2^\lambda$. Moreover, no classical algorithm does better than this. But there is a *quantum* algorithm (Grover search) that makes t calls to h and finds such an x with probability $\Omega(t^2|S|/2^\lambda)$.

In general, a proof-of-work scheme may not have this form; indeed, the alternative constructions described above are quite different. Our key observation is that the Grover attack applies to all *proportional* proofs of work; i.e., where the probability of producing a valid proof scales *linearly* with the amount of work.

More precisely, let $\mathsf{Work}(c, t; r)$ denote the "honest" proof of work algorithm, for challenge c with time bound t using randomness r, and let $\mathsf{Verify}(c, \pi)$ be the verification algorithm. By proportionality, $\Pr_r[\mathsf{Verify}(c, \mathsf{Work}(c, t; r))] = \Theta(t)$.[4] To construct a quantum attack, we define a function $f_c(r) = \mathsf{Verify}(c, \mathsf{Work}(c, t_0; r))$, where t_0 is the smallest time such that Work outputs a proof with positive probability p. Then by running t iterations of Grover search on f_c we obtain with probability $\Omega(t^2)$ a string r such that $\mathsf{Work}(c, t_0; r)$ is a valid proof of work.

New Proof-of-Work Construction. We present a proof-of-work construction in the random beacon model which avoids both the Quantum Advantage and Superlinearity Problems. Similarly to Hashcash, we compute $h(x)$ for many random x. We store each pair $(x, h(x))$ in a data structure sorted by $h(x)$. When the beacon value $\beta \in \{0, \ldots, 2^\lambda - 1\}$ arrives, we search through the data structure for x such that $|\beta - h(x)|$ is minimized, and publish x as the proof. The verification algorithm accepts if $|\beta - h(x)|$ is below some specified difficulty threshold.

Intuitively, this circumvents the impossibility because proofs cannot be verified until after the beacon value arrives. We show this formally in Theorem 3 by modelling h as a quantum-accessible random oracle, using Zhandry's compressed oracle technique. In other words, we show that the honest classical mining algorithm is asymptotically optimal for both classical and quantum miners.

1.2 Summary of Contributions

1. We identify and initiate the study of the Quantum Superlinearity Problem.
2. *Impossibility.* We prove an impossibility, namely, that the Superlinearity Problem is inherent in a large class of proofs of work, encompassing all existing definitions and constructions to our knowledge (Sect. 2).
3. *Possibilities.* We analyse our impossibility theorem to systematically highlight new proof-of-work approaches and other alternatives that may avoid the Superlinearity Problem, as open directions for future work (Sect. 3).
4. *Construction.* We offer a new proof-of-work construction in a random-beacon model that provably avoids the Superlinearity Problem, and discuss remaining challenges of integrating it into a consensus protocol (Sect. 4).

---

[4] This is not strictly true: the left hand side is bounded by 1 whereas t grows without bound. A refined definition of proportionality (Definition 4) handles this issue.

2   The Quantum Superlinearity Problem Is Inherent

In this section, we show that the Superlinearity Problem is inherent in a broad class of proofs of work. Section 2.1 introduces the necessary definitions, and Sect. 2.2 presents the impossibility theorem and proof.

2.1   A Broad Definition of Proofs of Work

Our aim in this context is not to propose a canonical definition of proof of work that is somehow better than the scattered existing definitions in the literature, but rather, to be as *as inclusive as possible*—since the broader the definition, the stronger the impossibility.

Relation to Existing Proof-of-Work Definitions. Our definition generalizes many existing definitions of proofs of work from the literature, including Dwork and Naor's seminal "pricing functions" [22], Chen et al.'s "client puzzles" [16], Miller et al.'s "scratch-off puzzles" [35], Garay et al.'s "signatures of work" [26], and Ball et al's proofs of work [5].

Our definition is also compatible with Jakobsson and Juels' proofs of work [29], which additionally discusses *interactive* proofs of work. Our definition is incomparable with Stebila et al.'s "client puzzles" [49], which have a non-public verification algorithm. Section 3 provides further discussion of these and other model variants not captured by our definition.

Finally, our definition captures all proof-of-work constructions for blockchains of which we are aware, including Hashcash [4] and Equihash [8].

Definition 1. *A proof of work is parametrized by a proof space $\Pi = \{\Pi_\lambda\}_{\lambda \in \mathbb{N}}$ and a challenge space $\mathcal{C} = \{\mathcal{C}_\lambda\}_{\lambda \in \mathbb{N}}$, and consists of a triple of algorithms* POW = (Gen, Work, Verify) *with the following syntax.* Gen *and* Work *may be randomized;* Verify *is deterministic.* Gen *and* Verify *must be efficient (i.e., polynomial time).*

- Gen$(1^\lambda, \gamma)$ *takes as input a security parameter λ (in unary) and difficulty parameter $\gamma \in [0, 1]$ and outputs a challenge $c \in \mathcal{C}_\lambda$.*
- Work(c, t) *takes as input a challenge $c \in \mathcal{C}_\lambda$ and time parameter $t \in \mathbb{N}$, and outputs a proof of work $\pi \in \Pi_\lambda$. The time complexity of* Work *is $t \cdot W_\gamma(\lambda)$, where W_γ is a polynomial.*
- Verify(c, π) *takes as input a challenge $c \in \mathcal{C}_\lambda$ and a candidate proof of work $\pi \in \Pi_\lambda$ and outputs $b \in \{0, 1\}$.*

Remark 1. We can omit λ and γ from the input to Work, Verify since we can assume that c includes them both without loss of generality. We sometimes write Work$(c, t; r)$ to explicitly denote the randomness r of the Work algorithm.

Remark 2. $W_\gamma(\lambda)$ may be thought to represent the minimum time required to produce a valid proof for difficulty parameter γ with positive probability.

Next, we define the *reward function* of a proof of work (Definition 2), which relates the likelihood of obtaining a valid proof to (honest) work done.

Definition 2. *A proof of work* POW *has reward function ρ if the probability of generating a valid proof by running* Work *with time parameter t with respect to difficulty parameter γ is negligibly close to $\rho(\gamma, t)$ with overwhelming probability. That is, for any $\lambda, t \in \mathbb{N}$, $\gamma \in [0, 1]$, there exists a negligible function ε such that*

$$\Pr_{c \leftarrow \mathsf{Gen}(1^\lambda, \gamma)} \left[\left| \Pr_r \left[b = 1 : \begin{array}{l} \pi \leftarrow \mathsf{Work}(c, t; r) \\ b \leftarrow \mathsf{Verify}(c, \pi) \end{array} \right] - \rho(\gamma, t) \right| \geq \varepsilon(\lambda) \right] \leq \varepsilon(\lambda) . \quad (1)$$

The bound (1) states (in the contrapositive) that with all but negligible probability over challenges, the probability of obtaining a valid proof in time t is very close to $\rho(\gamma, t)$, where γ is the difficulty parameter.

Next, we define *smoothness* and *proportionality* of reward functions. Informally, a reward function is *smooth* if no matter how hard the difficulty is set ($\gamma \to 0$), there is a positive probability of obtaining a valid proof after one time-step of computation.[5] A reward function is *proportional* if for all small enough γ (i.e., for all hard enough difficulty settings), the probability of obtaining a valid proof scales approximately linearly with computation, up to a positive upper bound.[6] Note that proportionality implies smoothness.

Definition 3. *For $\alpha, \beta \in (0, 1]$, we say a reward function ρ is (α, β)-smooth if for any $\gamma \in [0, \beta]$, $\rho(\gamma, 1) \geq \alpha \cdot \gamma$.*

Definition 4. *We say a reward function ρ is* proportional *if there exist $\alpha, \beta \in (0, 1]$ such that for any $\gamma \in [0, \beta]$, $\alpha \cdot \min(\gamma t, 1) \leq \rho(\gamma, t) \leq \gamma t$.*

Remark 3. Hashcash-like "progress-free" [8] proofs of work have $\rho(\gamma, t) = 1 - (1 - \gamma)^t$: a proportional reward structure according to our definition.

Finally, we define the *hardness* of a proof of work. Informally, POW is *classically (resp., quantumly) (μ_C, ρ')-hard* if any classical (resp. quantum) algorithm running in time μ_C computes a valid proof of work with probability ρ'.

Definition 5 (Classical hardness). *A proof of work* POW *is classically (μ_C, ρ')-hard if for any classical two-part adversary $\mathcal{A} = (\mathcal{A}_1, \mathcal{A}_2)$ such that $\mathcal{A}_1$ runs in polynomial time and $\mathcal{A}_2$ runs in time at most $\mu_C(t)$, for any $t \in \mathbb{N}$, and $\gamma \in [0, 1]$, there is a negligible function ε such that*

$$\Pr \left[b = 1 : \begin{array}{l} z \leftarrow \mathcal{A}_1(1^\lambda, t, \gamma) \\ c \leftarrow \mathsf{Gen}(1^\lambda, \gamma) \\ \pi \leftarrow \mathcal{A}_2(z, c) \\ b \leftarrow \mathsf{Verify}(c, \pi) \end{array} \right] \leq \rho'(\gamma, t) + \varepsilon(\lambda) . \quad (2)$$

Definition 6 (Quantum hardness). *A proof of work* POW *is quantumly (μ_C, ρ')-hard if for any quantum adversary $\mathcal{A} = (\mathcal{A}_1, \mathcal{A}_2)$ such that $\mathcal{A}_1$ runs in polynomial time and $\mathcal{A}_2$ runs in time at most $\mu_Q(t)$, for any $t, n \in \mathbb{N}$ and $\gamma \in [0, 1]$, there is a negligible function ε such that (2) holds.*

---

[5] This rules out deterministic proofs of work (whose reward functions are 0–1).
[6] The upper bound is necessary since probabilities are upper-bounded by 1.

Definition 7 (Hardness). *A proof of work POW is* (μ_C, μ_Q, ρ')-*hard if it is classically* (μ_C, ρ')-*hard and quantumly* (μ_Q, ρ')-*hard.*

2.2   Impossibility Result

Our impossibility result relates reward functions to achievable quantum speedup. Any proof of work with a smooth reward function must allow quantum adversaries a probability of obtaining a valid proof that is quadratic in work done (Theorem 1). It follows that any proof of work with a *proportional* reward function must admit a quadratic quantum speedup (Corollary 1).

Theorem 1. *If a proof of work with an* (α, β)-*smooth reward function is quantum* (μ_Q, ρ')-*hard then there exists* $\kappa \in [0,1]$ *such that for all* $\gamma \in [0, \beta]$ *and all sufficiently large* $t \in \mathbb{N}$, $\rho'(\gamma, t) \geq \kappa \cdot \min(\mu_Q(t)^2 \alpha \gamma, 1)$.

Proof. Let POW $=$ (Gen, Work, Verify) be a proof of work with reward structure ρ. A quantum attack on POW proceeds as follows. Consider the algorithm $f_c(r) = \mathsf{Verify}(c, \mathsf{Work}(c, 1; r))$. A single invocation of f_c runs in time $\mathsf{poly}(\lambda)$. By Eq. (1), $\Pr_r[f_c(r) = 1] \geq p(\gamma, 1) - \mathsf{negl}(\lambda)$; denote this probability by p_0.

We use Grover search to find r such that $f_c(r) = 1$, stopping at time $\mu_Q(t)$. This algorithm makes $\mu_Q(t)/\mathsf{poly}(\lambda)$ queries to the f_c-oracle. Denote the probability that this algorithm finds a winning choice of r by $p(\lambda, \gamma, t)$. By the standard analysis of Grover search, we have that $p(\lambda, \gamma, t) \geq \kappa(\lambda) \cdot \min(\mu_Q(t)^2 p_0, 1)$ for some $\kappa(\lambda)\colon \mathbb{N} \to [0,1]$ and all sufficiently large t.

Suppose that POW is (μ_Q, ρ')-hard; then there exists λ_0 such that for all $\lambda \geq \lambda_0$ and all γ, t it holds that $p(\lambda, \gamma, t) \leq \rho'(\gamma, t)$. Hence in particular for all sufficiently large t it holds that $\rho'(\gamma, t) \geq \kappa(\lambda_0) \cdot \min(\mu_Q(t)^2 p_0, 1)$. Noting that $p_0 \geq p(\gamma, 1)/2$ for large enough λ yields the theorem.

Corollary 1. *If a proof of work with proportional reward function* ρ *is quantum* (μ_Q, ρ)-*hard then* $\mu_Q = O(\sqrt{t})$.

Proof. Let POW be a proof of work with proportional reward function ρ that is quantum (μ_Q, ρ)-hard. Let α, β be as in Definition 4. By Theorem 1, there exist $\kappa \in [0,1], t_0 \in \mathbb{N}$ such that for all $\gamma \in [0, \beta]$ and $t \geq t_0$, $\gamma t \geq \rho(\gamma, t) \geq \kappa \cdot \min(\mu_Q(t)^2 \cdot \alpha \cdot \gamma, 1)$. Setting $\gamma = 1/\mu_Q(t)^2$ we see that there exists t_0' such that for all $t \geq t_0'$, $t \geq \kappa \cdot \mu_Q(t)^2$.

3   Towards Bypassing the Superlinearity Problem

In this section, we analyze the scope of our impossibility to identify potential paths forward. Informally restated, Theorem 1 tells us that the Superlinearity Problem is inherent in any proof of work that has *all* of the following properties:

1. the prover takes some input,
2. then performs classical computational work for a time t
3. to output a proof π of polynomial size,

4. which verifies successfully with a probability (over Work) increasing in t,
5. using a verification algorithm that is deterministic, runs in polynomial time, and takes (only) c and π as input,
6. in the standard model or a quantum-accessible-oracle-based model.

Towards bypassing the Superlinearity Problem, then, we consider how proofs of work could be designed *not* to satisfy any of the properties listed above—since such proof-of-work schemes would fall outside the scope of Theorem 1.

Let us consider each of the listed properties in turn. Property 1—namely, that the prover takes some input—admits no meaningful modification.

Property 2 is arguably inherent to the concept of a proof of (classical computational) work; as such, it highlights the possibilities of avoiding the Superlinearity Problem by turning to proofs of resources other than classical computational work. One option is to consider proofs of *quantum* computational work; this would preclude classical mining, of course, but might be acceptable in scenarios where efficient quantum computers are sufficiently widely available. More broadly, as also noted in Sect. 1, proof-of-work alternatives are an already thriving research area for which our results offer novel additional motivation.

Property 3 states that there is a proof string of polynomial size, raising the possibilities of having an interactive proof or having a proof string of superpolynomial size. Interactive proofs are not suitable for existing blockchain-based consensus systems, and would often incur prohibitive communication overhead; that said, interactive proofs of work could still be an interesting direction for future work.[7] Superpolynomial size, however, is unacceptable for efficiency.

Property 4 states the chance of obtaining a valid proof increases with work, a condition that seems inherent to the notion of a proof of work in the blockchain context. That is, for incentive-compatible mining in blockchain systems, the probability of obtaining a valid proof must increase with work. Property 4 raises the possibility of a proof of work where the probability of obtaining a valid proof still increases with work, but does not depend only on the random coins of Work. (For example, it might also depend on a miner's private information or on the randomness of an oracle.)

Property 5 seems arguably necessary in the blockchain context as existing blockchain networks rely crucially on verification being efficiently publicly computable and agreed on by everyone. Still, alternative models where Verify is not publicly computable (say, because it is keyed) may be worth exploring.[8]

Property 6 means that oracle-based cryptographic models such as the random oracle model and the common reference string (CRS) model will not take us outside the scope of Theorem 1's impossibility. However, other common nonstandard cryptographic models could—such as a timed random beacon model or assuming a sybil-free public-key infrastructure (PKI)—as could oracle-based models that are not quantum-accessible. The latter would include, for example, oracles implemented under certain trusted hardware models, or oracles implemented by third parties (or networks of parties).

---

[7] Jakobsson and Juels proposed a definition that includes interactive protocols [29].

[8] Stebila et al. proposed a definition where verification is keyed [49].

In summary, we have highlighted the following preliminary avenues for exploration towards designing a proof of work that falls outside the scope of our impossibility result (and thus may not suffer from the Superlinearity Problem). In Sect. 4, we elaborate a preliminary proposal based on F.

A. Proofs of quantum work
B. Proof-of-work alternatives
C. Interactive proofs of work
D. Probability of obtaining a valid proof does not depend only on Work
E. Proofs of work with non-public verification
F. Non-standard non-oracle-based cryptographic models (e.g., beacon; PKI)
G. Oracle-based cryptographic models that are not quantum-accessible

4   A New Proof of Work in a Random Beacon Model

We provide a proof-of-work construction in a timed random beacon model that provably avoids the Superlinearity Problem. Our protocol relies on the existence of a "beacon" that outputs a random string at regular time intervals. We prove our protocol's security in the quantum random oracle model (QROM). Then, in Sect. 4.1, we highlight the significant challenges that seem inherent in integrating our proof of work into a realistic blockchain.

Model. We define variants in the random beacon model of *proof of work* (Definition 8), *reward structure* (Definition 9), and (ρ, μ)-*hardness* (Definition 10).

Definition 8 (Proof of work with beacon). *A* proof of work *is parametrized by a* proof space Π *and a* challenge space $\mathcal{C}$, *and consists of a triple of algorithms* POW = (Gen, Work, Verify) *with the following syntax. All the algorithms may be randomized.* Gen *and* Verify *must be efficient;* Work *need not be.*

- Gen$(1^\lambda, \gamma)$ *takes as input a security parameter* λ *(in unary) and public parameters* $\gamma \in [0, 1]$ *and outputs a challenge* $c \in \mathcal{C}$.
- Work(c, t) *takes as input a challenge* $c \in \mathcal{C}$ *and* time parameter $t \in \mathbb{N}$, *runs for time at most* $t \cdot W_\gamma(\lambda)$ *for some polynomial* W_γ, *and outputs a private state* $\mathcal{D} \in \{0, 1\}^*$.
- Choose$^{\mathcal{D}}(\beta)$ *takes as input a state* $\mathcal{D}$ *(as an oracle) and an auxiliary input* $\beta \in \{0, 1\}^{\mathsf{poly}(\lambda)}$ *and outputs a proof of work* $\pi \in \Pi$.
- Verify(c, π, β) *takes as input a challenge* $c \in \mathcal{C}$, *a candidate proof of work* $\pi \in \Pi$, *beacon input* $\beta \in \{0, 1\}^{\mathsf{poly}(\lambda)}$ *and outputs* $b \in \{0, 1\}$.
- Beacon(1^λ) *takes as input security parameter* λ *(in unary) and outputs a beacon value* $\beta \in \{0, 1\}^{\mathsf{poly}(\lambda)}$.

Definition 9 (Reward function with beacon). *A proof of work and allocation algorithm* POW *has reward function* ρ *if for any* $t \in \mathbb{N}$ *and* $\gamma \in [0, 1]$, *there is a negligible function* ε *such that*

$$\Pr_{c \leftarrow \mathsf{Gen}(1^\lambda, \gamma)} \left[\left| \Pr \left[b = 1 : \begin{array}{l} \mathcal{D} \leftarrow \mathsf{Work}(c, t) \\ \beta \leftarrow \mathsf{Beacon}(1^\lambda) \\ \pi \leftarrow \mathsf{Choose}^{\mathcal{D}}(\beta) \\ b \leftarrow \mathsf{Verify}(c, \pi, \beta) \end{array} \right] - \rho(\gamma, t) \right| > \varepsilon(\lambda) \right] < \varepsilon(\lambda) . \quad (3)$$

Definition 10 (Hardness with beacon). *A proof of work with beacon* POW *is classically* $(\mu_{C,2}, \mu_{C,3}, \rho')$*-hard if for any classical three-part adversary* $\mathcal{A} = (\mathcal{A}_1, \mathcal{A}_2, \mathcal{A}_3)$ *such that* $\mathcal{A}_1$ *runs in polynomial time,* $\mathcal{A}_2$ *runs in time at most* $\mu_{C,2}(t) \cdot W(\lambda)$ *and* $\mathcal{A}_3$ *runs in time at most* $\mu_{C,3}(t) \cdot W(\lambda)$*, and* $\gamma \in [0,1]$*, there is a negligible function* ε *such that*

$$\Pr\left[b = 1 : \begin{array}{l} z_1 \leftarrow \mathcal{A}_1(1^\lambda, \gamma) \\ c \leftarrow \mathsf{Gen}(1^\lambda, \gamma) \\ z_2 \leftarrow \mathcal{A}_2(z_1, c) \\ \beta \leftarrow \mathsf{Beacon}(1^\lambda) \\ \pi \leftarrow \mathcal{A}_3^{z_2}(c, \beta) \\ b \leftarrow \mathsf{Verify}(c, \pi, \beta) \end{array} \right] < \rho'(\gamma, t) + \varepsilon(\lambda) \ . \tag{4}$$

We define quantum $(\mu_{Q,2}, \mu_{Q,3}, \rho')$*-hardness analogously.*

Next we give our construction of a proof of work in the random beacon model, and then prove that it satisfies Definitions 9 and 10.

Construction 2 *Challenge space* $\mathcal{C} = \{0,1\}^\lambda \times \mathbb{N}$*; proof space* $\Pi = \{0,1\}^{2\lambda}$.

- $\mathsf{Gen}(1^\lambda, \gamma)$ *samples uniform* $\alpha \leftarrow \{0,1\}^\lambda$*, computes* $\tau = \gamma \cdot 2^{\lambda-1}$*, and outputs* $c = (1^\lambda, \tau, \alpha)$.
- $\mathsf{Work}(c, t)$ *repeats the following* t *times: choose a random nonce* $r \in \{0,1\}^\lambda$*, compute* $y = h_\alpha(r)$*, and store* (r, y) *in a table* $\mathcal{D}$ *sorted by* y *(interpreted as an integer). It then outputs* $\mathcal{D}$.
- $\mathsf{Choose}^{\mathcal{D}}(\beta)$ *outputs* $\pi = \arg\min_{(r,y) \in \mathcal{D}} |y - \beta|$ *(interpreting* y, β *as integers).*
- $\mathsf{Verify}(c, (r, y), \beta)$ *accepts if* $y = h_\alpha(r)$ *and* $|y - \beta| < \tau$.
- $\mathsf{Beacon}(1^\lambda)$ *outputs uniformly random* $\beta \in \{0,1\}^\lambda$.

Lemma 1. *When* h *is pseudorandom and runs in time* $t_h(\lambda)$*, Theorem 2 is a proof of work with reward structure* $\rho(\gamma, t) = 1 - (1 - \gamma)^t$*, which achieves proportional representation.*

Proof. We show that replacing h_α with a random function h yields reward structure ρ. For a random h, the probability that for a random r and any β that $|h(r) - \beta| < \tau$ is γ. The probability that at least one proof succeeds out of t is then $1 - (1 - \gamma)^t$, since these are independent events. We now show that ρ achieves proportional representation. For the upper bound, observe that for all γ, t, $\rho(\gamma, t) \le \gamma t$. For the lower bound, suppose first that $\gamma \ge 1/t$; then $(1 - \gamma)^t \le (1 - 1/t)^t \le 1/e$. Now suppose instead that $\gamma t < 1$; then $1 - (1 - \gamma)^t \ge \gamma t - \frac{1}{2}(\gamma t)^2 \ge \gamma t / 2$.

QROM Preliminaries. We introduce the technical background for our security proof in the quantum random oracle model (QROM) [11]. We omit standard quantum information definitions (e.g., states, unitaries) (see [40, §I.2]).

Let $\mathcal{A}$ be an algorithm that makes t quantum queries to an oracle $h \colon X \to \{0,1\}^\lambda$ and outputs a pair $(x, y) \in X \times \{0,1\}^\lambda$. Then there exist unitary transformations $U_1, \ldots, U_t$ and a quantum state $|\psi_0\rangle$ such that for any h, x, y,

$$\Pr[(x, y) \leftarrow \mathcal{A}^h] = \| \langle x, y | \, U_t O_h U_{t-1} O_h \cdots U_1 O_h \, |\psi_0\rangle \|^2 \ ,$$

where O_h is the unitary with action $O_h \ket{x, y} = \ket{x, y \oplus h(x)}$ for all x, y and $\oplus$ is the bitwise XOR.

Compressed Oracle Technique. We make use of Zhandry's compressed oracle technique [53]. Let $X \rightharpoonup \{0,1\}^\lambda$ be the set of partial functions from X to $\{0,1\}^\lambda$. For $D \colon X \rightharpoonup \{0,1\}^\lambda$, let $\mathsf{supp}(D)$ be the set of $x \in X$ for which $D(x)$ is defined. Let $\mathcal{D}$ be a quantum register supported on states $\ket{D}$ for $D \colon X \rightharpoonup \{0,1\}^\lambda$. The key lemma of the compressed oracle technique follows.

Lemma 2 ([53]). *There exists a unitary $\mathcal{O}$ such that for all $R \subseteq X \times \{0,1\}^\lambda$, letting $\Pi_R = \sum_{D, \exists (x,y) \in R, D(x) = y} \ket{D}\bra{D}_{\mathcal{D}}$, $\mathcal{A}^{\mathcal{O}} = U_t \mathcal{O} \cdots U_1 \mathcal{O}$:*

$$\Pr \left[\begin{array}{c|c} (x, y) \in R & h \leftarrow (X \to \{0,1\}^\lambda) \\ \wedge\, h(x) = y & (x, y) \leftarrow \mathcal{A}^h \end{array} \right] \leq \| \Pi_R \mathcal{A}^{\mathcal{O}} \ket{\psi_0} \ket{\perp}_{\mathcal{D}} \|^2 + O(2^{-\lambda}) \ .$$

Moreover, let $p_R = \max_x \Pr_y[(x, y) \in R]$. Then $\| [\Pi_R] \mathcal{O} \| = O(\sqrt{p_R})$.

Theorem 3. *In the (quantum) random oracle model, Theorem 2 is (ρ, μ_C, μ_Q)-hard for $\mu_{C,2}, \mu_{C,3} = \Theta(t)$, $\mu_{Q,2} = \Theta(t), \mu_{Q,3} = \Theta(\sqrt{t})$.*

Proof. The classical hardness proof is straightforward, and so we omit it.

Let $\mathcal{A} = (\mathcal{A}_1, \mathcal{A}_2, \mathcal{A}_3)$ be quantum oracle algorithms making at most t_1, t_2, t_3 queries respectively. Let $R(\alpha, \beta) = \{((\alpha, x), y) : |y - \beta| \leq \tau\}$; note that for all α, β, $p_{R(\alpha,\beta)} = p_R = 2\tau/2^\lambda$. By Lemma 2 the probability that $\mathcal{A}$ produces a valid proof of work is at most

$$\delta = \mathsf{E}_{\alpha,\beta} \| \Pi_{R(\alpha,\beta)} \mathcal{A}_3^{\mathcal{O}}(c, B) \mathcal{A}_2^{\mathcal{O}}(c) \mathcal{A}_1^{\mathcal{O}} \ket{\psi_0} \ket{\perp} \|^2 + O(2^{-\lambda}) \ .$$

Let $S(\alpha) = \{((\alpha, x), y) : x, y \in \{0,1\}^\lambda\}$ and $\bar{\Pi} = I - \Pi$. Then

$$\| \Pi_{R(\alpha,\beta)} \mathcal{A}_3^{\mathcal{O}}(\alpha, \beta) \mathcal{A}_2^{\mathcal{O}}(\alpha) \mathcal{A}_1^{\mathcal{O}} \ket{\psi_0} \ket{\perp} \|$$
$$\leq \| \Pi_{R(\alpha,\beta)} \mathcal{A}_3^{\mathcal{O}}(\alpha, \beta) \bar{\Pi}_{R(\alpha,\beta)} \mathcal{A}_2^{\mathcal{O}}(\alpha) \mathcal{A}_1^{\mathcal{O}} \ket{\psi_0} \ket{\perp} \|$$
$$+ \| \Pi_{R(\alpha,\beta)} \mathcal{A}_2^{\mathcal{O}}(\alpha) \bar{\Pi}_{S(\alpha)} \mathcal{A}_1^{\mathcal{O}} \ket{\psi_0} \ket{\perp} \| + \| \Pi_{S(\alpha)} \mathcal{A}_1^{\mathcal{O}} \ket{\psi_0} \ket{\perp} \|$$

by the triangle inequality. Now we bound each term in turn. For all α, β,

$$\| \Pi_{R(\alpha,\beta)} \mathcal{A}_3^{\mathcal{O}}(\alpha, \beta) \bar{\Pi}_{R(\alpha,\beta)} \mathcal{A}_2^{\mathcal{O}}(\alpha) \mathcal{A}_1^{\mathcal{O}} \ket{\psi_0} \ket{\perp} \|$$
$$\leq \| \Pi_{R(\alpha,\beta)} \mathcal{A}_3^{\mathcal{O}}(\alpha, \beta) \bar{\Pi}_{R(\alpha,\beta)} \|$$
$$\leq \| \mathcal{A}_3^{\mathcal{O}}(\alpha, \beta) \Pi_{R(\alpha,\beta)} \bar{\Pi}_{R(\alpha,\beta)} \| + t_3 \cdot \| [\Pi_R] \mathcal{O} \| = O(t_3 \sqrt{p_R}),$$

where the final equality follows by Lemma 2 and because $\Pi_{R(\alpha,\beta)} \bar{\Pi}_{R(\alpha,\beta)} = 0$.

For the second term, observe that for any α and any state $\ket{\varphi}$ in the image of $I - \Pi_{S(\alpha)}$, the support of $\mathcal{D}$ in $\mathcal{A}_2^{\mathcal{O}}(\alpha) \ket{\varphi}$ is contained in the set

$$S = \{D : |\mathsf{supp}(D) \cap \{\alpha \| x : x \in \{0,1\}^\lambda\}| \leq t_2\} \ .$$

Hence if we measure $\mathcal{D}$, we obtain $D \in S$ with probability 1. For all such D, $\Pr_\beta[\exists x, D(\alpha \| x) = \beta] \leq t_2 \cdot p_R$. Hence for all α,

$$\mathsf{E}_\beta \| \Pi_{R(\alpha,\beta)} \mathcal{A}_2^{\mathcal{O}}(\alpha) \bar{\Pi}_{S(\alpha)} \mathcal{A}_1^{\mathcal{O}} \ket{\psi_0} \ket{\perp} \|^2 \leq t_2 \cdot p_R \ .$$

A similar argument shows that $\mathsf{E}_\alpha \|\Pi_{S(\alpha)} \mathcal{A}_1^{\mathcal{O}} |\psi_0\rangle |\bot\rangle\|^2 = O(t_1/2^\lambda)$. Then

$$\delta = O((t_1 + \tau t_2 + \tau t_3^2)/2^\lambda) = O((t_2 + t_3^2) \cdot \frac{\tau}{2^\lambda}) + \mathsf{negl}(\lambda) \ .$$

4.1 Challenges of Protocol Integration

Given our new proof-of-work construction, one might hope to "plug it in" to a Bitcoin-like protocol and thus resolve the Quantum Superlinearity Problem. Unfortunately, integrating our proof of work into a decentralised consensus protocol seems to present non-trivial further challenges. Next, we briefly elaborate on these, guided by sketches of simple but natural failed attempts.

Why not, for instance, rely on the beacon to keep time (say, one block per beacon output) and have miners publish proofs of work after each beacon value?

A fundamental issue with this approach is takeover attacks: a malicious miner could create an alternate history on a fork or an entire alternate chain knowing the beacon values after the fact, and obtain a chain indistinguishable from—or of higher quality than—the honestly derived chain for any network participant who is newly joining or joining after an offline period. This problem seems difficult to mitigate when network participants are not almost always online.

Inspired by this observation, we might propose a variant protocol that requires miners to publish commitments to their candidate proofs in each time-step, and only considers valid those proofs that miners can prove were committed "on-chain". To achieve this, individual miners must be able to decommit their own proofs (in a publicly verifiable way). This constraint appears to preclude the natural approach of committing to all miners' commitments with a single Merkle root. But then, storing commitment information on-chain that scales with the total number of miners would incur an impractical bandwidth cost.

When the validity of a proof of work is effectively dependent on when it was computed, and participants are not always online, it is arguably inherent that a consensus protocol dependent on such a proof of work must record some timing information. The problem we have highlighted lies in recording timing information *even for unsuccessful attempts* at block mining, which creates impractical bandwidth demands. We would be interested to see future work exploring new approaches to integrating timing-dependent proofs of work into blockchains.

5   Conclusion

We have identified the Quantum Superlinearity Problem in post-quantum proof-of-work blockchains and proven that it is inherent in a large class of proofs of work encompassing existing approaches. By analyzing our impossibility result, we have suggested a range of approaches or alternatives to proofs of work that may have the potential to avoid the Superlinearity Problem. We have explored one such approach in more detail, proposing a new proof-of-work construction in a random-beacon model that provably avoids the Superlinearity Problem;

and we provide discussion of the significant challenges that seem to remain in integrating our new proof of work into a realistic consensus protocol.

Finally, we have highlighted several open problems and directions for future research to improve our understanding of post-quantum blockchains in light of the Superlinearity Problem, as follows.

1. Explore new models of proofs of work that avoid the Superlinearity Problem (including, but not limited to, the directions A–G noted in Sect. 3).
2. Explore how such new proofs of work (including, but not limited to, our construction in Sect. 4) can be integrated into decentralised consensus protocols that avoid the Superlinearity Problem.
3. Explore post-quantum implementations of a public random beacon.

Acknowledgments. We are grateful to Thaddeus Dryja for the conversation that sparked this research, and to Chris Peikert for a helpful discussion at early stages of the work.

SP's work on this project was supported by a 2021–22 Computing Innovation Fellowship, funded by the National Science Foundation under Grant #2127309 to the Computing Research Association, by Cornell Tech's Digital Life Initiative, and by the MIT Media Lab's Digital Currency Initiative.

References

1. Aggarwal, D., Brennen, G., Lee, T., Santha, M., Tomamichel, M.: Quantum attacks on bitcoin, and how to protect against them. Ledger 3 (2018). https://doi.org/10.5195/ledger.2018.127, https://www.ledgerjournal.org/ojs/ledger/article/view/127
2. Arnosti, N., Weinberg, S.M.: Bitcoin: a natural oligopoly. Manag. Sci. **68**(7), 4755–4771 (2022). https://doi.org/10.1287/mnsc.2021.4095
3. Arute, F., et al.: Quantum supremacy using a programmable superconducting processor. Nature **574**(7779) (2019). https://doi.org/10.1038/s41586-019-1666-5
4. Back, A.: Hashcash - a denial of service counter-measure (2002). http://www.hashcash.org/papers/hashcash.pdf
5. Ball, M., Rosen, A., Sabin, M., Vasudevan, P.N.: Proofs of work from worst-case assumptions. In: Shacham, H., Boldyreva, A. (eds.) CRYPTO 2018, Part I. LNCS, vol. 10991, pp. 789–819. Springer, Cham (2018). https://doi.org/10.1007/978-3-319-96884-1_26
6. Barton, R.E., McNamara, C.J., Ward, M.C.: Are cryptocurrencies securities? the SEC is answering the question. Reuters (2022). https://www.reuters.com/legal/transactional/are-cryptocurrencies-securities-sec-is-answering-question-2022-03-21 [https://perma.cc/32DQ-PB4J]
7. Behnia, R., Postlethwaite, E.W., Ozmen, M.O., Yavuz, A.A.: Lattice-based proof-of-work for post-quantum blockchains. In: Garcia-Alfaro, J., Muñoz-Tapia, J.L., Navarro-Arribas, G., Soriano, M. (eds.) DPM CBT 2021. LNCS, vol. 13140, pp. 310–318. Springer, Cham (2021). https://doi.org/10.1007/978-3-030-93944-1_21
8. Biryukov, A., Khovratovich, D.: Equihash: asymmetric proof-of-work based on the generalized birthday problem. Ledger **2**, 1–30 (2017). https://doi.org/10.5195/ledger.2017.48, https://ledger.pitt.edu/ojs/ledger/article/view/48

9. Blinder, M.: Making cryptocurrency more environmentally sustainable. Harvard Business Review (Online) (2018). https://hbr.org/2018/11/making-cryptocurrency-more-environmentally-sustainable

10. Bolfing, A.: Post-Quantum Blockchains. In: Cryptographic Primitives in Blockchain Technology: A Mathematical Introduction. Oxford University Press (2020)

11. Boneh, D., Dagdelen, Ö., Fischlin, M., Lehmann, A., Schaffner, C., Zhandry, M.: Random oracles in a quantum world. In: Proceedings of the 17th International Conference on the Theory and Application of Cryptology and Information Security. ASIACRYPT 2011, pp. 41–69 (2011)

12. Bonneau, J., Miller, A., Clark, J., Narayanan, A., Kroll, J.A., Felten, E.W.: SOK: research perspectives and challenges for bitcoin and cryptocurrencies. In: 2015 IEEE Symposium on Security and Privacy, SP 2015, San Jose, CA, USA, 17–21 May 2015, pp. 104–121. IEEE Computer Society (2015). https://doi.org/10.1109/SP.2015.14

13. Buser, M., et al.: Post-quantum verifiable random function from symmetric primitives in pos blockchain. In: Atluri, V., Pietro, R.D., Jensen, C.D., Meng, W. (eds.) ESORICS 2022, Part I. LNCS, vol. 13554, pp. 25–45. Springer, Cham (2022). https://doi.org/10.1007/978-3-031-17140-6_2

14. Böhme, R., Christin, N., Edelman, B., Moore, T.: Bitcoin: economics, technology, and governance. J. Econ. Perspect. **29**(2), 213–38 (2015). https://doi.org/10.1257/jep.29.2.213

15. Castor, A.: Why Ethereum is switching to proof of stake and how it will work (2022). https://www.technologyreview.com/2022/03/04/1046636/ethereum-blockchain-proof-of-stake [https://perma.cc/U957-V7X7]

16. Chen, L., Morrissey, P., Smart, N.P., Warinschi, B.: Security notions and generic constructions for client puzzles. In: Matsui, M. (ed.) ASIACRYPT 2009. LNCS, vol. 5912, pp. 505–523. Springer, Heidelberg (2009). https://doi.org/10.1007/978-3-642-10366-7_30

17. Chen, X., Papadimitriou, C.H., Roughgarden, T.: An axiomatic approach to block rewards. In: AFT, pp. 124–131. ACM (2019)

18. Cohen, B., Pietrzak, K.: The chia network blockchain (2019). https://www.chia.net/wp-content/uploads/2022/07/ChiaGreenPaper.pdf

19. CoinMarketCap: Today's cryptocurrency prices by market cap (2022). https://coinmarketcap.com [https://perma.cc/9ARA-AXBQ]

20. Cojocaru, A., Garay, J., Kiayias, A., Song, F., Wallden, P.: Post-quantum blockchain proofs of work (2020). https://arxiv.org/abs/2012.15254

21. Council of the European Union: Digital finance: agreement reached on european crypto-assets regulation (mica). Press release (2022). https://www.consilium.europa.eu/en/press/press-releases/2022/06/30/digital-finance-agreement-reached-on-european-crypto-assets-regulation-mica [https://perma.cc/36NR-DQVQ]

22. Dwork, C., Naor, M.: Pricing via processing or combatting junk mail. In: Brickell, E.F. (ed.) CRYPTO 1992. LNCS, vol. 740, pp. 139–147. Springer, Heidelberg (1993). https://doi.org/10.1007/3-540-48071-4_10

23. Ethereum.org: Proof-of-stake (pos). https://ethereum.org/en/developers/docs/consensus-mechanisms/pos [https://perma.cc/FB7M-SZU2]

24. Eyal, I., Sirer, E.G.: Majority is not enough: bitcoin mining is vulnerable. Commun. ACM **61**(7), 95–102 (2018). https://doi.org/10.1145/3212998

25. Fernández-Caramés, T.M., Fraga-Lamas, P.: Towards post-quantum blockchain: a review on blockchain cryptography resistant to quantum computing attacks. IEEE Access **8**, 21091–21116 (2020)

26. Garay, J.A., Kiayias, A., Panagiotakos, G.: Consensus from signatures of work. In: Jarecki, S. (ed.) CT-RSA 2020. LNCS, vol. 12006, pp. 319–344. Springer, Cham (2020). https://doi.org/10.1007/978-3-030-40186-3_14

27. Gencer, A.E., Basu, S., Eyal, I., van Renesse, R., Sirer, E.G.: Decentralization in bitcoin and Ethereum networks. In: Meiklejohn, S., Sako, K. (eds.) FC 2018. LNCS, vol. 10957, pp. 439–457. Springer, Heidelberg (2018). https://doi.org/10.1007/978-3-662-58387-6_24

28. Griffith, E., Yaffe-Bellany, D.: Bitcoin plummets below $20,000 for first time since late 2020. New York Times (2022). https://www.nytimes.com/2022/06/18/technology/bitcoin-20000.html

29. Jakobsson, M., Juels, A.: Proofs of work and bread pudding protocols. In: Preneel, B. (ed.) Secure Information Networks: Communications and Multimedia Security, IFIP TC6/TC11 Joint Working Conference on Communications and Multimedia Security (CMS 1999), September 20–21, 1999, Leuven, Belgium. IFIP Conference Proceedings, vol. 152, pp. 258–272. Kluwer (1999)

30. King, S., Nadal, S.: PPCoin: peer-to-peer crypto-currency with proof-of-stake (2012). https://bitcoin.peryaudo.org/vendor/peercoin-paper.pdf

31. Kleinman, Z.: Bitcoin: Why is the largest cryptocurrency crashing? BBC (2022). https://www.bbc.co.uk/news/technology-61796155 [https://perma.cc/6PNV-9AZ7]

32. Küfeoğlu, S., Özkuran, M.: Bitcoin mining: a global review of energy and power demand. Energy Res. Soc. Sci. **58**, 101273 (2019). https://doi.org/10.1016/j.erss.2019.101273

33. LaMacchia, B.: The long road ahead to transition to post-quantum cryptography. Commun. ACM **65**(1), 28–30 (2021). https://doi.org/10.1145/3498706

34. Long, S., Basu, S., Sirer, E.G.: Measuring miner decentralization in proof-of-work blockchains. CoRR abs/2203.16058 (2022). https://doi.org/10.48550/arXiv.2203.16058

35. Miller, A., Kosba, A.E., Katz, J., Shi, E.: Nonoutsourceable scratch-off puzzles to discourage bitcoin mining coalitions. In: Ray, I., Li, N., Kruegel, C. (eds.) Proceedings of the 22nd ACM SIGSAC Conference on Computer and Communications Security, Denver, CO, USA, October 12–16, 2015. pp. 680–691. ACM (2015). https://doi.org/10.1145/2810103.2813621

36. Mosca, M., Piani, M.: 2021 quantum threat timeline report (2021). https://globalriskinstitute.org/publications/2021-quantum-threat-timeline-report [https://perma.cc/8AU5-2JDC]

37. Nakamoto, S.: Bitcoin: a peer-to-peer electronic cash system (2009). http://www.bitcoin.org/bitcoin.pdf

38. National Institute of Standards and Technology (NIST): Post-quantum cryptography (2022). https://csrc.nist.gov/projects/post-quantum-cryptography [https://perma.cc/6U4S-VEDW]

39. Nerem, R.R., Gaur, D.R.: Conditions for advantageous quantum bitcoin mining (2021). https://doi.org/10.48550/ARXIV.2110.00878

40. Nielsen, M.A., Chuang, I.L.: Quantum Computation and Quantum Information (10th Anniversary edition). Cambridge University Press, Cambridge (2016)

41. Nxt Community: Nxt whitepaper (2014). https://www.jelurida.com/sites/default/files/NxtWhitepaper.pdf

42. Osborne, M.: Bitcoin could rival beef or crude oil in environmental impact. Smithsonian Magazine (2022). https://www.smithsonianmag.com/smart-news/bitcoin-could-rival-beef-or-crude-oil-in-environmental-impact-180980877 [https://perma.cc/8WJH-NVPU]
43. Park, S., Kwon, A., Fuchsbauer, G., Gazi, P., Alwen, J., Pietrzak, K.: Spacemint: a cryptocurrency based on proofs of space. In: Meiklejohn, S., Sako, K. (eds.) FC 2018. LNCS, vol. 10957, pp. 480–499. Springer, Cham (2018). https://doi.org/10.1007/978-3-662-58387-6_26
44. Pietrzak, K.: Proofs of catalytic space. In: Blum, A. (ed.) 10th Innovations in Theoretical Computer Science Conference, ITCS 2019, January 10–12, 2019, San Diego, California, USA. LIPIcs, vol. 124, pp. 59:1–59:25. Schloss Dagstuhl - Leibniz-Zentrum für Informatik (2019). https://doi.org/10.4230/LIPIcs.ITCS.2019.59
45. Protocol Labs: Filecoin: A decentralized storage network (2017). https://filecoin.io/filecoin.pdf
46. Quisquater, J.-J., Delescaille, J.-P.: How easy is collision search. New results and applications to DES. In: Brassard, G. (ed.) CRYPTO 1989. LNCS, vol. 435, pp. 408–413. Springer, New York (1990). https://doi.org/10.1007/0-387-34805-0_38
47. Shi, E., Stefanov, E., Papamanthou, C.: Practical dynamic proofs of retrievability. In: Sadeghi, A., Gligor, V.D., Yung, M. (eds.) 2013 ACM SIGSAC Conference on Computer and Communications Security, CCS 2013, Berlin, Germany, 4–8 November 2013, pp. 325–336. ACM (2013). https://doi.org/10.1145/2508859.2516669
48. Shinobi: How centralized is bitcoin mining really? Bitcoin Magazine (2021). https://bitcoinmagazine.com/business/is-bitcoin-mining-centralized
49. Stebila, D., Kuppusamy, L., Rangasamy, J., Boyd, C., Gonzalez Nieto, J.: Stronger difficulty notions for client puzzles and denial-of-service-resistant protocols. In: Kiayias, A. (ed.) CT-RSA 2011. LNCS, vol. 6558, pp. 284–301. Springer, Heidelberg (2011). https://doi.org/10.1007/978-3-642-19074-2_19
50. Vranken, H.: Sustainability of bitcoin and blockchains. Current Opinion Environ. Sustain. 28, 1–9 (2017). https://doi.org/10.1016/j.cosust.2017.04.011
51. Wagstaff, J.: Subspace: a solution to the farmer's dilemma. https://drive.google.com/file/d/1v847u_XeVf0SBz7Y7LEMXi72QfqirstL/view [https://perma.cc/W33J-CQNK]
52. White House Office of Science and Technology Policy (OSTP): Climate and energy implications of crypto-assets in the united states (2022). https://www.whitehouse.gov/wp-content/uploads/2022/09/09-2022-Crypto-Assets-and-Climate-Report.pdf [https://perma.cc/7DDQ-KYX9]
53. Zhandry, M.: How to record quantum queries, and applications to quantum indifferentiability. In: Boldyreva, A., Micciancio, D. (eds.) CRYPTO 2019. LNCS, vol. 11693, pp. 239–268. Springer, Cham (2019). https://doi.org/10.1007/978-3-030-26951-7_9

Fair Delivery of Decentralised Randomness Beacon

Runchao Han[1,2]($\boxtimes$) and Jiangshan Yu[1]

[1] Monash University, Melbourne, Australia
me@runchao.rocks, jiangshan.yu@monash.edu
[2] CSIRO-Data61, Melbourne, Australia

Abstract. The security of many protocols such as voting and blockchains relies on a secure source of randomness. Decentralised Randomness Beacon (DRB) has been considered as a promising approach, where a set of participants jointly generates a sequence of random outputs. While the DRBs have been extensively studied, they failed to capture the advantage that some participants learn random outputs earlier than other participants. In time-sensitive protocols whose execution depends on the randomness from a DRB, such an advantage allows the adversary to behave adaptively according to random outputs, compromising the fairness and/or security in these protocols.

In this paper, we formalise a new property, *delivery-fairness*, to quantify the advantage. In particular, we distinguish two aspects of delivery-fairness, namely *length-advantage*, i.e., how many random outputs an adversary can learn earlier than correct participants, and *time-advantage*, i.e., how much time an adversary can learn a given random output earlier than correct participants. In addition, we prove the lower bound of delivery-fairness showing optimal guarantee. We further analyse the delivery-fairness guarantee of state-of-the-art DRBs and discuss insights, which, we show through case studies, could help improve delivery-fairness of existing systems to its optimal.

1 Introduction

Decentralised Randomness Beacon (DRB) is a protocol where a set of participants jointly generates a sequence of random outputs. It has been a promising approach to provide secure randomness to other protocols and applications. There have been emerging DRB proposals [6,20,26,37] and deployed DRB systems [3,5], and DRBs have been used by many high-financial-stake applications such as blockchains [19,27,30,32], lotteries [11], games [14,17], and non-fungible tokens (NFTs) [1,4].

Applications have two common approaches to use a DRB, namely 1) by using a random output at a certain height which the DRB has not reached yet, and 2) by using a random output produced near a certain time in the future. For example, Polygon Hermez [13] and Celo [2] used the 697500-th random

© International Financial Cryptography Association 2024
F. Baldimtsi and C. Cachin (Eds.): FC 2023, LNCS 13950, pp. 218–234, 2024.
https://doi.org/10.1007/978-3-031-47754-6_13

output [10] and the random output produced near 29/10/2021 9am UTC [12] of Drand [6] for their zkSNARK trusted setup, respectively.

Existing DRBs are designed with three main security properties in consideration, namely *consistency*, *liveness* and *unpredictability* [20,26]. Consistency states that all correct participants (who generate random outputs) share the same view on a unique ledger, i.e., sequence of random outputs. Liveness states that all correct participants produce random outputs no slower than a certain rate. Unpredictability states that no participant can distinguish a future random output from a uniformly sampled random string of the same length.

However, existing adversary models and security properties do not cover the unfair case resulted by the difference in the timing of learning a random output. In particular, when a random output is generated, the first "creator", or "observer", learns its value earlier than others. Such an advantage is not desired in practice. In time-sensitive protocols whose execution depends on the randomness from a DRB, the advantage allows an adversary to behave adaptively according to random outputs, compromising the fairness and/or security in these protocols. In the above example of zkSNARK trusted setup, if the adversary learns the random output before the trusted setup starts, then Hermez's and Celo's trusted setup will be insecure against an adaptive adversary [10,15,22]. Another example is the on-chain lottery which determines the winner out of all players by using random outputs from a DRB. If the adversary learns the random output before the lottery starts, then it learns whether it will win the lottery in advance, and thus can decide whether to participate in the lottery according to its outcome.

1.1   Related Works

A systematic and formal study on the advantage of learning random outputs faster in DRB is still missing. Existing DRB models only focus on certain attacks leading to certain aspects in this advantage [20,27]. Related security properties in other primitives do not cover this advantage, as they either concern eventual delivery without quantifying the advantage [24], or concern the advantage among correct participants excluding Byzantine participants [25,33–35].

Related Properties in DRBs. Previous research either informally studies such advantage, or formally studies certain attacks leading to this advantage. Ouroboros Praos [27] states that a DRB is leaky if the leader can learn the random output in the next epoch. However, the "leaky" definition is embedded in the ideal functionality of DRB rather than stated separately, disallowing specific analysis.

RandPiper [20] combines the "leaky" property into the unpredictability property, yielding d-unpredictability. It states that in the beginning of an epoch, the adversary can learn at most d future random outputs in advance. However, d-unpredictability only captures *length-advantage*, i.e., how many random outputs the adversary can learn earlier than correct participants, but not *time-advantage*, i.e., how much time the adversary can learn a given random output earlier than correct participants. In addition, RandPiper only studies d-unpredictability under the private beacon attack where the adversary solely samples random outputs, neglecting other possible attacks on delivery-fairness.

SPURT [26] defines the "nearly simultaneous beacon output" as a part of the unpredictability property. It states that all correct participants learn a random output within a constant time after the adversary learns it. The "nearly simultaneous" notion only captures the time-advantage but not the length-advantage. It also falls short of quantifying the time-advantage only asymptotically, and thus does not support concrete analysis.

Guaranteed Output Delivery and Fairness in Multiparty Computation. Guaranteed output delivery (GOD) and fairness are properties of multiparty computation (MPC) protocols, where participants jointly compute a function of their inputs securely under a subset of corrupted participants. GOD specifies that corrupted participants cannot prevent the correct participants from receiving the function's output. Fairness specifies that corrupted participants should receive the function's output if and only if correct participants receive it. GOD and fairness are equivalent when broadcast channels are accessible [24], which is our setting. However, these two properties are usually analysed under discrete time models which only concern eventual delivery, and thus do not allow quantitative analysis.

Consistent Length in Blockchain. Blockchain protocols allow participants to jointly maintain a blockchain. The consistent length property [25,33–35] of blockchain protocols specify that if a correct participant's blockchain is of length ℓ at time t, then any correct participant's blockchain at time $t + \psi$ is of length at least ℓ. Blockchains trivially satisfy the property in synchronous networks, as a correct participant will send its chain to other correct participants within the synchronous latency Δ.

Adapting the consistent length property from blockchain protocols to DRBs suffers from two limitations. First, it only considers the advantage between correct participants rather than the advantage of an adversary. In particular, the adversary may grow its blockchain faster than correct participants, while withholding its blockchain. This makes it a liveness property rather than a security property. Second, it only concerns the time advantage, i.e., how much time the adversary learns blocks earlier than correct participants, but does not concern how many blocks the adversary can learn earlier than correct participants.

1.2 Our Contributions

In this paper, we initiate the study of *delivery-fairness*, a new security property capturing the advantage that some participants learn random outputs earlier than other participants in DRBs. We formalise delivery-fairness, prove its lower bound, and analyse the delivery-fairness guarantee of state-of-the-art DRBs, including Drand [6], HydRand [37], GRandPiper [20] and SPURT [26]. Through the analysis, we identify attacks on delivery-fairness and obtain several insights

Table 1. Summary of evaluation results under synchronous networks.

	Protocol	No DKG	Fault tolerance	Comm. compl.		Latency		Delivery-fairness¶	
				Best	Worst	Best	Worst	ω	ψ
Existing work	Drand [6]	✗	$n = 2f+1$	$O(n^2)$	$O(n^2)$	δ	Δ	$\frac{\Delta}{\delta} - 1$	$\Delta - \delta$
	Lock-step Drand [7]	✗	$n = 2f+1$	$O(n^2)$	$O(n^2)$	Δ	Δ	1	$\Delta - \delta$
	HydRand [37]	✓	$n = 3f+1$	$O(n^2)$	$O(n^3)$†	3δ	3Δ	$\frac{\Delta}{3\delta} + f$	$(3f+1)\Delta - \delta$
	GRandPiper [20]	✓	$n = 2f+1$	$O(n^2)$	$O(n^2)$	11Δ	11Δ	$f+1$	$(11f+1)\Delta - \delta$
	SPURT [26]	✓	$n = 3f+1$	$O(n^2)$	$O(n^2)$	7δ	$(f+7)\Delta^*$	$\frac{\Delta}{7\delta}$	$\Delta - \delta$
This paper	Lock-step HydRand	✓	$n = 3f+1$	$O(n^2)$	$O(n^3)$†	3Δ	3Δ	$f+1$	$(3f+1)\Delta - \delta$
	Lock-step SPURT	✓	$n = 3f+1$	$O(n^2)$	$O(n^2)$	7Δ	$(f+7)\Delta^*$	1	$\Delta - \delta$

¶ In (ω, ψ)-delivery-fairness (Definition 5), the delivery-fairness is better when ω and ψ are smaller. When $\omega = 1$ and $\psi = \Delta - \delta$, the delivery-fairness is optimal, where δ and Δ are the actual network latency and the latency upper bound, respectively. In practice, $\delta << \Delta$.
† In the worst case, the adversary does not reveal its committed secrets for f consecutive epochs. In the next epoch, the correct leader needs to broadcast f $O(n)$-size recovery certificates to all participants, leading to $O(n^3)$ communication complexity.
* In the worst case, the adversary controls f consecutive leaders and aborts these f consecutive epochs before a correct epoch with 7Δ, leading to $(f + 7)\Delta$ worst-case latency.

for improving delivery-fairness. The insights allow us to suggest lock-step variants for HydRand and SPURT with better delivery-fairness (where SPURT achieves the optimal value), without affecting system models or security properties. Table 1 summarises our results.

Delivery-Fairness and Its Lower Bound. We base our study on existing DRB models [20, 26, 28]. As specified in Sect. 2, we consider a fixed set of n participants and an adversary who can corrupt up to f of them, where f is protocol-specific. The network is synchronous, where messages are delivered in at least the actual network latency δ and at most a known upper bound Δ. Participants jointly execute the DRB protocol to agree on a unique ledger containing a sequence of random outputs securing three properties, namely consistency, liveness and unpredictability.

Atop the DRB model, we provide the first formal definition of delivery-fairness in Sect. 3. The delivery-fairness concerns two aspects of advantage, namely the *length-advantage*, i.e., how many random outputs an adversary can learn earlier than correct participants, and the *time-advantage*, i.e., how much time an adversary can learn a given random output earlier than correct participants.

Definition 1 (Delivery-fairness, informal; formalised in Definition 5). *A DRB protocol satisfies (ω, ψ)-delivery-fairness if the following holds for any two participants (p_i, p_j) and any time t, except for negligible probability:*

- ω-**length-advantage**: *at time t, p_i's ledger pruning the last ω random outputs precedes or is equal to p_j's ledger; and*
- ψ-**time-advantage**: *p_i's ledger at time t precedes or is equal to p_j's ledger at time $t + \psi$.*

When ω and ψ are smaller, the length-advantage and time-advantage of any participant over the other participants are smaller, thus the DRB provides better delivery-fairness. We stress that delivery-fairness is achievable in synchronous networks, where messages are delivered in at least the actual network latency δ and at most a known upper bound Δ. Otherwise, the adversary can arbitrarily delay messages in asynchronous networks or the asynchrony period in partially synchronous networks, increasing ω and ψ to values that are impractical.

We then prove the lower bound of delivery-fairness in synchronous networks, where ω and ψ are at least 1 and $\Delta - \delta$, respectively. The intuition behind the proof is that, if the time difference of learning a random output between any two participants is smaller than $\Delta - \delta$, then the group of Byzantine participants can produce valid random outputs without communicating with correct participants, contradicting to unpredictability or consistency.

Theorem 1 (Delivery-fairness lower bound, informal; formalised in Theorem 2). *There does not exist a secure DRB protocol that achieves (ω, ψ)-delivery fairness with $\omega < 1$ or $\psi < \Delta - \delta$ under synchronous networks.*

Analysis of Delivery-Fairness of Existing DRBs. With the formalisation, we analyse the delivery-fairness of state-of-the-art DRB protocols, namely Drand [6], HydRand [37], GRandPiper [20] and SPURT [26], in Sect. 4. Table 1 summarises the results. Through the analysis, we identify attacks on delivery-fairness and obtain several insights for improving delivery-fairness. Specifically, we identify a new attack called *latency manipulation attack* that can weaken the delivery-fairness in the original versions of Drand, HydRand and SPURT. This attack is rooted in their non-lock-step design that participants can make progress once receiving sufficient messages, without the need of waiting for a fixed time period. Following this observation, we suggest lock-step variants for HydRand and SPURT that resist against the latency manipulation attack and thus achieve the better delivery-fairness (where SPURT achieves the optimal value), without affecting system models or security properties. In addition, a previously known unpredictability-focused attack, which we call *private beacon attack*, can also weaken the delivery-fairness of HydRand and GRandPiper. The private beacon attack is rooted in their design that the epoch leader solely samples the entropy for the random output. To resist against the attack, the entropy should instead be sampled by a group of at least $f + 1$ participants, where f is the number of Byzantine participants.

2   Model

2.1   System Model

Participants. We consider a fixed number of n participants. Each participant $p_k \in [p_n]$ generates a pair of secret key and public key (sk_k, pk_k), and is uniquely identified by its public key in the system. We assume each participant has the knowledge of other participants' public keys.

Adversary. We consider a static adversary $\mathcal{A}$. In the beginning of the protocol, $\mathcal{A}$ can corrupt at most f participants, where f is a corruption parameter subjected to the protocol design. After that, $\mathcal{A}$ cannot change the set of corrupted participants or corrupt more participants. $\mathcal{A}$ fully controls corrupted participants, including observing the participant's internal state and controlling its messages and outputs, without any latency. $\mathcal{A}$ can read all messages between participants, but cannot modify or drop messages sent by correct participants. We also refer to a corrupted participant as *Byzantine* participant. We assume $\mathcal{A}$ is probabilistically polynomial-time (PPT), and thus cannot break standard cryptographic primitives.

Network Model. We assume synchronous networks: $\mathcal{A}$ can decide to deliver any message in at least the actual network delay δ and at most a known upper bound Δ. In practice, $\delta << \Delta$.

We will conduct analysis assuming synchronous networks for all DRBs, although some of them can work in relaxed network models. The reason is that the delivery-fairness is a concrete measure and is meaningful only in synchronous networks. Otherwise, in asynchronous networks or the asynchrony period in partially synchronous networks, the adversary can arbitrarily delay messages to increase its advantage, leading to impractical delivery-fairness guarantee. Consequently, applications that require time-sensitive random outputs will be insecure or unfair. Thus, when the application scenarios demand a delivery-fair DRB, the application and DRB have to be deployed in synchronous networks.

2.2 Components of DRBs

The set of n participants continuously execute the DRB protocol Π to produce a sequence of random outputs. Specifically, participants jointly produce and agree on a ledger formed as a sequence of blocks. Each agreed block has to meet a verification predicate. Each block deterministically derives a random output, which can be extracted via a random output extraction function. The verification predicate and random output extraction function are accessible to anyone inside and outside the system, and their instantiation depends on the concrete protocol design.

Ledger. A ledger T is formed as a sequence of blocks. Let $T[e]$ be the e-th block in the ledger T. Let $|T|$ be the length of ledger T. Let $T[p:q]$ be the ledger from p-th block to $(q-1)$-th block of ledger T. Parameter p and q can be set empty, indicating the beginning and the end of the ledger, respectively. Let $T^{\lceil \ell} = T[:-\ell]$ be the ledger from pruning the last ℓ blocks of ledger T. We denote a ledger T is a prefix of or equals to another ledger T' as $T \preceq T'$.

Epoch. DRBs are executed in epochs. In each epoch, participants are expected to produce and agree on a new block. The time period of an epoch can be fixed by the protocol design, or be variant depending on Byzantine behaviours and/or actual network delay. In leader-based DRBs, in each epoch, a leader is elected to drive the protocol execution. In some leader-based DRBs (e.g., SPURT [26]), a Byzantine epoch leader can abort the protocol, so that no block is produced in that epoch.

Verification Predicate. To be agreed, a block has to meet the verification predicate $F_V(\cdot)$. In $F_V(\kappa, T, B) \to \{0, 1\}$, given security parameter κ, ledger T and block B as input, outputs 1 if B is a valid successor block of T. A ledger T is valid in κ if for all $\ell \in [|T| - 1]$, $F_V(\kappa, T[: \ell], T[\ell]) = 1$. Let T_i^t be participant p_i's longest valid ledger at time t.

Random Output Extraction Function. Each block contains a random output, which can be extracted by the random output extraction function $F_R(\cdot)$. In $F_R(\kappa, T) \to R_e$, given security parameter κ and a ledger T of length $|T| = (e - 1)$ as input, $F_R(\kappa, T)$ can derive a random output R_e. That is, every block B_e is associated with a random output R_e.

2.3 Security Properties of DRBs

A DRB protocol Π should satisfy the following properties, namely consistency, liveness, and unpredictability.

Consistency. Consistency ensures that correct participants agree on a unique ledger, and thus a unique sequence of random outputs. The consistency definition follows the common prefix property in blockchain protocols [29], where the ledgers of any two correct participants are same except for the last ℓ blocks.

Definition 2 (ℓ-consistency, from [29]). *For any κ, there exists a negligible function* negl$(\cdot)$ *such that the following holds except for probability* negl(κ). *For any two correct participants p_i and p_j ($i = j$ is possible) at time t,*

$$(T_i^t)^{\lceil \ell} \preceq T_j^t \vee (T_j^t)^{\lceil \ell} \preceq T_i^t$$

Liveness. Liveness ensures that correct participants produce new random outputs at an admissible rate. The liveness definition follows the chain growth property in blockchain protocols [31], where for any period of t time a correct participant's ledger grows at least $t \cdot \tau$ blocks.

Definition 3 ((t, τ)-liveness, from [31]). *For any κ, there exists a negligible function* negl$(\cdot)$ *such that the following holds except for probability* negl(κ). *For any correct participant p_i and time $t' \geq t$,*

$$|T_i^{t'}| - |T_i^{t'-t}| \geq t \cdot \tau$$

Unpredictability. Each random output should be *unpredictable*: given an agreed ledger, the adversary cannot predict the next random output before it is produced. If the adversary can predict future random outputs, then it may take advantage in randomness-based applications. The unpredictability definition follows the paradigm that without protocol transcripts from correct participants, no adversary can distinguish between a future random output of the DRB and a randomly sampled string of the same length [26,28].

Definition 4 (Unpredictability, from [26]**).** *A DRB protocol Π is unpredictable if for every κ, there exists a negligible function $\mathsf{negl}(\cdot)$ such that the following holds. Assuming all participants have agreed on a ledger of e consecutive random outputs $R_1, \ldots, R_e$. For any future random output $R_{e'}$ where $e' > e$ and any probabilistic polynomial-time (PPT) adversary $\mathcal{A}$, if $\mathcal{A}$ does not have the knowledge of protocol transcripts associated with $R_{e'}$ from correct participants, then*

$$|\Pr[\mathcal{A}(R_{e'}) = 1] - \Pr[\mathcal{A}(r) = 1]| \leq \mathsf{negl}(\kappa)$$

, where r is a randomly sampled κ-bit string, and $\mathcal{A}(x) \rightarrow \{0,1\}$ outputs 1 if $\mathcal{A}$ guesses x to be the random output in epoch e' and otherwise 0.

2.4 Performance Metrics

DRBs concern two performance metrics, namely communication complexity and latency.

Communication Complexity. Communication complexity is the total amount of communication required to complete a protocol [39]. In DRBs, the communication complexity is quantified as the amount of bits transferred among participants for generating a random output. A protocol may have different communication complexity in the best-case and worst-case executions.

Latency. Latency is the time required to complete a protocol. In the context of DRBs, the latency is quantified as the time participants take to generate a random output. Similarly, a protocol may have different latencies in the best-case and worst-case executions.

3 Delivery-Fairness Property

In this section, we formally define the delivery-fairness property. The delivery-fairness concerns two aspects of the advantage: *length-advantage* and *time-advantage*. Length-advantage concerns how many random outputs the adversary can learn earlier than correct participants. Time-advantage concerns how much time the adversary can learn a random output earlier than correct participants. We also prove the lower bound of the delivery-fairness, representing the optimal guarantee.

3.1 Defining Delivery-Fairness

We define delivery-fairness through two strawman definitions that are intuitive but incomplete. We begin with the *fairness* notion in multiparty computation (MPC) protocols that, if the adversary receives the output, then correct participants eventually receive the output [36]. We then generalise the fairness notion to the continuous time model, making it consistent with the DRB settings.

Attempt #1: Time Advantage. We first consider relaxing the round-based fairness definition to the continuous time model by introducing a time parameter

ψ. Namely, if a participant learns a random output at time t, then all other participants learn this random output no later than time $t + \psi$. However, this definition fails to capture that the adversary may learn more than one random outputs in advance than correct participants.

Attempt #2: Length and Time Advantage. We then consider capturing both length and time advantage. Let ω be the length parameter and ψ be the time advantage parameter. A DRB protocol satisfies (ω, ψ)-delivery-fairness if for any two participants p_i, p_j: 1) p_i's ledger is longer than p_j's ledger by no more than ω random outputs, and 2) p_j's ledger at time $t + \psi$ is no shorter than p_i's ledger at time t.

However, the definition does not specify whether the last ω random outputs of p_j at time $t + \psi$ should be identical to the last ω random outputs of p_i at time t or not. If not, then this contradicts to the consistency property.

Final Definition: Length and Time Advantage with Consistency. We then add the consistency guarantee to the definition in attempt #2, leading to our final definition. Specifically, delivery-fairness concerns the adversary's length advantage and time advantage, parameterised by ω and ψ, respectively. The ω-length-advantage states that the longest valid ledger pruning the last ω blocks is a prefix of the valid ledger in any participant's view at any time. The ψ-time-advantage states that the shortest valid ledger at time t should "catch up with" all participants' ledgers at time t after the time period of ψ. When ω and ψ are smaller, the DRB provides stronger delivery-fairness guarantee.

Definition 5 ((ω, ψ)-Delivery-Fairness). *A DRB protocol Π satisfies (ω, ψ)-delivery-fairness if for every κ, there exists a negligible function $\mathsf{negl}(\cdot)$ such that the following holds for any two participants p_i, p_j and any time t except for probability $\mathsf{negl}(\kappa)$:*

- *ω-length-advantage:* $(\mathcal{T}_i^t)^{\lceil \omega} \preceq \mathcal{T}_j^t$
- *ψ-time-advantage:* $\mathcal{T}_i^t \preceq \mathcal{T}_j^{t+\psi}$

3.2   Lower Bound of Delivery-Fairness

We prove that $(1, \Delta - \delta)$-delivery-fairness is the optimal delivery-fairness guarantee. Specifically, we prove the following theorem.

Theorem 2 (Delivery-fairness lower bound of DRB). *There does not exist a DRB protocol that simultaneously satisfies the following in synchronous networks:*

- *consistency, liveness and unpredictability as in Sect. 2; and*
- *(ω, ψ)-delivery fairness with $\omega < 1$ or $\psi < \Delta - \delta$*

Proof. Assuming such a DRB protocol exists. Assuming at time t, all participants have agreed on a ledger of e consecutive random outputs $R_1, \ldots, R_e$, and start producing R_{e+1}. $\mathcal{A}$ sets the latency among correct participants to be Δ, the latency of messages from any corrupted participant to any correct participant to be Δ, and the latency of messages from any correct participant to any corrupted participant to be δ. By unpredictability, without messages from correct participants, corrupted participants cannot learn the value of R_{e+1}. Thus, the fastest possible way for corrupted participants to learn a random output is to get messages from correct participants, which is at least $t + \delta$. Given the latency set by $\mathcal{A}$, a correct participant receives messages only at $t + \Delta$.

By the assumption that the time-advantage between correct and corrupted participants is smaller than $\Delta - \delta$, correct participants learn the random output R_{e+1} before $t + \Delta$. Thus, a correct participant has to learn the random output R'_{e+1} that satisfies the verification predicate. If $R'_{e+1} = R_{e+1}$, then this means that a participant can solely produce random outputs without interacting with the other participants. Thus, f corrupted participants can also produce random outputs without interacting with the other correct participants, contradicting to the unpredictability property. If $R'_{e+1} \neq R_{e+1}$, then this means that f corrupted participants can produce valid random outputs conflicted with those from the other participants, contradicting to the consistency property.

4   Delivery-Fairness Analysis of Existing DRBs

4.1   Drand

Summary of Design. Drand a DRB protocol based on the BLS threshold signature [21]. It allows a threshold number of participants in a group to jointly sign a message, where the signature is publicly verifiable.

In Drand design, participants perform a distributed key generation (DKG) to generate secret keys, and agree on an initial signature σ^0. Then, for each epoch e, participants jointly generate a BLS threshold signature σ^e over e and the last epoch's BLS signature σ^{e-1} (or σ^0 at the first epoch). An epoch's random output R_e is the calculated as $H(\sigma^e)$, where $H(\cdot)$ is a hash function. Drand requires a DKG due to the usage of threshold signature, and achieves the fault tolerance capacity of $n = 2f + 1$.

Drand has two variants, namely the non-lock-step Π_{Drand} specified in the documentation [8] and the lock-step $\Pi_{\text{Drand}}^{\text{LS}}$ in the actual implementation [7]. Compared to Π_{Drand}, $\Pi_{\text{Drand}}^{\text{LS}}$ requires participants to wait for a time period during the phase of broadcasting signatures for each epoch e. In synchronous networks, the time period is at least Δ. In Drand's implementation $\Pi_{\text{Drand}}^{\text{LS}}$ [7], the default time period (named `DefaultBeaconPeriod`) is 60 s.

Latency Manipulation Attack. We identify a new attack *latency manipulation attack* that can increase the adversary's advantage of delivery-fairness in the non-lock-step Π_{Drand}. The latency manipulation attack only requires the adversary to manipulate the latency among participants (subjected to the network model), and does not require equivocating or withholding messages. Thus, the attack is unaccountable and does not affect other security properties or performance metrics (Fig. 1).

In the beginning of the DRB protocol, the adversary $\mathcal{A}$ does the follows.

1. $\mathcal{A}$ chooses $n - 2f$ correct participants.
2. $\mathcal{A}$ sets the latency of messages among f corrupted participants and $n - 2f$ correct participants to be δ.
3. $\mathcal{A}$ sets the latency of messages from, to and among the other f correct participants to be Δ.

Fig. 1. Latency manipulation attack on leaderless DRBs.

The adversary $\mathcal{A}$ follows the protocol with $n - 2f$ (which is 1 in Drand) correct participants while delaying all messages from and to the other f correct participants. During the first Δ under latency manipulation attack, $\mathcal{A}$ and $n-2f$ correct participants learn a random output for every δ, while the other f correct participants learn a random output only at the end of this Δ.

Delivery-Fairness of Non-Lock-Step Drand. At the end of this Δ, $\mathcal{A}$ and $n-2f$ correct participants have learned $\frac{\Delta}{\delta}+1$ random outputs, while the other f correct participants only learn two random outputs, leading to length-advantage degree $\omega = \frac{\Delta}{\delta} - 1$. In real-world networks, $\Delta >> \delta$, which leads to large value of ω. For each of these random outputs (except for the first one), $\mathcal{A}$ and $n - 2f$ correct participants learn it earlier than the other f correct participants by $\Delta - \delta$, leading to time-advantage degree $\psi = \Delta - \delta$. Therefore, the non-lock-step Drand Π_{Drand} achieves (ω, ψ)-delivery-fairness where $\omega = \frac{\Delta}{\delta} - 1$ and $\psi = \Delta - \delta$.

Delivery-Fairness of Lock-Step Drand. We analyse the delivery-fairness guarantee of $\Pi_{\text{Drand}}^{\text{LS}}$, and show that $\Pi_{\text{Drand}}^{\text{LS}}$ achieves optimal $(1, \Delta - \delta)$-delivery-fairness. The improvement compared to the non-lock-step Π_{Drand} is due to the lock-step design, where correct participants will wait for Δ before entering the next epoch and broadcasting signature shares, even learning the random output of this epoch in advance.

Gained Insights. Through the analysis, we obtain an insight on improving the delivery-fairness. Namely, the lock-step execution is necessary to bound the adversary's length-advantage to 1. Otherwise, without the lock-step execution, the latency manipulation attack can always allow the adversary to grow its ledger faster than correct participants within a Δ, and thus increase its advantage in length and time.

4.2   HydRand and GRandPiper

We analyse the delivery-fairness of HydRand [37] and GRandPiper [20], two DRB protocols based on the rotating leader paradigm and PVSS. We observe that a previously known unpredictability-focused attack, which we call *private beacon attack*, weakens the delivery-fairness of HydRand and GrandPiper. The attack is rooted in their design is that the entropy of a random output is solely

In the beginning of the DRB protocol, the adversary $\mathcal{A}$ does the follows.

1. $\mathcal{A}$ chooses $n - 2f$ correct participants.
2. $\mathcal{A}$ sets the latency of messages among f corrupted participants and $n - 2f$ correct participants to be δ.
3. $\mathcal{A}$ sets the latency of messages from, to and among the other f correct participants to be Δ.
4. Upon a new random output R_e, $\mathcal{A}$ calculates the next leader l_{e+1} based on Π_{LE}. If l_{e+1} is the participant with δ latency, then keep running the attack, otherwise stop the attack.

Fig. 2. Latency manipulation attack on leader-based DRBs. Extra specification compared to the latency manipulation attack on leaderless DRBs is labelled in blue. (Color figure online)

provided by the epoch leader. To resist against the attack, the entropy should instead be provided by a group of at least $f + 1$ participants.

Summary of HydRand. HydRand is a DRB protocol based on leader election, accumulator and publicly verifiable secret sharing (PVSS) [23,38]. Leader election allows a group of participants to elect a leader for every epoch. Accumulator [18] allows to compress a set of values into a short accumulation value, and prove the inclusion of each value given the accumulation value and a short witness. PVSS [23,38] allows one to distribute a secret with a group of participants, in which a threshold number of participants can collaboratively reconstruct the secret.

In HydRand design, participants employ the round-robin leader election to elect a leader for every epoch. In each epoch, the leader solely samples a random input, generates the commitment of this random input, uses PVSS to generate secret shares for this random input, and use the accumulator to generate an accumulation value for these secret shares. Then, the leader broadcasts the commitment, a secret share, and the accumulation value to each participant. Meanwhile, the leader can choose whether to reveal its last random input, which, together with the last f random outputs, determines this epoch's random output. If the leader is Byzantine and does not reveal it, then all participants reconstruct the last random input via broadcasting secret shares. HydRand does not require distributed key generation and achieves the fault tolerance capacity of $n = 3f + 1$.

The original HydRand protocol Π_{HydRand} in the paper [37] and implementation [9] is non-lock-step. We also study its lock-step variant $\Pi_{\text{HydRand}}^{\text{LS}}$ that resists against the latency manipulation attacks and achieves better delivery-fairness.

Latency Manipulation Attack on Leader-Based DRBs. Recall that the latency manipulation attack on leaderless DRBs (e.g., Drand) allows the adversary $\mathcal{A}$ to learn random outputs faster than f correct participants with Δ latency, within a time period of Δ. However, the latency manipulation attack in leader-based DRBs faces a different scenario: during this Δ, if one of these f correct

While following the DRB protocol, the adversary $\mathcal{A}$ does the follows.

1. Upon a new random output R_e, $\mathcal{A}$ calculates the next leader l_{e+1} based on Π_{LE}.
2. If the next leader l_{e+1} is a Byzantine participant, $\mathcal{A}$ follows the protocol to sample the random output R_{e+1} locally and repeats step 1.

Fig. 3. Private beacon attack on DRBs.

participants becomes the leader in an epoch, then $\mathcal{A}$ cannot learn any new random output until this leader reaches this epoch. Consequently, $\mathcal{A}$ has to stop the attack, leading to less advantage compared to the attack in leaderless protocols like Drand. Figure 2 presents the latency manipulation attack on leader-based DRBs.

Private Beacon Attack. Bhat et al. [20] observes an attack on the unpredictability of HydRand and GRandPiper. This attack, which we call *private beacon attack*, can also weaken the delivery-fairness of HydRand (including both Π_{HydRand} and $\Pi_{\mathsf{HydRand}}^{\mathsf{LS}}$) and GRandPiper. In this attack, the adversary grows its own ledger to learn random outputs earlier than correct participants. As HydRand allows the epoch leader to solely sample the entropy, the epoch leader can learn the random output instantly without communicating with others. When c consecutive leaders are corrupted, the adversary can learn c future random outputs. With round-robin leader election used in HydRand, GRandPiper and SPURT, c is at most f. Same as the latency manipulation attack, the private beacon attack does not require equivocating or withholding messages, and thus remains unaccountable. The private beacon attack is presented in Fig. 3.

Delivery-Fairness of Non-Lock-Step HydRand. Both the latency manipulation attack and the private beacon attack can be applied to the non-lock-step Π_{HydRand}. Under both attacks, the non-lock-step Hydrand Π_{HydRand} achieves (ω, ψ)-delivery-fairness where $\omega = \frac{\Delta}{3\delta} + f$ and $\psi = (3f + 1)\Delta - \delta$.

Delivery-Fairness of Lock-Step HydRand. The lock-step execution rules out the latency manipulation attack. Under the private beacon attack, the lock-step HydRand $\Pi_{\mathsf{HydRand}}^{\mathsf{LS}}$ achieves (ω, ψ)-delivery-fairness where $\omega = f + 1$ and $\psi = (3f + 1)\Delta - \delta$.

Summary of GRandPiper. GRandPiper is a DRB based on leader election, Byzantine broadcast and publicly verifiable secret sharing (PVSS). Byzantine broadcast Π_{BB} allows a designated broadcaster broadcasts a value to a group of participants, such that all correct participants will commit the same value. If the broadcaster is correct, then all correct participants will commit the broadcasted value. GRandPiper employs a Byzantine broadcast protocol with $O(n^2)$ communication complexity and latency $t_{\mathsf{BB}} = 11\Delta$.

GRandPiper [20] follows the HydRand's approach with three major modifications. First, GRandPiper enforces participants to recover the secret random input committed by the leader, without allowing the leader to reveal it by itself. Second, GRandPiper replaces the Acknowledge and Vote-confirm phase in HydRand with an explicit Byzantine broadcast protocol Π_{BB}. Note that the Byzantine broadcast and the round-robin leader election constitute a SMR protocol, as described in the RandPiper paper. Third, GRandPiper formalises the Hydrand's idea of separating the process of committing and revealing random inputs as a queue-based mechanism, where each participant buffers previously committed secret values and pops one value to reconstruct for each epoch. GRandPiper does not require distributed key generation and achieves the fault tolerance capacity of $n = 2f + 1$.

Delivery-Fairness of GRandPiper. GRandPiper is lock-step and thus rules out the latency manipulation attack. Under the private beacon attack, GRand-Piper achieves (ω, ψ)-delivery-fairness where $\omega = f + 1$ and $\psi = (11f + 1)\Delta - \delta$.

Gained Insights. In HydRand and GRandPiper, the entropy of a random output is provided by a sole leader. In this case, the adversary can always launch the private beacon attack as long as the leader is Byzantine. To mitigate the private beacon attack, the protocol should prevent the adversary from controlling the entropy for a random output. To this end, the entropy should instead be provided by a group of at least $f + 1$ participants rather than a single participant.

4.3   SPURT

Summary of Design. SPURT is a DRB based on leader election, Byzantine broadcast, and a specialised PVSS protocol $\Pi_{\text{PVSS}}^{\text{uniform}}$. The used Byzantine broadcast protocol a variant of HotStuff [40] with best-case latency of 4δ and worst-case latency $t_{\text{BB}} = 4\Delta$.

In the SPURT design, each participant samples a random input, uses PVSS to generate secret shares, encrypted secret shares and inclusion proofs of this random input, and sends all encrypted shares and inclusion proofs to the leader elected via a round-robin leader election. Then, the leader homomorphically aggregates all received commitments and inclusion proofs column-wise, and triggers a Byzantine broadcast over the aggregated encrypted shares and inclusion proofs, such that all participants agree on the entropy for the random output. After Byzantine broadcast, each participant decrypts one of the encrypted shares and broadcasts the decrypted share, such that all participants can reconstruct the secret from received decrypted shares. SPURT [26] does not require distributed key generation and achieves the fault tolerance capacity of $n = 3f + 1$.

The original SPURT protocol Π_{SPURT} in the paper [26] and implementation [16] is non-lock-step. We also study its lock-step variant $\Pi_{\text{SPURT}}^{\text{LS}}$ that resists against the latency manipulation attacks and achieves optimal delivery-fairness.

Delivery-Fairness of Non-Lock-Step SPURT. SPURT resists against the private beacon attack, as the entropy of a random output is jointly provided by $f + 1$ participants. However, similar to HydRand, the non-lock-step Π_{SPURT} does not resist against the latency manipulation attack in Fig. 2. Specifically, $\mathcal{A}$ sets the latency among its corrupted participants and $n - 2f = f + 1$ correct participants as δ, while the latency from, to and among the rest correct participant as Δ. Recall that SPURT achieves the 7δ best-case latency and 7Δ worst-case latency. Similar to non-lock-step HydRand Π_{HydRand}, after a Δ of the latency manipulation attack, $\mathcal{A}$ and $f + 1$ correct participants learn $\frac{\Delta}{7\delta} + 1$ random outputs, while the rest correct participant only knows a single random output, leading to $\frac{\Delta}{7\delta}$ length-advantage and $\Delta - \delta$ time-advantage. Thus, the non-lock-step Π_{SPURT} achieves (ω, ψ)-delivery-fairness with $\omega = \frac{\Delta}{7\delta}$ and $\psi = \Delta - \delta$.

Delivery-Fairness of Lock-Step SPURT. We then analyse the delivery-fairness guarantee of $\Pi_{\text{SPURT}}^{\text{LS}}$, and show that $\Pi_{\text{SPURT}}^{\text{LS}}$ achieves the optimal $(1, \Delta - \delta)$-delivery-fairness.

References

1. 16 Ways to Create Dynamic Non-Fungible Tokens (NFT) Using Chainlink Oracles. https://blog.chain.link/create-dynamic-nfts-using-chainlink-oracles/
2. Celo: Mobile-First DeFi Platform for Fast, Secure, and Stable Digital Payments https://celo.org/
3. Chainlink VRF. https://docs.chain.link/docs/chainlink-vrf/
4. CryptOrchids: NFT plants that must be watered weekly. https://cryptorchids.io/
5. Distributed Randomness Beacon — Cloudflare,.https://www.cloudflare.com/leagueofentropy/
6. Drand - Distributed Randomness Beacon. https://drand.love/
7. Drand: A Distributed Randomness Beacon Daemon - Go implementation. https://github.com/drand/drand
8. Drand Specification. https://drand.love/docs/specification
9. HydRand: Python implementation of the HydRand protocol. https://github.com/PhilippSchindler/HydRand
10. Join Hermez Trusted Setup Phase 2 Ceremony! https://blog.hermez.io/hermez-trusted-setup-phase-2/
11. PancakeSwap Lottery. https://pancakeswap.finance/lottery
12. Phase 2 setup random beacon of Celo. https://github.com/celo-org/celo-bls-snark-rs/issues/227
13. Polygon Hermez. https://hermez.io/
14. PolyRoll: Decentralized Games. https://polyroll.org/
15. Reinforcing the Security of the Sapling MPC. https://electriccoin.co/blog/reinforcing-the-security-of-the-sapling-mpc/
16. SPURT implementation, forked from HydRand. https://github.com/sourav1547/HydRand
17. The Economic Impact of Random Rewards in Blockchain Video Games. https://blog.chain.link/the-economic-impact-of-random-rewards-in-blockchain-video-games/
18. Barić, N., Pfitzmann, B.: Collision-free accumulators and fail-stop signature schemes without trees. In: Fumy, W. (ed.) EUROCRYPT 1997. LNCS, vol. 1233, pp. 480–494. Springer, Heidelberg (1997). https://doi.org/10.1007/3-540-69053-0_33
19. Benet, J., Greco, N.: Filecoin: a decentralized storage network. In: Protocol Labs, pp. 1–36 (2018)

20. Bhat, A., Shrestha, N., Luo, Z., Kate, A., Nayak, K.: RandPiper-reconfiguration-friendly random beacons with quadratic communication. In: Proceedings of the 2021 ACM SIGSAC Conference on Computer and Communications Security, pp. 3502–3524 (2021)

21. Boneh, D., Lynn, B., Shacham, H.: Short signatures from the weil pairing. In: Boyd, C. (ed.) ASIACRYPT 2001. LNCS, vol. 2248, pp. 514–532. Springer, Heidelberg (2001). https://doi.org/10.1007/3-540-45682-1_30

22. Bowe, S., Gabizon, A., Miers, I.: Scalable multi-party computation for ZK-snark parameters in the random beacon model. Cryptology ePrint Archive (2017)

23. Cascudo, I., David, B.: SCRAPE: scalable randomness attested by public entities. In: Gollmann, D., Miyaji, A., Kikuchi, H. (eds.) ACNS 2017. LNCS, vol. 10355, pp. 537–556. Springer, Cham (2017). https://doi.org/10.1007/978-3-319-61204-1_27

24. Cohen, R., Lindell, Y.: Fairness versus guaranteed output delivery in secure multiparty computation. J. Cryptol. 30(4), 1157–1186 (2017)

25. Daian, P., Pass, R., Shi, E.: Snow white: robustly reconfigurable consensus and applications to provably secure proof of stake. In: Goldberg, I., Moore, T. (eds.) FC 2019. LNCS, vol. 11598, pp. 23–41. Springer, Cham (2019). https://doi.org/10.1007/978-3-030-32101-7_2

26. Das, S., Krishnan, V., Isaac, I.M., Ren, L.: Spurt: scalable distributed randomness beacon with transparent setup. In: 2022 IEEE Symposium on Security and Privacy (SP), pp. 1380–1395. IEEE (2022)

27. David, B., Gaži, P., Kiayias, A., Russell, A.: Ouroboros Praos: an adaptively-secure, semi-synchronous proof-of-stake blockchain. In: Nielsen, J.B., Rijmen, V. (eds.) EUROCRYPT 2018. LNCS, vol. 10821, pp. 66–98. Springer, Cham (2018). https://doi.org/10.1007/978-3-319-78375-8_3

28. Galindo, D., Liu, J., Ordean, M., Wong, J.M.: Fully distributed verifiable random functions and their application to decentralised random beacons. In: European Symposium on Security and Privacy (2021)

29. Garay, J., Kiayias, A., Leonardos, N.: The bitcoin backbone protocol: analysis and applications. In: Oswald, E., Fischlin, M. (eds.) EUROCRYPT 2015. LNCS, vol. 9057, pp. 281–310. Springer, Heidelberg (2015). https://doi.org/10.1007/978-3-662-46803-6_10

30. Hanke, T., Movahedi, M., Williams, D.: Dfinity technology overview series, consensus system. arXiv preprint arXiv:1805.04548 (2018)

31. Kiayias, A., Panagiotakos, G.: Speed-security tradeoffs in blockchain protocols. IACR Cryptol. ePrint Arch. 2015, 1019 (2015)

32. Kiayias, A., Russell, A., David, B., Oliynykov, R.: Ouroboros: a provably secure proof-of-stake blockchain protocol. In: Katz, J., Shacham, H. (eds.) CRYPTO 2017. LNCS, vol. 10401, pp. 357–388. Springer, Cham (2017). https://doi.org/10.1007/978-3-319-63688-7_12

33. Pass, R., Seeman, L., Shelat, A.: Analysis of the blockchain protocol in asynchronous networks. In: Coron, J.-S., Nielsen, J.B. (eds.) EUROCRYPT 2017. LNCS, vol. 10211, pp. 643–673. Springer, Cham (2017). https://doi.org/10.1007/978-3-319-56614-6_22

34. Pass, R., Shi, E.: Hybrid consensus: efficient consensus in the permissionless model. In: 31st International Symposium on Distributed Computing (DISC 2017). Schloss Dagstuhl-Leibniz-Zentrum fuer Informatik (2017)

35. Pass, R., Shi, E.: Thunderella: blockchains with optimistic instant confirmation. In: Nielsen, J.B., Rijmen, V. (eds.) EUROCRYPT 2018. LNCS, vol. 10821, pp. 3–33. Springer, Cham (2018). https://doi.org/10.1007/978-3-319-78375-8_1

36. Pass, R., Shi, E., Tramèr, F.: Formal abstractions for attested execution secure processors. In: Coron, J.-S., Nielsen, J.B. (eds.) EUROCRYPT 2017. LNCS, vol. 10210, pp. 260–289. Springer, Cham (2017). https://doi.org/10.1007/978-3-319-56620-7_10

37. Schindler, P., Judmayer, A., Stifter, N., Weippl, E.: HydRand: efficient continuous distributed randomness. In: 2020 IEEE Symposium on Security and Privacy (SP), pp. 32–48

38. Schoenmakers, B.: A simple publicly verifiable secret sharing scheme and its application to electronic voting. In: Wiener, M. (ed.) CRYPTO 1999. LNCS, vol. 1666, pp. 148–164. Springer, Heidelberg (1999). https://doi.org/10.1007/3-540-48405-1_10

39. Yao, A.C.C.: Some complexity questions related to distributive computing (preliminary report). In: Proceedings of the Eleventh Annual ACM Symposium on Theory of Computing, pp. 209–213 (1979)

40. Yin, M., Malkhi, D., Reiter, M.K., Gueta, G.G., Abraham, I.: Hotstuff: Bft consensus with linearity and responsiveness. In: Proceedings of the 2019 ACM Symposium on Principles of Distributed Computing, pp. 347–356 (2019)

Bicorn: An Optimistically Efficient Distributed Randomness Beacon

Kevin Choi[1(✉)] , Arasu Arun[1] , Nirvan Tyagi[2] , and Joseph Bonneau[1,3]

[1] New York University, New York City, USA
kc2296@nyu.edu
[2] Cornell University, Ithaca, USA
[3] a16z crypto research, Ithaca, USA

Abstract. We introduce Bicorn, an optimistically efficient distributed randomness protocol with strong robustness under a dishonest majority. Bicorn is a "commit-reveal-recover" protocol. Each participant commits to a random value, which are combined to produce a random output. If any participants fail to open their commitment, recovery is possible via a single time-lock puzzle which can be solved by any party. In the optimistic case, Bicorn is a simple and efficient two-round protocol with no time-lock puzzle. In either case, Bicorn supports open, flexible participation, requires only a public bulletin board and no group-specific setup or PKI, and is guaranteed to produce random output assuming any single participant is honest. All communication and computation costs are (at most) linear in the number of participants with low concrete overhead.

1 Introduction

Distributed randomness beacons (DRBs) aim to enable a group of n participants to jointly compute a random output (which we denote Ω) such that no participant or coalition of participants can predict or influence the outcome. Among many other applications, they are useful for cryptographically verifiable lotteries or leader election in efficient distributed consensus protocols.

A classic approach is *commit-reveal* [9]. First, all participants publish a commitment $c_i = \mathsf{Commit}(r_i)$ to a random value r_i. Next, participants reveal their r_i values and the result is $\Omega = \mathsf{Combine}(r_1, \ldots, r_n)$ for some suitable combination function (such as exclusive-or or a cryptographic hash). Commit-reveal protocols are simple, efficient, and secure as long as one participant chooses a random r_i value—assuming all participants open their commitments. However, the output can be biased by the last participant to open their commitment (a so-called *last-revealer attack*), as that participant will know all other r_i values and can compute Ω early. If the last revealer doesn't like the impending value of Ω, they can refuse to open, forcing the protocol to abort. Even if the last revealer is removed from subsequent protocol runs, this enables one bit of bias.

Related Work. Several approaches exist to avoid last-revealer attacks. Commit-reveal-punish protocols impose a financial penalty on any participant who fails

© International Financial Cryptography Association 2024
F. Baldimtsi and C. Cachin (Eds.): FC 2023, LNCS 13950, pp. 235–251, 2024.
https://doi.org/10.1007/978-3-031-47754-6_14

to open their commitment. This penalty can be automatically enforced using modern cryptocurrencies [2,32], but this requires locking up capital and security relies on economic assumptions about the value of manipulation to the attacker.

Other protocols relax the security model of commit-reveal and assume an honest majority of participants. Many constructions enable a majority of participants to recover the input of a malicious minority of participants [7,8,19,20, 24,26,27,34,35,37], using cryptographic tools such as publicly verifiable secret sharing (PVSS). Typically, these constructions can tolerate some threshold t of malicious participants failing to complete the protocol, with the trade-off that any coalition of $t+1$ participants can (secretly) learn the impending output early and potentially bias the protocol, leading to a requirement that $t < \frac{n}{2}$ (honest majority). These protocols are also often quite complex, with communication and computation costs superlinear in n. Another approach is to rely on threshold cryptography for participants to jointly compute a cryptographic function which produces Ω, such as threshold signatures in Dfinity [18], threshold encryption [22], or threshold inversion in RSA groups [3,4]. The drand DRB [1], which uses a chain of threshold BLS signatures, is now deployed publicly with a group of 16 participating nodes producing a new random output every 30 s.

A very different approach to constructing DRBs uses time-based cryptography, specifically using *delay functions* to prevent manipulation. The simplest example is Unicorn [28], a one-round protocol in which participants directly publish (within a fixed time window) a random input r_i. The result is computed as $\Omega = \mathsf{Delay}(\mathsf{Combine}(r_1, \ldots, r_n))$. By assumption, a party cannot compute the Delay function before the deadline to publish their contribution r_i and therefore cannot predict Ω or choose r_i in such a way as to influence it. This protocol retains the strong $n - 1$ (dishonest majority) security model of commit-reveal, but with no last-revealer attacks. It is also simple and, using modern verifiable delay functions[1] (VDFs) [10], the result can be efficiently verified. The downside is that a delay function must be computed for every run of the protocol.

Our Approach. We introduce the Bicorn family of DRB protocols, which retain the advantages of Unicorn while enabling efficient computation of the result (with no delay) if all participants act honestly. The general structure is:

- Each of n participants chooses a random value r_i and publishes $c_i = \mathsf{TCom}(r_i)$ using a timed commitment scheme [14] TCom before some deadline T_1.
- In the optimistic case, every participant opens their commitment by publishing r_i. The DRB output is $\Omega = \mathsf{Combine}(r_1, \ldots, r_n)$. In this case, the protocol is equivalent to a classic commit-reveal protocol.
- If any participant does not publish their r_i value, it can be recovered by computing $r_i = \mathsf{ForceOpen}(c_i)$, a slow function requiring t steps of sequential work which cannot be evaluated quickly enough for a malicious coalition of participants to learn honest participants' committed values early. The result Ω is the same as in the optimistic case, even if all participants don't reveal their committed values.

---

[1] The original Unicorn proposal used modular square roots in a prime-order group. We consider using a modern VDF instead.

This protocol structure was used in a recent proposal by Thyagarajan et al. [38]. They observe that by using a homomorphic commitment scheme, the commitments can be combined and only a single forced opening is required, instead of opening every withholding participant's commitment separately. Asymptotically, their protocols require linear $(O(n))$ communication and computation costs when run with n participants.

However, Thyagarajan et al. use a general-purpose CCA-secure timed commitment scheme suitable for committing to arbitrary messages, which introduces significant practical complexity and overhead. Our key insight is that constructing a DRB does not require a general-purpose commitment scheme; it is sufficient to use a special restricted commitment scheme which only enables committing to a pseudorandom message. As a result, our protocols are considerably simpler and offer much better concrete performance.

Contributions. We introduce the Bicorn family of protocols, which comes in three flavors with slightly different security proofs and practical implications:

- Bicorn-ZK, which requires each participant to publish a zero-knowledge proof of knowledge of exponent. This imposes the highest practical overhead but offers the simplest security proof.
- Bicorn-PC, in which participants "pre-commit" their contribution before the protocol. This is the simplest version, though it adds an extra communication round (which can be amortized over multiple runs).
- Bicorn-RX, which utilizes a randomized exponent to prevent manipulation attacks. This is the most efficient version in practice, though the security proof relies on stronger assumptions.

In Sect. 3, we prove security of our constructions by reducing to the RSW assumption [33] in the algebraic group model (AGM) [25], except for Bicorn-ZK where we assume a zero-knowledge proof of knowledge of exponent (ZK-PoKE) exists. The Bicorn-RX variant assumes a random oracle. In Sect. 6, we report on concrete implementations of these protocols in Ethereum, showing that our constructions are practical and incur 3–8× increase in per-user cost compared to commit-reveal (but with no manipulation due to aborts) and 5–7× compared to Unicorn (but with no delay function required in the optimistic case).

2 Overview

2.1 Protocol Outline

We specify all three of our protocol variants in Protocol 1. Our protocols are initialized via a security parameter λ and a delay parameter t, and work over a *group of unknown order*, which we denote $\mathbb{G}$ (see preliminaries in Sect. 3). In addition to the group $\mathbb{G}$, the public parameters include a pair (g, h), where g is a generator of the group and $h = g^{2^t}$. If desired, a Wesolowski [41] or Pietrzak [30] proof of exponentiation can enable efficient verification that h was computed correctly. Note that this setup only needs to be run once ever (for a specific delay parameter t) and can be used repeatedly (and concurrently) by separate protocol instances; the number of participants does not need to be known and may dynamically change over time.

The common structure of Bicorn protocols is:

- Each of n participants chooses a random value α_i and publishes $c_i = g^{\alpha_i}$. The value c_i can be viewed as the input to a VDF whose output is $(c_i)^{2^t}$, with α_i serving as a trapdoor to quickly compute $(c_i)^{2^t} = (g^{\alpha_i})^{2^t} = (g^{2^t})^{\alpha_i} = h^{\alpha_i}$. Without knowledge of α_i this value is slow to compute. Depending on the security assumptions made, α_i can be sampled from different distributions. We abstract this choice by parameterizing by a uniform distribution $\mathcal{B}$ from which α_i is sampled.
- Participants "open" their commitment c_i by revealing a value $\tilde{\alpha}_i$. It can be quickly verified that $\tilde{\alpha}_i$ is the correct α_i by verifying that $c_i = g^{\tilde{\alpha}_i}$.
- *Optimistic case:* Given all correct α_i values, the DRB output Ω is the product $\Omega = \prod_{i \in [n]} h^{\alpha_i}$, which is unpredictable as long as at least one of the α_i values was randomly chosen and is easy to compute if all α_i values are correctly revealed.
- *Pessimistic case:* If any participant withholds α_i (or chose c_i without knowledge of the corresponding α_i), then the missing value h^{α_i} can be recovered (slowly) by computing $h^{\alpha_i} = (c_i)^{2^t}$, equivalent to evaluating a VDF. If multiple participants withhold α_i, naively one must compute each missing value h^{α_i} individually. A more efficient approach (which works even if all participants withhold α_i) is to first combine each participant's contribution into the value $\omega = \prod_{i \in [n]} c_i$. The output can then be computed via a single slow computation as $\Omega = \omega^{2^t}$, which is identical to the output $\Omega = \prod_{i \in [n]} h^{\tilde{\alpha}_i}$ computed in the optimistic case.

By itself this protocol is insecure, because a malicious participant need not choose c_i by choosing a value α_i and computing g^{α_i}. An adversary j who has pre-computed a desired output $\Omega_* = (\omega_*)^{2^t}$ and is able to publish last can compute a malicious contribution:

$$c_j = \omega_* \cdot \left(\prod_{i \in [n], i \neq j} c_i \right)^{-1} \tag{1}$$

This will cancel out every other participant's contribution and force the output value Ω_*. There are three ways to prevent this attack, each leading to a protocol variant with slightly different properties, which we will present in the following subsections. We present the protocols combined for comparison in Protocol 1.

Setup(λ, t)		(run once for all protocol runs)

1. Run $(\mathbb{G}, g, A, B) \xleftarrow{\$} \mathsf{GGen}(\lambda)$ to generate a group of unknown order
2. Compute $h \leftarrow g^{2^t}$, optionally with $\pi_h = \mathsf{PoE}(g, h, 2^t)$
3. Output $(\mathbb{G}, g, h, \pi_h, A, B)$

Prepare()		(run by each participant i)

$\alpha_i \xleftarrow{\$} \mathcal{B}$	$\alpha_i \xleftarrow{\$} \mathcal{B}$	$\alpha_i \xleftarrow{\$} \mathcal{B}$
$c_i \leftarrow g^{\alpha_i}$	$c_i \leftarrow g^{\alpha_i}$	$c_i \leftarrow g^{\alpha_i}$
$\pi_i \leftarrow \mathsf{ZK\text{-}PoKE}(g, c_i, \alpha_i)$	$d_i \leftarrow H(c_i)$	

Precommit(d_i)		(run by each participant i)

–	Publish d_i	–

$\cdots\cdots\cdots\cdots\cdots\cdots\cdots\cdots\cdots\cdots\cdots\cdots\cdots\cdots\cdots\cdots\cdots\cdots\cdots\cdots\cdots\cdots$ *deadline T_0* $\cdots$

Commit(c_i, π_i)		(run by each participant i)

Publish c_i, π_i	Publish c_i	Publish c_i

$\cdots\cdots\cdots\cdots\cdots\cdots\cdots\cdots\cdots\cdots\cdots\cdots\cdots\cdots\cdots\cdots\cdots\cdots\cdots\cdots\cdots\cdots$ *deadline T_1* $\cdots$

Reveal(α_i)		(run by each participant i)

Publish α_i	Publish α_i	Publish α_i

Finalize($\{(\tilde{\alpha}_i, c_i, d_i, \pi_i)\}_{i=1}^n$)		(optimistic case, once per protocol run)

1. $\forall_j$ Verify proof π_j	1. $\forall_j$ Verify $d_j = H(c_j)$	1. $b_* \leftarrow H(c_1 \|\ldots\| c_n)$
–else: remove user j	–else: remove user j	2. $\forall_j$ Verify $c_j = g^{\tilde{\alpha}_j}$
2. $\forall_j$ Verify $c_j = g^{\tilde{\alpha}_j}$	2. $\forall_j$ Verify $c_j = g^{\tilde{\alpha}_j}$	–else: go to Recover
–else: go to Recover	–else: go to Recover	$\Omega = \prod_{i \in [n]} \left(h^{H(c_i \| b_*)} \right)^{\tilde{\alpha}_i}$
$\Omega = \prod_{i \in [n]} h^{\tilde{\alpha}_i}$	$\Omega = \prod_{i \in [n]} h^{\tilde{\alpha}_i}$	

Recover($\{(c_i, d_i, \pi_i)\}_{i=1}^n$)		(pessimistic case, once per protocol run)

$\Omega = \left(\prod_{i \in [n]} c_i \right)^{2^t}$	$\Omega = \left(\prod_{i \in [n]} c_i \right)^{2^t}$	$\Omega = \left(\prod_{i \in [n]} c_i^{H(c_i \| b_*)} \right)^{2^t}$

Protocol 1: All Bicorn protocol variants: Bicorn-ZK (left column), Bicorn-PC (center column), and Bicorn-RX (right column).

2.2   Bicorn-ZK: Using Zero-Knowledge Proofs

The conceptually simplest fix is for each user to publish, along with their commitment c_i, a zero-knowledge proof-of-knowledge $\pi_i = \mathsf{ZK\text{-}PoKE}(g, c_i, \alpha_i)$ of the discrete logarithm of c_i to the base g_i (i.e. α_i). This version (Bicorn-ZK) is specified in Protocol 1 (left). This removes the attack above, as an adversary who computes c_j via Eq. 1 will not know the discrete log of c_j to the base g. Such proofs can be done in groups of unknown order particularly efficiently in this case. The use of a fixed base g enables the simpler ZKPoKRep protocol of Boneh et al. [11] (possibly in combination with their proof aggregation PoKCR protocol).

Participants publishing invalid proofs are removed, and the protocol can continue and still produce output. Attempting to participate with an invalid proof is equivalent to not participating at all (though participants who do so might need to be blocked or penalized financially to deter denial-of-service attacks).

It might be tempting to optimize the protocol by not verifying each proof π_i in the optimistic case, instead checking directly that $c_i = g^{\tilde{\alpha}_i}$ using the revealed value $\tilde{\alpha}_i$. However, this would introduce a subtle attack: a malicious participant could publish a correctly generated $(c_i, \tilde{\alpha}_i)$ pair but with an invalid proof $\tilde{\pi}_i$. Next, after all other participants have revealed their α values, the attacker can compute the impending result Ω with their own contribution included, as well as the alternative Ω' if it is removed. They could then choose which output is produced, introducing one bit of bias into the protocol: by publishing $\tilde{\alpha}_i$, they will remain in the protocol (as $\tilde{\pi}_i$ is not checked) and Ω will result, whereas by withholding $\tilde{\alpha}_i$ they will force the pessimistic case, in which they will be removed on account of the faulty $\tilde{\pi}_i$ and Ω' will result. Thus, it is important to verify every participant's proof π_i in both cases to prevent this attack.

2.3   Bicorn-PC: Using Precommitment

Another approach to prevent manipulation is to add an initial precommitment round where participants publish $d_i = H(c_i)$, preventing them from choosing c_i in reaction to what others have chosen. This version (Bicorn-PC) is specified in Protocol 1 (center). Participants can decline to reveal their committed c_i, in which case they are removed and the protocol can continue safely. Because participants will not have time to compute the impending output before choosing whether to reveal, this does not introduce any opportunity for manipulation.

Note that the precommitted values d_i can be published at any point prior to T_0 (the point at which participants start revealing their actual commitment c_i). If the protocol is run iteratively, it is possible for participants to publish any number of precommitments d_i in advance (or a single commitment to a set of d_i values using a set commitment construction such as a Merkle Tree), making the protocol a two-round protocol on an amortized basis.

Table 1. A brief comparison of the Bicorn variants. See Fig. 1 for notation ($\langle \mathbb{G} \rangle$ and $\langle \mathcal{B} \rangle$ are the sizes of elements from $\mathbb{G}$ and $\mathcal{B}$, respectively) and Sect. 3 for a background on the RSW assumptions, the algebraic group model (AGM), the random oracle model (ROM), and zero-knowledge proof of knowledge of exponent (ZK-PoKE).

	Protocol	Rounds	Communication	Assumptions
Sect. 2.2	**Bicorn-ZK**	2	$n(\langle \mathbb{G} \rangle + \langle \mathcal{B} \rangle + |\pi|)$	RSW, ZK-PoKE
Sect. 2.3	**Bicorn-PC**	3	$n(\langle \mathbb{G} \rangle + \langle \mathcal{B} \rangle + \lambda)$	RSW, AGM
Sect. 2.4	**Bicorn-RX**	2	$n(\langle \mathbb{G} \rangle + \langle \mathcal{B} \rangle)$	RSW, AGM, ROM

2.4 Bicorn-RX: Using Pseudorandom Exponents

Finally, we can prevent manipulation by raising each participant's contribution c_i to a unique (small) exponent which depends on all other participants' contributions. Specifically, we define b_* to be the hash of all c_i values: $b_* = H(c_1||c_2||\ldots||c_n)$. We then raise each value c_i to the pseudorandom exponent $b_i = H(c_i \,\|\, b_*)$. The intuition is that modifying any contribution c_i will induce new exponents on each participant's contribution which prevents an adversary from forcing the value $\omega = \prod_{i \in [n]} c_i^{H(c_i\|b_*)}$ to a fixed value. A similar technique was used by Boneh et al. [13] to prevent rogue-key attacks in BLS multi-signatures. This version (Bicorn-RX) is specified in Protocol 1 (right) (Table 1).

2.5 Comparison

Each of these leads to a secure protocol, albeit reducing to slightly different computational assumptions, as we will prove in Sect. 5. All of our protocols reduce to the RSW assumptions with Bicorn-PC and Bicorn-RX requiring the algebraic group model (AGM) for the security reductions and Bicorn-RX also assuming a random oracle. Bicorn-ZK doesn't require the AGM explicitly but instead assumes a secure zero-knowledge proof of knowledge of exponent (ZK-PoKE) for which efficient existing protocols are proven secure only in the AGM [11].

Each protocol also offers slightly different performance trade-offs, though asymptotically all require $O(n)$ broadcast communication by participating nodes and $O(n)$ computation to verify the result. While Bicorn-PC incurs an extra round, Bicorn-ZK incurs extra computational overhead which may be significant in some scenarios (e.g. smart contracts). Bicorn-RX requires only two rounds and does not require the user to produce proofs but requires extra group exponentiations which incur slightly higher costs than Bicorn-PC.

3 Preliminaries

Algebraic Group Model. In some of our security proofs, we consider security against *algebraic* adversaries which we model using the algebraic group model,

$\mathcal{G}^{\text{C-RSW}}_{\mathcal{A},t,\text{GGen}}(\lambda)$	$\mathcal{G}^{\text{C-RSW}^e}_{\mathcal{A},t,\text{GGen}}(\lambda)$	$\mathcal{G}^{\text{D-RSW}}_{\mathcal{A},t,b,\text{GGen}}(\lambda)$
$(\mathbb{G}, g, A, B) \xleftarrow{\$} \text{GGen}(\lambda)$	$(\mathbb{G}, g, A, B) \xleftarrow{\$} \text{GGen}(\lambda)$	$(\mathbb{G}, g, A, B) \xleftarrow{\$} \text{GGen}(\lambda)$
$\sigma \leftarrow \mathcal{A}_0(\mathbb{G}, g, A, B)$	$\sigma \leftarrow \mathcal{A}_0(\mathbb{G}, g, A, B)$	$\sigma \leftarrow \mathcal{A}_0(\mathbb{G}, g, A, B)$
$x \xleftarrow{\$} \mathbb{G}$	$x \xleftarrow{\$} \mathbb{G}$	$x \xleftarrow{\$} \mathbb{G};\ \tilde{y}_1 \leftarrow x^{2^t};\ \tilde{y}_0 \xleftarrow{\$} \mathbb{G}$
$\tilde{y} \xleftarrow{\$} \mathcal{A}_1(\sigma, x)$	$(e, \tilde{y}) \xleftarrow{\$} \mathcal{A}_1(\sigma, x)$	$b' \xleftarrow{\$} \mathcal{A}_1(\sigma, x, \tilde{y}_b)$
Return $\tilde{y} = x^{2^t}$	Return $\tilde{y} = (x^e)^{2^t}$	Return $b = b'$

Fig. 1. Security games for the repeated squaring hardness assumptions: computational RSW (left), computational power-of-RSW (center), and decisional RSW (right).

following the treatment of [25]. We call an algorithm $\mathcal{A}$ *algebraic* if for all group elements Z that are output (either as final output or as input to oracles), $\mathcal{A}$ additionally provides the representation of Z relative to all previously received group elements. The previously received group elements include both original inputs to the algorithm and outputs received from calls to oracles. More specifically, if $[X]_i$ is the list of group elements $[X_0, \ldots, X_n] \in \mathbb{G}$ that $\mathcal{A}$ has received so far, then, when producing group element Z, $\mathcal{A}$ must also provide a list $[z]_i = [z_0, \ldots, z_n]$ such that $Z = \prod_i X_i^{z_i}$.

Groups of Unknown Order and RSW Assumptions. Our protocols will operate over cyclic groups of unknown order. We assume an efficient group generation algorithm $\text{GGen}(\lambda)$ that takes as input security parameter λ and outputs a group description $\mathbb{G}$, generator g, and range $[A, B]$ where A, B, and $B - A$ are all exponential in λ; the group $\mathbb{G}$ has order in range $[A, B]$. We assume efficient algorithms for sampling from the group ($g \xleftarrow{\$} \mathbb{G}$) and for testing membership.

There are a few currently known options with which to instantiate a group of unknown order. One option that requires only a transparent setup is through class groups of imaginary quadratic order [15]. However, class groups typically incur high concrete overheads. Instead, one may opt for more efficient RSA groups, which require a trusted setup or multiparty computation "ceremony" [21] to compute the modulus $N = pq$ without revealing safe primes p, q. Looking forward, we will require our group to additionally be cyclic and satisfy the low order assumption [12]. So instead we will use the group $\mathbb{QR}_N^+$, the group of signed quadratic residues modulo N (we refer to Pietrzak for more details [30]).

The security of our constructions is based on the assumption, originally proposed by RSW [33], that, given a random element $x \in \mathbb{G}$, the fastest algorithm to compute $y = x^{(2^t)}$ takes t sequential steps. We use three RSW assumptions; we provide security games in Fig. 1.

Randomizing Exponent Sizes. We recall a useful lemma for randomizing group elements [29].

Lemma 1. *For any cyclic group* $\mathbb{G}$ *and generator* g, *if* $r \xleftarrow{\$} \mathcal{B}$ *is chosen uniformly at random, then the statistical distance between* g^r *and the uniform distribution over* $\mathbb{G}$ *is at most* $\frac{|\mathbb{G}|}{2|\mathcal{B}|}$.

Looking forward, we will use this lemma in our security proofs to replace a generator taken to the power of a large exponent of size $|\mathcal{B}| \approx 2^{2\lambda} \cdot |\mathbb{G}|$ with a random element. Alternatively, one may opt for the stronger *short exponent indistinguishability (SEI) assumption* [23] which asserts that an adversary cannot computationally distinguish between a uniformly random element of $\mathbb{G}$ and g^r for $r \xleftarrow{\$} [0, 2^{2\lambda}]$. The latter assumption enables significant efficiency gains in practice, with participants publishing 32-byte α values instead of 288 bytes.

Non-interactive Zero-knowledge Proofs. A *non-interactive proof system* for a relation $\mathcal{R}$ over *statement-witness* pairs (x, w) enables producing a proof, $\pi \leftarrow$ Prove(pk, x, w), that convinces a verifier $\exists w : (x, w) \in \mathcal{R}, 0/1 \leftarrow$ Verify(vk, π, x); pk and vk are proving and verification keys output by a setup, $(pk, vk) \leftarrow$ Keygen$(\mathcal{R})$. A *non-interactive argument of knowledge* further convinces the verifier not only that the witness w exists but also that the prover *knows* w, and if proved in *zero-knowledge*, the verifier does not learn any additional information about w. In this work, we will make use of proof systems for two relations. First, we use PoE for the following relation for proofs of exponentiation in groups of unknown order [11,30,41]: $\{((x, y \in \mathbb{G}, \alpha \in \mathbb{Z}), \bot) : y = x^\alpha\}$. Second, we use ZK-PoKE (realized by ZKPoKRep from [11]) for zero-knowledge proofs of knowledge of exponent in groups of unknown order: $\{((x, y \in \mathbb{G}), \alpha \in \mathbb{Z}) : y = x^\alpha\}$.

4   Timed DRBs: Syntax and Security Definitions

We first define a timed DRB using a generalized syntax which captures all of our protocol variants. A timed DRB protocol DRB with time parameter t is a tuple of algorithms (Setup, Prepare, Finalize, Recover). We describe them below for a run of the protocol with n participants:

- Setup$(\lambda, t) \xrightarrow{\$}$ pp: The setup algorithm takes as input a security parameter λ and a time parameter t and outputs a set of public parameters pp.
- Prepare(pp) $\xrightarrow{\$} (\alpha_i, c_i, d_i, \pi_i)$: The prepare algorithm is run by each participant and outputs a tuple of opening, commitment, precommitment, and proof. The precommitment is contributed during the Precommit phase (see Protocol 1). The commitment and proof are contributed during the Commit phase, and the opening is contributed during the Reveal phase. The length of the Commit phase is dictated by the time parameter t.
- Finalize(pp, $\{(\alpha_i, c_i, d_i, \pi_i)\}_{i=1}^n) \to \Omega$: The finalize algorithm is run after the Reveal phase and verifies the contributions of participants to optimistically produce a final output Ω or returns $\bot$ indicating the need to move to the pessimistic case.
- Recover(pp, $\{(c_i, d_i, \pi_i)\}_{i=1}^n) \to \Omega$: The recover algorithm performs the timed computation to recover the output Ω without any revealed α values.

$\underline{\mathcal{G}^{\text{consist}}_{\mathcal{A},t,n,\mathsf{DRB}}(\lambda)}$

$\mathsf{pp} \xleftarrow{\$} \mathsf{Setup}(\lambda, t)$
$(\alpha_1, c_1, d_1, \pi_1) \xleftarrow{\$} \mathsf{Prepare}(\mathsf{pp})$
$(\sigma, \{d_i\}_{i=1}^{n'}) \xleftarrow{\$} \mathcal{A}_0(\mathsf{pp}, d_1)$
$\{(\alpha_i, c_i, \pi_i)\}_{i=2}^{n} \xleftarrow{\$} \mathcal{A}_1(\sigma, c_1, \pi_1)$
$\Omega \leftarrow \mathsf{Finalize}(\mathsf{pp}, \{(\alpha_i, c_i, d_i, \pi_i)\}_{i=1}^{n})$
Return $\bigwedge \begin{pmatrix} \Omega \neq \perp \\ \Omega \neq \mathsf{Recover}(\mathsf{pp}, \{(c_i, d_i, \pi_i)\}_{i=1}^{n}) \end{pmatrix}$

$\underline{\mathcal{G}^{\text{unpred}}_{\mathcal{A},t,n,\mathsf{DRB}}(\lambda)}$

$\mathsf{pp} \xleftarrow{\$} \mathsf{Setup}(\lambda, t)$
$(\alpha_1, c_1, d_1, \pi_1) \xleftarrow{\$} \mathsf{Prepare}(\mathsf{pp})$
$(\sigma, \{d_i\}_{i=1}^{n'}) \xleftarrow{\$} \mathcal{A}_0(\mathsf{pp}, d_1)$
$(\tilde{\Omega}, \{(c_i, \pi_i)\}_{i=2}^{n}) \xleftarrow{\$} \mathcal{A}_1(\sigma, c_1, \pi_1)$
Return $\tilde{\Omega} = \mathsf{Recover}(\mathsf{pp}, \{(c_i, d_i, \pi_i)\}_{i=1}^{n})$

$\underline{\mathcal{G}^{\text{indist}}_{\mathcal{A},t,n,b,\mathsf{DRB}}(\lambda)}$

$\mathsf{pp} \xleftarrow{\$} \mathsf{Setup}(\lambda, t)$
$(\alpha_1, c_1, d_1, \pi_1) \xleftarrow{\$} \mathsf{Prepare}(\mathsf{pp})$
$(\sigma_0, \{d_i\}_{i=1}^{n'}) \xleftarrow{\$} \mathcal{A}_0(\mathsf{pp}, d_1)$
$(\sigma_1, \{(c_i, \pi_i)\}_{i=2}^{n}) \xleftarrow{\$} \mathcal{A}_1(\sigma_0, c_1, \pi_1)$
$\Omega_1 \leftarrow \mathsf{Recover}(\mathsf{pp}, \{(c_i, d_i, \pi_i)\}_{i=1}^{n})$
$\Omega_0 \xleftarrow{\$} \mathbb{G}$
$b' \xleftarrow{\$} \mathcal{A}_2(\sigma_1, \Omega_b)$
Return $b = b'$

Fig. 2. Security games for our three main security properties: consistency (left), t-unpredictability (center), and t-indistinguishability (right).

We require Finalize to be a deterministic algorithm running in time $\mathsf{polylog}(t)$ (the fast optimistic case), and Recover to be a deterministic algorithm running in time $(1+\epsilon)t$ for some small ϵ. We also require the following security properties of a timed DRB (given in pseudocode in Fig. 2):

Consistency. Our first security property is a form of correctness. We require that it is not possible for the optimistic and pessimistic paths to return different outputs. The adversary is tasked with providing an accepting set of contributions that results in different outputs from Finalize and Recover. We define the advantage of an adversary as $\mathsf{Adv}^{\text{consist}}_{\mathcal{A},t,n,\mathsf{DRB}}(\lambda) = \Pr\left[\mathcal{G}^{\text{consist}}_{\mathcal{A},t,n,\mathsf{DRB}}(\lambda) = 1\right]$.

t-Unpredictability. The t-unpredictability game tasks an adversary with predicting the final output Ω exactly, allowing it control of all but a single honest protocol participant (which publishes first). We define the advantage of an adversary as $\mathsf{Adv}^{\text{unpred}}_{\mathcal{A},t,n,\mathsf{DRB}}(\lambda) = \Pr\left[\mathcal{G}^{\text{unpred}}_{\mathcal{A},t,n,\mathsf{DRB}}(\lambda) = 1\right]$.

t-Indistinguishability. The t-unpredictability property does not guarantee the output is indistinguishable from random. For that, we provide a stronger t-indistinguishability property in which the adversary must distinguish an honest output from a random output, again allowing the adversary control of all but one participant. We define the advantage of an adversary as: $\mathsf{Adv}^{\text{indist}}_{\mathcal{A},t,n,\mathsf{DRB}}(\lambda) = \left|\Pr\left[\mathcal{G}^{\text{indist}}_{\mathcal{A},t,n,1,\mathsf{DRB}}(\lambda) = 1\right] - \Pr\left[\mathcal{G}^{\text{indist}}_{\mathcal{A},t,n,0,\mathsf{DRB}}(\lambda) = 1\right]\right|$. A timed DRB that satisfies t-unpredictability can be transformed generically into one with t-indistinguishability by applying a suitable randomness extractor [39,40] or hash function (modeled as a random oracle) to the output. A nice feature of our DRBs is that they satisfy t-indistinguishability with respect to the group output space (without applying a randomness extractor) under the suitable decisional RSW assumption.

Discussion. In t-unpredictability and t-indistinguishability, the adversaries $\mathcal{A}_1$ and $\mathcal{A}_2$ are restricted to run in fewer than t sequential steps. This is a slight simplification of the (p, σ)-sequentiality assumption in VDFs [10], which is suitable for working in the AGM in which parallelism is not helpful in computing group operations.

Note that our syntax and security definitions encompass all three of our protocol variants. Except for Bicorn-ZK, the proofs π_i can be set to $\perp$ and are ignored; except for Bicorn-PC, the precommitment values d_i can be set to $\perp$ and are ignored. Also note that there are n' ($\geq n$) values of d_i output by the adversary; they have the option in Bicorn-PC to choose which to use in later steps. The implementation of Recover is unique to each protocol.

We observe that the consistency property holds unconditionally for all Bicorn variants, as Finalize and Recover are deterministic and algebraically equivalent. It remains to prove unpredictability and indistinguishability for each variant.

5   Security of Bicorn-RX

We present a proof of t-unpredictability for Bicorn-RX here, as it is representative of the techniques used for all other proofs.

Theorem 1 (t-Unpredictability of Bicorn-RX). *Let $\mathcal{A}_{\mathrm{brx}} = (\mathcal{A}_{\mathrm{brx},0}, \mathcal{A}_{\mathrm{brx},1})$ be an algebraic adversary against the t-unpredictability of BRX with random exponent space $\mathcal{B} = [2^{2\lambda} \cdot B]$ where hash function H is modeled as a random oracle. Then we construct an adversary $\mathcal{A}_{\mathrm{rsw}} = (\mathcal{A}_{\mathrm{rsw},0}, \mathcal{A}_{\mathrm{rsw},1})$ such that*

$$\mathsf{Adv}^{\mathrm{unpred}}_{\mathcal{A}_{\mathrm{brx}},t,n,\mathsf{BRX}}(\lambda) \leq \mathsf{Adv}^{\mathrm{C\text{-}RSW}^e}_{\mathcal{A}_{\mathrm{rsw}},t,\mathsf{GGen}}(\lambda) + \frac{2(\mathsf{q}^2_{\mathrm{ro}} + n) + 1}{2^{2\lambda+1}} + \prod_{i=1}^{\ell} I_{\frac{1}{p_i}}(r_i, n),$$

and where $\mathsf{GGen} \xrightarrow{\$} (\mathbb{G}, g, A, B)$ generates the group of unknown order ($|\mathbb{G}| = \prod_{i=1}^{\ell} p_i^{r_i}$ for distinct primes $p_1, \ldots, p_\ell$) used by BRX, q_{ro} is the number of queries made to the random oracle, n is the number of participants, and $I_{\frac{1}{p}}(r, n) = (1 - \frac{1}{p})^n \sum_{j=r}^{\infty} \binom{n+r-1}{r} p^{-j}$ is the regularized beta function. The running time of $T(\mathcal{A}_{\mathrm{rsw},0}) \approx T(\mathcal{A}_{\mathrm{brx},0}) + 2t$ and $T(\mathcal{A}_{\mathrm{rsw},1}) \approx T(\mathcal{A}_{\mathrm{brx},1})$.

Proof. At a high level, our proof strategy will be to replace the initial commitment c_1 provided by the single honest participant with a random group element. If $\mathcal{A}_{\mathrm{brx}}$ can win with non-negligible probability, then we show that due to unpredictability of the random exponents applied in Bicorn-RX, it must be that a nontrivial large exponent of c_1 was computed which we can use to win the computational power-of-RSW game.

More specifically, we bound the advantage of $\mathcal{A}_{\mathrm{brx}}$ by bounding the advantage of a series of game hops, using the fundamental lemma of game playing and its identical-until-bad argument [6]. We define $\mathcal{G} = \mathcal{G}^{\mathrm{unpred}}_{\mathcal{A}_{\mathrm{brx}},t,n,\mathsf{BRX}}(\lambda)$ and hybrids $\mathcal{G}_1, \mathcal{G}_2, \mathcal{G}_3$ for which we justify the following claims leading to the inequality above:

- $|\Pr[\mathcal{G}(\lambda) = 1] - \Pr[\mathcal{G}_1(\lambda) = 1]| \leq \frac{1}{2^{2\lambda+1}}$
- $|\Pr[\mathcal{G}_1(\lambda) = 1] - \Pr[\mathcal{G}_2(\lambda) = 1]| \leq \frac{\mathsf{q}^2_{\mathrm{ro}}}{2^{2\lambda}}$
- $|\Pr[\mathcal{G}_2(\lambda) = 1] - \Pr[\mathcal{G}_3(\lambda) = 1]| \leq \frac{n}{2^{2\lambda}} + \prod_{i=1}^{\ell} I_{\frac{1}{p_i}}(r_i, n)$
- $\Pr[\mathcal{G}_3(\lambda) = 1] = \mathsf{Adv}^{\mathrm{C\text{-}RSW}^e}_{\mathcal{A}_{\mathrm{rsw}},t,\mathsf{GGen}}(\lambda)$

$\mathcal{G} \to \mathcal{G}_1$. Hybrid $\mathcal{G}_1$ is defined the same as $\mathcal{G}$ except $\mathcal{G}_1$ samples c_1 in Prepare at random from $\mathbb{G}$ instead of through an exponent sampled from $\mathcal{B}$. By Lemma 1, the statistical distance between $\mathcal{G}$ and $\mathcal{G}_1$ is at most $1/2^{2\lambda+1}$.

We can view $\mathcal{G}_1$ as computing the beacon output Ω using the representations of $\{c_i\}_{i=2}^n$ provided by the algebraic adversary. Since $\mathcal{A}_{\text{brx}}$ is algebraic, it will provide a representation for each c_i in terms of elements (c_1, g, h). That is, the adversary outputs $[(e_{i,0}, e_{i,1}, e_{i,2})]_{i=2}^n$ such that $c_i = c_1^{e_{i,0}} g^{e_{i,1}} h^{e_{i,2}}$.

Given a value $\hat{h} = h^{2^t}$, we can compute Ω as follows. Consider the random exponents $b_i = H(c_i \parallel b_*)$ where $b_* = H(c_1 \parallel \ldots \parallel c_n)$, and let $\mathbf{b} = (b_1, \ldots, b_n)$. Using these, we have:

$$\Omega = \left(\prod_{i=1}^n c_i^{b_i} \right)^{2^t} = \left(c_1^{b_1} \cdot \prod_{i=2}^n \left(c_1^{e_{i,0}} g^{e_{i,1}} h^{e_{i,2}} \right)^{b_i} \right)^{2^t}$$

$$= \left(c_1^{b_1 + \sum_{i=2}^n b_i e_{i,0}} g^{\sum_{i=2}^n b_i e_{i,1}} h^{\sum_{i=2}^n b_i e_{i,2}} \right)^{2^t}$$

By letting $\mathbf{e} = (1, e_{2,0}, \ldots, e_{n,0})$, $m_1 = \sum_{i=2}^n b_i e_{i,1}$, and $m_2 = \sum_{i=2}^n b_i e_{i,2}$,

$$= \left(c_1^{\langle \mathbf{b}, \mathbf{e} \rangle} g^{m_1} h^{m_2} \right)^{2^t} = (c_1^{2^t})^{\langle \mathbf{b}, \mathbf{e} \rangle} \cdot h^{m_1} \cdot \hat{h}^{m_2}$$

Thus if $\mathcal{A}_{\text{brx}}$ wins, i.e., $\tilde{\Omega} = \Omega$, then we have

$$(c_1^{2^t})^{\langle \mathbf{b}, \mathbf{e} \rangle} = \tilde{\Omega} \cdot h^{-m_1} \cdot \hat{h}^{-m_2}$$

and we build $\mathcal{A}_{\text{rsw}}$ to win the computational power-of-RSW game by setting c_1 equal to challenge element x and returning this value along with $\langle \mathbf{b}, \mathbf{e} \rangle$. All that is left to show is that $\langle \mathbf{b}, \mathbf{e} \rangle \neq 0$ which we can do through an application of the Schwartz-Zippel lemma modulo a composite [17,36,43]. Define a non-zero polynomial $f(x_1, \ldots, x_n) = x_1 + \sum_{i=2}^n x_i e_{i,0}$. Note that $f(\mathbf{b}) = \langle \mathbf{b}, \mathbf{e} \rangle$.

$\mathcal{G}_1 \to \mathcal{G}_2$. To apply the Schwartz-Zippel lemma modulo a composite, we must first have that the evaluation point $\mathbf{b}$ does not coincide with values precomputed by the adversary. To do this, we step through $\mathcal{G}_2$ in which we disallow the output of the random oracle H from colliding with (the trailing substring of) any previous inputs to the random oracle. This ensures that the adversary has not made any previous queries that include b_* and ultimately ensures that the b_i values are chosen randomly *after* the polynomial is decided. We can apply a standard birthday analysis to bound the probability of collision among the q_{ro} queries made to $\mathsf{q}_{\text{ro}}^2/2^{2\lambda}$, to bound the distinguishing advantage between $\mathcal{G}_1$ and $\mathcal{G}_2$.

$\mathcal{G}_2 \to \mathcal{G}_3$. After we have that the evaluation point $\mathbf{b}$ does not coincide with precomputed values, we transition to $\mathcal{G}_3$ which is identical to $\mathcal{G}_2$ except it aborts if $f(\mathbf{b}) = 0$. We bound the distinguishing advantage to probability $\frac{n}{2^{2\lambda}} + \prod_{i=1}^\ell I_{\frac{1}{p_i}}(r_i, n)$ by applying Schwartz-Zippel modulo a composite [17]. Adversary $\mathcal{A}_{\text{rsw}}$ can simulate $\mathcal{G}_3$ perfectly, simulating the setup and computing $\hat{h}$ with $2t$ work, and wins the RSW game with the same advantage as $\mathcal{G}_3$.

Table 2. Ethereum gas costs and main operations involved for each Bicorn variant as well as Unicorn and Commit-Reveal DRBs. For Bicorn-PC, the Commit cost is split to show Precommit and Commit costs. The operations are: store$_{\mathbb{G}/2\lambda}$, storing a group element or 2λ-bit value; mul, multiplication of two group elements; exp, raising a group element to a power of size 2λ bits; poe.v and zk-poke.v, verifying a proof of exponentiation and proof of knowledge of exponent, respectively. Concrete costs are given with $\mathbb{G} = \mathbb{QR}_N^+$ within an RSA-2048 group and $\lambda = 128$.

		Gas Costs ($\times 10^3$), Operations Involved					
		Commit/user		Reveal/user		Recover	
	Commit-Reveal		store$_{2\lambda}$	60	xor, hash	-	
[28]	**Unicorn**	55	store$_{2\lambda}$		-	$30n$ | n·hash	}$+2{,}330$ poe.v
Sect. 2.2	**Bicorn-ZK**	2,950	zk-poke.v, store$_{\mathbb{G}}$	300	exp, mul	(*negligible*)	
Sect. 2.3	**Bicorn-PC**	155; 180	mul, store$_{\mathbb{G}}$	300	exp, mul	(*negligible*)	
Sect. 2.4	**Bicorn-RX**	145	mul, store$_{\mathbb{G}}$	425	2·exp, mul	$170n$ | n·exp	

6 Implementation

We implemented all three variants of Bicorn in Solidity and measured the associated gas costs in Ethereum [42]. Our results are presented in Table 2. We instantiate $\mathbb{G}$ as an RSA group with a 2048-bit modulus (specifically, it is the quadratic residue subgroup $\mathbb{QR}_N^+$ [30]). Multiplying two group elements costs $\sim$90,000 gas and raising a group element to a power of size 32 bytes costs $\sim$150,000 gas. As mentioned in Sect. 3, we use the short exponent indistinguishability (SEI) assumption [23] to reduce the size of the exponent required in practice from 288 to 32 bytes. The largest costs for each protocol are verifying a proof of exponentiation (PoE) for the VDF computation in the pessimistic Recover case and verifying a zero-knowledge proof of knowledge of exponent needed for each commitment in Bicorn-ZK. We implemented both proofs using non-interactive variants of Wesolowski proofs (ZKPoKRep from [11] for the latter), which requires a prime challenge to be sampled. Verifying this "hash-to-prime" operation costs between 2.3–4 million gas.[2]

Comparison to other DRBs. *Per-user Costs:* We find that the user operations for Bicorn-RX are practical on Ethereum with them costing 3× for Commit and 7× for Reveal when compared to the standard Commit-Reveal and Unicorn protocols. In total, the sum of these operations per user per run comes to under 600,000 gas, or $6 USD when 1 Eth = $1,000 USD and 1 gas = 10 Gwei.

Pessimistic Costs: In the pessimistic case, a single call to Recover is required in all versions of Bicorn, costing millions of gas. This pessimistic case is roughly equivalent to *every* run of Unicorn. As the number of users grows large and the chances of Bicorn's optimistic case occurring decrease though, at some point it

---

[2] Verifying "hash-to-prime" involves testing the primality of a number on-chain using Pocklington certificates. This costs between 2.3–4 million gas, depending on the size of the certificate. Table 2 reports costs with the smallest possible certificate.

may make more sense to switch to Unicorn and avoid the overheads of Commit and Reveal that Bicorn protocols incur.

7   Discussion

Last Revealer Prediction. All Bicorn variants come with a fundamental security caveat: if participant j withholds their α_j value, but all others publish, then participant j will be able to simulate the optimistic case and learn Ω quickly, while the honest participants will need to execute the pessimistic case and compute the delay function to complete before learning Ω. Similarly, a coalition of malicious participants can share their α values and privately compute Ω. This issue appears fundamental; in any protocol with a fast optimistic case and a slow pessimistic case, a unified malicious coalition can simulate the optimistic case.

This does not undermine t-unpredictability or t-indistinguishability and does not allow an adversary to manipulate the outcome. As a result, any protocol built on top of Bicorn should consider the output Ω to be potentially available to adversaries as of the deadline T_1, even if the result is not publicly known until $T_1 + t$ if the pessimistic case is triggered. For example, in a lottery application all wagers must be locked in before time T_1.

Incentives and Punishment. While all Bicorn variants ensure malicious participants cannot manipulate the output, they can waste resources by forcing the protocol into the more-expensive recovery mode. The protocol provides accountability as to which nodes published an incorrect α_i value or other minor deviations which lead to removal (i.e. publishing an incorrect c_i such that $H(c_i) \neq d_i$ in Bicorn-PC or publishing an incorrect π_i in Bicorn-ZK). If signatures are added to each message, efficient fraud proofs are possible. In a blockchain setting, financial penalties can be used to punish incorrect behavior.

Batch Verification Optimization. In the optimistic case, the n exponentiations required to verify that $c_i = g^{\tilde{\alpha}_i}$ for each participant can be streamlined via batch verification [5,16]. The general idea is that $g^x = 1 \wedge g^y = 1$ can be verified more efficiently by checking $g^{r \cdot x + y} = 1$ for a random $r \xleftarrow{\$} \mathcal{R}$, as the latter equation implies the former with high probability given a large enough $\mathcal{R}$. In our case, to verify that $c_1 = g^{\tilde{\alpha}_1} \wedge c_2 = g^{\tilde{\alpha}_2} \wedge \ldots \wedge c_n = g^{\tilde{\alpha}_n}$, we generate random values $r_i \xleftarrow{\$} \mathcal{R}$ and verify that $g^{\sum r_i \cdot \tilde{\alpha}_i} = \prod c_i^{r_i}$. Thus, instead of computing n exponentiations each with an exponent of size $|\mathcal{B}|$, verification requires only one exponentiation with an exponent of size $n|\mathcal{B}||\mathcal{R}|$ and one n-way multi-exponentiation [31].

Lowering Costs with Rollup Proofs. Practical costs can become significant if all users must post data to the blockchain to participate. For example, each run of Bicorn-RX costs about $6 USD per user even in the optimistic case. An alternative solution is to perform Bicorn mediated via a *rollup server* (Rollup-Bicorn) which gathers every participant's c_i value and publishes:

- A commitment $s = \mathsf{SetCommitment}(C)$ to the set $C = \{c_1, \ldots, c_n\}$ of all participant contributions. For example, s might be a Merkle Tree root.
- The value $c_* = \prod_{i \in [n]} c_i$, the product of all participants' commitments.
    - For Bicorn-RX, c_* will be adjusted with each party's exponent $H(c_i \| b_*)$.
- A succinct proof (SNARK) $\pi_{\text{rollup-commit}}$ that c_* has been computed consistently with the set S. This proof does not need to be zero-knowledge.
    - For Bicorn-ZK, the proof must recursively check each proof π_i.
    - For Bicorn-PC, the proof must check c_i was correctly precommitted.
    - For Bicorn-RX, the proof must check c_i was raised to the power b_i.

In the optimistic case, if all participants reveal their private value α_i, then the rollup server can finalize the protocol by posting:

- The output Ω and a succinct proof (SNARK) $\pi_{\text{rollup-finalize}}$ that states that:
    - The prover knows a set $A = \{\alpha_1, \ldots, \alpha_n\}$
    - For each $c_i \in C$, it holds that $c_i = g^{\alpha_i}$
    - The output Ω was computed correctly given the set A.

In the pessimistic case, if the rollup server goes offline without supplying the second proof (or some participants don't publish α_i), anybody can still compute $\Omega = c_*^{(2^t)}$. A single proof could be used which is a disjunction of verifying the rollup server's proof $\pi_{\text{rollup-finalize}}$ or verifying a PoE proof that $\Omega = c_*^{2^t}$. The end result is that Bicorn can be run with $O(1)$ cost for any number of participants.

Lowering Cost with Delegation. While the rollup approach requires only constant overhead on the blockchain regardless of the number of participants, the primary downside (in common with most rollup systems) is that the rollup server can *censor* by refusing to include any participant's c_i in the protocol. In the worst case, a malicious rollup server might only allow participants from a known cabal to participate, who are then able to manipulate the DRB output.

To achieve the best of both worlds (the efficiency of rollup servers for large protocol runs as well as robustness against censorship), we might design a *delegated* Bicorn protocol. In a delegated protocol, users can choose between multiple rollup servers or directly participate as an untrusted (possibly singleton) rollup server. This works like delegated proof-of-stake protocols: participants can delegate for efficiency if they want or participate individually if no server is considered trustworthy. This is straightforward for Bicorn-PC and Bicorn-ZK, as each rollup server can simply compute a partial product c_* which are multiplied together to obtain the final output Ω. Such a protocol for Bicorn-RX would require additional rounds of exponent randomization, to ensure each user's exponent is randomized by contributions from users at other rollup servers.

Acknowledgments. Kevin Choi, Arasu Arun and Joseph Bonneau were supported by DARPA under Agreement No. HR00112020022. Nirvan Tyagi was supported via a Facebook Graduate Fellowship, and part of this work was done while he was a visiting student at Stanford University. Joseph Bonneau and Arasu Arun were also supported by a16z crypto research. Any opinions, findings and conclusions or recommendations expressed in this material are those of the authors and do not necessarily reflect the views of the United States Government, DARPA, a16z, Facebook or any other supporting organization.

References

1. Drand. https://drand.love/
2. Andrychowicz, M., Dziembowski, S., Malinowski, D., Mazurek, L.: Secure multi-party computations on bitcoin. In: IEEE Security & Privacy (2014)
3. Beaver, D., et al.: Strobe: stake-based threshold random beacons. Cryptology ePrint Archive (2021)
4. Beaver, D., So, N.: Global, unpredictable bit generation without broadcast. In: Eurocrypt (1993)
5. Bellare, M., Garay, J.A., Rabin, T.: Fast batch verification for modular exponentiation and digital signatures. In: Eurocrypt (1998)
6. Bellare, M., Rogaway, P.: The security of triple encryption and a framework for code-based game-playing proofs. In: Vaudenay, S. (ed.) EUROCRYPT 2006. LNCS, vol. 4004, pp. 409–426. Springer, Heidelberg (2006). https://doi.org/10.1007/11761679_25
7. Bhat, A., Kate, A., Nayak, K., Shrestha, N.: OptRand: optimistically responsive distributed random beacons. Cryptology ePrint Archive, Paper 2022/193 (2022)
8. Bhat, A., Shrestha, N., Kate, A., Nayak, K.: RandPiper - reconfiguration-friendly random beacons with quadratic communication. Cryptology ePrint Archive, Paper 2020/1590 (2020)
9. Blum, M.: Coin flipping by telephone a protocol for solving impossible problems. In: ACM SIGACT News (1983)
10. Boneh, D., Bonneau, J., Bünz, B., Fisch, B.: Verifiable delay functions. In: CRYPTO (2018)
11. Boneh, D., Bünz, B., Fisch, B.: Batching techniques for accumulators with applications to IOPs and stateless blockchains. In: CRYPTO (2019)
12. Boneh, D., Bünz, B., Fisch, B.: A Survey of Two Verifiable Delay Functions. Cryptology ePrint Archive, Paper 2018/712 (2018)
13. Boneh, D., Drijvers, M., Neven, G.: Compact multi-signatures for smaller blockchains. In: Asiacrypt (2018)
14. Boneh, D., Naor, M.: Timed commitments. In: Annual International Cryptology Conference (2000)
15. Buchmann, J., Hamdy, S.: A survey on IQ cryptography. In: Public-Key Cryptography and Computational Number Theory (2011)
16. Bünz, B., Bootle, J., Boneh, D., Poelstra, A., Wuille, P., Maxwell, G.: Bulletproofs: Short proofs for confidential transactions and more. In: IEEE Security & Privacy (2018)
17. Bünz, B., Fisch, B.: Schwartz-zippel for multilinear polynomials mod n. Cryptology ePrint Archive, Paper 2022/458 (2022)
18. Camenisch, J., Drijvers, M., Hanke, T., Pignolet, Y.A., Shoup, V., Williams, D.: Internet computer consensus. In: ACM PODC (2022)
19. Cascudo, I., David, B.: Scrape: scalable randomness attested by public entities. In: ACNS (2017)
20. Cascudo, I., David, B.: Albatross: publicly attestable batched randomness based on secret sharing. In: Asiacrypt (2020)
21. Chen, M., et al.: Diogenes: lightweight scalable RSA modulus generation with a dishonest majority. In: IEEE Security & Privacy (2021)
22. Cherniaeva, A., Shirobokov, I., Shlomovits, O.: Homomorphic encryption random beacon. Cryptology ePrint Archive, Paper 2019/1320 (2019)

23. Couteau, G., Klooß, M., Lin, H., Reichle, M.: Efficient range proofs with transparent setup from bounded integer commitments. In: Eurocrypt (2021)
24. Das, S., Krishnan, V., Isaac, I.M., Ren, L.: Spurt: scalable distributed randomness beacon with transparent setup. Cryptology ePrint Archive, Paper 2021/100 (2021)
25. Fuchsbauer, G., Kiltz, E., Loss, J.: The algebraic group model and its applications. In: CRYPTO (2018)
26. Guo, Z., Shi, L., Xu, M.: SecRand: a secure distributed randomness generation protocol with high practicality and scalability. IEEE Access **8**, 203917–203929 (2020)
27. Kiayias, A., Russell, A., David, B., Oliynykov, R.: Ouroboros: a provably secure proof-of-stake blockchain protocol. In: CRYPTO (2017)
28. Lenstra, A.K., Wesolowski, B.: A random zoo: sloth, unicorn, and TRX. Cryptology ePrint Archive, Paper 2015/366 (2015)
29. Micciancio, D.: The RSA group is pseudo-free. In: CRYPTO (2005)
30. Pietrzak, K.: Simple verifiable delay functions. In: ITCS (2018)
31. Pippenger, N.: On the evaluation of powers and monomials. SIAM J. Comput. **9**(2), 230–250 (1980)
32. Qian, Y.: Randao: Verifiable random number generation (2017). https://randao.org/whitepaper/Randao_v0.85_en.pdf
33. Rivest, R.L., Shamir, A., Wagner, D.A.: Time-lock puzzles and timed-release crypto (1996)
34. Schindler, P., Judmayer, A., Stifter, N., Weippl, E.: Hydrand: efficient continuous distributed randomness. In: IEEE Security & Privacy (2020)
35. Schoenmakers, B.: A simple publicly verifiable secret sharing scheme and its application to electronic voting. In: CRYPTO (1999)
36. Schwartz, J.T.: Fast probabilistic algorithms for verification of polynomial identities. J. ACM (JACM) **27**(4), 701–717 (1980)
37. Syta, E., et al.: Scalable bias-resistant distributed randomness. In: IEEE Security & Privacy (2017)
38. Thyagarajan, S.A.K., Castagnos, G., Laguillaumie, F., Malavolta, G.: Efficient CCA timed commitments in class groups. Cryptology ePrint Archive, Report 2021/1272 (2021)
39. Trevisan, L.: Extractors and pseudorandom generators. J. ACM **48**(4), 860–879 (2001)
40. Trevisan, L., Vadhan, S.: Extracting randomness from samplable distributions. In: FOCS (2000)
41. Wesolowski, B.: Efficient verifiable delay functions. In: Eurocrypt (2019)
42. Wood, G., et al.: Ethereum: a secure decentralised generalised transaction ledger. In: Ethereum Project Yellow Paper (2014)
43. Zippel, R.: Probabilistic algorithms for sparse polynomials. In: Symbolic and Algebraic Manipulation (1979)

McFly: Verifiable Encryption to the Future Made Practical

Nico Döttling[1]([⊠]) [iD], Lucjan Hanzlik[1], Bernardo Magri[2] [iD],
and Stella Wohnig[1,3]([⊠]) [iD]

[1] CISPA Helmholtz Center for Information Security, Saarbrücken, Germany
{doettling,hanzlik,stella.wohnig}@cispa.de
[2] The University of Manchester, Manchester, UK
bernardo.magri@manchester.ac.uk
[3] Saarland University, Saarbrücken, Germany

Abstract. Blockchain protocols have revolutionized how individuals
and devices interact and transact over the internet. More recently, a
trend has emerged to harness blockchain technology as a catalyst to
enable advanced security features in distributed applications, in particular fairness. However, the tools employed to achieve these security
features are either resource wasteful (e.g., time-lock primitives) or only
efficient in theory (e.g., witness encryption). We present McFly, a protocol that allows one to efficiently "encrypt a message to the future" such
that the receiver can efficiently decrypt the message at the right time.
At the heart of the McFly protocol lies a novel primitive that we call
signature-based witness encryption (SWE). In a nutshell, SWE allows to
encrypt a plaintext with respect to a tag and a set of signature verification keys. Once a threshold multi-signature of this tag under a sufficient
number of these verification keys is released, this signature can be used
to efficiently decrypt an SWE ciphertext for this tag. We design and
implement a practically efficient SWE scheme in the asymmetric bilinear
setting. The McFly protocol, which is obtained by combining our SWE
scheme with a BFT blockchain (or a blockchain finality layer) enjoys a
number of advantages over alternative approaches: There is a very small
computational overhead for all involved parties, the users of McFly do
not need to actively maintain the blockchain, are neither required to
communicate with the committees, nor are they required to post on the
blockchain. To demonstrate the practicality of the McFly protocol, we
implemented our SWE scheme and evaluated it on a standard laptop
with Intel i7 @2,3 GHz.

1 Introduction

Blockchain protocols have become increasingly popular as they revolutionized
the way peer-to-peer transactions can be made. In their most basic form, block-

N. Döttling—Funded by the European Union (ERC, LACONIC, 101041207). Views
and opinions expressed are however those of the author(s) only and do not necessarily
reflect those of the European Union or the European Research Council. Neither the
European Union nor the granting authority can be held responsible for them.

© International Financial Cryptography Association 2024
F. Baldimtsi and C. Cachin (Eds.): FC 2023, LNCS 13950, pp. 252–269, 2024.
https://doi.org/10.1007/978-3-031-47754-6_15

chain protocols are run by independent parties, the so-called miners, that keep their own copy of the blockchain and verify the contents of all transactions they receive before appending them to their own copy of the blockchain. The fact that the content of the transactions can be verified *before* its inclusion in the blockchain is fundamental to the validity of the transactions and the consistency of the blockchain. However, there are many scenarios where one would like to keep the contents of a transaction secret for some time even *after* inclusion in the blockchain. One simple example is running sealed-bid auctions on the blockchain; one would like for its bid to be included in the blockchain, but at the same time such a bid should remain hidden until the end of the auction.[1] Another example that recently became very relevant with the popularization of decentralized exchanges (DEX) is the hurtful practice of transaction *frontrunning*, where malicious actors try to profit by taking advantage of possible market fluctuations that could happen after some target transaction is added to the ledger. To exploit this, the adversary tries to get its own transaction included in the ledger *before* the target transaction, by either mining the block itself and changing the order of transactions, or by offering considerably more fees for its own transaction. Hiding parts of the content of the transactions until they are final in the ledger would make it harder for adversaries to target those transactions for frontrunning. A more general application for such a mechanism, that can keep the contents of a blockchain transaction secret for some pre-defined time, would be to simply use it as a tool to realize timed-release encryption [24] without a trusted third party.

In previous works [3,15], solutions to the problems above were based on time-lock primitives, such as time-lock puzzles (TLP) or verifiable delay functions (VDF). An inherent problem of time-lock type primitives is that they are wasteful in terms of computational resources and notoriously difficult to instantiate with concrete parameters. Usually, a reference hardware is used to measure the "fastest possible" time that it takes to solve a single operation of the puzzle (e.g., modular squaring) and this reference number is used to set the security parameters. Moreover, in a heterogeneous and decentralized system such as a blockchain, where different hardware can have gaps in speed of many orders of magnitude, an approach like this could render the system impractical. An operation that takes one time unit in the reference hardware could take 1000 time units on different hardware used in the system.

Moreover, the environmental problems that proof-of-work blockchains, where miners invest computation power to create new blocks, can cause have been intensively debated by the community and regulators. This made the majority of blockchain systems adopt a proof-of-stake (PoS) consensus for being a much more sustainable solution. In PoS systems, typically a subset of users is chosen as a committee, which jointly decides which blocks to include in the chain. This selection can be by a lottery with winning probability proportional to the amount

---

[1] Clearly, the auction should run on an incentive-compatible transaction ledger, where transactions paying the required fees are guaranteed to be included in the ledger within some fixed time.

of coins parties hold on the chain or by the parties applying by locking a relatively big amount of their coins, preventing them from spending them. In light of that, any solution employing a time-lock type primitive completely defeats the purpose of achieving a more resource-efficient and environmentally conscious system.

1.1   Our Contributions

In that vein, we diverge from the time-lock primitive approach and propose McFly, an efficient protocol to keep the contents of a message (e.g., a blockchain transaction) secret for some pre-specified time period. McFly is based on a new primitive that we call signature witness encryption (SWE), that combined with a byzantine fault tolerance (BFT) blockchain or with any blockchain coupled with a finality layer such as Ethereum's Casper [11] or Afgjort [16] allows users to encrypt messages to a future point in time by piggybacking part of the decryption procedure on the tasks already performed by the underlying committee of the blockchain (or the finality layer) - namely voting for and signing blocks. In BFT blockchains this happens for every new potential block to reach consensus, while in a finality layer this is done for blocks at regular intervals to make them "final". We detail our contributions next.

Signature Witness Encryption. We formally define a new primitive that we call signature-based witness encryption (SWE). To encrypt a message m, the encryption algorithm takes a set of verification keys for a (potentially aggregatable) multi-signature scheme[2] and a reference message r as an input and produces a ciphertext ct. The witness to decrypt ct consists of a multi-signature of the reference message r under a threshold number of keys. We instantiate SWE with an aggregatable multi-signature scheme that is a BLS scheme [6] with a modified aggregation mechanism. We show, that this signature scheme fulfills the same security notions as previous aggregatable BLS multi-signatures.

Concretely, the guarantees for SWE are that (1) it correctly allows to decrypt a ciphertext given a multi-signature on the underlying reference and (2) if the adversary does not gain access to a sufficient number of signatures on the reference then ciphertext-indistinguishability holds. The security guarantee is conceptually closer related to that of identity-based encryption, rather than that of fully-fledged witness encryption; decryption is possible when a threshold number of key holders participate to unlock. We achieve this in the bilinear group setting from the bilinear Diffie-Hellman assumption. Also, unlike general witness encryption constructions [19] that are highly inefficient, we demonstrate SWE to be practicable. To ensure that decryption is always possible we make SWE verifiable by designing specially tailored proofs to show well-formedness of ciphertexts as well as additional properties of the encrypted message.

McFly Protocol. We build an "encryption to the future" protocol by combining SWE with a BFT blockchain or a blockchain finality layer. The main idea of this

---

[2] This type of signature schemes allows to compress multiple signatures by different signers on the same messages into just one verifiable signature. In aggregatable schemes, this works even on different messages.

is to leverage the existing committee infrastructure of the underlying blockchain that periodically signs blocks in the chain to piggyback part of the decryption procedure of the SWE scheme. At a high level, a message is encrypted with respect to a specified block height of the underlying blockchain (representing how far into the future the message should remain encrypted) and the set of verification keys of all the committee members that are supposed to sign the block at that height; once the block with the specified height is created by the committee, it automatically becomes the witness required to decrypt the ciphertext. We have the following requirements on the underlying blockchain:

- **BFT-Style or Finality Layer.** Every (final) block in the chain must be signed by a committee of parties. These committees are allowed to be static or dynamic, with the only requirement that the committee responsible for signing a block at a particular height must be known *some time* in advance. How much "time in advance" the committee is known is what we call horizon (following the nomenclature of [20]). For simplicity, we will explicitly assume that all blocks are immediately finalized, but our results can be easily adapted to the more general setting where the height of the next final block is known.
- **Block Structure.** We assume that blocks have a predictable header, which we will model by a block counter, and some data content. When finalizing a block the committee signs the block as usual, but additionally, it also signs the block counter separately.[3]
- **Public Key Infrastructure.** The public keys of the committee members must have a proof of knowledge. This can be achieved, e.g., by registering the keys with a PKI.
- **Honest Majority Committee.**[4] The majority of the committee behaves honestly. That is, there will not be a majority of committee members colluding to prematurely sign blocks.
- **Constant Block Production Rate.** To have a meaningful notion of "wall-clock time", the blocks must be produced at a near constant rate.

A blockchain functionality modelling the above requirements and an analysis on how to integrate our scheme with a modified version of Ethereum 2.0 can be found in the full version. Intuitively, to make Ethereum 2.0 running with Casper [11] compatible with our model we only need to add the public key infrastructure and require the committee members to sign a block counter separately for each finalized block. This enables encryption up to the horizon where a future committee is already known. Unfortunately, in Ethereum 2.0 this leads to a maximum horizon of 12.8 minutes. If we use "sync committees" instead, which

---

[3] They use the same keys for this. This is safe whenever the underlying signature is a hash-and-sign scheme as is commonly the case.

[4] The honest majority requirement must be strengthened to honest supermajority (i.e. at least 2/3 of members being honest) if the underlying blockchain or finality layer considers a partially synchronous network model. For simplicity, we choose to describe it in the synchronous network model where honest majority plus PKI is sufficient.

were only introduced in Ethereum Altair [10], we can have a horizon of up to 27 hours. However, it is unclear whether sync committees enjoy the same level of trust as standard ones.

Implementation. To demonstrate the practicality of McFly, we implement the SWE scheme and run a series of benchmarks on a standard Macbook Pro with an Intel i7 processor @2,3 GHz. Details can be found in the full version.

1.2   Technical Overview

As detailed above, the key ingredient and main technical challenge of the McFly protocol is *Signature Witness Encryption* (SWE). In the following, we will provide an outline of our construction of practically efficient SWE.

SWE Based on BLS. Our construction of Signature-based Witness Encryption is based on the BLS signature scheme [7] and its relation to identity-based encryption [5]. Recall that BLS signatures are defined over a bilinear group, i.e. we have 3 groups $\mathbb{G}_1, \mathbb{G}_2, \mathbb{G}_T$ (with generators g_1, g_2, g_T) of prime-order p and an efficiently computable bilinear map $e : \mathbb{G}_1 \times \mathbb{G}_2 \to \mathbb{G}_T$. A verification key vk is of the form $\mathsf{vk} = g_2^x$, where $x \in \mathbb{Z}_p$ is the corresponding signing key. To sign a message $T \in \{0,1\}^*$, we compute $\sigma = H(T)^x$, where $H : \{0,1\}^* \to \mathbb{G}_1$ is a hash function (which is modeled as a random oracle in the security proofs). To verify a signature σ for a message T, all we need to do is check whether $e(\sigma, g_2) = e(H(T), \mathsf{vk})$. The BLS signature scheme is closely related to the identity-based encryption scheme of Boneh and Franklin [5]. Specifically, in the IBE scheme of [5] BLS verification keys take the role of the master public key, the signing key takes the role of the master secret key and signatures take the role of identity secret keys, where the signed messages correspond to the identities, respectively. In this sense, the BF scheme can be seen as a witness encryption scheme that allows to encrypt plaintexts m with respect to a verification key vk and a message T, such that anyone in possession of a valid signature of T under vk will be able to decrypt the plaintext m. Specifically, we can encrypt a message $m \in \{0,1\}$ by computing $\mathsf{ct} = (g_2^r, e(H(T), \mathsf{vk})^r \cdot g_T^m)$. Given a signature $\sigma = H(T)^x$, we can decrypt a ciphertext $\mathsf{ct} = (c_1, c_2)$ by computing $d = c_2/e(\sigma, c_1)$ and taking the discrete logarithm of d with respect to g_T (which can be done efficiently as $m \in \{0,1\}$).

SWE for BLS Multi-signatures. The BLS scheme can be instantiated as an aggregatable multi-signature scheme [6]. Specifically, assume that for $i = 1, \ldots, n$ we have messages T_i with a corresponding signature σ_i with respect to a verification key vk_i. Then we can combine the signatures $\sigma_1, \ldots, \sigma_n$ into a *single* compact aggregate signature $\sigma = \prod_{i=1}^n \sigma_i$. Verifying such a signature can be done by checking whether $e(\sigma, g_2) = \prod_{i=1}^n e(H(T_i), \mathsf{vk}_i)$, where correctness follows routinely. We can adapt the BF IBE scheme to aggregate signatures in a natural way: To encrypt a plaintext $m \in \{0,1\}$ to messages $T_1, \ldots, T_n$ and corresponding verification keys $\mathsf{vk}_1, \ldots, \mathsf{vk}_n$ compute a ciphertext ct via $\mathsf{ct} = (g_2^r, (\prod_{i=1}^n e(H(T_i), \mathsf{vk}_i))^r \cdot g_T^m)$. Such a ciphertext $\mathsf{ct} = (c_1, c_2)$ can be decrypted analogously to the above by computing $d = c_2/e(\sigma, c_1)$ and taking the discrete logarithm with respect to g_T. To decrypt ct we need an aggregate signature σ of *all* T_i under their respective verification keys vk_i. For our envisioned applications this requirement is too strong, instead, we need a *threshold* scheme where a t-out-of-n aggregate signature suffices as a witness to decrypt a ciphertext. Thus, we will rely on Shamir's secret sharing scheme [25] to implement a t-out-of-n access structure. This, however, leads to additional challenges. Recall that Shamir's secret sharing scheme allows us to share a message $r_0 \in \mathbb{Z}_p$ into shares $s_1, \ldots, s_n \in \mathbb{Z}_p$, such that r_0 can be reconstructed via a (public) linear combination of any t of the s_i, while on the other hand, any set of less than t shares s_i reveals no information about r_0. The coefficients L_{i_j} of the linear combination required to reconstruct r_0 from a set of shares $s_{i_1}, \ldots, s_{i_t}$ (for indices $i_1, \ldots, i_t$) can be obtained from a corresponding set of Lagrange polynomials. Given such L_{i_j}, we can express r_0 as $r_0 = \sum_{j=1}^{t} L_{i_j} s_{i_j}$. We can now modify the above SWE scheme for aggregate signatures as follows. To encrypt a plaintext $m \in \{0, 1\}$, we first compute a t-out-of-n secret sharing $s_1, \ldots, s_n$ of the plaintext m. The ciphertext ct is then computed by $\mathsf{ct} = (g_2^r, (e(H(T_i), \mathsf{vk}_i)^r \cdot g_T^{s_i})_{i \in [n]})$. Security of this scheme can be established from the same assumption as the BF IBE scheme, namely from the bilinear Diffie-Hellman (BDH) assumption [21]. We would now like to be able to decrypt such a ciphertext using an aggregate signature. For this purpose, however, we will have to modify the aggregation procedure of the aggregatable multi-signature scheme. Say we obtain t-out-of-n signatures σ_{i_j}, where σ_{i_j} is a signature of T_{i_j} under vk_{i_j}. Let L_{i_j} be the corresponding Lagrange coefficients. Our new aggregation procedure computes $\sigma = \prod_{j=1}^{t} \sigma_{i_j}^{L_{i_j}}$. That is, instead of merely taking the product of the σ_{i_j} we need to raise each σ_{i_j} to the power of its corresponding Lagrange coefficient L_{i_j}. We can show that this modification does not hurt the security of the underlying aggregatable BLS multi-signature scheme. To decrypt a ciphertext $\mathsf{ct} = (c_0, c_1, \ldots, c_n)$ using such an aggregate signature σ, we compute $d = \prod_{j=1}^{t} c_{i_j}^{L_{i_j}}/e(\sigma, c_0)$ and take the discrete logarithm of d with respect to g_T. Correctness follows routinely.

Moving to the Source Group. While the above scheme provides our desired functionality, implementing this scheme leads to a very poor performance profile. There are two main reasons: (1) Each ciphertext encrypts just a single bit. Thus, to encrypt any meaningful number of bits we need to provide a large number of ciphertexts. Observe that each ciphertext contains more than n group elements. Thus, encrypting k bits would require a ciphertext comprising kn group elements, which would be prohibitively large even for moderate values of k and n. (2) Both encryption and decryption rely heavily on pairing operations and operations in the target group. From an implementation perspective, pairing operations and operations in the target group are typically several times slower than operations in one of the source groups.

To address these issues, we will design a scheme that both allows for *ciphertext packing* and shifts almost all group operations into one of the two source groups (in our case this will be $\mathbb{G}_2$). This scheme is provided in Sect. 2.1 and we will only highlight a few aspects here.

- Instead of computing a secret sharing of the plaintext m, we compute a secret sharing of a random value $r_0 \in \mathbb{Z}_p$. The value r_0 can be used to randomize many batch-ciphertext components, leading to ciphertexts comprising only $O(k + n)$ group elements.
- We encrypt each share s_i in the source group $\mathbb{G}_2$ instead of $\mathbb{G}_T$. That is, we compute the ciphertext-component c_i via $c_i = \mathsf{vk}_i^r \cdot g_2^{s_i}$. This necessitates a corresponding modification of the decryption algorithm and requires that all messages T_i are identical, but this requirement is compatible with our envisioned applications. Somewhat surprisingly, this modification does not necessitate making a stronger hardness assumption, but only requires a rather intricate random-self-reduction procedure in the security proof. That is, even with this modification we can still rely on the hardness of the standard BDH assumption.
- Instead of encrypting single bits $m \in \{0, 1\}$, we allow the message m to come from $\{0, \ldots, 2^k - 1\}$. This will allow us to pack k bits into each ciphertext component. Recall that decryption requires the computation of a discrete logarithm with respect to a generator g_T. We can speed up this computation by relying on the Baby-Step-Giant-Step (BSGS) algorithm [27] to $O(2^{k/2})$ group operations. This leads to a very efficient implementation as a discrete logarithm table for the fixed generator g_T can be precomputed.

A Compatibility-Layer for Efficient Proof Systems. Our scheme so far assumes that encryptors behave honestly, i.e. the ciphertext ct is well-formed. A malicious encryptor, however, may provide ciphertexts that do not decrypt consistently, i.e. the decrypted plaintext m may depend on the signature σ used for decryption. Furthermore, for several of the use cases, we envision it is crucial to ensure that the encrypted message m satisfies additional properties. To facilitate this, we provide the following augmentations in the full version.

- We provide an efficient NIZK proof[5] in the ROM which ensures that ciphertexts decrypt consistently, i.e. the result of decryption does not depend on the signature which is used for decryption.
- We augment ciphertexts with efficient *proof-system enabled commitments* and provide very efficient plaintext equality proofs in the ROM. In essence, we provide an efficient NIZK proof system that allows to prove that a ciphertext ct and a Pedersen commitment C commit to the same value.
- We can now rely on efficient and succinct proof systems such as Bullet-proofs [9] to establish additional guarantees about the encrypted plaintext. For instance, we can rely on the range-proofs of [9] to ensure that the encrypted messages are within a certain range to ensure that our BSGS decryption procedure will recover the correct plaintext.

---

[5] Technically speaking, since our systems are only computationally sound, we provide non-interactive argument systems. However, to stay in line with the terminology of [9,18] we refer to them as proof systems.

To make this construction efficient, we add redundancy to include homomorphic commitments into SWE ciphertexts.

1.3   Related Work

Timed-Release Crypto and "Encryption to the Future". The notion of timed-release encryption was proposed in the seminal paper by Rivest, Shamir and Wagner [24]. The goal is to encrypt a message so that it cannot be decrypted, not even by the sender, until a pre-determined amount of time has passed. This allows to "encrypt messages to the future". In [24] the authors propose two orthogonal directions for realizing such a primitive. Using trusted third-parties to hold the secrets and only reveal them once the pre-determined amount of time has passed, or by using so-called time-lock puzzles, which are computational problems that can not be solved without running a computer continuously for at least a certain amount of time.

An interesting example of the latter are timed commitments [8], which are commitments with an additional forced opening phase that requires a specified (big) amount of computation time. This is useful in an optimistic setting, where cooperation is usually the case, as an honest party can convince the receiver of the comitted value without needing to do the timely decryption step. This is indeed also possible for our SWE scheme, as its ciphertexts constitute a statistically binding commitment, but that is not our focus, as our decryption is efficient enough to be run. In case of one party aborting, timed commitments share all drawbacks of time-lock puzzles, whereas our protocol works efficiently.

Our approach is closer to the paradigm of using a trusted party as in [13,14]. Simply put, these approaches set up a dedicated server that outputs tokens for decryption at specified times. We could deploy SWE in such a scenario as well, with the tokens being aggregated signatures on predictable messages. Specifically both [13] and our scheme achieve that no communication needs to take place between the trusted server and other entities. However, complete trust in a single (or multiple) servers is a strong assumption, thus we re-use the decentralized architecture, computation and trust structure already present in blockchains.

With the advent of blockchains, multiple proposals to realize timed-release encryption using the blockchain as a time-keeping tool emerged, already. These previous results, presented here, are all more of theoretical interest, while we demonstrate practical efficiency of our scheme.

In [22] the authors propose a scheme based on extractable witness encryption using the blockchain as a reference clock; messages are encrypted to future blocks of the chain that once created can be used as a witness for decryption. However, extractable witness encryption is a very expensive primitive. Concurrently to this work, [12] proposes an "encryption to the future" scheme based on proof-of-stake blockchains. Their approach is geared at transmitting messages from past committee members to future slot winners of the proof-of-stake lottery and requires active participation in the protocol by the committee members. Our results differ from this by enabling encrypting to the future even for encryptors and decryptors that only read the state of the blockchain and we require no active participation of the committee beyond their regular duties, assuming, that predictable messages like a block header are already signed in each (finalized) block. Otherwise, all committees need to only include this one additional signature, irrespective of pending timed-encryptions, so there is no direct involvement between users of McFly and committees.

Another related line of work is presented in [2], where a message is kept secret and "alive" on the chain by re-sharing a secret sharing of the message from committee to committee. This allows to keep the message secret until an arbitrary condition is met and the committee can reveal the message. A more general approach is the recent YOSO protocol [20] that allows to perform secure computation in that same setting, by using an additive homomorphic encryption scheme, to which committees hold shares of a secret key and continuously re-share it. While these approaches realize some form of encryption to the future, they require massive communication from parties and are still far from practical.

A spin on timed commitments is also available using blockchains; in [1], a blockchain contract is introduced, that locks assets of the commitment sender for a set time based on a commitment. If the sender fails to open the commitment within that time, their assets are made available to the receiver as a penalty - however the commitment is not opened in that case.

BLS Signatures and Identity-Based Encryption (IBE). The BLS signature scheme, introduced in [7], is a pairing-based signature scheme with signatures of one group element in size. Additionally, it is possible to aggregate signatures of multiple users on different messages, thus saving space as shown in [6]. Due to the very space-efficient aggregation, BLS signatures are used in widely deployed systems such as Ethereum 2.0 [17]. Aggregation for potential duplicate messages is achieved in [4,23].

Identity based encryption was first introduced by Shamir [26]. The initial idea was to use the identity - e.g. a mailing address - as a public key that messages can be encrypted to. In a sense, our scheme can be seen as a threshold IBE, as we encrypt with respect to a committee and can only decrypt if a threshold of the committee members collaborate.

1.4   Contents

This is a shortened conference-version of this paper including an overview of our results, the construction of our modified BLS multi-signature scheme, as well as definitions and constructions for both our basic SWE and McFly. Due to space limitations, we refer readers to the full version for more details including:

- The construction of a proof compatibility layer to add verifiability to SWE.
- A blockchain functionality rigorously modelling the requirements on the blockchain that are outlined above.
- Details and evaluations of an implementation of our scheme.
- Discussions of applications of our scheme in decentralized auctions and randomness beacons.

1.5   Preliminaries

We denote by $\lambda \in \mathbb{N}$ the security parameter and by $x \leftarrow \mathcal{A}(\text{in}; r)$ the output of the randomized algorithm $\mathcal{A}$ on input in with $r \leftarrow \{0,1\}^*$ as its randomness. We omit this randomness when it is obvious or not explicitly required. By $\mathcal{A}^O$ we denote, that we run $\mathcal{A}$ with oracle access to O. We denote by $x \leftarrow_\$ S$ an output x being chosen uniformly at random from a set S. We denote the set $\{1, \ldots, n\}$ by $[n]$. PPT denotes probabilistic polynomial time. Also, $poly(x), negl(x)$ respectively denote any polynomial or negligible function in parameter x.

We assume familarity with the following cryptographic notions, for which full definitions are included in our full version: Aggregateable multi-signatures, Cryptographic Hash functions, Pseudo-random functions, commitment schemes, Zero-Knowledge Proofs (of Knowledge), Secret Sharings, Reed-Solomon Codes, Lagrange Interpolation, Bilinear Maps as well as the Co-Diffie-Hellman and Bilinear Diffie-Hellman Assumptions.

2   Signature-Based Witness Encryption

In this section we introduce the new cryptographic primitive SWE that is the core technical component of the McFly protocol. We formally define it next.

Definition 1 (Signature-Based Witness Encryption). *A t-out-of-n SWE for an aggregate signature scheme* Sig = (KeyGen, Sign, Vrfy, Agg, AggVrfy, Prove, Valid) *is a tuple of two algorithms* (Enc, Dec) *where:*

- ct $\leftarrow$ Enc($1^\lambda, V = (\mathsf{vk}_1, \ldots, \mathsf{vk}_n), (T_i)_{i \in [\ell]}, (m_i)_{i \in [\ell]}$): *Encryption takes as input a set V of n verification keys of the underlying scheme* Sig, *a list of reference signing messages T_i and a list of messages m_i of arbitrary length $\ell \in poly(\lambda)$. It outputs a ciphertext* ct.
- m $\leftarrow$ Dec(ct, $(\sigma_i)_{i \in [\ell]}, U, V$): *Decryption takes as input a ciphertext* ct, *a list of aggregate signatures $(\sigma_i)_{i \in [\ell]}$ and two sets U, V of verification keys of the underlying scheme* Sig. *It outputs a message m.*

We require such a scheme to fulfill robust correctness and security.

Definition 2 (Robust Correctness). *A t-out-of-n SWE scheme* SWE = (Enc, Dec) *for an aggregate signature scheme* Sig = (KeyGen, Sign, Vrfy, Agg, AggVrfy, Prove, Valid) *is correct if for all $\lambda \in \mathbb{N}$ and $\ell = poly(\lambda)$ there is no PPT adversary $\mathcal{A}$ with more than negligible probability of outputting an index* ind $\in [\ell]$, *a set of keys $V = (\mathsf{vk}_1, \ldots, \mathsf{vk}_n)$, a subset $U \subseteq V$ with $|U| \geq t$, message lists $(m_i)_{i \in [\ell]}, (T_i)_{i \in [\ell]}$ and signatures $(\sigma_i)_{i \in [\ell]}$, such that* AggVrfy($\sigma_{\mathsf{ind}}, U, (T_{\mathsf{ind}})_{i \in [|U|]}$) = 1, *but* Dec(Enc($1^\lambda, V, (T_i)_{i \in [\ell]}, (m_i)_{i \in [\ell]}), (\sigma_i)_{i \in [\ell]}, U, V$)$_{\mathsf{ind}} \neq m_{\mathsf{ind}}$.

Definition 3 (Security). *A t-out-of-n SWE scheme* SWE = (Enc, Dec) *for an aggregate signature scheme* Sig = (KeyGen, Sign, Vrfy, Agg, AggVrfy, Prove, Valid) *is secure if for all $\lambda \in \mathbb{N}$, such that $t = poly(\lambda)$, and all $\ell = poly(\lambda)$,* *subsets $SC \subseteq [\ell]$, there is no PPT adversary $\mathcal{A}$ that has more than negligible advantage in the experiment $\mathsf{Exp}_{\mathsf{Sec}}(\mathcal{A}, 1^\lambda)$. We define $\mathcal{A}$'s advantage by $\mathsf{Adv}_{\mathsf{Sec}}^{\mathcal{A}} = |\Pr\left[\mathsf{Exp}_{\mathsf{Sec}}(\mathcal{A}, 1^\lambda) = 1\right] - \frac{1}{2}|$.*

Experiment $\mathsf{Exp}_{\mathsf{Sec}}(\mathcal{A}, 1^\lambda)$

1. *Let H_{pr} be a fresh hash function from a keyed family of hash functions, available to the experiment and $\mathcal{A}$.*
2. *The experiment generates $n - t + 1$ key pairs for $i \in \{t, \ldots, n\}$ as $(\mathsf{vk}_i, \mathsf{sk}_i) \leftarrow \mathsf{Sig.KeyGen}(1^\lambda)$ and provides vk_i as well as $\mathsf{Sig.Prove}^{H_{pr}}(\mathsf{vk}_i, \mathsf{sk}_i)$ for $i \in \{t, \ldots, n\}$ to $\mathcal{A}$.*
3. *$\mathcal{A}$ inputs $VC = (\mathsf{vk}_1, \ldots, \mathsf{vk}_{t-1})$ and $(\pi_1, \ldots, \pi_{t-1})$. If for any $i \in [t-1]$, $\mathsf{Sig.Valid}(\mathsf{vk}_i, \pi_i) = 0$, we abort. Else, we define $V = (\mathsf{vk}_1, \ldots, \mathsf{vk}_n)$.*
4. *$\mathcal{A}$ gets to make signing queries for pairs (i, T). If $i < t$, the experiment aborts, else it returns $\mathsf{Sig.Sign}(\mathsf{sk}_i, T)$.*
5. *The adversary announces challenge messages m_i^0, m_i^1 for $i \in SC$, a list of messages $(m_i)_{i \in [\ell] \setminus SC}$ and a list of signing reference messages $(T_i)_{i \in [\ell]}$. If a signature for a T_i with $i \in SC$ was previously queried, we abort.*
6. *The experiment flips a bit $b \leftarrow_\$ \{0,1\}$, sets $m_i = m_i^b$ for $i \in SC$ and sends $\mathsf{Enc}(1^\lambda, V, (T_i)_{i \in [\ell]}, (m_i)_{i \in [\ell]})$ to $\mathcal{A}$.*
7. *$\mathcal{A}$ gets to make further signing queries for pairs (i, T). If $i \geq t$ and $T \neq T_i$ for all $i \in SC$, the experiment returns $\mathsf{Sig.Sign}(\mathsf{sk}_i, T)$, else it aborts.*
8. *Finally, $\mathcal{A}$ outputs a guess b'.*
9. *If $b = b'$, the experiment outputs 1, else 0.*

Definition 4 (Verifiable Signature-Based Witness Encryption). *A scheme $\mathsf{SWE} = (\mathsf{Enc}, \mathsf{Dec}, \mathsf{Prove}, \mathsf{Vrfy})$ is a verifiable SWE for relation $\mathcal{R}$, if $\mathsf{Enc}, \mathsf{Dec}$ are as above and $\mathsf{Prove}, \mathsf{Vrfy}$ are a NIZK proof system for a language given by the following induced relation $\mathcal{R}'$, where $V = (\mathsf{vk}_1, \ldots, \mathsf{vk}_n)$ is a set of keys:*

$$(V, (T_i)_{i \in [\ell]}, \mathsf{ct}), ((m_i)_{i \in [\ell]}, w, r)) \in \mathcal{R}' \Leftrightarrow$$
$$\mathsf{ct} = \mathsf{Enc}(1^\lambda, V, (T_i)_{i \in [\ell]}, (m_i)_{i \in [\ell]}); r) \text{ and } (m = \sum_{i \in [\ell]} 2^{(i-1)k} m_i, w) \in \mathcal{R}$$

2.1 Construction

In the following, we describe a t-out-of-n SWE. Let two base groups $\mathbb{G}_1, \mathbb{G}_2$ of prime order p with generators g_1, g_2 which have a bilinear map $e : \mathbb{G}_1 \times \mathbb{G}_2 \rightarrow \mathbb{G}_T$ into a target group $\mathbb{G}_T$ with generator g. Also, we assume full-domain hash functions $H : \{0,1\}^* \rightarrow \mathbb{G}_1$, $H_2 : \{0,1\}^* \rightarrow \mathbb{Z}_p$ and $H_{pr} : \{0,1\}^* \rightarrow \mathbb{Z}_p$.

First, let us describe the underlying signature scheme Sig'.

Protocol Sig′

Sig′.KeyGen(1^λ): Randomly pick $x \leftarrow_\$ \mathbb{Z}_p$ and output ($\mathsf{vk} = g_2^x$, $\mathsf{sk} = x$).

Sig′.Sign(sk, T): Output $H(T)^{\mathsf{sk}}$.

Sig′.Vrfy(vk, T, σ): If ($e(\sigma, g_2) = e(H(T), \mathsf{vk})$), output 1, else output 0.

Sig′.Agg($(\sigma_1, \ldots, \sigma_k), (\mathsf{vk}_1, \ldots, \mathsf{vk}_k)$):
- Compute $\xi_i = H_2(\mathsf{vk}_i)$ for $i \in [k]$.
- Compute $L_i = \prod_{j \in [k], i \neq j} \frac{-\xi_j}{\xi_i - \xi_j}$ for $i \in [k]$.
- Output $\sigma \leftarrow \prod_{i \in [k]} \sigma_i^{L_i}$.

Sig′.AggVrfy($\sigma, (\mathsf{vk}_1, \ldots, \mathsf{vk}_k), (T_1, \ldots, T_k)$):
- If $e(\sigma, g_2) = \prod_{i \in [k]} e(H(T_i), \mathsf{vk}_i)^{L_i}$, output 1. Output 0 otherwise.

Sig′.Prove(vk, sk): Output Schnorr.Prove$^{H_{pr}}(\mathsf{vk}, \mathsf{sk})$.

Sig′.Valid(vk, π): Output Schnorr.Valid$^{H_{pr}}(\mathsf{vk}, \pi)$.

Here, Schnorr.Prove, Schnorr.Valid are the non-interactive variant of the well-known Schnorr proofs due to Fischlin [18]. As shown in [18], they constitute an online-extractable proof of knowledge for the key relation $\mathcal{K} = \{(g^x, x) : x \in \mathbb{Z}_p\}$.

Theorem 1. *Sig′ is a correct aggregatable multi-signature scheme. Sig′ is unforgeable, assuming that H is modelled as a random oracle and that the computational Co-Diffie-Hellman assumption holds for $(\mathbb{G}_1, \mathbb{G}_2)$.*

The proof is given in the full version only, due to space restrictions. Now, we can give the construction of our SWE scheme.[6]

Protocol SWE for signature scheme Sig′

SWE′.Enc($1^\lambda, (\mathsf{vk}_j)_{j \in [n]}, (T_i)_{i \in [\ell]}, (m_i)_{i \in [\ell]}$):
- Choose random $r, r_j \leftarrow_\$ \mathbb{Z}_p$ for $j \in \{0, \ldots, t-1\}$.
- Let $f(x) = \sum_{j=0}^{t-1} r_j \cdot x^j$. This will satisfy $f(0) = r_0$.
- For $j \in [n]$, set $\xi_j = H_2(\mathsf{vk}_j)$, $s_j = f(\xi_j)$.
- For $i \in [\ell]$ choose random $\alpha_i \leftarrow_\$ \mathbb{Z}_p$.
- Compute $c = g_2^r$, $a_i = c^{\alpha_i}$, $t_i = H(T_i)^{\alpha_i}$ for $i \in [\ell]$.
- Choose $h \leftarrow \mathbb{G}_2$ uniformly at random.
- Compute $c_0 = h^r \cdot g_2^{r_0}$.
- For $j \in [n]$, compute $c_j = \mathsf{vk}_j^r \cdot g_2^{s_j}$.
- For $i \in [\ell]$, set $c_i' = e(t_i, g_2^{r_0}) \cdot g_T^{m_i}$.
- Output $\mathsf{ct} = (h, c, c_0, (c_j)_{j \in [n]}, (c_i', a_i, t_i)_{i \in [\ell]})$.

SWE.Dec($\mathsf{ct}, (\sigma_i)_{i \in [\ell]}, U, V$):
- Parse $\mathsf{ct} = (h, c, c_0, (c_j)_{j \in [n]}, (c_i', a_i, t_i)_{i \in [\ell]})$.
- Parse $V = (\mathsf{vk}_1, \ldots, \mathsf{vk}_n)$, $U = (\mathsf{vk}_1', \ldots, \mathsf{vk}_k')$.
- If $k < t$ or $U \not\subseteq V$, abort.
- Define as I the indices $j \in [n]$ s.t. $\mathsf{vk}_j \in U$.

---

[6] Notice that a previous version of this manuscript provided a slightly different protocol, which had the caveat, that all T_i needed to be distinct.

- Compute $\xi_j = H_2(\mathsf{vk}_j)$ for $j \in I$.
- Compute $L_j = \prod_{i \in I, i \neq j} \frac{-\xi_i}{\xi_j - \xi_i}$ for $j \in I$.
- Compute $c^* = \prod_{j \in I} c_j^{L_j}$.
- For $i \in [\ell]$, compute
  $z_i = c_i' \cdot e(\sigma_i, a_i)/e(t_i, c^*)$.
- For $i \in [\ell]$, compute $m_i' = \mathsf{dlog}_{g_T}(z_i)$.
- Output $(m_i')_i$.

Notice, that we only do the expensive computation of c^* in SWE.Dec once.[7] Further, we require that all T_i are from the range $\{0, \dots, 2^k - 1\}$ for some k to enable efficient discrete log computation via the baby-step giant-step method.

Theorem 2. *The following statements hold:*

1. SWE *for the signature scheme* Sig' *has robust correctness, given that H_2 is collision resistant.*
2. *Assume that the hash functions H, H_2, H_{pr} are modelled as random oracles. Then* SWE *for the signature scheme* Sig' *is secure under the BDH assumption in* $(\mathbb{G}_1, \mathbb{G}_2, \mathbb{G}_T)$. *The security reduction is tight.*
3. *There are protocols* SWE.Prove, SWE.Vrfy *which extend* SWE *to be verifiable.*

The proofs of statement 1, 2 are found in the full version only, due to space restrictions. For statement 3, the full version includes a full construction and proofs of SWE.Prove, SWE.Vrfy which closely follows the outline given in Sect. 1.2.

Efficiency of SWE. Our construction is specifically optimized to push as many operations as possible into the source group $\mathbb{G}_2$. This leads to significant performance improvements over a naive approach if we choose $\mathbb{G}_2$ to be the one of the two source groups with cheaper group operations. In Table 1, we briefly analyze the number of group operations in each group required for encryption and decryption. We regard the numbers n, ℓ to be fixed and give upper bounds on the operations needed. Note also, that the extraction of the discrete logarithm does not cause a large overhead as we use the baby-step giant-step methodology. More details and a concrete performance evaluation for an implementation of our scheme can be found in the full version.

---

[7] In case the sets of signers are the same for all T_i. Otherwise we compute it once per relevant set U of signers.

Table 1. Analysis of SWE Efficiency in Group Operations

		encryption	decryption
Evaluations of H, H_2		ℓ, n	$0, n$
Multiplications, Exponentiations	in $\mathbb{G}_1$	$0, \ell$	$0, 0$
	in $\mathbb{G}_2$	$n, 2 + 2n + \ell$	$n - 1, n$
	in $\mathbb{G}_T$	ℓ, ℓ	$2\ell, 0$
Pairing Evaluations		ℓ	2ℓ
dlog in $\mathbb{G}_T$		0	ℓ

3   The McFly Protocol

In this section, we describe how to build a general-purpose time-release encryption mechanism, that we call McFly, by integrating a verifiable signature-based witness encryption SWE with a blockchain. The time-release mechanism is available to all users of the underlying blockchain.

3.1   Formal Model and Guarantees

In the full version we introduce a simplified model for blockchains in the form of the $\mathcal{BC}_{\lambda,H}$ functionality reflecting the requirements introduced in Sect. 1.1. It essentially runs a blockchain with a static committee of size $n = poly(\lambda)$. The public interface allows to retrieve the committee keys and the published blocks. The adversary is allowed a (static) corruption threshold $c < n/2$. They may control c committee members and choose the block contents to be signed.

Protocol Guarantees. Let $\mathcal{L}_0$ be an NP language defined by relation $\mathcal{R}_0$ via $m \in \mathcal{L}_0 \Leftrightarrow \exists w$ s.t. $(m, w) \in \mathcal{R}_0$. Our protocol McFly consists of five algorithms (Setup, Enc, Dec, Prove, Vrfy) in a hybrid model where access to the public interface of $\mathcal{BC} = \mathcal{BC}_{\lambda,H}$ is assumed. The syntax of these algorithms is as follows:

CRS $\leftarrow$ Setup(1^λ): Setup takes a security parameter λ. It outputs a common reference string CRS.

ct $\leftarrow$ Enc$^{\mathcal{BC}}(1^\lambda, m, d)$: Encryption takes a security parameter λ, a message m and an encryption depth d. It outputs a ciphertext ct.

$m \leftarrow$ Dec$^{\mathcal{BC}}(\text{ct}, d)$: Decryption takes a ciphertext ct and an encryption depth d. It outputs a message m.

$\pi \leftarrow$ Prove$^{\mathcal{BC}}(1^\lambda, \text{CRS}, \text{ct}, m, d, w_0, r)$: The proving algorithm takes a security parameter λ, CRS, a message m, an encryption depth d, a witness w_0 and randomness r. It outputs a proof π.

$b \leftarrow$ Vrfy$^{\mathcal{BC}}(\text{CRS}, \text{ct}, \pi, d)$: The verification algorithm takes CRS, a ciphertext ct, a proof π and an encryption depth d. It outputs a bit b.

We prove the following security guarantees for McFly, which are inspired by traditional time-lock puzzles:

Definition 5 (Correctness). *A protocol* McFly = (Setup, Enc, Dec, Prove, Vrfy) *is correct, if for any parameter* λ*, message* m*, depth* d*, and algorithm* $\mathcal{A}$ *running the adversarial interface in* $\mathcal{BC}$*, if* ct $\leftarrow$ Enc$^{\mathcal{BC}}(1^\lambda, m, d)$ *is run at any point and* McFly.Dec$^{\mathcal{BC}}$(ct, d) *is run, when the number of finalized blocks* $\mathcal{BC}$.QueryTime *is at least* d*, it will output* m*, except with negligible probability.*

Definition 6 (Security). *A protocol* McFly = (Setup, Enc, Prove, Vrfy, Dec) *is secure, if for any parameter* λ *and committee size* $n = poly(\lambda)$*, corruption threshold* $c < n/2$ *there is no PPT adversary* $\mathcal{A}$ *with more than negligible advantage* Adv$_{\mathsf{Lock}}^{\mathcal{A}}$ = | Pr [$b = b'$] − $\frac{1}{2}$| *in the experiment* Exp$_{\mathsf{Lock}}(\mathcal{A}, 1^\lambda)$.

Experiment Exp$_{\mathsf{Lock}}(\mathcal{A}, 1^\lambda)$

1. *The experiment computes* CRS $\leftarrow$ Setup(1^λ) *and outputs it to* $\mathcal{A}$.
2. $\mathcal{A}$ *gets to use the adversarial interface in* $\mathcal{BC}$*, which is run by the experiment.*
3. *At some point,* $\mathcal{A}$ *sends two challenge messages* m_0, m_1 *and a depth* $d > 0$. $|m_0| = |m_1|$ *must hold.*
4. *The experiment draws* $b \leftarrow_\$ \{0, 1\}$.
5. *Run* ct $\leftarrow$ Enc$^{\mathcal{BC}}(1^\lambda, m_b, d)$ *and send* ct *to* $\mathcal{A}$.
6. $\mathcal{A}$ *can submit a bit* b' *while the number of finalized blocks* ctr < d *in* $\mathcal{BC}$.
7. *Once* ctr $\geq d$ *on* $\mathcal{BC}$ *with no prior input from* $\mathcal{A}$*,* $b' \leftarrow_\$ \{0, 1\}$ *is set instead.*

Definition 7 (Verifiability). *A protocol* McFly = (Setup, Enc, Dec, Prove, Vrfy) *is verifiable for an NP language* $\mathcal{L}_0$ *with witness relation* $\mathcal{R}_0$*, if* (Prove, Vrfy) *is a NIZK proof system for a language* $\mathcal{L}'$ *given by the following relation* $\mathcal{R}'$:

$$(V = (\mathsf{vk}_1, \ldots, \mathsf{vk}_n), d, \mathsf{ct}), (m, r, w_0)) \in \mathcal{R}' \Leftrightarrow$$
$$\mathsf{ct} = \mathsf{McFly.Enc}(1^\lambda, m, d; r, V) \wedge (m, w_0) \in \mathcal{R}_0.$$

Enc($\ldots; r, V$) denotes, that the randomness used is r and the committee keys obtained from the blockchain are V. Note that this guarantees that (1) a receiver of a verifying pair (ct, π) can be sure to retrieve an output in $\mathcal{L}_0$ after block d was made and (2) outputting π alongside ct reveals no further information.

3.2 Protocol Description

Let COM = (Setup, Commit, Vrfy) be a Pedersen commitment, H be the hash function in $\mathcal{BC}$ and H_2 be another hash function. H, H_2 are implicitly made available in all calls to SWE, which is set up for parameters $t = n/2$ out of n. k is the upper bound on the message lengths for SWE. We now describe McFly:

Protocol McFly

$\mathsf{Setup}(1^\lambda)$: Return $\mathsf{COM.Setup}(1^\lambda)$.

$\mathsf{McFly.Enc}^{\mathcal{BC}}(1^\lambda, m, d)$:
  - Get the commitee keys V by calling $\mathsf{QueryKeys}$ to $\mathcal{BC}$.
  - Split $m = (m_i)_{i\in[\ell]}$ for $m_i \in \{0,\ldots,2^k - 1\}$ s.t. $m = \sum_{i\in[\ell]} 2^{(i-1)k} m_i$.
  - Output $\mathsf{ct} \leftarrow \mathsf{SWE.Enc}(1^\lambda, V, (H(d))_{i\in[\ell]}, (m_i)_{i\in[\ell]})$.

$\mathsf{McFly.Dec}^{\mathcal{BC}}(\mathsf{ct}, d)$:
  - If $\mathsf{QueryTime}$ returns less than d, abort.
  - Get (σ, U) by calling $(\mathsf{QueryAt}, d)$ and V by calling $\mathsf{QueryKeys}$ to $\mathcal{BC}$.
  - Call $(m_i)_{i\in\ell} \leftarrow \mathsf{SWE.Dec}(\mathsf{ct}, (\sigma)_{i\in[\ell]}, U, V)$.
  - Output $m = \sum_{i\in[\ell]} 2^{(i-1)k} m_i$.

$\mathsf{McFly.Prove}^{\mathcal{BC}}(1^\lambda, \mathsf{CRS}, \mathsf{ct}, m, d, w_0, r)$:
  - Get the keys V by calling $\mathsf{QueryKeys}$ to $\mathcal{BC}$.
  - Split $m = (m_i)_{i\in[\ell]}$ s.t. $m = \sum_{i\in[\ell]} 2^{(i-1)k} m_i$.
  - Output $\pi \leftarrow \mathsf{SWE.Prove}(\mathsf{CRS}, V, (H(d))_{i\in[\ell]}, \mathsf{ct}, (m_i)_{i\in[\ell]}, w_0, r)$.

$\mathsf{McFly.Vrfy}^{\mathcal{BC}}(\mathsf{CRS}, \mathsf{ct}, \pi, d)$:
  - Get the keys V by calling $\mathsf{QueryKeys}$ to $\mathcal{BC}$.
  - Output $b \leftarrow \mathsf{SWE.Vrfy}(\mathsf{CRS}, V, (H(d))_{i\in[\ell]}, \mathsf{ct}, \pi)$

Theorem 3. McFly *is correct, given that* SWE *has robust correctness.* McFly *is secure given that* SWE *is secure and H is collision resistant.* McFly *is verifiable, given that* SWE *is a verifiable SWE.*

The proofs are only included in the full version due to space restrictions.

Extension for Dynamic Committees. In our model, we assumed static committees. However, finality layers advocate for a short-lived dynamic committee, as committee members usually become targets of attacks. We can safely regard a committee as known and static during its lifetime. Thus, our model naturally extends as long as we only encrypt messages as far into the future as the committees are currently known.

References

1. Andrychowicz, M., Dziembowski, S., Malinowski, D., Mazurek, L.: Secure multi-party computations on bitcoin. In: 2014 IEEE Symposium on Security and Privacy, pp. 443–458. IEEE Computer Society Press, May 2014. https://doi.org/10.1109/SP.2014.35
2. Benhamouda, F., et al.: Can a public blockchain keep a secret? In: Pass, R., Pietrzak, K. (eds.) TCC 2020. LNCS, vol. 12550, pp. 260–290. Springer, Cham (2020). https://doi.org/10.1007/978-3-030-64375-1_10
3. Boneh, D., Bonneau, J., Bünz, B., Fisch, B.: Verifiable delay functions. In: Shacham, H., Boldyreva, A. (eds.) CRYPTO 2018. LNCS, vol. 10991, pp. 757–788. Springer, Cham (2018). https://doi.org/10.1007/978-3-319-96884-1_25

4. Boneh, D., Drijvers, M., Neven, G.: Compact multi-signatures for smaller blockchains. In: Peyrin, T., Galbraith, S. (eds.) ASIACRYPT 2018. LNCS, vol. 11273, pp. 435–464. Springer, Cham (2018). https://doi.org/10.1007/978-3-030-03329-3_15

5. Boneh, D., Franklin, M.: Identity-based encryption from the weil pairing. In: Kilian, J. (ed.) CRYPTO 2001. LNCS, vol. 2139, pp. 213–229. Springer, Heidelberg (2001). https://doi.org/10.1007/3-540-44647-8_13

6. Boneh, D., Gentry, C., Lynn, B., Shacham, H.: Aggregate and verifiably encrypted signatures from bilinear maps. In: Biham, E. (ed.) EUROCRYPT 2003. LNCS, vol. 2656, pp. 416–432. Springer, Heidelberg (2003). https://doi.org/10.1007/3-540-39200-9_26

7. Boneh, D., Lynn, B., Shacham, H.: Short signatures from the weil pairing. In: Boyd, C. (ed.) ASIACRYPT 2001. LNCS, vol. 2248, pp. 514–532. Springer, Heidelberg (2001). https://doi.org/10.1007/3-540-45682-1_30

8. Boneh, D., Naor, M.: Timed commitments. In: Bellare, M. (ed.) CRYPTO 2000. LNCS, vol. 1880, pp. 236–254. Springer, Heidelberg (2000). https://doi.org/10.1007/3-540-44598-6_15

9. Bünz, B., Bootle, J., Boneh, D., Poelstra, A., Wuille, P., Maxwell, G.: Bulletproofs: short proofs for confidential transactions and more. In: 2018 IEEE Symposium on Security and Privacy, pp. 315–334. IEEE Computer Society Press, May 2018. https://doi.org/10.1109/SP.2018.00020

10. Buterin, V.: Hf1 proposal. https://notes.ethereum.org/@vbuterin/HF1_proposal

11. Buterin, V., Griffith, V.: Casper the friendly finality gadget (2019)

12. Campanelli, M., David, B., Khoshakhlagh, H., Konring, A., Nielsen, J.B.: Encryption to the future: A paradigm for sending secret messages to future (anonymous) committees. Cryptology ePrint Archive, Report 2021/1423 (2021). https://ia.cr/2021/1423

13. Cathalo, J., Libert, B., Quisquater, J.J.: Efficient and non-interactive timed-release encryption. In: Qing, S., Mao, W., López, J., Wang, G. (eds.) ICICS 05. LNCS, vol. 3783, pp. 291–303. Springer, Heidelberg (2005)

14. Cheon, J.H., Hopper, N., Kim, Y., Osipkov, I.: Provably secure timed-release public key encryption. ACM Trans. Inf. Syst. Secur. **11**(2) (2008). https://doi.org/10.1145/1330332.1330336

15. Deuber, D., Döttling, N., Magri, B., Malavolta, G., Thyagarajan, S.A.K.: Minting mechanism for proof of stake blockchains. In: Conti, M., Zhou, J., Casalicchio, E., Spognardi, A. (eds.) ACNS 20, Part I. LNCS, vol. 12146, pp. 315–334. Springer, Heidelberg (2020). https://doi.org/10.1007/978-3-030-57808-4_16

16. Dinsdale-Young, T., Magri, B., Matt, C., Nielsen, J.B., Tschudi, D.: Afgjort: a partially synchronous finality layer for blockchains. Cryptology ePrint Archive, Report 2019/504 (2019). https://ia.cr/2019/504

17. ethereum.org: Ethereum 2.0 keys (2022). https://kb.beaconcha.in/ethereum-2-keys

18. Fischlin, M.: Communication-efficient non-interactive proofs of knowledge with online extractors. In: Shoup, V. (ed.) CRYPTO 2005. LNCS, vol. 3621, pp. 152–168. Springer, Heidelberg (2005). https://doi.org/10.1007/11535218_10

19. Garg, S., Gentry, C., Sahai, A., Waters, B.: Witness encryption and its applications. In: Boneh, D., Roughgarden, T., Feigenbaum, J. (eds.) 45th ACM STOC, pp. 467–476. ACM Press, June 2013. https://doi.org/10.1145/2488608.2488667

20. Gentry, C., Halevi, S., Krawczyk, H., Magri, B., Nielsen, J.B., Rabin, T., Yakoubov, S.: YOSO: you only speak once. In: Malkin, T., Peikert, C. (eds.) CRYPTO 2021. LNCS, vol. 12826, pp. 64–93. Springer, Cham (2021). https://doi.org/10.1007/978-3-030-84245-1_3

21. Joux, A.: A one round protocol for tripartite Diffie–Hellman. In: Bosma, W. (ed.) ANTS 2000. LNCS, vol. 1838, pp. 385–393. Springer, Heidelberg (2000). https://doi.org/10.1007/10722028_23

22. Liu, J., Jager, T., Kakvi, S.A., Warinschi, B.: How to build time-lock encryption. Des. Codes Cryptogr. **86**(11), 2549–2586 (2018). https://doi.org/10.1007/s10623-018-0461-x

23. Ristenpart, T., Yilek, S.: The power of proofs-of-possession: securing multiparty signatures against rogue-key attacks. In: Naor, M. (ed.) EUROCRYPT 2007. LNCS, vol. 4515, pp. 228–245. Springer, Heidelberg (2007). https://doi.org/10.1007/978-3-540-72540-4_13

24. Rivest, R.L., Shamir, A., Wagner, D.A.: Time-lock puzzles and timed-release crypto. Technical report, Massachusetts Institute of Technology, USA (1996)

25. Shamir, A.: How to share a secret. Communications of the Association for Computing Machinery **22**(11), 612–613 (1979)

26. Shamir, A.: Identity-based cryptosystems and signature schemes. In: Blakley, G.R., Chaum, D. (eds.) CRYPTO 1984. LNCS, vol. 196, pp. 47–53. Springer, Heidelberg (1985). https://doi.org/10.1007/3-540-39568-7_5

27. Shanks, D.: Class number, a theory of factorization, and genera. In: Proc. of Symp. Math. Soc., 1971, vol. 20, pp. 41–440 (1971)

Eagle: Efficient Privacy Preserving Smart Contracts

Carsten Baum[1]($\boxtimes$)(iD), James Hsin-yu Chiang[1](iD), Bernardo David[2],
and Tore Kasper Frederiksen[3](iD)

[1] Technical University of Denmark, Kongens Lyngby, Denmark
cabau@dtu.dk, jachiang@ucla.edu
[2] IT University of Copenhagen, Copenhagen, Denmark
bernardo@bmdavid.com
[3] Alexandra Institute, Aarhus, Denmark

Abstract. The proliferation of Decentralised Finance (DeFi) and
Decentralised Autonomous Organisations (DAO), which in current form
are exposed to front-running of token transactions and proposal voting,
demonstrate the need to shield user inputs and internal state from the
parties executing smart contracts. In this work we present "Eagle", an
efficient UC-secure protocol which efficiently realises a notion of privacy
preserving smart contracts where both the amounts of tokens and the
auxiliary data given as input to a contract are kept private from all parties but the one providing the input. Prior proposals realizing privacy preserving smart contracts on public, permissionless blockchains generally
offer a limited contract functionality or require a trusted third party to
manage private inputs and state. We achieve our results through a combination of secure multi-party computation (MPC) and zero-knowledge
proofs on Pedersen commitments. Although other approaches leverage
MPC in this setting, these incur impractical computational overheads
by requiring the computation of cryptographic primitives within MPC.
Our solution achieves security without the need of any cryptographic
primitives to be computed inside the MPC instance and only require a
constant amount of exponentiations per client input.

Keywords: Blockchain · DeFi · MPC · Privacy

Carsten Baum: Part of the work was carried out while the author was visiting Copenhagen University and supported by Partisia. Any opinions, findings and conclusions
or recommendations expressed in this material are those of the author and do not
necessarily reflect the views of Partisia.
Bernardo David: The project was supported by the Concordium Foundation, by the
Independent Research Fund Denmark (IRFD) grants number 9040-00399B (TrA^{2}C),
9131-00075B (PUMA) and 0165-00079B, and by Copenhagen Fintech.
Tore Kasper Frederiksen: The work was carried out while at the Alexandra Institute,
supported by Copenhagen Fintech as part of as part of the "National Position of
Strength programme for Finans & Fintech" funded by the Danish Ministry of Higher
Education and Science.

© International Financial Cryptography Association 2024
F. Baldimtsi and C. Cachin (Eds.): FC 2023, LNCS 13950, pp. 270–288, 2024.
https://doi.org/10.1007/978-3-031-47754-6_16

1 Introduction

Ethereum introduced the first implementation of Turing-complete smart contracts for blockchains, widely adopted for financial and contracting applications since its introduction in 2015. Smart contracts offer auditability and correctness guarantees, and as a consequence expose both their state and any submitted inputs to all participants of the blockchain network. This lack of privacy not only leaks user data but also gives rise to concrete attacks. For example, current Decentralised Finance (DeFi) and Decentralised Autonomous Organisations (DAO) are vulnerable to front-running [23] in token transactions and proposal voting. This motivates the need to shield user inputs and internal contract state from the very parties who execute smart contracts in a decentralized environment.

Challenges. Hawk [37] introduced the first notion of general-purpose privacy preserving smart contracts, which required users to privately submit both input strings and confidential balances to a trusted contract manager. Upon evaluation of the contract over private inputs, the contract manager settles the confidential outputs to a confidential ledger, proving in zero knowledge that these outputs have been obtained according to the contract's instructions. Importantly, in order to accommodate real-world applications such as DeFi or DAO's, we must extend the Hawk notion of confidential contracts as follows:

1. Distribute the role of the trusted third party in an efficient manner, avoiding a single point of failure without significantly sacrificing performance.
2. Only require clients to be online during a short input phase; as in the standard client-blockchain interaction model, clients only broadcast signed inputs.
3. Allow privacy preserving smart contracts to be long-running applications over indefinite rounds, as is the case in standard, public smart contracts.

Our Contributions. In this work we present "Eagle", a Universally Composable [17] protocol for achieving efficient privacy preserving smart contracts, which handles all the three challenges explained above: (1) is achieved by evaluating the contract's instructions via an *outsourced* secure multi-party computation (MPC) protocol [31], where clients provide private inputs and servers execute the bulk of the protocol to compute a function on these inputs without learning them. We use a MPC protocol, known as *insured MPC*, which allows a public verifier to identify servers aborting at the output phase, so that cheating servers can be identified and financially punished, incentivizing fairness (*i.e.* if a server gets the output, all servers/clients also get it) [7]. That is, by combining outsourced and insured MPC we get a protocol where client computation and interaction is independent of the circuit computed in MPC and where *reliability* is incentivized and *security* is obtained as long as only a single MPC is honest. (2) is accomplished with a novel input protocol which pre-processes data necessary for the servers to generate private outputs (*e.g.* token amounts) that are posted directly to the public ledger but can only be read by specific clients. (2) facilitates (3), realized by a *reactive* version of our MPC protocol, which maintains a secret off-chain state over multiple rounds. Here, we contribute a model of long-running, privacy preserving contracts, which at the onset of each round accepts new inputs from any subset of clients. At the end of each round, clients get public outputs and servers keep a secret internal state, allowing evaluation to take place in a continuous, *multi-round* fashion, even if clients are offline (2).

Applications. Several general applications for privacy preserving smart contracts have already been proposed. **Auctions:** can be realized securely on-chain with privacy preserving smart contracts, as auctions implemented without privacy are vulnerable to front-running (miners can trivially observe individual bids posted to the ledger). **Identity management:** Decentralized Identity (DID) management considers the setting where user-attributes are posted to a ledger, in a certified, yet hidden manner. DID implemented with privacy preserving smart contracts enables proofs and computations on private identity attributes, facilitating their integration with blockchain applications. **KYC Mixing:** We can construct a privacy preserving smart contract to realize a mixer that enforces Anti Money Laundering (AML) policies. For example, such a mixer could use DID to integrate Know Your Customer (KYC) information to either limit user permissions or the quantity of mixed tokens allowed per month. **Side-chains:** The MPC servers alone could be considered a privacy preserving side-chain. Multiple sets of MPC servers could work together with a single smart contract to realize a privacy preserving sharding scheme on any layer 1 chain with Turing complete smart contracts. **AMMs and DeFi via Cross-chain contracts:** Using ideas of P2DEX [9], we show that the MPC servers can interact with smart contracts on many different ledgers. Hence, privacy preserving smart contracts can work *across* multiple ledgers and different native tokens. This realizes cross-chain, front-running resistant automated market makers (AMMs) with strong privacy guarantees. We discuss these applications in more detail in the full version [6].

Our Techniques. We sketch our protocol in Fig. 1. This only considers execution of a *single* instance of a privacy preserving smart contract for simplicity. We discuss the multi-round setting in the full version [6]. where computations are executed continuously with different sets of clients. We assume a set of clients $\mathcal{C}$ and MPC servers $\mathcal{P}$, both interacting with a ledger functionality $\mathcal{F}_{\mathsf{Ledger}}$. The ledger hosts two deployed smart contract instances: $\mathcal{X}_{\mathsf{CLedger}}$ maintains a confidential ledger and is extended with $\mathcal{X}_{\mathsf{Lock}}$, which locks and redistributes confidential balances, output and jointly signed, by the MPC servers. Concretely our protocol runs the following phases:

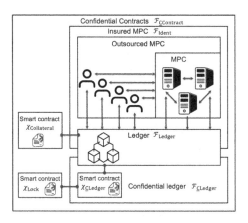

Fig. 1. Outline of our protocol for confidential contracts. The wrapping and interaction of functionalities are shown.

Init. Before any execution, the servers setup the system by sampling a threshold signature key pair and provide sufficient collateral for the insured MPC execution, and setup smart contact $\mathcal{X}_{\mathsf{Lock}}$, administered by the distributed signature key. We note that in the multi-round setting this only needs to be executed *once* for the specific set of MPC servers, and is thus independent of the clients and the amount of computations that will get carried out later.

Enroll. When a privacy preserving smart contract is to be executed, each client who wish to participate transfers confidential tokens to $\mathcal{X}_{\mathsf{CLedger}}$ which they wish to use as input to the confidential smart contract $\underline{C}$Contract. The client then gives any auxiliary input, along with the opening information to the commitment containing their confidential balance v, to the insured MPC functionality $\mathcal{F}_{\mathsf{Ident}}$ from the work of Baum *et al.* [7,9], extended with a secure client input interface to allow for outsourced MPC [31] and described in detail in the full version [6]. Each client constructs an appropriate amount of "mask" commitments; one for each round of confidential contract computation, for which they wish their input to be used. A masking commitment is simply a commitment to a random value.

Verify Input. The servers validate the input received from the clients using outsourced MPC, and ensure that $\mathcal{X}_{\mathsf{Lock}}$ has also received the appropriate confidential tokens. The servers and the clients also execute a proof to ensure that the opening information supplied by clients are indeed valid for the confidential token commitments. They do this following a standard Σ-protocol where each client commits to a random commitment a and servers select a random challenge γ and ask the client to open $\mathrm{com}(c) = \mathrm{com}(a) \oplus (\gamma \odot \mathrm{com}(v))$. Similarly the servers use MPC to securely open $[c] = [a] + \gamma \cdot [v]$ and check consistency[1].

Evaluate. After the checks are completed the servers evaluate the circuit expressing the private smart contract $\underline{C}$Contract, using insured MPC. For the clients who are supposed to get output from this round of computation, shares of messages and randomness for a new commitment for *each* client are computed, and blinded with the "masking" values the clients provided during *Enroll*. If this goes well, the servers distributedly sign a message saying that they have reached this stage and post it to $\mathcal{X}_{\mathsf{Lock}}$.

Open. For clients that receive output after this round of computation the servers open the masked output. They publish these values and sign them, as part of the transcript of the current round execution, and post this to $\mathcal{X}_{\mathsf{Lock}}$. Note that $\mathcal{X}_{\mathsf{Lock}}$ can generate the output coins in commitment form, due to the homomorphism of the commitments and since it obtained the mask commitments from the clients in *Enroll*. $\mathcal{X}_{\mathsf{Lock}}$ can then transfer the new confidential tokens back to the client's address. We show an extension to our protocol in the full version [6]) that ensures no token minting can occur even if all servers are corrupted.

Withdraw. Based on the masks they constructed, the clients who are supposed to receive outputs can compute the coin commitment openings from their masked outputs signed and posted to $\mathcal{X}_{\mathsf{Lock}}$ by servers during *Open*.

---

[1] In our full protocol we optimize this by batching client input checks.

Abort. In case a server stops responding or acts maliciously, an honest server can request the entering of an abort phase. Any server can do this, either by submitting a proof that the malicious server sent wrong information or by requesting missing information from the accused servers. At this point the accused malicious server has a constant amount of time left to prove to the smart contract that they did not abort, by submitting the message that the accusing server claims they didn't get. If they don't, they will have their collateral revoked and it will be shared among the honest servers and clients, and the contract state will roll back one round, i.e. to the contract state preceding *Evaluate*. Concretely $\mathcal{X}_{\mathsf{Lock}}$ will refund the clients their input funds, plus a compensation obtained from the cheating servers' collateral.

Related Works. A long line of work realizes notions of privacy preserving smart contracts that sacrifice privacy [21,32,35,37,41,46–48] or flexibility [14,15]. Zexe [14] extends the ZCash model of confidential transactions to enable Bitcoin Script-like stateless privacy preserving smart contracts supporting only very simple logic. Zether [15] implements confidential transactions on top of Ethereum, allowing for very simple privacy preserving applications (*e.g.* auctions). Zkay [47] allows for computing on encrypted private inputs by means of keeping data encryption on the blockchain, and using NIZKs to validate that any updates done to the encrypted is carried out correctly. Follow-up work, Zeestar [46] uses additively homomorphic encryption to allow for *limited* private computation on data from multiple owners, without them having to share their private data with each other. Secret Network [48] and Ekiden [21] implement general purpose contracts but rely on notoriously vulnerable trusted execution environments (*e.g.* Intel SGX [42]) for privacy and correctness. Arbitrum [32] relies on a full quorum of parties (the servers in our setting) being honest to achieve privacy for general purpose contracts. Finally, Kachina [35] subsumes these approaches with a framework based on state oracles [41] that yields privacy preserving smart contracts, where either flexibility is limited (*i.e.* contract state is only updated by one client's private input at a time) or privacy is compromised (*i.e.* a trusted third party must learn clients' private inputs in order to update the state). The ideal functionality of Kachina is designed to permit *input concurrency*, allowing honest inputs to be finalized on a global ledger in a different order as their generation; the Kachina protocol requires private inputs to be accompanied with NIZKs proving a valid update of the private state fragment. Here, the NIZKs are not bound to a specific, public contract state and thus remain valid even if the public contract state observed by the user was updated by another user input in the meantime.

Combining MPC with blockchain based cryptocurrencies and smart contracts has been investigated in a long line of works [1,2,7–12,22,27,36,38–40] aiming at achieving fairness in the dishonest majority setting via financial punishments. The core idea of these works is having all parties, who execute the MPC protocol, provide a collateral deposit, which is taken from them in case they are caught cheating. Thus incentivizing honest behavior. However, this approach publicly reveals the amount of collateral deposited by each party, which falls short of achieving our notion of privacy preserving smart contracts, where both auxiliary data *and* the amount of tokens given as input to the contract must remain private. Notice that revealing the deposit amount is an issue in applications where this amount is directly related to the client's private input, *e.g.* in sealed-bid auctions, where the collateral deposit must be equal to at least the client's private bid. An auction protocol using collateral deposits with private amounts was proposed in [28] but it cannot be generalized to other tasks.

Hawk [37, App. G] does suggest to use MPC to achieve a decentralized confidential smart contracts on both token amount and auxiliary input. However, Hawk works in the ZCash model and thus their MPC solution would require the computation of SNARKs to realize the ZCash transactions, within the MPC circuit. Although it has been shown [33,43] that integrating NIZKs with MPC can be done without degrading performance too much, there is still a performance hit. Since the construction of a single ZCash transaction SNARK still takes a non-negligible amount of time plain, this would naturally be inefficient to realize in MPC, as MPC is orders of magnitude slower than regular computation. Furthermore, they need *all* users to take part in the MPC computation. zkHawk [4] improves upon this, by forgoing the need of doing SNARKs in MPC, but still require *all* users taking part in a confidential smart contract to facilitate an MPC computation which *must* compute Schnorr style ZKPs on Pedersen commitments to the bit-decomposition of the amount of coins each of them hold. While V-zkHawk [5] forgoes the need of proofs of the bit-decomposed commitments, they replace it with the computation of commitments in a larger fields and a signature, in MPC instead. While more efficient, this approach would still require MPC over a large domain and contributes non-negligible overhead. In the full version [6]. we further discuss related works.

2   Preliminaries

Let $y \leftarrow\!\!\$\, F(x)$ denote running the randomized algorithm F with input x and implicit randomness, and obtaining output y. Similarly, $y \leftarrow F(x)$ is used for a deterministic algorithm. For a set $\mathcal{X}$, let $x \leftarrow\!\!\$\, \mathcal{X}$ denote x chosen uniformly at random from $\mathcal{X}$. s denotes the computational and κ the statistical security parameter. Let $[x]$ denote secret x maintained in an MPC instance: we lift the $[\cdot]$ notation to any object that can be encoded over secrets securely input to an MPC scheme, e.g. $[g]$, where g is an arithmetic circuit

Table 1. Notation.

$\mathcal{P}$	The set of servers
$\mathcal{C}$	The set of clients
n	Number of servers $n = |\mathcal{P}|$
m	Number of clients; $m = |\mathcal{C}|$
l	Number of bits representing balances
z	Number of input/output per client
κ	Computational security parameter
s	Statistical security parameter
$\mathcal{F}$	An ideal functionality
Π	A protocol
$\mathcal{L}$	A ledger map indexed by vk
$\mathcal{X}$	A smart contract program
g	A smart contract in circuit form
vk	A public key for signature verification
x	A client input
y	A client output
$\bar{v}$	A token balance
$\bar{v}_{\max}$	The maximum permitted balance
$\bar{\mathbf{v}}_{\max}$	A vector of the maximum permitted balance

over field $\mathbb{F}$. We use a group $\mathbb{G}$ where the discrete log problem is hard, and which is a source group of pairing scheme. For simplicity we assume $|\mathbb{G}| = |\mathbb{F}| = p$. Unless noted otherwise we use log to denote the logarithm to base 2, rounded up. We use $\bar{v}_{\mathsf{max}}$ to denote the maximum amount of tokens we want to represent and say $l = \log(\bar{v}_{\mathsf{max}})$. For simplicity, we assume $|\mathcal{C}| \cdot \bar{v}_{\mathsf{max}} < |\mathbb{G}|$, where $\mathcal{C}$ is the set of participating clients. We denote set $\{1, 2, \ldots, n\}$ by $[n]$ and vectors by bold faced Latin letters, e.g. $\mathbf{v}, \mathbf{w}$.

2.1   Security Model and Building Blocks

We analyse our results in the the (Global) Universal Composability or (G)UC framework [18,20]. We consider static malicious adversaries. Our protocols work in a synchronous communication setting, which is modeled by assuming parties have access to a global clock ideal functionality $\mathcal{F}_{\mathsf{Clock}}$ as seen in multiple works [3,34,36]. The core component of our protocols is publicly verifiable MPC with cheater identification in the output phase, which is modelled as an ideal functionality $\mathcal{F}_{\mathsf{Ident}}$, which can be realized as described by Baum *et al.* [7,9]. This functionality produces a proof that either a certain output was obtained after the MPC or that a certain party has misbehaved in the output phase, while cheating before the output phase causes an abort without cheater identification. We further extend this functionality to handle reactive computation [25,26] and an *outsourced* computation with inputs provided by clients and computation done by servers [24,31]. Moreover, we use Pedersen Commitments [44], digital signatures represented by an ideal functionality $\mathcal{F}_{\mathsf{Sig}}$ as in [19], threshold signatures represented by an ideal functionality $\mathcal{F}_{\mathsf{TSig}}$ as defined by Baum *et al.* [9] and non-interactive zero knowledge proofs represented by $\mathcal{F}_{\mathsf{NIZK}}$ as defined by Groth [30]. Further discussion on our security model and building blocks are presented in the full version [6].

2.2   Ledgers and Smart Contracts

We model a ledger functionality $\mathcal{F}_{\mathsf{Ledger}}$ in the full version [6]. featuring a smart contract virtual machine which is adapted from an authenticated, public bulletin board functionality, an approach adopted from the work of Baum *et al.* [7,9]. For this work, we emphasize accurate modelling of confidential balances, which are implemented on a public ledger, and omit the full consensus details in our UC model, similar to previous works [3,36].

Token Universe. $\mathcal{F}_{\mathsf{Ledger}}$ supports a token universe consisting of t token types: $\mathbb{T} = (\tau_1, \ldots, \tau_t)$. A ledger in $\mathcal{F}_{\mathsf{Ledger}}$ maintains a map from signature verification key to balances of each token type: $\mathcal{L} : \{0,1\}^* \to \mathbb{Z}^t$. We write $\bar{\mathbf{v}} = (v_1, \ldots, v_t)$ for a balance over all supported token types. In addition to balances associated to signature verification keys, $\mathcal{F}_{\mathsf{Ledger}}$ also maintains token balances for each deployed smart contract instance. The ledger functionality enforces the preservation of token supplies over $\mathbb{T}$.

Overview of Smart Contracts. In this work, we present smart contracts as human-readable programs and assume the presence of a compiler which translates program $\mathcal{X}$ to a valid circuit T and initial state γ_{init}. The following smart contract programs are deployed in the protocol which realizes the proposed confidential contract functionality $\mathcal{F}_{\underline{C}Contract}$.

- $\mathcal{X}_{\underline{CL}edger}$ (described in the full version [6]) describes a smart contract which implements a confidential token wrapper for each token in $\mathbb{T}$ supported on the base ledger $\mathcal{F}_{Ledger}$.
- $\mathcal{X}_{Lock}$ (described in the full version [6]) is an extension to $\mathcal{X}_{\underline{CL}edger}$. It permits the locking and redistribution of confidential balances authorized by verifying threshold signatures generated by the servers (via global functionality $\mathcal{F}_{TSig}$).
- $\mathcal{X}_{Collateral}$ (described in the full version [6]) accepts collateral deposits from servers, which upon being identified as cheating parties lose their collateral to clients.

2.3 Confidential Ledgers from $\mathcal{F}_{Ledger}$

We briefly describe a confidential ledger functionality $\mathcal{F}_{\underline{CL}edger}$, presented in full detail in the full version [6], that can be implemented from a hybrid $\mathcal{F}_{Ledger}$ functionality, enabling both confidential balances and the confidential transfer of default tokens types $\mathbb{T}$ exposed by the underlying public ledger $\mathcal{F}_{Ledger}$. This modeling choice maximizes the generality of our construction, as it can be implemented on any standard ledger and a basic smart contract machine.

Confidential Ledger. Confidential coins in $\mathcal{F}_{\underline{CL}edger}$ are identifiable by a unique public id, and a confidential balance $\bar{\mathbf{v}}$ over $\mathbb{T}$, as in [45]. Each confidential token is publicly associated with an account verification key vk, owned by a party that generated it with GENACCT. A confidential transfer consumes two input coins (id_1, id_2) with confidential balances $(\bar{\mathbf{v}}_1, \bar{\mathbf{v}}_2)$ and mints fresh output coins (id'_1, id'_2) with confidential balances $(\bar{\mathbf{v}}'_1, \bar{\mathbf{v}}'_2)$, such that $(\bar{\mathbf{v}}_1 + \bar{\mathbf{v}}_2 = \bar{\mathbf{v}}'_1 + \bar{\mathbf{v}}'_2)$. Here, coin id'_1 is now held by the owner of the receiving account, who also learns the confidential amount $\bar{\mathbf{v}}'_1$.

Functionality $\mathcal{F}_{\underline{CL}edger}$ exposes MINT and REDEEM interfaces: a mint activation *locks* a public amount of tokens $\mathbb{T}$ and generates a fresh confidential token of the same balance. Conversely, a redeem activation will *release* the balance of a confidential coin back to the public ledger.

Realizing a Confidential Ledger. A confidential token is realized in protocol $\Pi_{\underline{CL}edger}$ with Pedersen Commitments [44], described in full detail in the full version [6]. Let $g, g_1, ..., g_t, h$ denote generators of group $\mathbb{G}$ of safe prime order p, such that s_i in $g_i = g^{s_i}$ and w in $h = g^w$ are given by $\mathcal{F}_{Setup}$ (parameterized with $g \in \mathbb{G}$) that publicly outputs $g_1, ..., g_t, h$. The commitment to a balance $\bar{\mathbf{v}} = (v_1, ..., v_t)$ over tokens $\mathbb{T}$ with blinding r is $\mathsf{com}(\bar{\mathbf{v}}, r) = \mathbf{g}^{\bar{\mathbf{v}}} h^r = g_1^{v_1} ... g_t^{v_t} h^r$. Pedersen commitments are additively homomorphic: $\mathsf{com}(\bar{\mathbf{v}}_1, r_1) \circ \mathsf{com}(\bar{\mathbf{v}}_2, r_2) = \mathsf{com}(\bar{\mathbf{v}}_1 + \bar{\mathbf{v}}_2, r_1 + r_2)$. Thus, during a confidential transfer, the sum equality between consumed input and freshly constructed output coin commitments holds if total token balances are preserved and r'_1 and r'_2 are correlated such that $r_1 + r_2 = r'_1 + r'_2$.

$$\mathsf{com}(\bar{\mathbf{v}}_1, r_1) \circ \mathsf{com}(\bar{\mathbf{v}}_1, r_1) = \mathsf{com}(\bar{\mathbf{v}}'_1, r'_1) \circ \mathsf{com}(\bar{\mathbf{v}}'_2, r'_2) \qquad (1)$$

However, since the equality above holds for any $\bar{\mathbf{v}}_1 + \bar{\mathbf{v}}_2 \equiv \bar{\mathbf{v}}'_1 + \bar{\mathbf{v}}'_2 \mod p$ and correlated r'_1, r'_2, an additional p units of each token in $\mathbb{T}$ can be minted: $\bar{v}_1 + \bar{v}_2 + p \equiv \bar{v}'_1 + \bar{v}'_2 \mod p$. Thus, each confidential token is associated with NIZK π which proves $\mathcal{R}(c; \bar{\mathbf{v}}, r) = \{c = \mathsf{com}(\bar{\mathbf{v}}, r) \wedge \bar{\mathbf{v}} \le \bar{\mathbf{v}}_{\max} = 2^l - 1\}$, such that such wrap-around never occurs undetected.

We note that $\Pi_{\underline{\mathsf{CLedger}}}$ in itself affords a fully decentralized layer 2 confidential token transfer solution, since it is independent of the MPC servers. Thus allowing client's to send a receive confidential tokens in a peer-to-peer manner. This is needed to prevent leakage of exchange orders after-the-fact by analysing client's non-confidential tokens given as input and withdrawn as output from a privacy preserving smart contract execution. By allowing the privacy preserving smart contract executions to integrate in a greater payment ecosystem reasonably ensures that it is possible to hide token inputs and outputs from a privacy preserving smart contract execution by using them for confidential payment, similar to other confidential token systems.

We present a protocol $\Pi_{\underline{\mathsf{CLedger}}}$ which GUC-realizes $\mathcal{F}_{\underline{\mathsf{CLedger}}}$ in the full version [6], where we also prove the following statement:

Theorem 1. *Protocol $\Pi_{\underline{\mathsf{CLedger}}}$ GUC-realizes functionality $\mathcal{F}_{\underline{\mathsf{CLedger}}}$ in the $\mathcal{F}_{\mathsf{Clock}}$, $\mathcal{F}_{\mathsf{Ledger}}$, $\mathcal{F}_{\mathsf{NIZK}}$, $\mathcal{F}_{\mathsf{Setup}}$, $\mathcal{F}_{\mathsf{Sig}}$-hybrid model against any PPT-adversary corrupting any minority of committee $\mathcal{Q}$.*

3   Confidential Contracts

We present our formal model of confidential contracts. We assume m clients $\{C_1, \ldots, C_m\}$ and servers $\{P_1, \ldots, P_n\}$ that interact with $\mathcal{F}_{\underline{\mathsf{CContract}}}$, which extends $\mathcal{F}_{\underline{\mathsf{CLedger}}}$. For simplicity of presentation, we first present a single-round confidential contract functionality in Fig. 2, and subsequently illustrate how it is easily extended to a multi-round contract functionality where clients can selectively choose to participate in specific rounds.

The choice of modelling $\mathcal{F}_{\underline{\mathsf{CContract}}}$ as an extension of $\mathcal{F}_{\underline{\mathsf{CLedger}}}$ arises from the relation between underlying protocols: confidential coins in $\Pi_{\underline{\mathsf{CLedger}}}$ that are committed to a confidential contract evaluation must be *locked* and subsequently *replaced* by a new set of output coins reflecting a new distribution of balances, determined by $\Pi_{\underline{\mathsf{CContract}}}$. However, this requires verification operations over the homomorphic *commitment* representation of coins in $\Pi_{\underline{\mathsf{CLedger}}}$, which are not exposed by $\mathcal{F}_{\underline{\mathsf{CLedger}}}$.

We provide a brief sketch of the interface exposed by $\mathcal{F}_{\underline{\mathsf{CLedger}}}$. Upon initialization with an arithmetic circuit g encoding only the contract logic, users can enroll, specifying input string x and a confidential coin to input, identified by its id. Upon a completed *Enroll*, the functionality is prompted by servers to evaluate circuit g on both client input strings, interpreted as numerical values, and input balances, with checks to ensure g does not mint tokens. $\mathcal{F}_{\underline{C}Ledger}$ permits clients to withdraw anytime to retrieve the private output string and output balance. $\mathcal{F}_{\underline{C}Contract}$ permits the simulator to abort and indicate cheating servers, which are then penalized by the functionality.

Functionality $\mathcal{F}_{\underline{C}Contract}$, extends $\mathcal{F}_{\underline{C}Ledger}$

$\mathcal{F}_{\underline{C}Contract}$ interacts with clients $\mathcal{C} = \{C_1, ..., C_m\}$ and servers $\mathcal{P} = \{P_1, ..., P_n\}$. The functionality exposes interfaces and and accesses the state of $\mathcal{F}_{\underline{C}Ledger}$. It is parameterized with max. circuit depth d_T, and collateral balance $\bar{\mathbf{v}}_{coll}$.

Init: On (INIT, sid, g) from $P_i \in \mathcal{P}$ forward messages to $\mathcal{S}$. If $\mathcal{S}$ continues.
1. Run **GenAcct** and **Init** procedures on $\mathcal{F}_{\underline{C}Ledger}$.
2. Assert that g is a circuit and that $\mathsf{depth}(g) \leq d_T$, store g.
3. Assert $\mathsf{vk} \in \mathcal{K}[P_i]$ and $\mathcal{L}[\mathsf{vk}] \geq \bar{\mathbf{v}}_{coll}$.
4. Set $\mathcal{L}[\mathsf{vk}] \leftarrow \mathcal{L}[\mathsf{vk}] - \bar{\mathbf{v}}_{coll}$.
   - If all servers have successfully called **Init**, set state to **enroll**, tick $\mathcal{F}_{Clock}$.

Enroll: Upon input (ENROLL, $sid, x, \mathsf{id}, \mathsf{vk}$) from client $C_j \in \mathcal{C}$,
1. Assert $\mathsf{vk} \in \mathcal{K}[C_j]$ and $\langle \mathsf{id}, \bar{\mathbf{v}} \rangle \in \mathcal{L}[\mathsf{vk}]$.
2. Forward (ENROLL, $sid, \mathsf{id}, \mathsf{vk}$) to $\mathcal{S}$, if $\mathcal{S}$ aborts, run **Abort**. Otherwise, continue.
3. Assert state is in **enroll** and $\exists \langle \mathsf{id}, \bar{\mathbf{v}} \rangle \in \mathcal{L}_{Conf}[\mathsf{vk}]$: then remove $\langle \mathsf{id}, \bar{\mathbf{v}} \rangle$.
4. Store input $(x_j, \bar{\mathbf{v}}_j)$.
   - If all clients have successfully called **Enroll**, tick $\mathcal{F}_{Clock}$.

Execute: Upon input (EXECUTE, sid) from $P_i \in \mathcal{P}$,
1. If EXECUTE received from all $\mathcal{P}$ and $\mathcal{F}_{Clock}$ ticked since state update to **enroll**, forward (EXECUTE, sid) to $\mathcal{S}$ and wait for *Ok* or *Abort*. If *Ok*, continue.
   a. Evaluate circuit g over current user inputs $\{(x_j, \bar{\mathbf{v}}_j)\}_{j \in [m]}$ and client state.
   c. Store client states $\{(y_j, \bar{\mathbf{w}}_j)\}_{j \in [m]}$ read from output gates of g.
      - Assert $\sum_{j \in [m]} \bar{\mathbf{v}}_j = \sum_{j \in [m]} \bar{\mathbf{w}}_j$. Tick $\mathcal{F}_{Clock}$.
2. Forward (EVALUATE, sid) to $\mathcal{S}$ and wait for *Ok* or *Abort*.
   - If *Ok* returned, set state to **evaluated** and tick $\mathcal{F}_{Clock}$.
3. Send (OUTPUT, $sid, \{y_j, \bar{\mathbf{w}}_j\}_{j \in [m]}$) to $\mathcal{S}$ and wait for *Ok* or *Abort*.
   - If $\mathcal{S}$ aborts, it provides cheating server set $\mathcal{J}$, run **Abort** with $\mathcal{J}$.
4. For $j \in [m]$, get a unique id'_j from $\mathcal{S}$, and set $\mathcal{L}_{Conf}[\mathsf{vk}_j] \leftarrow \mathcal{L}_{Conf}[\mathsf{vk}_j] \cup \{\langle \mathsf{id}'_j, \bar{\mathbf{w}}_j \rangle\}$.
5. Set state to **enroll** and tick $\mathcal{F}_{Clock}$.

Withdraw: Upon (WITHDRAW, sid) from $C_j \in \mathcal{C}$, obtain newly stored outputs since last *Withdraw* by $C_j \in \mathcal{C}$. Return $((y_{j,1}, \langle \mathsf{id}'_{j,1}, \bar{\mathbf{w}}_{j,1} \rangle), ..., (y_{j,l}, \langle \mathsf{id}'_{j,l}, \bar{\mathbf{w}}_{j,l} \rangle))$.

Abort: Tick $\mathcal{F}_{Clock}$,
a. If state is **enroll**, return server and client funds: update $\mathcal{L}, \mathcal{L}_{Conf}$.
b. Else if state in **evaluated**, obtain cheating servers $\mathcal{J}$ from $\mathcal{S}$:
   - If $\mathcal{J} \neq \emptyset$, reimburse clients $\mathcal{C}$ and honest servers $\mathcal{P} \backslash \mathcal{J}$, then distribute $\mathcal{J}$'s collateral amongst $\mathcal{C}$: update $\mathcal{L}, \mathcal{L}_{Conf}$ accordingly.
   - Else if $\mathcal{J} = \emptyset$, obtain $\{(y_j, \bar{\mathbf{v}}_j)\}_{j \in [m]}$ from last evaluation of circuit g.
      - For $C_j \in \mathcal{C}'$, sample $\mathsf{id}_j \leftarrow_\$ \mathbb{F}$ and set $\mathcal{L}_{Conf}[\mathsf{vk}_j] \leftarrow \mathcal{L}_{Conf}[\mathsf{vk}_j] \cup \{\langle \mathsf{id}_j, \bar{\mathbf{v}}_j \rangle\}$.
      - Return collateral for all $\mathcal{P}$: update $\mathcal{L}$ accordingly.
c. Terminate.

Fig. 2. Functionality for Confidential Contracts

Model of Confidential Contracts. Unlike public smart contracts deployed to $\mathcal{F}_{\mathsf{Ledger}}$, an instance of $\mathcal{F}_{\mathsf{Ident}}$ permits the computation of any arithmetic circuit on both private and public inputs. We model a confidential contract as an arithmetic circuit over a field $\mathbb{F}_p$ consistent with the domain that $\mathcal{F}_{\mathsf{Ident}}$ is realized with. A well-formed confidential contract permits the writing of both *numerical* and *financial* inputs from each client to its input gates. Further, we enforce a maximum circuit depth d_T prior to the circuit evaluation to bound the rounds of interaction in the MPC instance.

$$\big(([\,y_1\,],[\,\bar{\mathbf{w}}_1\,]),...,([\,y_m\,],[\,\bar{\mathbf{w}}_m\,])\big) \leftarrow \mathsf{eval}_g\big(([\,x_1\,],[\,\bar{\mathbf{v}}_1\,])....,([\,x_m\,],[\,\bar{\mathbf{v}}_m\,])\big)$$

Upon confidential evaluation of a contract circuit g with well-formed depth and gates, the following assertion must be performed at each run-time over confidential inputs and outputs of evaluated g: namely, that token supplies have been preserved.

$$\sum_{i \in [m]} [\,\bar{\mathbf{v}}_i\,] =^? \sum_{i \in [m]} [\,\bar{\mathbf{w}}_i\,] \tag{2}$$

One-Round Client-Server Interaction. Upon providing inputs to a confidential contract execution, clients can go off-line and retrieve confidential outputs with *Withdraw* at any later point in time.

Collateral. Our need for collateral follows the same logic as in Insured MPC [7]. The collateral contract incentivizes the servers to continue to participate in the privacy preserving smart contract computation, and behave honestly as they would otherwise suffer a financial loss. While the underlying maliciously secure MPC system will ensure that a server acting maliciously will cause an abort except with negligible probability, such an abort the adversary might have learned the output of the computation. This can in some situations have high value. Thus we require each server to give as collateral, strictly *more* than the maximum value they could gain from learning the output of a privacy preserving computation.

3.1   Realizing the Confidential Contract Functionality

Overview of Protocol. Having provided a high-level overview of the protocol phase in Sect. 1, we now proceed to detail the individual protocol phases for the single-round privacy preserving smart contract execution and refer to the full version [6] for the full protocol description and UC-security proof.

Setup of Contracts. Servers deploy instances of $\mathcal{X}_{\mathsf{Lock}}[\mathcal{X}_{\underline{\mathsf{CLedger}}}]$, $\mathcal{X}_{\mathsf{Collateral}}$ on $\mathcal{F}_{\mathsf{Ledger}}$. Since wrapper $\mathcal{X}_{\mathsf{Lock}}$ extends $\mathcal{X}_{\underline{\mathsf{CLedger}}}$, both are deployed and initialized as a single contract instance on $\mathcal{F}_{\mathsf{Ledger}}$ with shared contract id ($\mathsf{cn}_{\mathsf{Lock}}$) and shared state such as the confidential ledger ($\mathcal{L}_{\mathsf{Conf}}$). Here, the function of $\mathcal{X}_{\mathsf{Lock}}$ is to lock the confidential coins of clients input to the confidential contract evaluation, and to *replace* these with a new confidential distribution according to result of the contract evaluation. Further, $\mathcal{X}_{\mathsf{Lock}}$ is initialized with a threshold signature verification key $\mathsf{vk_{TSig}}$, jointly generated by all servers via $\mathcal{F}_{\mathsf{TSig}}$: whenever servers agree on a new status of the contract evaluation in $\mathcal{F}_{\mathsf{Ident}}$, this agreement can be settled in $\mathcal{X}_{\mathsf{Lock}}$ with a threshold signature jointly generated via global functionality $\mathcal{F}_{\mathsf{TSig}}$. $\mathcal{X}_{\mathsf{Collateral}}$ is parameterized by $\mathsf{cn_{Lock}}$ and is activated each time $\mathcal{F}_{\mathsf{Clock}}$ progresses: it obtains collateral from all participating servers. It observes any recorded cheating servers $\mathcal{J}$ stored in the state of contract instance $\mathsf{cn_{Lock}}$ and enforces penalties accordingly.

Client Enrollment. Clients interact with $\mathcal{X}_{\mathsf{Lock}}$ to enroll a confidential coin it controls to the contract evaluation, and send both the coin commitment opening and numerical input x to an instance of $\mathcal{F}_{\mathsf{Ident}}$. Enrolled coins are removed from the confidential ledger $\mathcal{L}_{\mathsf{Conf}}$ maintained by $\mathcal{X}^{\mathcal{L}_{\mathsf{Ledger}}}$ and moved to a dedicated ledger $\mathcal{L}_{\mathsf{Lock}}$ for funds committed to a pending MPC computation in $\mathcal{F}_{\mathsf{Ident}}$.

Clients must also commit to a *output mask* during enrollment, which enables the subsequent redistribution of confidential coins without client interaction in the output phase of the contract evaluation. Here each client with confidential coin input c and numerical input x performs the following:

- Samples $\hat{y} \leftarrow_\$ \mathbb{F}$ as a numerical output mask and sends to $\mathcal{F}_{\mathsf{Ident}}$.
- Samples $\hat{\mathbf{w}} \leftarrow_\$ \mathbb{F}^{|\mathbb{T}|}$, $\hat{s} \leftarrow_\$ \mathbb{F}$, and computes mask commitment $\hat{c} \leftarrow \mathsf{com}(\hat{\mathbf{w}}, \hat{s})$.
- Sends mask commitment $\hat{c}$ to $\mathcal{X}_{\mathsf{Lock}}$ on $\mathcal{F}_{\mathsf{Ledger}}$.
- Sends mask commitment openings $(\hat{\mathbf{w}}, \hat{s})$ of $\hat{c}$ to $\mathcal{F}_{\mathsf{Ident}}$.

Here clients can also give any auxiliary input, x, needed for the privacy preserving smart contract computation.

Input Verification. Upon enrollment of clients, servers must verify that the confidential coin c and mask commitment $\hat{c}$ sent to $\mathcal{X}_{\mathsf{Lock}}$ are consistent with their respective openings $(\bar{\mathbf{v}}, \bar{r})$ and $(\hat{\mathbf{v}}, \hat{r})$ sent to $\mathcal{F}_{\mathsf{Ident}}$ during enrollment. For simplicity of presentation, we illustrate the batched input verification of input confidential coins and their openings assuming a token universe size of

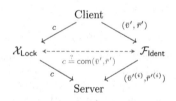

$|\mathbb{T}| = 1$, such that $c = g^{\bar{v}} h^{\bar{r}}$. Input verification for output masks $\hat{c}$ and their openings submitted to $\mathcal{F}_{\mathsf{Ident}}$ follow similarly.

Each server obtains both confidential coin c from $\mathcal{X}_{\mathsf{Lock}}$ and *additive shares* of submitted openings thereof from $\mathcal{F}_{\mathsf{Ident}}$, namely $(\bar{v}'^{(i)}, \bar{r}'^{(i)})$. We write $\bar{v}'^{(i)} = (\bar{v} + \epsilon)^{(i)}$ and similarly for $\bar{r}'^{(i)}$, where the ϵ denotes the error or discrepancy that the adversary can introduce to $\bar{v}$. We employ a standard technique of evaluating a random linear combination over client inputs to verify consistency.

1. Servers jointly sample $\gamma, \alpha, \beta \leftarrow_\$ \mathbb{F}$ and open γ.
2. Each server locally computes the following on the inputs from m clients.
   - $\bar{v}'^{(i)}_{\mathsf{lin}} = \alpha^{(i)} + \gamma \, \bar{v}'^{(i)}_1 + ... + \gamma^m \, \bar{v}'^{(i)}_m$ and $r'^{(i)}_{\mathsf{lin}} = \beta^{(i)} + \gamma \, r'^{(i)}_1 + ... + \gamma^m \, r'^{(i)}_m$
   - Subsequently, it sends $\bar{v}'^{(i)}_{\mathsf{lin}}$ and $\bar{v}'^{(i)}_{\mathsf{lin}}$ to all other servers.
3. Each server locally reconstructs $\bar{v}'_{\mathsf{lin}} = \prod_{i \in [n]} \bar{v}'^{(i)}_{\mathsf{lin}}$ and $r'_{\mathsf{lin}} = \prod_{i \in [n]} r'^{(i)}_{\mathsf{lin}}$

4. Servers locally verify: $\prod_{i \in [n]} g^{\alpha^{(i)}} h^{\beta^{(i)}} \prod_{j \in [m]} c_j^{\gamma^j} \overset{?}{=} g^{\bar{v}'_{\mathsf{lin}}} h^{r'_{\mathsf{lin}}}$

Note that $\bar{v}'^{(i)}_{\mathsf{lin}}$ and $r'^{(i)}_{\mathsf{lin}}$ are shares held by servers and do not reveal the values of user inputs. We write $\bar{v}'_{\mathsf{lin}} = \alpha + \gamma (\bar{v}_1 + \epsilon_{\bar{v}_1}) + ... + \gamma^m (\bar{v}_m + \epsilon_{\bar{v}_m})$ and similarly for r'_{lin} to expose ϵ's introduced by the adversary. If ϵ values are committed to by the adversary before α, β, γ are sampled, we can interpret $\bar{v}'_{\mathsf{lin}} - \bar{v}_{\mathsf{lin}} = 0$ and $r'_{\mathsf{lin}} - r_{\mathsf{lin}} = 0$ as m - degree polynomials with coefficients chosen by the adversary that are later evaluated at some random coordinate γ: since verification step (4) implies exactly these assertions, the probability for an undetected non-zero error is therefore $m/|\mathbb{G}|$, where m is the number of polynomial roots, by the Schwartz-Zippel Lemma.

Execute. Servers call the **Evaluate** interface on $\mathcal{F}_{\mathsf{Ident}}$ to evaluate circuit g with input gates set to client inputs.

$$([x_1], [\hat{y}_1], [\bar{\mathbf{v}}_1], [r_1], [\hat{\mathbf{w}}_1], [\hat{s}_1]), ..., ([x_m], [\hat{y}_m], [\bar{\mathbf{v}}_m], [r_m], [\hat{\mathbf{w}}_m], [\hat{s}_m])$$

Upon secure evaluation, outputs in form of numerical values and balances are written to the output gates of g: $\big(([y_1], [\bar{\mathbf{w}}_1]), ..., ([y_m], [\bar{\mathbf{w}}_m])\big)$. Before masking these for opening, the servers then perform a confidential consistency check to ensure the preservation of tokens as shown in Eq. (2).

Masked output values are obtained by applying the masking values input by users, $[y'_j] = [y_j] + [\hat{y}_j]$ and similarly for balances, $[\bar{\mathbf{w}}'_j] = [\bar{\mathbf{w}}_j] + [\hat{\mathbf{w}}_j]$ and generating a joint signature $\sigma_{\mathsf{vkTSig}}(\mathsf{evaled})$ via $\mathcal{F}_{\mathsf{TSig}}$, that is sent to $\mathcal{X}_{\mathsf{Lock}}$ on $\mathcal{F}_{\mathsf{Ledger}}$. Upon verification, the $\mathcal{X}_{\mathsf{Lock}}$ contract updates the state of protocol execution, reflecting completion of the *Execute* phase.

Open. Servers run **Optimistic Reveal** in $\mathcal{F}_{\mathsf{Ident}}$ to open masked numerical outputs and balances $\big((y'_1, \bar{\mathbf{w}}'_1), ..., (y'_m, \bar{\mathbf{w}}'_m)\big)$. Should all servers agree on the successful completion of the contract evaluation, they jointly sign all *masked* outputs and send these to $\mathcal{X}_{\mathsf{Lock}}$ (on $\mathcal{F}_{\mathsf{Ledger}}$), which then computes the *unmasked* confidential coins for clients with the newly computed distribution as follows. Given the masked output balance $\bar{\mathbf{w}}'$ from $\mathcal{F}_{\mathsf{Ident}}$ and the coin mask $\hat{c}$ sampled by a client in **Enroll**, contract $\mathcal{X}_{\mathsf{Lock}}$ computes

(a) The masked confidential coin: $c^{\mathsf{out}\prime} \leftarrow \mathbf{g}^{\bar{\mathbf{w}}'} h^0$
(b) The <u>unmasked</u> confidential coin: $c^{\mathsf{out}} \leftarrow c^{\mathsf{out}\prime} \cdot \hat{c}^{-1}$

We rewrite (b) as $c^{\mathsf{out}} = \mathbf{g}^{\bar{\mathbf{w}}' - \hat{\mathbf{w}}} h^{-\hat{s}} = \mathsf{com}(\bar{\mathbf{w}}, -\hat{s})$ to expose the unmasking of the output coin without any knowledge of the final balance. $\mathcal{X}_{\mathsf{Lock}}$ subsequently stores unmasked output coin c^{out} in the confidential ledger in $\mathcal{X}_{\mathsf{CLedger}}$, thereby settling the output balance distribution read from output gates of contract circuit g. Should $\mathcal{X}_{\mathsf{Lock}}$ successfully verify the signed outputs, $\mathcal{X}_{\mathsf{Collateral}}$ will infer from the state of $\mathcal{X}_{\mathsf{Lock}}$ the completion of a successful round and return the deposited collateral to the servers.

Withdraw. Upon a successful **Open**, the output of the confidential contract evaluation has completed. Each client can obtain their masked output $(y', \bar{\mathbf{w}}')$

from $\mathcal{X}_{\text{Lock}}$ and newly minted c_{out} from $\mathcal{X}_{\text{CLedger}}$ anytime following a success-ful execution of a contract evaluation. Let $\hat{y}$ and $(\hat{\mathbf{w}}, \hat{s})$ be the output masks generated by the client in **Enroll**. The withdrawing client obtains

(a) The numerical output: $y \leftarrow y' - \hat{y}$
(b) The opening of the output coin: $(\bar{\mathbf{w}}, s) \leftarrow (\bar{\mathbf{w}}' - \hat{\mathbf{w}}, -\hat{s})$

Thus, their the tokens are still confidential and that clients can transfer or redeem these using Π_{CLedger} described in the full version [6].

Abort. If the protocol aborts prior to the completion of the **Execute** phase, client funds are simply returned by $\mathcal{X}_{\text{Lock}}$ and collateral deposited to $\mathcal{X}_{\text{Collateral}}$ is returned. If servers have agreed upon the completion of **Execute**, honest servers can interact with $\mathcal{F}_{\text{Ident}}$ to either (a) obtain shares that are verifiable and enable reconstruction of the output or (b) identify cheating servers (functionality described in the full version [6]). Thus, $\mathcal{X}_{\text{Lock}}$ as a registered public verifier, can identify cheating servers by either verifying shares with $\mathcal{F}_{\text{Ident}}$, or obtaining the identities of servers $\mathcal{J}$ that refuse to participate in revealing their shares and allowing their verification. Cheating servers lose their collateral held by $\mathcal{X}_{\text{Collateral}}$ which is redistributed to clients.

We present the full protocol $\Pi_{\text{CContract}}$ which GUC-realizes $\mathcal{F}_{\text{CContract}}$ in the full version [6] and prove the following statement.

Theorem 2. $\Pi_{\text{CContract}}[\Pi_{\text{CLedger}}]$ *realizes* $\mathcal{F}_{\text{CContract}}[\mathcal{F}_{\text{CLedger}}]$ *in the* $\mathcal{F}_{\text{Clock}}$, $\mathcal{F}_{\text{Ident}}$, $\mathcal{F}_{\text{Ledger}}$, $\mathcal{F}_{\text{NIZK}}$, $\mathcal{F}_{\text{Setup}}$, $\mathcal{F}_{\text{Sig}}$, $\mathcal{F}_{\text{TSig}}$-*hybrid model against any PPT-adversary cor-rupting at most* $n - 1$ *of the* n *servers* $\mathcal{P}$ *statically and any minority of* $\mathcal{Q}$.

4   Efficiency

We note that since previous works focus on using zero knowledge proofs and a trusted contract manager, we refrain from directly comparing our efficiency to their works. The closest previous works to ours is the Hawk family [4,5,37]. Unfortunately neither of the works provide an efficiency analysis, making it hard to provide a meaningful comparison. However, we note they all require computation of cryptographic primitives (commitments and ZKPs) in MPC. Thus requiring strictly more MPC computation, *along* with a larger (and hence) slower field of computation, as this field is needed to facilitate *computational* security of the cryptographic primitives they compute in MPC. In the following analysis, we assume Bulletproofs for range proofs and standard Fiat-Shamir Schnorr proofs of knowledge of exponents using elliptic curves. Although neither of these are UC-secure since knowledge extraction requires rewinding, there is evidence [29] that these techniques can be made non-malleable in the algebraic group model. Hence, for the purpose of efficiency we believe it is reasonable to forgo the formal UC security in this section. We use BLS threshold signatures and for simplicity we assume the size of the group used for BLS and commitments is the same, although it will in practice be slightly larger for BLS.

Table 2. Complexity of our protocol when executing one $\underline{C}$Contract, *excluding* the computation of contract circuit g in MPC. We assume $|\mathcal{C}|z > s$ for statistical security parameter s, where z is the amount of input/output for each client in the set of clients $\mathcal{C}$, including the hidden token amount. $n = |\mathcal{P}|$ is the amount of servers and **mult** denotes the number of multiplications in MPC.

		Init	Execution	Abort
User	**exp**	2	2	0
Server	**exp**	$2 + 2(n-1)$	$6|\mathcal{C}| + 2$	0
	pair	0	$n-1$	0
	mult	0	$z|\mathcal{C}|$	0
SC comp.	**exp**	0	$2|\mathcal{C}|z$	$|\mathcal{C}|$
	pair	0	2	0
SC call space	#$\mathbb{G}$ elem.	3	$|\mathcal{C}|z$	$O(n|\mathcal{C}|z)$
Comm	#$\mathbb{G}$ elem.	$O(n)$	$O(n^2 \cdot z \cdot |\mathcal{C}|)$	$O(n^2 \cdot z \cdot |\mathcal{C}|)$

We outline the amount of heavy computations needed for our core protocol in Table 2, *except* what is needed by the underlying MPC computation computing the contract circuit g, reflecting the privacy preserving smart contract $\underline{C}$Contract. Concretely we count the amount of group exponentiations when assuming that the Pedersen commitments are realized using elliptic curves, along with pairings assuming BLS [13] has been used for realizing distributed signatures. The table only contains the complexity of executing one instance of $\underline{C}$Contract, but we note that execution of multiple contracts is slightly sublinear in the complexity of a single execution. The *Abort* column illustrates the *additional* overhead associated with a cheating party.

Table 3. Complexity of $\underline{C}$Ledger in group exponentiation and amount of group elements stored, when $\bar{v}_{\mathsf{max}}$ is the maximum amount of allowed tokens (Recall $|\mathcal{C}| \cdot \bar{v}_{\mathsf{max}} < |\mathbb{G}|$).

	Mint	ConfTransfer	Redeem
User	4	$O(\log(\bar{v}_{\mathsf{max}}) \cdot \log(\log(\bar{v}_{\mathsf{max}})))$	3
SC comp	3	$O(\log(\bar{v}_{\mathsf{max}}))$	3
SC space	3	$2\log(\bar{v}_{\mathsf{max}}) + 10$	4

When it comes to our confidential token layer, we outline the complexity in Table 3. We note that the constant in the complexity of *Confidential Transfer* reflects two range proofs over $\log(|\mathbb{G}|/2)$, under the assumption that BulletProofs are used [16]. Although if the domain of the token amounts is further limited from $\mathbb{G}$ to $\bar{v}_{\mathsf{max}} < |\mathbb{G}|/|\mathcal{C}|$ then they can be reduced to range proofs of $[0; \bar{v}_{\mathsf{max}} - 1]$ and thus complexity $O(\bar{v}_{\mathsf{max}} \cdot \log(\bar{v}_{\mathsf{max}}))$.

In both tables the amount of smart contract space is only what needs to be submitted. The persistent space use needed is only $3 + 3|\mathcal{C}|$ group elements, if we assume that the storage used when posting to $\mathcal{X}_{\mathsf{Lock}}$ in *evaluate* and *open* gets overwritten the next time the servers call these methods.

The round complexity for all steps of both the confidential token layer protocols and our core protocol is constant, assuming g has constant multiplicative depth. Otherwise, the computation of g dominates the round complexity.

References

1. Andrychowicz, M., Dziembowski, S., Malinowski, D., Mazurek, Ł: Fair two-party computations via bitcoin deposits. In: Böhme, R., Brenner, M., Moore, T., Smith, M. (eds.) FC 2014. LNCS, vol. 8438, pp. 105–121. Springer, Heidelberg (2014). https://doi.org/10.1007/978-3-662-44774-1_8

2. Andrychowicz, M., Dziembowski, S., Malinowski, D., Mazurek, L.: Secure multiparty computations on bitcoin. In: 2014 IEEE Symposium on Security and Privacy, pp. 443–458. IEEE Computer Society Press (2014). https://doi.org/10.1109/SP.2014.35

3. Badertscher, C., Maurer, U., Tschudi, D., Zikas, V.: Bitcoin as a transaction ledger: a composable treatment. In: Katz, J., Shacham, H. (eds.) CRYPTO 2017. LNCS, vol. 10401, pp. 324–356. Springer, Cham (2017). https://doi.org/10.1007/978-3-319-63688-7_11

4. Banerjee, A., Clear, M., Tewari, H.: zkhawk: practical private smart contracts from mpc-based hawk. In: 2021 3rd Conference on Blockchain Research & Applications for Innovative Networks and Services (BRAINS), pp. 245–248. IEEE (2021). https://doi.org/10.1109/BRAINS52497.2021.9569822

5. Banerjee, A., Tewari, H.: Multiverse of HawkNess: A Universally-Composable MPC-based Hawk Variant. Cryptology ePrint Archive (2022). https://eprint.iacr.org/2022/421

6. Baum, C., yu Chiang, J.H., David, B., Frederiksen, T.K.: Eagle: efficient privacy preserving smart contracts. Cryptology ePrint Archive, Paper 2022/1435 (2022). https://eprint.iacr.org/2022/1435,

7. Baum, C., David, B., Dowsley, R.: Insured MPC: efficient secure computation with financial penalties. In: Bonneau, J., Heninger, N. (eds.) FC 2020. LNCS, vol. 12059, pp. 404–420. Springer, Cham (2020). https://doi.org/10.1007/978-3-030-51280-4_22

8. Baum, C., David, B., Dowsley, R., Nielsen, J.B., Oechsner, S.: CRAFT: composable randomness and almost fairness from time. Cryptology ePrint Archive, Report 2020/784 (2020). https://eprint.iacr.org/2020/784

9. Baum, C., David, B., Frederiksen, T.K.: P2DEX: privacy-preserving decentralized cryptocurrency exchange. In: Sako, K., Tippenhauer, N.O. (eds.) ACNS 2021. LNCS, vol. 12726, pp. 163–194. Springer, Cham (2021). https://doi.org/10.1007/978-3-030-78372-3_7

10. Benhamouda, F., Halevi, S., Halevi, T.: Supporting private data on hyperledger fabric with secure multiparty computation. IBM J. Res. Dev. **63**(2/3), 1–3 (2019). https://doi.org/10.1147/JRD.2019.2913621

11. Bentov, I., Kumaresan, R.: How to use bitcoin to design fair protocols. In: Garay, J.A., Gennaro, R. (eds.) CRYPTO 2014. LNCS, vol. 8617, pp. 421–439. Springer, Heidelberg (2014). https://doi.org/10.1007/978-3-662-44381-1_24

12. Bentov, I., Kumaresan, R., Miller, A.: Instantaneous decentralized poker. In: Takagi, T., Peyrin, T. (eds.) ASIACRYPT 2017. LNCS, vol. 10625, pp. 410–440. Springer, Cham (2017). https://doi.org/10.1007/978-3-319-70697-9_15

13. Boneh, D., Lynn, B., Shacham, H.: Short signatures from the Weil pairing. J. Cryptol. **17**(4), 297–319 (2004). https://doi.org/10.1007/s00145-004-0314-9

14. Bowe, S., Chiesa, A., Green, M., Miers, I., Mishra, P., Wu, H.: ZEXE: enabling decentralized private computation. In: 2020 IEEE Symposium on Security and Privacy, pp. 947–964. IEEE Computer Society Press (2020). https://doi.org/10.1109/SP40000.2020.00050

15. Bünz, B., Agrawal, S., Zamani, M., Boneh, D.: Zether: towards privacy in a smart contract world. In: Bonneau, J., Heninger, N. (eds.) FC 2020. LNCS, vol. 12059, pp. 423–443. Springer, Cham (2020). https://doi.org/10.1007/978-3-030-51280-4_23

16. Bünz, B., Bootle, J., Boneh, D., Poelstra, A., Wuille, P., Maxwell, G.: Bulletproofs: short proofs for confidential transactions and more. In: 2018 IEEE Symposium on Security and Privacy, pp. 315–334. IEEE Computer Society Press (2018). https://doi.org/10.1109/SP.2018.00020

17. Canetti, R.: Universally composable security: a new paradigm for cryptographic protocols. In: 42nd FOCS, pp. 136–145. IEEE Computer Society Press (2001). https://doi.org/10.1109/SFCS.2001.959888

18. Canetti, R.: Universally composable security: a new paradigm for cryptographic protocols. In: Proceedings 42nd IEEE Symposium on Foundations of Computer Science, pp. 136–145. IEEE (2001), https://doi.org/10.1109/SFCS.2001.959888

19. Canetti, R.: Universally composable signature, certification, and authentication. In: 17th IEEE Computer Security Foundations Workshop, (CSFW-17 2004), 28–30 June 2004, Pacific Grove, CA, USA, p. 219. IEEE Computer Society (2004). https://doi.org/10.1109/CSFW.2004.24, http://doi.ieeecomputersociety.org/10.1109/CSFW.2004.24

20. Canetti, R., Dodis, Y., Pass, R., Walfish, S.: Universally composable security with global setup. In: Vadhan, S.P. (ed.) TCC 2007. LNCS, vol. 4392, pp. 61–85. Springer, Heidelberg (2007). https://doi.org/10.1007/978-3-540-70936-7_4

21. Cheng, R., et al.: Ekiden: a platform for confidentiality-preserving, trustworthy, and performant smart contracts. In: 2019 IEEE European Symposium on Security and Privacy (EuroS&P) (2019). https://doi.org/10.1109/EuroSP.2019.00023

22. Choudhuri, A.R., Green, M., Jain, A., Kaptchuk, G., Miers, I.: Fairness in an unfair world: fair multiparty computation from public bulletin boards. In: Thuraisingham, B.M., Evans, D., Malkin, T., Xu, D. (eds.) ACM CCS 2017. pp. 719–728. ACM Press (2017). https://doi.org/10.1145/3133956.3134092

23. Daian, P., et al.: Flash boys 2.0: frontrunning in decentralized exchanges, miner extractable value, and consensus instability. In: 2020 IEEE Symposium on Security and Privacy, pp. 910–927. IEEE Computer Society Press (2020). https://doi.org/10.1109/SP40000.2020.00040

24. Damgård, I., Damgård, K., Nielsen, K., Nordholt, P.S., Toft, T.: Confidential benchmarking based on multiparty computation. In: Grossklags, J., Preneel, B. (eds.) FC 2016. LNCS, vol. 9603, pp. 169–187. Springer, Heidelberg (Feb 2016). https://doi.org/10.1007/978-3-662-54970-4_10

25. Damgård, I., Keller, M., Larraia, E., Pastro, V., Scholl, P., Smart, N.P.: Practical covertly secure MPC for dishonest majority – or: breaking the SPDZ limits. In: Crampton, J., Jajodia, S., Mayes, K. (eds.) ESORICS 2013. LNCS, vol. 8134, pp. 1–18. Springer, Heidelberg (2013). https://doi.org/10.1007/978-3-642-40203-6_1

26. Damgård, I., Pastro, V., Smart, N., Zakarias, S.: Multiparty computation from somewhat homomorphic encryption. In: Safavi-Naini, R., Canetti, R. (eds.) CRYPTO 2012. LNCS, vol. 7417, pp. 643–662. Springer, Heidelberg (2012). https://doi.org/10.1007/978-3-642-32009-5_38

27. David, B., Dowsley, R., Larangeira, M.: Kaleidoscope: an efficient poker protocol with payment distribution and penalty enforcement. In: Meiklejohn, S., Sako, K. (eds.) FC 2018. LNCS, vol. 10957, pp. 500–519. Springer, Heidelberg (2018). https://doi.org/10.1007/978-3-662-58387-6_27

28. David, B., Gentile, L., Pourpouneh, M.: FAST: fair auctions via secret transactions. In: Ateniese, G., Venturi, D. (eds.) ACNS 2022. LNCS, vol. 13269, pp. 727–747. Springer, Heidelberg (Jun 2022). https://doi.org/10.1007/978-3-031-09234-3_36

29. Ganesh, C., Orlandi, C., Pancholi, M., Takahashi, A., Tschudi, D.: Fiat-shamir bulletproofs are non-malleable (in the algebraic group model). In: Dunkelman, O., Dziembowski, S. (eds.) EUROCRYPT 2022, Part II. LNCS, vol. 13276, pp. 397–426. Springer, Heidelberg (2022). https://doi.org/10.1007/978-3-031-07085-3_14

30. Groth, J., Ostrovsky, R., Sahai, A.: New techniques for noninteractive zero-knowledge. J. ACM (JACM) **59**(3), 1–35 (2012). https://doi.org/10.1145/2220357.2220358

31. Jakobsen, T.P., Nielsen, J.B., Orlandi, C.: A framework for outsourcing of secure computation. In: Ahn, G., Oprea, A., Safavi-Naini, R. (eds.) Proceedings of the 6th edition of the ACM Workshop on Cloud Computing Security, CCSW 2014, Scottsdale, Arizona, USA, 7 November 2014, pp. 81–92. ACM (2014). https://doi.org/10.1145/2664168.2664170

32. Kalodner, H.A., Goldfeder, S., Chen, X., Weinberg, S.M., Felten, E.W.: Arbitrum: scalable, private smart contracts. In: Enck, W., Felt, A.P. (eds.) USENIX Security 2018, pp. 1353–1370. USENIX Association (Aug 2018)

33. Kanjalkar, S., Zhang, Y., Gandlur, S., Miller, A.: Publicly auditable mpc-as-a-service with succinct verification and universal setup. In: IEEE European Symposium on Security and Privacy Workshops, EuroS&P 2021, Vienna, Austria, 6–10 September 2021, pp. 386–411. IEEE (2021). https://doi.org/10.1109/EuroSPW54576.2021.00048

34. Katz, J., Maurer, U., Tackmann, B., Zikas, V.: Universally composable synchronous computation. In: Sahai, A. (ed.) TCC 2013. LNCS, vol. 7785, pp. 477–498. Springer, Heidelberg (2013). https://doi.org/10.1007/978-3-642-36594-2_27

35. Kerber, T., Kiayias, A., Kohlweiss, M.: KACHINA - foundations of private smart contracts. In: Küsters, R., Naumann, D. (eds.) CSF 2021 Computer Security Foundations Symposium, pp. 1–16. IEEE Computer Society Press (2021). https://doi.org/10.1109/CSF51468.2021.00002

36. Kiayias, A., Zhou, H.-S., Zikas, V.: Fair and robust multi-party computation using a global transaction ledger. In: Fischlin, M., Coron, J.-S. (eds.) EUROCRYPT 2016. LNCS, vol. 9666, pp. 705–734. Springer, Heidelberg (2016). https://doi.org/10.1007/978-3-662-49896-5_25

37. Kosba, A.E., Miller, A., Shi, E., Wen, Z., Papamanthou, C.: Hawk: the blockchain model of cryptography and privacy-preserving smart contracts. In: 2016 IEEE Symposium on Security and Privacy, pp. 839–858. IEEE Computer Society Press (May 2016). https://doi.org/10.1109/SP.2016.55

38. Kumaresan, R., Bentov, I.: Amortizing secure computation with penalties. In: Weippl, E.R., Katzenbeisser, S., Kruegel, C., Myers, A.C., Halevi, S. (eds.) ACM CCS 2016, pp. 418–429. ACM Press (2016). https://doi.org/10.1145/2976749.2978424

39. Kumaresan, R., Moran, T., Bentov, I.: How to use bitcoin to play decentralized poker. In: Proceedings of the 22nd ACM SIGSAC Conference on Computer and Communications Security, pp. 195–206 (2015). https://doi.org/10.1145/2810103.2813712

40. Kumaresan, R., Vaikuntanathan, V., Vasudevan, P.N.: Improvements to secure computation with penalties. In: Weippl, E.R., Katzenbeisser, S., Kruegel, C., Myers, A.C., Halevi, S. (eds.) ACM CCS 2016, pp. 406–417. ACM Press (2016). https://doi.org/10.1145/2976749.2978421

41. Lee, J., Nikitin, K., Setty, S.T.V.: Replicated state machines without replicated execution. In: 2020 IEEE Symposium on Security and Privacy, pp. 119–134. IEEE Computer Society Press (2020). https://doi.org/10.1109/SP40000.2020.00068

42. Nilsson, A., Bideh, P.N., Brorsson, J.: A survey of published attacks on intel SGX. CoRR abs/ arXiv: 2006.13598 (2020)

43. Ozdemir, A., Boneh, D.: Experimenting with collaborative zk-SNARKs: Zero-knowledge proofs for distributed secrets. Cryptology ePrint Archive, Report 2021/1530 (2021). https://eprint.iacr.org/2021/1530

44. Pedersen, T.P.: Non-interactive and information-theoretic secure verifiable secret sharing. In: Feigenbaum, J. (ed.) CRYPTO 1991. LNCS, vol. 576, pp. 129–140. Springer, Heidelberg (1992). https://doi.org/10.1007/3-540-46766-1_9

45. Abe, M., Ohkubo, M., Suzuki, K.: 1-out-of-n signatures from a variety of keys. In: Zheng, Y. (ed.) ASIACRYPT 2002. LNCS, vol. 2501, pp. 415–432. Springer, Heidelberg (2002). https://doi.org/10.1007/3-540-36178-2_26

46. Steffen, S., Bichsel, B., Baumgartner, R., Vechev, M.: ZeeStar: private Smart Contracts by Homomorphic Encryption and Zero-knowledge Proofs. In: 2022 IEEE Symposium on Security and Privacy (SP), pp. 1543–1543. IEEE Computer Society (2022). https://files.sri.inf.ethz.ch/website/papers/sp22-zeestar.pdf

47. Steffen, S., Bichsel, B., Gersbach, M., Melchior, N., Tsankov, P., Vechev, M.T.: zkay: specifying and enforcing data privacy in smart contracts. In: Cavallaro, L., Kinder, J., Wang, X., Katz, J. (eds.) ACM CCS 2019, pp. 1759–1776. ACM Press (2019). https://doi.org/10.1145/3319535.3363222

48. Team, T.S.N.: Secret network: a privacy-preserving secret contract & decentralized application platform (2022). https://scrt.network/graypaper

Provably Avoiding Geographic Regions
for Tor's Onion Services

Arushi Arora[1]([✉]) [iD], Raj Karra[1] [iD], Dave Levin[2] [iD], and Christina Garman[1] [iD]

[1] Purdue University, West Lafayette, IN 47906, USA
{arora105,karra0,clg}@purdue.edu
[2] University of Maryland, College Park, MD 20742, USA
dml@cs.umd.edu

Abstract. Tor, a peer-to-peer anonymous communication system, is one of the most effective tools in providing free and open communication online. Many of the attacks on Tor's anonymity occur when an adversary can intercept a user's traffic; it is thus useful to limit how much of a user's traffic can enter potentially adversarial networks. Recent work has demonstrated that careful circuit creation can allow users to provably avoid geographic regions that a user expects to be adversarial. These prior systems leverage the fact that a user has complete control over the circuits they create. Unfortunately, that work does not apply to onion services (formerly known as "hidden services"), in which no one entity knows the full circuit between user and hidden service. In this work, we present the design, implementation, and evaluation of DeTor_{OS}, the first provable geographic avoidance system for onion services. We demonstrate how recent work to build and deploy programmable middleboxes onto the Tor network allows us to take existing techniques like these and deploy them in scenarios that were not possible before. DeTor_{OS} is immediately deployable as it is built using programmable middleboxes, meaning it does not require either the Tor protocol or its source code to be modified. This work also raises a number of interesting questions about extensions of provable geographical routing to other scenarios and threat models, as well as reinforces how the notion of programmable middleboxes can allow for the deployment of both existing and new techniques in novel ways in anonymity networks.

Keywords: Programmable anonymity networks · Tor · Onion Services · Privacy

1 Introduction

The ability to achieve freedom of speech anonymously and access resources privately has now become an important part of our society. Tor, one of the most popular and widely used anonymous communication networks today, is used by people across the globe who wish to share or access systems without revealing their identity. In addition, Tor's *onion services* let users host content anonymously (i.e. without disclosing the host server's IP). This is critically important

© International Financial Cryptography Association 2024
F. Baldimtsi and C. Cachin (Eds.): FC 2023, LNCS 13950, pp. 289–305, 2024.
https://doi.org/10.1007/978-3-031-47754-6_17

not just in the face of internet censorship and hosting of services like anonymous dropboxes for whistleblower submissions, but also for regular users who might want to protect their privacy online.

Tor is designed under the realistic assumption that no adversary has a *global* view of the network [5]. However, even under this relaxed threat model, there are still very powerful *routing-capable* nation-state adversaries that can manipulate, inspect, and correlate traffic crossing their borders. In other words, these attackers can censor Tor traffic and launch powerful deanonymization attacks against Tor users (including onion service hosts). Some of the first known attacks on onion services include timing analysis, service location attacks, and distance attacks, which expose the location of a server hosting an onion service [12,20]. Further, circuit fingerprinting attacks [14] attempt to recognize the circuits involved in communicating with an onion service and then perform a website fingerprinting attack [27] on the identified circuits to deanonymize the target service with high accuracy.

While, for Tor clients, some work has sought to deal with such attackers by making traffic appear innocuous to them, others have proposed avoiding these attackers altogether [13,15,17]. Although the Tor protocol provides a way to allow users to specify certain countries to avoid, this avoidance is not certain [21]. For instance, one study found that circuits excluding US Tor nodes only bypassed the US 12% of the time [17].

These efforts have led to techniques that allow users to specify *forbidden* geographic regions, and to construct circuits that *provably* bypass these regions. After a round-trip of communication, the idea is to return a proof verifying that packets could not have traversed the forbidden region. This proof combines proof of some of the places where the packet *did* go, combined with the fact that information cannot travel faster than the speed of light as an "alibi," thereby showing where the packet *could not* have gone.

Unfortunately, no prior work has managed to extend these provable avoidance techniques to onion services. In general, extending such architectures to onion services seems to inherently be a hard problem given the design of the interaction between clients and an onion service. As shown in Fig. 1, there is a 6-hop circuit between a client and an onion service, of which both the parties know only their side of the respective 3-hop circuit. Since both parties involved are unaware of the other side's respective circuit to ensure anonymity, it is a challenge for either side to gain assurances of the other half without a loss of anonymity.

Our proposed approach, which we call $DeTor_{OS}$, allows an onion service host as well as their respective users to verify whether their traffic successfully evaded certain regions. We are able to extend this functionality to onion services by leveraging recent advances that introduce programmability to Tor (and other similar anonymity systems), which allows a user to upload and execute code on willing Tor relays [22]. This paradigm allows us to do something that was not possible before: build $DeTor_{OS}$ as a (trusted) function which can compute on data from both parties in a confidential manner. Our design also has the benefit of being immediately deployable. Because $DeTor_{OS}$ leverages programmable

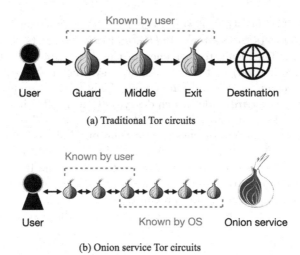

Fig. 1. Whereas a user knows every hop in the circuit they create, circuits to onion services are created collaboratively, and thus no one entity knows the full circuit. This makes provable avoidance difficult to achieve.

anonymity networks, no changes are required to the underlying Tor source code or protocol. We also show that, under reasonable assumptions, it protects the anonymity of both the onion services and their users.

Contributions. Our contributions in this work are as follows. We aim to improve the usability of Tor's onion services for its host as well as its respective users. We achieve this by providing the first realization for provable geographic avoidance for onion services that is immediately deployable and requires no changes to the underlying Tor code. We present the design, implementation, and evaluation of $\texttt{DeTor}_{OS}$, a set of techniques that aim to provably guarantee avoidance for onion services. While we leverage existing techniques to provide provable avoidance, we are the first to demonstrate how this can be done for onion services.

Roadmap. The organization of this paper is as follows. In Sect. 2, we provide a brief discussion on related work and background knowledge of the core ideas in the paper, as well as discuss the threat model for our architecture. Next, we discuss the design of $\texttt{DeTor}_{OS}$ in Sect. 3 and its security analysis in Sect. 4. We evaluate our work in Sect. 5. We discuss the implications of our design and pave a path for future directions in Sect. 6, discuss ethical considerations in Sect. 7, and conclude in Sect. 8.

2   Background and Related Work

Tor. Tor is a peer-to-peer overlay network based on onion routing that allows its users to browse the internet anonymously. This low-latency TCP-based communication service lets a client, who runs an Onion Proxy (OP), build a *circuit*

(3-hop by default) consisting of volunteer Tor relays called an Onion Router (OR)- *guard* (connects the source), *middle*, and *exit* (connects the destination) nodes. See Fig. 1a. The idea is to then encrypt the client's message (that needs to be sent to the destination) first with the unique symmetric key shared with the *exit* node followed by *middle* and *guard* node. This triple-encrypted ciphertext is then passed to the *guard* node, which decrypts ("peels off") it using the same shared symmetric key. The *middle* and *exit* nodes then "peel off" their respective layers until the message reaches the destination. This technique, therefore, maintains the confidentiality of the message, obscuring it from anyone trying to intercept it between two ORs. The Tor protocol by default prioritizes high-bandwidth relays for circuit construction and selects them from different subnets. The client constructs these circuits preemptively and is aware of all the chosen relays, whereas the ORs are only aware of their immediate successor or predecessor in the circuit. The OP is responsible for multiplexing TCP streams across circuits. Many such streams can share the same circuit. Tor protocol chooses ORs (almost) uniformly at random to construct its circuits.

Onion Services. An onion service allows its host to share information across the internet while maintaining its anonymity i.e. without revealing the identity or location of the host server. To establish an onion service, its host *Alice* first generates a public key pair and selects Tor relays to be its introduction points (IPs). *Alice* then publicizes her service (signing it with her private key) and forms a circuit to her IPs. *Bob*, who wants to visit *Alice*'s service, does so via Tor. To establish a connection to the onion service, first, he would select an onion router (OR), which is a Tor relay, to be his rendezvous point (RP). *Bob* then sends a cookie to the RP and builds a circuit to *Alice*'s IP sending it a message encrypted with *Alice*'s public key and starting a DH (Diffie Hellman) handshake. This message, which contains *Bob*'s cookie, and information about himself and RP, is forwarded to *Alice* who can then connect with *Bob* anonymously by building a circuit to RP. In this case, *Alice* would send the second half of the DH handshake, cookie, and hash of the session key. This establishes the anonymous stream between *Alice* and *Bob*. See Fig. 1b.

Bento. Bento [22] introduces programmability to anonymity networks (Tor as of now) by allowing users to execute tiny code snippets (called *functions*) on Tor relays thus improving a user's anonymity and performance and Tor's usability. This architecture runs on top of Tor and is immediately deployable. These in-network middleboxes can support numerous jobs like load-balancing, sending cover traffic, sharding files, and browsing the web with just a few lines of code. Bento also introduces a middlebox node policy that specifies resources and tasks that a Bento server can provide to its users. This ensures that Tor relays enacting as Bento servers are protected from the functions they run. Similarly, this system considers that some Tor relays support trusted execution environments (TEEs) which therefore prevent a third-party Bento server to introspect on any user function or its relevant data, as well as enforce correctness of execution for the function [8].

Provable Geographical Avoidance. Powerful nation-state adversaries can influence Tor routing into and out of their borders [26]. This allows them to censor and deanonymize traffic through correlation attacks [10,16]. Li et al. [17] introduced DeTor, a technique for constructing Tor circuits that provably avoids geographic regions of the user's choosing, based on Alibi routing [15]. Kohl et al. [13] and Ryan et al. [25] overcame some of DeTor's limitations by extending to asymmetric paths and providing more accurate node locations, which was later further refined by Ryan et al. [25]. At a high level, all of these make use of the same basic proof structure: clients prove where the traffic *did* go (based on the locations of the relays on the circuit), and combine that with latency information to infer where the traffic *could not have* gone (based on the fact that information cannot travel faster than the speed of light).

These proofs are calculated as

$$\min_{f \in F}[R(s,f) + R(f,a)] + R(a,t) \geq$$
$$\frac{3}{2c} \cdot \left(\min_{f \in F}[2 \cdot D(s,f) + 2 \cdot D(f,a)] + 2 \cdot D(a,t) \right) \tag{1}$$

where $D(x,y)$ is the great circle distance between hosts located at x and y; $R(x,y)$ denotes the RTT between x and y; F represents a forbidden region and $f \in F$ refers to a forbidden geographic coordinate; a is a relay that is not in F; s and t represent a source and destination node respectively.

DeTor provides proof for two modes of avoidance [17]. *Never-once*, which desires to fight fingerprinting [14] and censorship attacks [19] by verifying that a packet, passing through a Tor circuit, never transited a particular geographic region, even once. And *Never-twice*, which aims to resist deanonymization attacks [3,9,10,18], wherein an adversary needs to witness a packet twice: at the entry leg (from client to entry node) and the exit leg (from exit to destination). This technique confirms that an adversary does not appear on two non-contiguous portions of the Tor circuit.

2.1 Threat Model

Our network-level threat model is similar to Tor's. We consider our attacker to be a powerful nation-state adversary. Such a routing-capable adversary is unable to have a global view of the Tor traffic, but can observe, control and censor traffic in their respective local geographic regions. They may be able to achieve this by advertising themselves as Tor relays. In addition, this adversary is not restricted to a specific region or nation and may be able to collude with other (non-neighboring) countries.

Bento involves executing *functions* on a third-party machine (the Bento server). Following the original Bento design, we assume that the host node itself could be malicious, meaning that it can both try to tamper with or gain information about the avoidance computation and its inputs and outputs, as well as try to manipulate the inputs to alter the results. We assume that some of these servers will have secure TEEs, such as Intel SGX[1], prohibiting the host machine to access the executing *function* and its relevant data, as well as ensuring correctness of execution. As thus far all known TEE vulnerabilities have been patched by their respective vendors, we therefore assume that these TEEs are not fundamentally flawed, and that such an environment can indeed provide a secure enclave and is safe for running code, denying a malicious attacker/host the ability to introspect the executing *function*. We discuss the implications of the use of TEEs further in Sect. 6, but note that in this work we do not rely on any additional assumptions from the TEE, and inherit (and can make use of) Bento's support for remote attestation [1,11], which allows a client to verify that the Bento server is truly running inside an enclave and that the current TCB version as been patched against all known vulnerabilities.

The DeTor$_{OS}$ architecture itself employs an honest-but-curious model for the client and server. We therefore assume that both the client and the onion service are faithful to the DeTor$_{OS}$ protocol even though they attempt to learn what information they can.

3   DeTor$_{OS}$ Design

DeTor$_{OS}$ extends the DeTor proofs and computations [17] to onion services. This work introduced the idea of never-once proofs, which involved calculating $D_{\min}(x_1, \ldots, x_n)$: the shortest possible great-circle (geographic) distance along a circuit $x_1 \rightarrow \cdots \rightarrow x_n$, and converting this into the shortest possible traversal time by dividing it by $2c/3$ (the fastest speed at which information travels on the Internet). They also introduced never-twice proofs, which involve computing geographic ellipses denoting where in the world the packets could have traversed over each leg of the circuit, and then determining whether the entry and exit leg ellipses intersect. If they did not intersect, then never-twice avoidance was successful (see [17] for more details on the exact calculations). Performing these computations requires knowing the precise locations of each hop on the circuit. While this is straightforward for traditional Tor circuits as the client chooses these nodes, when working with onion services, the client cannot know the entire combined circuit (namely the onion service's half of the circuit is hidden from them), making this a hard problem. This section presents the solution for this problem, that is, the design for the DeTor$_{OS}$ never-once and never-twice functions.

3.1   DeTor$_{OS}$ Overview

The central idea behind DeTor$_{OS}$ is to use a semi-trusted Bento function that sits between the client and onion service to which both can upload their half-knowledge of the circuit, and that can then perform the computations and determine whether the circuit achieved never-once or never-twice avoidance. Critically,

---

[1] We note that, as discussed in [22], the Bento architecture is not bound to SGX and can work with any TEE that supports similar functionality [2].

although the function reveals whether or not avoidance was achieved, it does not reveal either side's inputs (much like secure multiparty computation). The overall design is presented in Fig. 2.

We break this design down into two different sub-functions, one for never-once avoidance and one for never-twice avoidance, though the core protocol is the same for both. A client, Alice, first either identifies a `Bento` node that is running the DeTor$_{OS}$ function or else uploads it to a chosen node. Before running the DeTor$_{OS}$ protocol, both Alice and Bob first perform a TLS handshake with the DeTor$_{OS}$ function to establish a secure channel against a malious node operator (see Sect. 3.4), and, optionally, ask the `Bento` server to attest to the correctness of its code base. This provides them with strong guarantees of the correctness and confidentiality of their subsequent proofs of avoidance. Alice would then run the desired DeTor$_{OS}$ protocol (presented in detail in Sects. 3.2 and 3.3) as part of connection establishment with Bob's onion service before communicating with it further[2].

Computation Models. We also introduce two different models of computation: the `Bento`-*side computation* model and the *local computation* model. In the `Bento`-side computation model, the client and OS simply upload all necessary circuit information to the DeTor$_{OS}$ function, which then performs the computations and returns the result. In the local computation model, the client and OS perform the bulk of the avoidance proof locally and then upload only their results to the DeTor$_{OS}$ function, which then computes the final result. We discuss each of these models further in the respective never-once and never-twice sections. These different models trade off trust in the DeTor$_{OS}$ function and `Bento` server for increased computation for the client and OS.

3.2 DeTor$_{OS}$ Never-Once function

The main objective of the never-once avoidance technique is to gain assurance that a packet or its response could not have passed a user-specified forbidden region F during a round-trip transmission. The idea is to first obtain the end-to-end round-trip time R_{e2e} of packets traversed through the selected Tor relays (entry (e), middle (m), and exit (x)). We also take into consideration the case where the packets could have gone through the forbidden region, calculating the shortest possible time necessary to go through each circuit and the forbidden region R_{min} as

$$R_{min} = \frac{3}{2c} \cdot \min \begin{cases} 2 \cdot D_{min}(s, F, e, m, x, t) \\ 2 \cdot D_{min}(s, e, F, m, x, t) \\ 2 \cdot D_{min}(s, e, m, F, x, t) \\ 2 \cdot D_{min}(s, e, m, x, F, t) \end{cases} \tag{2}$$

---

[2] Assuming Bob's OS supports the DeTor$_{OS}$ protocol. In our current honest-but-curious model, we can provide no guarantees if the OS refuses to participate.

where δ acts as an extra buffer against irregular delays. We then check if

$$(1 + \delta) \cdot R_{e2e} < R_{min} \tag{3}$$

is satisfied, which, therefore, proves that the packets could not have possibly transmitted through F. Otherwise, one cannot decipher if the packets traversed the F or simply suffered a delay. We now present our never-once design for onion services and how it incorporates these computations, referencing the steps in Fig. 2.

The DeTor$_{OS}$ never-once function, when loaded and executed by a client on a Bento server, first accepts both client- and onion service-side circuits. In other words, a client Alice, who wishes to communicate with Bob's onion service, would first send her entry and middle nodes and the RP to the DeTor$_{OS}$ function that she has uploaded to a Bento server, along with her desired forbidden regions. Simultaneously, Bob would also send his part of the circuit, comprising of his entry, middle, and exit nodes to the DeTor$_{OS}$ function (*Step 1*). The DeTor$_{OS}$ function then performs the aforementioned never-once computations for the forbidden region as specified by the client (*Step 2*). The function then attests to whether Alice's communication with Bob would avoid the forbidden region as specified by her (*Step 3*). Alice would then receive an attestation of avoidance. Alice and Bob communicate normally after a successful attestation (*Step 4*). This realizes our Bento-*side computation* model.

Optionally, Alice and Bob may also choose to perform the never-once computations locally (the *local computation* model), and then only upload the result of this in *Step 2*. This trades off trust in the DeTor$_{OS}$ function and Bento server (as neither party needs to send their circuit information now) for increased computation (as they must now do the calculations on their own).

3.3   DeTor$_{OS}$ Never-Twice function

The main objective of the never-twice avoidance technique is to gain assurance that a packet or its response could not have passed a user-specified forbidden country C on both the entry (C_e) and exit legs (C_x) of the Tor circuit. To prove this case, one needs to verify that the entry (focal point s and e and radius $\frac{3}{c} \cdot (R_{e2e} - R_m) - D(x,t)$, where $R_m = \frac{3}{c} \cdot D(e,m,x)$) and exit leg (focal point x and t and radius $\frac{3}{c} \cdot (R_{e2e} - R_m) - D(s,e)$) ellipses do not intersect, thereby, denying the possibility for the same country to have been traversed twice. If these entry and exit leg ellipses intersect then one must additionally verify the following condition to prove that same countries were not traversed twice.

$$\forall F \in C_e \cap C_x : (1+\delta) \cdot R_{e2e} < \frac{3}{c} \cdot (D_{min}(s,F,e) + D(e,m,x) + D_{min}(x,F,t)) \tag{4}$$

Similar to never-once, we accomplish never-twice avoidance for onion services by building it as a function that is uploaded to a Bento server. The DeTor$_{OS}$ never-twice function first accepts both the entry legs of the client- and onion service-side circuits (*Step 1*). The DeTor$_{OS}$ function then computes the set of

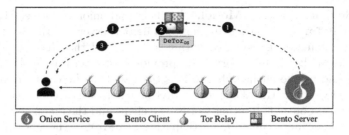

Fig. 2. The DeTor$_{OS}$ Protocol for never-once and never-twice avoidance. Both parties send their circuit information to a **Bento** server which is running the DeTor$_{OS}$ function. The server then computes the desired avoidance proof and sends it to the client. If successful, the client then begins communicating with the onion service.

countries that Alice and Bob's entry legs could have gone through (*Step 2*), and then returns the intersection of the two sets (*Step 3*). Alice then receives the intersection. If this intersection is empty, Alice and Bob communicate normally (*Step 4*), otherwise Alice can choose to run never-once for the countries in the intersection to gain additional information.

In the case of the *local computation* model, the client and onion service each compute the set of countries that the entry legs of their circuits go through and upload these sets to the function (*Step 2*), which then computes the intersection.

3.4 Ensuring Correctness of Input Data

As we do assume the **Bento** operator (i.e., the host Tor node and other networking infrastructure) itself can be malicious, we must also ensure that the correct data and circuit information is able to reach our DeTor$_{OS}$ function, and that a corrupt operator cannot substitute it for their own data and thus corrupt the enclave calculations. We can achieve this by simply having the client and OS both establish a TLS connection with the DeTor$_{OS}$ function (running in the protected enclave[3]) prior to passing in the circuit information, thus allowing them to pass all data directly to the enclave and DeTor$_{OS}$ through this secure channel. This can be done as part of the initial (pre-computation) setup process, in addition to the optional attestation process which ensures both client and OS that the **Bento** node is patched and up-to-date. This additional communication does not alter or affect anything with the underlying Tor protocol, as all information is just passed as data through established Tor circuits to the **Bento** node.

4   Security Analysis

In this section, we discuss the security implications of our proposal and argue that it inherits strong guarantees of correctness, confidentiality, and integrity from its design.

---

[3] That has been provisioned with a TLS certificate as part of the **Bento** setup.

Bento-Side Computation Model. The client and onion service send their circuits to the $DeTor_{OS}$ function running on a `Bento` server. By the `Bento` design, the $DeTor_{OS}$ function is executed within a TEE, and the server is, therefore, unable to learn the circuit information provided (or even the result of the calculation). And as the client only receives the result of the calculation, neither the onion service nor the client learn anything new about each other beyond the computation output. In other words, the client and the onion service do not compromise their anonymity by participating in $DeTor_{OS}$ (beyond the obvious and unavoidable fact that in never-once the client learns that the onion service cannot be in the forbidden region).

It is worth noting that a curious client could try to use this fact to attempt to locate an onion service. Through numerous never-once queries with different forbidden regions, a client can attempt to learn which regions an onion service might be near based on what regions it cannot avoid. To thwart such an attack, one could envision extending the never-once function in such a way that it is able to let an onion service know if a single client has made numerous never-once queries about it; the onion service could then choose not to participate in future never-once queries to protect its privacy. We leave such an extension for future work at this time, but discuss potential solutions in more depth in Sect. 6.

Local Computation Model. In our second scenario, much of the sensitive computation is done on the client and onion service respectively, which allows all involved parties to never need to export their circuit information to anyone. For never-once avoidance, the client and the onion service calculate never-once on their own circuits and send only the result of this computation (a boolean which denotes whether avoidance was achieved or not) to the `Bento` server. Thus even if the `Bento` server was not using a TEE, it only learns the boolean values and the result of the AND. This decreases the level of trust required in the $DeTor_{OS}$ function, but comes at a cost of increased computation for both parties involved. In never-twice avoidance, even though much of the computation is done client-side on the respective circuits, we still rely on the `Bento` server to compute the intersection of the countries and return the result. Thus we again lean on the fact that our $DeTor_{OS}$ function will be running in a TEE, protecting the confidentiality of any data.

Integrity and Correctness. The final important properties that we must guarantee are integrity of the data and correctness of the avoidance computation. We again rely heavily on the guarantees provided to us by the programmable `Bento` architecture. Because $DeTor_{OS}$ is running within a TEE on a `Bento` node, data (such as circuit and relay information) is protected from any tampering by the middlebox operator. This model also allows both the client and onion service to be assured of the correctness of the computation on the given data, as the $DeTor_{OS}$ function must be correctly executed. Additionally, we must ensure the correctness of the inputs to the avoidance computation. As both the client and OS have established a TLS connection that terminates inside the enclave where the $DeTor_{OS}$ function is running, this provides a secure channel for both to transfer information to DeTor$_{OS}$ while preventing tampering by the node operator.

5   Evaluation

In this section, we present the evaluation of DeTor$_{OS}$ for both never-once and never-twice avoidance. We aim to show that these techniques are feasible for 6-hop circuits, that is, that even with these provable avoidance techniques in place, a client still is able to (easily) find a circuit to connect to the onion service. For both never-once and never-twice avoidance, we use the same experimental setup and dataset as Li et al. [17], i.e., choosing our source-destination pairs from the Ting set of 50 relays and utilizing their latency measurements [4], but we do so for circuits with 6 hops to replicate the connection to a Tor onion service. Because adding three extra hops to a circuit exponentially increases the number of possible circuits to test[4], we elect to randomly sample one million circuits per source-destination pair (where each end of these pairs resides in a different country) rather than evaluating every possible circuit. We assume that Bento nodes have roughly the same geographic distribution as regular Tor relays.

5.1   Never-Once

We evaluate how successful DeTor$_{OS}$ is at avoiding various regions around the world, using a δ of 0.5 (recall that δ is a user configurable value $0 \leq \delta \leq 1$ where the higher the δ, the fewer potential compliant circuits will exist because of the higher burden of proof of avoidance). We do so by considering eight countries that are either very prominent for being on common routes, have many Tor relays, or are known to practice censorship, and comparing their success rates for the source-destination pair. Note that except for China, Japan, and North Korea, our results (i.e. success/failure) are proportional to [17], even if the overall success rates are slightly lower due to the 6-hop architecture.

We present our success rates in Fig. 3. Each bar represents, for one of the aforementioned forbidden regions, the fraction of source-destination pairs that: successfully avoid the forbidden region over at least one circuit (*green*); terminate in the forbidden region and thus cannot achieve provable avoidance (*black*); and circuits that fail provable avoidance with real RTTs (although they theoretically avoid the forbidden region) (*red*).

Overall, our success rates are slightly lower than for DeTor's original evaluation over three-hop circuits. This is to be expected though. In the onion service setting, we are traversing six hops, and adding more hops in the circuit increases the chances that it will cross a forbidden region. Additionally, because of the extra time it takes for a packet to cross the six hop circuit, we are less certain of a circuit's ability to avoid the forbidden region. The fact that we are able

---

[4] Since there are 50 possible Tor relays in the dataset and we choose 6 without replacement, this gives us over 36 billion circuits, which was infeasible to evaluate for never-once.

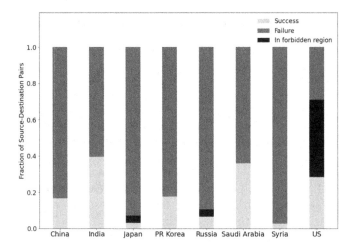

Fig. 3. Success of DeTor$_{OS}$ at never-once avoidance of various forbidden regions. Each bar represents the avoidance rate of the given country for the one million sampled source-destination pairs.

to achieve even modest success rates for many forbidden regions is surprisingly positive. It is also worth noting that as we randomly sampled circuits to achieve a feasible experimental setup, this dataset is a small fraction of the actual Tor relays that are deployed today. Because the overall Tor network is denser and has a larger diversity of hosts, we anticipate that DeTor$_{OS}$ will actually perform much better in practice.

We also note that the Ting dataset is modeled based on the real configuration of the Tor network (albeit a slightly older configuration). This, of course, means that a large portion of this dataset has relays that reside in locations like the United States and Europe. As a result of this, it is difficult to, for example, find circuits that avoid the United States. However, it is worth noting that of the circuits where the entry and exit node are not in the United States, DeTor$_{OS}$ avoids the United States around 50% of the time, which is quite encouraging.

5.2   Never-Twice

We evaluate how successful DeTor$_{OS}$ is at never-twice avoidance by generating candidate circuits for our one million previously sampled source-destination pairs from the Ting dataset [4] where both the source and destination are in different countries, as never-twice is impossible when the source and destination nodes are in the same country.

We then sample 1000 circuits from each source-destination pair and see if they can provide a proof of never-twice avoidance. Doing this showed that 72.4% of our sampled source-destination pairs have a successful proof of never-twice avoidance. While this number is very encouraging, it too is lower than in DeTor's original three-hop experiments (which achieved about 98% success rates for a similar never-twice avoidance experiment). This, too, is expected; with the extra three nodes added to a circuit, if the ellipses' of a circuit's entry and exit legs go through at least one common country, the added round trip time due to various network factors increases the difficulty of providing a proof of avoidance. We also hypothesize that we would have better performance if deployed on the live Tor network as the set of clients and destinations are exponentially greater than the combinations within the dataset.

5.3 Performance

We finish our evaluation by briefly discussing the performance of $\texttt{DeTor}_{OS}$ and its potential impacts on latency.

The use of $\texttt{DeTor}_{OS}$ will add additional connection establishment latency for a user who wishes to run it before they connect to an onion service. To test this, we ran our $\texttt{DeTor}_{OS}$ function ten times on a $\texttt{Bento}$ node running in the US, using randomly generated circuits with actual Tor relays, with a client located in the US and an OS located in Germany. On average, it took 64.85 s for our function to compute the never-once avoidance proof. While this time is not insignificant, as our function must take various network timing measurements for six Tor relays and then also compute the avoidance proof, we note that a user will only need to run this once for a specific circuit/OS pair (and that it often takes this long to access an onion service itself even without these computations). Besides the additional computational overhead incurred by using $\texttt{DeTor}_{OS}$ to verify never-once or never-twice for both the onion service and the client, there is next to no additional latency involved. In fact, as observed in [17], because circuits with a lower round trip time are more likely to be $\texttt{DeTor}_{OS}$ compliant, there is likely less latency than if the client were to use a Tor generated circuit to connect to the onion service.

A potential source of additional performance overhead (and hence latency) is the use of $\texttt{Bento}$ (and hence conclaves and SGX) to realize $\texttt{DeTor}_{OS}$. We note that the overhead induced by this should be nominal on $\texttt{DeTor}_{OS}$ itself. SGX runs computations at essentially native speed, which means that it has little effect on the performance of $\texttt{DeTor}_{OS}$ computations. The largest overhead incurred for this model is context switching, and a comprehensive analysis of conclaves and SGX overhead in [7] demonstrated that this overhead was reasonable for even a CDN-like latency sensitive application[5]. As such, we believe that such minimal overhead should not be impactful or add to the overall latency induced by $\texttt{DeTor}_{OS}$.

6   Discussion and Future Work

Provable geographic avoidance for onion services was once thought to be impossible, since no one entity was able to safely know and evaluate every hop on

---

[5] Given this, we do not repeat similar experiments here and instead refer the interested reader to [7,22] for more information.

the path. We have demonstrated that through the application of secure, programmable middleboxes, provable avoidance is possible and surprisingly effective. We believe this opens up several interesting and immediate avenues for future work.

First, our current protocol only operates under the honest-but-curious model, assuming that the onion service correctly reports its path to the DeTor_{OS} function and does not lie to the client or try to actively subvert the protocol in some way. While in practice there are likely large numbers of honest onion services that are deployed to benefit users and will follow such a protocol, and we believe it is valuable to demonstrate that geographical avoidance is possible at all with onion services, we also desire our geographical avoidance protocol to work in the face of active adversarial involvement. While this could be trivially addressed by also requiring a TEE on the onion service side that could directly communicate with the `Bento` function, this is a strong assumption that we would like to avoid. Without the use of TEEs, this seems like a challenging problem to address, and one that might involve inherent changes to the underlying DeTor_{OS} protocol and computations.

Second, we inherit the use of TEEs from the design of `Bento` and rely on them to ensure the privacy and correctness of the computations. While we have seen a number of attacks on TEEs thus far, we have also seen TEE vendors provide patches and updates for all such attacks, and remote attestation mechanisms allow for users to gain assurance that a computer is fully patched against all known vulnerabilities. However, we still briefly discuss the impacts of a TEE compromise on DeTor_{OS} . Since we rely on the TEE for both correctness and confidentiality, a breach would likely harm both of these properties, resulting in the potential leakage of circuit information to the node operator and a weakening of the correctness guarantees of the computations. This is where the difference in the `Bento`-side versus local computation model can be beneficial, as the information leakage can be minimized with local computation (though we still lose strong correctness guarantees on the returned result). As such, an interesting avenue of future work would be to explore mechanisms, such as multi-party computation, that would allow us to still leverage the idea of programmable anonymity networks, without relying on the need for TEEs.

Third, as we discussed briefly in Sect. 4, our current protocol does not protect an onion service from a malicious client that wishes to try to deanonymize it through repeated queries about avoidance of distinct geographic regions. We envision that one simple way to mitigate this would be to extend the DeTor_{OS} function to track the number of times a user invokes it with regards to a specific onion service, and either rate-limit queries or notify the onion service of repeated queries, allowing it to decide whether to participate in the protocol or now. One way to achieve this rate-limiting in a privacy-preserving manner would be through issuing k-show anonymous credentials [6,24]. A client wishing to visit an onion service would then first obtain an anonymous credential (which refreshes every day) from the issuer (which could be a `Bento` server). The client would then show this anonymous token every time she wants to execute DeTor_{OS}. This limits the client's access to the onion service since the client can execute $DeTor_{OS}$ only k times per day. However, as the $DeTor_{OS}$ function is user-controlled, the onion service itself would also need to, through the Bento attestation process or other mechanism, ensure itself that the deployed function it is interacting with contains these protections. Another interesting piece of future work would be to investigate if there are other avenues to thwart such an attack.

Fourth, while the results of both never-once and never-twice for $DeTor_{OS}$ are promising, it is critical to come up with ways to reduce the additional latency added by adding the three extra hops required to connect to a hidden service. It is also imperative to find new ways to speed up the calculations that $DeTor_{OS}$ (and the original detor paper [17]) use in order to reduce the computational overhead required.

Finally, taking a step back, Bento's programmable middleboxes made provable avoidance possible by outsourcing a sensitive computation to a mutually trusted third party. We wonder: what other services could be run in a similar fashion? Perhaps it is possible to build disaggregated services on top of a programmable anonymity network by disseminating pieces of code across the network, so that even if one part of it is compromised other parts can replicate and recover. Perhaps it is possible to randomize where any computation in the network occurs, so that the onion service is hidden even from the user who is running it. Our hope is that this work spurs such considerations, and to assist in future work we have made our code publicly available[6].

7   Ethical Considerations

All of the data in our experiments comprised only our own traffic: not any actual users' data. Our never-once performance evaluation was performed on the actual Tor network. However, this only involved collecting latency times for various nodes and circuits on the network, and data was gathered in a rate-limited fashion to ensure that our experiments would not impact the performance of the Tor network. Also, we deployed both our own Tor node and Bento node, which was limited to only our own traffic so as not to affect the larger Tor network.

8   Conclusion

In this work we present $DeTor_{OS}$, the first technique that is able to provide provable geographic avoidance for onion services. We achieve this by leveraging recent advances in programmable anonymity networks, which allow the user and onion service to jointly compute on their circuits, without leaking information to the other party. While we implement this work primarily with the Bento architecture, we believe the overall design of $DeTor_{OS}$ can be used with any architecture that supports such programmability in anonymity networks [23]. We showed that our design and implementation is able to achieve never-once and

---

[6] https://bento.cs.umd.edu.

never-twice avoidance at rates that are encouraging. We also discuss a number of avenues of future work that this first deployment opens up.

Acknowledgments. We thank the anonymous reviewers for their helpful comments. Arushi Arora and Christina Garman's work was partially supported by NSF grant CNS-1816422. Dave Levin's work was partially supported by NSF grant CNS-1943240.

References

1. Anati, I., Gueron, S., Johnson, S., Scarlata, V.: Innovative technology for CPU based attestation and sealing. In: International Workshop on Hardware and Architectural Support for Security and Privacy (HASP) (2013)
2. ARM security technology: building a secure system using TrustZone technology. http://infocenter.arm.com/help/topic/com.arm.doc.prd29-genc-009492c/PRD29-GENC-009492C_trustzone_security_whitepaper.pdf
3. Arp, D., Yamaguchi, F., Rieck, K.: Torben: a practical side-channel attack for deanonymizing tor communication. In: Proceedings of the 10th ACM Symposium on Information, Computer and Communications Security, pp. 597–602 (2015)
4. Cangialosi, F., Levin, D., Spring, N.: Ting: measuring and exploiting latencies between all tor nodes. In: Proceedings of the 2015 Internet Measurement Conference, pp. 289–302 (2015)
5. Dingledine, R., Mathewson, N., Syverson, P.: Tor: the second-generation onion router. Technical report (2004)
6. Garman, C., Green, M., Miers, I.: Decentralized anonymous credentials. Cryptology ePrint Archive (2013)
7. Herwig, S., Garman, C., Levin, D.: Achieving keyless CDNs with conclaves. In: USENIX Security Symposium (2020)
8. Intel: L1 Terminal Fault (2018). http://software.intel.com/content/www/us/en/develop/articles/software-security-guidance/advisory-guidance/l1-terminal-fault.html
9. Jansen, R., Tschorsch, F., Johnson, A., Scheuermann, B.: The sniper attack: anonymously deanonymizing and disabling the tor network. Techncial report, Office of Naval Research Arlington VA (2014)
10. Johnson, A., Wacek, C., Jansen, R., Sherr, M., Syverson, P.: Users get routed: traffic correlation on tor by realistic adversaries. In: Proceedings of the 2013 ACM SIGSAC Conference on Computer and Communications Security, pp. 337–348 (2013)
11. Johnson, S., Scarlata, V., Rozas, C., Brickell, E., Mckeen, F.: Intel Software Guard Extensions: EPID Provisioning and Attestation Services (2016)
12. Karunanayake, I., Ahmed, N., Malaney, R., Islam, R., Jha, S.: Anonymity with tor: a survey on tor attacks. arXiv preprint arXiv:2009.13018 (2020)
13. Kohls, K., Jansen, K., Rupprecht, D., Holz, T., Pöpper, C.: On the challenges of geographical avoidance for tor. In: Network and Distributed System Security Symposium (NDSS) (2019)
14. Kwon, A., AlSabah, M., Lazar, D., Dacier, M., Devadas, S.: Circuit fingerprinting attacks: passive deanonymization of tor hidden services. In: USENIX Security Symposium (2015)
15. Levin, D., et al.: Alibi routing. ACM SIGCOMM Comput. Commun. Rev. (2015)

16. Levis, P.: The collateral damage of internet censorship by DNS injection. ACM SIGCOMM CCR **42**(3), 10–1145 (2012)
17. Li, Z., Herwig, S., Levin, D.: Detor: Provably avoiding geographic regions in tor. In: USENIX Security Symposium (2017)
18. Nasr, M., Bahramali, A., Houmansadr, A.: DeepCorr: strong flow correlation attacks on tor using deep learning. In: Proceedings of the 2018 ACM SIGSAC Conference on Computer and Communications Security, pp. 1962–1976 (2018)
19. Nebuchadnezzar, H.: The collateral damage of internet censorship by DNS injection. ACM SIGCOMM CCR **42**(3), 10–1145 (2012)
20. Overlier, L., Syverson, P.: Locating hidden servers. In: IEEE Symposium on Security and Privacy (2006)
21. Project, T.T.: Tor Manual (2022). http://2019.www.torproject.org/docs/tor-manual.html.en
22. Reininger, M., et al.: Bento: safely bringing network function virtualization to tor. In: ACM SIGCOMM (2021)
23. Rochet, F., Bonaventure, O., Pereira, O.: Flexible anonymous network. arXiv preprint arXiv:1906.11520 (2019)
24. Rosenberg, M., White, J., Garman, C., Miers, I.: zk-creds: Flexible anonymous credentials from zksnarks and existing identity infrastructure. Cryptology ePrint Archive (2022)
25. Ryan, M.J., Chowdhury, M., Jiang, F., Doss, R.: Avoiding geographic regions in tor. In: 2020 IEEE 19th International Conference on Trust, Security and Privacy in Computing and Communications (TrustCom) (2020)
26. Schuchard, M., Geddes, J., Thompson, C., Hopper, N.: Routing around decoys. In: Proceedings of the 2012 ACM Conference on Computer and Communications Security, pp. 85–96 (2012)
27. Wang, T., Cai, X., Nithyanand, R., Johnson, R., Goldberg, I.: Effective attacks and provable defenses for website fingerprinting. In: USENIX Security Symposium (2014)

Decentralized Finance

R2: Boosting Liquidity in Payment Channel Networks with Online Admission Control

Mahsa Bastankhah[1]($\boxtimes$)(ID), Krishnendu Chatterjee[2](ID),
Mohammad Ali Maddah-Ali[3](ID), Stefan Schmid[4](ID), Jakub Svoboda[2](ID),
and Michelle Yeo[2](ID)

[1] Sharif University of Technology, Tehran, Iran
mahsa.bastankhah@ee.sharif.edu
[2] ISTA, Klosterneuburg, Austria
[3] University of Minnesota Twin Cities, Minneapolis, USA
[4] TU Berlin, Berlin, Germany

Abstract. Payment channel networks (PCNs) are a promising technology to improve the scalability of cryptocurrencies. PCNs, however, face the challenge that the frequent usage of certain routes may deplete channels in one direction, and hence prevent further transactions. In order to reap the full potential of PCNs, recharging and rebalancing mechanisms are required to provision channels, as well as an admission control logic to decide which transactions to reject in case capacity is insufficient. This paper presents a formal model of this optimisation problem. In particular, we consider an online algorithms perspective, where transactions arrive over time in an unpredictable manner. Our main contributions are competitive online algorithms which come with provable guarantees over time. We empirically evaluate our algorithms on randomly generated transactions to compare the average performance of our algorithms to our theoretical bounds. We also show how this model and approach differs from related problems in classic communication networks.

1 Introduction

Blockchain consensus protocols are notoriously inefficient: for instance, Bitcoin can only support 7 transactions per second on average which makes it unrealistic to use in everyday situations. Payment channel networks like Bitcoin's Lightning Network [17] and Ethereum's Raiden [1] have been proposed as scalability solutions to blockchains. Instead of sending transactions to the blockchain and waiting for the entire blockchain (which can comprise of millions of users) to achieve consensus, any two users that wish to transact with each other can simply open a payment channel between themselves. Opening a payment channel requires an initial funding transaction on the blockchain where both users lock some funds only to use in the channel. Once a payment channel is opened, the channel acts as a local, two-party ledger: payments between the users of channel simply involve decreasing the balance of the payer by the payment amount, and

© International Financial Cryptography Association 2024
F. Baldimtsi and C. Cachin (Eds.): FC 2023, LNCS 13950, pp. 309–325, 2024.
https://doi.org/10.1007/978-3-031-47754-6_18

increasing the balance of the payee correspondingly. As these local transactions only involve exchanging signatures between the two users and do not involve the blockchain at all, they can be almost instantaneous. As long as there is sufficient balance, payments can occur indefinitely between two users, until the users decide to close the channel. This would involve going back to the blockchain and takes, in the worst case, a small constant number of transactions. Thus, with only a small constant number of on-chain transactions, any two users can potentially make arbitrarily many costless transactions between themselves.

Apart from joining a payment channel network to efficiently transact with other users, an additional financial incentive to joining the network is to profit from forwarding transactions. Any two users that are not directly connected can transact with each other in a multi-hop fashion as long as they are connected by a path of payment channels. To incentivise the intermediary nodes on the path to forward the payment, the network typically allows these nodes to charge a transaction fee. Thus, it is common for users to join the network specifically to play the role of an intermediary node that routes transactions, creating channels and fees optimally and selecting the most profitable transactions to maximise their profit from transaction fees [4,10].

However, greedily accepting and routing incoming transactions could rapidly deplete a user's balance in their channels. In particular, if certain routes are primarily used in one direction, their channels can get depleted, making it impossible to forward further transactions. Accounting for this problem can be non-trivial since demand patterns are hard to predict and often confidential.

To resolve this issue, PCNs typically support two mechanisms:

- *On-chain recharging:* A user can close and reopen a depleted channel with more funds on-chain.
- *Off-chain rebalancing:* An alternative solution is to extend the lifetime of a depleted channel without involving the blockchain, by finding a cycle of payment channels in the network to shift funds from one channel to another.

Both cases, however, entail a cost. Intermediaries need to consider the tradeoff between admitting transactions and potential recharging and rebalancing costs. This decision making process is especially important to big routers which are the primary maintainers of payment channel networks like the Lightning Network.

In this work, we focus on the problem of admission control, recharging and rebalancing in a single payment channel from the perspective of an intermediary node that seeks to route as many transactions as possible with minimal costs. Specifically, we address the following research question:

Can we design efficient online algorithms for deciding when to accept/reject transactions, and when to recharge or rebalance in a single payment channel?

We seek to address this problem with as few restrictions on user actions in order to ensure that our work remains realistic. Thus, we assume a fixed PCN topology with some recharging and rebalancing costs, and a global fee function that is linear in the transaction size. We also assume users incur a rejection cost in the form of opportunity cost when they reject to route a transaction.

We are interested in robust solutions which do not depend on any knowledge or assumptions on the demand. Accordingly, we assume that transactions can arrive in an arbitrary order at a channel, and aim to design online algorithms which provide worst-case guarantees. We are in the realm of competitive analysis, and assume that an adversary with knowledge of our algorithms chooses the most pessimal online transaction sequence. Our objective is to optimise the *competitive ratio* [7]: we compare the performance of our online algorithms (to which the transaction sequence is revealed over time) with the optimal offline algorithm that has access to the entire transaction sequence in advance.

1.1   Our Contributions

We initiate the study of a fundamental resource allocation problem in payment channel networks, from an online algorithms perspective. Our main result is a competitive online algorithm to admit transaction streams arriving at both sides of a payment channel, and also to recharge and rebalance the channel, in order to maximise the throughput over the channel while accounting for costs. In particular, our algorithm achieves a competitive ratio of $7 + 2\lceil \log C \rceil$ where $C + 1$ is the length of the rebalancing cycle used to replenish the funds on the channel off-chain. We also provide lower bounds on the amount of funds needed in a channel in order to ensure our algorithm is c-competitive for $c < \frac{\log C}{\log \log C}$.

In order to prove our main theorem, we decompose the problem into two simpler sub problems that may also be of independent interest:

1. *Sub problem 1:* The first and most restrictive sub problem considers a transaction stream coming only from one direction across a payment channel, and users do not have the option to reject incoming transactions. We present a 2-competitive algorithm for this problem, which is optimal in the sense that no deterministic online algorithm can achieve a lower competitive ratio.
2. *Sub problem 2:* As a relaxation, our second sub problem allows users to reject transactions although all transactions are still restricted to come from one direction along a payment channel. We show that our algorithm achieves a competitive ratio of $2 + \frac{\sqrt{5}-1}{2}$ for this sub problem. We stress that our lower bound of 2 we achieve in sub problem 1 also holds in this sub problem, hence our competitive ratio of $2 + \frac{\sqrt{5}-1}{2}$ is close to optimal.

All intermediate and main results are summarised in Table 1. The algorithms and analysis designed to address these sub problems are eventually used as building blocks for our main algorithm and main theorem.

We complement our theoretical worst-case analysis by performing an empirical evaluation of the performance of our algorithm on randomly generated transaction sequences. We observe that our algorithms perform much better on average compared to our theoretical worst-case bound.

Table 1. Summary of the theoretical results in our paper. The first column presents each sub problem we analyse in our paper and the second column shows the competitive ratio achieved by our algorithms for each sub problem

Sub problem	Competitive ratio
Unidirectional stream without rejection	2
Unidirectional stream with rejection	$2 + \frac{\sqrt{5}-1}{2}$
Bidirectional stream	$7 + 2\lceil \log C \rceil$

1.2   Related Work

Maintaining Balanced Payment Channels. As channel balances are typically private, classic transaction routing protocols on payment channel networks like Flare [18], SilentWhispers [15] and SpeedyMurmurs [19] focus mainly on throughput and ignore the issue of balance depletion. Recently, several works shift the focus on maintaining balanced payment channels for as long as possible while ensuring liveness of the network. Revive [12] initiated the study rebalancing strategies, Spider [21] uses multi-path routing to ensure high transaction throughput while maintaining balanced payment channels, the Merchant [9] utilises fee strategies to incentivise the balanced use of payment channels, and [13] uses estimated payment demands along channels to plan the amount of funds to inject into a channel during channel creation, to just give a few examples. Our work focuses on minimising costs incurred in the process of handling transactions across a channel and thus we also indirectly seek to maintain balanced payment channels. Moreover, in contrast to previous works which typically assume some form of offline knowledge of the transaction flow in the network, we provide an algorithm which comes with provable worst-case guarantees.

Off-Chain Rebalancing. Off-chain rebalancing has been studied as a cheaper alternative to refunding a channel by closing and reopening it on the blockchain. In the Lightning Network, there are already several off-chain rebalancing plugins for c-lightning[1] and lnd[2]. An automated approach to performing off-chain rebalancing using the imbalance measure as a heuristic has been proposed in [16]. Our work similarly studies when to rebalance payment channels, however we make the decision in tandem with other decisions like accepting or rejecting transactions. Recently, [5] and [12] propose a global approach to off-chain rebalancing where demand for rebalancing cycles is aggregated across the entire network and translated to an LP which is subsequently solved to obtain an optimal rebalancing solution. These approaches are orthogonal and complementary to ours as our focus concerns decision making in a single payment channel and not the entire network.

---

[1] https://github.com/lightningd/plugins/tree/master/rebalance.
[2] https://github.com/bitromortac/lndmanage.

Online Algorithms for Payment Channel Networks. Online algorithms for payment channel networks have also been studied in [3] and [11]. Avarikioti et al. [3] establish impossibility results against certain classes of adversaries, however they only consider a limited problem setting where their algorithms can only accept or reject transactions (with constant rejection cost). Fazli et al. [11] considers the problem of optimally scheduling on-chain recharging given a sequence of transactions. In contrast to previous work, our work considers a more general problem setting where our algorithms can not only accept or reject transactions, but also recharge and rebalance channels off chain. We also extend the cost of rejection to take into account the size of the transaction.

Relationship to Classic Communication Networks. Admission control problems such as online call admission [2,14] are fundamental and have also received much attention in the context of communication networks. However, in classic communication networks the available capacity of a link in one direction is independent of the flows travelling in the other direction, and moreover, link capacities are only consumed by the currently allocated flows. In contrast, the capacities of links in payment-channel networks are permanently reduced by transactions flowing in one direction, but can be topped up by flows travelling in the other direction. The resulting rebalancing opportunity renders the underlying algorithmic problem significantly different.

2   Model

Payment Channels. We model the payment channel network as an undirected graph $G = (V, E)$. A payment channel between users ℓ (left) and r (right) in the network is an edge $(\ell, r) \in E$. We denote the balance of user ℓ (resp. r) in the channel (ℓ, r) by $b(\ell)$ (resp. $b(r)$). The *capacity* of the channel is the total amount of funds locked in the channel. That is, for a channel (ℓ, r), the capacity of (ℓ, r) is $b(\ell) + b(r)$. A left-to-right transaction of amount x decreases ℓ's balance by x and increases r's balance by x and vice versa for a right-to-left transaction of x.

Recharging and Rebalancing Payment Channels. When a user in a channel does not have sufficient funds to accept a transaction, the user can either reject the transaction, recharge the channel, or rebalance the channel. Recharging the channel happens on-chain and corresponds to closing the payment channel on the blockchain and opening a new channel with more funds. In contrast, rebalancing the channel happens entirely off-chain (refer to Fig. 1 for an example). Here, users find a cycle of payment channels to shift funds from one of their other channels to refund the depleted channel.

Transactions. We consider a transaction sequence $X_t = (x_1, ..., x_t)$, $x_i \in \mathbb{R}^+$, that arrives at a payment channel online. Each transaction x_i has both a value and a direction along a payment channel. The value of a transaction is simply the amount that is being transferred. The direction of a transaction across a payment channel (ℓ, r) determines who is the sender and who is the receiver. When we have a sequence of transactions that go in both directions along a payment channel, we use $\vec{x}$ to denote a transaction that goes from left-to-right and $\overleftarrow{x}$ to denote a transaction that goes from right-to-left. We say a user, wlog ℓ, *accepts* a transaction of size x coming from the left to right direction along the channel (ℓ, r) if ℓ agrees to forward x to r. Similarly, we say a user ℓ *rejects* a transaction x coming from the left to right direction along the channel (ℓ, r) when ℓ does not forward the transaction to r. When it is clear which channel and direction we are referring to, we simply say ℓ accepts or rejects x.

Costs. We consider three types of costs in our problem setting:

1. **Rejecting transactions:** For a user ℓ, the revenue in terms of transaction fees from forwarding a payment of size x is $Rx + f_2$, where $R, f_2 \in \mathbb{R}^+$. Consequently, the cost of rejecting a transaction of size x is simply the opportunity cost of gaining revenue from accepting the transaction, i.e. $Rx + f_2$.
2. **On-chain recharging:** For any user ℓ, the cost of recharging a channel on-chain is $F + f_1$, where F is some function of the amount of funds ℓ puts into the new channel (this captures the opportunity cost of locking in the funds in the channel) and $f_1 \in \mathbb{R}^+$ is an auxiliary cost independent of F which captures the on-chain recharging transaction fee.
3. **Off-chain rebalancing:** For any user ℓ, the cost of off-chain rebalancing for an amount x is $C \cdot (Rx + f_2)$, where C is the length of the cycle along which funds are sent -1. In the example of off-chain rebalancing in Fig. 1, the length of the rebalancing cycle is 3 and thus $C = 2$.

Let us denote by OFF the optimal offline algorithm and ON an online deterministic algorithm. We denote by $\text{COST}_{\text{ON}}(X_t)$ (resp. $\text{COST}_{\text{OFF}}(X_t)$) the total cost of ON (resp. OFF) given the transaction sequence X_t.

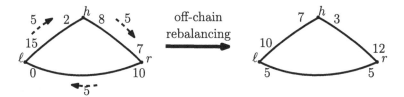

Fig. 1. Example of off-chain rebalancing with users ℓ, h, and r. The graph on the right depicts the channel balances after off-chain rebalancing.

Competitive Ratio. We say an online algorithm ON is *c-competitive* if for every transaction sequence X_t generated by the adversary,

$$\text{COST}_{\text{ON}}(X_t) \leq c \cdot \text{COST}_{\text{OFF}}(X_t)$$

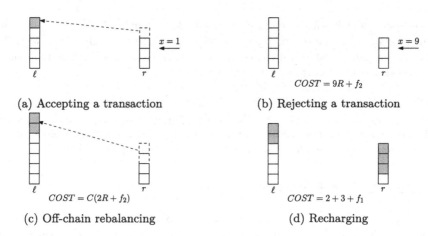

(a) Accepting a transaction   (b) Rejecting a transaction

(c) Off-chain rebalancing   (d) Recharging

Fig. 2. Example of actions users ℓ and r can take in the general bidirectional stream setting. Each square represents 1 coin.

Main Problem. Our main problem is to design a competitive deterministic online algorithm that determines when to accept/reject transactions and when to recharge or rebalance the channel given a bidirectional stream of transactions across a payment channel. More precisely, we consider a stream of transactions that can arrive from both right to left or left to right in a given payment channel (ℓ, r). ℓ (resp. r) can choose to accept or reject transactions coming in the left-to-right (resp. right-to-left) direction in the stream. Either user would incur a cost of $Rx + f_2$ for rejecting a transaction of size x. Both users can also recharge the channel on-chain at any point, incurring a cost of $F_\ell + F_r + f_1$ where F_ℓ and F_r are functions of the funds put into the channel by ℓ and r respectively. Since transactions are streaming in both directions in this model, both users would incur costs in this setting. Thus, we seek to design an algorithm that minimises the cost of the *entire* channel. Refer to Fig. 2 for examples of the actions that a user can take in our main bidirectional transaction stream setting.

To this end, we give a formal definition of two sub problems of decreasing restrictiveness on user actions. We present these sub problems as the algorithms and analysis used to solve these sub problems are used in developing the algorithm and analysis for our main problem.

Unidirectional Stream without Rejection. In this model, transactions stream only in one direction along a given payment channel. Here, we assume users cannot reject incoming transactions. Formally, given a channel (ℓ, r) and a transaction stream from wlog left to right, user ℓ only accepts a transaction x if $b(\ell) > x$. Otherwise, ℓ has to recharge the channel on-chain with more funds, incurring a cost of $F + f_1$ where F is some function of the amount of funds ℓ adds to the channel. As we only consider transactions streaming in one direction, only one user would incur costs in this setting (the user that has to decide whether to accept or reject transactions). A real world example that motivates this setting is a company which wants to position itself as a "routing hub" in a payment channel network, providing a routing service in return for transaction fees. As such, the company would want to accept as many transactions possible to acquire the reputation of a hub that is constantly available.

Unidirectional Stream with Rejection. In this model, we still restrict the transaction stream from wlog left to right in a payment channel (ℓ, r). However, in addition to accepting transactions and recharging, ℓ can now also reject transactions, incurring a rejection cost of $Rx + f_2$ for a transaction of size x.

3   Algorithmic Building Blocks

Before we describe and analyse the performance of our algorithms in the various problem settings, we first introduce two algorithmic building blocks that we use extensively in our work. The first building block is an algorithm FUNDS. It takes a sequence of transactions as an input and returns the amount of funds that an optimal algorithm uses on this sequence. The purpose of the algorithm is to track the funds OFF has in their channel assuming that the sequence of transactions ends at this point. For the first two sub problems we show how to compute FUNDS. For the main problem, we propose a dynamic programming approach. The second building block is a general recharging online algorithm that calls FUNDS as a subroutine and uses the output to decide when and how much to recharge the channel. The intuition behind the recharging online algorithm is to recharge whenever the amount of funds in OFF's channel "catches up" to the amount of funds ON has in their channel.

Building Block 1: Tracking Funds of OFF. For a given transaction sequence $X_t = (x_1, \ldots, x_t)$, let us denote $A(X_i)$ to be the amount of funds OFF would use in the channel if OFF gets the sequence $X_i = (x_1, \ldots, x_i)$ (i.e. the length i prefix of X_t) as input. By appending subsequent transactions $x_{i+1}, \ldots, x_t$ from X_t to X_i, we can view $A(X_i)$ as a partial solution to the online optimisation problem that gets updated with any new transaction. In the unidirectional transaction stream (with or without rejection) setting, $A(X_i)$ refers to the funds a user locks into a payment channel. In the bidirectional transaction stream setting, $A(X_i)$ refers to the total balance of both users in the channel. We assume that given an input sequence X_t, FUNDS(X_t) performs the necessary computations and returns $A(X_t)$. For our main problem, computing FUNDS(X_t) is generally NP-hard, but we can approximate it to a constant factor, see [20] for more details.

Building Block 2: Using Tracking for Recharging. In Algorithm 1, we describe an online (γ, δ)-recharging algorithm ON that uses FUNDS as a subroutine to decide when and how much to recharge the channel. ON is run by one user (wlog ℓ) in a payment channel (ℓ, r). ON calls FUNDS after each transaction to check if the new transaction sequence results in a significant increase in the amount of funds OFF has in their channel. Whenever ON notices that OFF's funds have increased above a threshold (Line 4), ON recharges the channel with an amount of $\gamma(A(X_i) + \delta)$ where $A(X_i)$ is the amount of funds OFF has in their channel.

Algorithm 1: (γ, δ)-recharging

Initialise: $F_{tracker}, X \leftarrow 0, \emptyset$

1 **for** *transaction x in order of arrival* **do**
2 $\quad$ concatenate x to X
3 $\quad$ $F'_{tracker} \leftarrow$ Funds(X)
4 $\quad$ **if** $F'_{tracker} > F_{tracker}$ **then**
5 $\quad\quad$ $F_{tracker} \leftarrow F'_{tracker} + \delta$
6 $\quad\quad$ recharge to $\gamma F_{tracker}$

Let us denote $A_t := \max_{i \leq t} A(X_i)$. Now we state (proof in our extended version [6]) two important properties of the (γ, δ)-recharging algorithm.

Lemma 1. *Algorithm 1 with parameters* (γ, δ) *ensures that* ON *always has at least* γ *times the amount of funds* OFF *has and ensures that* ON *incurs a cost of at most* $\gamma(A_t + \delta) + f_1 \cdot \lceil \frac{A_t}{\delta} \rceil$.

Next, we show a simple lower bound in terms of A_t for the cost of OFF given a sequence of transactions X_t.

Lemma 2. *If* $A_t > 0$, *then* $\text{COST}_{\text{OFF}}(X_t)$ *is at least* $A_t + f_1$.

4 Unidirectional Transaction Stream Without Rejection

In this section we consider the first sub problem where, given a payment channel (ℓ, r), transactions stream along the channel in only one direction (wlog left to right). Moreover, ℓ has to accept an incoming transaction of size x and forward it to r if ℓ's balance $b(\ell) \geq x$. Otherwise, ℓ needs to recharge the channel on-chain (and accept the transaction after).

The optimal offline algorithm OFF follows a simple strategy: since it knows the entire stream of transactions in advance, it makes a single recharging action at the beginning of the transaction sequence X_t of size $\sum_{i=1}^{t} x_i$. The cost incurred by OFF is thus $f_1 + \sum_{i=1}^{t} x_i$.

Now, we present in Line 2 a 2-competitive online algorithm ON for this sub problem. ON uses (γ, δ)-recharging with parameters $\gamma = 1$ and $\delta = f_1$. The algorithm accepts all transactions and the recharging ensures that ON always has enough funds.

Theorem 1. *The algorithm described above is 2-competitive in the unidirectional transaction stream without rejection.*

In addition, we note that ON is optimal in this setting. The next theorem (proof in our extended version [6]) proves that no deterministic algorithm can achieve a strictly smaller competitive ratio compared to ON. In particular, our proof shows that ON cannot lock too much funds into the channel, otherwise ON's cost is too high, but if ON locks too little funds, it needs to recharge often.

Algorithm 2: Unidirectional transaction stream without rejection

Initialise: tracker $F_{tracker}, X \leftarrow 0, \emptyset$
Initialise: balance $b = 0$
1 **for** *transaction x in order of arrival* **do**
2   concatenate x to X
3     $F'_{tracker} \leftarrow \text{FUNDS}(X)$
4   **if** $F'_{tracker} > F_{tracker}$ **then**
5        $F_{tracker} \leftarrow F'_{tracker} + f_1$
6   recharge to $F_{tracker}$
7   Accept x

Theorem 2. *There is no deterministic algorithm that is c-competitive for $c < 2$ in the unidirectional transaction stream without rejection sub problem.*

5 Unidirectional Transaction Stream with Rejection

In this section we consider the second sub problem where transactions are still streaming along a given payment channel (ℓ, r) in one direction (wlog left to right). This time though, a user can choose to reject incoming transactions. We describe an algorithm Algorithm 3 with competitive ratio $2 + \frac{\sqrt{5}-1}{2}$. We note that the competitive ratio for this setting is larger than the competitive ratio we achieve in the previous setting as OFF has a wider range of decisions.

Let us call a transaction of size x *big* if $x > Rx + f_2$ and *small* otherwise. We first observe that OFF in this setting always rejects big transactions.

Lemma 3. OFF *rejects all big transactions in the unidirectional transaction stream with rejection.*

Thus, the strategy of OFF in this setting is to simply reject all big transactions. Moreover, if there are sufficiently many small transactions in the sequence to offset the cost of recharging, OFF makes a single recharging action at the beginning of the sequence of size $\sum_{x \in X_t, x \text{ is small}} x$ for a cost of $f_1 + \sum_{x \in X_t, x \text{ is small}} x$.

The online algorithm performs $(1, \frac{\sqrt{5}-1}{2} f_1)$-recharging and it accepts a transaction x if it has enough funds and x is small. The following theorem (proof in our extended version [6]) states that ON is $(2 + \frac{\sqrt{5}-1}{2})$-competitive in this problem setting.

Theorem 3. *The algorithm described above is $(2 + \frac{\sqrt{5}-1}{2})$-competitive in the unidirectional transaction stream with rejection sub problem.*

Algorithm 3: Unidirectional transaction stream with rejection

---

Initialise: tracker $F_{tracker}, X \leftarrow 0, \emptyset$
Initialise: balance $b = 0$
1 **for** *transaction x in order of arrival* **do**
2   concatenate x to X
3      $F'_{tracker} \leftarrow \text{FUNDS}(X)$
4   **if** $F'_{tracker} > F_{tracker}$ **then**
5         $F_{tracker} \leftarrow F'_{tracker} + \frac{\sqrt{5}-1}{2} f_1$
6   recharge to $F_{tracker}$
7   **if** $b \geq x$ and x is small **then**
8   Accept x
9   **else**
10   Reject x

Before analysing the optimality of ON, we first observe, as a simple corollary of Theorem 2, that the lower bound of 2 also holds for this sub problem.

Corollary 1. *There is no deterministic algorithm that is c-competitive for $c < 2$ in the unidirectional transaction stream with rejection sub problem.*

We conjecture that no other deterministic algorithm can perform better that ON in this setting. Moreover, we sketch an approach to prove the conjecture in our extended technical report [6].

Conjecture 1. There is no deterministic algorithm that is c-competitive for $c < 2 + \frac{\sqrt{5}-1}{2}$ in the unidirectional transaction stream with rejection setting.

6   Bidirectional Transaction Stream

In this section, we consider the most general problem setting, where for a given payment channel (ℓ, r), transactions stream along the channel (ℓ, r) in both directions. A user ℓ (resp. r) can accept or reject incoming transactions that stream from left to right (resp. right to left). Either user would incur a cost of $Rx + f_2$ for rejecting a transaction of size x. ℓ does not need to take any action when encountering transactions that stream from right to left as they simply increase the balance of ℓ in the channel (ℓ, r). Both users can also decide at any point to recharge their channel on-chain, or rebalance their channel off-chain.

Our main online algorithm ON for the bidirectional transaction stream setting is detailed in Algorithm 6. For simplicity, we assume that $R = 0$ in the rejection cost. This means that the cost of rejecting a single transaction of size x is simply f_2, and rebalancing an amount of x off-chain now only incurs a cost of Cf_2. Our algorithm is run by both users on a payment channel and is composed of three smaller algorithms: the first is a recharging algorithm to determine when and how much to recharge the channel on-chain. The second algorithm (Algorithm 4) decides whether to accept or reject new transactions and when to perform off-chain rebalancing. The last algorithm (Algorithm 5) describes how to store the funds received from the other user of the channel.

$(4+2\lceil \log C \rceil, f_1)$-*recharging*. ON runs an on-chain recharging algorithm similar to Algorithm 1 (see Line 3 and Line 6 in Algorithm 6) but with parameters $\gamma = 4+2\lceil \log C \rceil$ and $\delta = f_1$. Since we are in the bidirectional transaction stream setting, FUNDS returns the amount of funds OFF has inside the entire channel (i.e. $b(\ell) + b(r)$) given a transaction sequence.

Let us look at the period between the on-chain recharging instances of ON. From Line 6 in Algorithm 6, we know that ON ensures that it has more than $4 + 2\lceil \log C \rceil$ times more funds than OFF locked in the channel. These funds are distributed in the following way: ON initialises $\lceil \log C \rceil + 2$ "buckets" on each end of the channel. We denote set of left-side buckets as B^ℓ and it consists of $B_s^\ell, B_1^\ell, \ldots, B_{\lceil \log C \rceil}^\ell, B_o^\ell$. Likewise, the set of right-side buckets is B^r and it consists of $B_s^r, B_1^r, \ldots, B_{\lceil \log C \rceil}^r, B_o^r$.

After recharging, users decide how to distribute funds in the channel, so the buckets B_s^ℓ and B_s^r are filled with $2F_{tracker}$ funds. Buckets B_o^ℓ and B_o^r are empty (0 funds). Other buckets contain $F_{tracker}$ funds.

Looking ahead, the funds in the i-th bucket on both sides are used to accept transactions x with a size in the interval $\left[\frac{F_{tracker}}{2^i}, \frac{F_{tracker}}{2^{i-1}}\right)$. The funds in B_s are used to accept transactions with a size less than $\frac{F_{tracker}}{C}$. Finally, B_o stores excess funds coming from payments from the other side when all other buckets are full.

Transaction Handling. When a transaction arrives at the channel, based on the direction of the transaction, either ℓ or r executes Algorithm 4 to decide whether to accept the transaction. Wlog let us assume ℓ encounters transaction $\overrightarrow{x}$. If $\frac{F_{tracker}}{2^i} < x \leq \frac{F_{tracker}}{2^{i-1}}$ for some $i \in [\lceil \log C \rceil]$ and B_i^ℓ has sufficient funds, the funds from B_i^ℓ are used to accept the transaction. If B_i^ℓ lacks sufficient funds for accepting x, ℓ rejects x.

Now, we consider the case where $x \leq \frac{F_{tracker}}{C}$. If B_s^ℓ has sufficient funds, ℓ uses the funds from B_s^ℓ to accept x. If B_s^ℓ has insufficient funds to accept x, ℓ performs off-chain rebalancing with an amount such that after deducting x from B_s^ℓ, there would still be $2F_{tracker}$ funds left in B_s^ℓ. ℓ subsequently accepts x. The required funds for off-chain rebalancing are transferred from B_o^r and B_s^r (see Line 15 and Line 16 in Algorithm 4). Whenever $B_o^\ell > 0$ and some bucket in B^ℓ gets under its original capacity, funds are reallocated from B_o^ℓ to fill the bucket.

Handling Funds Coming from the Other Side. When a transaction x is accepted by wlog ℓ, ON calls Algorithm 5 to distribute the transferred funds among r's buckets in the following way: r first uses x to fill B_s^r up to its capacity of $2F_{tracker}$ (see Line 2 in Algorithm 5). If there are still funds left, r refills the B_i^r buckets in descending order from $i = \lceil \log C \rceil$ to $i = 1$. Intuitively, the reason why buckets are refilled in descending order is due to our simplified cost model for this problem where we assume the cost of rejection for any transaction is f_2. Thus, rejecting three small transactions size x costs thrice as much as rejecting

---

Algorithm 4: Decision on transaction

---

1 DECIDE$(F_{tracker}, x, B^{sdr}, B^{rcv})$

2    $Status \leftarrow$ Accept

3   **if** $\frac{F_{tracker}}{2^i} < x \leq \frac{F_{tracker}}{2^{i-1}}$ *and* $x \leq B_i^{sdr}$ **then**

4 | Accept x

5 | $X \leftarrow \min(F_{tracker}, B_i^{sdr} - x + B_o^{sdr})$

6 | $B_o^{sdr} \leftarrow \max(0, B_i^{sdr} - x + B_o^{sdr} - F_{tracker})$

7 | $B_i^{sdr} \leftarrow X$

8   **else if** $x_i \leq \frac{F_{tracker}}{C}$ *and* $x \leq B_s^{sdr}$ **then**

9 | Accept x

10 | $X \leftarrow \min(2F_{tracker}, B_s^{sdr} - x + B_o^{sdr})$

11 | $B_o^{sdr} \leftarrow \max(0, B_s^{sdr} - x + B_o^{sdr} - 2F_{tracker})$

12 | $B_s^{sdr} \leftarrow X$

13   **else if** $x_i \leq \frac{F_{tracker}}{C}$ *and* $x > B_s^{sdr}$ **then**

14 | Do off-chain rebalancing to fill B_s and pay $f_2 C$.

15 | $B_o^{rcv} \leftarrow B_o^{rcv} - (2F_{tracker} - B_s^{sdr})$.

16 | $B_s^{rcv} \leftarrow B_s^{rcv} - x$.

17 | Accept x

18 | $B_s^{sdr} \leftarrow 2F_{tracker}$.

19   **else**

20 | Reject x

21 | $Status \leftarrow$ Reject

22   **return** $(B^{sdr}, B^{rcv}, Status)$

---

a larger transaction of size $3x$. Finally, if there are still some funds left, they are added to B_o^r.

Algorithm 5: Handling funds coming from the other side

---

1 HANDLEFUNDS$(F_{tracker}, x, B)$

2    $X \leftarrow \min(2F_{tracker}, B_s + x)$

3    $x \leftarrow \max(x + B_s - 2F_{tracker}, 0)$

4    $B_s \leftarrow X$

5   **for** $i \in [\lceil \log C \rceil]$ *in decreasing order* **do**

6 | **if** $x > 0$ **then**

7 | | $X \leftarrow \min(F_{tracker}, B_i + x)$

8 | | $x \leftarrow \max(x + B_i - F_{tracker}, 0)$

9 | | $B_i \leftarrow X$

10   $B_o \leftarrow B_o + x$ **return** (B)

Algorithm 6: Main algorithm

    Initialise: left side buckets B^ℓ
    Initialise: right side buckets B^r
    Initialise: tracker $F_{tracker}, X \leftarrow 0, \emptyset$
1 **for** *transaction x in order of arrival* **do**
2   concatenate x to X
3     $F'_{tracker} \leftarrow \text{FUNDS}(X)$
4   **if** $F'_{tracker} > F_{tracker}$ **then**
5         $F_{tracker} \leftarrow F'_{tracker} + f_1$
6   recharge to $2(2 + \lceil \log C \rceil) F_{tracker}$
7     $sdr, rcv \leftarrow \ell, r$
8   **if** *x is from right to left* **then**
9         $sdr, rcv \leftarrow r, \ell$
10    $B^{sdr}, B^{rcv}, Status \leftarrow \text{DECIDE}(F_{tracker}, x, B^{sdr}, B^{rcv})$
11   **if** $Status ==$ `Accept` **then**
12        $B^{rcv} \leftarrow \text{HANDLEFUNDS}(F_{tracker}, x, B^{rcv})$

Our main theorem (proof in our extended version [6]) shows that our main algorithm is $7 + 2\lceil \log C \rceil$ competitive.

Theorem 4. *Algorithm 6 is* $7 + 2\lceil \log C \rceil$ *competitive.*

Finally, we also analyse in the next lemma (proof in our extended version [6]) how much funds ON needs to lock in the channel to have a chance to be c-competitive. We make the construction for A, the amount of funds that OFF locked in the channel. Observe that OFF would rather reject transactions that have average size $> \frac{A}{C}$ than perform off-chain rebalancing to accept them.

Lemma 4. *For any A, if* ON*'s cost for rejection is at most c times* OFF*'s cost for rejection (for $c < \frac{\log C}{\log \log C}$), any deterministic* ON *needs to lock at least $\sigma = A \cdot \left(\frac{\frac{1}{c+1} \log C}{\log c + 1} + 1 \right)$ funds in the channel.*

Theorem 5. *There is no deterministic c-competitive algorithm for $c \in o(\sqrt{\log C})$.*

Proof. From Lemma 4 for any A, ON needs $A \cdot (\frac{\frac{1}{c+1} \log C}{\log c + 1} + 1)$ funds to have its rejection cost c-competitive. But ON also needs to lock some funds in the channel. The total cost is then $c + A(\frac{\frac{1}{c+1} \log C}{\log c + 1} + 1)$, which is bigger than $\mathcal{O}(\sqrt{\log C})$.

7 Empirical Evaluation

Methodology. We consider the performance of Algorithm 6 on randomly generated transaction sequences. We compare it with the optimal offline algorithm

OFF. Since computing the optimal solution is NP-hard [20], we use dynamic programming to compute the cost (see the full algorithm in our extended version [6]).

Average Performance of ON. We sample 50 random transaction sequences of length 50 each. In each sequence, transaction sizes are sampled independently from a folded Gaussian with mean 0 and standard deviation 3, and then we assign its direction (left-to-right or right-to-left) uniformly at random. Finally, we quantise the size of the transaction to the closest integer. We run both OFF and ON on the generated sequences and compute five important metrics.

We present our results in Table 2. As we can see from the cost of ON vs OFF in Table 2, the competitive ratio is generally lower than the $7+2\lceil \log C \rceil$ bound as suggested by our conservative worst-case analysis in Theorem 4. In addition, we notice that when we use some heuristics to make further minor modifications to ON, we achieve even better performance. In our extended technical report [6], we also compare the average-case performance of ON and OFF with these modified algorithms, and also on sequences sampled from different distributions.

Table 2. Comparison between OFF and ON for $f_1 = 3$ and $R = 0$. $A(X)$ is the total amount of funds in the channel. "Accept rate" shows the fraction of transactions that were accepted. "Off-chain rebalancing" shows how much funds on was moved along the channel using off-chain rebalancing. "Rechargings" shows the number of rechargings performed. Note that OFF recharges only once.

Param		OFF					ON				
C	f_2	Cost	$A(X)$	Accept rate	Off-chain rebalancing	Rechar-gings	Cost	$A(X)$	Accept rate	Off-chain rebalancing	Rechar-gings
2	0.5	15.02	6.4	0.78	0.8	1	63.3	44.26	0.50	0.9	2.18
8	0.5	15.21	6.38	0.77	0	1	87.79	69.06	0.50	0	2.04
2	2	23.6	14.26	0.95	5.36	1	127.02	100.2	0.91	0.38	5.86
8	2	24.5	13.9	0.92	0	1	184.32	156.6	0.9	0	5.84

Case Study: Lightning Network. We conclude our evaluation section with a case study of the Lightning network. We first run our experiments with realistic parameters taken from Lightning Network data. In the Lightning Network, f_1 is the on-chain transaction fee (roughly 1000 satoshi) which is a lot larger than f_2, the base fee one receives when forwarding a payment (around 1 satoshi).

From analysis of the Lightning Network (We use snapshot from September 2021) [8], we know that the average cycle length is 4.15 (after excluding roughly 10% of vertices that are not part of any cycle). That means the value of C in Theorem 4 is just slightly above 4. Details are in Table 3.

Table 3. Frequency of the length of shortest cycle between all users in the Lightning Network. The last column shows the frequency of channels that are not part of any cycle (N.A. not applicable) The average cycle length is 4.15

Cycle length	≤ 4	5	6	7	N.A
Frequency	$49,424(77.44\%)$	$7,758(12.16\%)$	$469(0.73\%)$	$12(0.02\%)$	$6,157(9.65\%)$

8 Conclusion

This paper presents competitive strategies to maintain minimise cost while maximising liquidity and transaction throughput in a payment channel. Our algorithms come with formal worst-case guarantees, and also perform well in realistic scenarios in simulations.

We believe that our work opens several interesting avenues for future research. On the theoretical front, it would be interesting to close the gap in the achievable competitive ratio, and to explore the implications of our approach on other classic online admission control problems. Furthermore, while in our work we have focused on deterministic algorithms, it would be interesting to study the power of randomised approaches in this context, or to consider different adversarial models.

Acknowledgements. Supported by the German Federal Ministry of Education and Research (BMBF), grant 16KISK020K (6G-RIC), 2021–2025, and ERC CoG 863818 (ForM-SMArt).

References

1. Raiden network (2017). https://raiden.network/
2. Aspnes, J., Azar, Y., Fiat, A., Plotkin, S., Waarts, O.: On-line routing of virtual circuits with applications to load balancing and machine scheduling. J. ACM (JACM) **44**(3), 486–504 (1997)
3. Avarikioti, G., Besic, K., Wang, Y., Wattenhofer, R.: Online payment network design. CoRR abs/1908.00432 (2019). http://arxiv.org/abs/1908.00432
4. Avarikioti, Z., Heimbach, L., Wang, Y., Wattenhofer, R.: Ride the lightning: the game theory of payment channels. In: Bonneau, J., Heninger, N. (eds.) FC 2020. LNCS, vol. 12059, pp. 264–283. Springer, Cham (2020). https://doi.org/10.1007/978-3-030-51280-4_15
5. Avarikioti, Z., Pietrzak, K., Salem, I., Schmid, S., Tiwari, S., Yeo, M.: HIDE & SEEK: privacy-preserving rebalancing on payment channel networks. CoRR abs/2110.08848 (2021). https://arxiv.org/abs/2110.08848
6. Bastankhah, M., Chatterjee, K., Maddah-Ali, M.A., Schmid, S., Svoboda, J., Yeo, M.: Online admission control and rebalancing in payment channel networks. CoRR abs/2209.11936 (2022). https://doi.org/10.48550/arXiv.2209.11936
7. Borodin, A., El-Yaniv, R.: Online Computation and Competitive Analysis. Cambridge University Press, Cambridge (2005)
8. Decker, C.: Lightning network research; topology, datasets. https://github.com/lnresearch/topology, https://doi.org/10.5281/zenodo.4088530. Accessed 01 Apr 2022
9. van Engelshoven, Y., Roos, S.: The merchant: avoiding payment channel depletion through incentives. In: 2021 IEEE International Conference on Decentralized Applications and Infrastructures (DAPPS), pp. 59–68 (2021)
10. Ersoy, O., Roos, S., Erkin, Z.: How to profit from payments channels (2019)
11. Fazli, M., Nehzati, S.M., Salarkia, M.: Building stable off-chain payment networks. CoRR abs/2107.03367 (2021). https://arxiv.org/abs/2107.03367

12. Khalil, R., Gervais, A.: Revive: rebalancing off-blockchain payment networks. IACR Cryptol. ePrint Arch. p. 823 (2017). http://eprint.iacr.org/2017/823
13. Li, P., Miyazaki, T., Zhou, W.: Secure balance planning of off-blockchain payment channel networks. In: 39th IEEE Conference on Computer Communications, INFO-COM 2020, Toronto, ON, Canada, 6–9 July 2020, pp. 1728–1737. IEEE (2020). https://doi.org/10.1109/INFOCOM41043.2020.9155375
14. Lukovszki, T., Schmid, S.: Online admission control and embedding of service chains. In: Scheideler, C. (ed.) SIROCCO 2014. LNCS, vol. 9439, pp. 104–118. Springer, Cham (2015). https://doi.org/10.1007/978-3-319-25258-2_8
15. Malavolta, G., Moreno-Sanchez, P., Kate, A., Maffei, M.: SilentWhispers: enforcing security and privacy in decentralized credit networks. In: 24th Annual Network and Distributed System Security Symposium, NDSS 2017, San Diego, California, USA, February 26 - March 1, 2017. The Internet Society (2017)
16. Pickhardt, R., Nowostawski, M.: Imbalance measure and proactive channel rebalancing algorithm for the lightning network. In: IEEE International Conference on Blockchain and Cryptocurrency, ICBC 2020, Toronto, ON, Canada, 2–6 May 2020, pp. 1–5. IEEE (2020). https://doi.org/10.1109/ICBC48266.2020.9169456
17. Poon, J., Dryja, T.: The bitcoin lightning network: scalable off-chain instant payments (2015). https://lightning.network/lightning-network-paper.pdf
18. Prihodko, P., Zhigulin, S.N., Sahno, M., Ostrovskiy, A.B., Osuntokun, O.: Flare : an approach to routing in lightning network white paper (2016)
19. Roos, S., Moreno-Sanchez, P., Kate, A., Goldberg, I.: Settling payments fast and private: efficient decentralized routing for path-based transactions. In: 25th Annual Network and Distributed System Security Symposium, NDSS 2018, San Diego, California, USA, 18–21 February 2018. The Internet Society (2018)
20. Schmid, S., Svoboda, J., Yeo, M.: Weighted packet selection for rechargeable links: complexity and approximation (2022). https://doi.org/10.48550/ARXIV.2204.13459
21. Sivaraman, V., et al.: High throughput cryptocurrency routing in payment channel networks. In: Bhagwan, R., Porter, G. (eds.) 17th USENIX Symposium on Networked Systems Design and Implementation, NSDI 2020, Santa Clara, CA, USA, 25–27 February 2020, pp. 777–796. USENIX Association (2020)

Complexity-Approximation Trade-Offs in Exchange Mechanisms: AMMs vs. LOBs

Jason Milionis[1(✉)] , Ciamac C. Moallemi[2(✉)] ,
and Tim Roughgarden[1,3(✉)]

[1] Department of Computer Science, Columbia University, New York, NY 10027, USA
{jm,tr}@cs.columbia.edu
[2] Graduate School of Business, Columbia University, New York, NY 10027, USA
ciamac@gsb.columbia.edu
[3] a16z, Crypto, New York, NY 10010, USA

Abstract. This paper presents a general framework for the design and analysis of exchange mechanisms between two assets that unifies and enables comparisons between the two dominant paradigms for exchange, constant function market markers (CFMMs) and limit order books (LOBs). In our framework, each liquidity provider (LP) submits to the exchange a downward-sloping demand curve, specifying the quantity of the risky asset it wishes to hold at each price; the exchange buys and sells the risky asset so as to satisfy the aggregate submitted demand. In general, such a mechanism is budget-balanced (i.e., it stays solvent and does not make or lose money) and enables price discovery (i.e., arbitrageurs are incentivized to trade until the exchange's price matches the external market price of the risky asset). Different exchange mechanisms correspond to different restrictions on the set of acceptable demand curves.

The primary goal of this paper is to formalize an approximation-complexity trade-off that pervades the design of exchange mechanisms. For example, CFMMs give up expressiveness in favor of simplicity: the aggregate demand curve of the LPs can be described using constant space (the liquidity parameter), but most demand curves cannot be well approximated by any function in the corresponding single-dimensional family. LOBs, intuitively, make the opposite trade-off: any downward-slowing demand curve can be well approximated by a collection of limit orders, but the space needed to describe the state of a LOB can be large.

This paper introduces a general measure of *exchange complexity*, defined by the minimal set of basis functions that generate, through their conical hull, all of the demand functions allowed by an exchange. With this complexity measure in place, we investigate the design of *optimally expressive* exchange mechanisms, meaning the lowest complexity mechanisms that allow for arbitrary downward-sloping demand curves to be approximated to within a given level of precision. Our results quantify the fundamental trade-off between simplicity and expressivity in exchange mechanisms.

As a case study, we interpret the complexity-approximation trade-offs in the widely-used Uniswap v3 AMM through the lens of our framework.

Keywords: Blockchain · Decentralized Finance · Automated Market Makers

© International Financial Cryptography Association 2024
F. Baldimtsi and C. Cachin (Eds.): FC 2023, LNCS 13950, pp. 326–343, 2024.
https://doi.org/10.1007/978-3-031-47754-6_19

1   Introduction

Decentralized exchanges are now an integral part of the broader ecosystem of blockchains, as evidenced by their ever growing volume of transactions [24]. On model centralized exchanges, the exchange of a risky asset for a numéraire is typically carried out by an exchange mechanism known as an electronic limit order book (LOB), in which market participants specify quantities of shares of the risky asset they would like to trade at specified prices. Trades then occur as orders are matched in a greedy way: whenever there is overlap between bid and ask prices (i.e., between a buy and a sell), a trade is executed, and the matched orders are cleared from the LOB. LOBs therefore maintain and update a list of all the currently outstanding buy and sell orders.

LOBs face two types of challenges in an decentralized environment such as the Ethereum blockchain. First, because storage and computation in such an environment tend to be so scarce, implementing an LOB can be prohibitively expensive. Second, LOBs are well known suffer from liquidity problems in thin markets (markets with few buyers or sellers), for example, for "long-tail" crypto assets.

These challenges have motivated an alternative exchange design that has become very widely used in blockchains: automated market makers (AMMs) and, in particular, constant function market makers (CFMMs). Uniswap [1,2] is the most well known and widely used example of a CFMM.

AMMs address the second challenge above by offering guaranteed liquidity, meaning at all times there is a spot price between 0 and ∞ at which the AMM is willing to buy or sell. AMMs like Uniswap address the first challenge by using only simple calculations and data structures. For example, for the canonical ("$xy = k$") constant product market maker, the state of mechanism can be described by two numbers (the quantities x and y held by the pool), and there is a simple closed-form formula (requiring only a small number of additions, multiplications, divisions, and square roots) for computing the quantity of the risky asset received in exchange for a specified amount of the numéraire(as a function of x and y).

In this paper, we provide a general framework for describing and reasoning about exchange mechanisms, which enables "apples-to-apples" comparisons between LOBs and AMMs on metrics such as complexity and expressiveness. More specifically, our contributions can be delineated as follows:

1. We provide a **common framework** for describing exchange mechanisms that encompasses both CFMMs and LOBs. In our general model, liquidity providers (LPs) submit to the exchange their preferences (in the form of what we define as **demand curves** for the risky asset) along with appropriate deposits of the risky asset and numéraire (see Sect. 2 for details).
2. We formalize the sense in which some methods of exchange are simpler than others, introducing a general notion of **exchange complexity**. Exchange complexity is defined by the minimal set of basis functions that generate, through their conical hull, all of the demand functions allowed by an exchange.

We classify the complexity of all the prominent types of exchange mechanisms (see Sect. 3 for details).

3. We characterize the **fundamental trade-off** between the *complexity* of an exchange (in a sense that we define) and the *expressibility* of an exchange as measured by its ability to approximate arbitrary preferences of the LPs (i.e., arbitrary demand curves). In particular, we prove matching (up to constant factors) upper and lower bounds on the minimum exchange complexity necessary to attain a specified approximation error (see Sect. 4 for details).

4. As a case study, we interpret the complexity-approximation trade-offs in the widely-used Uniswap v3 AMM through the lens of our framework (see Sect. 5 for details).

1.1 Literature Review

The use of AMMs for decentralized exchange mechanisms was first proposed by Buterin [12] and Lu and Köppelmann [27]. The latter authors suggested a constant product market maker, which was first analyzed by Angeris et al. [7]. Angeris et al. [4,5] define and use a reparameterization of a CFMM curve (established by Angeris and Chitra [3]) in terms of portfolio holdings of the pool with respect to the price as a tool to replicate payoffs and compute the pool's value function; we use this same reparameterization for different purposes, to define a general (i.e., not AMM-specific) framework of exchange and identify fundamental complexity-approximation trade-offs in exchange design.

A separate line of work seeks to design specific CFMMs with good properties by identifying good bonding functions, variations and combinations of CFMMs in a dynamic setting with a specific focus on optimizing fees, and minimizing arbitrage and slippage [6,15–17,19,20,23,25,28,29,33,36,37]. While fees could be easily integrated into our model, they have no bearing on complexity-approximation trade-offs and thus we generally ignore them in this paper for simplicity.

Some previous papers propose generalizations of CFMMs to somewhat wider classes of exchanges [11,38] without considering LOBs.

CFMMs and LOBs have been compared before (in ways orthogonal to the questions studied here) [10,13,26]. Most of these works either compare the observed liquidities and the price efficiency of these mechanisms [13,26] or study the same through the lens of arbitrage bounds [10]. Young [40] argues that AMMs can be interpreted as "smooth order books" and notes a type of non-uniform converse (with each possible state of a smooth order book represented using a different AMM). Chitra et al. [14] compare CFMMs and LOBs in terms of the number of arbitrage transactions necessary to recover from a liveness attack on the underlying blockchain.

Another line of work analyzes competition between CFMMs and LOBs and the consequent liquidity properties of both at equilibrium [8,9,13]. Goyal et al. [21] consider the computational complexity of computing such equilibria.

There is a large literature on the market microstructure of limit order books; see the textbook by O'Hara [32] and references therein. There are some examples of on-chain LOBs on high-throughput blockchains [30,35].

Finally, Adams et al. [2] suggest that Uniswap v3's key feature is that "LPs can approximate any desired distribution of liquidity on the price space," with empirical backing provided by Huynh [22]; one application of our work is to put this intuition on sound mathematical footing. There is also work on Uniswap v3 from the LP perspective, such as how beliefs about future prices should guide the choice of an LP's demand curve [18,31,39].

2 Model

2.1 Model Primitives

We begin by describing our framework for exchange design. While this paper uses this framework specifically to study fundamental complexity-approximation trade-offs in exchange mechanisms, we believe it can serve also as a starting point for many future investigations.

Suppose there are two assets, a risky asset and a numéraire asset. Each LP comes separately to the exchange, and declares the amount of risky asset they would like to hold at each possible price p, i.e., a non-increasing, non-negative function $g_i \colon (0, \infty) \to \mathbb{R}^+$. We call the function $g_i(\cdot)$ the ith LP's **demand curve** for the risky asset, because it refers to the demand of the LP for the risky asset (i.e., we are considering the perspective of the LP). Assuming that the current price is p_0, the LP simultaneously deposits a quantity $g_i(p_0)$ of the risky asset in the common pool, along with an amount of numéraire given by the Riemann-Stieltjes integral

$$- \int_0^{p_0} p \, dg_i(p) \,. \tag{1}$$

Note that this integral is well-defined (though possibly infinite) since $g_i(\cdot)$ is monotonic. Moreover, the integral is non-negative since $g_i(\cdot)$ is non-increasing. In cases where $g_i(p)$ is differentiable, the differential takes the form $dg_i(p) = g_i'(p) \, dp$. We will show later that this deposit of numéraire is necessary and sufficient for the exchange to be budget-balanced or solvent, i.e., the exchange system does not extend credit.

The exchange mechanism maintains the demand curves of the LPs, along with the current price p_0. Assuming that n liquidity providers have contributed to the exchange their demand curves along with respective payments of risky asset and numéraire, the *aggregate demand curve* (i.e., the total quantity of risky asset that the exchange will hold at any given price) is given by the non-increasing function

$$g(p) = \sum_{i=1}^n g_i(p) \,. \tag{2}$$

Addition and removal of liquidity (LP "mints" and "burns", as they are known in practice) simply occur through additions and removals of particular g_i's to the aggregate demand curve of the exchange. These demand curves of the LPs can arise through *bonding curves* of traditional CFMMs (i.e., functions f such that the holdings of the joint pool (x, y) satisfy $f(x, y) = c$ for some c) but this is not necessary; i.e., the exchange mechanisms defined by our framework strictly generalize AMMs.

Trading. A liquidity demanding trader who wants to trade with the exchange will do so by specifying a target (new) price $p_1 \neq p_0$. The trader gets a quantity $g(p_0) - g(p_1)$ of risky asset, and pays the following amount in numéraire:

$$- \int_{p_0}^{p_1} p \, dg(p) \,, \tag{3}$$

as determined by the aggregate liquidity of the exchange $g(p)$ of Eq. 2. As was the case for Eq. 1, this integral is well-defined, it is non-negative if $p_1 \geq p_0$, and non-positive if $p_1 \leq p_0$.

Uniswap v2 Example. To give a simple example, the particular case of a constant product market maker (CPMM), such as Uniswap v2, arises from our mechanism as follows: restrict the set of allowable demand curves g_i that an LP may submit to the form

$$g_i(p) = \frac{c_i}{\sqrt{p}} \,,$$

for some constant $c_i > 0$. Then, the aggregate demand curve of the exchange will be of the form

$$g(p) = \sum_{i=1}^{n} g_i(p) = \frac{c}{\sqrt{p}} \,,$$

for $c = \sum_{i=1}^{n} c_i > 0$. A trader who will trade with this exchange at a current price p_0 with a target price p_1 (or equivalently, with a specific quantity of risky asset to be purchased, since there a one-to-one correspondence) will obtain a quantity $g(p_0) - g(p_1) = c \left(\frac{1}{\sqrt{p_0}} - \frac{1}{\sqrt{p_1}} \right)$ of risky asset, and pay in numéraire

$$- \int_{p_0}^{p_1} p g'(p) \, dp = \int_{p_0}^{p_1} \frac{c}{2\sqrt{p}} \, dp = c \left(\sqrt{p_1} - \sqrt{p_0} \right) .$$

Comparing this to the same expressions for an "$xy = k$" CPMM, the trader gets exactly the same quantity of risky asset and pays exactly the same amount of numéraire as they would in the "$xy = k$" CPMM, with $k = c^2$. Essentially, the curve $g(p)$ above is just a reparameterization of the CPMM curve $xy = k$ in terms of prices [5] where the risky asset is available in quantity x in the pool and the amount of numéraire is y[1].

---

[1] In particular, $x = g(p) = c/\sqrt{p}$ and $y = c\sqrt{p}$ at all times in the pool for the corresponding defined price p.

Significance of LPs' Demand Curves. In this mechanism, we view the individual demand curves chosen by the LPs as their *ideal preferences* with respect to risky asset holdings at each price in regards to their market making activity. They are in some sense "forced" to make the market —this is tautologically the reason that they participate in the exchange as LPs[2]— but *exactly how* they do this is specified by the shape of their demand curves. The requirement that each g_i be non-increasing can be explained through this argument: each demand curve of any LP has to always correspond to making the market; as the price of the risky asset increases, a market maker may only decrease their holdings of the asset (i.e., sell the asset), because if at any given price their holdings as defined in the exchange mechanism marginally increased (i.e., the LP would buy the risky asset at the marginal price), then any trader would sweep such a marginal quantity as it is to their advantage.

2.2 Price Discovery and Budget Balance

In the previous section, we defined a framework for an exchange mechanism. In order for an exchange to be reasonable, two properties would be necessary: (1) price discovery should occur, i.e., given an outside market with a fixed external market price, the exchange's price should eventually become identical to the market price; and (2) the exchange should at no point in time become insolvent, i.e., any feasible trade should always keep the amount of numéraire non-negative. (Because demand curves are non-negative, the amount of the risky asset is automatically non-negative.) Equivalently, the second property is broadly known in financial markets as a "no credit" requirement, i.e., that the exchange does not incorporate the ability of LPs to take credit. In the remainder of the section, we formalize and prove these properties for our model.

Proposition 1. (Price discovery). *If there exists an outside market with fixed external market price p of the risky asset with respect to the numéraire, then external market participants (arbitrageurs) always have financial incentive to trade with an exchange defined as per the framework of Sect. 2.1 until the price of such exchange becomes equal to the external market price.*

Proposition 2. (Budget balance). *An exchange defined as in the framework of Sect. 2.1 is budget-balanced or solvent, i.e., the amount of numéraire that the joint pool contains at all times (with any sequence of feasible trades, or liquidity additions/removals) is non-negative.*

We defer the full proofs of these two propositions to Appendix A.

---

[2] Note that LPs may also hold other portfolios of the risky asset, which of course need not be restricted to be non-increasing in the asset price, but their individual demand curves when they participating in an exchange mechanism need to reflect exactly and only the activity of making the market.

3 Exchange Description Complexity and Examples

Our general model in Sect. 2.1 allows LPs to submit arbitrary downward-sloping demand curves. Such curves are not generally representable in a finite amount of space, so practical considerations suggest restricting the space of demand curves that LPs are allowed to submit. We will say that an *exchange mechanism* is a restriction of the general exchange framework of Sect. 2.1 in which each LP demand curve is required to belong to a set of allowable demand curves, i.e., $g_i \in \mathcal{G}$ for some class $\mathcal{G}$ of non-increasing, non-negative functions over the positive reals. An exchange mechanism, then, is defined by the choice of class $\mathcal{G}$.

Towards defining a measure of exchange complexity, we will be interested in succinct ways of representing all the demand functions g in a class $\mathcal{G}$. Specifically, given an arbitrary such class $\mathcal{G}$, we can consider its conical hull. This is the smallest convex cone that contains[3] $\mathcal{G}$ or, equivalently, the closure of $\mathcal{G}$ under finite non-negative linear combinations:

$$\text{cone}(\mathcal{G}) = \left\{ \sum_{i=1}^{k} c_i g_i(p) : g_i(p) \in \mathcal{G}, c_i \geq 0, k \in \mathbb{N} \right\}.$$

In our context, non-negative linear combinations can be interpreted as aggregations of multiple LP positions.

A *basis* of a cone is a minimum-cardinality set of elements that generates the cone, meaning a set $\mathcal{S}$ such that $\text{cone}(\mathcal{S}) = \text{cone}(\mathcal{G})$. We then define the **exchange complexity** of an exchange (i.e., a choice $\mathcal{G}$ of allowable demand functions) as the cardinality of a basis for $\text{cone}(\mathcal{G})$.[4] By definition, if a set $\mathcal{G}$ of demand functions has exchange complexity k, every function of $\mathcal{G}$ can be represented by a k-tuple of non-negative real numbers (one coefficient for each of the basis functions).[5]

Our measure of exchange complexity is, by design, well defined for an arbitrary collection $\mathcal{G}$ of allowable demand functions. In all the real-world examples that we are aware of, this set $\mathcal{G}$ is already closed under non-negative linear combinations (i.e., is a cone). In this case, exchange complexity effectively counts an exchange's "primitive" LP positions from which all possible aggregations of LP positions can be derived.

---

[3] This definition makes sense because the intersection of convex cones is again a convex cone; see, e.g., Rockafellar [34] for further background.

[4] While our formalism in principle accommodates exchanges with infinite exchange complexity, any practical exchange needs to be defined by a finite basis on any compact (sub-)domain. Additionally, our results only make use of exchanges that have a finitely generated conic closure to approximate any demand curve within a finite approximation error under reasonable assumptions about the error metrics.

[5] The focus of this work is on information-theoretic complexity – approximation trade-offs, and we do not explicitly model computation. However, our positive results only make use of mechanisms for which computation with basis functions is straightforward.

This definition of exchange complexity allows us to formalize the intuition that some exchanges are easier to represent than others (e.g., that CFMMs are simpler than LOBs). Next, we evaluate the exchange complexity of all of the most popular types of exchanges used to trade crypto assets.

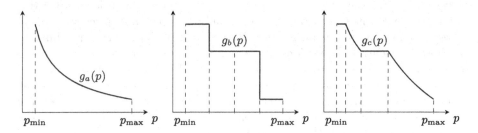

Fig. 1. $g \in \text{cone}(\mathcal{G})$ for three typical cases: (a) CPMM, (b) LOB, (c) Uniswap v3

CFMMs. CFMMs are generated by the restriction to non-negative scalar multiples of a *single* basis function, i.e., $\mathcal{G} = \{c \cdot g(p) : c \geq 0\}$, where $g(p)$ is *one* reference demand curve, out of all the possible curves of the CFMM. The coefficient c of this basis function can then be interpreted as the liquidity parameter. As an example, for the CPMM, we can choose $g(p) = 1/\sqrt{p}$ (cf., Fig. 1a); the coefficient can be interpreted as $\sqrt{k}$ for the k in "$xy = k$." In general, irrespective of the bonding curve, the exchange complexity of a CFMM is 1. Under standard assumptions (e.g., as in Angeris et al. [4]) on a CFMM's bonding curve f, the corresponding basis function g can be derived from f in a mechanical way, through optimization.

LOBs. Limit order books consist of limit orders, which are (buy or sell) orders of quantities of the risky asset at some price. The predetermined prices at which limit orders can be specified are called *ticks*. In our framework, limit orders can be represented by a set of basis functions in which each function corresponds to a limit order at a specific tick (i.e., a step function, where the step occurs at the tick). According to our definition of exchange complexity above, then, the exchange complexity of a limit order book (cf., Fig. 1b) with k ticks is k. If we restrict our attention to a price range $[p_{\min}, p_{\max}]$ with ticks $p_{\min}, p_{\min} + \epsilon$, $p_{\min} + 2\epsilon, \ldots, p_{\max}$, the exchange complexity of such a LOB would be $(p_{\max} - p_{\min})/\epsilon$.

There is a superficial difference in convention between traditional LOBs and our model of them in the preceding paragraph, concerning the *default action* after a trade that crosses the price of a limit order. In an LOB, the matching limit order would be automatically removed from the order book, whereas in our framework here the corresponding LP would, in effect, automatically place a new limit order in the opposite direction at the same price. In other words, a LOB basis function is equivalent to both a limit buy and a limit sell at the tick price, and which one takes effect depends on the current price p_0 and the trade to be executed. Because limit orders can be easily added to or removed from traditional LOBs, and because our model accommodates LP mints and burns, there is no material difference between the two viewpoints.

Uniswap v3. Uniswap v3 (cf., Fig. 1c) can be viewed as a hybrid of a CFMM and a LOB, with the CPMM curve applied only within a short price interval (in between two of the pre-defined ticks). By allowing multiple intervals, Uniswap v3 allows concentrated positions in the spirit of LOBs, a property known as *concentrated liquidity.* If there are k ticks contained in the interior of an interval $[p_{\min}, p_{\max}]$, then Uniswap v3's complexity on this interval is k. (There is one basis function for each price segment $[t_i, t_{i+1}]$ between two successive ticks; the function is constant up until the interval, decreases as in a CPMM within the interval, and is zero after the interval, as in Eq. 4).

$$g_i(p) = \begin{cases} \frac{1}{\sqrt{t_i}} - \frac{1}{\sqrt{t_{i+1}}}, & \text{for } p \leq t_i \\ \frac{1}{\sqrt{p}} - \frac{1}{\sqrt{t_{i+1}}}, & \text{for } t_i \leq p \leq t_{i+1} \\ 0, & \text{for } p \geq t_{i+1} \end{cases} \tag{4}$$

Thus, the exchange complexity of both LOBs and Uniswap v3 is controlled by the number of ticks (independent of the spacing between them). In practice, ticks are sparser in Uniswap v3 than in a traditional LOB, and the former accordingly has lower exchange complexity than the latter. For an example calculation, if the ticks in Uniswap v3 are assumed to be of the form 1.0001^i, and $p_{\min} = 1.0001^s$, $p_{\max} = 1.0001^{s+t}$, then Uniswap v3's complexity in the price interval $[p_{\min}, p_{\max}]$ is

$$t = \frac{\log(p_{\max}/p_{\min})}{\log 1.0001} \approx 10000.5 \log(p_{\max}/p_{\min}).$$

We note that range orders in Uniswap v3 correspond to sums of single-interval positions (with one position per interval in the range) and are therefore automatically included in the cone generated by the basis functions defined above.

4   Complexity – Approximation Trade-Offs

4.1   Notions of Approximation

Having defined the complexity of an exchange mechanism, we turn to defining the *expressiveness* of such a mechanism and proving fundamental trade-offs between complexity and expressiveness. Informally, we will measure the expressiveness of an exchange mechanism via the extent to which its allowable demand curves (i.e., the functions in the class $\mathcal{G}$) can represent arbitrary LP preferences (i.e., an arbitrary demand curve).

Precisely, denote by $\mathcal{F}$ the class of all non-increasing functions $f : [p_{\min}, p_{\max}] \to [f_{\min}, f_{\max}]$. This is the most general class of bounded demand curves according to our framework. Any arbitrary (bounded) preference of an LP will be some specific non-increasing function $f \in \mathcal{F}$.[6] We next define the extent to which some allowable demand curve $g \in \mathcal{G}$ (with the same domain and range) approximates f. (In this section we use g rather than g_i to denote an arbitrary function of $\mathcal{G}$.)[7]

First, we introduce the weighted ℓ_p norm in the function space as a distance metric; without loss of generality, assume we have a normalized (and integrable) weight function $w : [p_{\min}, p_{\max}] \to \mathbb{R}^+$ such that $\int_{p_{\min}}^{p_{\max}} w(p)\, dp = 1$. Then, the weighted ℓ_p distance of two functions $f, g \in \mathcal{F}$ is

$$d(f, g) = \left(\int_{p_{\min}}^{p_{\max}} w(s)\, |f(s) - g(s)|^p\, ds \right)^{1/p}.$$

The weight function w can be interpreted as a measure on the price space, for example reflecting a belief (by an LP, the AMM designer, or the community) that some prices may be more relevant than others. On a first read, we encourage the reader to take w to be the constant function $w(s) = 1/(p_{\max} - p_{\min})$ for all $s \in [p_{\min}, p_{\max}]$.

Given this definition, we define the **approximation error** of the exchange defined by $\mathcal{G}$ as the worst-case (over arbitrary LP preferences/demand curves $f \in \mathcal{F}$) distance from the best-case approximation (over allowable functions $g \in \mathrm{cone}(\mathcal{G})$) of f, as above:

$$\mathrm{err}(\mathcal{G}) = \sup_{f \in \mathcal{F}} \left\{ \inf_{g \in \mathrm{cone}(\mathcal{G})} d(f, g) \right\}. \tag{5}$$

4.2 Upper and Lower Bounds

From the AMM designer's perspective, an "optimal" AMM would enable LPs to have their preferences expressed closely; a bit more formally, the worst-case approximation error through the AMM for arbitrary LP demand curves should

---

[6] Note that in what follows f is a demand curve, as defined in Sect. 2.1, and not a bonding curve of a CFMM.

[7] The restricting to a bounded domain and range is convenient but can be relaxed considerably. The fundamental issue is that, to meaningfully speak about function approximations and avoid infinite distances between distinct functions, we need to impose constraints on allowable demand functions and/or the choice of distance function and underlying measure (on prices). Functions with bounded domain and range are convenient because they are integrable no matter what the distance notion and measure. Our results can be generalized by considering combinations of demand function classes and classes of measures for which the same integrability properties are guaranteed.

Additionally, it will be apparent from our lower bound (Theorem 2) that, if the family of functions $\mathcal{F}$ was not bounded by some finite bound $f_{\max} < \infty$, there would be no finite approximation error guarantee with any finite complexity (under any natural notion of approximation error).

be low, and intuitively should decrease with the complexity of the exchange mechanism: the higher exchange complexity should result in a payoff of lower worst-case approximation error. The results below characterize this trade-off, by identifying the best-possible worst-case approximation error as a function of the exchange complexity. For example, for the special case in which the approximation metric between two functions is the (unweighted) ℓ_1 distance, an exchange complexity (equivalently, number of basis functions) of $\Theta(1/\epsilon)$ is necessary and sufficient to achieve an ϵ worst-case approximation error.

Our upper bound argument also implies the (intuitive but previously unformalized) fact that limit order books at appropriately defined price ticks attain the optimal approximation error guarantee for a given level of exchange complexity (up to a factor of 2). In other words, when computation and storage are not first-order constraints, LOBs are nearly optimally expressive exchange mechanisms.

Theorem 1. (Upper bound). *For every $\epsilon > 0$, there exists a limit order book (LOB) exchange mechanism $\mathcal{G}$ with exchange complexity $k = O(1/\epsilon^p)$ that attains approximation error*

$$err(\mathcal{G}) \le \epsilon \cdot \frac{f_{max} - f_{min}}{2}.$$

Theorem 2. (Lower bound). *For every $\epsilon > 0$, every exchange mechanism $\mathcal{G}$ with exchange complexity $O(1/\epsilon^p)$ suffers approximation error*

$$err(\mathcal{G}) \ge \epsilon \cdot \Omega(f_{max} - f_{min}).$$

For the detailed proofs of Theorems 1, and 2 we refer to Sects. 6.1 and 6.2 respectively.

5   Uniswap V3

Next, we answer the question: to what extent do various formats in practice come close to this complexity – approximation trade-off? Historically, constant product market makers (CPMMs) were first built for gas efficiency purposes [1], but when it was realized that this came often at the expense of capital efficiency, the proposal of Uniswap v3 came around [2], which trades like a CPMM curve inside tight intervals at a pre-defined tick spacing, which are otherwise independent. In this section, we consider Uniswap v3, which is at the time of writing a widely used AMM, as an enlightening example to showcase how our theory can be applied to formally prove approximation guarantees for AMMs employed in practice.

More specifically, we can prove that —under a particular assumption of the returns distribution with maximum entropy, i.e., a uniform prior in the returns space— a variation of Uniswap v3 with variable tick spacing δ achieves an approximation error that matches (up to a constant multiplicative factor) the lower bound in Theorem 2. The precise formulation follows.

Theorem 3. *For every $\epsilon > 0$, there exists a Uniswap v3-like exchange mechanism $\mathcal{G}$ with $n = O(1/\epsilon^p)$ ticks at prices $p_{min}(1+\delta)^i$ for $i \in \{0, 1, \ldots, n\}$ where $\log(1+\delta) = \epsilon^p \log(p_{max}/p_{min})$, that attains approximation error according to Eq. 5 with a normalized weight function $w(p)$ which assigns measure at most $O(1/n)$ to each of the intervals defined by these ticks, of*

$$err(\mathcal{G}) \leq O(\epsilon \cdot (f_{max} - f_{min})).$$

The detailed proof of Theorem 3 is relegated to Sect. 6.3.

6   Proofs

6.1   Proof of Theorem 1

Let $\epsilon > 0$, and a normalized weight function $w \colon [p_{min}, p_{max}] \to \mathbb{R}^+$ such that $\int_{p_{min}}^{p_{max}} w(p)\, dp = 1$. Then, since $w(p) \geq 0 \; \forall p \in [p_{min}, p_{max}]$, split the interval $[p_{min}, p_{max}]$ into $n = 1/\epsilon^p$ equal measure (according to the weight function) sub-intervals $[t_i, t_{i+1}]$, $\forall i \in \{1, 2, \ldots, n\}$, i.e., such that $\int_{t_i}^{t_{i+1}} w(p)dp = \frac{1}{n}$. Define the limit order book (LOB) exchange mechanism $\mathcal{G} = \text{cone}(\mathcal{G})$ as the conical hull of the following set of basis functions: each basis function represents a limit order at each price point t_i above, i.e., the basis function is a unit step function dropping from 1 to 0 at price t_i. The exchange complexity of this $\mathcal{G}$ is therefore $1/\epsilon^p$.

Consider any $f \in \mathcal{F}$, and define the following $g_f \in \text{cone}(\mathcal{G})$ that will "approximate" this f:

$$\forall p \in (t_i, t_{i+1}), \; g_f(p) = \frac{f(t_i) + f(t_{i+1})}{2}. \tag{6}$$

It is true that this $g_f \in \text{cone}(\mathcal{G})$, because g_f is piecewise constant, with function value drops occurring only at the prices t_i (see Fig. 1b for an example representation).

We have that

$$\forall p \in (t_i, t_{i+1}), \; |f(p) - g_f(p)| \leq \frac{f(t_i) - f(t_{i+1})}{2},$$

since f is non-increasing, and by the definition of g_f in Eq. 6.

Hence, we obtain the desired result:

$$
\begin{aligned}
\mathrm{err}(\mathcal{G}) = \sup_{f \in \mathcal{F}} \left\{ \inf_{g \in \mathrm{cone}(\mathcal{G})} d(f,g) \right\} &\leq \sup_{f \in \mathcal{F}} \left(\sum_{i=1}^{n} \int_{t_i}^{t_{i+1}} w(s) \, |f(s) - g_f(s)|^p \, ds \right)^{1/p} \\
&\leq \sup_{f \in \mathcal{F}} \left(\sum_{i=1}^{n} \int_{t_i}^{t_{i+1}} w(s) \left(\frac{f(t_i) - f(t_{i+1})}{2} \right)^p ds \right)^{1/p} \\
&= \frac{1}{2n^{1/p}} \sup_{f \in \mathcal{F}} \left(\sum_{i=1}^{n} [f(t_i) - f(t_{i+1})]^p \right)^{1/p} \\
&\leq \frac{1}{2n^{1/p}} \sup_{f \in \mathcal{F}} \sum_{i=1}^{n} [f(t_i) - f(t_{i+1})] \\
&\leq \epsilon \cdot \frac{f_{\max} - f_{\min}}{2},
\end{aligned}
$$

where the second-to-last inequality follows from the inequality between ℓ_1 and ℓ_p norms in the function space.

6.2   Proof of Theorem 2

Let $\epsilon > 0$, and a normalized weight function $w \colon [p_{\min}, p_{\max}] \to \mathbb{R}^+$ such that $\int_{p_{\min}}^{p_{\max}} w(p) \, dp = 1$. Similarly to the upper bound, but with double the amount of intervals, split the interval $[p_{\min}, p_{\max}]$ into $2(n+2)$ (where $n = 1/\epsilon^p$) equal measure (according to the weight function) sub-intervals $[t_i, t_{i+1}]$, $\forall i \in \{1, 2, \ldots, 2n+4\}$, i.e., such that $\int_{t_i}^{t_{i+1}} w(p) dp = \frac{1}{2(n+2)}$. Now, consider any exchange mechanism $\mathcal{G}$ with exchange complexity $\leq \frac{1}{\epsilon^p} - 1$, i.e., such that $\mathrm{cone}(\mathcal{G})$ is generated by $\leq \frac{1}{\epsilon^p} - 1$ basis functions; suppose without loss of generality that these are $g_1, g_2, \ldots, g_{n-1} \in \mathrm{cone}(\mathcal{G})$.

Lemma 1. *For every basis function g_i (where $i \in \{1, 2, \ldots, n-1\}$ as above), there exists at most one interval of the form $[t_{2l+1}, t_{2l+3}]$ for some $l \in \{1, \ldots, n\}$ (where t's are defined as in the above paragraph) such that*

$$
g_i(t_{2l+1}) - g_i(t_{2l+3}) > \frac{g_i(t_3) - g_i(t_{2n+3})}{2}.
$$

Proof. Let g_i be any basis function. Assume that the lemma's hypothesis is not true, i.e., there exist at least two intervals $[t_{2l+1}, t_{2l+3}]$ and $[t_{2m+1}, t_{2m+3}]$ for some l, m such that the lemma's equation holds for each of these intervals. But since g_i is non-increasing, this would necessitate that

$$
\begin{aligned}
g_i(t_3) - g_i(t_{2n+3}) &\geq \left[g_i(t_{2l+1}) - g_i(t_{2l+3}) \right] + \left[g_i(t_{2m+1}) - g_i(t_{2m+3}) \right] \\
&> g_i(t_3) - g_i(t_{2n+3}),
\end{aligned}
$$

which completes the proof by contradiction.

From Lemma 1 and the pigeonhole principle (there exist n odd-indexed intervals of the form $[t_{2l+1}, t_{2l+3}]$ for some $l \in \{1, \ldots, n\}$, but only $n-1$ basis functions), we get that there exist at least one interval of the form $[t_{2l+1}, t_{2l+3}]$ (for some $l \in \{1, \ldots, n\}$) such that for all $i \in \{1, 2, \ldots, n-1\}$,

$$g_i(t_{2l+1}) - g_i(t_{2l+3}) \leq \frac{g_i(t_3) - g_i(t_{2n+3})}{2},$$

and because $\mathrm{cone}(\mathcal{G})$ is finitely generated, it holds that for all $g \in \mathrm{cone}(\mathcal{G})$,

$$g(t_{2l+1}) - g(t_{2l+3}) \leq \frac{g(t_3) - g(t_{2n+3})}{2}. \tag{7}$$

Note that the interval is not the leftmost $[t_1, t_3]$ or the rightmost $[t_{2n+3}, t_{2n+5}]$ interval.

Consider the following specific $f_a \in \mathcal{F}$:

$$f_a(p) = \begin{cases} f_{\max}, & \text{for } p_{\min} \leq p < t_{2l+2} \\ f_{\min}, & \text{for } t_{2l+2} \leq p \leq p_{\max} \end{cases}.$$

Consider any $g \in \mathrm{cone}(\mathcal{G})$. We distinguish a few cases for the extreme values of g outside of the outermost odd-indexed intervals, i.e., $g(t_3)$ and $g(t_{2n+3})$:

- If $g(t_3) \geq f_{\max} + \frac{f_{\max} - f_{\min}}{4}$, then

$$\int_{t_1}^{t_3} w(s) |f_a(s) - g(s)|^p \, ds \geq \frac{(f_{\max} - f_{\min})^p}{(n+2) \cdot 4^p}.$$

- If $g(t_{2n+3}) \leq f_{\min} - \frac{f_{\max} - f_{\min}}{4}$, then

$$\int_{t_{2n+3}}^{t_{2n+5}} w(s) |f_a(s) - g(s)|^p \, ds \geq \frac{(f_{\max} - f_{\min})^p}{(n+2) \cdot 4^p}.$$

- Otherwise, we have that $g(t_3) - g(t_{2n+3}) < \frac{3}{2}(f_{\max} - f_{\min})$. We now distinguish 3 sub-cases:

  - If $g(t_{2l+1}) \geq f_{\max}$, then $g(t_{2l+2}) \geq g(t_{2l+3}) \geq \frac{f_{\max} + 3f_{\min}}{4}$ by Eq. 7, thus

$$\int_{t_{2l+2}}^{t_{2l+3}} w(s) |f_a(s) - g(s)|^p \, ds \geq \frac{(f_{\max} - f_{\min})^p}{(n+2) \cdot 2^{1+2p}}.$$

  - If $g(t_{2l+3}) \leq f_{\min}$, then $g(t_{2l+2}) \leq g(t_{2l+1}) \leq \frac{3f_{\max} + f_{\min}}{4}$ by Eq. 7, thus

$$\int_{t_{2l+1}}^{t_{2l+2}} w(s) |f_a(s) - g(s)|^p \, ds \geq \frac{(f_{\max} - f_{\min})^p}{(n+2) \cdot 2^{1+2p}}.$$

  - Otherwise, for some $\delta_1, \delta_2 > 0$ we have that $f_{\min} < f_{\min} + \delta_2 = g(t_{2l+3}) \leq g(t_{2l+1}) = f_{\max} - \delta_1 < f_{\max}$; then by Eq. 7 we get $\delta_1 + \delta_2 \geq \frac{f_{\max} - f_{\min}}{4}$, therefore

$$\int_{t_{2l+1}}^{t_{2l+3}} w(s) |f_a(s) - g(s)|^p \, ds \geq \frac{\delta_1^p + \delta_2^p}{2(n+2)} \geq \frac{(\delta_1 + \delta_2)^p}{(n+2) \cdot 2^p} \geq \frac{(f_{\max} - f_{\min})^p}{(n+2) \cdot 8^p},$$

where the second-to-last inequality follows from Hölder's inequality.

Hence, we obtain the desired result:

$$\text{err}(\mathcal{G}) = \sup_{f \in \mathcal{F}} \left\{ \inf_{g \in \text{cone}(\mathcal{G})} d(f,g) \right\} \geq \inf_{g \in \text{cone}(\mathcal{G})} \left(\int_{p_{\min}}^{p_{\max}} w(s) \, |f_a(s) - g(s)|^p \, ds \right)^{1/p}$$

$$\geq \epsilon \cdot \Omega(f_{\max} - f_{\min}).$$

6.3   Proof of Theorem 3

Let $\epsilon > 0$, and consider ticks $t_i = p_{\min}(1 + \delta)^i$ for $i \in \{0, 1, \ldots, n\}$ where $\log(1 + \delta) = \epsilon^p \log(p_{\max}/p_{\min})$, and $n = \log(p_{\max}/p_{\min}) / \log(1 + \delta)$, so that $t_0 = p_{\min}$ and $t_n = p_{\max}$. Consider the normalized weight function $w \colon [p_{\min}, p_{\max}] \to \mathbb{R}^+$ such that $\int_{p_{\min}}^{p_{\max}} w(p) \, dp = 1$, with the property that for some constant $C > 0$, $\forall i \in \{0, 1, \ldots, n-1\}$, $\int_{t_i}^{t_{i+1}} w(p) \, dp \leq \frac{C^p}{n}$. Our Uniswap v3-like exchange mechanism $\mathcal{G} = \text{cone}(\mathcal{G})$ is described with the following $n + 1$ basis functions: one basis function for each of the intervals $[t_i, t_{i+1}]$ for $i \in \{0, 1, \ldots, n-1\}$ defined by

$$g_i(p) = \begin{cases} \frac{1}{\sqrt{t_i}} - \frac{1}{\sqrt{t_{i+1}}}, & \text{for } p_{\min} \leq p \leq t_i \\ \frac{1}{\sqrt{p}} - \frac{1}{\sqrt{t_{i+1}}}, & \text{for } t_i \leq p \leq t_{i+1} \\ 0, & \text{for } t_{i+1} \leq p \leq p_{\max} \end{cases},$$

along with the additional basis function $g_n(p)$ that is everywhere 1[8].

Consider any $f \in \mathcal{F}$, and define the following $g_f \in \text{cone}(\mathcal{G})$ that will "approximate" this f:

$$g_f(p) = f(p_{\max})g_n(p) + \sum_{i=0}^{n-1} \frac{f(t_i) - f(t_{i+1})}{\frac{1}{\sqrt{t_i}} - \frac{1}{\sqrt{t_{i+1}}}} g_i(p).$$

Then, it holds that

$$\forall p \in (t_i, t_{i+1}), \ |f(p) - g_f(p)| \leq f(t_i) - f(t_{i+1}).$$

Hence, we obtain the stated result by a similar argument to that of Sect. 6.1.

Disclosures. The first author is a Research Fellow with automated market making protocols, including ones mentioned in this work. The second author is an advisor to fintech companies. The third author is Head of Research at a16z crypto, which reviewed a draft of this article for compliance prior to publication and is an investor in various decentralized finance projects, including Uniswap, as well as in the crypto ecosystem more broadly (for general a16z disclosures, see https://www.a16z.com/disclosures/).

Acknowledgments. We would like to thank Neel Tiruviluamala for helpful comments on the proof of our lower bound. We also thank anonymous reviewers of the Financial

---

[8] Note that this additional basis function is always necessary whenever $f_{\min} \neq 0$ to obtain an *arbitrarily good* approximation of any curve, due to the construction of the Uniswap curves to end at exactly 0 at the end of each interval.

Cryptography and Data Security conference for useful suggestions. The first author is supported in part by NSF awards CNS-2212745, CCF-2212233, DMS-2134059, and CCF-1763970. The second author is supported by the Briger Family Digital Finance Lab at Columbia Business School. The third author's research at Columbia University is supported in part by NSF awards CNS-2212745, and CCF-2006737.

A   Deferred Proofs of Section 2.2

Proof. (rice discovery) Assume that the current price of the exchange is $p_0 \neq p$. Suppose that an external market participant comes to the exchange and is willing to trade to some price p_1, and then uses the external market to trade back. We prove that the maximum profits will be obtained at $p_1 = p$; therefore, if the trader does not maximize their profits, other external market participants will continue to have an incentive to trade until the price of the exchange is p and the conclusion follows.

Due to Eq. 3, the external market participant's optimization problem for their profit is:

$$\max_{p_1 \in \mathbb{R}^+} p(g(p_0) - g(p_1)) + \int_{p_0}^{p_1} pdg(p) = \max_{p_1 \in \mathbb{R}^+} (p_1 - p)g(p_1) - \int_0^{p_1} g(p)dp$$

First-order conditions then prove that the optimum is attained at $p_1 = p$.

Proof. (Budget balance). Assume that the current price of the exchange is p_0. First, we note that liquidity additions and removals, due to the linear nature of the aggregate demand curves and the numéraire contributed/removed by Eq. 1 with respect to the curves $g_i(p)$, do not affect the rest of the joint pool, i.e., if the amount of numéraire was non-negative before the operation, so it is after it. Trading is the only action which is yet unclear how it affects the amount of numéraire in the pool. In aggregate, the joint pool contains a quantity $g(p_0)$ of risky asset, and in numéraire by Eq. 1:

$$\sum_{i=1}^{n} - \int_0^{p_0} pdg_i(p) = - \int_0^{p_0} pdg(p) \geq 0,$$

because g is non-increasing (as the sum of non-increasing functions) and $p_0 \geq 0$. Suppose that a trader comes and moves the pool price to p_1. The new amount of numéraire contained in the pool by the above equation and Eq. 3 is

$$- \int_0^{p_0} pdg(p) - \int_{p_0}^{p_1} pdg(p) = - \int_0^{p_1} pdg(p) \geq 0,$$

thereby completing our argument.

References

1. Adams, H., Zinsmeister, N., Robinson, D.: Uniswap v2 core (2020)
2. Adams, H., Zinsmeister, N., Salem, M., Keefer, R., Robinson, D.: Uniswap v3 core (2021)

3. Angeris, G., Chitra, T.: Improved price oracles: constant function market makers. In: Proceedings of the 2nd ACM Conference on Advances in Financial Technologies, pp. 80–91 (2020)
4. Angeris, G., Evans, A., Chitra, T.: Replicating market makers. arXiv preprint arXiv:2103.14769 (2021)
5. Angeris, G., Evans, A., Chitra, T.: Replicating monotonic payoffs without oracles. arXiv preprint arXiv:2111.13740 (2021)
6. Angeris, G., Evans, A., Chitra, T., Boyd, S.: Optimal routing for constant function market makers. In: Proceedings of the 23rd ACM Conference on Economics and Computation, pp. 115–128 (2022)
7. Angeris, G., Kao, H.T., Chiang, R., Noyes, C., Chitra, T.: An analysis of uniswap markets. arXiv preprint arXiv:1911.03380 (2019)
8. Aoyagi, J.: Liquidity provision by automated market makers. SSRN 3674178 (2020)
9. Aoyagi, J., Ito, Y.: Coexisting exchange platforms: Limit order books and automated market makers. SSRN 3808755 (2021)
10. Barbon, A., Ranaldo, A.: On the quality of cryptocurrency markets: Centralized versus decentralized exchanges. arXiv preprint arXiv:2112.07386 (2021)
11. Bichuch, M., Feinstein, Z.: Axioms for automated market makers: a mathematical framework in fintech and decentralized finance (2022). 10.48550/ARXIV.2210.01227. https://arxiv.org/abs/2210.01227
12. Buterin, V.: Let's run on-chain decentralized exchanges the way we run prediction markets, October 2016. https://www.reddit.com/r/ethereum/comments/55m04x/lets_run_onchain_decentralized_exchanges_the_way/
13. Capponi, A., Jia, R.: The adoption of blockchain-based decentralized exchanges. arXiv preprint arXiv:2103.08842 (2021)
14. Chitra, T., Angeris, G., Evans, A.: How liveness separates cfmms and order books (2021)
15. Ciampi, M., Ishaq, M., Magdon-Ismail, M., Ostrovsky, R., Zikas, V.: Fairmm: a fast and frontrunning-resistant crypto market-maker. In: International Symposium on Cyber Security, Cryptology, and Machine Learning, pp. 428–446. Springer, Cham (2022). https://doi.org/10.1007/978-3-031-07689-3_31
16. Engel, D., Herlihy, M.: Composing networks of automated market makers. In: Proceedings of the 3rd ACM Conference on Advances in Financial Technologies, pp. 15–28 (2021)
17. Engel, D., Herlihy, M.: Presentation and publication: Loss and slippage in networks of automated market makers. arXiv preprint arXiv:2110.09872 (2021)
18. Fan, Z., Marmolejo-Cossío, F.J., Altschuler, B., Sun, H., Wang, X., Parkes, D.: Differential liquidity provision in uniswap v3 and implications for contract design. In: Proceedings of the Third ACM International Conference on AI in Finance, ICAIF 2022, pp. 9–17. Association for Computing Machinery, New York (2022). https://doi.org/10.1145/3533271.3561775. https://doi.org/10.1145/3533271.3561775
19. Felekis, G., Kristensen, J.: λ - constant function markets generalizing and mixing automated market makers. In: 2022 IEEE International Conference on Blockchain (Blockchain), pp. 290–297 (2022). https://doi.org/10.1109/Blockchain55522.2022.00047
20. Forgy, E., Lau, L.: A family of multi-asset automated market makers. arXiv preprint arXiv:2111.08115 (2021)
21. Goyal, M., Ramseyer, G., Goel, A., Mazières, D.: Batch exchanges with constant function market makers: axioms, equilibria, and computation. arXiv preprint arXiv:2210.04929 (2022)

22. Huynh, Y.: Providing liquidity in uniswap v3 (2022)
23. Jensen, J.R., Pourpouneh, M., Nielsen, K., Ross, O.: The homogenous properties of automated market makers. arXiv preprint arXiv:2105.02782 (2021)
24. Kaiko: Crypto Markets Recover Despite 9.1% Inflation, July 2022. https://blog.kaiko.com/crypto-markets-recover-despite-9-1-inflation-9d7db87ab83f
25. Krishnamachari, B., Feng, Q., Grippo, E.: Dynamic automated market makers for decentralized cryptocurrency exchange. In: 2021 IEEE International Conference on Blockchain and Cryptocurrency (ICBC), pp. 1–2 (2021). https://doi.org/10.1109/ICBC51069.2021.9461100
26. Lehar, A., Parlour, C.A.: Decentralized exchanges. Technical report, Working paper (2021)
27. Lu, A., Köppelmann, M.: Building a Decentralized Exchange in Ethereum, March 2017.   https://blog.gnosis.pm/building-a-decentralized-exchange-in-ethereum-eea4e7452d6e
28. Milionis, J., Moallemi, C.C., Roughgarden, T.: Extended abstract: the effect of trading fees on arbitrage profits in automated market makers. In: Essex, A., et al. (eds.) FC 2023. LNCS, vol. 13953, pp. 262–265. Springer, Cham (2024). https://doi.org/10.1007/978-3-031-48806-1_17
29. Milionis, J., Moallemi, C.C., Roughgarden, T., Zhang, A.L.: Quantifying loss in automated market makers. In: Proceedings of the 2022 ACM CCS Workshop on Decentralized Finance and Security, DeFi 2022, Los Angeles, CA, USA, pp. 71–74. Association for Computing Machinery, New York (2022). https://doi.org/10.1145/3560832.3563441. ISBN: 9781450398824
30. Moosavi, M., Clark, J.: Lissy: experimenting with on-chain order books. arXiv preprint arXiv:2101.06291 (2021)
31. Neuder, M., Rao, R., Moroz, D.J., Parkes, D.C.: Strategic liquidity provision in uniswap v3. arXiv preprint arXiv:2106.12033 (2021)
32. O'Hara, M.: Market microstructure theory. Mass., repr. edn, Blackwell, Malden (2011)
33. Port, A., Tiruviluamala, N.: Mixing constant sum and constant product market makers. arXiv preprint arXiv:2203.12123 (2022)
34. Rockafellar, R.T.: Convex analysis. Princeton Landmarks in Mathematics and Physics, Princeton University Press, Princeton, NJ, December 1996
35. Shuttleworth, D.: Serum: A Decentralized On-Chain Central Limit Order Book | ConsenSys Cryptoeconomic Research (2022). https://consensys.net/blog/cryptoeconomic-research/serum-a-decentralized-on-chain-central-limit-order-book/
36. Wang, S., Krishnamachari, B.: Optimal trading on a dynamic curve automated market maker. In: 2022 IEEE International Conference on Blockchain and Cryptocurrency (ICBC), pp. 1–5 (2022). https://doi.org/10.1109/ICBC54727.2022.9805489
37. Wu, M., McTighe, W.: Constant power root market makers. arXiv preprint arXiv:2205.07452 (2022)
38. Xu, J., Paruch, K., Cousaert, S., Feng, Y.: Sok: decentralized exchanges (dex) with automated market maker (amm) protocols. arXiv preprint arXiv:2103.12732 (2021)
39. Yin, J., Ren, M.: On liquidity mining for uniswap v3. arXiv preprint arXiv:2108.05800 (2021)
40. Young, J.E.: On equivalence of automated market maker and limit order book systems (2020)

Mitigating Decentralized Finance Liquidations with Reversible Call Options

Kaihua Qin[1,4], Jens Ernstberger[2,4], Liyi Zhou[1,4], Philipp Jovanovic[3], and Arthur Gervais[3,4]($\boxtimes$)

[1] Imperial College London, London, UK
kaihua.qin@imperial.ac.uk
[2] Technical University Munich, Munich, Germany
[3] University College London, London, UK
arthur@gervais.cc
[4] Berkeley Center for Responsible, Decentralized Intelligence (RDI), Berkeley, USA

Abstract. Liquidations in Decentralized Finance (DeFi) are both a blessing and a curse—whereas liquidations prevent lenders from capital loss, they simultaneously lead to liquidation spirals and system-wide failures. Since most lending and borrowing protocols assume liquidations are indispensable, there is an increased interest in alternative constructions that prevent immediate systemic-failure under uncertain circumstances.

In this work, we introduce *reversible call options*, a novel financial primitive that enables the seller of a call option to terminate it before maturity. We apply reversible call options to lending in DeFi and devise MIQADO, a protocol for lending platforms to replace the liquidation mechanisms. To the best of our knowledge, MIQADO is the first protocol that actively mitigates liquidations to reduce the risk of liquidation spirals. Instead of selling collateral, MIQADO incentivizes external entities, so-called *supporters*, to top-up a borrowing position and grant the borrower additional time to rescue the debt. Our simulation shows that MIQADO reduces the amount of liquidated collateral by 89.82% in a worst-case scenario.

Keywords: DeFi · Liquidation · Reversible call option

1 Introduction

Recently, there has been an increasing interest in Decentralized Finance (DeFi), a financial ecosystem where users exercise cryptographic control over their financial assets. Commonly, DeFi is enabled by blockchains that support smart contracts (e.g., Ethereum), and financial primitives are instantiated as publicly accessible decentralized applications. A wide variety of traditional financial services that are implemented in DeFi, ranging from asset exchanges, to market making, as well as lending and borrowing platforms [15]. DeFi differs from the traditional, centralized financial system in multiple aspects. For instance, most DeFi services are open-source, such that traders can inspect the protocol rules encoded within immutable smart contracts.

With over 15B USD of total value locked (TVL), DeFi's lending and borrowing services account for 30% of DeFi's locked up assets. Just as in the traditional

© International Financial Cryptography Association 2024
F. Baldimtsi and C. Cachin (Eds.): FC 2023, LNCS 13950, pp. 344–362, 2024.
https://doi.org/10.1007/978-3-031-47754-6_20

centralized finance domain, debt in DeFi is prone to *liquidation events* upon price-swings of the debts' security deposit (subsequently referred to as collateral). A borrowing position becomes "unhealthy" (i.e., liquidatable), whenever the collateral is deemed insufficient to cover the debt, corresponding to a *health factor* inferior to one. The most prevalent liquidation mechanism, fixed spread liquidation (FSL), allows a *liquidator* to repay a fraction of the borrower's debt and acquire its collateral at a discount. The fraction at which the borrowers' debt is repaid in a liquidation is limited to an upper bound, commonly referred to as the *close factor* (e.g., 50%). As such, liquidations intend to protect the lender by preventing a loss of capital by selling a sufficient amount of collateral. However, liquidations serve as a double-edged sword. Selling off collateral causes a price decrease, which potentially leads to further liquidations and market-wide panic [11]. Quantifying the extent of liquidations in DeFi, a recent two-year longitudinal study (April 2019 to April 2021) by Qin *et al.* [16] finds that liquidation events on the Ethereum blockchain amount to over 800M USD in volume, yielding a staggering 64M USD profit to liquidators. Such liquidation profit constitutes a source of miner extractable value (MEV) [5], which grants miners a risk-free opportunity to extract financial profit. MEV, however, negatively affects blockchain consensus security by incentivizing blockchain forks [17].

In this work, we propose MIQADO, a mechanism designed to mitigate liquidation events to *(i)* protect borrowers from excessive collateral liquidation, *(ii)* alleviate MEV sourcing, and *(iii)* mitigate liquidation spirals. To this end, we introduce *reversible call options*, a novel financial primitive that enables the seller of a call option to terminate it at a premium before reaching maturity. MIQADO applies reversible call options to incentivize external support for "unhealthy" borrowing positions, while the original borrower is granted additional time to protect its borrowing position and limit the potential loss.

Thereby, we summarize the contributions of this work as follows.

1. **Quantifying Liquidation Spiral.** We quantify the liquidation spiral caused by the FSL mechanism by analyzing 48,364 past liquidation events over a time-frame of 41 months, capturing 2.32B USD of collateral liquidated. We find the existence of 18,305 short liquidations, where a liquidator immediately sells the acquired collateral. These liquidations account for 1.33B USD sold collateral and a maximal collateral price decline of 26.90%.
2. **A Novel Financial Primitive.** We introduce reversible call options, a novel financial primitive where the seller of a European call option can pay a premium to the buyer to terminate the option before its maturity.
3. **A Protocol for Liquidation Mitigation.** We propose MIQADO, the first protocol that protects DeFi borrowers from excessive liquidation losses. By realizing a reversible call option, MIQADO incentivizes external actors to support "unhealthy" borrowing positions, mitigating liquidations by design. MIQADO serves as a plug-and-play mechanism, which can be integrated into any existing lending platform. We evaluate MIQADO by simulating how it would have performed in past liquidation events. We find that MIQADO reduces the amount of liquidated collateral by 89.82% in a worst-case scenario.

2   Background

2.1   Blockchain and Smart Contract

In essence, a blockchain is a distributed ledger operating on top of a peer-to-peer (P2P) network [4]. The core blockchain functionality is that participants can transfer financial assets (i.e., cryptocurrencies) without any trusted third-party custodian [13]. To send cryptocurrencies, one broadcasts a signed transaction through the blockchain P2P network. The so-called *miners* collect, verify and package transactions into a block which is appended onto the already confirmed blocks forming a linear chain. All peers in the blockchain network are expected to follow a specific consensus mechanism (e.g., Nakamoto consensus [13]) to achieve the consistency of the ledger.

Beyond the simple cryptocurrency transfer, more versatile blockchains (e.g., Ethereum [23]) enable advanced transaction logic through pseudo-Turing complete smart contracts. Similar to regular user accounts, smart contracts can own cryptocurrencies. In addition, every smart contract is bound to a piece of immutable code upon its creation. Users can send a transaction to a smart contract account and trigger the execution of the associated smart contract code. We refer readers to [4] for more detailed explanations of blockchains and smart contracts.

2.2   Decentralized Finance

Smart contracts enable the creation of cryptocurrencies (also known as tokens) on a blockchain in addition to the native cryptocurrency (e.g., ETH on Ethereum). A token smart contract serves as a balance sheet recording the balance of every token holder account. Smart contracts also allow anyone to create any type of imaginable financial product on-chain, by enforcing the rules through the smart contracts' immutable code. The ecosystem as a whole, composed of these tokens and smart contract-based financial products, is referred to as DeFi. At the time of writing, the scale of DeFi has reached over 50B USD, with an abundance of applications such as exchanges, lending platforms, and derivatives.[1]

2.3   Lending/Borrowing in DeFi

Lending and borrowing, with over 15B USD TVL, is one of the most popular DeFi use cases. In a DeFi lending system, a smart contract called *lending pool*, manages the borrowing positions. Lenders provide assets to the lending pool to earn interests from borrowers. To minimize the lenders' risk of losing funds, every borrower is required to provide *collateral* as a guarantee. The lending and borrowing interests are programmatically determined by the contract code.

Lending in DeFi can be divided into *over-collateralized* and *under-collateralized* lending. In over-collateralized lending, the borrower provides a security deposit (i.e., collateral) which *exceeds* the lent assets by a factor of 1.1× to

---

[1]   https://defillama.com/.

2× depending on the respective protocol [16]. The borrower may then choose to freely use the lent asset in any capacity. Contrary to over-collateralized lending, in under-collateralized lending, the borrower only provides a fraction of the lent assets as security, hence achieving a leverage factor beyond 1×. For this leveraged borrowing to remain secure, the assets granted through under-collateralization can only be utilized in very specific, hard-coded settings encoded in immutable smart contracts, such that the lending pools stay in control of the lent assets. In this work, we primarily focus on over-collateralized lending.

We refer to the debts of a borrower together with the collateral securing these debts as a *borrowing position*. Due to asset price fluctuations, the collateral of a borrowing position may become insufficient to cover the debt. Therefore, lending pools typically set a threshold for the borrowing positions, at which a position becomes liquidatable. When the collateral value of a borrowing position declines below this threshold, lending pools can then allow the so-called liquidators, to repay the debt for the position, commonly referred to as liquidation. In return, the liquidator is eligible to acquire parts of the collateral from the borrowing position. The acquired collateral exceeds the repaid debt in value, which incentivizes the liquidator to realize a profit.

2.4 Call Options

Call options are financial contracts that grant buyers the right, but not the obligation, to buy an underlying asset (e.g., stocks) at an agreed-upon price (i.e., the exercise price or strike price) and date (i.e., the expiration date or maturity) [8,20]. In general, options are priced using a mathematical model, such as the Black-Scholes [3] or the Binomial pricing model [19]. On a high level, an options price is determined by *(i)* its intrinsic value and *(ii)* its time value. The intrinsic value is a measure of the profitability of an option if it were to be exercised immediately. The time value measures the value of an option arising from the time left to maturity (i.e., volatility). When the strike price of an option increases, the price of the call option consequently increases as well. In traditional finance, there are two styles of option contracts: *(i)* American options can be executed (or exercised) at any time up to the expiration date; *(ii)* European options can be exercised only on the expiration date [8].

3 Preliminaries

In the following, we formalize a collateralized debt model and the fixed spread liquidation, which is the prevalent DeFi liquidation mechanism.

3.1 Collateralized Debt Model

We assume the existence of an on-chain lending pool $\mathcal{L} = \{P_1, P_2, ..., P_n\}$, where P_i is the i-th borrowing position in the lending pool. Each borrowing position $P = \langle D_t, C_t \rangle$ is parametrized by the debt D_t the borrower owes, and the collateral C_t the borrower owns at time t. We denote the price of the debt cryptocurrency towards the collateral cryptocurrency, provided by an oracle [7], as p_t. In the following, we consider the case where each borrowing position consists of a single debt cryptocurrency and a single collateral cryptocurrency. In practice, a lending pool may allow for mixed borrowing positions by including multiple cryptocurrencies as either debt or collateral. We further assume that a borrower only opens a single borrowing position.

Whether or not a borrowing position is *liquidatable* is determined by the *health factor*.

$$HF_t(P) = \frac{C_t \cdot p_t \cdot \theta}{D_t} \tag{1}$$

$C_t \cdot p_t$ represents the value of the collateral, whereas D_t represents the value of the debt denoted in the same cryptocurrency. θ is the collateral discount, s.t. $0 < \theta < 1$. The collateral discount is configured as a safety margin to ensure the over-collateralization of a position, i.e., the value of the collateral is discounted when calculating the health factor. If $HF_t(P) < 1$, e.g., due to price fluctuations, P is deemed "unhealthy" making it available for liquidations under existing prevalent designs of DeFi lending protocols. Internally, the health factor of a borrowing position relies on the *collateralization ratio*

$$CR_t(P) = \frac{C_t \cdot p_t}{D_t}. \tag{2}$$

The collateralization ratio determines whether a position is over-collateralized or under-collateralized. If $CR_t(P) > 1$ at time t, a position is over-collateralized, and under-collateralized otherwise.

3.2   Fixed Spread Liquidation

We denote a decentralized application for lending and borrowing that applies a fixed spread liquidation mechanism as protocol prot_{FSL}. For ease of exposition, we assume that prot_{FSL} hosts a single lending pool $\mathcal{L}$. The liquidation of a position $P = \langle D_t, C_t \rangle$ is determined by a set of variables, including the previously introduced collateral discount θ, the close factor k_{CF} (s.t. $0 < k_{CF} \leq 1$) and the liquidation spread S.

$$\text{prot}_{FSL} = \langle \mathcal{L}, \theta, k_{CF}, S \rangle \tag{3}$$

The close factor k_{CF} describes the percentage of debt that the liquidator can repay in a single fixed spread liquidation. The spread S is the discount at which the liquidator can obtain the collateral. S is fixed throughout the execution of the protocol (i.e., the name *fixed spread liquidation*). With the liquidation spread, one can calculate the maximal collateral claimable by the liquidator $\mathcal{Q}$ as $(D_t \cdot k_{CF}) \cdot (1 + S)$. Without consideration of gas fees, the maximal obtainable profit by $\mathcal{Q}$ is $(D_t \cdot k_{CF}) \cdot S$. As the protocol is overall a zero-sum game, and under the assumption of non-existant slippage, the profit of the liquidator is equivalent to the borrowers loss, if denoted in the same cryptocurrency.

Other liquidation mechanisms, though operated differently from the fixed spread liquidations, follow similar high-level designs—debts are repaid in exchange for collateral from the liquidated borrowing position. For example, in MakerDAO auction liquidations, liquidators bid for the liquidation opportunity by submitting transactions [16]. In such a setting, the liquidation spread can hence be considered dynamic during the auction execution.

4 Motivation

We proceed to outline the design flaws of liquidation mechanisms and motivate why mitigating liquidations is necessary.

1. **Over-Liquidation.** DeFi borrowers are exposed to an unnecessarily overwhelming liquidation risk. In regular FSL configurations, $50\% \sim 100\%$ of a borrowing position is liquidated within a single transaction [16, 21].
2. **MEV.** Liquidation is one of the major sources of MEV, which disrupts miner incentives and endangers the consensus security of a blockchain [17].
3. **Liquidation Spiral.** A liquidation increases the supply of the collateral cryptocurrencies available for sale. This supply inflation imposes a negative impact on the collateral prices [22] and may result in further liquidations (possibly liquidation spiral [11]). We provide a case study of a real liquidation event to present the impact of liquidations on collateral prices.

Fig. 1. A real liquidation event with a subsequent downward price trend of the collateral asset. The liquidator $\mathcal{Q}$ immediately sold parts of the redeemed ETH collateral from a Compound liquidation, which decreased the ETH price on Uniswap by 6.95%.

Case Study 1 (Liquidation Spiral). *As shown in Fig. 1, two DeFi platforms were involved in this liquidation: (i) Compound, an over-collateralized lending platform; (ii) Uniswap, an on-chain exchange. USDC is a stablecoin, of which the value is pegged to USD.[2] In the studied liquidation, the liquidator mainly took the following three steps.*

1. *The liquidator repaid $4.61M$ USDC for a Compound borrowing position.*
2. *In return, the liquidator was allowed to redeem $2,034.64$ ETH of collateral.*
3. *The liquidator bought $1,933.43$ ETH from the redeemed collateral and exchanged the ETH for $4.61M$ USDC to cover its repayment cost in Step 1. The liquidator realized a profit of 101.20 ETH through this liquidation.*

In the third step, the exchange from ETH to USDC on Uniswap USDC/ETH triggered a price decline from $2,477.96$ USDC/ETH to $2,305.85$ USDC/ETH (-6.95%). This event shows that even a single liquidation can decrease the collateral price significantly.

---

[2] Transaction hash: 0xe7b6fac6502be7c6659880ff5d342ec470429c6f49cd457945bf07266 67eb689. Note that we ignore the irrelevant execution details to ease understanding.

Why Collateralization Instead of Liquidation? In this work, MIQADO requires additional collateral to be locked in the lending pool, reducing the liquid collateral asset supply. Hence, we conclude that MIQADO behaves more positively than a liquidation mechanism on stabilizing lending markets, effectively acting like a price "softening buffer". We empirically confirm this effect in Sect. 6.

5   Miqado

In this section, we introduce MIQADO. MIQADO is a debt management mechanism for DeFi lending protocols. It mitigates liquidations through a set of incentives that decrease the likelihood of liquidation spirals. MIQADO relies on *supporters*, which are entities that are willing to top up unhealthy borrowing positions. To enable MIQADO, we introduce *reversible call options*, a novel financial primitive where the seller of a call option can pay a premium to terminate the contract before maturity.

5.1   Reversible Call Option

Recall the notion of European call options as introduced in Sect. 2.4. In a European call option, the seller offers the option contract whereas the buyer acquires the option to exercise the right to buy an asset at a specific price by buying said option at a premium (i.e., the option price). The outcome of a European call option contract at maturity is binary—*(i)* the buyer exercises its right to buy or *(ii)* the buyer does not exercise its right to buy. We now introduce the *reversible* European call option, which augments the traditional European call option with an additional outcome to the option contract, where the seller is able to terminate the contract at a premium.

We say that a reversible European call option contract gives the buyer $\mathcal{C}_B$ the option, but not the obligation, to buy a specified amount N of an asset A at a specified price K at maturity T, and the seller $\mathcal{C}_S$ the option to terminate the contract at pre-Maturity $t_0 < t < T$. The buyer $\mathcal{C}_B$ pays a premium ϕ at t_0 for the option to exercise the contract at maturity T.

Formally, we define reversible call option as follows:

Definition 1 (Reversible Call Option). *A reversible call option is parameterized by an asset A, the asset amount N, the strike price K, the reimbursement factor k, and the time of maturity T. The mechanics are as follows:*

t_0: (i) *The contract is agreed upon between $\mathcal{C}_B$ and $\mathcal{C}_S$.*
    (ii) *The buyer $\mathcal{C}_B$ pays a premium ϕ to the seller $\mathcal{C}_S$.*
$t_0 < t < T$: *The seller $\mathcal{C}_S$ of the option can choose to terminate the contract by reimbursing the buyer $\mathcal{C}_B$ with $\phi \cdot k$.*
T: *The buyer $\mathcal{C}_B$ can acquire N units of asset A at strike price K.*

Payoff Analysis. The buyer $\mathcal{C}_B$ is the entity which is entitled to execute the option contract at maturity. We assume that $\mathcal{C}_B$ always acts rationally, such that

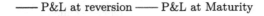

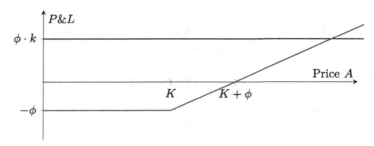

Fig. 2. Payoff & Loss (P&L) analysis for the Buyer $\mathcal{C}_B$ of the reversible call option. In case of reversion, the payoff for the $\mathcal{C}_B$ is constant. In case of maturity, the payoff is equal to a traditional call option.

their financial benefit is maximized. In the case of a reversible call option, the payoff which $\mathcal{C}_B$ receives can be categorized into two cases—*(i)* $\mathcal{C}_S$ terminates the option at pre-maturity or *(ii)* the contract is not terminated until maturity at time T. In the first case, the payoff for $\mathcal{C}_B$ is constant, as the seller $\mathcal{C}_S$ reimburses the buyer $\mathcal{C}_B$ with $\phi \cdot k$, where $k > 1$. If the seller $\mathcal{C}_S$ does not terminate the contract, the payoff for $\mathcal{C}_B$ is equivalent to

$$P_{\mathcal{C}_B} = \begin{cases} A(T) - K - \phi & \text{if } A(T) \geq K \\ -\phi & \text{if } A(T) < K \end{cases} \tag{4}$$

Note, that the payoff in this case is equivalent to a traditional European style call option. The visualized payoff curves for $\mathcal{C}_B$ are presented in Fig. 2.

5.2 The Miqado Protocol

We present the MIQADO protocol in the following. On a high-level, MIQADO seeks to mitigate liquidations through supporters that top-up the collateral of an unhealthy borrowing position (i.e., the health factor declined below one). MIQADO allows any external entity to become such a supporter. We start with an overview of MIQADO by outlining the equivalence to reversible call options.

Overview. An overview of MIQADO is presented in Fig. 3. On a high-level, MIQADO is separated into three phases—*(i)* Initialization, *(ii)* pre-Maturity, and *(iii)* Maturity. We first assume that MIQADO replaces the liquidation mechanism in our exemplary lending/borrowing protocol. We defer practical considerations for co-existence of MIQADO and liquidations to Sect. 5.4.

1) Initialization. We assume the existence of an on-chain lending pool $\mathcal{L}$ with a single borrowing position $P = \langle D_t, C_t \rangle$ initialized by the borrower $\mathcal{B}$. The supporter can engage at time t_0, if the following condition holds:

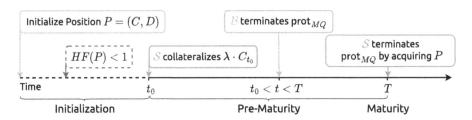

Fig. 3. High-level overview of the MIQADO protocol which realizes a reversible call option in DeFi. Once the borrowing position opened by the borrower B is unhealthy, yet not liquidated, the supporter S is able to top up the collateral in position P.

$$HF_{t_0}(P) = \frac{C_{t_0} \cdot p_{t_0} \cdot \theta}{D_{t_0}} < 1 \qquad (5)$$

In words, the health factor should be lower than one. Note that the position may be over-collateralized ($CR_{t_0}(P) > 1$) or under-collateralized ($CR_{t_0}(P) < 1$), depending on the steepness of the price decline that yields a borrowing position unhealthy. At this point, S buys a reversible call option by topping-up $\lambda \cdot C_{t_0}$ into P, which grants the right to take over the borrowing position P at maturity T. The price of the reversible call option hence is $\lambda \cdot C_{t_0}$. Note that the premium factor λ is a protocol parameter that can be ruled in the lending pool contract. To decide whether to deposit, a supporter would need to price the reversible call option and estimate its potential profitability, which we detail in Sect. 5.3.

2) **pre-Maturity.** Once S acquires a MIQADO option with maturity T, the pre-maturity stage starts. At any point $t_0 < t < T$, the borrower B can terminate the MIQADO protocol by repaying S the premium $\lambda \cdot C_{t_0}$ multiplied by a constant factor k_{re} that incentivizes the initial support of S, hence

$$C_{re} = \lambda \cdot C_{t_0} \cdot (1 + I_{\mathcal{L}}) \cdot k_{re} \qquad (6)$$

where $0 < I_{\mathcal{L}} < 1$ is the interest rate which B agreed to pay for its loan when initiating the position P. The factor $0 < k_{re} < 1$ is implementation dependent and should account for the risk S has to take when supporting a position.

3) **Maturity.** At Maturity, there are two possible options how the MIQADO protocol may terminate. The payoff for the supporter S in the case of maturity is depicted in Fig. 2.

    1. **Full Takeover.** In general, MIQADO option contracts have an "Out-of-the-Money" strike price K, such that the strike is greater than the collateralization ratio upon initiation of the position P by B. Essentially, as the health factor is lower than one, the intrinsic value of the option is low, whereas the time value based on volatility and time of expiration is high.

    2. **Default.** The supporter defaults and does not exercise the option, hence loses the premium ϕ (cf. Fig. 2), if the price at Maturity is below the

strike price K. In this case, where MIQADO fully replaces the liquidation mechanism, another round of Miqado initiates. Rational supporters initiate a MIQADO session if the condition presented in *1.) Initialization* is fulfilled.

Incentive Discussion. A common question is why a supporter would actually engage in the MIQADO protocol and top up liquidity positions that are unhealthy. In general, whether a supporter is incentivized to engage in a MIQADO option in a FSL liquidity pool depends on the price volatility and the selected strike price. Given the volatility of various cryptocurrencies, it is infeasible to draw a general conclusion fitting all scenarios. Supporters can price the MIQADO options and compare to the required cost (i.e., the premium) to evaluate the potential risks. We outline a pricing model for reversible call options in Sect. 5.3. In practice, we assume that supporters taking a low risk will face termination at pre-maturity by $\mathcal{B}$, yielding a smaller payoff for $\mathcal{S}$. We empirically evaluate MIQADO's ability to prevent liquidation spirals by replacing the liquidation mechanism in Sect. 6.

5.3 Pricing Reversible Call Option

The reversible call option is equivalent to an European call option in the case of maturity. Therefore, we can apply the widely adopted Black-Scholes pricing model [8] for European call options to MIQADO. We outline the B-S model details in Appendix A. We assume that at initialization t_0, the supporter $\mathcal{S}$ buys a MIQADO option by supplying $\lambda \cdot C_{t_0}$ of additional collateral priced at $\lambda \cdot C_{t_0} \cdot p_{t_0}$. The spot exchange rate is equivalent to p_{t_0}, whereas the domestic interest rate r is equivalent to the borrowing interest rate of the protocol $I_{\mathcal{L}}$. The foreign interest rate r_f remains the same. The volatility σ can be calculated from the price history. Henceforth, the optimal factor λ^* following the B-S model can be calculated as

$$\lambda^* = \frac{p_{t_0} e^{-r_f \cdot T} N(d_1) - K e^{-I_{\mathcal{L}} \cdot T} N(d_2)}{C_{t_0} \cdot p_{t_0}} \tag{7}$$

with equations for d_1 and d_2 outlined in Appendix A. A supporter then compares the actual premium factor λ set by the lending protocol to λ^* and evaluates the profitability. In practice, a supporter would have a personalized pricing model based on the supporter's predictions on the price dynamics and risk preference.

5.4 Practical Instantiation

When there is no supporter $\mathcal{S}$ willing to purchase a reversible call option or when a supporter defaults, the lender $\mathcal{E}$ faces a loss as the borrower $\mathcal{B}$ is not incentivized to repay the outstanding debt and $\mathcal{S}$ is not incentivized to take over the position P. In a practical instantiation (cf. Fig. 4), a protocol operator may want to operate MIQADO options on top of a traditional liquidation mechanism

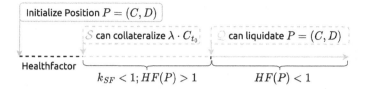

Fig. 4. Practical Instantiation of MIQADO on top of a traditional liquidation mechanism. The supporter $\mathcal{S}$ has an advantage over the liquidator $\mathcal{Q}$ to support a temporarily unhealthy position.

in order to prevent this. As such, the protocol can employ a buffer to derive an additional *support factor* k_{SF}, such that $\mathcal{S}$ can engage in a MIQADO option if

$$k_{SF} = CR_{t_0}(P) \cdot (\theta + B) < 1 \tag{8}$$

where B is the buffer parameter, s.t. $B > 1$.

A liquidator can additionally engage when the health factor is lower than one, as traditionally assumed and presented in Eq. 5. With this construction, the supporter has an advantage over the liquidator to support a temporarily unhealthy position and make a profit. Effectively, this construction similarly mitigates liquidation spirals, dependent on the buffer B.

5.5 Remarks

MIQADO enhances Fixed Spread Liquidations in the following aspects:

Rescue Opportunity. The reversible call option of MIQADO offers a time window for a borrower to rescue its borrowing position. With a fixed spread liquidation, the close factor is usually larger than necessary such that more collateral is sold off at a discount, which negatively impacts the borrowers financial interests. With MIQADO options, this risk is alleviated, such that over-liquidation is not a concern and the borrower has to pay less to rescue its position.

Collateral Restraint. MIQADO absorbs additional collateral and locks it in the lending pool until the reversible call option's maturity. This mitigates the possible liquidation spiral, which we quantitatively show in Sect. 6.

MEV Mitigation. FSL liquidations provides deterministic and cost-free opportunities for miners to profit through manipulating transaction order and front-running other liquidators. In MIQADO, if a miner deems a reversible call option profitable, it still has an advantage over other supporters. This is because a miner can single-handedly front-run any competing transaction and be the first to initiate MIQADO. Nevertheless, as shown in Sect. 6.2, a MIQADO reversible call option does not guarantee a profit. Moreover, a supporter bears a capital cost while locking the premium in the lending pool. We hence conclude that MIQADO mitigates the MEV problem.

6   Empirical Evaluation

In this section, we evaluate the MIQADO protocol by comparing MIQADO to the dominant liquidation mechanism FSL. To this end, we collect all liquidation events on Aave (both V1 and V2) and Compound from the 1st of May, 2019 to the 30th of September, 2022. Aave and Compound are the top two lending protocols on Ethereum in terms of TVL, according to defillama.com. Both of the two lending protocols follow the FSL mechanism (cf. Sect. 3.2). In total, we collect 48,364 liquidations (Aave V1: 5,765; Aave V2: 25,576; Compound: 17,023).

6.1   Quantifying Liquidation Spiral

Collateral Release. A lending protocol that applies FSL directly sells the liquidated collateral to the liquidator at a discount. This aggravates the price downtrend of the liquidated cryptocurrency as liquidators may immediately sell of the acquired collateral, which was locked in the lending protocol, to secondary markets. Precisely measuring the impact of FSL on the liquidated collateral price is challenging. We need to devise an accurate economic model to exclude the impact of other factors, such as the demand change for the collateral. We also need to model the liquidity dynamics on various centralized and decentralized exchanges at the time of liquidation. These challenges are however beyond the scope of this study and are left for future work. Therefore, we choose to present the value of collateral that is released in the FSL liquidations (cf. Metric 1) to intuitively quantify the liquidation spiral introduced by the FSL mechanism.

Metric 1 (FSL Collateral Release). *The value of collateral released to the markets in a FSL liquidation.*

Figure 5 presents the monthly collateral release in the past 48,364 FSL liquidations. The total collateral release amounts to 2.32B USD over the 41 months.

Direct Price Decline. In Case Study 1 (cf. Sect. 4), we show that a liquidator can choose to sell the collateral acquired from the borrower within the liquidation transaction. We observe that such a "sell-after-liquidation" strategy is prevalent, which we define as a short liquidation (cf. Definition 2).

Definition 2 (Short Liquidation). *In a short liquidation, Q sells (fully or partially) the collateral acquired from B within the liquidation transaction.*

To identify a short liquidation, we first gather the ERC-20 transfer and asset swap events from a liquidation transaction.[3] With these events, we then filter

---

[3] ERC-20 is a fungible token standard, which is extensively adopted in the Ethereum DeFi ecosystem. An event refers to a log emitted by a smart contract during its execution. These events are identifiable by a unique topic hash and can represent various actions, such as an asset swap on a decentralized exchange. In this work, for asset swap events, we captured the most liquid exchanges on Ethereum including Uniswap V1, V2, V3, Sushiswap, and Curve.

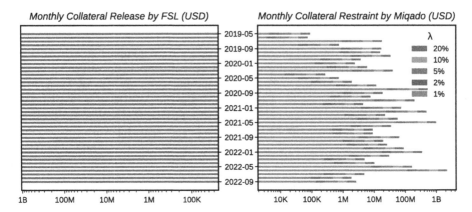

Fig. 5. Over a time-frame of 41 months (from the 1st of May, 2019 to the 30th of September, 2022), the collateral release by the FSL mechanism accumulates to 2.32B USD, with a monthly peak of 653.11M USD in May, 2021. On the contrary, our MIQADO protocol restrains additional collateral in the lending pool instead of releasing and further mitigates the liquidation spiral. The accumulative collateral restraint by MIQADO (cf. Metric 3, Sect. 6.2) amounts to 5.63B USD when the premium factor λ is set to 20%.

the exchange contracts that are potentially used for collateral selling. The filtering process is based on two criteria: *(i)* the contract emits an asset swap event during the transaction execution; *(ii)* the contract receives the liquidated collateral token (fully or partially). If such an exchange contract is detected, the liquidation transaction is classified as a short liquidation. From the 48,364 studied liquidations, we identify 18,305 short liquidations. In total, 1.33B USD of collateral is sold directly by the liquidators in these short liquidations. We find that in 3,365 of the short liquidations, the acquired collateral is fully sold. On average, 95.95% of the collateral is sold in a short liquidation.

A short liquidation directly leads to a collateral price decline on the exchange where the liquidator sells the acquired collateral. Although a significant price change in a single market will eventually be evened out by arbitrageurs[4] among all available markets, while the negative impact on the collateral price remains. We therefore apply such a price decline as a metric of how FSL liquidations destabilize lending protocols (cf. Metric 2).

Metric 2 (Direct Price Decline). *In a short liquidation, the spot price decline on the exchange where the liquidator sells the acquired collateral.*

We find that the average collateral price decline led by the 18,305 short liquidations is 0.38%, while the maximal decline reaches 26.90%.[5]

---

[4] Entities who profit by leveraging price differences across different markets.
[5] Cf. 0xff2d484638b846a46b203a22b02d71df44bf78346c72b954ad0ad05f34b134c8.

6.2 Miqado Evaluation

In the following, we assume that Aave and Compound had adopted MIQADO and simulate how MIQADO could have outpaced FSL in the past liquidation events. Our simulation is constrained to every single liquidation event, while ignoring the long-term impact of MIQADO. For example, MIQADO mitigates the price downtrend and hence could have prevented follow-up liquidations in a liquidation spiral, which we leave for future research.

The performance of MIQADO is influenced by its parameters. In our simulation, we assume that MIQADO follows the corresponding lending protocol's configuration for the collateral discount θ at the time of each liquidation. This implies that MIQADO shares the same triggering condition as FSL (i.e., when the health factor declines below one) and hence applies to every liquidated borrowing position. We also need to parameterize the premium factor λ and the time to maturity ΔT for the reversible call option. Similar to how the parameters for lending protocols evolve,[6] these two parameters need to be empirically determined and dynamically adjusted given various market conditions (e.g., the price volatility). We therefore simulate on various specific settings to show how MIQADO performs under different configurations.

Collateral Restraint. MIQADO absorbs additional collateral, which is restrained in the lending pool during the protocol execution. This collateral restraint, contrary to FSL's supply release (cf. Metric 1), imposes a positive impact on stabilizing collateral price (cf. Metric 3).

Metric 3 (Miqado Collateral Restraint). *The value of collateral deposited by the supporter in a* MIQADO *execution.*

We visualize the monthly comparison between the collateral restraint by MIQADO and the collateral release by FSL in Fig. 5. The accumulative collateral restraint with different parameters is outlined in Table 1, Appendix B. We find that when λ is 20%, the accumulative collateral restraint reaches 5.63B USD. Notably, as a by-product, the restrained additional collateral is counted towards the lending pool's TVL, which is a common protocol success metric.

Health Factor Recovery. One shared target of MIQADO and FSL is to increase the health factor of a borrowing position. In Fig. 6, we present the health factor distributions before and after the studied FSL liquidations. We further simulate how MIQADO could have increased the health factor with different parameters. We find that, 82.25% of the liquidated positions become healthy (the health factor is increased above one) after a FSL liquidation. When λ is set to 5%, MIQADO achieves the same performance (82.22% of the borrowing positions become healthy after the supporter deposits).

---

[6] https://docs.aave.com/risk/asset-risk/risk-parameters.

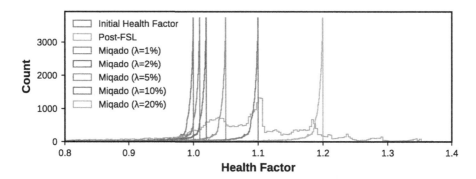

Fig. 6. The health factor distributions pre- and post-FSL liquidations. We also visualize how MIQADO increases the health factor with different premium factors.

Payoffs for Supporter. We proceed to simulate the payoffs of MIQADO supporters. In this section, we assume that the borrowers would not terminate the reversible call options. We parameterize ΔT to 1, 6, and 24 hours and apply the real market price to value every reversible call options at maturity. A supporter then chooses to exercise the option when the value of collateral exceeds the outstanding debt at maturity, and defaults otherwise (cf. Fig. 2). In Table 2, Appendix B, we outline the probability that a supporter *(i)* exercises the call option and profits, *(ii)* exercises the call option but loses, *(iii)* defaults, under different parameters. We also present the average profit for every supporter. We show that, to our surprise, the MIQADO premium factor does not impact the probability of the reversible call option in practice. Notably, in Table 2, we assume that the borrowers would not rescue their debts and therefore conjecture that the actual payoffs for supporters would be lower than the presented results.

Collateral Release Reduction. In practice, the probability that a MIQADO supporter may default on the reversible call option is up to 13.48%. This implies that the associated borrowing position is under-collateralized at maturity and may be further available for FSL (cf. Sect. 5.4). We simulate that, in the worst case, the collateral release by FSL after MIQADO (cf. Metric 1) amounts to 236.40M USD, which is a reduction of 89.82% compared the 2.32B USD collateral release by FSL only (cf. Sect. 6.1).

7   Related Work

Various works in DeFi focus on lending & borrowing protocols from diverse perspectives such as economics, security and formal modeling. Kao *et al.* [9] evaluate the economic security of Compound by using agent-based simulation.

Darlin *et al.* [6] investigate the optimal bidding strategies for auction liquidations. Perez *et al.* [14] present an empirical analysis of liquidations on Compound. Qin *et al.* [16] perform a longitudinal study on the liquidation events of four major Ethereum lending pools (i.e., Aave, Compound, dYdX, and MakerDAO), while showing the over-liquidation problem of the fixed spread liquidations. In this work, we show that the proposed MIQADO protocol mitigates these problems. Bartoletti *et al.* systematize DeFi lending pools [2] and further provide a formal analysis of DeFi lending pools [1]. Wang *et al.* [21] study under-collateralized DeFi lending platforms showing the three main risks of a leverage-engaging borrower, namely, impermanent loss, arbitrage loss, and collateral liquidation. Select stablecoin designs leverage lending and borrowing mechanisms (e.g., DAI from MakerDAO), as studied in [10–12].

Besides DeFi lending and borrowing, further studies focus on decentralized exchanges and the security of the DeFi ecosystem [5,17,18,24,25]. Most recently, Zhou *et al.* [25] systematize attacks on DeFi and highlight the need for further research on the protocol layer due to 59% of attacks on lending & borrowing platforms yielding from insufficient protocol design.

Further, there are various non-academic works that offer call options in decentralized applications. Hegic offers gas-free option trading for ETH and BTC. Ribbon supports on-chain options, where the option price, or premium, is set through an auction. However, none of the existing decentralized applications applies an equivalent financial primitive to lending & borrowing platforms to mitigate liquidations.

8   Conclusion

We presented MIQADO, the first liquidation mitigation protocol. Whereas existing lending and borrowing protocols rely on plain liquidation mechanisms, MIQADO secures borrowing positions by incentivizing external entities to provide additional collateral. To facilitate MIQADO, we introduce reversible call options, a novel financial primitive with promising properties for application in MIQADO. To highlight the need for MIQADO, we show that fixed spread liquidations trigger liquidation spirals and destabilize lending markets. We evaluate MIQADO by executing MIQADO logic on past blockchain states. We show that by applying MIQADO, the amount of liquidated collateral can be reduced by 89.82%. By providing a plug-in replacement to existing liquidation mechanisms, MIQADO can prevent systemic-failures without extensive overhead.

Acknowledgements. We thank the anonymous reviewers for the thorough reviews and helpful suggestions that significantly strengthened the paper. This work is partially supported by Lucerne University of Applied Sciences and Arts, the Federal Ministry of Education and Research of Germany (in the programme of "Souverän. Digital. Vernetzt.". Joint project 6G-life, project identification number: 16KISK002), and the Algorand Centres of Excellence programme managed by Algorand Foundation.

A   Black-Scholes Model

We apply the Black-Scholes model [3] to price call options under optimal assumptions, such as the non-existence of dividend payouts. The option premium is calculated for European call options on a per-share basis. The payoff for $\mathcal{C}_S$ introduced in Fig. 2 is trivial to grasp but it does not yield any insights on the pricing of the option. With the BS model for a European call option determines the option price as

$$c = S_0 e^{-r_f \cdot T} N(d_1) - K e^{-r \cdot T} N(d_2) \tag{9}$$

where

$$d_1 = \frac{\ln(S_0 K) + (r - r_f + \sigma^2 2) \cdot T}{\sigma \cdot \sqrt{T}} \tag{10}$$

and

$$d_2 = d_1 - \sigma \cdot \sqrt{T}. \tag{11}$$

S_0 is the spot exchange rate, r_f is the foreign interest rate, r is the domestic interest rate and σ is the volatility of the underlying asset. For a detailed introduction to the Black-Scholes pricing model for European call options, we refer the interested reader to [8].

We remark that the B-S model does not take into account the decrease in risk and lowered average payoff due to termination by $\mathcal{C}_S$. We defer a more precise pricing model for reversible call options that to future work.

B   Tables

Table 1. Accumulative collateral restraint by MIQADO over a time-frame of 41 months.

MIQADO Premium Factor λ	1%	2%	5%	10%	20%
Accumulative Collateral Restraint (USD)	281.70M	563.40M	1.41B	2.82B	5.63B

Table 2. Payoffs for MIQADO supporters at maturity assuming that borrowers would not rescue. We present the probability that a supporter *(i)* exercises the call option and profits, *(ii)* exercises the call option but loses, *(iii)* defaults. We also simulate the average profit for supporters. our simulations are based on the real market prices.

λ	1%	2%	5%	10%	20%	ΔT
+	87.46%	87.46%	87.46%	87.46%	87.46%	1 hour
−	0.29%	0.58%	1.41%	2.47%	4.14%	
#	12.25%	11.96%	11.13%	10.08%	8.41%	
$	125.51K±1.52M	125.51K±1.52M	125.50K±1.52M	125.49K±1.52M	125.48K±1.52M	
+	87.19%	87.19%	87.19%	87.19%	87.19%	6 h
−	0.30%	0.60%	1.50%	2.68%	4.44%	
#	12.51%	12.21%	11.31%	10.13%	8.37%	
$	154.01K±2.19M	154.01K±2.19M	154.00K±2.19M	154.00K±2.19M	154.98K±2.19M	
+	85.95%	85.95%	85.95%	85.95%	85.95%	24 h
−	0.56%	1.03%	2.16%	3.62%	5.59%	
#	13.48%	13.02%	11.89%	10.42%	8.45%	
$	144.42K±1.83M	144.40K±1.83M	144.36K±1.83M	144.32K±1.83M	144.29K±1.83M	

+ exercise and profit   − exercise but lose # default
$ average profit for supporters in USD (mean±std)

References

1. Bartoletti, M., Chiang, J., Junttila, T., Lluch Lafuente, A., Mirelli, M., Vandin, A.: Formal analysis of lending pools in decentralized finance. In: Margaria, T., Steffen, B. (eds.) ISoLA 2022 Part III. LNCS, vol. 13703, pp. 335–355. Springer, Cham (2022). https://doi.org/10.1007/978-3-031-19759-8_21
2. Bartoletti, M., Chiang, J.H., Lafuente, A.L.: SoK: lending pools in decentralized finance. In: Bernhard, M., et al. (eds.) FC 2021. LNCS, vol. 12676, pp. 553–578. Springer, Heidelberg (2021). https://doi.org/10.1007/978-3-662-63958-0_40
3. Black, F., Scholes, M.: The pricing of options and corporate liabilities. J. Polit. Econ. **81**(3), 637–654 (1973)
4. Bonneau, J., Miller, A., Clark, J., Narayanan, A., Kroll, J.A., Felten, E.W.: Sok: research perspectives and challenges for bitcoin and cryptocurrencies. In: 2015 IEEE Symposium on Security and Privacy (SP), pp. 104–121. IEEE (2015)
5. Daian, P., et al.: Flash boys 2.0: frontrunning in decentralized exchanges, miner extractable value, and consensus instability. In: 2020 IEEE Symposium on Security and Privacy (SP), pp. 910–927. IEEE (2020)
6. Darlin, M., Papadis, N., Tassiulas, L.: Optimal bidding strategy for maker auctions. arXiv preprint arXiv:2009.07086 (2020)
7. Eskandari, S., Salehi, M., Gu, W.C., Clark, J.: Sok: oracles from the ground truth to market manipulation. In: Proceedings of the 3rd ACM Conference on Advances in Financial Technologies, pp. 127–141 (2021)
8. Hull, J.C.: Options Futures and Other Derivatives. Pearson Education India, Noida (2003)
9. Kao, H.T., Chitra, T., Chiang, R., Morrow, J.: An analysis of the market risk to participants in the compound protocol. In: Third International Symposium on Foundations and Applications of Blockchains (2020)

10. Klages-Mundt, A., Harz, D., Gudgeon, L., Liu, J.Y., Minca, A.: Stablecoins 2.0: economic foundations and risk-based models. In: Proceedings of the 2nd ACM Conference on Advances in Financial Technologies, pp. 59–79 (2020)

11. Klages-Mundt, A., Minca, A.: (In) stability for the blockchain: Deleveraging spirals and stablecoin attacks. arXiv preprint arXiv:1906.02152 (2019)

12. Klages-Mundt, A., Minca, A.: While stability lasts: a stochastic model of noncustodial stablecoins. Math. Financ. (2022)

13. Nakamoto, S.: Bitcoin: a peer-to-peer electronic cash system (2008)

14. Perez, D., Werner, S.M., Xu, J., Livshits, B.: Liquidations: DeFi on a knife-edge. In: Borisov, N., Diaz, C. (eds.) FC 2021. LNCS, vol. 12675, pp. 457–476. Springer, Heidelberg (2021). https://doi.org/10.1007/978-3-662-64331-0_24

15. Qin, K., Zhou, L., Afonin, Y., Lazzaretti, L., Gervais, A.: CeFi vs. DeFi-comparing centralized to decentralized finance. arXiv preprint arXiv:2106.08157 (2021)

16. Qin, K., Zhou, L., Gamito, P., Jovanovic, P., Gervais, A.: An empirical study of DeFi liquidations: incentives, risks, and instabilities. In: Proceedings of the 21st ACM Internet Measurement Conference, pp. 336–350 (2021)

17. Qin, K., Zhou, L., Gervais, A.: Quantifying blockchain extractable value: how dark is the forest? In: 2022 IEEE Symposium on Security and Privacy (SP), pp. 198–214. IEEE (2022)

18. Qin, K., Zhou, L., Livshits, B., Gervais, A.: Attacking the DeFi ecosystem with flash loans for fun and profit. In: Borisov, N., Diaz, C. (eds.) FC 2021. LNCS, vol. 12674, pp. 3–32. Springer, Heidelberg (2021). https://doi.org/10.1007/978-3-662-64322-8_1

19. Shreve, S.: Stochastic Calculus for Finance I: The Binomial Asset Pricing Model. Springer, New York (2005). https://doi.org/10.1007/978-0-387-22527-2

20. Stoll, H.R.: The relationship between put and call option prices. J. Financ. **24**(5), 801–824 (1969)

21. Wang, Z., Qin, K., Minh, D.V., Gervais, A.: Speculative multipliers on DeFi: quantifying on-chain leverage risks. In: Eyal, I., Garay, J. (eds.) FC 2022. LNCS, vol. 13411, pp. 38–56. Springer, Cham (2022). https://doi.org/10.1007/978-3-031-18283-9_3

22. Whelan, J., Msefer, K., Chung, C.V.: Economic Supply & Demand. MIT, Cambridge (2001)

23. Wood, G., et al.: Ethereum: a secure decentralised generalised transaction ledger. Ethereum project yellow paper **151**(2014), 1–32 (2014)

24. Zhou, L., Qin, K., Torres, C.F., Le, D.V., Gervais, A.: High-frequency trading on decentralized on-chain exchanges. In: 2021 IEEE Symposium on Security and Privacy (SP), pp. 428–445. IEEE (2021)

25. Zhou, L., et al.: Sok: decentralized finance (DeFi) attacks. arXiv preprint arXiv:2208.13035 (2022)

Short Paper: DeFi Deception—Uncovering the Prevalence of Rugpulls in Cryptocurrency Projects

Sharad Agarwal[1]([✉]) [iD], Gilberto Atondo-Siu[2] [iD], Marilyne Ordekian[1] [iD],
Alice Hutchings[2] [iD], Enrico Mariconti[1] [iD], and Marie Vasek[1] [iD]

[1] University College London, London, UK
{sharad.agarwal,marilyne.ordekian.21,e.mariconti,m.vasek}@ucl.ac.uk
[2] University of Cambridge, Cambridge, UK
{jga33,ah793}@cl.cam.ac.uk

Abstract. DeFi has attracted legitimate investors and scammers alike. The paper presents an empirical investigation into the prevalence of rugpulls, a scam where cryptocurrency project developers exit without fully delivering and leave investors in the wind. Using forum data, 101 rugpulls from 6 different types of DeFi services are documented. ICOs form the majority of the rugpulls, most of which were active for less than six months before scamming out. ICOs rugpulled in 2021 were active for a much longer time than those that were rugpulled later on, perhaps pointing to new entrants intending to pull the rug. Through qualitative thematic analysis, we discover that these schemes primarily use authoritative and financial lures at the announcement stage of the project to mimic legitimate projects.

Keywords: cryptocurrency fraud · DeFi · cybercrime measurement · Ethereum

1 Introduction

With the rise of many types of cryptocurrency projects, it has become increasingly difficult for ordinary consumers to assess the validity of any particular project. With decentralized finance (DeFi) becoming increasingly popular, more and more consumers are brought to the cryptocurrency ecosystem. In turn, scammers have capitalized on investment scams, using consumers' lack of knowledge and the relative lack of consumer protections to earn millions of dollars.

Exit scams are scams where project developers abandon the project and run away with investors' funds. Unlike Ponzi schemes, these do not offer ludicrous rates of returns as a whole. Rather, they promise a good or service that they do not deliver. **Rugpulls** are exit scams in DeFi.

Exit scams, more broadly, are quite profitable – Chainalysis found that 37% of scam revenue in 2021 was from exit scams [2]. In 2021, operators of a Turkish cryptocurrency exchange, Thodex, ran away with $2 billion after closing

© International Financial Cryptography Association 2024
F. Baldimtsi and C. Cachin (Eds.): FC 2023, LNCS 13950, pp. 363–372, 2024.
https://doi.org/10.1007/978-3-031-47754-6_21

overnight. In March 2022, the US Department of Justice charged two people in a rugpull NFT scam that they anticipated would earn around $1.5M [17].

Our work investigates the incidences of rugpulls over time across different categories of projects in DeFi. To measure this comprehensively across these different categories, we use reports of rugpulls from a discussion forum to create a list of 101 different services which were rugpulled, mostly from 2020–2022. We provide the following contributions:

- We detail our comprehensive methodology that identifies rugpulls across six different categories of projects over more than two years in Sect. 3. The dataset is available at https://doi.org/10.7910/DVN/SMGMW8.
- We show the variety of types of rugpulls in Sect. 4. We relate this back to other occurrences in the ecosystem during this time to decipher why this happens.
- Using qualitative thematic analysis, we work towards understanding the lures when the projects are first announced in Sect. 5. This helps explain how scam projects draw in victims.

2   Related Work

There exists a burgeoning research direction in measuring exit scams on blockchains. Mazorra et al. [9] and Xia et al. [19] both detect over 10,000 rugpull scam tokens on the Uniswap platform, which defrauds users out of millions of dollars. Trozze et al. investigate five of these rugpulled tokens using investigative tools [16].

Mackenzie analyzes cryptocurrency scams through a criminological lens and divides rugpulls into two types: slow and fast [8]. Slow rugpulls are scams where the organizers start, e.g., an Initial Coin Offering (ICO), premine a large sum of the currency, and then slowly sell off their stock of coins. This contrasts with fast rugpulls of the sort that Mazorra et al. and Xia et al. uncover, which exploit quick liquidity hits on DeFi platforms like Uniswap. Xu et al. formalizes fast rugpulls [22]. Our work collects information on primarily the slower type.

Others have explored different areas in the cryptocurrency ecosystem and showed the impact of exit scams. Soska and Christin showed the impact of exit scam behavior both by exchange operators and on individual vendors on the reputation of the dark net market ecosystem [13]. In 2020, Xia et al. found that many COVID-influenced ICOs ended up performing exit scams [20]. Oosthoek and Doerr and Moore et al. separately analyzed security behavior on cryptocurrency exchanges and considered (but did not independently measure) exit scams [10,12]. This work fits broadly into the literature on cryptocurrency scams [1,5,18,21].

3   Methodology

In this section, we describe our approach to collecting our rich dataset on reported rugpulls.

3.1   Quantitative Methods

Collecting Rugpulls. Rugpulls are a relatively new form of cryptocurrency fraud, and no comprehensive list of these exists. To curate a more diverse listing of these scams, we use the discussion forum, bitcointalk.org. This forum, started by Satoshi themself, has historically been used to talk about cryptocurrencies more broadly. Currently, it remains a source for cryptocurrency beginners and often attracts scammers (and then talks about scams). This source is by no means comprehensive, but it does yield an insight into scams particularly targeting new users. We evaluated other open source listings of rugpull scams and could not find another set of listings of not just large rugpulls that make the news, but also smaller ones that influence not just new users' wallets, but also their trust in the community.

We use the Google Custom Search API[1] and identify all posts between Jan 2018 and Sept 2022 which include the keywords "rug pull" or "rugpull." We find 551 pages consisting of 335 distinct threads. For each thread, we fetch a local copy of all the posts in that thread.

Rugpull is a relatively new term and many users used it out of context, increasing the number of false positive threads. For instance, some threads speculate if a particular project will rugpull in the future, new users ask advice on various identification strategies for a rugpull, and investment advertisements claim to be 'rugpull proof.' Therefore, we manually review all the 335 distinct threads and identify 101 unique rugpulled projects. By inspecting the related threads and archived versions of the linked project websites, we categorize them into six different service categories. Table 1 shows an overview of the collected information.

Table 1. DeFi service types by quantity of observed rugpulls ($N = 101$).

Service Type	Definition	Obs.
Initial Coin Offerings (ICO)	Raising money to create a new ERC20 token	73
Yield farms	Lending crypto assets to earn interest on the loan	16
Exchanges	Platforms for users to buy/sell cryptocurrency	5
Non-Fungible Tokens (NFT)	Unique, non-interchangeable digital asset that can be bought and sold	5
Initial Dex Offerings (IDO)	Similar to ICO, but on a decentralized exchange	1
Cloud mining	Fractional shares of a mining operation	1

Collecting Supplementary Data. To find the corresponding start date of each project (since many projects did not exist on third-party aggregator websites), we collect the dates when the services were first introduced on the forum. These project announcements, aka ANN threads, are threads where people announce their upcoming projects. Users often link the ANN threads in the same thread

---

[1] https://developers.google.com/custom-search/v1/overview.

where the rugpull was reported. Other times, rugpull report thread is an ANN thread where the incidence of rugpull was mentioned in a later post on the thread. For the remainder, we query the bitcointalk forum using the rugpull's name to find its first occurrence. We manually verify that the mentioned service was indeed the same. To this end, we identify 63 rugpulls' first occurrence date.

To supplement our data on rugpulled services, we collect data on ICOs, the most common identified rugpull. We collate 2177 ICOs introduced between 2014 and September 2022 from the aggregator website coincodex.com. We omit 57 without a start date. We augment this with the available listings on coinmarketcap.com, resulting in 2227 total ICOs. Additionally, we use the historical data for the price of Bitcoin and Ethereum in USD from coincodex.com.

3.2   Qualitative Thematic Method

Cybercriminals use social engineering techniques to attract and deceive investors. It is essential to understand these techniques so investors can detect and avoid falling prey to fraudulent schemes. Therefore, we perform a qualitative thematic analysis [6] of project announcements in bitcointalk before they are reported to be rugpulled. We extract the content of posts identified as rugpulls and perform a manual thematic categorization of the text used in the announcement of these projects. We compare this to an analysis of an equal number of project announcements, selected from similar date ranges, that were not claimed to have been rugpulled. We use one coder to classify the data following a "concept-driven" [6] approach and adapt Stajano and Wilson's [14] scam lure principles as the framework for our analysis. We apply this framework's seven principles (shown in Table 2) as the codebook used for matching announcements; our results in Sect. 5 have been paraphrased to anonymize the source.

Table 2. Description of lure principles adapted from Stajano and Wilson [14]

Lure Principle	Description
Authority	Cybercriminals aim to provide trust to investors by showing technical knowledge and making references to legitimate entities
Dishonesty	Fraudsters invite users to participate willingly and knowingly into a fraudulent scheme
Distraction	Scammers aim to confuse users by giving many unrelated details
Financial	Cybercriminals leverage users' 'greed' and offer attractive monetary benefits, so users make an investment
Herd	Scammers encourage investors to not miss out on opportunities by relating to the popularity of the scheme
Kindness	Fraudsters leverage the willingness of people to help others
Time	Scammers pressure users to make decisions quickly

Ethical Considerations: We constructed our study design and data collection to minimize harm to forum participants. We did not store potential PII. We went through the ethics oversight process through the department of Security and Crime Science at UCL and received approval.

4   Quantitative Findings

While almost every cryptocurrency platform has had scam services confusing potential customers, scams tend to concentrate on specific sectors based on the scam type. Rugpulls are, by definition, related to DeFi services which naturally limits their scope. However, we wish to uncover which services disproportionately fall prey to this scam and if this trend changes as new technology in the DeFi space is released over time or if other factors, such as the price of Ethereum, change the incentives for scammers to decide to pull the rug at a given time.

4.1   Rugpulls over Time and by Service

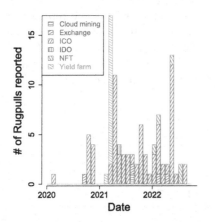

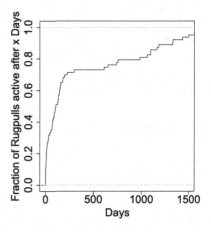

Fig. 1. Rugpulls reported between Jan 2020 and Sept 2022 ($N = 98$), split by type of service.

Fig. 2. Cumulative distribution for the number of days rugpull services were active ($N = 63$).

We start by understanding how reports of rugpulls have evolved. There were four reported rugpulls before mid-2020: one exchange and three ICOs. However, the start of this phenomenon really kicks off starting the second half of 2020, as shown in Fig. 1. This follows the rise of DeFi services; scammers enter the market after its popularity increases, and new services (which might have otherwise failed) "cash out" using this scam.

Yield farming services suddenly gained attraction in the summer of 2020 [3]. We see a peak in yield farm rugpulls in March 2021 after fifteen such scams were reported in a single thread on the forum. We only observed one other occurrence of rugpulls of yield farming services beyond this. This is likely an artifact of our data – bitcointalk tends towards less sophisticated users. For instance, an aggregator website of yield farming scams[2] lists 41 different scams (ranging from fake air drops to rugpulls) from Oct 2020 through Jan 2021.

To understand the number of days between the projects being announced and subsequently rugpulled, we analyze the distribution of their lifetime as seen in Fig. 2[3]. While 68% of the rugpulled projects were active for less than six months, 23.8% were active for more than two years. We hypothesize that the longer-running projects wait for a reasonable ETH exchange rate before pulling the rug. We observe this in Fig. 4. The positive Spearman's correlation coefficient between the monthly price of Ethereum and the monthly frequency of rugpull projects supports this hypothesis ($r_s = 0.606, p < 0.001$).

We also find that the projects rugpulled before September 2021 were active for a long time (median 384 d): the most long-lasting project was active for 2551 d. However, in 2022, rugpulled projects were active for only a short time (< 180 days, median 110.5 d). This likely demonstrates that these products started to engage in a rugpull scam after seeing the earlier success of their pre-2022 analogues. For instance, 'WX Coin' started in 2018 with some reputation mechanisms like a GitHub repo and whitepaper, but after 3 years, were possibly tempted by financial gains and rugpulled. On the other hand, 'Squid Coin,' based on a famous TV show in Oct 2021, was designed to attract investors and then rugpull within days once the token's price dramatically increased [15].

4.2   Rugpulls in ICOs

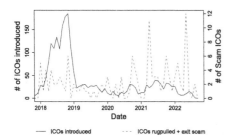

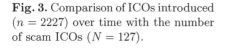

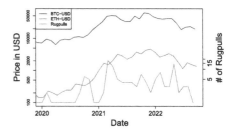

Fig. 3. Comparison of ICOs introduced ($n = 2227$) over time with the number of scam ICOs ($N = 127$).

Fig. 4. Exchange rate of Bitcoin and Ethereum compared to rugpulls ($N = 98$) between Jan 2020 to Sept 2022.

---

[2] https://defiyield.info/yield-farming-scam-database.
[3] We only consider those that we have start dates for. See Sect. 3.1.

ICOs form the majority of the rugpulls in our data. Most of these are considered in the literature to be slow rugpulls [8], where the scam is rolled out over periods of months or years rather than hours. However, this term used to discuss token ICOs is relatively new, and ICOs are becoming less frequent with time.

The word "rugpull" is a relatively new term whose usage can overlap colloquially with the word "exit scam" since rugpulls are a subset of exit scams that particularly refer to DeFi projects. Using the same methodology described in Sect. 3.1, we collect the posts on bitcointalk using the keyword "exit scam" and find 940 unique threads between 2018 and 2022. We further refine to find the ones that contain the keyword "ICO". After a manual review of these threads, we identify 54 exit scam ICOs.

To understand this interaction, we compare the number of ICOs introduced with ICOs rugpulled over time. We find that the increase in rugpulled ICOs broadly follows the increase in ICOs introduced, as seen in Fig. 3. We observe that while the peak in ICO announcements occurred in October 2018, rugpulls started to peak two years later. This could be due to the lifetime of a legitimate ICO – it takes time for projects to turn a product and similarly, scammers can then accept money for longer periods of time. We also hypothesize this could be due to companies that started with legitimate, but perhaps overhyped and underresourced ideas, and ended up selling to scammers to get out. We also see from Trozze et al. how token scams are often interconnected [16] and this post 2020 peak could be due to increased activity elsewhere.

We find that the number of rugpulled ICOs has decreased since the second half of 2022. This is likely due to the decrease of the popularity of ICOs waning with time with scammers and legitimate project owners moving other to new DeFi attractions like IDOs and NFTs. This could also be due to volatility.

5   Qualitative Thematic Analysis

As mentioned in Sect. 4.2, many rugpull projects are associated with ICOs, which use marketing tools to attract investors and provide credibility. ICO rugpulls also aim to follow these processes, at least to some extent, to convince potential victims of their purported legitimacy.

We identify the authority principle being used in some of these projects. Our dataset includes schemes that provide details of their corresponding founders, proposed algorithms, and links to code in GitHub repositories. Many include this information in whitepapers, some of which turn out to be plagiarized [11]. For example, one project claims to provide a better consensus protocol. Another project claims to be sponsored by reputable fund providers. We found similar examples of legitimate projects that provide analogous information when they are introduced in the forum. This shows the difficulty that investors might have to differentiate scams from legitimate projects when scammers use this principle.

We also uncover the financial principle in rugpulled projects. For instance, one promises an outstanding rate of passive return on a guaranteed and effortless basis. We discover a combination of the time and herd principles used in some other projects. For example, one of the schemes encourages users not to miss an opportunity to see their tokens' price increase, which will happen if more people join the project. We did not find these types of strategies used to advertise legitimate projects. Therefore, these examples provide some indications of the warnings that investors should be aware of to avoid falling prey to rugpulls.

Our analysis shows that investors should be skeptical of projects that employ financial, time, and herd principles to lure investors since these are not frequently found in legitimate projects. We do not observe the use of dishonesty, distraction, or kindness principles in the rugpulled project announcements. This fits into the work of Jahani et al. on discussions about "less serious" coins on bitcointalk where users hype up the coin rather than seeking for truth about it [7].

6 Conclusion

We have presented the dynamics of rugpull scams using a mixed method approach, with the aim of empirically analyzing the phenomena. While the early rugpull scams were using services that have been active for a long time, the later peaks have consisted of very new services. This indicates that, while at the beginning rugpull scams were perhaps not planned but rather opportunistic, more recent scams were likely planned and operated with malicious intent due to the easy earnings. This highlights not only how users flock to invest in DeFi after particular types of services are hyped, but also how scammers follow the money.

In this paper, we have established the prevalence of rugpull scams during the prolonged regulatory void. However, the situation is expected to change with the upcoming MiCA (Markets in Crypto-Assets [4]) regulation which is set to harmonize rules for cryptocurrencies across the EU. The framework intends to alleviate existing uncertainties in many ways, including the enhancement of consumer protection and bringing those such as token issuers under a proper form of standards. In particular, the rules will require issuers to be legal entities that draft, notify, and publish a detailed whitepaper that not only includes clear and transparent information about the project and the marketing communications[4], but also on the issuers/offerors themselves (art. 4, 5, 6, 7, 8). MiCA will also grant consumers[5] the right to withdraw their funds or even be reimbursed when possible (art. 12). Consequently, it will be harder for scammers to run and get away with schemes such as rugpulls.

In the interim, our qualitative analysis highlights how criminals use the promise of financial gain (financial principle) and the unmissable opportunity (time principle) to lure investors and scam them. Note that these principles are of differing effectiveness as some savvy investors highlight these lures as suspicious behavior. We encourage those operating platforms for beginning investors,

---

[4] Marketing must also follow the notification and publication process where applicable.

[5] The right to withdraw and reimbursement only applies to retail holders and not to qualified investors.

such as those moderating discussion forums to alert novices to these potential
lures and exercise caution.

Acknowledgements. We would like to thank the reviewers for their helpful comments and the FC attendees for their insightful questions. MO is supported by the UK Engineering and Physical Sciences Research Council [grant number EP/S022503/1]. GAS and AH are supported by the European Research Council (ERC) under the European Union's Horizon 2020 research and innovation programme [grant agreement No. 949127].

References

1. Atondo Siu, G., Hutchings, A., Vasek, M., Moore, T.: "Invest in crypto!": an analysis of investment scam advertisements found in Bitcointalk. In: 2022 APWG Symposium on Electronic Crime Research (eCrime). IEEE (2022)
2. Chainalysis: The Biggest Threat to Trust in Cryptocurrency. Rug pulls put 2021 cryptocurrency scam revenue close to all-time highs. https://blog.chainalysis.com/reports/2021-crypto-scam-revenues/
3. Cousaert, S., Xu, J., Matsui, T.: SOK: yield aggregators in DeFi. In: 2022 IEEE International Conference on Blockchain and Cryptocurrency (ICBC), pp. 1–14 (2022)
4. European Commission. Proposal for a regulation of the European parliament and of the council on markets in crypto-assets, and amending Directive (EU) 2019/1937 (2022). https://eur-lex.europa.eu/legal-content/EN/TXT/?uri=CELEX%3A52020PC0593
5. Foley, S., Karlsen, J.R., Putniņš, T.J.: Sex, drugs, and bitcoin: how much illegal activity is financed through cryptocurrencies? Rev. Financ. Stud. **32**(5), 1798–1853 (2019)
6. Gibbs, G.: Analyzing qualitative data. The SAGE Qualitative Research Kit. SAGE, London (2007)
7. Jahani, E., Krafft, P.M., Suhara, Y., Moro, E., Pentland, A.S.: Scamcoins, s*** posters, and the search for the next bitcoin^{TM}: collective sensemaking in cryptocurrency discussions. In: Proceedings of the ACM on Human-Computer Interaction, vol. 2(CSCW), pp. 1–28 (2018)
8. Mackenzie, S.: Criminology towards the metaverse: cryptocurrency scams, grey economy and the technosocial. Br. J. Criminol. (2022)
9. Mazorra, B., Adan, V., Daza, V.: Do not rug on me: leveraging machine learning techniques for automated scam detection. Mathematics **10**(6) (2022)
10. Moore, T., Christin, N., Szurdi, J.: Revisiting the risks of bitcoin currency exchange closure. ACM Trans. Internet Technol. **18**(4), 50:1–50:18 (2018)
11. Morin, A., Vasek, M., Moore, T.: Detecting text reuse in cryptocurrency whitepapers. In: 2021 IEEE International Conference on Blockchain and Cryptocurrency (ICBC), pp. 1–5 (2021)
12. Oosthoek, K., Doerr, C.: From hodl to heist: analysis of cyber security threats to bitcoin exchanges. In: 2020 IEEE International Conference on Blockchain and Cryptocurrency (ICBC), pp. 1–9. IEEE (2020)
13. Soska, K., Christin, N.: Measuring the longitudinal evolution of the online anonymous marketplace ecosystem. In: Proceedings of the 24th USENIX Security Symposium, Washington, DC, pp. 33–48 (2015)

14. Stajano, F., Wilson, P.: Understanding scam victims: seven principles for systems security. Commun. ACM **54**(3), 70–75 (2011)
15. Stokel-Walker, C.: How a Squid Game crypto scam got away with millions. https://www.wired.co.uk/article/squid-game-crypto-scam
16. Trozze, A., Davies, T., Kleinberg, B.: Of degens and defrauders: using open-source investigative tools to investigate decentralized finance frauds and money laundering (2023). https://arxiv.org/abs/2303.00810
17. US Department of Justice. Two defendants charged in non-fungible token fraud and money laundering scheme. https://www.justice.gov/usao-sdny/pr/two-def endants-charged-non-fungible-token-nft-fraud-and-money-laundering-scheme-0
18. Vasek, M., Moore, T.: There's no free lunch, even using bitcoin: tracking the popularity and profits of virtual currency scams. In: Böhme, R., Okamoto, T. (eds.) FC 2015. LNCS, vol. 8975, pp. 44–61. Springer, Heidelberg (2015). https://doi.org/10.1007/978-3-662-47854-7_4
19. Xia, P., et al.: Trade or trick? Detecting and characterizing scam tokens on Uniswap decentralized exchange. Proc. ACM Measur. Anal. Comput. Syst. **5**(3), 1–26 (2021)
20. Xia, P., et al.: Don't fish in troubled waters! characterizing coronavirus-themed cryptocurrency scams. In: 2020 APWG Symposium on Electronic Crime Research (eCrime), pp. 1–14. IEEE (2020)
21. Xia, P., et al.: Characterizing cryptocurrency exchange scams. Comput. Secur. **98**, 101993 (2020)
22. Xu, J., Paruch, K., Cousaert, S., Feng, Y.: SOK: decentralized exchanges (DEX) with automated market maker (AMM) protocols (2021). https://arxiv.org/abs/2103.12732

Author Index

© International Financial Cryptography Association 2024
F. Baldimtsi and C. Cachin (Eds.): FC 2023, LNCS 13950, pp. 373–375, 2024.
https://doi.org/10.1007/978-3-031-47754-6